Weaned on Carrot Juice

by
Gerardo Joffe

Advance Books
San Francisco

Weaned on Carrot Juice

or
How I survived the Nazis and landed at the Golden Gate via the tin mines of Bolivia and the oil fields of Arkansas.

by
Gerardo Joffe

- Founder and president emeritus of Haverhills
- Founder and president of FLAME (Facts and Logic about the Middle East)
- President Emeritus of Friends of the Danish Jewish Museum

Advance Books
San Francisco

Books by Gerardo Joffe:

- How You Too Can Make at Least a Million Dollars (but probably much more) in the Mail-Order Business
- Anagraphics I
- How to Build a Great Fortune in Mail Order (a 7-volume course)
- How You Too Can Develop a Razor-Sharp Mind and a Steel-Trap Memory
- Weaned on Carrot Juice

This book is dedicated to:

Priscilla – *my loving and beloved companion for most of this journey*
Michael – *who is always in my heart*
Rachel and Joe – *always hanging in there for Dad*

ISBN Number: 0-930992-0-67
Library of Congress Control Number: 2003091792

Publishers: Jomira/Advance, Advance Books Division
               470 Third Street, #211
               San Francisco, CA 94017

FOREWORD

Dear Readers, dear Friends:

This is the story of my life – my reminiscences. I guess you could call it an "autobiography," but I think that is a somewhat pretentious term.

I am now over eighty years old. There are five distinct "chapters" in my life – the first is my growing up in Germany where, fortunately, I got away from the Nazis just before the Holocaust, if not on the last boat, then very close to it.

The second part of my life took place in Bolivia where I worked in the tin and tungsten mines for almost eight years. As you will see, it was a most interesting time.

The third part took place in the Untied States. I worked in the mines and in the oil fields and acquired a substantial education.

The final two parts tell of my adventures in business and in philanthropy.

I think you might find all of this quite interesting, sometimes funny, and perhaps even instructive and helpful in your own life.

Everything in this book is true. I have changed some names and some addresses, for reasons that you will find easy to understand.

I wish to express my thanks to Eve Ward for her invaluable help in producing the typescript. I just couldn't have done it without her.

Thank you – I hope you will enjoy reading this story of my life.

Gerardo Joffe

P.S.: Oh yes, there's one more thing: I really would like to hear from you and have your views of what you think of this book – both accolades and brickbats would be welcomed. Also, if you find that I have committed any errors, any inconsistencies or any typos, please let me know and I shall correct them in the next edition of this book. Thank you very much for your help. G.J.

Table of Contents

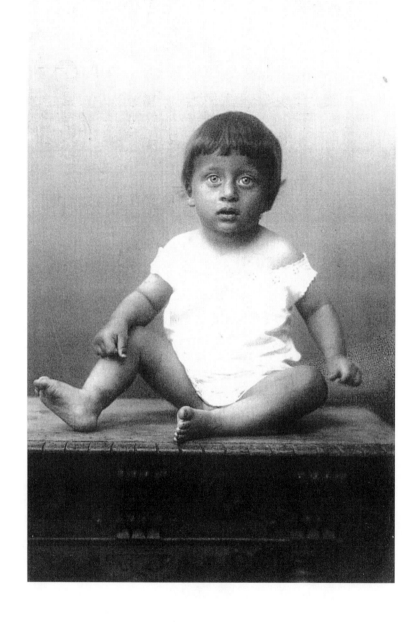

Here I am, about 15 months old. I look pretty filled out, don't I?
It looks as though Dr. Finkelstein (the "*coryphaeus*") knew what
he was doing.

Part I

GOOD RIDDANCE TO NAZI GERMANY

What is the very earliest thing you can remember? Was it the candles on the cake on your third birthday? Was it the fireworks on the Fourth of July when you were about two-and-one-half years old? Or, was it your mother telling you, "Sweetheart, you are now old enough to go to the potty by yourself, but don't forget to wipe."?

I remember distinctly my mother holding me in her arms while we were riding in a taxicab. I must have been three or four weeks old. Of course, I did not know at the time where we were going. I know now. We were going to the hospital because apparently I was a very sick baby.

And the reason that I was such a sick baby was that I wouldn't take my mother's milk. At that time – I was born in 1920 – no suitable formulas were available; therefore, a baby that wouldn't take its mother's milk was in serious trouble.

My mother always told me that the *Kinderarzt*, the pediatrician, who attended me, was Professor Finkelstein, whom she described as a *coryphaeus*, a Greek word meaning "leader of the chorus." To my mother, it meant an outstanding member of his profession. Dr. Finkelstein might indeed have been such an outstanding professional, but I remember that all the doctors whom my mother consulted on behalf of our family were given such an honorary appellation. Only the best!

In any case, Professor Finkelstein somehow kept me alive. My mother said he did it on carrot juice, but I never really entirely believed that. So, he must have had some "secret formula," some magic concoction that he mixed with that carrot juice in order to keep me alive.

While I wasn't sickly, I was not a very tall child. For many years in school, I was always the runt of the class. The lack of proper nursing was probably the cause of this. By the way, I still can't stand milk. The very look and smell of it make me sick. On the other hand, I am very fond of cheese and ice cream. Go figure!

I was born on Tuesday, June 22, 1920 and, as was the custom in those days, my mother had me at home in the matrimonial bed, Dr. Jacques Peltesohn attending. Everything seemed to have gone well. Dr. Peltesohn, by the way, was the only person with the first name of Jacques that I ever met in Germany.

We were Jewish, and being Jewish really permeated our whole life. There was never a big deal made of it, but we were always conscious of being Jewish and therefore somewhat "different" from the gentiles around us. The family was not religious, and as far as I can remember, we attended synagogue only on the High Holy Days or for weddings, bar mitzvahs, and other such special occasions. Bat mitzvahs and similar coming-of-age ceremonies for girls did not exist in those days.

My mother, while I would not call her religious in the conventional sense of the word, did, however, attend services every Sabbath. She also followed many of the Jewish customs and rituals that she had learned in her parents' home. Going to synagogue on the Sabbath was to her very much a social occasion as well, because on that day she got together with her brother and sisters, all but two of whom lived in Berlin; after services, she went to visit my Uncle Wilhelm and my Aunt Jenny, who lived close by. Aunt Jenny was the sister of my grandmother – my mother's mother.

Since my mother would not drive or ride in any conveyance on the Sabbath, she would walk to synagogue and back. It was at least thirty blocks each way, but that was her routine.

Uncle Wilhelm and Aunt Jenny were very religious and spent much time in religious practice. They were totally observant and followed all religious laws meticulously and to the letter. They were quite poor and lived in only one room that served as living room, bedroom, and kitchen. Aunt Jenny, a lovely old lady, was very deaf. She listened through a large black horn that apparently captured and concentrated the sound. It fascinated me; I had never seen anyone else using an instrument like it.

The most lovable thing about Aunt Jenny was this: At the birthday of any of her children, grandchildren, nieces, nephews, grandnieces, and grandnephews she would bake a chocolate fish, a delightful confection of chocolate, nuts, almonds, dried fruit, and, I always thought, various mysterious and secret ingredients. She would wrap that fish in gold foil and bring it to the birthday child on his or her day. She would do this without fail. If the birthday fell on the Sabbath she would walk, no matter how far it was, because as a strictly religious woman, she would not drive or ride in any conveyance under any circumstance. The distance to our house was about forty blocks. She would valiantly walk there and back, and she would never fail. What a lady!

As another part of our lifestyle, we kept a strictly kosher household. That meant primarily that we had two sets of dishes, one for dairy foods and the other set (I remember it had a gold rim around it) for meat foods. Many foods, of course, were what is called *parve* – neither dairy nor meat. *Parve* foods could be eaten on either set of dishes and could be eaten together with anything else. Dairy food and meat were never mixed and never served at the same meal. For this purpose, to keep a kosher home, two sets of pots and pans, and two sets of flatware were also required.

On Passover, all dishes, all pots and pans, and all flatware were put away and two whole new sets of dishes, and everything else, one for dairy and one for meat, were broken out for this eight-day festival. It was quite a production.

My mother had other such observances, some of which exasperated me. For instance, under no circumstances would she do any sewing on the Sabbath. I remember one time; I was about nine years old and had a Scout meeting, I needed a button sewed on in the worst possible way. She absolutely refused to do this and it frustrated me badly. I had to hold my pants together with a safety pin.

My mother had strict rules as to when the Sabbath would begin and when it would end. As I recall, there was something about three stars being in the sky. When they were visible, the Sabbath would begin or end. Another test was whether two threads, a black one and a white one, could or could not be distinguished in the natural light.

Naturally, the most serious offense in a kosher household, the one unpardonable sin, was the consumption of pork and pork products, especially ham. My father respected my mother's dietary rules, but did not feel himself bound by them and had a predilection for eating smoked ham. Every once in a while he would indulge himself. I am quite sure that my mother knew about that, but she never acknowledged it. The routine was that my father would sit down at the breakfast table while my mother went to the bathroom. The way our apartment was arranged, she had to go through the dining/living room in order to get to the bathroom.

My father would then say, "Gerhard, run down to Pfeiffers." Pfeiffers was the non-kosher butcher store on the ground floor of our house. "Get me an A*chtel*, an eighth of a pound, of smoked ham." It cost 35 *pfennig* and he'd give me a 50-*pfennig* piece. I could keep the 15-*pfennig* change. I often thought of it as my bribe. My mother, of course, would hear me running down the stairs and coming back up. She knew what was going on.

My father would then tell me to bring him a *fleischige* plate, one of those destined for meat, because by some crazy logic, ham, of course, could not be put on a dairy plate. He would then spread the butcher paper on the plate so that the ham would not touch it. He would then eat the ham, crumple up the paper, give it to me, and ask me to take it to the kitchen and put it in the trash.

My mother would call from the bathroom periodically, "Max, Max, are you through with breakfast yet?"

He would say, "Not yet, dear."

A while later, "Max, Max, are you through with breakfast?"

"Yes, I'm through with breakfast, sweetheart."

I had, in the meantime, thrown the butcher paper into the trash. Everyone knew what had happened. Nobody talked about it. I was a coconspirator.

The neighborhood in which we lived was called the *Bayrisches Viertel***, at the** center of which was the *Bayrischer Platz*, a small park with meadows and fountains – very pretty! It was a fairly upscale neighborhood, with a rather heavy upper-middle-class Jewish population. The closer one lived to the *Platz* itself, the fancier were the apartment buildings, the higher the social/income level. We lived at the very fringes of that district. I wouldn't say that my parents were upper-middle class.

They were, at best, middle-middle class. But in any case, we belonged to that quarter.

When I was little, my mother would often walk with me the five or six blocks to the *Platz*. There was the Lachmann lending library close by. She liked to sit on one of the chairs that framed the *Platz*, and read what she called her "good book." I remember that the chairs cost five *pfennig* per hour. An official-looking man in a green uniform came by periodically to collect. She always paid that small fee rather grudgingly. She felt that it should be a free service. I think she was right.

Every afternoon, punctually at 3 o'clock, a distinguished-looking gentleman appeared on the *Platz*. He was about fifty years old, at least that's what he looked like to me. He walked with his hands clasped behind his back and he looked to the ground while he walked, as though he was deep in thought. He probably was. His most outstanding feature, as far as I was concerned, was his hair. It stood straight up, as if electrified, and he reminded me of the *Struwelpeter*, who was on the cover of the most popular German children's book. The *Struwelpeter's* hair, too, stood straight up.

My mother told me, "Gerdchen, this is Dr. Einstein; he is a very famous physicist."

"*Mutti*, what is a physicist?" I asked

"Well," she answered, "he thinks about speed, time, gravity and things like that." That didn't strike me as highly unusual, because those were things that I thought of myself quite often. "Dr. Einstein is a very famous man," she continued. "You will remember that you met him. He won the Nobel Prize in physics – the highest honor one can get." Then she added, "He's Jewish." That was important. She, and I suppose all of us, kept score of things like that.

Another place I visited with my mother almost daily, but closer to home, was the *Kleist Park*. *Kleist* was a famous German author and poet whom I learned to admire when I was in school. *Kleist Park* was a rather grandiose affair with extensive meadows and shrubbery, riding paths, cycling paths, and sandboxes for us little children. I liked to go there with my bucket, play with other children, and build sand castles. The greatest attraction at the *Kleist Park*, however, as far as I was concerned, was the photographer. He stood at the entrance of the park with his wooden tripod and wooden camera. He had a sign, which proclaimed as follows:

> *Urahne, Grossmutter, Mutter und Kind*
> *Beim Kleist Park Photographen versammelt sind.*

That sign was accompanied by a picture of four women – an old lady, a middle-aged lady, a young woman, and her small girl child. Translated into English, the caption read:

> Great-grandmother, Grandmother, Mother and Child
> are gathered at the *Kleist Park* Photographer.

I thought that it was very clever.

A picture cost one *mark*. Every day that I went there I begged and begged my mother to allow me to have my picture taken by that photographer. She was a thrifty lady and times were rough. A *mark* was quite a bit of money to her. She never gave me permission. I was disappointed about it. One day, while my mother was sitting on a bench reading her "good book" (at the *Kleist Park* seating was free), I approached the photographer with my bucket in my hand and told him that I wanted to have my picture taken.

"Have you talked to your mother about that?" he asked.

"Yes," I lied, "and she has approved of it."

"How is that possible? She has never let you have your picture taken before?"

"I talked to her and she has now allowed it," I continued lying.

"Are you sure?"

"Yes, I am sure."

I don't know whether he actually believed me or not, but in any case, he positioned me in front of his camera and took my picture. It was going to be ready the next day.

My mother had been looking for me at the sandbox and when I reappeared she asked, "Where have you been?"

I confessed, "I have been to the photographer and had my picture taken."

She was very, very unhappy with me and gave me the worst scolding that I ever had in my life. *"Du ungezogener Junge!* You bad boy, you shouldn't have done that at all. I am very angry with you."

The next day we went back to the park and there was the photographer with the picture. My mother looked at it and her heart melted. She gave the photographer the *mark* and a 25-*pfennig* tip. It was an unusual thing for her to do. I was impressed. She had tears in her eyes. "You are a lovely child," she said. I still have the picture. The last time I saw my mother she brought the picture with her from Buenos Aires where she then lived. She wanted me to keep it.

She said, "I know I scolded you at the time, but this picture is now one of my most precious souvenirs." Then, somewhat hyperbolically, she added, "I wouldn't take a million dollars for it." Well, nobody would have given her a million dollars, but I know that she was really happy to have that little picture.

Here is another incident with my mother that quite shook me up at the time: I was about five years old and had a piggy bank in which I accumulated *"sechsers"* (which was what the Berliners curiously called a 5-*pfennig* coin) and *"groschen"* (10-*pfennig* coins) that I had received from my parents and from my uncles and aunts from time to time. There were no larger coins in my piggy bank. Somehow, over the course of the year or more, I had accumulated over twelve *marks*. It was rather a minor fortune to me. My mother had a birthday coming up. I wanted to get something really nice for her.

My first big lie. I told the photographer that my mother had authorized this picture, but of course she hadn't. She scolded me severely. But later in life she told me that she would not take "a million dollars" for this picture.

That's me, about three years old, with my brother Heinz (who eventually became Enrique). It got mighty cold in Berlin, so my mother bundled us up.

I broke the piggy bank and counted the coins. I had been right. There were 12 *marks* and 25 *pfennig*. I put all the coins into a paper bag and went to the Kadewe, the fancy department store in West Berlin, which is still in operation today. I thought what my mother really wanted was an elegant purse, since she always carried the same purse for all occasions. I went to the ladies' purse department and talked to the saleslady.

"What do you want, little fellow," she asked.

"I want to buy a really nice purse for my mother."

"How much can you spend?"

"I have 12 *marks* and 25 *pfennig*," I said, forgetting that I needed ten *pfennig* for the streetcar to get back home.

"Well," she says, "we have a really nice purse here but it costs 15 *marks* 75. But, you know what, if you take it I will let you have it for 12 *marks* 25."

I didn't negotiate. She offered it. She brought out the purse. I was absolutely stunned. It was about six inches wide and about eight inches deep. It was made out of the softest blue glove leather. It was embroidered on the front with a beautiful picture of a languorous lady. The most miraculous aspect, however, was that when you opened the purse there were three different compartments. One was lined in gray leather, the second in white leather, and the third in a beautiful brown fabric. I didn't understand and still don't to this day, what these three different compartments were for, but I thought that it was the most beautiful thing I had ever seen. I thanked the lady for kindly letting me have this beautiful purse for 12 *marks* and 25 *pfennig*, and asked her to gift wrap it in the most beautiful paper she had. She did this for me and assured me that my mother would really like it. I didn't have the nerve to ask her for a reduction of ten *pfennig*, which would have enabled me to take the streetcar home. I didn't really care. I was happy and elated with my purchase and didn't really mind walking home. It was about thirty-five blocks.

Well, I kept it in my secret drawer for a week until my mother's birthday. On the morning of her birthday, I wakened her. I gave her a kiss and said, "Mutti, happy birthday, and here's a present for you."

She was very astonished because she didn't think I was going to give her anything. After all, I had no money at all. She opened the package and saw the purse. She was really astonished. Then she looked at me sharply and said, "Where did you get the money to buy this purse?"

I said, "Mutti, I broke my piggy bank and I bought it with that money."

I thought that she would praise me, and kiss me, and thank me for my thoughtfulness and for the beautiful purse, but she did nothing of the sort. She scolded me for having broken the piggy bank. I was not supposed to do that and I had done a very wrong thing. This totally shattered me. I was so unhappy I went to my room and cried. My mother was a wonderful lady, but I don't think that she was a great child psychologist.

She kept that purse all of her life. And again, on her last trip to San Francisco, when she was seventy-eight years old, and at the same time that she showed me that picture from the *Kleist Park* that she had scolded me about and now was so proud of, she said, "Gerdchen (that was her pet name for me even when I was fifty years old), this purse you gave me is the most beautiful thing I have ever had. I have treasured it all my life. I know that I scolded you when you bought it. I am still so sorry about that. It was a very dumb thing of me to do."

I thought it was just wonderful that after all those years she had not only forgiven me but had praised me and understood the loving thing that I had done.

About 650,000 Jews lived in Germany at that time.   **That was about one per** cent of the total population. The Jewish population of Berlin was about 250,000 out of 4 million, about six per cent. I would say that the proportion of Jews in the *Bayrisches Viertel* was perhaps fifteen per cent. It was a nice neighborhood. We lived at *Grunewaldstrasse* #80, in one of four adjoining apartment buildings. Numbers 78 and 79 shared a courtyard and numbers 80 and 81 shared a courtyard. Each of the buildings had eight apartments facing the street and sixteen apartments facing the courtyard. The people in the front part of the building, the *Vorderhaus*, were middle-class people, mostly small merchants.   Those in the back, the *Hinterhaus*, were mostly blue-collar workers. There was little contact between the front and the back. In fact, there was not too much contact among any of the neighbors. Also, each of the apartment buildings had two stores on the ground floor. Those in our building were a toy store and that non-kosher butcher shop, where I occasionally bought that forbidden smoked ham for my father. The toy store, with an apartment behind it, was owned by a Herr Stein and his wife, who were Jewish. They had a daughter, about two years younger than I, whose name was Irma. During the Holocaust, all three of them were deported by the Nazis to Riga and killed there.

About once a day, a man with a hand organ would appear in the courtyard to play popular tunes. He expected or hoped that people would throw coins down to him from the windows. The usual donation was a *sechser* (a 5-*pfennig* piece) or, for the big spenders, a *groschen* (a 10-*pfennig* piece). The coins would be wrapped in a piece of newspaper so they wouldn't bounce too much. One time the hand-organ man came with a little monkey dressed in a tiny red suit and with a red-and-gold fez on his head. He retrieved the coins. The monkey was a sensation and his presence added to the harvest of coins.

I remember one of the popular tunes the hand-organ man played. The words went as follows:

> *Du kannst nicht treu sein,*
> *Nein, nein das kannst Du nicht,*
> *Wenn auch Dein Mund mir wahre Liebe verspricht.*
> *In Deinem Herzen hast Du für viele Platz,*
> *Darum bist Du auch nicht für mich der richtige Schatz.*

In translation it went like this:

You cannot be true,

No, no you cannot be,
Even though your mouth promises true love.
In your heart there is room for many,
Therefore you are not the right sweetheart for me.

I found it very touching.

I have an older brother – Heinz, now called Enrique. Heinz is six years my senior. I did not have too much contact with him when we were children, partly because he was so much older, but mostly because it became clear from the very beginning that our interests and temperaments were quite different. Now that we both are so much older, we have become very good friends. As of this writing, he lives in Argentina and we try to visit at least once a year.

My brother did like to tell me stories (in all likelihood apocryphal), which impressed me greatly and which I totally believed. I remember two of them. Here is the first one:

Kaiser Wilhelm II of Germany, who abdicated in 1918 (after the disastrous World War I), had a court dinner for the king of some exotic country, I don't remember which. My brother described lovingly and in great detail the golden plates, goblets, knives and forks, and all the other costly appurtenances, and also that a golden finger bowl with lukewarm water was put in front of each guest. When the meal ended, the royal guest of honor, not knowing the protocol and never having seen a finger bowl before, put the bowl to his lips and drank the water. All the other guests had in the meantime cleaned their greasy fingers in their bowls. In order not to embarrass the guest, the Kaiser passed a stern look around the table and he, too, put the bowl to his lips and drank the water. All of the other guests immediately drank the dirty water in their bowls. I though it was hilarious.

Another story had to do with King Amanullah of Afghanistan. I remember the name distinctly. The king had come to visit the president of the United States, I believe it must have been Mr. Hoover. Afghanistan at the time was not very interesting or important to the United States. In fact, my brother told me confidentially that Mr. Hoover didn't really know where it was and had to be shown Afghanistan in an atlas. Of course, Mr. Hoover was very friendly to the royal visitor and at the end of the visit asked him if there was anything else in the United States that he wanted to see. "Yes," King Amanullah answered through his interpreter, "I have heard so much about the Ford Motor Company and I would like to go to Detroit and see that."

"That can easily be arranged," Mr. Hoover said. He called Henry Ford right then and there and said, "Henry, I have Amanullah, the King of Afghanistan, here. He wishes to come to Detroit to see your factory. Please, have someone show him your place and give him a good reception."

King Amanullah and his entourage, which of course included an interpreter, went to Detroit, and an executive vice president of the Ford Motor Company gave him a tour of the Lincoln plant. Mr. Ford himself joined the party at the end of the tour where the brand-new Lincolns rolled off the assembly line. "Welcome, your Majesty," he said.

"Rabokie nam hallah naksooki," said His Majesty.

The interpreter translated, "His Majesty is very happy to be here."

Then Mr. Ford said, "Your Majesty, on behalf of the Ford Motor Company I would like to give you this brand-new Lincoln limousine as a present and as a souvenir of the United States."

The interpreter translated this to the king.

"Ramfa kabomkah rumtucky," said the king.

The interpreter translated, "His Majesty says that his position and his religion do not allow him to accept any gifts."

"No problem," said Mr. Ford. "I shall sell it to him for $10."

The translator conveyed the message to His Majesty.

Thereupon, the king took his wallet out of his pocket, extracted a $20 bill and said, "Furfty meh tak." ("Give me two.")

I thought it was the funniest story I had ever heard.

My mother was a stickler for good manners.   Little boys, when introduced to any adult, had to put their heels together (didn't actually have to click them), shake hands, and make a bow. I knew quite well how to do this, but my mother never really gave me a chance to show what I could do, that I could do it right. Every time we met someone new, she'd push my head forward and say, "Make a bow." This annoyed me very much. But even though I complained about that habit of hers many times, I could not keep her from doing that.

A small ordeal of my childhood was having her buy clothes for me. Her favorite store for that purpose was Peek & Kloppenburg, which had a boys' department that she liked. I would have to stand on a box and a salesman would produce the kind of garment my mother had in mind.   All discussions and negotiations about the garment took place between her and the salesman. I don't recall ever once having been asked whether I liked it or not. An important concept in purchasing clothes for me was that they be *auf Zuwachs*, which meant I could grow into them, and that they would last, hopefully, for two or three years. And, actually, they were always a little bit too large for me and I was not entirely comfortable; no sooner did I grow into them, I began to grow too large for the clothes and the cycle would start over again.

One of my favorite articles of clothing, at least until I was about five years old, was my "Mozart suit." It was made of green velveteen, had short pants, of course, and a coat that was buttoned at the collar and then opened up to a ruffled white shirtfront, very much like little Lord Fauntleroy.

My father (Max) was the oldest of four children. There was a sister, Selma, and a brother, Bernhard, both of whom lived in Berlin. There was also another sister, Helene. As a young girl Helene apparently had eloped and married a Russian man, had gone to Russia with him, and had disappeared from sight. She came visiting once about forty years later. She was a total stranger to all of us and spoke German with some difficulty. My father and his siblings were born in Berlin. His parents had migrated from Russia to Germany as young people. I am not sure whether they were already married or met and married in Berlin. They settled in a fringe neighborhood of Berlin, which was essentially a self-imposed Jewish ghetto centered around the *Grenadier Strasse.*

My grandfather, Zemach, was a very simple and uneducated man. He was a barber and pulled teeth and put on leeches if required. Like many poor people, he had a fantasy of some day perhaps striking it rich. Together with his friend Abe, a shoemaker, he religiously played the Prussian State Lottery every month. They had their "lucky number," which one could reserve and get for every drawing. The tickets could be bought whole or in halves, quarters, or eighths. My grandfather and Abe the shoemaker always bought a one-eighth ticket together, which I believe in those days cost five *marks*, a substantial sum for poor people. They never, of course, won anything. My grandmother always scolded him for wasting his money on such frivolities. She needed the money to feed and clothe her family. At the end, he gave in and Abe the shoemaker had to buy the eighth ticket by himself or find another partner. So, being convinced that he had a lucky number, he brought an extra sacrifice and, probably making his wife very angry, bought the whole eighth ticket by himself. Well, you know of course what would happen. The very first time that my grandfather did not participate, Abe the shoemaker won 10,000 *marks* on his one-eighth lottery ticket. It was an incredible sum of money in those days, and especially for poor people. Abe the shoemaker propelled himself into a totally different social category. He moved away from the self-imposed ghetto to some fancy part of the city, probably to the *Bayrischer Platz* neighborhood. My father told me that my grandfather never quite forgave his wife for having given him such poor advice.

Because of the peculiar laws in Germany and I believe in all of Europe at that time, my father and his siblings, even though born in Berlin and not knowing any other country or speaking any other language, were not German citizens. One had the nationality or citizenship of one's parents. So, my father was a Russian citizen until early into World War I. In 1915, I believe, the German government, probably in order to make more people eligible for military service, gave German-born people with foreign nationality the option to become Germans. My father opted for that. He did not, however, serve in World War I. He had flat feet or something like that.

My mother came from a quite different background. She was born in the city of Posen, a city in Upper Silesia, a part of Germany. After Germany lost World War I, that part of the country was ceded to Poland and the city was renamed Poznan, a name which it still holds today.

My grandfather and his family, and, as far as I can tell, virtually all other German-speaking Jewish families moved to Germany proper, mostly to Berlin. They just couldn't stand to be living in Poland. Like most Germans, they held the Poles in contempt. In the end, of course, it didn't make any difference at all.

My grandfather on my mother's side, Samuel Brandt, had a small shoe factory. As my mother explained it to me, he only made the uppers of shoes. The soles, apparently, were made by a different firm, and a third firm put all of it together to make the complete shoe. I don't know how big an operation it was, but he must have done fairly well, because there were seven children, five girls and two boys. Each of the girls received a dowry of 20,000 gold *marks*. Comparing this sum to today's values, I would say that this was roughly equivalent to $200,000 – a very tidy sum, especially multiplied by five. My mother, Hedwig, was the fourth of the five girls.

The oldest daughter, Sarah, married Uncle Max Hirsch, who was the "rich man" of the family. He and his partner, Herr Zander, owned a men's suit factory. When I was older, about fourteen, I had suits made to measure by his firm. It was wonderful. There was a wrinkle, however. One of the stories or myths my brother told me was that a gentleman always had real functioning sewn buttonholes on his sleeves.

"Why would gentlemen want that?" I asked.

"So they could unbutton the lower part of their sleeves," my brother patiently explained to me, "and could play pool without having to take off their coats."

That struck me as perfectly logical. Uncle Max's factory did not provide real buttonholes on the sleeves of their coats. I so totally insisted on that, however, in fact I remember throwing somewhat of a fit. As a special favor to my mother, but mostly perhaps to shut me up, he would have a tailor put a few buttonholes in the sleeves. I was satisfied and very proud.

Uncle Max and Aunt Sarah had three children: Erich, Edith, and Steffie, all of whom, as well as their parents, later went to Argentina.

The second of the Brandt sisters was Hanne. She was married to Uncle Oscar Gans. Gans means goose in German and I always thought that was a funny name. He was a traveling shoe salesman and had a very hard time providing for his family, I believe. He died fairly young and left Aunt Hanne with two daughters, Liese and Ruth. The three of them eventually wound up in New York.

My Aunt Hanne had an apparent predilection for the macabre. I remember a poem she composed about the Jewish cemetery in Weissensee in Berlin. I didn't think it was a very good poem (though it rhymed), but mostly I thought it was a weird topic. Also, in her living room she had a picture that fascinated me. It showed four skulls on a table. Underneath it was printed

> *Wer war der Tor, wer Weiser,*
> *Wer Bettelmann, wer Kaiser?*

which translated means:

> Who was the fool, who the wise man,
> who was the beggar, who the emperor?

Then beneath that was the line:

> *Ob arm, ob reich,*
> *Im Tode gleich.*

> Whether poor or rich,
> in death all are the same.

I thought it was a peculiar thing to hang in one's living room.

The Gans girls were quite a bit older than I. Liese was about fifteen years older and Ruth was about ten years older. Even as a little boy I could tell that they were not very attractive and might therefore have a hard time finding husbands. Finding a husband was the all-important thing. The whole family was concerned. The usual ways that we know now how to meet prospective spouses, such as dating, were not available. In our circles, virtually all marriages were somehow arranged – either "informally," through friends and family, or "formally," by engaging a marriage broker.

One day it was announced that Liese had a suitor. It was an arranged deal. A marriage broker – a so-called *shadchen*, had located a prospect in a small town in southern Germany. Herr Goldheimer, whom we got to meet, turned out to be a very nice man. It was whispered that he was very rich. That made him particularly eligible, of course. There was one problem: He was very, very short, I would say not over 5'2". Liese was a fairly tall girl. Well, nothing is perfect!

One day (as my father reported to my mother and as I overheard) Herr Goldheimer unexpectedly appeared at my father's business. My father was somewhat surprised but very cordial, of course. After all, he was a prospective member of the family.

"How can I help you, Max?" he asked. (Herr Goldheimer's first name, just like my father's, was also Max.)

"Herr Joffe, I have an unusual request. I must ask you a very serious, confidential question."

"Out with it, Max. What is it? I'll answer it if I can."

"Is Liese a virgin?" he asked.

My father was absolutely stunned. He thought he had not understood well.

"I beg your pardon, Max, what was the question?"

"I would like to know whether she is a virgin."

Of course, in those days everyone was a virgin. Not being a virgin was virtually unheard of. Certainly the Gans girls had no prior experience, had never dated, certainly had no history of carousing.

"Max," my father said, "I am quite sure that she is a virgin."

"I am pretty sure too, but I have to make absolutely sure," Goldheimer replied.

"How can you do that?" my father asked."

"I must insist that she submit to a medical examination and that the doctor will certify to her virginity."

"That may be impossible," my father said. "I don't think that my sister-in-law would ever agree to that, nor would Liese."

"Well, I'm so sorry. I really would like to marry her. She is a wonderful girl, but that is the one condition I must insist on."

"Well," my father said, "I'll talk with Hanne." When he told my mother the story she was appalled, but after some thought and discussion she decided to tell Hanne and Liese about it. Hanne was outraged, indignant and Liese cried. Of course she was a virgin, but it became clear that nothing but the medical certificate would suffice. So Liese went to a doctor who made the pertinent examination. Everything was in place, a certificate was issued, and the wedding took place very soon thereafter.

After a few years, Max and Liese, her mother and her sister all emigrated to the United States. I think Liese had a good marriage and was quite happy. They had one son, Michael, who now lives in the San Francisco Bay Area and whom we see from time to time.

I got to be quite friendly with Max in the last years of his life. He was a secretive man. As far as I could tell, he never really worked a day in his life. From the day he arrived in the United States, he seems to have played the stock market. Apparently, he knew what he was doing and was very successful at it. He refused to tell his wife or his only son how much money he had and after getting over her shock of suddenly being a widow, Liese was very pleased about how rich she was.

My Aunt Martha, the sister immediately older than my mother was my favorite aunt. For many years she lived in Cologne, which is on the Rhine River, about 400 miles from Berlin. She and her husband, Gustav, later moved to Berlin. Uncle Gustav was also a traveling shoe salesman. He also had to struggle and needed periodic financial support from the family. Martha, I always thought, was sort of a cut above the rest of the family, always ready for a joke and for a good time.

She had been married to Gustav for fifteen years. There were no children. Suddenly she was pregnant and I had a new cousin by the name of Klaus. He was six years younger than I. Klaus looked like nobody else in our family. He was tall and blond and the most un-Jewish-looking Jew I'd ever seen. Even as a child I thought that there was something fishy. And, there was some whispering. Whenever my father and mother wanted to keep some secrets from me, they would always speak in very rudimentary French. I usually got the gist of it. On her last visit to San Francisco my mother felt that she might never see me again (she was right) and decided to reveal all the family secrets to me, let all the family skeletons out of the closet.

She told me that she and Martha were on a cruise on Lake Constance in southern Germany. Martha had engaged in a "relationship" with the ship's doctor – and voilá. I have to hand it to Uncle Gustav: He treated Klaus as though he were his own flesh and blood, and Klaus loved him as a father. While I did not know the details, that really didn't come as a total surprise to me. Klaus surely would also have had questions about his provenance. Uncle Gustav was not a very impressive man – physically and otherwise – but I always admired him for how he handled this.

Several times, when Martha was living in Cologne, my mother and I went to visit her. It was about a six-hour trip by train.

I loved my aunt's apartment, especially one room that she called her Biedermeyer room. Apparently, Biedermeyer was a special furniture style of a previous century. Everything in that room, which was like a museum, never used, looked totally impractical to me but it was very beautiful. The main attraction to me was that it had a spinning wheel in it. I spent hours and hours trying to produce a thread but never succeeded.

One year, when I was five years old, my mother had to return to Berlin for some reason, and I was left alone with Aunt Martha to spend another week. I was quite happy about that. Uncle Gustav was away on a business trip. On the third day of this extended stay, I realized that it was Yom Kippur, the holiest day in the Jewish calendar. We were supposed to go to the synagogue and, of course, to fast. Uncle Gustav was very observant and even though Aunt Martha had the same background as my mother she seemed to be oblivious of the day and the holiness of it.

When she served breakfast I said, "Aunt Martha, I can't eat breakfast. Today is Yom Kippur and we have to fast. Don't you know that."

"Eat your breakfast," she said, "it's good for you."

So, of course, I had to obey my aunt and I ate the breakfast.

Some time later in the day, she said, "Gerdchen, there's a wonderful movie playing at the local theatre. I'd like to see it and you'd really like it too."

I thought she had lost her mind. How could anybody go see a movie on Yom Kippur. I said, "Aunt Martha, we can't do that; it would be a very bad sin. We cannot go to a movie on Yom Kippur. We are supposed to go to the synagogue and to fast."

"God will forgive us," she said.

"Yes," I replied, "God may forgive us, but what will Uncle Gustav do when he finds out?"

"He's not going to find out," she said, "because I am not going to tell him and you aren't either, are you?"

We did go to the movie. We enjoyed it very much, and neither she nor I were ever punished by God which, as I thought for many years, we surely deserved.

Another time that my mother and I were visiting in Cologne, I was allowed to attend the carnival celebration for children. My mother and my aunt sewed up a beautiful costume for me, namely as a domino. It was a silky one-piece suit with wide pants gathered at the ankles, with black and yellow lozenges all over, and with yellow-and-black buttons in front. I also had a black-and-yellow pointed hat. I was ecstatic. I thought it was the most wonderful day in my life. We were so happy and sang songs that I remember to this day. One of them went as follows:

Mit der Liebe darf man nicht scherzen,
Denn die Liebe kommt vom Herzen,
Und bist Du tot, dann ist's vorbei,
Dann ist das kleine Herz entzwei.

Translation:

With love you must not toy,
Because love comes from the heart,
And when you're dead it's all over,
And your little heart is broken.

I thought it was very beautiful. It made me cry.

The youngest of the sisters was Rosa.   She was not very good-looking and, apparently, there was a problem in finding a husband for her. Finally, again through the intermediacy of a marriage broker, they found a Jewish man in the unlikely city of Quedlinburg in the Harz Mountains. I was amazed how they found him, but there was obviously some kind of network among the brokers, some listing service, just as in real estate. This man's name was Konrad Hesse, but everyone called him Uncle Kern. He was a very nice, pot-bellied man. I liked him very much. He opened a hardware store in a little town by the name of Blankenburg, also in the Harz Mountains, and until the dreadful things happened in Germany they lived a nice life.

They had two children, my cousin Franz, one year younger than I, and Gerda, six years younger than I. When he was eleven years old, Franz became very ill. He was brought to Berlin to be attended by fine physicians, but he died from some kind of blood cancer. It was a terrible tragedy and everyone in the family was in mourning.

I loved to visit my aunt and uncle in Blankenburg. I was seven years old when I was first allowed to travel by myself. When I went to Blankenburg I always had a wonderful time. My aunt introduced me to *pommes frites*, crispy fried potatoes, which I had never tasted at home.

Uncle Kern was the most "un-Jewish" person of the whole family. I was totally aghast when, one winter when I was staying with them, he erected a Christmas tree and gave presents to his children and also to me. I remember my cousin Franz getting an electric train. Uncle Kern had, of course, bought it wholesale, being in this kind of business. I had never seen anything as exciting as that train. We played with it all day long.

Aunt Rosa, Uncle Kern, and Gerda eventually wound up in Israel – the only ones from the family and as far as I could tell, the most unlikely candidates for that destination.

Then there was my Uncle Siegfried. He was the only son (there was actually another one – I'll talk about him in later) and the oldest. He remained a bachelor his whole life, but he was straight. He was the tyrant of the family, and all of his sisters, even when they were grown women with children, and to some degree even their husbands, stood in awe of him. The sisters were scandalized because, while not married, he lived with a Frau Jacobsohn who had two very attractive teenage daughters. It was a most "unconventional" situation at the time, certainly in our circles. Frau Jacobsohn never got invited to any family occasion.

One of the unbroken and unbreakable routines of our household was that Uncle Siegfried would come every Friday night for Sabbath dinner. My father would make the *Kiddush*, the blessing and opening of the Sabbath ceremony, and then my mother would serve a very nice dinner. But what should and could have been a weekly happy occasion was almost invariably destroyed by Uncle Siegfried's ranting and raving about something or another – usually about a member of the family, like some brother-in-law who didn't pull his weight or needed money, and so on. I regretted it and so did my parents, but nothing could be done about it. It was an established routine that could not be broken.

Our living-dining room was heated by a large coal-fired tile stove. On this particular Friday, Uncle Siegfried was throwing one of his fits, and my mother stood by or perhaps even cowered against the stove, warming herself. Uncle Siegfried was ranting and raving and then he walked over to my mother and shook his fist in her face; I thought he might be going to hit her. Suddenly, my father had enough. He rang the bell for the maid and said, "Gertrud, Mr. Brandt wishes to go home now. Please give him his hat and his walking stick."

She did as she was told. Uncle Siegfried, nonplused, left without saying goodbye. He was back the next week.

Another Friday night, the established routine began as usual. That evening we were all there – Father, my brother, I, Uncle Siegfried…but no Mother. Where was she? It was most unusual. We waited until 7:30, then we waited until 8 o'clock. At 8:30 we were seriously concerned. It was totally against all custom and experience. About a quarter to nine, my mother waltzed in. I thought she looked very beautiful and I noticed that her hair looked different. She had been to the beauty parlor. The operator had put a touch of henna (red) into her hair. I thought it looked very good. My father, usually the most mild-mannered of men, was livid. He started a harangue, close to a fit. He told her strongly that he did not marry a red-headed woman, and that he did not want to have a red-headed woman now. He told her to go back to the beauty parlor immediately and to have the red rinsed out.

My mother started crying. She told him how impossible it would be, even if she were willing, to have it done at this time in the evening. But my father insisted. So she went back to the beauty parlor and had it rinsed out. She was finally home by 10 o'clock. It was a most abbreviated and subdued Sabbath dinner that evening.

As I said, my father was the most mild-mannered and even-tempered man that one could imagine. I cannot recall his ever raising his voice to my mother or to my brother or to me. But he did have fixed ideas, peculiarities I thought, which could not be shaken. Not having a red-headed wife seems to have been one of them.

Here's another example: His fixed plan was that my brother should become a doctor and that I should become an attorney. I don't recall that either my brother or I were ever consulted about these career choices. My brother did indeed eventually study at Berlin University in a pre-med program. I am not sure that he enjoyed it very much.

I might perhaps have made a pretty good attorney. I ultimately got a law degree, but never took the bar or practiced the profession.

Another one of his ideas – I don't know where he got them – was that the older son had to learn to play the piano and the younger son should learn to play the violin. My brother learned to play the piano, but he never showed much enthusiasm for it and as far as I could tell he wasn't very good at it. But he took lessons for about three years, I believe.

My brother had really wanted to learn to play the cello. Why, I don't know. But, that was his wish. That, however, was a totally un-acceptable instrument to my father. Only people who worked in orchestras played the cello and that was not the career choice he had planned for my brother. So, it was the piano for him.

When my turn came – I believe I wanted to begin a music program when I was about twelve years old – I did want to play the piano but, of course, I had been destined to play the violin. I absolute refused to learn to play the violin. I threw several fits and finally, and surprising to me, my father relented and allowed me to take piano lessons. That didn't last very long either because my mind wandered to how the piano notes, the different intervals, related to each other. What combination of frequencies made a harmony? I never gained any proficiency in playing the instrument although, even today, I can pick out almost any tune.

Another thing: My brother secretly practiced how to handle a salad fork and a salad spoon in one hand, just as he had seen the headwaiter do it in a movie. Only I was allowed to be present when he was secretly practicing. He tried very hard to master this and finally he succeeded. A few days later, when my mother had a salad on the table, he asked to be allowed to serve it and he showed off his newly acquired skill. My father stopped him immediately. "Only waiters serve salad like that," he said. "Don't you ever do that in this house."

I thought it was crazy, but that's the way it was.

My mother agreed with everything. My father was sweet and accommodating, but he just had some of these funny and very fixed ideas.

One more: One time my brother took it into his head to part his hair in the middle, rather than on the side. He was about sixteen years old. He thought he looked very *soigné*. I thought so too. My father had one look at him and told him to immediately go back to his room and part his hair on the side. The stated reason? Only gigolos part their hair that way. I didn't know what a gigolo was. I looked it up in the dictionary. I was impressed.

But back to Uncle Siegfried. I kind of liked him in a way. I think he was a nice man when he did not fly into one of his rages. One day, when I was in his neighborhood, I decided to pay him an impromptu visit. He was sitting at his desk, playing solitaire (a habit I must have inherited from him). He seemed to be happy to see me. He asked me good questions about school and so on. I was ready to leave when he pulled out his wallet and gave me a 20-*mark* note. It was the most money I'd ever had.

Uncle Siegfried, a tall, nice looking man, had been an officer in the German army in World War I, a relatively rare thing for a Jew. He received the Iron Cross First Class for valor, of which he liked to wear a miniature in his buttonhole. We had a picture of him at home in uniform, in a martial pose.

When the Nazis came to power, he believed that because of his service, having been an officer and having received the Iron Cross, he would be spared unpleasantness and humiliation. He was wrong. One day when he was walking in the street, a Nazi thug came and ripped the Iron Cross out of his buttonhole. I don't think he ever quite got over that. Uncle Siegfried died a terrible death. He had suffered a stroke and was clubbed to death in his bed by Nazi assailants. As dreadful as it was, he was the only one of our close relatives to die in the Holocaust. It was most unusual to lose only one family member to the Nazis.

Most of our family social life took place with my mother's family. My father's family played a minor role. And that had to do, sad to say, with the fact that my mother really felt herself and her family to be "superior" and, though she made some attempt to hide it, looked with a certain degree of disdain on my father's family. That was because of the general attitude of the German Jews toward the so-called *Ostjuden*, the Jews that had come themselves or whose forebears had migrated a generation or two earlier from eastern Europe. They came mostly from what was then called "Russian Poland," from where they had fled to escape both anti-Semitism and the pogroms that took place there with numbing regularity and from the ensuing untenable economic conditions. My father's parents belonged to that disdained group. I always wondered why my mother would have married into such a family that she thought unworthy, or certainly socially beneath her.

My mother complained about and sometimes even mimicked what she thought was the improper use of the German language or the foreign intonation of my father's mother. I thought that my grandmother was a lovely old lady and I was totally unaware of her having any kind of foreign accent or that she spoke German any differently from any of us.

This disdain or mistrust had one particularly unpleasant consequence. My Uncle Siegfried, who was "the man" in his family after his father had died, oversaw the distribution of the dowries to his sisters. He decided not to give my father the 20,000 gold *marks* that he had been promised. Instead, not entirely trusting him, he gave him 20,000 *marks* of City of Posen municipal bonds, which matured within five years. My parents got married in 1913. World War I broke out in 1914, which made the municipal bonds worth only the paper they were printed on. My father kept the bonds in his desk drawer. He let me look at them and handle them a few times. He smiled ruefully at the loss he had suffered, but he had no bitterness against Uncle Siegfried because of it. My father was just a very nice man.

All his life, my father subsidized his younger brother Bernhard, who could barely eke out a living by being a representative of some small fabric companies. He was not a very talented man.

My father's sister, Selma, was married to Salo, a tailor. They also lived in very poor conditions. My father was the constant support of his brother, his sister, and of his mother, who had no income at all.

Bernhard was married to a very nice lady by the name of Nanny. They had no children. Bernhard was divorced and had previously been married to a woman whose name was also Nanny.

I remember the first Nanny only very vaguely. They had a son by the name of Manfred. The first Nanny had emigrated with her next husband to, of all places, Yugoslavia. They all perished in the Holocaust.

My father and his partner, Herr Borger, had a wholesale fabric, mostly silk, business. They had many customers, mostly small retail businesses, dressmakers, or peddlers. The main problem with the business, which was clear to me even when I was a little boy, and which permeated my father's unending concern and which was a source of constant conversation at the dinner table was the creditworthiness or, rather, creditunworthiness of his customers. A disproportionate number of them went bankrupt, especially as the depression took hold in Germany. Each loss was a terrible blow to my father and his partner. In the end, their business too went bankrupt.

There was much monetary loss, anguish and humiliation for my parents. I felt very sorry for them. I did realize, however, even as a child, that my father's business had no real economic justification. From what I could see and understand, the only customers that he had were those who were unable to buy directly from the manufacturers. And the reason that they could not buy directly from the manufacturers, the textile mills, was that they either had very small demand or had bad credit and usually both. I was surprised that my father never seemed to identify this problem or, as a matter of denial, refused to identify it.

After suffering the bankruptcy of their business, my father separated from Herr Borger and started exactly the same type of business again, but this time as sole proprietor. His separation from Herr Borger was a friendly one. They each just thought that they could do better by themselves. He worked very hard, was constantly worried, and didn't make a whole lot of money. He was able, however, to maintain for himself and for his family a decent middle-class life and, of course, also to assist his brother, his sister, and his mother and – in some cases – members of my mother's family. It was a remarkable accomplishment for a very small businessman, especially during the depression, which was just as bad in Germany as it was in the United States.

I remember distinctly that my father had two monthly nuts to crack, namely to produce 1,000 *marks* for his business overhead and 600 *marks* for my mother's household money. He always succeeded in doing that, but it was a struggle every month. It seemed that nothing was ever left over.

My mother, who had learned thrift in her mother's home, kept a *Haushaltbuch* – a book of household expenditures, in which she entered every expense, even the smallest one. The book was kept in a locked drawer, which could only be opened with a key on her key ring. I was not allowed to see it. Occasionally, however, especially when she was in the bathroom I would take the key ring, and open the drawer to study the book. I was impressed by her meticulousness and how she always managed to stay just under her 600 *marks* monthly limit. The monthly household expenditures usually amounted to 520 *marks*, 567 *marks* or something like that, but never, never exceeded her 600-*mark* allotment.

One of the monthly expenditures was the payment of the rent. My parents had lived in their apartment since the day they were married in March of 1913. The monthly rent was 89.50 *marks*, an amount that never varied during that entire time that they lived there. The owner of the four buildings was a Herr Weissmüller. On the first day of each month, from the time that I was six years old, my mother would send me with the rent money in cash to Herr Weissmüller, who lived in #78, one of the four buildings. I would walk up to the third floor, ring the bell, and Frau Weissmüller, a buxom and very kindly lady, would open the door and direct me to Herr Weissmüller's study. Invariably, Herr Weissmüller was seated at his desk, profiled against the window. I never saw him standing up or walking. He would take the money, count it, and then sign the receipt in the blue rent book that my mother had given me. He always said something nice to me or asked me a good question, usually about school. More often than not, he would give me a 25-*pfennig* piece as his little gift. He was a person deserving of enormous respect, as far as I was concerned.

I enjoyed dealing with the trades people in our neighborhood. All of them were very nice to me. There was of course the large and very busy butcher shop in our building, and Herr Pfeiffer and his son, who owned and were in charge of the store and were always most cordial to me on the occasions I went down and bought that surreptitious smoked ham for my father. At each visit, they offered me a piece of sausage or something like that, but of course I always declined with thanks. I wouldn't eat that *tref* meat

I have already mentioned Herr Stein and his toy store. I spent much time in the store and did crossword puzzles with Herr Stein. Of course, my mother bought all my toys from him.

Then there was the baker, Herr Erich, to whom my mother sent me every morning to buy fresh bread and rolls, which had a delicious hard crust and a distinctive cut down the center. Rolls were called *Schrippen*, a term used only in Berlin, even today. All bread was made of rye. A few times, Herr Erich would let me go with him to the basement of his store, where he had the ovens and where the bread, the rolls, and the pastry were baked every day. I remember the strong smell of yeast and was fascinated by the intense heat and the wonderful aroma.

Invariably, Herr Erich would put the wooden paddle in the oven and would pull out a freshly baked *Schnecke*, a delightful, very Berlin pastry for me. I was in seventh heaven.

Then there was Herr Ball, who had what the Germans oddly called a *Kolonialwarengeschäft* – a store handling "colonial" goods. It was an odd name because such a store only sold non-perishable groceries. Most of the things were in cans. I was a special favorite of Frau Ball. She would always give me a piece of dried fruit when I came to buy something in her store.

Next door was a bicycle shop, owned by Herr and Frau Schiller. They were nice people who let me play in their workshop. When the time came, my father eventually bought my first bicycle from them.

Across the street was a tavern, what the Berliners call a *Kneipe*, where my father would send me once a week or so to buy him a bottle of beer. That was another small source of income for me. My father would give me a *mark* and I could always keep the 25-*pfennig* change.

My favorite place was the shop of Herr Scheunemann, the shoemaker. It was also across the street from our apartment building. Herr Scheunemann and his assistant sat on little three-legged stools by a low table on which they fastened soles and heels with wooden nails that they kept in their mouths. I thought it was marvelous that they never seemed to swallow even one of those nails. Whenever I came to visit, Herr Scheunemann allowed me to sit on the third unoccupied, three-legged little stool by that table. I could watch him and his assistant at work. When my mother needed a pair of shoes soled, Herr Scheunemann would bring out several large pieces of sole leather, would explain the respective qualities to my mother and then, between the two of them, they would make a choice. Right then and there, Herr Scheunemann would draw the outline of the shoe on the leather and cut it out with a special very sharp knife. My father and mother had great respect for Herr Scheunemann because he was able to give his only son an academic education. The son became a dentist and thus had reached a higher rung on the social ladder than his father. It was a fairly unusual thing in Germany at the time.

Before I started school I would accompany my mother on her daily shopping. Just like everyone else that I knew, we had no refrigeration. There were things that we bought every day. I usually bought the breakfast rolls in the morning, but more often than not, there would be an additional stop by the shop of Herr Erich, the baker. We would then go to the dairy store and to the greengrocers and to the kosher butcher, Herr Rosenbaum. Herr Rosenbaum was a tall, bony, and very kindly man. He had a bushy mustache that I found very impressive. He gave me a slice of salami every time my mother made a purchase. I liked this tasty salami very much and, of course, I could eat it because it didn't contain any pork. That was a real treat. One thing that puzzled me endlessly was this: Herr Rosenbaum sliced the salami on the bias, diagonally, so that the slices were oval rather than round. It was clear to me that an oval slice contained more meat than a round one of the same thickness. I wondered how it was possible that a cylinder, which was the shape of the salami, could yield more meat if slices of the same thickness were cut on the bias than if cut perpendicular to its axis. I asked my mother, but she did not know; she didn't understand what I was talking about. She thought I was a strange child. She may have been right. I thought about this question very much and very hard. It took me years to figure it out.

Once a week, my mother went to the open-air market, which took place in a square not too far from our home. There she bought mostly fresh fruit that was not usually available at the greengrocers, but primarily fresh fish. The live fish swam around in large tubs, made more beguiling to me because of the pumps that supplied the tubs with air. My mother would select the fish – often having it netted and inspected it, then discarding it for another specimen. I never quite understood what her selection criteria were. The fishmonger would then kill the fish by hitting it on the head with a wooden mallet and eviscerate it right then and there. It fascinated me to watch the whole process. For some reason, however, the scales of the fish were removed at home. My mother had a special tool for that and it went pretty quickly.

The main fish were two that are deprecated to this day in the United States for food, namely carp and pike. I thought they tasted just great, though both of them were a little bony.

Herr Rosenbaum also provided the weekly chicken. Chicken was the standard Sabbath and weekend bird, except for the month of December, when it was goose. I suppose that was an unintentional "assimilation" gesture, because gentiles, of course, would not do without that classic bird, the Christmas goose.

The chicken was dead, it was hanging by is neck on a hook, but that was just about all. All the rest had to be done at home. My mother and the maid would pluck the chicken, then they would sear it over the fire to remove all the little pinfeathers. Then my mother would open the chicken and would examine its innards for possible imperfections. I don't really know to this day what she was looking for and I don't think she really did either, but it seems that if the organs were not in the proper place or if something else did not look right, the chicken could not be considered kosher. It never happened.

For some reason that I never understood, and that my mother was never able to explain to me, she cut a cross on each side of the chicken's gizzard before she sliced it, and exposed its contents, which mostly seemed to consist of gravel. She removed the contents and also peeled off the tough skin on the inside of the gizzard. I was very fond of the gizzard and all the other odds and ends, which came under the heading of *Hühnerklein*, chicken giblets.

Once every week or so, my mother would do some baking. She would either make a pie or some butter cookies. I preferred the latter. I loved to watch her make the dough, roll it out, and then cut the dough with cookie cutters. She had a heart shaped cookie cutter, a diamond, a circle, and, my favorite, a little man. I got to eat the leftover dough, of course.

My brother was in school, so I had my mother mostly to myself. I loved to go shopping with her and go on the walks with her to the *Kleist Park* or to the *Bayrischer Platz.*

Once a week, my mother and her sisters living in Berlin at the time would meet at my grandmother's house. I was the only kid and was usually sent off to another room where I played with the toys that I had brought or read one of my books. I had no problem entertaining myself. I had no interest in the endless chattering and gossiping of my mother, her sisters, and their mother.

The women, usually four or five, chattered endlessly. Occasionally they even raised their voices, though never really in anger. One day, it must have been in 1925, my grandmother bought a radio, the first in the family. It was a very primitive set. A station had to be located by tickling a crystal with a copper whisker. There was no loudspeaker, only earphones. Programs were broadcast irregularly but, as I recall, a music program came on at 3 p.m. At that time, all conversation ended and all women present, my grandmother, my mother, and my aunts, kept the earphones glued to their ears, listening intently to the music and to what the announcer had to say. They shushed me every time if I tried to interrupt their reverie.

The programs were broadcast irregularly. Sometimes a program would terminate, say, at 3:55, with a new program not beginning until 4 o'clock. In the five-minute interval, the station would transmit the station's signal, which was a four-tone bell tune that was repeated every ten seconds. I was allowed to listen to the bell tune, but as soon as the 4 o'clock music program came on, I was commanded to immediately turn the earphones over to my grandmother, my mother and my aunts. Once, when I attempted to listen to the music, I was sternly reprimanded. I never got to listen to a program or even to any part of it.

I wonder even now how come that these very nice people had so little understanding of what today we would call child psychology. The term and, I believe, even the concept of child psychology were totally unknown to my mother (a loving woman), my aunts, and my grandmother, or anyone else of their generation in Germany.

Here's another example. One time we had a big family dinner, I believe it was my Aunt Sarah's twenty-fifth wedding anniversary or something like that. We all got together in my grandmother's house. There was a long table – I would guess seating perhaps twenty people altogether. I was the youngest person there. There were also my brother and four or five cousins, but they were all at least six or eight years older than I was. At the time I was about six years old.

My grandmother had set the table beautifully with her fanciest linen, her finest china and crystal. Though I had to sit on a pillow in order to reach the proper height, I had the same place setting in front of me as all the others. There was one small difference, however. There was a beautiful thick slice of Swiss cheese on my plate. Nobody else had it. My grandmother said, "Gerdchen, I know how much you like to eat cheese." She was right. I did love cheese and still do.

"I bought this special slice of cheese just for you, so you could eat it before we start our dinner."

"Thank you, grandmother," I said. I took the slice and bit into it. Imagine my horror, anguish and anger when I found out that they had played a joke on me. That was no cheese, it was a piece of soap in the form of cheese. I felt cheated and humiliated and I started crying. Everyone else around the table, including my parents, laughed. They thought it was very funny. As I said, child psychology was not a strong suit.

I was able to read pretty well from the time I was five years old. By the time I was six, I read the interesting parts of the newspaper every day and by the time I was seven I was a regular patron of the local branch of our public library. The librarian was a lovely young woman. She looked very much like Marian the librarian from the Music Man. They could have patterned Marian after her.

I got all of my books from the so-called Section for Young Readers, but I was becoming pretty bored with that. One day, as I was checking out a book, the librarian said to me, "Gerhard, I see that you are such a good reader. May I recommend something else to you? Have you ever read any of the foreign authors? There are some I can recommend very much."

"Like what, for instance?" I asked.

"The first I would recommend is Mark Twain. He has two books, Tom Sawyer and Huckleberry Finn that I think you would enjoy very much."

So I checked them out. I really liked them. I thought Mark Twain was the most wonderful writer I had ever read. I also read The Prince and the Pauper. The next thing I read was his Sketchbook which has all kinds of interesting stories. There was another Mark Twain story I read later. I'll tell you about that.

Then the librarian turned me on to Jules Verne. I absolutely devoured every one of his books. From In 80 Days Around the World to Voyage to the Center of the Earth, From the Earth to the Moon, and all the others. What an imagination, I thought, and I was convinced that many of the things that Jules Verne wrote about would become reality during my lifetime. Some of the most unbelievable ones have indeed become reality, such as his story about the voyage to the moon.

Finally, the librarian recommended that I read Charles Dickens. That was already a little more difficult because of the many different characters and the conditions of Dickens's England, which were totally strange to me. I read Oliver Twist, David Copperfield, The Pickwick Papers, and a few others. Reading these novels gave me a view of a wonderful new world.

When I was seven years old, even though times were pretty tough, my parents sent me to a *Kinderheim*, a youth home, in Norderney, which is a beautiful island off the North Sea coast of Germany. It was a Jewish institution. I enjoyed the sea, swimming in the ocean, and getting to know all the animals that I had never seen before, though I'd heard about them, such as the starfish and most fascinating of all, the jellyfish. I learned how to eat shrimp. It was something totally new and, of course, I did not realize that it was not kosher.

I still love shrimp today. My mother, in whose universe of abominations the shrimp played no role at all, never told me otherwise.

What I didn't like so much was that it was an institutional arrangement almost like a benevolent prison. There was a section for boys and a separate one for girls. We were about sixty boys and all of us slept in one very large hall, thirty beds on each side. At the end of the room there was a big window behind which was the office of the supervisor, a lady who would sit there all night long, awake I suppose, watching us to be sure we were not doing anything that we should not be doing. The girls had a similar arrangement.

I made many friends and mostly had a good time.

I was so enchanted by the ocean and by the life in Norderney that I composed a poem, the first stanza of which went, in German, as follows:

> *Die Wogen rauschen laut und wild,*
> *Es ist ein malerisches Bild.*
> *Sie wälzen sich dem Strande zu*
> *Und haben weder Rast noch Ruh.*

Obviously, since I was only seven years old there was not much depth to it. I was intent only that it should rhyme. It did. The translation of the first few lines states approximately that the waves thunder loud and wild and are a picturesque thing to behold. They come toward the coast and never seem to rest, etc., etc.

I recited it at the farewell party, got much applause, and won some kind of a prize.

The next year, my parents wanted to send me to the same home, but I demurred. I told them that, yes, I wanted to go back to Norderney, but to some place that was smaller and not so regimented. Even though it was more expensive, my parents acceded and I went to another Jewish home in Norderney, a much smaller one than the one of the previous year. In this one, I shared a room with just two other boys. There were not more than perhaps twenty-five kids in the whole home – about half of them boys and half of them girls.

There was one girl, Vera Vogel, who was about a year or two older than I. Vera was tall and (what I considered) statuesque; she had straight black hair and was, I thought, very beautiful. We became great friends. I remained good friends with her until I finally left Germany. During the months and years in which I spent much time alone at home and had interesting wrestling matches with Eva Siegler and Cilly Steinfeld, (about whom I shall tell you later), Vera also came to visit me quite often. We were always pals. I realize later that she would have been the one who would have been most amenable to any sexual exploration, but somehow it never occurred to me, although it did perhaps to her, I later supposed. Her father had a chain of kosher butcher shops. Every time she came to visit she would bring some frankfurters that we would cook and eat.

Knowing how fond I was of Mark Twain, she brought me a beautiful book one time (in German, of course) The Man That Corrupted Hadleyburg. This is one of Mark Twain's lesser known but really exquisite little stories. I thoroughly enjoyed it. I still have the book.

From about the age of four, I looked forward very much to starting school. I could read pretty well by the time I was five years old and I thought that it would be great fun to learn to read better and to learn about numbers in an organized environment. Until then I had only learned to read from what my brother and my mother had taught me. I was a good student, however.

The school year in Germany started in April. There was no kindergarten. So, at the age of six, we started right away in the first grade. Here's how the system worked: Grade school had eight grades – from the first grade to the eighth grade. After the fourth grade, however, one could make a choice – either to continue in the grade school for another four years or go to a *Gymnasium* (for boys) or a *Lyceum* (for girls). The first four years, however, were the same for all. The concept of private schools barely existed. Later, when it became very difficult for Jews in Germany, there were special private schools for Jews in Berlin and, I believe, in other cities also. When I began school in 1926, that was not a problem.

The municipal authorities, in their wisdom, had established a special experiment in our school district, namely, a school for Catholic children only. To the best of my knowledge, it was the only such school in the whole city. Even though the emphasis was on Catholicism, it was not a parochial school. It was a public school. Attendance in that school was voluntary for Catholic children. If their parents wished, they could also go to the other school in our school district.

And then, by some kind of peculiar logic, the authorities decided to establish a special class only for Jewish children in that Catholic school. That attendance was also voluntary. My parents decided to put me in that school and in that class. I would say that the ratio of Catholic children to Jewish children in the school was about 4 to1. The experiment, for no good reason that I knew of, was abolished after three years. The school was converted to a fully Catholic one. There was one other thing. There were both boys and girls in the Jewish class, but the Catholic part of the school was only for boys. Strange!

For months before I started school my mother had admonished me to sit still, not to fidget, to be good, to pay attention to the teacher, not to talk back and to follow instructions, and by all means to avoid the worst fate of all, namely being put in the corner. That was the accepted punishment for serious misbehavior. Of course, it didn't occur to me that I would do anything that would put me in that dreaded corner.

On the first day of school, my mother took me to the front gate. She kissed me goodbye and wished me luck. She admonished me once again to be good. She told me that she would pick me up after school, which on this first day lasted only 30 minutes.

For the first time, all by myself, I timidly and hesitantly entered the classroom that had been assigned and looked at all the strange faces, boys and girls. There were about thirty of us. I didn't know a single person.

A few minutes later a tall and somewhat bony woman entered the room. I noticed that she had no discernible bosom. As my parents had told me to do, I and all the other children stood up. She said, "Sit down, children."

Then she asked, "Can any of you read?" and a few raised their hands. She said, "My name is Fräulein Phillips," and she put the word Phillips in block letters on the blackboard. "I'm not going to be your regular teacher," she said, "only for the first few days until a homeroom teacher, a Jewish teacher, will be assigned to you."

"But right now, I'd like to see how smart you kids are."

"How many ears do you have?" she asked.

All thirty of us grabbed our earlobes and said, "Two."

"Very good," she said. "How many eyes do you have?"

Again, all of us pointed to our eyes and said, "Two."

"I can see this is a very smart class. We shall try a few more. How many hands do you have?"

We all raised our hands and said, "Two."

"Very good," Fräulein Phillips said. "This seems to be a very smart class. O.K.," she said, "one more. How many feet do you have?"

All the kids said "two," but I was not sure exactly what she wanted and put my feet on the desk and pointed to them and said, "Two."

Her back stiffened. Her face became a frozen mask. She pointed at me. She said, *"Wie heisst du?"* ("What is your name?")

I knew that I was in trouble, but I didn't know why. "Gerhard Joffe," I said.

"Komm mal her," ("Come here.") she said.

That was awful. I had done something wrong, and I had no idea what it was. She said, "You will stand now in the corner," and she pointed to the corner next to her desk. I was speechless, dumbfounded, and horrified. The worst possible fate of having to stand in the corner had befallen me within the first five minutes of my school career.

I was crying and sobbing. After about two or three minutes I half turned around and said, "Fräulein Phillips, how long do I have to stand in the corner?"

And she said, *"Bis du manierlich bist."* ("Until you are mannerly.")

I had absolutely no idea what *manierlich* (mannerly) was. It was a word I hadn't heard before. I wanted to be *manierlich* in the worst possible way, in order to be released from that horrible corner, but I didn't know how to go about it. So I stood crying in that corner the whole time until, about twenty minutes later, I was released by the bell. It was the worst day in my young life. I was totally shaken. My mother waited for me at the schoolhouse door. When she saw me there she knew that something was very wrong.

"How did it go, darling?" she asked.

"Mutti, I had to stand in the corner the whole time," I said crying.

"Why?" she asked.

In tears, I explained to her what had happened. She was astonished, and said, "I am certainly glad that this dreadful woman is not going to be your teacher. She is the dumbest person I've ever heard about."

My mother and her four sisters – she is the second youngest and the third from the left.
Each of the girls got a dowry of 20,000 gold marks. But my father wound up with zilch.

This is my third grade class – only Jewish children – in a Berlin public school. Can you find me? I am in the fourth row, the second from the right.

I was so happy that she agreed with me and that she didn't scold me for my "unmannerly" behavior.

But my troubles weren't over. That day, which I had looked forward to for months as one of the happiest in my young life, turned out to be one of the worst. It was a custom in Germany, and I think it is still a custom there today, that a child, on his first day of school, receives a so-called *Zuckertüte*; this is really a long, cardboard cone, which was supposed to be filled with candy to the very top. Times were pretty hard in Germany and I didn't get too much candy, so I had been looking forward to that day and to the *Zuckertüte*, and had fantasized about it for months. Sure enough, there was my mother with the *Zuckertüte* in her hand. I wanted to grab it right away. "Just a minute, darling," she said, "we have to take your photograph first."

So we went to the square next to our home, the square on which the Apostle Paulus Church stood, and which, just like the *Kleist Park*, had a permanent photographer. I posed rather unhappy and grim-looking, with the *Zuckertüte* in my hand, and had the picture taken. As soon as that was over, I reached into the *Zuckertüte* for my first piece of candy. It was delicious. But then I noticed with horror that the cone, instead of being filled with candy from top to bottom, was filled mostly with shredded paper and that there was only a very thin layer of candy at the top – not more than two pieces deep. I was shattered; all of my great illusions had been destroyed. Can you imagine what this meant to a little boy – first the terrible scene on his first day of school, of having to spend all the time in the corner and crying, and then this great disappointment with the *Zuckertüte*! It was just awful.

There is a happy sequel to this however and I must now fast-forward about fifty years.

We had a German friend by the name of Sylvia. She was the third (or fourth) wife of a psychologist friend of ours. One day, when we were exchanging old memories, I told her this story. She took notice but didn't say anything. About three months later she had to go to Germany on a family visit. When she came back she brought me a brand-new *Zuckertüte*. It was beautiful. It was blue and it had a net with a string on top so things wouldn't fall out. The cone was filled from top to bottom with the most delicious candy and with little toys. Even though I was, by that time, over sixty years old, I thought that it was the most thoughtful present I had ever received. Her sweet and tender thoughtfulness and the gift itself went very far to nearly assuage the unhappiness of that dreadful day.

My Uncle Max Hirsch and my Aunt Sarah had three children. The oldest was Erich, who was about twenty years older than I. My mother treated him more as a cousin than a nephew, because he wasn't that much younger than she.

Erich was very talented. He effectively ran his father's business and brought it to a higher level of success. When he was younger he had been a member of *Blau-Weiss* (Blue-White), the first Zionist youth organization. I admired him and learned a lot from him.

He was married to a charming woman, Mia. She was the assistant to a theater impresario and often gave me tickets to shows in which she thought I would be interested – and which she thought to be suitable for me. They had no children. But they had a terrier by the name of Schnappsy, a very talented dog, which they treated like a child. I loved that dog.

Edith was Erich's younger sister. She was a tall, elegant woman, engaged to be married. Two months before the wedding, it turned out that her intended had tuberculosis and the wedding was canceled. It was a great family tragedy. There was another sister, Steffie. She had the reputation of being somewhat of a *femme fatale*. I always thought that the reputation might have been justified.

The whole family Hirsch wound up in Buenos Aires. Erich and Mia had done something very daring. The Nazis, and I'll have more to say about that, had totally forbidden anyone to take jewels or anything of value out of the country. The penalties were terrible: concentration camp if you were lucky and death if you were not. Erich had the enormous daring of hiding three large diamonds in a tube of toothpaste and thus smuggling them out of Germany. He turned them into cash as soon as he arrived Buenos Aires. That money enabled him to open an elegant and prosperous business in Calle Florida, the main shopping street in Buenos Aires. Its name was "Sporting Stepper." He did very well. Unfortunately, he died of heart disease at just under fifty years of age.

Until I went to school, I spent a lot of time with my mother. One day I asked, "Mutti, where do babies come from?" She was prepared for that.

She said, "When mothers and fathers love each other very much the baby grows inside the mother."

I thought about this splendid explanation and it sufficed for a quite a few years. The mechanics of how love could put the baby inside the mother did not interest me at the time.

My mother liked to take a nap every afternoon and I was admonished not to wake her up under any circumstances. One day, I believe I was looking for a toy, I woke her up to ask her if she had seen it. She didn't get really angry with me, but she admonished me severely.

"The sleep of a mother is sacred," she said. I thought she overstated that a little bit, but I let it go. "Let me tell you a little story," she continued. "My father told me this story."

> "My grandfather took an afternoon nap every day. One day, while he was asleep, a man came to the door with a very important business proposition that could have made my grandfather rich. He told my father to wake him up; he said it was very important. My father told him that the sleep of a parent was sacred and he could not wake him up. The man left. When my grandfather awakened, my father told him what had happened and my grandfather praised him for being such a good son and for not having wakened him."

I thought it was the dumbest story I had ever heard, that both my grandfather and my great-grandfather were not very smart having let a great business opportunity go by because somebody took a nap. My mother did not agree with my analysis.

There were two things that she really detested, that she could not abide and that she was forcefully against: long-distance telephone calls and taxis. The only exceptions for long-distance calls that she would make would be on selected occasions when she called my Aunt Martha in Cologne or my Aunt Rosa in Blankenburg; she made sure that no long-distance call lasted for more than three minutes, the minimum time billed by the German telephone service.

As to taxicabs, no matter what the urgency of the occasion, we would always take the streetcar. In addition to my earliest recollection of riding in a taxicab, cradled in my mother's arms, there were only three other occasions and I shall talk about those later.

But even the streetcar, which cost ten *pfennig*, could be a matter of some argument. Winters in Berlin could be awfully cold. There were many times when the weather was 30 degrees Fahrenheit below zero or colder. Regardless of the weather, I had to walk to school about six blocks away. I remember only one occasion, when there was about three feet of snow on the ground, that she gave me ten *pfennig* to take the streetcar to school – and that was after some discussion.

There were two things about which she admonished me severely – in fact, she made me promise about them, and they were – One: Never to eat *tref* (*tref* is that which is not kosher); and, Two: Never to marry a *shiksa*. For those who don't know, a *shiksa* is a non-Jewish woman. Neither of the two seemed to be severe restrictions, and I had no problem promising to follow her admonitions – I was six years old. I had never eaten anything that was not kosher and had no particular desire to do so. I had no desire to emulate my father's peculiar predilection for the occasional "treat" of smoked ham. My mother's admonition regarding not eating *tref* food made such a strong impression on me that, even today, I won't eat pork. It has absolutely no religious connotation for me; it is just (to quote Leviticus) an abomination, as far as I am concerned. No question: My mother implanted that abhorrence in me. This has an interesting sequel and I will tell you about it later in this story.

But there is another aspect of kosher that my mother never dealt with. As far as she, and therefore I, was concerned, only pork was not kosher. But like most everyone else in Berlin, my mother had never seen or barely heard of other "abominations," such as lobster or shrimp or caviar, eels or any other such things. All of those are not kosher, but they played no role in my mother's gastronomical universe. While even today I can't make myself eat pork, I have no problem at all eating all those other "forbidden" things, because my mother never told me about them and that they were truly abominations and forbidden.

As far as not marrying a *shiksa*, I didn't think of that as a severe restriction. In the first place I was, at the age of six, not giving much thought to marriage. I had never known a Jewish man who was married to a gentile woman, so I didn't think that this was a problem at all and I had no trouble giving my mother the assurance that I would follow her admonition. As it turned out, I broke that "promise."

My Uncle Max Hirsch, the husband of Aunt Sarah, was a sourpuss and a curmudgeon. I don't think I ever saw him smile or heard him say a kind word to me. Whenever he saw me he would say, "Here comes my little *retseach* (which was in contrast to the big *retseach*, his partner Mr. Zander). I always thought that *retseach* meant a pain in the butt or something like that and I am pretty sure that's the way Uncle Max meant it. But perhaps he didn't know that *retseach* is the word for murderer in Hebrew. I am sure he didn't mean that, however an unpleasant person he was.

One time I was alone with Aunt Martha in Cologne. It was the time we had gone to the movies on Yom Kippur. My mother had returned to Berlin because of some emergency – I believe my brother had fallen ill or something like that. So, when my vacation time was up. I had to return to Berlin by myself. My aunt took me to the station and put me on the express train to Berlin. But she didn't just put me on the train. She entrusted me to the matron on the train, the woman who took care of the restrooms and other such matters. Aunt Martha gave her a nice tip and told her not to leave me out of her sight, to take care of me. And, she told me that under no circumstances was I to move from the compartment assigned to the employees of the train, except to go to the bathroom. In addition to the matron, there was a conductor, an assistant conductor, and a handyman. The trip from Cologne to Berlin was about six hours on the express train.

After about two hours, the conductor returned from his rounds to the compartment and smoked a cigarette. He looked at me and said, "Gerhard, how would you like for me to take you to the locomotive and see how it works?"

I was fascinated by the exhilarating prospect of visiting the locomotive. To see the engineer and the fireman at work was an adventure totally beyond my imagining. None of my friends had ever done anything remotely like that and I didn't think that anybody ever would. I would be a sensation when I told my friends and classmates about it. But I remembered that I had promised my aunt not to move from the compartment, except to go to the bathroom and not let anybody talk me into going anyplace else. I told the conductor, "I'm very sorry, sir, but my aunt told me not to move from the compartment."

"Gerhard," he said, "Your aunt meant that you should not go with any strangers, but she entrusted you to us and if I want to take you to the see the locomotive you can go with me and I am sure she wouldn't mind.

I was incredibly tempted. At the end I said, "No, I am very sorry. I have to obey my aunt. I won't go."

I fretted about my decision, which was an unusual one for me – I still don't understand what made me be that obedient. For the rest of the trip I thought about telling the conductor that I had changed my mind, but I did not have the courage to do that. At the end of the trip, my mother was waiting for me at the station. I said, "Mutti, just a minute, I want to look at the locomotive."

"What for?" she said.

"I just want to look at it," I said and then I walked forward to the locomotive and looked at the beautiful sleek engine and at the engineer and at the fireman, who were still at their stations. Had I not been such a fool, I could have been with them for much of the trip and could have had a real adventure. I must say that I regretted my decision to obey my aunt for several years. I thought I had done a really dumb thing, missed a wonderful adventure.

Despite my very unpromising first day of school, and my unpleasant experience with Fräulein Phillips, I really enjoyed grade school very much.

Before I go on, perhaps I should explain how, at least in my day, schools in Germany worked:

Grade school had eight grades. If one completed those grades, one would have a very good education, although it would not involve foreign languages and math beyond basic algebra. Having completed those eight grades would qualify one for blue-collar work or for anything else not involving academia.

After four years, however, boys had the option of going to a *Gymnasium* and girls the option to go to a *Lyceum*. *Gymnasium* consisted of nine grades. After six years of *Gymnasium*, one would get a certificate of *Mittlere Reife* which means "middle maturity." That level also had the peculiar German word of *Einjähriges* which literally means "one yearer." This term was left over from the German Empire which ended with its defeat in World War I in 1918. *Einjäehriges* meant that a person with that degree of education had to serve only one year in the army, instead of two, and was entitled to become a noncommissioned officer. I understand that this term is still used, even today. I have asked several people, but nobody knows where it came from.

After nine years of *Gymnasium*, one would make the so-called *Abitur*, which was the final high school examination and which entitled one to enter a university anywhere in the country.

I enjoyed grade school very much, especially my teacher Herr Crain, who was truly a teacher, mentor, and friend to all of his students. Every one of us (about 26 boys and 10 girls) really loved him and his wife. They were wonderful people.

My best friends – they remained my best friends all through high school, were Heinz Vogel, Horst Peck, and Tommy Dyck. Under the German system, at least the system that was in vogue at the time, students were ranked by performance at the end of each year. I was always in competition with Heinz Vogel. Invariably, he was always number one and I was always number two. Some years I thought I might replace him as number one, but I never did.

The boys in my class were engaged in daily fights with the Catholic boys of the other classes in our grade. The fights were not really violent. They consisted of the smaller boys (like myself) riding piggy back on the bigger boys and the purpose of the fights was to pull the boys of the other team down. There was no violence and I don't think there was any grudge or hatred or anti-Semitism or anything like that involved. We were just rivals. Even though I was one of the smallest, I was the undisputed leader of our class team.

After that had been going on for quite some time, the principal decided to take exception to it. He called me to his office, which was a very big deal. He told me that I was the one who caused all the fighting in the schoolyard. He gave me a note to give to my father, asking him to come to the school at a certain date. In those days, being asked to come to the school for a conference about one's child was an unusual and important matter. Both my father and my mother were concerned about my misbehavior that made such a visit necessary.

On the appointed day, at the appointed hour, my father and I, both of us in somber anticipation and with great trepidation, went to the principal's office. My father was asked to sit down and I was kept standing.

"Herr Joffe, your son is the *Rädelsführer,* the gang leader of his class and the cause for constant fighting in the schoolyard. I shall have to punish him, and I shall administer ten strokes with the cane."

There wasn't very much my father could do about this. He said, in a rather noncommittal tone, "Herr Direktor, he is a good boy, please don't be too harsh on him." I had hoped that he would be a better and more forceful advocate for me, but I also realized that there wasn't really anything he could do to ameliorate my fate.

The principal took little note of my father's implied request for mercy. He told me to take a stool, step on that stool and look on the top of the closet that stood in the corner of the room. "Do you see those five canes on top of the closet?" he asked.

"Yes, sir, I do," I answered.

"Please pick them up and give them to me."

I did as I was told and gave him the five canes. He looked at them with the eye of a connoisseur and then he tested each one of them by whipping it through the air. They all looked the same to me and sounded the same but, apparently, he detected some small variances. He listened to the sound of the canes, just as I imagined a concertmaster of a great orchestra would listen to the sounds of several fine violins that had been brought to him for approval. He picked up cane number two and told me to lean over the chair. Mercifully, he did not ask me to take off my pants, which he could have done, I suppose. That would have added to my humiliation and also would have been a whole lot more painful. He administered ten hard blows to my buttocks. It was very painful, but I did not give him the satisfaction of crying out or weeping tears. My father sat stone-faced and didn't say a word. When the principal was finished with the procedure, he said to me, "Let this be a lesson to you, Gerhard."

I told him that it would be, but I wasn't entirely sure what the lesson was. In any case, the fights in the schoolyard continued.

None of the boys in our class (and none of the girls either, but we really were not too interested in them), was going to continue in the grade school beyond the fourth grade. Most of us boys were going to continue at the *Hohenzollern Gymnasium,* which was right across the street from the grade school. About a month before the end of the school year, Herr Crain sent us, in groups of four, across the street to introduce ourselves to the principal of the *Gymnasium*. He had the unusual name of Herr Warmbier, which means in German just what it sounds like, the same as in English, namely "warm beer."

Herr Warmbier, whom we had known by sight for years, was a man for whom we had enormous respect, of course. He was a classical scholar and had been principal of the school for many years. He was close to retirement at the time we were to enter the *Gymnasium*. He was tall, corpulent, and had a jowly face.

We four friends – Heinz Vogel, Horst Peck, Tommy Dyck, and I – went to visit Herr Warmbier as a group. We were dressed in our best clothes, consisting of short pants and clean white shirts. My mother had paid special attention that morning that my fingernails were scrubbed, that my ears were free of debris, and that my neck was clean. Those were the body parts to which she paid the closest attention.

We went across the street to the *Gymnasium* and walked up the two floors to Principal Warmbier's office. We knocked on the door. He said, "Come in, boys," and we entered. The four of us stood in front of Herr Warmbier's desk; we were nervous and most uncomfortable.

As we had been instructed, we stood with our feet together and with our hands clasped behind our backs. Herr Crain had sternly admonished us not to speak unless spoken to, and to answer questions firmly and briefly.

Herr Warmbier seemed to be a very kindly person. He really seemed to try to put us at ease. He spoke to us in generalities about the value of a good education and how the *Hohenzollern Gymnasium* was going to provide it, and how he expected us to be diligent in our studies, to be obedient to our teachers, and to comport ourselves in conformance with the traditions of the *Gymnasium*. We all nodded in agreement. Then he kindly dismissed us. He hadn't asked any questions. We were relieved.

While we were standing in front of his desk, about twenty feet away, I began to notice a peculiar odor which seemed to emanate from Horst Peck. It was not difficult to identify and I assumed that in his excitement and apprehension Horst had farted. Of course, it was not the thing to do, but it was understandable under the stressful circumstances. When we were outside the office, Horst said, "Gerhard, something terrible has happened."

I asked, "What has happened?"

He said, "I shit in my pants."

"You did what?" I asked.

"Yes, I shit in my pants. What should I do?

I really didn't know what to do either. Obviously, it was something totally new in our experience. I didn't know what I would have done under the circumstances. The way Horst solved his problem and the only thing he could think of doing was to take off his pants and his underpants. He then left the loaded underpants in front of Herr Warmbier's office and put his pants back on. He didn't know what else to do. He was in panic and none of us knew what and how to advise him. Of course, the proper advice would have been to tell him to go to the toilet to dispose of the loaded underpants. But it really didn't occur to us and, in any case, we didn't know where the toilet was. Most of all, we wanted to get the hell out of there as fast as we could. So he did what he did and we left hurriedly.

What worried me most was that Herr Warmbier, who inevitably would have found this "surprise" in front of his office, would not know which of the four of us had left that present. I thought of writing him a letter telling him that it was not I who had done it but I concluded that would not be fair. In any case, for the two years before his retirement, every time Herr Warmbier met me in the hall, he looked me in the eye and I always imagined that he asked himself, "Is he the one?" I wanted to shake my head and say, "Not me," but I never did.

The grades in German high schools (*Gymnasiums*) had peculiar names, mixtures of Latin and German. The first grade (the fifth school year) was the *Sexta*, the second grade was *Quinta*, and the third was *Quarta*; the fourth and fifth grades were *Untertertia* and *Obertertia*, respectively. The sixth and seventh grades were *Untersekunda* and *Obersekunda*, respectively. And the final two grades, the eighth and ninth, were *Unterprima* and *Oberprima*.

Most students wore the distinctive caps corresponding to their grade. Students in the first three grades, *Sexta, Quinta,* and *Quarta*, wore a blue velveteen cap. Students of the second three grades, *Untertertia* through *Untersekunda* had bright red cloth caps. The last three grades, *Obersekunda* through *Oberprima* wore the coveted white satin caps. The lowest grade in each of these three groups had a blue-white band around the cap, the second grade of each group had a blue-red band, and the third, a blue-yellow band. There were further distinctions. Those who went to a humanistic *Gymnasium*, a school emphasizing the classics and ancient languages, such as Latin and Greek, had a gold metallic border abound the cap. Those who went to a "realistic:" *Gymnasium*, with emphasis on modern languages math, and natural sciences, had a silver band around the cap. Finally, a student had a silver star on the right side of his cap for each modern language that he took and a gold star for each ancient language.

If you met another student on the street you could immediately tell what grade he was in, what kind of school he went to, and how many languages he took. It was quite a system. I must admit that the enthusiasm for the caps, which was almost universal in the lower grades, diminished as the years passed on.

In high school, I was thrown together for the first time with gentile boys. Until then all of my schoolmates had been Jewish. In the first grade of the *Gymnasium* (the *Sexta*) there were about thirty boys, ten of whom, classmates from grade school, were Jewish. In the early 1930's, even though the Nazis were already making a lot of noise in Germany, there was no trouble at all between the Jewish and the gentile boys. We did, however, not fraternize much and kept mostly to ourselves. Of course, we all sat together and had no problems. In looking back, I must say that, even until the very end when the Nazis were in government and anti-Semitism was the official policy, there were never any problems between the Jewish boys and the gentile boys in school.

Most of that, I am quite sure, was because, at least in the earlier days, the Nazis acted less brutally in Berlin – a city open to visitors and inspection by journalists from all over the world. They stepped very heavily in the rest of the country – especially in smaller towns, where dreadful brutalities against Jews started quite early.

I had no close gentile friends and was only invited twice to birthday parties of gentile classmates. Paul Pfeiffer invited me to his birthday party once – I believe when we were eleven years old. His mother served little ham sandwiches for refreshments. She said to me, "Gerhard, I know you don't eat ham, so I prepared some cheese sandwiches for you." She was a nice lady. I thought then and still think now that it was very thoughtful and considerate gesture of her.

Another birthday that is indelible in my mind was that of my friend Hans Guttmann. I believe we were twelve years old. He lived pretty much at the other end of Berlin and I had to take the #3 streetcar, which was called "*Der grosse Ring*" (the Big Circle) – which ran all around the periphery of western Berlin. It was a long trip to Hans's house. I took a nice present. There were about twenty kids there, all boys. We sat around a long table, on which Frau Guttmann had placed some very nice refreshments – cake, punch, ice cream and other good things. We made jokes, sang songs, played games, and had a very good time. For some reason, attention was focused on me. I was telling a good joke and everyone laughed. In doing so I rocked my chair back and forth and I suddenly lost balance and fell backwards. I grabbed onto the tablecloth for stability, but of course in vain. I pulled down the tablecloth and with it the cake, the ice cream, the punch, and several plates, all of which broke on the floor. To make things worse, I fell backward into Frau Guttmann's china closet, which was right behind me. Fortunately, I did not break any of her knick-knacks or figurines in the cabinet, but I did break the glass front. That was a terrible social situation, probably the worst I had found myself in up to that time.

Considering the circumstances, Frau Guttmann was very nice. She helped me get off the floor, wiped some ice cream off me and said, "I know you feel very bad about this, Gerhard. Maybe you should go home."

I was devastated and I did leave. I waited for the #3 streetcar and went the long way home. I told my mother about it. She called Frau Guttmann and asked her what she could do to make amends and restitution. Frau Guttmann told her not to worry, to forget it. I thought both women were very cool. I was proud of my mother, but I don't remember ever being invited to Hans Guttmann's house again.

The first foreign language we took, starting in the *Sexta*, was English. Somewhat in contrast to what happens in the United States, in Germany you were actually expected to be able to speak and write the foreign language after you had been learning it for a year or two. I remember the very first page of my first English book. It had a little poem as follows:

> Work while you work and play while you play,
> That is the way to be cheerful and gay.
> All that you do, do with your might,
> Things done by halves are never done right.

Strange as this may sound, I have been trying to make this simple doggerel one of my mottos all of my life.

In the Gymnasium, school was six days a week, Monday through Saturday, from 8 a.m. until 2:30 p.m. Each class lasted 50 minutes. There were ten minutes between classes and a 30-minute recess between the fifth and sixth class. We were expected to do at least three hours of homework every day.

The main emphasis was on the German language, rhetoric, composition, history (mostly German), and geography. Three times a week we had a gym class and twice a week we had music and drawing. It was a very full schedule.

In my second year (*Quinta*), English was taught by a retired German naval officer. Our textbook contained only stories of German naval battles of the First World War in which, invariably of course, the German Navy prevailed over the "perfidious" British. It was unusual, but by the time we got through with the year I believe I knew the English word for every part of a warship and every kind of ordnance and naval weaponry.

All of us knew the English word "people" even before we started with the language, and all of us were anxiously waiting for the teacher to pronounce it for the first time. The reason for our interest was that the word "people" means penis in German and is not a word that we were supposed to be using at home, of course, or in polite society. I had a feeling that our teacher delayed as long as possible to pronounce the fateful word because he knew what hilarity it would occasion. He had to go through that every year.

And finally, perhaps three or four months into the school year, we inevitably came across the word in a story, he said, "O.K., boys, here it comes. Laugh all you want but that's what they say in England and in America and in many others parts of the world where English is spoken. So please get your laughter out of your system and let's get on with our work."

Beginning with the third year (*Quarta*), our English teacher was a Herr Kuskopp. He was one of the most unusual people I had met until that time and perhaps ever since. By that time, we were pretty knowledgeable in English and could read and understand almost anything except perhaps the most difficult writing. Herr Kuskopp was not satisfied with English as presented in the standard textbook. He made up his own textbook, which he distributed to us. It consisted of short stories of his own composition, all of which, without exception, had terrible endings, resulting in death, dismemberment, or disfigurement for one or several of the protagonists.

Two stories stick in my mind, which I shall summarize so as to convey the flavor of the man and his stories.

The first one was about a little boy who played in the attic of his home and found an old painting that was stashed away. He took some paint and splashed it on top of that painting. When he didn't like what he had done, he took his pocketknife and sliced the painting up. A few weeks later an art connoisseur came to visit the house and for some reason or other headed up to the attic, where he spotted the painting that the boy had painted over and then slashed with his knife.

"Oh good Lord," the connoisseur said. "This is a genuine Franz Hals. If it had not been painted over and slashed, it would be worth at least two million *marks*. Now it is worthless."

When the father heard this he took a knife and stabbed his son to death. Obviously a very satisfying story for 11-year old boys.

The other story that I remember was this:

The employee of a commercial firm went to the bank for a transaction in which he was to receive 100 *marks*. After he left the window, he noticed that the clerk had erroneously given him 1,000 *marks*, instead of 100 *marks*. He want back to the window and said, "Excuse me, you made a mistake. You gave me 1,000 *marks* instead of 100 *marks*."

"Impossible," the teller told him. "We don't make any mistakes at the Deutsche Bank. I gave you the right amount of money. Now go away!"

"No," the man said. "Here are the 1,000 *marks*. Don't you see it?"

"Impossible," the teller said. "You brought it yourself. I gave you the right amount."

"O.K.," the man said and turned around and prepared to leave the bank. At that moment he heard a gun shot. He turned around and saw to his horror that the teller had shot himself because he knew that he had committed the error, had been unwilling to admit it, and would have to come up with the missing cash.

You get the idea; there were scores of grim stories just like that, many of them even worse.

We were so intrigued by Herr Kuskopp that we decided to visit him at his home. It was a most unusual thing to do. It was Horst Peck's idea, of course. He always came up with adventurous things like that to do. We knew where he lived and we went to his house one Saturday afternoon. Herr Kuskopp was surprised to see us, of course, but as always, he was most cordial and invited us to come in. He was a bachelor and, as far as we knew, he was straight, although that wasn't much of a concept to us at the time.

The furnishings in this apartment were unusual, to say the least. There were at least eight or ten human skulls around the house, on shelves and bookcases and on tables, and one full skeleton in the living room. The most unusual thing was his bedroom. In addition to the three or four skulls that he had around in various locations, he had, at the foot of his bed, a frame in the form of a cross. The cross was "dressed" in a formal evening coat with the crosspiece serving for the arms. There were white gloves at the ends. The costume included a white shirt front, on which Herr Kuskopp had meticulously drawn about one hundred small black gallows. There was a formal white bow tie, of course. The whole thing was topped off by a skull with a black top hat. There were two red bulbs in the eye sockets of the skull. Herr Kuskopp closed the door. It was pitch dark. Then he operated a switch by his bedside and the red lights in the eye sockets flashed off and on. It was the most scary and eerie thing that we had ever seen. That's how Herr Kuskopp felt comfortable and that's how he went to sleep. He certainly was an oddball. What a character!

Each of us boys kept a so-called friendship album in which, one for each page, friends and teachers would put their sentiments. I do not have the book any more and I don't remember any of the things in that book, except what Herr Kuskopp put. He quoted from Shakespeare's <u>Julius Caesar</u> as follows:

> There is a tide in the affairs of men,
> Which, taken at the flood, leads on to fortune.
> Omitted, all the voyage of their life
> Is bound in shallows and in miseries.

I was very impressed by that and took it seriously and have made it one of my guiding thoughts all of my life – I believe successfully so.

I did not realize until much later that this advice that Brutus gave Cassius turned out to have been very poor. They proceeded as Brutus had advised, and both of them, Brutus and Cassius, died by their own swords, defeated in the battle of Philippi, which Brutus had urged with his pretty words. But I lived by that motto and it has served me well. Had I been more schooled in Shakespeare and realized how poor that advice was, my life might have been different.

My mother belonged to what seems to have been an informal organization of women, which she called a *Kränzchen*, which literally means, "little wreath."

As best as I can recall, these women met once every week in the home of one of them, and about every other month or so it was my mother's turn to be the hostess. There were about eight or ten women. It was really noisy. Every one of the women brought some sewing or embroidery work with her. They also brought delicious cakes, cookies, and other things to eat. I always was allowed to partake of those. Until I was about five or six years old I was tolerated as I played in the corner of the room in which the event was held. Ultimately, however, I suspect when the gossip got pretty heavy and dealt with sexual peccadilloes, I was ordered out of the room and was told to play someplace else. On one of those occasions, having been banned into my parents' bedroom, I roamed though my father's medicine cabinet and found a beautiful purple-and-blue striped package. It was labeled *Fromms*. It contained balloons, each of them packed in individual small envelopes. I was delighted. I had never seen them before and my parents hadn't told me that they had anything like that. There were three of these balloons in the package. I blew them all up, knotted them to close them, and took them into the *Wohnzimmer*, the living room, where the ladies had their meeting.

My father and my mother in 1937.
Those were already grim times for Jews in Germany.
My father was 52 years old and my mother 47 when this picture was taken.

Here are my parents in 1938 on the day of their silver wedding anniversary. Things were terrible in Germany by then. This was just a few months before *"Kristallnacht"* – the night of the broken glass, when all synagogues and most Jewish businesses in Germany were destroyed.

As I entered with my three balloons, the chattering stopped abruptly and a deadly silence fell over the room. I had no idea why my mother blanched.

For the first time, I found her at a loss for words. When she recovered about ten or fifteen seconds later, she said, "Come here, Gerdchen."

I did. She took a fork and punctured my beautiful balloons and told me to throw them away and go back to play but not to blow up any more balloons. I did as I was told. As soon as I left the room, I could hear boundless laughter from the ladies, as if somebody had told the funniest joke. I didn't understand why I had caused such consternation and then so much laughter with my balloons.

Pesach (Passover) was the yearly big event in our home, as I believe it was in almost all Jewish homes in Berlin during that era and, gratifyingly, still is today also in the United States. In contrast to the customs of the Reformed, we had two seders, on the first and the second nights, which were identical in ritual and performance. As I understand it, the reason for that custom is that the rabbis were never quite sure exactly what the proper date for the holiday was. Therefore, in order to make sure, the seder had to be held on two consecutive evenings. In fact, as I understand it, really orthodox families celebrate, not just the first two days of Passover with a formal seder, but also the last two days. But we did not do that – it was just two nights and that, as far as I was concerned, was almost more than enough.

All vestiges of leavened bread, all vestiges of yeast had to be removed from the house. My mother was very thorough about that. Then, all pots, pans, dishes, silverware, etc. had to be rounded up and put away. A totally separate set of pots, pans, dishes, glasses and silverware would be produced, just for use for use during those eight days. And, of course, it goes without saying that we would eat only matzo for the eight-day holiday period, without a single crumb of bread available. Even my father, who came from a much more relaxed home, would adhere to this commandment.

It is considered a "*mitzvah*," a pious duty, to have guests on this occasion. We always had guests for the seder. There were usually at least six or eight guests for each of the two evenings in addition to the four members of our family. We invited not only friends, but also people who otherwise might not have had access to such a service and to such a festive meal.

I, always the youngest, would recite the traditional four questions. I learned to do that when I was about four years old and did it until the very end when we finally left Germany. The festive table was always decked with my mother's finest damask linen. Inevitably, and without fail, I would every year clumsily spill a glass of red wine on my mother's fine tablecloth. She sort of expected that and was reasonably cheerful and accepting about it. She had some secret recipe involving bleach, soda water and salt, I believe, to remove the wine stain from the tablecloth. For the next occasion it was again as white as freshly fallen snow.

Apart from Passover, there was little home entertaining. We had formal guests maybe two or three times a year. On each such occasion, which involved perhaps eight or ten people, the table again would be set with her fine tablecloth, her best china, and the sterling silverware. My mother and the maid would have been working long and hard all day long on creating this decor and enchanting atmosphere – and fine food, of course.

Being of somewhat mischievous disposition, I took my allowance, went to a magic store, and bought two items with which to mortify and agonize my mother. I used each of them on two separate occasions. The first one was an assortment of copper and brass plates which, when dropped on a wooden floor, sounded exactly as if a whole table setting of china was breaking. One evening, when the festive table for guests was prepared and my mother and the maid were in the kitchen for last touches, I dropped the trick plates on the dinning room floor, then went into the kitchen and said, "Mom, Mom, I'm so sorry. I really didn't mean it. It just happened."

My mother blanched and ran into the dinning room where, of course, she found all of the dishes as they had been. She gave me a good scolding but obviously was vastly relieved. I thought it was very funny. Since, for best effect, I decided I could use this trick only once, I gave the plates to my friend Horst Peck. Horst, you may remember, is the one who had the accident in Herr Warmbier's office and with whom I paid a visit to Herr Kuskopp's home.

Horst used the plates with good effect on his own mother, as he reported to me with great relish.

The second such "trick" was a pretend inkbottle, with a big artificial ink spot that was made of lacquered plastic. The artificial ink spot, which was to be put next to the overturned bottle, was really forbidding in size, perhaps one foot long and four inches wide. It looked perfectly natural. One evening, after my mother had lovingly and skillfully arranged the table for guests, and about fifteen minutes before their arrival, I ran into the kitchen and said, "Mom, Mom, I'm awfully sorry. I didn't mean to do it but I spilled a bottle of ink on your tablecloth."

She ran into the dining room and, sure enough, the tablecloth and the entire table arrangement were ruined by the enormous ink spot on the tablecloth. She was in despair and didn't really know how to remedy the situation at such a late moment. Then I went to the table and with a flourish lifted the bottle and the "ink spot" and everything was wonderful again. She gave an enormous sigh of relief. "You are going to be the death of me, yet," she said. "Why do you play these silly tricks on me! Can't you think of something constructive?"

I thought it was pretty constructive, but I didn't argue with her. The ink bottle and the spot also wound up with Horst who, without doubt, gave his mother a similar near heart attack.

I should tell you about the layout of our apartment. We lived on what the Germans call the second floor (we would call it the third floor) of the building. As in all Jewish homes and until the very end, there was a *mezuzah* at the front door. I saw later how easy it made it for the Nazis to kill us, since all Jewish homes were clearly marked by the *mezuzah*. That was quite in contrast to the Biblical story in which, as the tenth and last plague inflicted on the Egyptians, all their first-borns were slain. But the Angel of Death passed over the dwellings of the Jews, because their homes were clearly marked by the blood of the lamb which had been smeared on their door posts.

But even at the very end, my parents and, as far as I know, nobody else ever removed the *mezuzah* from the front door jamb.

When my parents finally left Germany, my mother (so my father told me – I was no longer there), cast one last tearful look at where she had lived for over twenty-five years and where she had raised her family, and on all the things she was forced to leave behind, had to abandon to the rapacious Nazis. Then, as a very last task, she told my father to take a screwdriver and remove the *mezuzah* from the door. She put it in her purse. The first thing she did, after she arrived in Buenos Aires and moved into the dingy apartment that was to be their home for the next few years, was to affix the *mezuzah* to the front door.

Speaking again of our home in Berlin, the front door of our apartment opened to a hall inside the apartment. There were two rooms to the right off the hall. The first was my parents' bedroom, a nice airy room, which ended in a balcony over the street. The second room was a so-called *Herrenzimmer* which literally means gentlemen's room and which I believe we would call a salon or a parlor. It was really very rarely used, except that after the age of six years, and until then having slept in my parents' bedroom, it was there that I slept. That room, also had windows to the street.

To the left of the hall there was the living/dining room where family life really took place. Its windows opened out to the courtyard. Beyond that room came another hallway. The first room off that was the maid's room, which one reached by climbing eight steps. Therefore, naturally, her bedroom did not have a very high ceiling. Next to that was the bathroom. Then came my brother's room, about 10 x 20 feet, and finally, the kitchen. The kitchen had access to the back stairs. After my brother left Germany, I inherited his room – finally a place of my own.

We had no running hot water and no central heating. The bathroom contained a sink, the bathtub, a hot-water stove, and a toilet. The hot-water stove had to be heated with coal briquettes, and bath day was once a week, on Saturdays. Since hot water was a difficult commodity, and to my constant annoyance, my brother always bathed first and I had to bathe in the same tub in the same water after he got through. It took me a couple of years and several fits to persuade my mother to change this terrible system. She consented at last to let me bathe in clean water, provided I would stoke my own fire for another round of hot water. Of course I was glad to do that.

A tall tiled stove stood unused in the living room during the summer – the very stove where Uncle Siegfried had menaced my mother, but was crackling in operation during the winter. Because there was no separate heat in any of the other rooms – except for whatever was going on in the kitchen – the doors of the living room were left open during the winter so that the heat from the stove could permeate the rest of the house.

The back stairs were important, because once a month or so during the winter months, 200 coal briquettes, each weighing 2 pounds, were delivered to the kitchen, where they were stored under the sink. I was fascinated by the men who did this work. They were big and strong. On each trip they carried 50 briquettes – 100 pounds, in a specially designed box on their backs. There were no elevators, they had to trudge up those back stairs with their heavy loads. When they were through – there were always two of them – my mother would always give each of them a 50-*pfennig* tip and a bottle of beer. That was the custom and that was expected.

There was no refrigeration and no ice. Food was stored in the *Speisekammer*, the "food chamber." It was ventilated by a small window. That was the reason that my mother had to go and buy groceries every day. Nothing could be kept for any length of time, especially, of course, during the summer.

Although it could get very cold in Berlin during the winter, the apartment was always comfortable. The walls were thick and all the windows were double-paned.

Like all families in our middle-class situation, we always had a live-in maid, a so-called *Mädchen vom Lande*, a girl from the country, usually eighteen or twenty years old, who was sent by her parents to the big city to learn city ways, to get some sophistication, and, hopefully, to find a husband. The girls were treated very well. They were considered pretty much like members of the family and they would almost always stay for several years. The maids were usually provided by an agency.

During the worst time of the depression in Germany, coincident pretty much with the depression in the United States, there was one instance in which my mother got a new maid through the agency. Her name, if I recall correctly, was Karen. I don't know what it was about her, but as far as I was concerned, with my nine-year-old sophistication, she looked different from any maid we had had before – in fact, she looked different from any woman I had ever seen. My mother instructed her what to do. She seemed to be accommodating and willing and did everything as she was told. After she was there for about ten days or two weeks, I walked in on her one day in the bathroom, which we shared and which she had not locked. She was peeing standing up. I knew that girls did not do that. I told my mother about it. There was a confrontation, though certainly not a hostile one. The "maid" confessed that she was really a man and that she had disguised herself as a woman in order to get the job. My mother expressed her regret about his plight but told him that he could not stay. She did a nice thing and gave him his full month's salary and sent him on his way with her best wishes. I thought that it was very sad. He/she was a nice person and we got along very well. I had pangs of conscience for having told my mother about the stand-up peeing, but she probably would eventually have found out anyway.

Now, of course, I believe that it wasn't quite that simple. "Karen" was probably a transvestite, a bisexual, a homosexual, or all of that.

The last maid we had was Gertrud Biastoch, who stayed with us for about seven years and until the Nazis prohibited any "Aryan" woman to live in a Jewish household where there were males under seventy-five years old. Gertrud was about five or six years older than I. I thought she was wonderful and I really loved her. I knew that she reciprocated my affection. After my father's bankruptcy, my mother started working in the business every day. She left with him in the morning and came back with him at night. I spent a great deal of time alone with Gertrud. She was, I'm totally sure, a virgin and I believe, had it not been a death sentence offense against the Nazi racial laws, that we would have initiated each other. We talked a lot about it. But it didn't happen.

Things were in turmoil in Germany. First there was the last World War. Then came the dreadful inflation, during which one (really!) needed a wheelbarrow full of money to buy a loaf of bread. There was wide-spread unemployment. About half of the able-bodied men were out of work and without any safety net. There were always battles in the streets between the Communists on one hand and the insurgent Nazis on the other. Governments came and fell. The Weimar Republic was in tatters, and the country's president, a "war hero," Paul von Hindenburg, was tottering and senile and did not know what to do. On January 30, 1933, he committed the unspeakable stupidity of appointing Adolf Hitler as Chancellor of Germany. It was without question the most fateful and disastrous decision in the history of Europe.

I remember the day distinctly. I was sick, with a cold I believe, and laid up in bed in my parents bedroom, with the door to the balcony open. Suddenly, shouts and singing arose in the streets. I realized that something momentous was going on. A few minutes later my brother came in and told me that Adolf Hitler had been appointed Chancellor. True, all of us were very unhappy, of course, because one of Hitler's main planks had been his rabid anti-Semitism. But we all assumed, that it was just so much sound and fury – anti-Semitism had been a recurring theme in Germany for a long time, and still, the condition of the Jews in Germany was quite bearable. We were pretty sure, with the burden of government on his shoulders and having so many other pressing and important things to deal with, that Hitler would forget about his anti-Semitism and would proceed to do whatever he thought best to govern Germany.

How terribly wrong we all were! To a degree that seemed impossible then and seems even more impossible today, Germany was totally transformed, literally from one day to the next. People in our building, our neighbors, and others we knew, who until yesterday had been active members of the Communist or of the Social Democratic party, appeared the next day in brown Nazi uniforms and strutted through the streets casting menacing glances on those whom they suspected to be of a different political persuasion or, worst of all, to be Jewish. Within a few months, the Reichstag, the German Parliament, went up in flames. They accused and convicted a demented Dutchman (surprisingly, not a Jew) of having set it on fire. Everyone knew that it was a lie. Everybody knew that Hitler's #2 man, Hermann Göring, had his henchmen set the fire in order to wipe out German democracy with one stroke and once and for all. Within a few months the President, Herr Hindenburg, died, at which time, totally contrary to the constitution, Hitler assumed the role of both President and Chancellor. He took on the title of *Führer*, "Leader of the German Nation," and had the armed forces swear loyalty to him personally.

Almost immediately, among many other happenings that were unimaginable only a short time earlier, such as book burnings and the installation of the first concentration camps, Jewish students were purged from German universities. My brother, who had followed my father's instructions to become a doctor, had started his pre-med studies at the University in Berlin. He had to leave the University and my parents sent him to London to continue his education.

All during my growing up, through puberty, and until leaving Germany, I enjoyed good health. I remember only five interactions with doctors.

The first was when I was about four years old. My parents decided that I had a curved spine. I don't know whether I did or I didn't, but in any case, they were convinced of that. My mother took me to an orthopedist who decided that, yes, there was some problem, but that he had the instruments to (literally) straighten it out. For about a year, I went twice a week to his office, where he had a special torture chamber for children like me. There were two torture instruments. In the milder one, I lay on a steep incline, I'd say about 70 degrees, with a harness around my head and weights on my feet. It pulled on my spine and was most uncomfortable. That lasted about 15 minutes. The next step was worse: Still with the harness around my neck I stood straight up and then, very slowly, the harness was raised until only my big toes, very slightly touched the ground. All of my weight was hanging from my head. That also lasted about 15 minutes. I wonder whether they are still allowed to do that. I thought it was a miracle that my head didn't snap off and that I didn't die by hanging.

Then, in 1926, when I was six years old and my brother twelve, my mother took both of us to Marienbad, a spa in the Sudetenland, the German-speaking part of western Czechoslovakia, which later gave rise to so much trouble. We stayed in a nice little hotel and had a large room with three beds, one for each of us.

One evening, my mother put both my brother and me to bed and went down to the dining room for dinner and, as I understood it, for a little dancing. While quite certainly within proper bounds, I always thought that my mother was somewhat of a flirt at the time. My brother and I were alone in the room and I started telling him ghost stories. Apparently, my stories and my powers of persuasion were such that I put him into hysterics of fear. We had to call my mother up from the dining room and she had to soothe him and put him back to sleep. I was amazed at what power I had over my older brother.

But this bad deed did not go unpunished. Within three days of this incident, I broke out in measles and my mother and brother had to move to another room. My room was totally darkened because the doctor told my mother that in measles, bright light could seriously and permanently damage the eyes. I ran a high fever and I was quite sick. But as usually happened, I overcame the measles and about a week or so later everything was fine. In any case, the vacation was ruined.

Here's the third sickness episode. One Sunday, when I was about seven years old, I was playing in our living room within about eight feet of my father, who was sitting in his favorite leather club chair. My father said something to me, but I paid no attention. He talked louder and I still didn't pay any attention. Then he hollered at me. I finally turned around and heard him. It turned out that I had suddenly lost most of my hearing. My parents were horrified. I was going deaf. Even though it was the weekend, my father called Dr. Lubinsky, a well-known ear-nose-throat man, another *coryphaeus* (just like Dr. Finkelstein, the extraordinary doctor who had nursed me into life by the magic of carrot juice), and made an appointment for me the following day.

Dr. Lubinsky's office was on the second floor of a building in the *Hauptstrasse* of *Schöneberg*. The receptionist was a jolly lady by the name of Elsa. Her outstanding feature, as far as I could tell, was a very ample and inviting bosom. In addition to being the receptionist, she had another duty, namely to hold children on her lap when Dr. Lubinsky did what he had to do. I did not mind sitting on Elsa's lap at all. I really enjoyed nestling my head in the sweet valley between her ample breasts.

Apparently I have been an obsessed breastman since early childhood.

Dr. Lubinsky didn't seem particularly concerned about my loss of hearing. He realized what my problem was before he even examined me. His examination confirmed that I had a middle ear infection, which in those days before penicillin, was the scourge of children and gave rise to much surgery. But, fortunately, we had caught it early enough to avoid surgery. He proceeded to puncture my eardrums. Then having told Elsa to close one of my nostrils, he put a hand pump in the other nostril and told me to say *Kakao*, which is cocoa in German. By the time I came to the second syllable, all important orifices in that region were open. He squeezed the pump and stuff started squirting out of my ears. Then he repeated the same thing with the other nostril and the other ear. It was a primitive method but it worked. I had to go back five times to repeat the procedure. He also gave my mother some kind of medicine for me to take orally, but obviously it was not an antibiotic. Those, of course, had not yet been invented. It think it was the blowing and saying *Kakao* that did it.

After five visits, when they thought I was completely well, my mother took me back to Dr. Lubinsky one more time. "What for, Mom?" I asked her.

"Oh," she said, but she didn't look me straight in the eye. "Dr. Lubinsky just wants to do one more checkup on you."

I knew her well. Something was fishy. She was obviously lying, but I didn't know what about. In any case, I had grave apprehensions. So we went to Dr. Lubinsky and entered the procedure room. As usual, Elsa put me on her lap and I rested my head in that comfy spot between her breasts. But something was different in the procedure room, something I had not seen before. Then I realized what it was.

There was a burner in the corner of the room with boiling water and instruments were in the pot being sterilized. I became very nervous and utterly concerned.

Dr. Lubinsky approached me and I noticed that Elsa's arms around me tightened. "Open your mouth, Gerhard," he said. That was something new. He never before had told me to open my mouth. All the procedures had been through my nose. But in any case, I obeyed and I opened my mouth. At that point, he took an instrument which looked to me like a knife and reached deeply in my throat with it. I panicked. I kicked Dr. Lubinsky in the crotch (I didn't know yet that that was a sensitive part of the male anatomy). I hit Elsa as hard as I could in her chest with my elbow. Both Dr. Lubinsky and Elsa gave out screams. I jumped up, out of the consultation room, down the stairs, and down the *Hauptstrasse*. Within seconds, my mother, Dr. Lubinsky and Elsa were in hot pursuit of me. Two blocks down the street, they eventually captured me and carried me back to the consultation room. By that time I was exhausted and I suppose so were Dr. Lubinsky and Elsa. In any case, Dr. Lubinsky put some kind of prop in my mouth to keep it open and proceeded to remove my tonsils.

It was very painful and very bloody. I thought I had been betrayed, because my mother had not told me about what was going to happen.

But it turned out very well because one of Dr. Lubinsky's prescriptions was that I could eat nothing but ice cream for the next week. Ice cream was a very, very rare treat for most people and for me too. I hardly ever got any. So I consoled myself and decided it was not too bad for the pain and scare that I had suffered.

The next medical episode came when I was about twelve years old. I developed an awful pain in my abdomen. Dr. Peltesohn was called in for consultation. He determined that I had appendicitis and that I had to have surgery. You may remember that one of my best friends was Heinz Vogel. His uncle, his mother's brother, was a Dr. Italiener, who was a urologist. He was well reputed and also performed urological surgery. But as far as my parents knew, he had never performed an appendectomy. Still, they had such confidence in him that they persuaded him to perform the appendectomy on me. I was put into a private hospital and he performed the surgery. It was quite uneventful. I do remember that as I was put under ether. I was told to count backwards from 100. I was determined to get all the way to zero. But, I didn't make it past 87.

I stayed for about a week in the hospital and shared a very large room with a man about twenty-five years old. His name was Hans Gerber. He was there because his lower jaw was broken in six places and he was totally wired up and could take only liquid nourishment through a straw. Of course, his speech was very much impaired. When I asked him how he had broken his jaw, he told me he had been ice sailing, had a collision with another ice sailor and had fallen to the ice at high speed. Thus, he had broken his jaw.

Some years later, my mother told me what had really happened. He had been beaten up by Nazi thugs, but he made my mother promise that she would not tell me because it would be dangerous for him to have it publicized. Hans Gerber had an interesting profession. He was a tobacco taster. He was employed by Muratti, one of the largest cigarette firms in Germany. He was responsible for one of their brands and had to make sure that the distinctive flavor of the brand would always remain the same. Every day, a messenger came from Muratti with a carton of cigarettes. Gerber opened each pack, and through his wired jaws and with clenched teeth, smoked only a few puffs from three or four cigarettes in each pack. He then made notations such as "add more of this," "take away some of that," etc. and gave these notes to the courier when he arrived the next day. I thought it was the most glamorous profession I had ever heard of. Of course, in those days it did not occur to anybody that one shouldn't smoke in a hospital (or anywhere else for that matter).

The last bout with a health problem occurred when I entered puberty at about thirteen, I began to develop a dreadful eczema covering my buttocks and the upper parts of the backs of my legs. It was pretty bad. The sores were painful and itchy, and they also oozed, so I had to change underwear two or three times a day. It was just awful.

My mother sent me to a very fine dermatologist (another *coryphaeus*), a Dr. Leider. He tried every medication in his arsenal to assuage my affliction. I remember one especially odious ointment, a thick white liquid, that had to be applied to the buttocks with a brush and then formed a white chalky crust. It had to be left on for a couple of days and was then removed with olive oil. My mother did that, and since I was a little shy I didn't like that too much. But even those heroic measures did not help. The eczema stayed the same or even got a little worse. Nothing seemed to help.

Dr. Leider said there was one more thing he could do. He described it as "the ultimate remedy."

"What is it?" I asked.

"We'll have to radiate you with X-rays. It's a new method, but I think it may help you. Before I do that, however, I think you should ask your parents to give me permission and please have them sign this form and return it to me if it is O.K. with them."

I talked with my parents and they saw no reason why they should not allow that.

Dr. Leider subjected me to eight sessions of fifteen minutes each of X-ray radiation. I lay prone on a table while he zapped me. The eczema disappeared. I didn't think about that episode until about twenty years later, when it occurred to me that all that radiation, especially into my genital area, might in all likelihood have made me sterile. Well, thank goodness, it didn't. I think that that was the real miracle of that heroic treatment.

Talking about doctors: Our dentist was a Dr. Laufer, a young man, a bachelor living with his widowed mother. He was a pretty good dentist, I suppose, because, despite the primitive equipment of the time – there were no dental X-rays and the drill was operated by a treadle – he kept the whole family in pretty good dental health. What fascinated me about him, however, was that he was an orthodox Jew – the first one that I had ever met. He wore a yarmulke while he worked, and his mother, who kept his books and opened the door for patients, wore a wig. As an orthodox woman, she wouldn't show her natural hair.

My mother was quite concerned about masturbation. While, of course, she never talked to me about anything like that, she gave me some very broad hints about the dreadful things that could befall me if I engaged in this odious practice. She might have found evidence that I was an occasional practitioner. Our neighbor on the floor just below us was a Herr Lubert. He and his wife owned a flower shop five blocks from our home. Herr Lubert had what appeared to be a very serious case of scoliosis, an extreme case of curvature of the spine. He was so bent over that his upper body formed almost a right angle to his legs. My mother would point him out to me and say, "Gerdchen, do you know why Mr. Lubert walks that way?"

"No, why?" I answered.

Then she looked at me, rolled her eyes significantly, and said, "Because of the sins of his youth – if you know what I mean."

I knew what she meant, but I also knew that she was misinformed about masturbation. I had studied it and knew that it was somewhat messy and disgusting, but that there was nothing really wrong with it, that it provided a great deal of entertainment for those who indulged in it and that it certainly did not pose any danger to health. If it did, all the boys in my class would have been deadly ill.

There was a small store at the end of our block. I can't recall what they sold beyond kerosene and laundry soap. The soap had the consistency of jelly. It had a marvelous smell that I can still vividly remember. The kerosene came out of a large barrel and the woman who owned the store would move a wooden lever back and forth, which pumped the kerosene into a large bottle on top of the barrel. When the bottle was full or filled to the degree required by the customer, the woman opened a spigot and the customer's container was filled.

But the main importance and attraction of the store, was the mangle in the back room. The maid (and I usually went with her) would take the sheets, pillowcases and other large items that had just emerged from the *grosse Wäsche* – the once-a-month big wash – and put them one by one into the mangle. It consisted of a very heavy box, about eight feet long, four feet wide, and four feet deep. It was operated by electricity and through a gearing arrangement that would move that box back and forth over two big wooden rollers and over a wooden bed. The trick was to put the sheets, or whatever, on the wooden bed when the box was on the far side and quickly remove one's hands before the box returned over the rollers so as to avoid being crushed by the mangle. I was fascinated and at the same time scared to death by the procedure and by the apparatus. I am surprised that nobody we knew ever got mutilated by the heavy mangle.

In the attic of our building where we lived was the *Waschküche*, the laundry room. My mother and the maid did the laundry once a month. One had to reserve the day in a special book kept by the janitor. The main feature of the laundry room was an enormous copper kettle into which all of our laundry was dumped. One brought one's own coal briquettes and stoked the fire beneath the kettle so it would bring the water to a boil. Then the clothes were taken out and, with the help of a washboard, washed by hand in a tub. I loved to watch it. It took all day long. At the end of the day, the clothes were wrung out by hand and hung up to dry in the attic.

Now you can see why the "trick" I played to pretend to spill ink on my mother's beautiful damask tablecloth (especially at a time when guests were due to arrive) might be such a dreadful event in a woman's life. It was because of that long and laborious process to get clothes and linen clean.

My job in this procedure was to put the clothes on the line in the attic, to apply the clothespins, pick up the clothes the next day when they were dry, and put them in a basket. I enjoyed doing it, especially the opportunity to look through the attic window down on the street, so many floors below. Everything, cars and people and horses, looked so much smaller than I had otherwise seen them.

One of the features of grade school was the weekly peeing contest of the boys in our class. That took place after school on Friday (in grade school we had no school on Saturday).

All the participants in this contest – about eight or ten of us – lined up at the curb to see who could pee the farthest. None of us went to the bathroom all through the morning because we wanted to leave enough "ammunition" to make a victory possible. I soon realized that body size and pressure played a great role in this contest. Since I was one of the smallest in the class, I didn't have much of a chance of winning. But then I made another discovery, a "secret" that every artillery officer knows and that even the archers of antiquity knew, namely that a missile goes farthest if launched at a 45-degree upward angle. So I did that and was victorious for a few weeks. But then the other, bigger boys caught up with me and my victorious days were over. By the way, the girls in the class thought that these contests were totally "gross and disgusting." I didn't think that I could entirely disagree with them. In those days, however, the opinions of "just girls" were of very little interest to us. And what's more, we had learned that they squatted to pee, and we couldn't think of anything grosser than that. Though we did not know the term, we were convinced that they suffered from penis envy.

Horst Peck, Heinz Vogel, and Tommy Dyck were my closest friends. From the first grade all the way through *Gymnasium* we thought of ourselves as the Four Musketeers. Interestingly, we were all quite different in personality, outlook, and abilities. My relations with Tommy could almost be described as symbiotic. He was a marvelous artist. Even as a young boy, Tommy could paint and draw beautifully and make wonderful sculptures. I was convinced that he would eventually become famous for his work. But he had no talent at all for anything else, and certainly not for mathematics. It was the exact opposite with me. I excelled in mathematics and had absolutely no talent for painting. Our art teacher was a Herr Kind. His idea of teaching art was to give us prints of old masters, which we then had to copy. I simply could not do that. I could not produce anything that would even remotely resemble the original, so Tommy always did it for me; I, in turn, did his math problems for him. It was a great arrangement for both of us. I suppose that that is indeed the essence of symbiosis.

What happened to Tommy? Tommy's father was the editor of the *8-Uhr Abendblatt*, the largest Berlin evening newspaper, the one my father read religiously every day when he came home from work. When the Nazis came to power, Tommy's father was unceremoniously thrown out of his job. Having few resources, he (he was divorced) and Tommy went to Paris, where he worked for some time in a German-language newspaper. Tommy, as I later learned, became involved in a love affair with a French woman. Things turned out badly, and at the age of twenty-one, he committed suicide over their affair. That was just awful. What a loss! He was such a nice boy and so talented.

Heinz Vogel was the cerebral type, all the way through school. Again, from the first grade through high school he was always the "primus," first in the class. I was always the "secundus," the second in the class. We had a friendly competition. I always tried to get the number one spot, but I never succeeded in getting ahead of him. There were no rancor, no hard feelings in that competition. It was a friendly one. Heinz's mother (Erna) was divorced. She was a school teacher. She taught French and English.

Once or twice a week, we went to each other's house to do schoolwork together, to play cards, or to read the young people's magazine *Fridolin*, to which he subscribed. We had much fun, but he was not at all adventurous. He was studious, and not much else.

Many years later, by chance, I got the address and the phone number of his uncle, Dr. Italiener, who had moved to New York. He was the doctor who, many years before, had performed the appendectomy on me. I called him. He was happy to hear from me. I asked Dr. Italiener about Heinz. He told me that he was a professor of chemistry at Rutgers University in New Jersey. That sounded like him. I made an effort to get in touch with him, but was unsuccessful. The University didn't know of him. Was Dr. Italiener in error? Or was he perhaps teaching at another university or under a different name? I made every effort I could, including through the Association of American College Professors, but could never locate him. It is possible that he could have changed his name. Perhaps to "Bird" which is English for Vogel. In any case, I never found him again.

Of the three, I was really closest to Horst Peck. He was the one who left that "souvenir" in front of Herr Warmbier's office and the one with whom I visited that chamber of horrors, Herr Kuskopp's apartment. Horst was always thinking of mischief and he was quite adventurous.

I was able to get him to join the Boy Scouts. He came to two meetings and went on three hikes. Then he had had enough. That was much too much discipline for him. He was a free spirit.

He and I liked to go to the *Schöneberg* (that was our district in Berlin) *Rathaus*, the municipal building. We had no interest in the municipal activities, but what fascinated us was the elevator in the building. It was a so-called *"paternoster"* which is an adaptation of the "…our Father..," the prayer spoken with the rosary. *Paternosters* did indeed resemble rosaries. They consisted of a set of wooden boxes stacked upon each other that slowly went from floor to floor – one side up and the other side down. There were no doors. You would step into the *paternoster*, say, on the fourth floor, and step out on the second floor or vice versa. We did a lot of that. But what fascinated us and made us come back again and again, was to find out what happened after any given box reached the top floor and then disappeared from sight and again reappeared after a while on the same floor on its way down. We wondered whatever happened in the loft or in the basement. It greatly preoccupied us. Did the box move sideways and then down again, or did it turn upside down? Also, we were concerned about the mechanism. Somehow, we visualized a giant gear that moved the box, and we didn't quite know if it would be dangerous or perhaps even fatal to anybody foolhardy enough to make the trip through the loft or through the basement. We absolutely needed to find out what happened. One of us needed to go to the loft or to the basement We argued endlessly about it. We could not decide which one of us should go.

Finally, when we were about nine years old, we decided to take the trip together. We stepped into the "up" box on the fifth floor, the uppermost floor. We were immediately enveloped in total darkness. We were scared. We held hands. We didn't know whether we would now be tumbled upside down or sideways and thrown down again, or whether we would be ground into a bloody pulp by that enormous gear that we envisioned. But nothing much happened. We came to the very top. The mechanism gently pushed us sideways in the box. A few second later we emerged again on the fifth floor on the way down – unscathed. We stepped out and congratulated each other. It was as if we had climbed Mt. Everest. It was the greatest adventure we had ever had and the scariest, bravest thing we had ever done. We promised each other not to tell our parents about it. We didn't.

Because of the peculiar citizenship laws in Germany, and perhaps in all of Europe at the time, Horst found out, to his enormous surprise, that he was a British "subject." His grandmother, it seems, had married an Englishman who was living in Germany at the time. So, being quite unaware of it, his father was also British; and so was Horst. It put him at an enormous advantage compared to everyone else. Next to United States citizenship, to be British was just about the best thing that could happen to a Jew in Germany. There was a somewhat comical aspect to that. After they became aware of their citizenship, Horst's father and mother went to the reception that the British Embassy threw for British residents in Berlin on the King of England's birthday. They felt a little isolated, they told me, because they were the only ones there who didn't speak a word of English.

Horst left for Canada – no problem for him, as a British "subject," at all. Somebody, I don't remember who, told me that he had eventually migrated to New York. On one of my trips to New York, I looked him up in the phonebook. He lived in the Bronx. He had changed his name from Horst to Horace. I called him up. I thought he would be overjoyed to hear from me. It had been over twenty years that we hadn't seen each other. After all, he had been my very closest friend for more than ten years. While he sounded pleased, he didn't sound as overjoyed as I had expected him to be. We exchanged some vital information. He told me that he was married, had two daughters and had a small electrical parts factory. He was vague and not specific, even under gentle questioning.

"Horst," I told him, "I am here with my wife. We are staying at the Hilton Hotel. Why don't you and your wife come down and let's have dinner together and talk about old times."

"Oh, that's very nice of you," he said, but I just can't do it tonight."

"No problem, we'll be here for three or four days. How about tomorrow or the day after?"

"Oh," he said, "I'm afraid I can't do that. I have appointments both evenings that I can't break."

It sounded weird to me. "How about lunch, Horst?" I asked him. "In fact, I can come up to the Bronx, no problem."

"No, I'm afraid lunch won't be convenient. In fact, I have some problems in my business that I have to take care of. Are you going to come back to New York?"

"Oh sure, within six months or so" I said, and I meant it.

"Please call me again and we'll get together then."

I did call him on my next trip, and essentially the same thing happened. Then I tried one more time, on my next visit to New York, but his number was no longer in service. I don't know where he went or what happened to him. It was strange and disconcerting.

I remember it was very cold one day when I was seven. I was on my way home from a visit to a friend. On a street corner, I saw a small crowd of people and, being curious, I joined them to see what was going on. There was a man with a small table and he was hawking something. I didn't know what it was. Since I was very small, I was able to wind my way through the other people and got very close to the demonstration. The man had a "magic" soap that he claimed could remove any stain at all, no matter how difficult it was. He asked the crowd, "What is the most difficult stain you can think of?"

One man in the back (obviously, as it turned out, he was a shill), said, "The most difficult stain is iodine."

"Iodine?" the hawker asked. "You may be right. Let me see if I have any iodine." He had some bottles on his table – inks, fruit juices and other stuff and, sure enough, there was a bottle of iodine. At that time, everyone knew what iodine was. It was the universal disinfectant for small wounds .Everyone knew what it looked like and what it smelled like. He took the bottle, opened it, and passed it around to the crowd for them to smell it. Yes, it was indeed iodine.

He unbuttoned the cuff of the left sleeve of his shirt, held the cuff in his hand, and, to the gasps of astonishment of the crowd, poured the iodine on his sleeve from top to bottom. It was an awful stain. He had a small bowl of water. He put his magic soap into it and washed his sleeve with it. Miraculously, the stain totally disappeared. The shirt was clean again. He said, "Folks, if my magic soap can remove an iodine stain, which is the toughest stain there is, you can be sure that it can remove any stain. No household should be without this wonderful product. I sell it for just 50 *pfennig*."

I didn't have 50 *pfennig*, I only had 40 *pfennig*, which I had saved from my last two allowances. But, I had to have that magic soap. I said to the man, "I only have 40 *pfennig*. Would you give me the soap for 40 *pfennig*?"

The man said, "All right, I'll do something for you, little fellow. I'll give you a special discount. Here's the soap, give me your 40 *pfennig*. Your mom will be very pleased."

I was delighted. I had struck an incredible bargain. I ran home as fast as I could.

My brother's bar mitzvah was pending and my mother had bought me a beautiful white shirt for the occasion. I was intent on giving a dramatic demonstration of the marvelous soap that I had bought and waited for my mother to come home. On my brother's desk I had found a bottle of black drawing ink. It was not just regular ink, but black drawing ink. It would be a stain almost as difficult, though not quite as difficult, as iodine. No doubt, the magic soap would handle it.

I put on the white shirt.

When my mother came home, I said, "Mom, I'm going to show you something totally extraordinary, but don't get freaked out. What I am going to show you is amazing." I did as the hawker had done. I unbuttoned the left cuff of my shirt, put the cuff in my left hand and poured the drawing ink over my sleeve from top to bottom. My mother almost fainted, but not quite.

"Are you out of your mind!" she screamed. "What's a matter with you, you dumb boy?"

"Relax, Mother, I bought some magic soap and I'm going to rub the stain out immediately." I did just like the hawker had done. I put the soap in a bowl of water and started rubbing on the ink spot. But, to my horror, instead of disappearing, as I firmly expected it would, it only seemed to spread it. By the time I was over with my demonstration my mother was furious and I was crying. She had to throw the shirt away.

It was not until years later, when I was studying chemistry in college, that I found out what this was all about. The soap consisted or had a strong component of sodium thiosulfate which is used as an analytical tool with iodine in chemical titration. It neutralizes iodine and makes it colorless. In other words, the only stain that the magical soap removed was iodine. To my amazement, about forty years later, I went to the *Fiera de Milano* – the Milan Fair, and saw exactly the same scam performed. I couldn't believe it.

Most of my early interactions were with my mother. Those became fewer by the time I was ten years old – when she started working every day in my father's business. I loved my father, but I had little real contact with him. When I was a little boy, he would let me ride piggyback with him and he would run around the dining room table with me. I would give him commands, "Spanish trot," or "Russian gallop," or "French canter," and he would perform various paces that he imagined would respond to that command. I had a great time.

But mostly I remember him sitting in his black easy chair when he came home from work and reading the *8-Uhr Abendblatt*, the evening paper, and smoking his cigar. He was always sweet and kind to me, but there was little contact.

One day I asked him, "Dad, what is a gentleman." I had heard the word, and the term is the same in German as in English.

"Why do you want to know that?" he asked.

"I heard somebody say that Herr so-and-so was a gentleman. What does it really mean, Dad?"

"Its difficult to explain," he said, "but I'll give you an example. Suppose you are at a party and a lady next to you audibly breaks wind. If you assume the responsibility and say, 'Excuse me,' to the assembled crowd, you are a gentleman."

"Dad, what do you mean by a lady breaks wind?"

"You know what I mean," he said, "she breaks wind."

"Well, what does it mean?"

"It means she farted," he said. "A gentleman says 'excuse me' when a lady farts. The lady is off the hook and he assumes the blame. That's what makes him a gentleman."

I thought it was a wonderful explanation and I spent years hoping that a lady in my neighborhood would fart so I could say "excuse me" and prove myself as a gentleman. That never happened.

Since all of us boys went on to the *Hohenzollern Gymnasium* after the fourth grade, and since the *Hohenzollern Gymnasium* was just across the street from us, we thought of it as sort of a "sister school." When I was in the second grade (seven years old) my brother was already in the *Gymnasium* in the *Untersekunda*. That year on *Verfassungstag* (Constitution Day – the birthday of the Weimar Republic) they had a presentation and performance in the *Aula,* the large assembly room of the *Gymnasium*. To show the connection between the two schools they invited several of the little boys to perform before the assembly. For some reason I was selected. I decided to recite a poem which my father had composed. I'll give it in the English translation which is very similar to the German original. It went as follows:

> My name is Fritz.
> Our dog's name is Spitz.
> MickyMatt is our cat.
> Mama is mama,
> And Papa is papa.
> My sister's name is Emily.
> And that's our whole family.

It was an important occasion for me, my first public performance. In order to lend more drama to the poem I prevailed on Herr Stein, the owner of the toy store in our building, to lend me a plush toy dog and a plush toy cat for the occasion. I pointed to the animals at the respective lines in the poem. When I talked about my parents and my imaginary sister Emily I pointed to someone in the audience. There were close to a thousand people in the audience and I received thunderous applause. It was until then my proudest and most successful day.

There is a sequel to this little story but, I have to fast-forward about seventy years. I saw an ad in a magazine by the "American Poetry Society." Their avowed purpose was to locate promising young American poets. They solicited readers to submit their creations and promised a first prize of (I believe) $5,000, a second prize of $2,500, and a third prize of $1,000 for the best poems. It was pretty clear to me that this was a phony deal, but to make quite sure I decided to submit my "Fritz" poem. Not too much to my surprise, I received a letter about two weeks later, from the president of the "American Poetry Society," telling me that I had "a rare talent," that my "poem showed signs of imagination and originality, and a keen sense of language and sensitivity." They also assured me that the board had decided to put me and my poem into the final selection and that I would be eligible for one of the prizes.

Of course, I knew for sure that this was a scam. And, sure enough, two weeks later, I got an invitation to buy their anthology in which my poem would appear. I believe the price of the anthology was $49.95 or something like that. I had been right. And, no, I did not buy the anthology and I did not win one of the prizes.

Until I was about eight years old, I did not compete with my brother at all. We simply lived in different worlds. But once I was closely ensconced in school and particularly, of course, after I entered the *Hohenzollern Gymnasium* when I was ten years old, I began to compete with him on some levels. He was very good in two things, namely German, which means rhetoric, composition – anything like that – and languages; he took English and French, I believe. But he was very poor in and simply could not get along with mathematics. It totally freaked him out. Ever since I can remember, he had to be tutored in mathematics to keep him afloat and advancing through the grades. If you got a "4" (*mangelhaft*, which meant deficient) in a "major," and math was a major, you could not advance to the next grade. It was a big and constant problem for him and for my parents.

So I decided that I would do better if I possibly could. It so happened that my math teacher, Herr Höntscher, was the same one that my brother had had six years ahead of me. Herr Höntscher told me how I was so very much smarter in math than my brother. Of course, I went gleefully home and told him about it. I really rubbed it in. And I also told my parents, of course. It was the first time I had ever bested him in anything.

Another area of competition was the Boy Scouts. The Jewish Boy Scouts were, as far as I could tell, the only Boy Scouts in Germany. I never saw any others although there surely must have been some. But somehow, Boy Scouts didn't seem to play the same role in gentile circles that they played with us. The Jewish Boy Scouts were an important movement and many of the Jewish kids belonged to it. When he was at the right age, about twelve years old, my brother joined the Boy Scouts, or rather my mother pushed him to join them. He joined the ninth troop, which was supposed to be the "elite" and which was distinguished by purple neckerchiefs.

He went on his first major hike, a six-week affair in southern Germany. After the third day he called home collect. He asked my father to send him some money to get home, because he had had enough. And he had made up his mind that the Boy Scout life was not for him. That was the end of that.

Naturally, that again gave me a special spur to also join the Boy Scouts when my time came. I indeed did just that when I was about nine years old.

I took to it like a duck takes to water or, as we would perhaps say today, like a dot takes to com. The Boy Scouts were the most formative influence in my young life. I stayed with them to the bitter end, until the Nazis effectively made it impossible for any Jewish organizations to function. That was about 1936 when I was sixteen years old.

When I was fifteen years old, I joined the Maccabi Jewish Boxing Club. I took the whole course of instruction. I worked with the bag, jumped rope and everything. I fought only one 3-round exhibition fight, in front of several hundred people. It was judged a draw. I didn't really think boxing was for me. I thought it was stupid sport and I gave it up.

My mother was supportive of me in my Boy Scout endeavors, because I believe she was a little disappointed that my brother hadn't made the grade with them. She gave me a generous allowance to go to the special Boy Scout outfitters and to buy everything I needed. I got a complete uniform including the coveted purple neckerchief, the special Boy Scout belt, and the shoulder strap. The most important piece of equipment was the military-style backpack because nothing else was allowed. Oddly, it was called an *Affe*, a monkey. I don't know why. Mine was especially pretty because it was covered with calfskin, hair and all.

The first thing we had to learn, before we even went on our first hike, was how to erect a tent. There were several types, the smallest one, a simple one made of two squares, held two boys. The next larger one was a pyramid-looking structure made of three tent squares. The next and largest was made of four squares. It had the shape of a gabled roof. Each was designed to carry one scout per tent square; each Scout, therefore, had to carry a tent square and a number of pegs, in addition to his sleeping bag, clothes, food, toiletries, and everything else. I thought it was wonderful.

About a year into the Boy Scouts, after I had learned all those wonderful songs, both in German and in Hebrew, I found that the most popular boys were those who could play the guitar to accompany the singing. Even though it is the same instrument, namely the guitar, the Germans differentiate between a guitar being played for "musical purposes" and a guitar that is being played to accompany songs just by strumming chords. Such a guitar is called a *Klampfe*. One of my older friends was Hubert Lehmann. He was the son of a pharmacist and lived with his parents in an apartment above the pharmacy. He knew how to play the *Klampfe* and he showed me how. It was really not too difficult. First I learned how to tune it and for that I had to remember a little mnemonic sentence. The sentence was: *Eine alte dumme Gans hat Eier*, which means "an old stupid goose has eggs" and which reminds one to tune *e, a, d, g, h , e*. H in German is what b would be in English. I only had to learn four keys, C and G major, and A and E minor, and only three chords in each of those. With those, I could accompany everything anybody would possibly sing. I mastered the *Klampfe* in about five lessons. Hubert sold me one of his used instruments. I practiced at home and then took my *Klampfe* with me on every one of our hikes. It made me even more popular and I liked that.

The routine of the Boy Scouts was essentially this: We would have an outing – a weekend hike each week. We would meet on Friday night (we were not religious and therefore had no problem with violating the Sabbath), or, if we had school, on Saturday night. We would travel to somewhere in the country, about 30 or 50 miles out of town that the leader (honestly, he was called *Führer* – until that became impossible and we called him by the Hebrew equivalent, *manheek*) had selected. After we arrived at the place that the *manheek* had pinpointed on his map, we usually marched about an hour or two until we came to the right place. Then we would camp – three boys to a tent – build a bonfire and sing songs.

The songs that we sang were the same as the gentile kids sang, perhaps only more of them. There were no patriotic songs but many, many songs of the *Landsknechte*, the mercenaries that fought in the Thirty-Year War and in so many of the other European wars. There were scores of these songs that were wonderful and even today I remember most of them – lyrics and all. Then there were so-called *Moritaten*, which were ballads of love or crime or of historical events. We had to learn the lyrics of all of these songs. But in addition to these German songs, we learned many Hebrew songs, because, from the very beginning, our identity as Jews was paramount and was strongly stressed.

Before, if I thought about it at all, I thought of myself as a German boy of the Jewish religion. Being in the Jewish Boy Scouts, however, I began more and more to think of myself as Jew who happened to live in Germany. That identification and self-image became more and more important as time went by. The Nazis methodically attempted and largely succeeded in robbing us Jews of our self-respect and our identity. By that time, however, the Boy Scouts had sufficiently imbued me with ethnic pride – *Selbstbewusstsein*, in German terms – that I really didn't care much about the insults and humiliations that the Nazis inflicted on us. I learned to despise the Germans and everything they stood for, and even when only thirteen or fourteen years old, made firm plans to emigrate to what was then called Palestine and to start my life anew in what I knew would be the Jewish State.

In addition to our weekly overnight hikes, there were also the weekly *Heimabende* (literally "home evenings") which took place in rotation in the homes of the troop members. The respective mother had the obligation to provide light refreshment for the occasion.   These weekly meetings usually took place on Wednesday afternoon and lasted about two or three hours.   There were presentations by our leader, such as slide shows, the singing of Hebrew and other songs, and discussions to further our Jewish identity.

Then we had the major encampments which coincided with school vacations.   The first of those in the year was at Easter.   That was usually for two weeks.   Most frequently we camped next to one of the beautiful lakes north of Berlin.

I remember my very first encampment when I was about nine years old. We did all of our own cooking and each boy had to bring certain provisions which, in most cases, included one hard salami.   The salamis contributed, usually a dozen or two dozen, were strung up on a tree so that the animals could not get to them.   That tree was called the salami tree.

As always, there was a campfire, and at night a boy had to stand guard for two hours, attend the fire, and watch the camp.   He was then relieved by another boy whose watch lasted for another two hours.

On my third day, I had the 2 a.m. to 4 a.m. watch and, quite frankly, did not feel completely at ease.   I was the only one awake.   There were strange noises from the woods and it was all a little eerie, but I did the best I could.   I walked around the camp and added wood to the fire.   About halfway through my watch, one of the older boys came out of his tent and inspected the campfire that I was keeping alive and told me that I should get more wood.

"Where do I get the wood?" I asked.

"Obviously by going into the forest and gathering some wood, dumb-dumb. It isn't going to fall from the sky.   Get a move on."

"Yes," I said.   With major trepidation I went into the forest.   I had barely gone about 100 feet when suddenly two people assaulted me from behind.   They threw a sack over my head and my shoulders and started pummeling me.   They didn't really hurt me, but they pushed me around quite a bit.   Instead of crying out, I started hitting and kicking and possibly even landed a couple of good blows.   At that point, the sack was pulled off my head.   The two "attackers" congratulated me and told me that I had passed the "test."   Apparently it was something that neophytes were subjected to.   Fortunately, I had acquitted myself with flying colors.

The next yearly event was *Pfingsten*, which is called Pentecost in English. It seems to be a much more important Christian holiday in Europe than it is in the United States.   Those vacations also lasted two weeks.   It was usually a hike through one of the beautiful regions of northern Germany.   Since it was only two weeks, we didn't go too far from Berlin.

The big deal of the year was the summer.   We would take the train to somewhere in southern Germany, usually the *Schwarzwald* (the Black Forest), or another of such beautiful places that abound in that part of the country.   We would usually hike ten to fifteen miles a day.   Then we would make camp, sit around the bonfire and sing our songs, sleep in our tents, keep those two-hour watches, and in general, enjoy nature and our wonderful camaraderie.

We had to bring some money, of course. As I recall it was about 100 *marks* each for the summer. That money was given to the leader who, in turn, gave it to two older and trusted boys who were named Finance Minister and Deputy Finance Minister, respectively. They kept the money in a pouch worn on a strap around their necks. They doled out the money as it was needed for various purposes. Then there was the Minister of the Exterior. His role was, on those occasions when we decided not to camp in our tents, to contact a farmer and persuade him to let us sleep in his barn. That wasn't really too difficult and most farmers readily agreed, because Boy Scouts were known to be orderly and respectful. There was never a touch of anti-Semitism, as far as I could tell.

A new boy was usually asked whether he wanted to be Minister of the Interior. The new boy, of course, was flattered by this attention and the honor and he always eagerly accepted. The role of the Interior Minister was to be the keeper of the toilet paper and to dole it out as it was needed.

Then there was the Minister of Gastronomy. He was the one who had the big cooking pot strapped to his backpack. Each boy carried his own military-style canteen on his backpack which contained sandwiches and other things and eating utensils.

Cooking was rotated on a daily basis. One of the favorite dishes and practically a daily standby was a dish called *Gureikawu*. This made-up word is a contraction of the German words *Gurke*, *Ei*, *Kartoffel*, and W*urst*. It is made of cucumber, eggs, potatoes, and salami sausage. It was an easy dish to prepare. The main protein was provided by the ever-present hard salami, which we always carried along.

I loved everything connected with the Boy Scouts – the hiking, the camaraderie, the singing, the campfires, the cooking, and truly, most of all, the emphasis on Judaism and the Zionist indoctrination which were always the main themes.

During the autumn vacation in late September, as long as it did not interfere with the Jewish holidays, we would have another encampment similar to that of Easter.

Finally, there was the winter journey. This was always a ski trip. We would go to what the Germans call the *Riesengebirge*, the Sudeten Mountains. We went to the Czechoslovakian side, the Sudetenland, where people were German-speaking. There were tiny villages. One we always used to go to was called *Ober Klein Aupa*, an unusual name. It wasn't even a village, just a cluster of farmhouses. We would rent one of them for the duration. The farmer and his family would move out and stay with relatives. They would come back once or twice a day to milk the cows and feed the chickens.

We would ski all day long on what was then really primitive equipment – wooden skis without edges and with leather-strap bindings. Nothing else being available, we would ski or attempt to ski in the Scandinavian style. Its main feature was the so-called *telemark* turn, which now looks very peculiar. But the Scandinavian style was the only style being taught at the time and perhaps the only style possible on those primitive skis.

There were no ski lifts. We would put our skis on our shoulders and trudge up the mountain all day long. Then we would wind up the day with one single run downhill. It was not very rewarding, considering the effort expended. Still, we had an exhilarating time. One day that I remember clearly we got up before dawn. We trudged up all the way to the top of the highest mountain of the range there, the *Schneekoppe*; which is 5,200 feet high. We had lunch at the *Baude*, the lodge, at the top, then skied down to our camp. We thought of it as a glorious day.

In 1932, my regular troop could, for some reason or other, not make the usual winter trip. I asked around for some other Jewish Boy Scout troop that I could join for the occasion. I did find one, but I was told that they were Communists. I had no interest in Communism at all, but it did not particularly bother me. What I wanted to do was to ski, and by going with this troop I would be able to do it.

On that occasion, instead of renting a farmhouse on the Czech side of the border, we rented a small house, a lodge, on the German side of the border. It was pretty comfortable, compared to the little farm houses that we were used to. There were two leaders whose names I remember until today: Hermann Feld and Rudy Kiefer. They were about twenty years old; I was twelve, and I was the youngest of about thirty boys.

There was a large courtyard, it may have been a parking lot, in the back of the lodge and there was a tall flagpole in the center of it. Herman and Rudy had brought a Soviet flag. It was red, with the hammer and sickle in the corner. I hadn't seen one before. The red flag was hoisted every morning. We all had to stand there with our clenched fist in the air and sing the international anthem: *Erwacht Verdammte dieser Erde...*, "Awake, you damned of this earth..." As far as I could tell, all the other boys took it very seriously and were quite devoted. I thought that it was a weird ritual, a silly song, and something that I didn't connect with at all. This group seemed to have no interest in Judaism or Zionism. They talked about class warfare, the liberation of the proletariat, and other such things. They did also, however, talk at great length about how to overcome the Nazis. I was interested in that.

The reality in Germany at that time was that the Communists, though ultimately unavailing, were the only ones who fought the Nazis and the only ones with any chance of success in possibly frustrating them. Of course, it didn't turn out that way. Hitler came to power in less than a month after I came home from that outing with the Communists. I told my parents about the Communist encampment. They were horrified and rightly worried that the "authorities" would discover what had happened and have me and all the other boys, especially Hermann Feld and Rudy Kiefer, arrested. It didn't happen. I don't know what ultimately happened to Rudy Kiefer, but I know that Hermann Feld later went and fought with the Loyalists in the Spanish Civil War and that he died in battle. He was a true believer and really an inspiring leader to a little boy like me. Despite his unusual beliefs, I liked and respected him very much.

Something quite significant happened on one of these winter trips two years later, when I was fourteen years old. We were in one of the farmhouses in *Ober Klein Aupa*. The farmer's daughter, whose name was Emma Schlopper, came twice a day to milk the cows and feed the chickens. She was sixteen years old. She was pretty, very nubile, and I liked her very much. It was clear to me that even though she was technically a Czech citizen, she was definitely considered a German by the Germans and that under no circumstances at all should I get involved with her in any way. I watched her milk the cows and she taught me how to do it. The activity involved a lot of touching, not only of the cows. Ultimately she told me that she was in love with me, and that she would do "anything" I wanted, and that she wanted to come to Berlin with me. Yes, that would have been a great prospect – just what my mother had in mind for me! When we left a week later, this winter romance, if it was one, was over – at least I thought it was. You'll hear more about Emma later in this story.

I was bar mitzvahed in June of 1933. As much as I try, and even though it was obviously an important event in my life, I can hardly remember anything about it. The only thing I do remember is that I was coached by Herr Margoliner, who was the main *shammes*, the #1 beadle, in the *Münchenerstrasse* Synagogue that we attended. He was the first among three. It was understood that he had studied to become a *chasen*, a cantor, but that his voice simply was not sufficient. Even so, when the regular *chasen* was sick or on vacation, Herr Margoliner would jump onto the breach and would conduct that part of the service. He was very knowledgeable. One of Herr Margoliner's jobs was to prepare boys for bar mitzvah. Of course, it was taken for granted that all of us could read Hebrew, so there was no problem with that. But, we had to learn the somewhat difficult cantilation which is a distinctive feature of Hebrew liturgy. The "notes" for the cantilation are diacritical marks that are attached at the bottom of the letters; each of these marks represents a "mini tune." These mini tunes are essential for the Torah readings – the first five books of Moses – and the Haftarah which are readings from the prophets – except, that the tune is in a major key for the Torah and in a minor key for the Haftarah.

I remember the portion I had to sing. It was from Judges Chapter 11, the story of Jephtach, the Gileadite ("son of a harlot"), who was a mighty warrior and who saved the Israelites from the Ammonites. He promised the Lord that, if he granted him victory in battle, he would sacrifice the very first thing that came to meet him when he returned home. He thought it would be his dog, but it was his daughter, whom he loved dearly. He fulfilled his promise and he sacrificed his daughter.

I very much wondered about that story. Why would God allow this young woman to be sacrificed? Why did He not stay Jephtach's hand, just as He had stayed Abraham's hand when he was about to sacrifice Isaac? And why did Jephtach not negotiate with God, because I had found that the Bible was full of such negotiations. I asked Herr Margoliner, but he dismissed my questions and instructed me to concentrate on my cantilations and not to question the stories in the Bible, certainly not to question God's judgment.

My fondest desire was to make "aliyah," emigration, "going up" to Israel, and I made formal application to the British government. According to my parents, a reply came from the British government while I was vacationing in Denmark. Under their White Paper, they severely restricted emigration to what was then called Palestine, and I was not accepted. I took my parents' word for it. I never questioned them. In later years, I began to wonder if they perhaps did not wish to send me into the constant upheaval of fighting with the Arabs and whether they had told me a white lie. I never found out. Somehow I never felt I could ask my mother, and I didn't think of it during her last visit, although I am pretty sure that she would by then have told me the truth.

Herr Margoliner prepared me well and I must have given a reasonable performance. I don't even remember any kinds of presents I received, except that my parents gave me my heart's desire, a small but complete Torah. I just can't remember what happened to that Torah. It is impossible that I would have willfully left it in Germany, but I don't have it any more. Could I have forgotten about it? It is possible.

I suppose that the reason that I can't remember my bar mitzvah is that in June 1933 the Nazis had been in power for about five months and the first onslaughts, totally unexpected, against the Jews had taken place. Everyone was most subdued.

In contrast, I remember in the minutest detail my brother's bar mitzvah which took place in 1927, when I was just seven years old. It was a very festive affair, catered in a substantial Jewish restaurant. I remember distinctly that all the guests, I would say about sixty of them, sat on both sides of a very long table. There was wonderful food, good wine, and great speeches, including one by the celebrant.

I was sitting next to a Fräulein Bernstein, a remote friend of my mother's. She was a big woman and I was particularly impressed by her big behind. It was of unusual size. She was sitting on my left. All during the festivities, I hoped fervently that she would fart or, as my father put it, that she would "break wind." I thought that, because of her big behind, she would be a good candidate for it. Why did I hope for that? I would immediately have jumped up and would have hollered, "I did it, I did it," so that everyone would know that I was a real gentleman. I had not forgotten my father's definition. To my regret, Fräulein Bernstein did not accommodate me in my quest.

I distinctly remember to this day the portion that my brother had to sing in Hebrew. It was from the 40th chapter of the Book of Isaiah: "Comfort, comfort my people." "*Nachamu, Nachamu, ami.*" I watched him practicing every opportunity I had and by the time his day arrived, I knew the portion as well as he did – cantilation and all. He was not aware of it. My secret dream was that, at the critical moment, he would suddenly be indisposed – nothing serious, of course, perhaps something like a mild laryngitis – that would make it impossible for him to perform. At that point, I planned to step forward, bow to the audience, and sing his portion. I would be greatly applauded. Well, it didn't happen. But there is a small "fast forward" to this one. When our son Joseph was bar mitzvahed in 1978, we invited my brother and his wife Lieschen to come from Buenos Aires and attend the festivities. They did that. What only I knew was that Joe's portion was the same one that Heinz had had more than fifty years earlier. He, of course, had forgotten all about it. But when Joe started singing, he recognized it, and he was very, very moved. I knew that it would be a wonderful surprise for him.

What most impressed me about my brother's bar mitzvah, and something which was a complete novelty for me, was that my parents had engaged a small combo consisting of piano, cello, and violin, and a male singer. There was no percussion. I watched them play and listened. One song impressed me so much that I asked them to repeat it twice. They accommodated me. The words, which I remember to this day, went as follows:

> *Oft, wenn sich die Schatten senken,*
> *Dein gedenken muss ich immerdar.*
> *Und im holden Traume halb verhüllt*
> *Zeigt sich mir Dein schönes Bild.*
> *Von vergang'nen Küssen willst Du nun nichts wissen*
> *Und Dein Herz bleibt stumm und kalt.*
> *Darum, willst Du bei mir weilen, musst Du eilen*
> *Ich entschwinde bald.*

In free translation, it means:

> Often when the shadows fall,
> Of you I must always think.
> And in my dreams, half uncovered,
> I see your beautiful image.
> Of kisses past you now don't wish to know.
> And your heart remains remote and cold.
> Therefore, if you wish to stay with me, you must hurry,
> Because I shall soon disappear.

I pondered the words but they never made any sense to me; even so, I was very impressed by the song and the mood it conveyed. Ah, well, grown ups!

And then there were my brother's bar mitzvah presents! He got at least four or five fountain pens which were, at least in those days – and I still think they are today – the classic bar mitzvah present. There were lots of books too, most of them dealing with Jewish themes such as *History of the Jews, The Wisdom of the Fathers, Jewish Holidays and their Significance*, etc. I was not too interested in those. I was already familiar with much of what they contained. But there was one book that immediately caught my rapt attention. It was called *Das Buch der Tausend Wunder, The Book of the Thousand Marvels*. It contained several sections such as "Marvels of Architecture," "Marvels of the Skies," "Marvels of the Earth," "Marvels of History," "Marvels of Myths," "Marvels of Science," and "Marvels of Mathematics." Even though I was only seven, I was fascinated by the book and most fascinated by the chapter on "Marvels of Mathematics."

Since my brother had so much, I decided he would not miss that book. He might not even know that he had received it. So I appropriated it, put my name on the flyleaf, and it became my "property" and my favorite book for years to come. What most intrigued me in the chapter on "Marvels of Mathematics," was the section called "Earth and Tennis Ball Belt." The problem was this: If one put a string snugly around the equator of a tennis ball, added one foot to that string and let it float around the equator just like the rings of Saturn, what would be the distance from the surface of the tennis ball to that string? It turned out that it was 1/2π feet. In other words, approximately two inches. What would happen, the problem continued, if one would put the same kind of string snugly around the equator of a smooth ball the size of Earth? That string would be about 24,000 miles long, the circumference of the Earth. What would happen if one added a foot to that string and also let it float around that huge ball? The amazing answer was that the distance from the surface of the huge ball to the string would be the same, 1/2π feet, just as with the tennis ball. It sounded incredible, marvelous indeed. I took it on faith. It took me about two years to understand the proof.

There was one thing, however, that concerned me about the book. Instead of 1,000 marvels, as promised in the title, it had only 363 marvels. I thought that it was somewhat of a gyp and I was a little disappointed. But it started me thinking of other marvels, and in my life so far, I have, indeed, found 1,000 marvels (and more).

The Berlin Zoo, the Zoological Garden, was one of the finest in Europe, perhaps in the entire world. Surprisingly, it did not belong to the city, but was a private corporation. My Aunt Sarah, my mother's older sister, owned shares in that corporation.

According to the bylaws of that corporation, any stockholder would get a one year's pass to the Zoo for every 100 or 1,000 shares he held. I don't remember the number. In any case, Aunt Sarah was a stockholder but had no interest in the Zoo, so she gave me her pass for two years in a row. I absolutely loved it. Almost every day after school, I took my bicycle and rode out to the Zoo. It was about a twenty-minute ride. I parked my bike, proudly showed my pass, and then went to one of the shady areas with benches, chairs and tables and did my homework. After having done my homework, I would go and visit the animals. There was also an aquarium that was especially well stocked with amphibians, reptiles, and of course every possible kind of fish. It was just wonderful.

I mostly liked the big cats, the tigers and the lions. I would often stand there for a long while and watch those animals. One day something really funny happened. An English lady wanted to take some pictures of the lions. She had a camera on a tripod about five feet away from the lions' cage. She wanted to photograph the male lion in some heroic pose, perhaps with its paws raised, giving a dreadful snarl or something of that order. But the lion just lay there. He wouldn't move. The lady approached the cage and, as if talking to a house cat said "meow, meow, meow" to the lion, hoping to get his attention and hoping to raise him. The lion just stared at her. She did it again. The lion stood up and looked at her. Then, so help me, the lion raised his leg and produced a powerful stream of urine, right at the English lady. It was the funniest thing I had ever seen. The lady was not amused.

One of my most enjoyable experiences with the Boy Scouts was in the summer of 1935. An appeal went out to those boys who were good cyclists and who wanted to participate in a bicycle trip from Berlin to Holland, then all around Holland and then back again to Berlin. It would take about five weeks and was about 1,000 miles altogether. Each day we would have to cycle between 30 and 50 miles. It included some mountainous regions in the southwestern part of Germany.

I enthusiastically signed up and got my parents' permission. Again, I was the youngest in the group – about twenty boys altogether.

In those days, we had very primitive bicycles. They were not geared, of course. They all had balloon tires. As long as we were fairly close to Berlin, say the first 200 miles or so, we were still in the flatlands of northern Germany. But then the hills and mountains began. It became at times quite difficult. It simply couldn't be managed on a bike that had no gears. So, for much of the trip we had to push the bike rather than ride it. We said: *"Wer sein Rad liebt, der schiebt"* – he who loves his bike pushes it.

On this trip, we did not make encampments every night. We couldn't carry the camping gear on the bike besides all the other things that we had to carry. We would be too tired at the end of each day and also, since we were on the highways rather than in the forests, the terrain did not lend itself to camping. Our leader had made arrangements with the Jewish community of every city in which we planned on staying the night to get us accommodations with families. When at the end of each day, we arrived in any of these cities, we would call on our contact and she – always a woman – would distribute all twenty of us in people's homes, two at a time.

I loved this trip and everything I saw. I was awed by the *Afslutdijk,* which is a long ribbon of concrete, a barrier that crosses the *Ijsselmeer* which connects the eastern to the western parts of Holland. It is about 20 miles long and you see only water to the right and left and in front of and behind you. It was quite eerie.

My mother loved to read. In fact, she had at least one book going at all times, but frequently two or three. But, as far as I can remember, we never bought any books. All books that she read came from the lending library at the *Bayrischer Platz,* which was owned by Mr. Lachmann. He had a bookstore in front, but it wasn't very busy. The real action was in the large backroom, at the lending library. All books, regardless of what they were, were bound in the same red heavy-duty linen binding. My father, quite in contrast to her, did not read anything, except the papers and magazines; only every once in a while my mother recommended a book that she thought he absolutely had to read and then he would do it.

So, we hardly ever bought books. But we did have a pretty large book closet in the *Herrenzimmer*, the "salon." It was a fairly magnificent affair with beveled glass doors. It was kept locked. Only my mother had the key but, of course, I was able to filch the key and open it whenever I wanted. It contained books that my parents had gotten as wedding presents, collected works of German classics, and also a beautiful leather-bound edition of Shakespeare, in German of course. Then there were odds and ends but mostly some German novels and reference works. I was particularly interested in one book that my parents had bought and the cover of which I had seen, but which was locked away from me. Its name was *The Perfect Matrimony*. It was by a Dutchman, whose name, I believe, was Van der Velde, or something very much like it. It explained in great deal and with wonderful graphs, the sex act and the techniques that had to be used. The most impressive was a graph showing the excitement levels during coitus, the diagonally ascending line of the male until reaching orgasm which then dropped in a vertical line after climax. That was in contrast to the excitement line of a woman, which ebbed off much more slowly after orgasm. (What was that?) I was very impressed, had no immediate application for this information, but remembered it for the rest of my life and tried to act on it.

I did not miss a single event, hike or excursion with the Boy Scouts until the summer of 1933. My mother and Aunt Martha had been approached by a travel agent, who explained that he could arrange a trip to Denmark for them. All the expenses of the trip could be paid in German *marks*. That was very important, of course, because no money beyond ten *marks* per month, per person, could be taken out of Germany. So, Mother and Aunt Martha accepted the deal. I was invited to go along. I agreed.

The normal way, in those days and even today, is to go straight north by train in order to travel from Berlin to Copenhagen, and then by ferry-train over to the Danish island of Sjaeland where Copenhagen is located. For some reason that wasn't and still isn't clear to me, we went instead by train to the port that was then called Stettin (it is now in Poland and called Szczecin) then took an overnight Danish vessel across the Baltic Sea to Copenhagen. On that trip, all of us were introduced for the first time to Scandinavian eating, especially to the famous smorgasbord. There was an incredible amount and variety of food, things that we had never seen before, such as shrimp, crab, lobster and all kinds of chicken dishes, beef and (of course) pork, and fruits, vegetables, an abundance of pastry and all kinds of cheeses and sweets. My mother and my aunt, declining only the forbidden pork, ate their fill of everything available and made themselves totally sick. They did not realize that lobster and all of the other shellfish also were not kosher. In addition to that, the sea was very rough and everyone became seasick. What was to have been a pleasure trip was not. It was a terrible sea journey and just the beginning of unpleasantness.

We arrived in Copenhagen. According to the organizer's program, we spent the night in a cheap hotel. The next morning we took a bus to our final destination, the little fishing village of Gilleleje. We went to the very pretty hotel right by the beach that the organizer had reserved for us, and looked forward to a wonderful vacation. We had beautiful rooms. I stayed in one room and my mother and my aunt stayed in another. The food, just as on the ship, was wonderful.

On the second day, the owner of the hotel, a stout lady by the name of Mrs. Olsen, asked my mother and my aunt to please come to her office. She said, "Mrs. Joffe, how are you planning to pay for your stay? I understand that you are not allowed to take any money out of Germany."

"Oh, Mrs. Olsen, that is no problem at all. You know that we are on a plan arranged by Mr. Hellsdorf. We paid him in German *marks*. He assured us that he would take care of paying for our stay here."

Mrs. Olsen said, "Mrs. Joffe, I've never heard of Mr. Hellsdorf before in my life and he has made no arrangements with me at all. He has defrauded you."

My mother said, *"Um Gottes Willen* – For heaven sake! What shall we now do?"

Mrs. Olsen looked at her and my aunt and said, "Mrs. Joffe, you and your sister look like honest women. I understand that you are planning on staying only ten days. You can stay here and then you can send me money from Germany, ten *marks* each month until I am paid. I trust you." Mrs. Olsen really did that. I was amazed. My mother and my aunt paid her off eventually, of course. It took almost two years, even with the help of friends, who made their ten-*marks* allotment per month available.

About the fourth day, we were sitting in the dining room partaking of that delicious smorgasbord to which we had by then gotten quite used. I noticed a woman, obviously Danish, I would say about thirty of thirty-five years old, who kept looking at me. I thought it was kind of strange.

After dinner I was roaming around the lobby. She approached me and said: "Come to my room. I am in number 127. I want to show you something interesting."

She spoke to me in halting German. I said, "O.K., I'll be there." I was very interested in what she was going to show me.

I somehow got rid of my mother and my aunt and told them that I wanted to go to bed early. I had told them that I was tired. I was lying. I said, "Goodnight."

I went to my room and for some reason decided to brush my teeth and to comb my hair. Then I went to room 127. The lady was there, but instead of German she started talking to me in Danish. I didn't understand a thing she was saying. Then she began to take off her blouse. I got the idea. I knew that was going to be IT. For some reason, I suppose by neglect, she had not locked the door. At that moment, just as in a cheap movie, my Aunt Martha burst into the room and loosed a stream of German invective on the poor woman. She didn't understand a word, but I am certain that she got the idea. My aunt hissed very stern words at me, which I clearly did understand, dragged me by the hand to my room, and ordered me to go to bed. The lady in number 127 left the next morning. I didn't see her again.

In the morning, my mother told me that I was a very bad boy, that this woman was a very evil and wicked woman, and that I was never, never again to do anything like that. Of course, I hadn't done anything. What surprised me about the whole thing was that my mother had not come herself, but that she had sent my aunt in her stead for this performance. Was she afraid of confronting me? Was she afraid of that woman? I never found out. My mother and my aunt never talked to me about that. The subject was never mentioned again.

About two days after my brief encounter with that beautiful seductress, something very extraordinary happened, which had an impact on me for the rest of my life. I met a little girl on the beach, who was about two years younger than I. I thought she was lovely. I spoke of course no Danish at all and very little English. She spoke very little German, just enough for us to communicate. We also used bits and pieces of English. The girls name was Ulla Hjalsted. She told me an interesting story:

Her father, Mr. Hjalsted, was a Danish Christian. Her mother, Ingrid, was Jewish. Mr. Hjalsted and Ingrid were friendly, mostly bridge buddies, with a Mr. and Mrs. Jespersen. One thing led to another. By the time the dust settled, Mr. Hjalsted had married Mrs. Jespersen, and Mr. Jespersen had married Mrs. Hjalsted, Ingrid – Ulla's mother, who was now the new Mrs. Jespersen. This "cross-marriage" was the most bizarre thing that I had ever heard.

Ulla and I really liked each other. We spent most of our first two days together. On the third day she asked me, "Would you like to meet my mom?"

"Of course," I said, "I would like to meet your mom."

"Come with me," she said. So, we walked down the beach for about half a mile until we came to a little cove. There were three women sitting there on easy chairs, all about thirty-five to forty years old and all of them naked from the waist up. Although I had been aware that there was probably something very interesting under women's and girls' blouses, I'd never, never seen a female breast. I almost fainted. It was a most wonderful but perturbing sight.

Sensing the source of my being so flustered, she covered herself up and gave me occasion to introduce myself formally. Ingrid Jespersen lived to be ninety-eight years old. She was my good friend and I think I was hers until the very end.

In any case, I was in love. Not just with Ulla, but also with her mother. I thought they were marvelous people and there was an air of luxury and elegance about them that I didn't find at home. I was enchanted.

Before my leaving for Germany, Ulla and I exchanged chaste kisses (my first ones) and promised to stay in touch with each other.

In those days people did not use long-distance telephones except in dire emergencies. In any case, that was one of my mother's great no-no's. So I wrote to Ulla perhaps every week or not less frequently than every other week and she responded in every case. We had beautiful correspondence, exchanged pictures, told about our lives and assured each other of our affection.

The next summer came around. Mrs. Jespersen wrote my mother and asked her if I could come visit with them in Copenhagen. My mother agreed, and again I went. That summer we spent in their home in Copenhagen, with excursions to the countryside, theatres, and all kinds of good things. Their home was beautifully appointed and was attended by two live-in servants. It was a degree of sophistication and luxury that I had never seen. Mrs. Jespersen noted that I did not have what she considered very good table manners. So one day she took me aside and taught me how to properly use a fork and knife. I didn't do it right because my mother hadn't properly taught me. I was a little embarrassed but also glad that I got to learn these things. Somehow, I resented my mother for not having taught me the fine points of table manners. When I later told my mother about that and tried to teach her how to hold a fork and knife properly, she just laughed and dismissed me by saying that, obviously, people in Denmark did things differently than they did in Germany. She might even have been right. Who knows? But apparently, she had pretty thick skin, certainly in her dealings with me. I didn't seem to have hurt her feelings by my pointing out, as I thought of them, her deficiencies.

In any case, I was quite enamored of Mrs. Jespersen and I believe that the feeling was reciprocated. She treated me like a son.

By the way, she spoke very good German. Her mother, who was called *mor-mor*, which means mother's mother in Danish, was born in Germany. So Mrs. Jespersen had heard much German at home and we had no trouble at all communicating with each other.

One day we were walking down the street when she told me out of a clear-blue sky and to my great surprise and some embarrassment that she didn't think that her husband – Jesper she called him – loved her at all. I don't know what brought that confession about. "Why do you think he does not love you?" I asked her. "He's always very nice to you."

"Oh yes, he's nice to me, but he doesn't really love me. And how do I know it?" she asked herself. "I know that when he lies on his deathbed he will not call my name. He will call the name of Jesus Christ."

I didn't know quite what to say about that and how to reply to it. I thought it was a most unusual statement.

The next year – by that time I was sixteen years old and Ulla was fourteen, I was invited again. On that occasion the family had rented a big house in a little fishing village, Liseleje, in the northern part of Sjaelland, the island on which Copenhagen is located. It was about twenty miles north of Gilleleje, the little village where we had first met. In addition to Mr. and Mrs. Jespersen, Ulla and myself and Ulla's little brother, Finn (about whom we will learn much more later in this story), there were two sons of Mr. Jespersen's first marriage, Sigurd and Vagn, a friend of Ulla's, Birgit Goldsmid, and two servants. Other relatives would float in and out, so there were always at least fifteen or twenty people. It was an absolutely wonderful vacation.

I shared a room with Vagn. He was twenty years old, about four years older than I.

Ulla and I spent all of our time with each other. One of our main delights was to go into the sea, dive and touch and kiss under water until we were out of breath. That was very exciting for both of us.

One night – it must have been about 2 or 3 o'clock in the morning and Vagn was snoring away in the other bunk bed in the room, I was stirred from my sleep by someone touching me. I turned around and I found that Ulla was in the bed with me. I was very excited and absolutely scared to death.

"What are you doing?" I asked her?

"I just want to be with you," she said.

"What do you want us to do?"

"Let's do whatever you want us to do," she said.

I knew very well what I wanted to do in the worst possible way, and I knew that she wanted exactly the same thing and just as much as I did – perhaps even more.

I was so excited it was almost unbearable. "Ulla," I said, "We cannot do that. What if your mother would come in and surprise us, and I don't have anything to protect us? What if you got pregnant?"

"You cannot get pregnant if it's the first time," she assured me.

I wasn't so sure about that at all, and as much as I wanted to make love with her, I knew we could not do that. If nothing else I knew there would be an awful mess in the bed and that we would be found out that way if no other way. "We can't do that, Ulla," I said, "please don't make it more difficult. Just leave."

So she said, "O.K., if that's the way you want it." She kissed me and she left.

As you can imagine, I have thought about this incident for more than sixty years. Did I do the right thing? Did I miss out on something precious?

Despite of what I thought of as my great love for Ulla, I wish I could say that I was faithful to her. Regrettably, that was not the case.

In the summer that I turned fifteen years old, my parents sent me to ballroom dancing school. It was one of the rites of passage; my brother had gone through the same thing. The school, attended only by Jewish boys and girls was owned by *Moniseur and Madame Mousson*. My brother swore the name had been *Mosessohn* and had been frenchified so as to make it more elegant. I think he was right.

My mother bought me a special blue suit for the occasion, because Herr Mousson had sent her a letter telling her that that was the prescribed uniform. All the girls were between fourteen and sixteen years old and wore very pretty dresses.

During the first session, the boys were lined up against one wall, the girls against the opposite wall. By coincidence, but probably by design, there were exactly the same number of boys and girls, namely twelve of each.

Herr Mousson gave us a little speech about ballroom manners, such as not to pick your nose and not to scratch your behind, and for the girls not to pull on their bra straps, and other such good advice. Then he told us to walk toward the girl exactly opposite us, make a bow, offer her our arm, walk around the room in a counterclockwise direction with her, and make small talk. I did that, including the small talk.

The girl I had chosen – or rather that was assigned to me was Cecily Steinfeld. She told me to call her Cilly. I did that. Cilly was very pretty, and I immediately noticed that she had a nice bosom. I decided that we were going to become great friends. I sensed that she was not opposed to that.

While Herr Mousson made some effort to teach us the rudiments of other dances such as the English (slow) waltz, the Viennese (fast) waltz, and the tango (Germanized version), the real emphasis was on the foxtrot. Herr Mossuon told us that if we mastered the foxtrot we would be considered accomplished ballroom dancers. We could always sit out the more difficult dances if we did not feel safe. It made a lot of sense.

The secret of the foxtrot, as he explained to us, was as follows: *einz, zwei – Wechselschritt,* which means one, two – changing step. What it boiled down to was make one step to the first beat, the second step to the second beat, and three steps to the next two beats. It wasn't difficult and I got it right very quickly.

He played the same piece over and over again until we got the hang of it. The piece went like this (translated into English):

> I wish I were a chicken,
> I didn't have much to do,
> I would lay an egg every morning
> And would have my afternoons free.

Herr Mousson stood in the middle of the room, the music would play and he'd clap his hands and say (in German, of course):

> I wish I were a Wechselschritt,
> I didn't have much to Wechselschritt,
> Etc.

Even now, more than sixty years later, every time I see a chicken I wonder whether it wishes to be a *Wechselschritt.*

There was another girl in the dancing class that I found quite interesting, but to whom I had never talked. I was preoccupied with Cilly. Her name was Eva Siegler. Eva was quite a different type. As Cilly was short, perky and brunette, Eva was tall and blond. She didn't seem to be all that perky. In any case, one evening we had *Damenwahl*, namely ladies choice. What do you know, Eva Siegler made a quick diagonal across the room and chose me as her partner, even though we had never talked to each other before. She was a little taller than I was, but that didn't make any difference to me. I decided that we were going to become great friends also.

By that time, of course, the boys in my class had become very interested in girls and in the mechanics of the sex act. This preoccupied us greatly. There was one consensus, namely that sex prowess was demonstrated, and that women admired it greatly, if man could perform the sex act quickly – 15 seconds maximum. We all thought that we could handle that. The location and the construction of the vagina were a great source of questions and discussion among us. Consensus was that the vagina was located in the middle of the female abdomen, for easy and convenient access. One of my friends, David Samter, the only one in our group who had a sister and was therefore considered somewhat of an authority on the female anatomy, claimed that the vagina had teeth, which, just as in a snake, were usually retracted. But when women got angry, those teeth could be brought out and inflict painful bites. Therefore, good behavior during the sex act and getting it over quickly were mandatory in order to avoid suffering painful injury.

And then there was the mystery of menstruation. We boys had heard about that, had some discussion about it, but then came to the conclusions that it had to be a myth because nothing so gross, so disgusting could actually be reality.

At that time, I spent much time home alone. My mother, of course, had been working in my father's business since the bankruptcy five or six years earlier. Gertrud had her own pursuits and spent many days out of the house. Then, in 1935, the Nazis issued their Nuremberg racial laws by which Jews with males under seventy-five years old in the household could not have any "Aryan" female servants younger than fifty years. That was the end of Gertrud with us. I was really very fond of her but she was forced by the Nazis to leave our house and I had to accept that. The advantage, of course, was that I had the house all to myself. Cilly came to visit at least two or three times a week. We always had something to eat, listened to some music and then engaged in increasingly heavy necking. All the necking was above the waist, because that's where she would draw an absolute line. By that time, I was fully prepared. I was not afraid of the teeth and always carried a condom with me in my wallet. My philosophy was that one never knew when fortune might strike and that one should be ready for that. I remembered Mr. Kuskopp's Shakespearean quote about the tide in the affairs of men. But no matter how much I wrestled with Cilly and how much she obviously enjoyed that, there was no way at all that she would possibly consent to having sex with me. It was out of the question. No way!

The reality was that, as far as I could tell, it was impossible in our circles, with "nice Jewish girls," to get sex. And nice Jewish girls were the only ones with whom we consorted. Even though there were quite a few braggarts among our friends, nobody ever had sex. My friend Werner Proskauer swore that he had done it with the maid. But he was not able to provide any details, so we knew he was a liar.

There was also heavy petting with Eva Siegler, but she drew the line even a few inches higher than Cilly. While I always hoped that Cilly would eventually yield, I never had such expectations with Eva.

On a few occasions it got to be pretty late and my parents came home. The girls, whether Cilly or Eva, would retire to the bathroom to freshen up a little, in order to make a good appearance to my parents. My mother, of course, was not fooled. She had a pretty good idea of what was happening. But whereas she did not like Cilly at all, because she considered her a vamp and a seductress, she thought of Eva as a "good girl."

Cilly had no father. I don't remember whether her mother was widowed or divorced. In any case, they lived in a small apartment in the Charlottenburg district. I went to visit there a few times but it was not very comfortable. It was clear that her mother viewed me as a potential seducer of her daughter. I don't know if she was aware of how unsuccessful I was.

Eva was an art student at an academy in Berlin. She came from a provincial town in central Germany. She shared a room with two other girls, close to the *Bayrischer Platz*. As Eva reported to me in disgust, the two other girls were lesbians and did weird things, including with dildos. It made Eva very uncomfortable, but she had no way of changing her situation.

One evening, in deep winter, she had been visiting and had dinner with us. She lived about eight blocks away and I was walking her home. There were about six inches of snow on the ground. While we were walking, I insisted, once more, on having sex with her, it was a way, the only way that she could show her love to me. I thought it was a very original line. In any case, I used it for the first time.

"I love you," she said, "but that I cannot do."

"Then what can you do?" I asked. "Show me something else."

"You tell me what you want me to do," she answered, "except having sex, and I'll do it for you."

I don't know what made me do it, but I said, "O.K., if you love me, take off your shoes and socks and walk home barefoot in the snow."

"I'll do it," she said.

She took off her shoes and her socks and walked barefoot for about one block. Then I took pity on her and told her how stupid that was and that she could possibly lose her feet by frostbite. I made her sit down on a bench nearby, rubbed her feet, which were ice cold, of course, put on her socks and her shoes, and said, "Now I know that you really love me."

It was one of the dumbest things I had ever done until that time.

After Gertrud Biastoch left our employ as a result of the Nuremberg Laws and since my mother was working all day long in my father's business, household help was needed. My mother scouted around and she found an elderly lady, Mrs. Schmidke, the wife of a municipal street worker, who lived in the upper reaches of our street. Mrs. Schmidke came in three afternoons a week to clean the house, and she did some laundry and some ironing. She was a nice lady. I liked her. Two days before Christmas, it was in 1937, she came to work, she had a black eye and looked otherwise beaten up.

"What's happened to you, Mrs. Schmidke?" asked my mother, quite alarmed

"Oh nothing," she said. "I fell down the stairs."

"Oh nonsense, you can't fool me. Tell me the truth. What happened?"

Then Mrs. Schmidke began to cry and told my mother that she had bought the traditional goose for Christmas and put it in the oven to roast. Somehow, she went to work, forgot about it and during her absence the goose had burned down to a black cinder. When her husband came home he smelled the stench of burnt meat and found the carbonized bird. Then, when Mrs. Schmidke came home from work at our house about an hour later, he screamed at her for being so careless and so stupid and then he hit her. Mrs. Schmidke was desperate. Not only had she been badly bandied about, but there couldn't be a Christmas without a goose and she had no money to buy another one. It was an expensive bird. My mother, always thrifty, the kind of woman who could bounce a *sechser*, a 5-*pfennig* piece, three times before she would spend it, immediately opened her purse and gave Mrs. Schmidke eight *marks*, the cost of a new bird. It was spontaneous. I was very proud of her for doing that nice thing for Mrs. Schmidke.

My parents having married in 1913, celebrated their silver wedding anniversary in March of 1938. Dark clouds overhung the Jewish community and all celebrations were subdued. Still, my parents had a small party for about eight couples. Despite peoples' worries and concerns, it was a nice occasion. I remember it quite well.

My father gave my mother a beautiful present on that occasion. It was not a surprise. On the contrary, it was something that they had talked about for a long time. He gave her a diamond wristwatch. I remember exactly what it cost, namely 3,000 *marks*. It was the equivalent of about $10,000 to $15,000 today. It was a beautiful piece. The laws against exporting jewelry were already in force. Therefore, it wasn't clear to me at all why they would have bought it. There was one important proviso that my mother hoped to be able to take advantage of. That proviso was so mean and so ridiculous that it is really hard to believe. It went like this: Jews could take their jewelry and have it appraised by one of the Nazis' designated estimators. The estimator would put a value on it, as high as he possibly could. He would then put the jewelry in a box and seal it with the Nazi seal. The applicant would then advise to where he or she was going to emigrate, and the package containing the jewelry would then be forwarded to the German embassy or German consulate in that city. In my parents' case it would be Buenos Aires. But in order to get one's jewelry back, in order to redeem it, one had to pay the appraised value in dollars at the German embassy or the consulate of the country of destination. In other words, if a person had bought a piece of jewelry for the equivalent of $3,000, and the appraiser had appraised it at that value, the person could pick it up from the German consulate in whatever city by paying $3,000. Can you imagine anything meaner then that? One had to pay the bastards to get one's own property back.

Shortly before my parents left Germany, and they left almost literally on the last boat, in June of 1939, my father went to one of the designated appraisers. It was in an office building in the *Friedrichstrasse*, a small room, with only the appraiser and the "client," sitting opposite each other across a table. The appraiser took the watch, put a loupe in his eye so as to evaluate each one of the many diamonds in the bracelet that formed the watchband. He looked at my father and said, "My God, man, that is a beautiful piece. How much did you pay for it?"

My father told the truth. A lie could have been fatal. "3,000 *marks*," he said.

"It's a bargain," the appraiser said, "It's worth much more. I would say at least 5,000 or 6,000 *marks*."

My father was afraid of just that because the appraisers always tried to put as high a value on the jewelry as possible, so as to get more money for the Nazis when the emigrants arrived at their destination.

My father tried a rear-guard action, "Oh no," he said, "I really think it isn't worth more than the 3,000 *marks* we paid for it."

The appraiser looked at him and he said, "Man, you look awfully familiar to me. What school did you go to?"

My father said, "I went to the *Gymnasium* in the *Grosse Hamburgerstrasse*."

The appraiser looked at him more thoughtfully. "What year were you born?"

My father said, "1885."

"Max, don't you recognize me? Don't you remember me? I'm Otto Hartmann. We were in the same class together in school."

My father said, "Otto, you are right. I wouldn't have remembered you. But now I do. You have a wonderful memory."

Otto said, "Those goddamn Nazis. I really feel ashamed that I have to do this shitty kind of work. I'll tell you what I'll do. I'll appraise this piece at 1,000 *marks*. That is my little present to you."

My father could not believe his good fortune. But that is what happened. Otto issued a certificate that the watch was worth 1,000 *marks*, put it in a box and sealed it with the Nazi seal – a spread eagle clutching the hated swastika in its claws. When my parents eventually went to Buenos Aires, my Aunt Sarah, who was already living there and already well established – in any case, her son Erich had a good business – she lent my mother the equivalent of 1,000 *marks*, about $250 at the time. She went to the German embassy, walked past the Nazi guards, up the marble stairs, showed her passport and immediately received her diamond watch against payment of the appraised value.

The beautiful watch with the diamond bracelet watchband is still in our family. My mother gave it to our daughter Rachel. Rachel took the watch itself out and discarded it. It was a bit old-fashioned and she replaced it with another diamond link. She wore the bracelet to her wedding and wears it to all wonderful occasions.

In Germany in those days, unusual things happened from time to time. I also had two such experiences, similar to that with the appraiser. Although I am getting a little ahead of myself, I am going to describe one of them right away. The other one, much more incredible, happened on my last day in Germany. I'll talk about it in a minute.

When I was ready to leave for South America in December of 1938, my mother bought me clothes and all other good things that one could take out of Germany, many more things than I could possibly use in the tough environment in which I would find myself. In any case, there were two large pieces of luggage. One was a steamer trunk, and the other one, which freely translated from the German would be a "wardrobe trunk." One could stand it up on its small end and open it like a wardrobe. One side had hangers for clothes and the other side had drawers. It was a very neat arrangement.

I was told to take the two trunks to the Anhalter Bahnhof Station for transport to Hamburg and then to my ship the SS AMMON. As a rare exception, I was allowed to take a cab and took one of the two trunks to the railroad station. It was about 10 o'clock in the evening.

When I arrived at the station, I pulled the trunk into the customs office. There was only an elderly man there. He was the inspector. He was reading a book when I came in. He looked at my steamship ticket and my passport and asked me what I had in the trunk.

I said, "Just my personal belongings, clothes and things like that."

"How about some jewelry and some sterling silver?"

"Oh no, nothing of the kind."

"Are you sure? Because frankly, I don't give a damn. I think the Nazis are a bunch of criminals. You guys should be able to take your property with you. This is outrageous."

I said, "No there's nothing in it. You can open it up and check yourself."

"No, I don't want to open the trunk and I don't want to check." He put a band around the trunk, again with that awful seal, and he said, "You have anything else?"

I said, "Yes, I am going to bring another trunk tomorrow."

He said quietly, "Take my advice, put your mother's jewelry in it and all the silverware that you can lay your hands on. I promise you that I am not going to open the trunk. I am just going to seal it. I promise you that. I am not going to cooperate with those bastards."

"Thank you," I said. "I'll see about it."

I was very excited about this. I went home on the streetcar and told my parents in detail what had happened.

They quizzed me over and over again – every word, every nuance was being discussed.

I said, "Mutti, put the bracelet in the trunk (this was before my father's encounter with Otto), and our good sterling. The man is not going to open the trunk."

My parents discussed that for at least an hour. Finally my father said, "This could be a trick. He is laying a trap for us, and if he does open the trunk and finds this stuff all of us will get killed." I suppose he made the right decision. So we put nothing of value in the trunk.

The next day I went to the railroad station and the same man was there. "Well, he said, here you are again. Did you follow my advice?"

"Which advice?" I asked innocently.

"I told you to put all your parents' jewelry and silver in that trunk. You guys must have plenty of that."

"We don't have anything like that. We follow the law and there is nothing in the trunk."

He said, "O.K., I believe you, but I told you that I was not going to open it." He put the strap with the hateful seal around the trunk and bid me good bye. "I see you are going to South America," he said. I've never been there. I always wanted to go there. I think it must be very beautiful. Good luck to you, my friend."

Well, I felt a little bit like a fool for not having believed him. But my father was right, we couldn't take the chance of being caught in a deadly trap. The only one I knew about who took the chance was my cousin Erich. I told you about him. He is the one who smuggled those three big diamonds out of Germany in a tube of toothpaste. It laid the basis for his fortune in South America.

Because of the weird rules that governed citizenship in Germany – the same rule that made my father a Russian citizen though he was born in Germany, Eva Siegler happened to be a Greek citizen. She had never been in Greece and, of course, could not speak one work of Greek. Her father was Greek and therefore she was a Greek. I believe that her father also had never been in Greece and did not speak a word of Greek. He probably got that citizenship from his father. It went through generations. This rule greatly benefited Horst Peck, who, to his surprise, turned out to be a British subject, and also gave cause to an interesting event with my friend Alfred Thursch.

At that time, Jews began to talk seriously about emigration – how to get out of Germany. They began to realize that things were getting worse and worse and that therefore leaving Germany would ultimately be inevitable.

One thing the Nazis had already decreed was that those who emigrated could not take anything with them, anything that they owned, if it had any value. There were meticulous regulations as to what personal possessions, furniture, etc. could be taken. But one thing was strictly forbidden and that was to take any jewelry out of the country. Jewelry had to be turned over to the state or had to be "redeemed" in dollars, just as with my mother's diamond bracelet. The only thing that could be kept were golden wedding rings.

Eva told my mother that she was planning on emigrating to Greece, which, since she was a Greek national, was very easy for her. As a Greek national, the jewelry laws did not apply to her.

My mother, after discussing the matter with my father and also with me, decided to entrust her remaining jewelry to Eva – to have her take it to Greece and eventually to send it to wherever my mother and father were going to wind up, probably in Buenos Aires.

Besides that diamond bracelet, my mother didn't have a great deal of jewelry. There were a few rings, a gold bracelet, my father's golden watch, which my mother had given him as a wedding present, two pendants and a brooch, but nothing extraordinary. My mother gave all of that to Eva and asked her to take it to Greece and then send it to her when the time came, and when she was settled in some foreign country. Eva took the jewelry and promised to do as she had been asked.

Eva Siegler left Germany with the jewelry my mother had given her and went to Greece. My mother gave her a big hug, took her address, and told her that she'd be in touch with her just as soon as she was settled, wherever it was going to be, so that Eva could forward the jewelry to her. Of course, the war broke out in the meantime. We never heard from Eva again. She was lost in the firestorm of the Holocaust just as so many other people. I am quite sure that some German matron, or several for that matter, are now adorned with my mother's jewelry that had been "liberated" in Adolf Hitler's glorious war.

While all the time maintaining my overarching love to Ulla Hjalsted, with whom I corresponded weekly, I was also deeply involved with Cilly Steinfeld. Mostly I suppose because I couldn't make a sexual conquest, I composed a tango for her which I still can sing today. The tune isn't really bad. I think it's better than some of the compositions of the Beetles, but of course, the Beetles didn't do tangos. The initial stanza went as follows:

> *Kleine Cilly, hast Du mich noch gerne,*
> *Kleine Cilly, hängst Du noch an mir.*
> *Denn weil ich auch jetzt in weiter Ferne,*
> *In Gedanken bin ich stets bei Dir.*

I won't bother you with the exact translations into English, but essentially the song described my (totally imaginary, of course) exploits with women in all major cities of the world. Interestingly, it had at least one Freudian component. The first city I mention in the second stanza is Copenhagen where, of course, Ulla lived. The other cities that I mentioned in this tango were totally alien to me at the time. The third stanza was even more lurid. In it, I describe my amorous exploits in the deserts and in the arctic regions. The refrain of all stanzas was that in every case I found that Cilly from the shores of the Spree (the river that flows through Berlin) was the most wonderful, the most beautiful, and the most sexy of them all.

Cilly appreciated my homage to her but still did not yield her virtue in return.

I continued to be fascinated with school and with the Boy Scouts. My good friend Heinz Vogel's mother, Erna, was a teacher of modern languages (though, of course, as a woman she could not possibly have taught at the *Hohenzollern Gymanisum*) and she decided that her son should become fluent in French. She felt that our learning English was not enough. In order to make it interesting for him, she decided to take me on also, so we both got French lessons from her. I went to Heinz's home three times a week for that. I didn't get very far and Heinz didn't either. I remember the very last sentence I learned. That was on page 5 of the textbook. It went as follows:

> *As-tu fait tes devoirs?*
> *Oui, c'est trés difficile,*
> *j'ai fait des bêtises.*

If you don't know French, it means:

> Have you done your homework?
> Yes, it is very difficult. I made mistakes."

That about told the story. I gave up learning French.

Fast forward: When I was forty-five years old and living in San Francisco, I was lying in bed one Sunday morning and reading the Sunday papers. They had one of those quizzes – twenty questions that had a Yes or No answer and you got points for the "right" answers. This particular quiz was about "Are you or are you not yet middle-aged?" At that time I had some serious doubts as to whether I was already middle aged so I wanted to be sure. I answered the questions as honestly as I could and found that I was indeed middle aged. I had "lost" by two points. I was unhappy about that and went back over the questions to see if I could honestly change any of my answers. One of the questions was: "Have you finally given up ever learning French?" I had answered with "Yes." I realized that if I had answered "No," I would have gotten three extra points and would not be considered middle-aged. I erased my "Yes" answer and changed it to "No." I was no longer middle-aged. But I had to keep myself honest, so the next day I went to the *Alliance Française* on Mason Street in San Francisco and enrolled in their French course for beginners. I stayed with it for two semesters. I actually acquired a pretty good working knowledge of French. In any case, when sometime later Priscilla and I went to France, I could communicate. It was gratifying. But of course, French should not have been too difficult a language for me since I had that background in Latin and since I was a fluent Spanish speaker.

My brother, who had interrupted his pre-med studies at the university in Berlin was sent by my parents to London to continue his studies at the university there. It was a major sacrifice for my parents because of the enormous difficulty of sending money abroad. As I recall, my brother needed 200 *marks* per month minimum to live and pay his student fees. The 200 *marks* was a substantial amount for my parents, but they could handle it. The difficulty was in transferring the money to London. Under the stringent currency laws introduced by the Nazis, each person could transfer only ten *marks* abroad per month. One would go to the post office and make such a transfer and the transfer was entered into one's passport. Everyone was scurrying around enlisting the help of other people to transfer ten *marks* to those who needed it. Relationships got strained. Everyone needed to send money abroad. Somehow or other, my parents, appealing to all our relatives and good friends, got the twenty people together every month to fulfill my brother's allowance.

There was another problem. My parents did not get satisfactory reports from my brother about his studies. There was no long distance telephone to London, or at least it wasn't used. Everything was by letters. Every time my parents asked him to be specific about what he was studying and about his progress, he seemed to be noncommittal and evasive. Eventually, his letters began to talk in somewhat lurid tones about a young woman with the unusual name of Salome who, I remember distinctly, was a waitress at Lyon's Teahouse. My parents were most alarmed. That was not at all what they had planned. Eventually, and after much discussion, my father decided to travel to London to confront my brother and to make a personal assessment of how things were going. In those days, the trip from Berlin to London was a major undertaking, involving permits, visas, travel by train and by ship across the channel, and, of course, being able to come up with enough foreign money to finance the trip. But my father did it. He did not speak one single solitary word of English.

When he arrived in London and managed to get to the address of my brother's lodgings, he found that he could somehow communicate with the Jewish landlady who spoke Yiddish, in addition to English. My father didn't speak a word of Yiddish. But Yiddish is very similar to German, so some primitive communication was possible. The landlady showed my father where my brother's room was and my father went and entered it. To his surprise, he found my brother asleep in his bed. He aroused him and questioned him. My brother told him some flimsy story about this being a day off. My father then asked him to take him to the university, because he wanted to see where he was studying. It became clear then that my brother had only the vaguest notion as to where the university was. It seems that he had spent the six months that he had been in London mostly in romancing Salome. My brother offered to introduce my father to Salome, but he declined. She did not sound like daughter-in-law material to him. I suppose he was right.

Having realized that the medical studies in London were not successful, my father decided that instead of medicine, my brother should study dentistry, that he should leave London to escape the clutches of Salome and move to Edinburgh in Scotland. My brother, of course, was not consulted as to his desire to become a dentist. Even then, I marveled at how my father arrived at such decisions. In any case, my brother went to Edinburgh, where he realized that he had no interest nor talent for dentistry. But, being apparently somewhat of a Lothario, he continued with his amorous pursuits by befriending a young woman by the name of Rose Rifkind. He sent us a picture of her. I thought she was quite ugly.

Many years later, in the 90's, a Mr. Rifkind became Britain's foreign secretary. I remembered the somewhat unusual name. I wrote to Mr. Rifkind, and described briefly how my brother and Rose Rifkind had been good friends those many years ago. There was no reply. Then, about two months later, I had a phone call from a Mr. Rifkind – not the foreign secretary, but his brother. He told me that his brother had asked him to call me and to tell me that Rose was their aunt. She had moved to Israel. Heinz, my brother, was touched by my having located his long-ago love. They had one round of correspondence sixty-five years after she and my brother had been lovers. I thought it was very romantic. Even Lieschen, Heinz's wife, thought it was quite charming and very sentimental.

My parents then decided that Heinz should terminate his studies, forget medicine and dentistry, and should emigrate to Argentina, where we had family. My cousin Edith, Aunt Sarah's older daughter, who had been engaged to the man who had died of T.B., was married to a Mr. Spatz, who had a prominent position in a large Argentine firm by the name of Bunge & Born. That firm dominated Argentine business to such an extent that it was called *"el pulpo"* – the octopus, because of its tentacles all over the country, both in industry and in agriculture. Mr. Spatz offered my brother a job. In what appears almost unbelievable in retrospect, Heniz returned from Edinburgh to Berlin – he could have been thrown into a concentration camp – my parents outfitted him and he took off to the new world to start his life in Argentina. As of this writing, he still lives there with his wife Lieschen. He stayed with Bunge & Born all of his working life, almost fifty years.

My brother, whom I go to visit from time to time in Buenos Aires, tells me that he does not feel that he would have been cut out to become a doctor or a dentist and he is still somewhat amused by my father's insistence that the first son, namely he, would become a doctor and, that the second son, namely I, should become an attorney. I might have perhaps made a pretty good attorney. But even though I acquired a law degree in a correspondence school, I never took the bar and I never practiced law. So, my father might have been right, at least about that.

I heard dreadful things about what the Nazis did to the Jews in the small towns in Germany, but really, there was no real hardship on us in Berlin. We were, of course, aware of some of the hateful things that were happening in the small towns and were much concerned. The newspapers were full of hateful articles about Jews. There was one paper, *Der Stürmer*, edited by the notorious, utterly loathsome Julius Streicher. *Der Stürmer* was dedicated solely to the disparagement of Jews and filled with the most vulgar and hateful stories and caricatures. Personally, we were not molested in Berlin. I suppose that was because Berlin was the showplace, hosting many foreign visitors. The Nazis did not wish to make too bad an impression, especially during the 1936 Olympics in Berlin. Also, I believe, the Berliners as a whole were not quite as enthusiastic about the Nazis as the people in the rest of the country. I certainly had no personal unpleasantness at all in school with my fellow students and not too much with teachers.

Within a few weeks of Hitler's coming to power, it was decreed that at the beginning of every school hour, every class, the teacher had to enter the room with outstretched arm and with the Hitler salute and we had to respond by saying, "Heil Hitler." We had always been used to standing up when the teacher entered the room, so that was just an addition to the usual routine, though a rather important one. Most of the teachers did not seem to be too enthusiastic about this new rule. As far as I could tell, they were not too interested in the Nazi regime and their "Heil Hitler" was careless and lackadaisical. But we had one teacher, Dr. Holöhr, who was a true believer, an enthusiastic Nazi and the only one who wore a swastika button on his lapel. When he entered the room he would click his heels, stretch out his arm at a stiff 45 degree angle, and shout "Heil Hitler" with full lung power. We had to respond with the same enthusiasm and at the same decibel level.

One day, my friend Alfred Thursch just stood there, did not raise his arm, and did not say "Heil Hitler." He was a Jewish boy. Dr. Holöhr asked him, "What's the matter with you, Thursch? Are you crazy? Say Heil Hitler like everyone else."

"I don't care to say Heil Hitler," said Thursch, "because I am Polish citizen." He was, indeed, for the same reason that my father had been a Russian citizen, Eva Siegler was a Greek citizen, and Horst Peck was a British subject. And of course, Polish citizens, just as all foreign nationals, were exempted from the obligation to give the Hitler salute. But it was a very daring thing for him to do, particularly, since the Poles were not considered as highly as say, the French, the British, the Americans or anybody else. They were, even before the war, very low on the Nazi Germany totem pole.

Dr. Holöhr told him in a very unfriendly manner, "Thursch, the next time I come into this class, I want you to say Heil Hitler or you will have to bear the consequences. You understand me?"

"Yes I do," Thursch said.

Next time Dr. Holöhr or any of the teachers entered the class, Thursch was right there with us giving the Hitler salute. In any case he had shown some independence .

I had the most ambivalent feelings about Dr. Holöhr. He taught us Latin and German history. I thought he was an absolutely magnificent teacher. He was totally knowledgeable in his fields and knew how to impart knowledge and information. But, of course, I also hated him because he was the only one of two convinced Nazis teachers. I'll talk about the other one in a minute.

One day, in Latin class, we came to the sentence in Latin: "*Ubi bene, ibi patria.*" "Where things are good, that's where my fatherland is." Dr. Holöhr gratuitously elaborated on this. He said, "This sentiment is typical of the Jews. They go wherever they think things will go well for them, and that's where they settle down and make their home. They have no loyalty, no roots anyplace and certainly not in Germany."

I, being imbued with Zionist convictions and zeal, could not tolerate that. I stood up and said, "Herr Doktor Holöhr, I do not agree with your statement at all. We Jews have a country. It is Palestine. Many Jews are there already, have developed that country, and are making it their home. I too will go there."

Dr. Holöhr looked at me nonplused. He had not expected anything like that. He deliberated for about five seconds and then he said, "Sit down, you idiot."

And I did sit down. I thought about that a little later and realized that my action had been much more daring than I had meant it to be. I had endangered myself and my parents; my statement could have had the most dreadful consequences. Still, Dr. Holöhr, even though an avowed Nazi, let the incident pass, I suppose because I was a very good student and the "primus," the best student, in his Latin class. Nothing else was ever said about it.

The only other Nazi teacher we had was our gym teacher. His name was Herr Krüger. He was not just a Nazi, he was also an SS man, part of the black-shirted and jack-booted murdering thugs who were Hitler's personal guard. He treated me pretty well. The reason was that he was sweet on Gertrud, our maid, whom he had met one day when I had forgotten my lunch and she brought it to school. It proved lucky for me that they met. He thought she was marvelous and, of course, I thought so too.

He even started to write letters to her, which I had to take to Gertrud and wait for her to write the reply. She sent one reply and it was to tell him to leave her alone. She told him that she wanted nothing to do with him. From that time on his attitude toward me totally changed.

One day he was the monitor for recess in the schoolyard. The schoolyard was about 250 x 250 feet, and I was close to one corner of it. Herr Krüger stood in the middle. He looked at me. I caught his eye and he crooked his finger, beckoning me to come to him. I wondered what in the world he wanted. I went to him at a fast pace, but not running. "Yes, Herr Krüger, what do you wish?" I asked.

He pointed to a piece of paper about 50 feet away that some student had dropped. "Pick it up, Joffe." I hesitated and thought that it was a most unreasonable request. I hadn't thrown the paper down, I was 200 feet away from it. Why, from about 500 boys, would he have asked me to pick up that paper. "Herr Krüger," I said, "I didn't throw it down and I don't really understand why you would call me from so far away to pick it up." At that, he hit me in the face with just enough strength not to seriously injure me. "When I tell you to do something, you'd better goddamn do it, without asking any stupid questions. This is Germany," he added incongruously. I knew where I was and I thought that this couldn't have happened anyplace else. I was pretty shaken up and almost (but not quite) blamed Gertrud. If she had been a little nicer to Herr Krüger this wouldn't have happened. I didn't tell my parents about this incident. It would have been too upsetting for them.

Here's another story about Herr Krüger.

My friend Horst Peck had a beef against Herr Krüger, not too surprising, because Krüger was really a bad guy, you might call him a sadist. I don't know what happened between them, but Herr Krüger probably had hit him also.

Understandably, it made Horst very mad. Krüger came to school every day on a motorcycle, which he parked in the basement garage of the school. Horst went down to the garage with an ice pick and punctured both of his tires. As you can imagine, Krüger was very, very unhappy and he knew that somebody in our class had done it. He told us all to stay in school after 2 o'clock, until he found out who of us had done this "fiendish deed," as he called it. We were all sitting in the classroom, all thirty-five of us, and everyone knew that it was Horst Peck who had done that. Even the boys from the Hitler Youth knew it. Krüger said, "The son-of-a-bitch who did this to my motorcycle is going to stand up and admit it. When he does, I'll let the rest of you go. If somebody knows who did it and tells me, then I will also let the rest of you go. If nobody tells me, I'll let you sit here until hell freezes over."

Horst, of course, was very scared because he knew that his punishment would be very severe if he were found out. In addition to everything else, Krüger would probably have beaten him half to death and he wouldn't be called to account for it – as an SS man he could do virtually anything he wanted. But nobody told on him, not even the Hitler Youth boys. We sat there for one hour and nothing happened. Then Krüger came back into the classroom. He ranted and raved and again told us that he would let us sit here forever if necessary. We sat there for another hour. Nobody said anything. At 4 o'clock, two hours after regular school time, he let us go and swore that he would sooner or later find the "bastard" who had done this. He never did. Nobody ever talked about it.

I thought it was kind of interesting that with all the anti-Semitism at the time, nobody would have betrayed Horst. Perhaps even then, being a rat-fink was the worst thing one could be.

I always had a theory that the human race survives because people like the food that their mothers prepare for them. I figured that if, say, a Hottentot child would have a hankering for kosher cornbeef sandwiches when his mother was giving him fried grasshoppers, he could not survive; that a child in the American South, with a preference for fried grasshoppers could not survive if his mother gave him sowbelly with red-eye gravy, collard greens and grits; and that a big-city Jewish kid could not survive if he hankered for that sowbelly and his mother insisted on giving him kosher cornbeef sandwiches. It made good sense to me. But I had a problem: I didn't really like my mother's cooking. I always thought that it was heavy, very "German," heavy on potatoes and green beans and red cabbage. I read in magazines recipes about fine French food and interesting recipes and I submitted them to my mother. She just laughed. "You'll eat what I give you," she said. "It will make you big and strong."

My reservations about her cooking became stronger after I went to Denmark and partook of Mrs. Jespersen's exquisite cuisine. Everything was so delicate, everything was so un-German. When I came back home I told my mother about the wonderful dishes that I'd eaten and how delicate everything was, how well seasoned, how dainty, and how delightful. She just laughed. "That was vacation food," she said. "Here at home you'll eat real food."

I really didn't mean to hurt my mother's feelings, but when I think about it I am surprised that I didn't. My comparing her to anybody else, especially to Mrs. Jespersen, just rolled off her back. She thought it was funny.

While we were certainly not "orthodox," there was heavy emphasis from the very beginning on Jewish education. For the first four years of my schooling, I was in a Jewish class (though in a Catholic school), and Jewishness permeated everything. Then, when I went to the *Hohenzollern Gymanisum*, we had two hours a week of religious instruction. The students were separated by religion. The Protestants had their teacher, the Catholic children had theirs, and we Jewish students had ours. Our teacher was a rabbi who, like all other teachers, was paid by the government. I remember Rabbi Nussbaum, who at that time was a very young man. He later became the chief rabbi of the largest Reform congregation in Beverly Hills, a very "prestigious" position.

What bemused me was that, even to the very last, the German government, which had sworn death to the Jews, made sure that Jewish children got instruction in their religion. *Ja, Ordnung muss sein* – there must be order.

But those two hours a week were not enough. In addition, I went two afternoons a week to a Jewish school for special instruction in Hebrew and the Hebrew of prayers and ritual. Our teacher was a Herr Kasper. Herr Kasper was a World War I veteran and had lost his right leg above the knee. He had a wooden leg and had great difficult in walking. He was quite fat, partly perhaps the result of his immobility. He was an absolute tyrant. We were all deadly afraid of him. If any of the boys (he did not touch the girls) ever did anything wrong, he said, "Come here." The boy, trembling, would walk up to him. When the boy got three or four feet away, Herr Kasper, though still sitting, would lunge forward like a tarantula, grab the boy by his shirt, and beat him as hard as he could. Sometimes he would even use his cane. For a long time I had been spared this punishment.

One day, however, I made a mistake in quotation or had forgotten a verse, or whatever, and Herr Kasper told me to come up to him. I responded, "Sir, I am not going to do that."

"What's the matter with you! Are you crazy! I told you to come here."

"I know," I said, "but I'm not going to do it because I know for certain that you will beat me up."

"Come here!" he repeated.

"No," I replied.

He then got totally red in his face, forcibly got out of his chair, grabbed his cane, and slowly walked toward me. But I had no problem getting away from him. I left the classroom and went to the next room, where Rabbi Arthur Levy, the principal of the school, had his office. "Rabbi," I said, "if you don't stop Herr Kasper from beating us up, I will never come back here again."

"He is not supposed to beat up on the children," the rabbi said. "That is totally out of the question." The rabbi knew, of course, about Herr Kasper's proclivity, but nobody had ever complained to him before. So the rabbi took me by the hand and walked back to the classroom with me and said, "Herr Kasper, leave Gerhard alone. I think he knows his lesson. He just got a little confused." But to my disappointment, he did not utter a general proscription against corporal punishment.

Herr Kasper was nonplused. He didn't know how to handle the rabbi's admonition, but from then on he never beat up on anybody again. I realized that I had attained a small triumph against child abuse.

As a result of all this Jewish education, I went to religious service every Saturday morning while I was still in grade school, because in grade school we had no classes on Saturday. One Saturday, when I came home from temple, nobody was home, and I didn't have a key. I was locked out, so I had to wait until my mother or the maid came home. I was out, on the street playing, when my eyes fell on a large coin. I couldn't believe my eyes. I couldn't believe my luck. Here was a big shiny one *mark* coin. It was just lying there, waiting for me to pick it up. I had never expected to find anything like that. It was a miracle, especially for someone like me who did not yet have a regular allowance. A whole *mark*! Why would I find that? Why would anybody drop that? Then it became clear to me. It was a sign from God. God wanted to tell me something. God wanted me to dedicate my life to Him. God wanted me to become a rabbi. I was nine years old.

When my parents came home, I was still very excited about what had happened. Not just about the money, but mostly because of the sign from God. I told them what had happened. I told my father that I had decided to become rabbi.

He told me that I would not become a rabbi. He said I would become an attorney.

"Dad," I said, "God has given me a sign and he wants me to become a rabbi. Why do you want me to become an attorney?"

"Because," he said, "the first son in our family becomes a doctor and the second becomes an attorney. That's the way I want it and that's the way it's going to be."

That was a real surprise to me, because there being so much Jewishness around the house I thought that he and my mother would be delighted by my decision to dedicate my life to God and to the Jewish religion.

Many, many years later I heard a bitter and self-deprecating Jewish joke that reminded me of this incident.

Three Jewish ladies tell each other about their sons. "What does your son do, Mrs. Goldsmith?"

"Oh, my son is an orthopedic surgeon. He is the head of medicine of Mt. Sinai Hospital and professor of medicine at the university."

"How marvelous," the other two women said.

"And how about your son, Mrs. Rosenbuam?"

"Oh, my son is a famous attorney," she said. "He is the managing partner of his firm, with a hundred and twenty attorneys, and he's accredited before the Supreme Court."

"Oh that's marvelous," the other two women said. "How wonderful for you."

Then they turned to the third woman. "Mrs. Lieberman, what does your son do?"

"My son is a rabbi," she said.

"A rabbi," the other two women cried out. "What kind of job is that for a Jewish boy?"

As I said, it's a bad and very bitter joke, but it very much reminded me of the incident with my father.

He was a most mild-mannered and accommodating man; he let my mother run the whole show. But he had some fixed ideas that nobody could change. One had to accept that for as long as my father lived.

There were two tracks at our school that separated after the *Untertertia*, **the** fourth *Gymnaisum* grade. One could either choose the "humanistic" track or the "realistic" track. The humanistic track was, in addition to everything else, heavy in old languages, Latin and Greek, and literature. There was only one modern language, namely English. The realistic track, on the other hand, had French in addition to English, and heavy emphasis on mathematics and natural sciences. Even though my brother was utterly untalented in math – as I said, he had to have tutors all along – my father insisted that he take the realistic track. I never really understood why he would have chosen that because for the medical career that had been destined for him, the humanistic track would have been the more appropriate.

I, on the other hand, showed an early talent for mathematics and for natural sciences, but my father decided that I should take the humanistic track.

"Why, Dad," I asked him, "I don't want to do that? I'm interested in math and modern languages. I don't want to learn any Latin or Greek."

"I don't care what you want," he said. "You are going to become an attorney. An attorney has to have a humanistic education."

I didn't like his decision but I didn't put up too much of a fight. I didn't really care all that much. In retrospect, my father did me a big favor, because I have all this Latin and Greek and literature under my belt, which turned out to be very satisfying and most helpful in later life, especially in my getting a quick grasp of Spanish. A thorough knowledge of Spanish turned out to be most important for me. I fully caught up with the math and the natural sciences later, so I really had the best of both worlds.

He had made the right decision for me, but for the wrong reasons.

The Nazis, totally besotted with the concept of race, introduced in the school curriculum a subject that had never before existed. This new subject was *Rassenkunde*, the "science" of race. It quickly became very important, and a grade in that subject counted highly. I thought the course was totally hilarious. One day, our teacher explained to us the characteristics of the different German "Aryan" races, in which, to my surprise and I suppose to the surprise of my fellow students, there were supposedly important differences. I thought they were all the same "master race," and that there were no distinctions. But there were.

As our teacher explained to us very earnestly, the highest level of the German race were the full Nordic types, those who most resembled the Swedes, the Danes and, most admired, the Norwegians and the "racially pure" Icelanders. Those paragons were obviously concentrated in the northern part of Germany. Then, the purity and quality of the race apparently deteriorated as one went south. The lowest of the German races, barely acceptable, were the so-called Alpine ones, those who lived in the mountainous regions of Bavaria. The teacher explained to us that they were inferior because, being weaker, they were driven up the mountains by their more successful rivals in the lowlands.

Cranial ratios and nasal cartilage played great roles in the determination of the subgroup to which one belonged. Jews, of course, just as some other races, including of course Negroes and gypsies, were classified as *Untermenschen*, those barely belonging to the human race. Most desirable was a long and narrow skull. The ratio between length and width should be at least 1.5 or more. The less that ratio, the less desirable a racial specimen one was.

All this nonsense was propagated with great earnestness and was taken very seriously by my classmates and, apparently, by almost everyone else.

I remember distinctly one of my fellow students by the name of Schumitz, whom the teacher one day called to the front of the classroom. The teacher applied his calibrating tool and told him with a straight face, "Schumitz, you are an example of the lowest level of the German race."

I thought it was very funny, but Schumitz didn't. Even though he was sixteen years old, he started crying in class. The teacher stated the result of his measurement as a matter of fact. That he could hurt Schumitz's feelings did not occur to him and, of course, he didn't care.

We got an assignment to take care of during our summer vacation, namely to prepare an *Ahnentafel*, a family tree. We were given a large form on heavy paper, with lots of boxes printed on it. We were given the assignment before we left for summer vacation. Each student was to place his name in the bottom box, with the two boxes above for his parents, the four boxes above that for his grandparents, eight boxes for his great-grandparents, etc. The top row, the fifth generation had thirty-two boxes. We had to put in the name, the place and date of birth and death in each box. Then there was an accompanying sheet in which each of our numbered ancestors had to be described. There were eight mental and eight physical characteristics for each, from which we had to pick, and room for special notations. Most of my classmates spent their vacation trying to complete this chart as best they could. Some of them traveled all over Germany to consult old church records, gravestones, city hall documents, and distant relatives.

I was on my third trip to Denmark, in order to be with Ulla and the Jespersen family and had forgotten all about this silly project. When I came back from my vacation, I remembered it and panicked. I was in big trouble. I told my father about it and he noted how upset I was. My punishment for not having done my research and not having filled out this chart and its attachment could be serious. My dad said not to worry and that he was going to help me. He told me about his father and his mother, but he knew very little if anything about his grandparents, my great-grandparents, who had been living in some remote place of a foreign country. The same was true with my mother, though she had some vague knowledge about her grandparents, certainly not anything that I could put on my chart. And how about those five generations?

My father said, "Don't worry about it. You and I are going to figure this thing out." He then proceeded to put in imaginary names and imaginary places and dates of birth and death in each one of these boxes – there were 63 of them altogether. He allowed approximately twenty-five to thirty years per generation, and with the help of the atlas, found places for birth and death in Russia and in Poland. I thought he did a very neat job, I hadn't realized that he was that imaginative. Then we had to go to the mental and physical qualities. He filled in those also for each one of the sixty-three boxes of the diagram. He had the good sense of putting just the name of the ancestors in a few of the boxes and remarked the dates and places of birth and death were unknown. He didn't want it to be "perfect." It would have been too pat. I thought it was a masterful job. Then he added a little flourish of his own in reference to his grandfather on his father's side. He made me put down that Gabriel Joffe was an adjutant to the Czar of Russia (yeah, that was just what the Czar was looking for, a Jewish adjutant!) and that he had died accompanying the Czar to a house of ill repute, where some aristocrat was trying to kill the Czar and that my great-grandfather had interposed his body and took the bullet for him. I though we could have done without that story but there it was.

I turned it in and I got an A grade on this project. The teacher said, "I have to hand it to these old Jewish families. They really take care of their ancestry. I wished some of our own people were that diligent." Then he said, "Joffe, I see one discrepancy here. I don't want to make any aspersions against your ancestors, but according to Mendel's Law, #43 should have brown eyes and she had blue eyes. How do you think that is possible?"

I said, "Mr. Boehm (that was his name), I really don't know. Either Mendel was wrong, or there are exceptions to his law or maybe we made a mistake. Some of our family records are a little musty."

He let it go, for which I was very grateful. I didn't think I could have stood up under more serious scrutiny.

In any case, I got an A in *Rassenkunde* – the only one in the class!

Almost to the exclusion of everything else, the discussion at home was interminably about the Nazis, the Jews, and the future, if any, of the Jews in Germany. Any time we met with other people, that was really all we ever talked about.

But nobody, nobody even in their wildest fantasy, could image what ultimately did happen to the Jews, not just in Germany, but all over Europe. Nobody foresaw that it was the purpose of the Nazis, a purpose in which they almost succeeded, to exterminate, to kill all of the Jews of Europe and, one must assume, to kill the Jews in the whole world, if victorious in their war.

After the promulgation of the Nuremberg Laws, many people came to the conclusion that there was no future in Germany any more for Jews and made preparations to emigrate. They were the smart ones. The others, and I suppose that also included my parents, believed that, though things were getting more and more dreadful every day, ultimately good sense and what they believed was the "innate decency" of the Germans would prevail. They believed, or rather hoped, that because of the Jews having so much contributed to Germany in every field of endeavor, that the *modus vivendi* would eventually prevail. Some even hoped that Hitler was ultimately going to be deposed or assassinated, but that hope became dimmer and dimmer because it was clear that his hold on all levels of the government was firm, becoming firmer by the day. It was also clear that the vast majority of the German people supported what the Nazis were doing, creating so many jobs, building those magnificent *Autobahnen*, and finally reoccupying the Rhineland, which had been demilitarized by the Treaty of Versailles. They were proud about the reassertion of German power and couldn't help noticing that other countries, including England, France, and the United States did not do anything about it, except for occasionally lodging some diplomatic complaints.

As for anti-Semitism, as far as I could tell, the great majority of the German people supported those measures, although some deplored "excesses" and maintained that the *Führer* did not know about what was happening and that it was his underlings who did those terrible things, of which he would certainly disapprove if he knew about them.

Jews who had little to lose, who perhaps just had a job, a small apartment and not too much property, decided to leave early in the game. Those who had big positions, medical or legal practices or who had businesses or nice homes and property were more reluctant. They left at the very last moment. Many of them, of course, did not manage to leave at all and found a terrible end. My parents, though they did not have a great deal of property, but had a business that supplied them with a livelihood, were reluctant to leave. I remember my father often quoting a German proverb, which in translation says: "Nothing is eaten as hot as it is being cooked," which means that in the end things usually turn out better than one had feared.

I felt very sorry for my parents, because I realized that their life was bound up with being Germans and being in Germany. I had very little such sentimental attachment.

Even today, I often wonder about how I could have felt that way. I was totally imbued with German language, with German literature, with German music, German songs, German food, everything German – except that I had developed my identity as a Jew. It was most important to me. I decided that I was going to leave Germany as soon as the occasion arose and that I would go to what was then called Palestine and which, of course, eventually became Israel. My parents were not too enthusiastic about that, because they felt it was too "dangerous," that there was "no future," and other such objections. My mind, however, was staunchly made up, and that was that.

In those days, in order to appease the Arabs, the British government had instituted a quota for Jewish emigration to Palestine and one had to make formal application to the British government to be considered. I made such application in 1937, when I was seventeen years old. I was told that it might take a little while before the application would be approved or rejected.

The efficient Germans had mail service twice every day, once in the morning and once in the afternoon and once on Saturday morning. There was no mail service on Sunday. One day in 1936, it was about 8 o'clock on a Saturday morning, and my parents were still in their beds, though not asleep, I went into their bedroom and we talked about this and that. Then I heard the mail falling through the mail slot. My father told me to go and pick it up to see what it was. There among the other mail was an official-looking envelope. It was bound not to contain any good news. I gave it to my father who opened it. He took out a letter, read it and blanched. He handed it to my mother. My mother read it and broke out in uncontrollable sobs. She just wouldn't stop. I took the piece of paper from her. The letter had only one paragraph. It informed my father and my mother that all of us, my parents, my brother and I had been deprived of German citizenship, that we would now be considered as "stateless," and that appropriate documents would be issued in due time.

My brother, of course, was in Argentina by that time. He couldn't care less. And it was a matter of indifference to me. I only hoped that being stateless would not offer additional difficulties to my emigration to Palestine. Between sobs, my mother told me how her father and grandfather and her great-grandfather had been loyal German citizens, as far back as records were available. She mumbled about her brother, Uncle Siegfried, who had been an officer in the First World War and had earned the Iron Cross First Class for bravery, of how she and her family had sacrificed everything after her hometown, Posen, was ceded to Poland, in order to be able to live in Germany. She was disconsolate.

My father, though born in Berlin and never having known anything else and did not speak any other language than German, took it much more in his stride. He certainly was not imbued with "Germanism" to the degree that my mother was. Perhaps he had been preparing himself, steeling himself for this to happen, over the previous few years.

In order to prepare me for my emigration to Palestine, my mother, at my insistence, had engaged a private Hebrew teacher who came twice a week to teach me modern spoken Hebrew. I had quite a bit of background in Hebrew because of the extensive Jewish education that I had received, but modern spoken Hebrew was something else again. I did reach a level of competence, which allowed me to read easy newspapers and carry on everyday conversations.

Hebrew, however, for somebody brought up in an Indo-European language, is so alien and so difficult that, unless one practices and practices it, is easily forgotten. That's what happened to me. Not using it and not immediately emigrating to Palestine, I forgot most of it. I certainly could no longer carry on any conversation.

Fast forwarding a little over fifty years: Even though I no longer intended to move to Israel I did decide that all Jews should at least have a working knowledge of Hebrew. I therefore engaged a Hebrew teacher and, once again, reached a level of moderate proficiency in the language. Ultimately, after about three years of private lessons, my teacher returned to Israel, and, once again, I forgot most of what I had learned. As I said, it is a very difficult language.

With the Nazi noose tightening, even my father had to concede that his dream of my becoming a lawyer in Germany was no longer realistic. I had to do something else to prepare myself for a livelihood abroad – for a life in Palestine. My purpose was to go to a kibbutz and to work on the land, in true pioneer fashion. My parents, who were never quite taken with the Palestine idea, suggested to me that I should go to an agricultural school in Palestine and I accepted that solution. But then they told me that I had to do "something" until I got the permit from the British to make *aliyah*, to "go up" to Israel. They persuaded me that I should go to an engineering school in Germany, which they had already selected for me. It was decided, and I agreed, that I should leave school after the *Einjaehriges*, after ten years of schooling, which the Germans called the "middle maturity" or the "one yearer."

My brother had finally finished high school. He had made the coveted *Abitur* and, quite frankly, I was a little envious of that. I would not be able to achieve that goal, but I accepted in good spirit to leave school and to go to the kind of engineering school to which my education entitled me. I would not be able to go to the *Technische Hochschule*, which was only available to those who had made the *Abitur*. The lesser school that was selected for me was in Mittweida, a little town in Saxony. I made some inquiries and found that it was well reputed and highly recommended, so I accepted that as an interim solution toward my ultimate goal.

One of the many hateful things the Nazis did in their very first year of being in government was to disenfranchise all Jewish physicians and attorneys, fire all Jewish teachers and all Jewish civil employees. In addition, they prohibited all Jewish artists – actors, directors, singers and everyone else – to perform in public. Thousands of wonderful artists, the cream of the German and primarily the Berlin cultural scene, were suddenly out of work.

The Berlin Jewish community, which was still very substantial – almost 200,000 people – decided to create cultural and artistic institutions of its own. Surprisingly, the Nazis permitted that. Berlin Jews formed the *Kulturbund*, the cultural society, in which most of the Jewish artists who were now out of work were employed. The *Kulturbund* bought or leased a large theater in which they put on the most marvelous performances, by far the best in Berlin. Every month we had two or three different operas or operettas, dramatic plays or comedies and concerts. The performances were absolutely wonderful. I especially remember seeing the "Bartered Bride" by Smetana and Mozart's "Marriage of Figaro" in absolutely first-rate performances. The stupid Nazis, having deprived themselves of the finest artists in Germany were left with mediocre performances. But by that time, they really didn't seem to care that much any more. They delighted in strutting around in their ridiculous uniforms, blowing their trumpets, and screaming "Sieg Heil."

There was an interesting wrinkle, which, I believe, strengthened solidarity in the beleaguered Jewish community. All tickets to the performances and concerts had the same price. Very old people, all those who could not see or hear very well, or had some other impediment, were allotted the front rows for all performances. All others got their seat assignments by turn. One month you would get an A ticket (the best seats), next month a B ticket, then a C ticket and, then a D ticket. Then the cycle would start over again. It was a great and very democratic system I thought.

In the spring of 1937, at the beginning of the school year I took the train from Berlin to Chemnitz. The station before Chemnitz was Mittweida and that's where I got off. I had been accepted by the school, so all I had to do was go to the registrar's office, fulfill some formalities and I was enrolled. The next order of the day was to find a place to live. The school had a bulletin board on which rooms for rent to students were advertised. I took down a few addresses within my price range and looked at the rooms.

I didn't like the first one because it was dank and dark and also didn't smell very good. So I told the lady that I was going to think about it and I was going to come back. I didn't like the second room because I thought the landlady was unfriendly and probably a Nazi. The third name on my list was a Fräulein Mieze. Her home was in a nice neighborhood on a pleasant tree-lined street. I walked up to the house and rang the bell. She opened the door and I liked her right away. She was obviously a nice lady and as I suspected, and later found out, a spinster. She took me to the room. It was absolutely beautiful. It had two big windows. It was large and sunny, very clean and, as a special "bonus," it had a drafting table, which a previous student had left. It was something I would need but now would not have to buy. I told her that I would take the room. The price was right too, 25 *marks* per month, just what I had budgeted.

But when I turned around, my heart froze. Over the bed there was a large picture of Adolf Hitler. I could not possibly be in that room, but I could not tell Fräulein Mieze that I didn't like the room, after I had told her that I did. It could have caused dreadful, unimaginable problems, not just for me, but also for my parents. Fräulein Mieze caught my glance and said, "You will like the room. I know you can make yourself comfortable here."

We understood each other perfectly well, though we did not say a word about it. I spent a happy school year there and the way I handled it, and I believe was the way Fräulein Mieze expected me to handle it, was to take the picture of Adolf Hitler off the wall the minute I came home from school and put it under the

Cilly Steinfeld – one of my adolescent amours. She liked
hugging and kissing, but she drew an iron curtain at the navel
– there was no way to get beyond it.

Seventeen years old, at my drafting table in Mittweida, in Fräulein Mieze's room. I look as though I knew what I was doing, but I was absolutely the worst draftsman in the world.

bed. I scotch taped a note on the door with the words "Don't Forget." That meant don't forget to put Adolf Hitler's picture back on the wall when I left the room in the morning. It would of course have been a major offense to put the *Führer's* picture under the bed. If Fräulein Mieze would have decided to denounce me, it would certainly have been the end of my school career and, who knows, the end of my life. But it didn't happen. I faithfully followed the routine every day: Come home, put the picture under the bed, leave the room in the morning, put the picture back on the wall.

I didn't think that Fräulein Mieze was a dedicated Nazi. She certainly was not ideologically motivated and, though we never talked about it, I am quite sure that she would have disapproved of the "excesses" (quite a remarkable word!) against the Jews. She did, however, have almost a schoolgirl's crush on Adolf Hitler, about whom she talked with me frequently, and whom she believed to be a Jesus-like figure and certainly the savior (from what?) of Germany.

One day, an *Autobahn* (a super highway) that ran within twenty miles of Mittweida was being inaugurated and the *Führer* himself was supposed to drive down the highway in an open car, greeting the adoring throngs that would gather on the sides of the road and on overpasses. The Mittweida municipality had arranged a bus service for the occasion and Fräulein Mieze got up very early in the morning and was driven to the overpass at which she could look at her beloved *Führer*. There was a long wait because the *Führer's* caravan was not on time and Fräulein Mieze had an urgent call of nature. She had to leave the overpass for about ten minutes. When she returned, the *Führer* had already passed. She hadn't been able to see him. Her unhappiness about having missed the great event and the great man was pitiful. She talked about it for weeks, and teared up every time she thought about it.

Fräulein Mieze, who I would guess was about fifty years old at the time and had never been married, subscribed to a lonely-hearts publication and had intensive correspondence with men all over Saxony. Sometimes she would consult me as to the suitability of prospective suitors, as much as one could tell from the ads that they had published and would reveal about themselves. Every other week or so, she would take a trip to meet somebody in one of the cities in Saxony, but she always came back disappointed. Nobody was just right. In fact, she confided to me that two of the prospects had had the temerity of suggesting sex in order to "get to know each other better." She was very indignant about such effrontery.

She was a nice lady, really. We never talked about the unspoken contract about Hitler's picture, and what's more, she provided me every morning with a continental breakfast, which was an "extra," not really part of the agreement.

Even so, the daily exercise with the Adolf Hitler picture made me uncomfortable and when my first vacation rolled around, I decided to seek other quarters.

I loved the school. One thing that immediately caught my attention was the exceptionally large number of foreigners who were enrolled, I would say at least a quarter of the student body. Virtually all of those foreigners were Scandinavians, mostly Norwegians and Danes. I realized that that was a great advantage to me and to the other Jewish students – there were about ten of us altogether, because the townspeople who depended on the school for their livelihood and the administration of the school would certainly refrain from doing anything nasty or violent in front of the foreign students. It might upset the foreigners and give the townspeople a bad reputation.

About that time, because of my interest in Ulla, I had become rather proficient in Danish. Danish is a relatively easy language for a German speaker to learn. I had made it a point to learn fifty new words every day and I practiced with the Danish students at the school, who became my good friends.

The only unpleasantness that I can remember was that when we returned for the second year of school, after summer vacation, we were told that all Jewish students had to sit in the back of the class in every course. It didn't bother me very much. This indifference was reflective, I suppose, of how inured and hardened we had become to slights and insults.

I did very well at all the courses, which were heavy on math, physics, and related subjects in the first two years. The only aspect in which I was a total failure was drawing. Any course that was related to drawing was a big problem and there was one class, engineering drawing, which was nothing else but that. When I thought I had completed a drawing – never very well, but I hoped perhaps satisfactorily, I would inevitably make a blob of ink on the most important part of the drawing. There were only two ways to remedy that, namely to start over again or to take a razor blade and carefully scrape away the damage. The first solution was unthinkable – simply too much work. The latter solution, which I always chose, never yielded satisfactory results. I got an *A* in all courses but a *D* in engineering drawing. As we go along in this story, you will see that my lack of ability to do engineering drawing haunted me later in life.

In addition to the few Danish friends with whom I was in connection mostly because of the language, I was friendly with all of the other Jewish boys in school. We found each other very quickly, sitting at the back of each class.

My best friend was Hans Lesser, who was also from Berlin and who had a steady girlfriend. He wrote impassioned letters to her, some of which he actually read to me. They were pretty steamy. One day, he also wrote a letter to his mother – (like my mother, most people simply didn't use long-distance telephoning) and happened accidentally to switch envelopes so that his mother got the letter destined to his girlfriend and vice versa. The girlfriend didn't mind, though she was somewhat concerned. She knew what had happened. The mother, however, was outraged about the explicitness in Hans's letter. From what he told me, there ensued a strong confrontation next time he went home.

The big city close to Mittweida – the third largest city in Saxony –was Chemnitz, which, when that part of Germany became "East Germany," was redubbed Karl-Marx Stadt. All of my Jewish friends, including Hans Lesser, had motorcycles. We frequently went on weekends to Chemnitz, which was only 35 miles away. We visited the youth organization of the local temple. I acquired a girlfriend by the name of Sonja. She was short, plump and kind of pretty, but nothing special. The interesting thing about her was that she was an honest-to-goodness Turk, i.e., not just by nationality of her parents, but she was actually born in Turkey and spoke Turkish. It fascinated me. I often asked her to say things in Turkish; they sounded strange and wonderful. I had never known anybody in Germany who was not born in Germany and whose native language was not German. But, nothing serious happened between her and me. We were just good pals. I had a feeling that she would have wanted the relationship to get a little deeper, but I was involved with my other *amours*. I didn't want to handle another "profound" relationship.

What bothered me was that all of my friends had motorcycles and I did not. I was dependent on their transportation if I wanted to go someplace, especially Chemnitz. So, I started a mail campaign with my parents to buy me a motorcycle. I knew that it was a totally outlandish thought, as far as they were concerned, and that my father would under no circumstances consent to it. But I kept insisting and insisting. One day, totally to my surprise, my father wrote me that he had bought a motorcycle for me and that next time that I came to Berlin I could pick it up.

I was utterly surprised, but very happy.

I made it a point, of course, to get back to Berlin just as quickly as possible, in fact the very next weekend. It was such an unusual thing for my father to offer the motorcycle that I asked him how he had acquired it. He told me that a customer with a bad debt had given him the motorcycle in payment. He also told me that whatever value I would assign to the motorcycle, it was only a fraction of what that person owed him.

"Where is the motorcycle, Dad?" I asked him. "I'd like to see it."

He handed me a piece of paper with an address written on it and told me that's where the motorcycle was stored. I called my friend Hans Lesser and we both went out to the place, which was at the very edge of Berlin. It turned out that it was a huge shed, perhaps 100,000 square feet, that had hundreds of cars and motorcycles stored in it. I didn't really know what it was. Perhaps it was storage for repossessed vehicles, or a dealer's inventory of used vehicles or something like that. My father had given me a stall number where my motorbike was stored and the keys. We located it quickly. It was so beautiful, I was utterly delighted. It had a big English engine with the unusual name of JAP. The body was of German manufacture. There was only one thing wrong with it as far as I was concerned: It had a sidecar. Obviously I did not want a motorcycle with a sidecar. That was sissy stuff. Even though I, myself, had never ridden a motorcycle, I thought of it as being pretty easy, that it would essentially be like a bicycle, only assisted by an engine. I was quite right about that, but I figured, that riding a motorbike with a sidecar was something quite different. I was right about that too.

In any case, despite my misgiving, I was very happy and very proud. I put the key in the ignition, turned it, and stepped on the kick starter. The engine roared into action but something else, something terrible, happened. The whole motorcycle burst into flames. It was until then absolutely the worst moment of my life. I had no way of saving the machine from the flames. I knew that in no time at all the entire shed, with perhaps 1,000 or more cars and bikes in it, would catch fire. I thought that I might as well stay there and perish with it. Worst of all, Hans Lesser, my trusted friend, ran away. "You bastard," I hollered. "What's the matter with you leaving me alone in this disaster!" But he didn't listen and kept running.

When I thought I was beyond all help he came running back and brought a fire extinguisher, which he had spotted stored at the front door as we were riding into the shed. We turned the extinguisher on to the flames and in no time at all we extinguished them. The whole thing had scared me to death. My motorcycle was totally blackened, but fortunately it was only surface damage. As I learned later, there was a lever which set the timing on the ignition, namely whether the spark would come early or late in the ignition cycle. That lever apparently was in the wrong position, and that caused the fire. It was really a terrible scare. It could have caused one of the worst disasters in German automotive history. I certainly didn't want that. I never told my parents about it, and I swore Hans to secrecy.

Still shaken, I decided to leave the motorcycle where it was because I did not feel confident about riding it with the sidecar, and I told my father about it. "Please, Dad, let me take the sidecar off. I really don't want it and I don't think it's safe, because it's too difficult to ride."

"No," my father says, "Three wheels are safer than two. I don't feel too good about this whole motorcycle business anyway, but if you are going to ride a motorcycle, you are not going to ride on two wheels, you are going to ride on three wheels."

There was no reasoning with him. He was immutable about it.

My father had only two full-time employees besides my mother, who also eventually worked full-time. There was Fräulein Sydow who was the bookkeeper and did what little secretarial work had to be done. She was a spinster, had been employed by my father for over ten years and seemed to be quite devoted to him. One day my father went to the backroom where the employees hung their clothes. It seems that Fräulein Sydow's coat had fallen to the floor and had revealed the underside of the lapel of her coat. There was a swastika button. Obviously, but until then unknown to my parents of course, she was a member of the Nazi party. My father and mother were most disturbed about that, but there was nothing they could do. They couldn't even mention it to her. But it very much colored the relationship from then on out.

The other full-time employee was a Herr Grambsch. He had also been there all along. His official title was *Hausdiener* which literally means house servant. His job was to ride his bicycle, fitted with a cargo tray, all over Berlin and deliver piece goods to my father's retail customers. He was a card-carrying member of the Communist Party. His open involvement, of course, terminated instantly when the Nazis came to power. Unlike so many others, however, he did have the good taste of not becoming a member of the Nazi party.

At the very end there was another employee, a young man by the name of Komorowski, who was the all-round utility man.

Even though most of my father's customers, as far as I could tell, were Jewish, he had a fair number of gentile customers and got along very well with them until the very end. The most unusual of those was a Herr Schneider who was a member of the SS, the feared and detested personal guard of Adolf Hitler. Usually, when he came into my father's business, he wore mufti, but occasionally he came in full uniform – the black tunic and riding breeches, the shiny black boots, the swastika armband, and the cap with the death head insignia. It made my father most uncomfortable, of course, every time that happened. But there was nothing that he could do about it.

One evening in 1937, Schneider called at home. That was a most unusual and totally unexpected event. He said, "Max, this is Schneider. Listen carefully. You and your son must leave the house immediately because we are making a raid on all Jewish homes tonight, in which there are men over sixteen years old. We are taking them to a concentration camp. So go someplace where there are no Jewish men. Do it immediately" Then he hung up.

Naturally, we took him by his word. My father and my mother spent that night and the following week with my Aunt Hanne, because she was widowed and only lived with her daughter Ruth. Liese was already married.. We thought it would be best if we split up. Where should I go? Of course, I went to Cilly Steinfeld and her mother. They had a very small apartment, but they put me up for that night and for the rest of the week. Frau Steinfeld didn't have to worry about her daughter's virtue being endangered. Cilly, much to my regret, took care of that herself.

There was indeed a raid on Jewish homes that night, just as Schneider had informed my father. He probably saved my father's life and mine also by warning us. He could have been severely punished if anybody had found out what he had done. We didn't know what happened with him later. He probably became a guard and executioner in one of the death camps. But he did do that fateful favor for my father – and of course for me as well.

My father then told me to go back to Mittweida by train and that his factotum, young Komorowski, would drive the motorcycle to Mittweida and then turn it over to me. So I went back to Mittweida and waited for the motorcycle to come. Herr Komorowski, just about five years older than I and a really nice guy, arrived three days later. The motorcycle had been all cleaned up and he explained to me carefully the matter of the ignition lever, a lesson that I made very sure to understand. He then said goodbye, wished me good luck, and left on the train back to Berlin.

As soon as I was by myself, I called my friends Hans Lesser and Gerhard Neumann. I told them about the motorcycle and that I was going to take it for a test run. I asked them to accompany me on my maiden ride. So, I took it out on the highway. with Hans and Gerhard close behind me. The sidecar was on the right. About 300 yards down the road there was a slight turn to the left. To my horror, the motorcycle would not follow my command to turn left and went straight ahead, across a ditch and into an open field. I did not know what might have happened.

Hans and Gerhard laboriously helped me to liberate the motorcycle and to get it back on the road. Gerhard was the most knowledgeable. He explained to me that, just as I had expected and had just experienced, a motorcycle with a sidecar was essentially much more difficult to handle than one without it. In a motorcycle without a sidecar, you would, just as in a bicycle, lean into the curve and take that curve easily. That was not possible with a sidecar, because you couldn't lean. In order to handle a left curve, one had to apply the brake so that the sidecar could go around you. On the other hand, in order to make a right turn, one had to accelerate to go around the sidecar. It was difficult in concept and even more difficult in application. Therefore, I had Gerhard ride the motorcycle back into town and he, being a skilled mechanic, took off the sidecar. There was my beautiful motorcycle, with only two wheels, just like those of the other fellows.

Another quick fast forward about Gerhard Neumann. Every week-end, unless he was out of town to Berlin visiting his parents or visiting his girlfriend, he would spread a blanket in his backyard and take his motorcycle apart virtually piece by piece. He would clean it, oil it, and then lovingly put it all back together. I thought he had the greatest skills and the finest mechanical mind I had ever known.

Decades later I caught up with him by reference. He had left Germany, just like all of us, and had gone to Shanghai, which was one of the last possible places of refuge. He found a job as a mechanical jack-of-all-trades with the American Air Force, which recognized his mechanical talents. Eventually, General Chenault, head of the Flying Tigers, got hold of him and Gerhard ultimately became the chief mechanic of his entire squadron, with many experienced mechanics under him. Chenault was so impressed with Gerhard that he managed to cut through red tape and got him a visa to the United States. He became a U.S. citizen by Congressional resolution. Gerhard went to work for General Electric and made a meteoric career. He eventually wound up as Executive Vice President of the corporation and Chief Executive Officer of General Electric's jet engine division, one of the most important jobs at GE and a top position in American industry.

Having decided that staying with Fräulein Mieze and with the daily ritual of Adolf Hitler's picture was becoming too complicated and would eventually lead me into trouble. I started looking for another place and found one with Herr and Frau Möbius. I had a very nice room. There was only one small problem, namely that the toilet was half a floor down from the Möbius apartment in which I had my room. It was not a major inconvenience, only a little awkward. But I was absolutely enchanted by the Möbius family. Herr Möbius told me immediately (and I thought somewhat imprudently, because it was really dangerous) that he was a long-time Social Democrat, that he was determined to foil the Nazis at every step, even though there was nothing much that he or anyone else could do about them. He was a convinced socialist and had been the leader of the tailors labor union in his district. I had many great conversations with him while he was sitting cross-legged on his tailor's table doing his work. His wife was a stout, motherly woman. She had two grown sons, twenty-three and twenty-five years old, who also lived in Mittweida and shared their parents' social and political opinions. Frua Möbius took a great liking to me. She treated me like a son. I was totally happy in their home.

One memorable evening I spent with the Möbius family was that of the second Max Schmeling-Joe Louis fight. It came on at about 4 o'clock in the morning in Germany. Herr Möbius and I stayed up to listen to the radio. The fight was preceded by Adolf Hitler haranguing Max Schmeling (who had defeated Joe Louis in the first bout), telling him that he carried the honor of Germany upon his shoulders and to demonstrate to the black African the superiority of the German master race. Poor Schmeling, of course, got knocked out in the first round and it was very funny and most satisfying to me to listen to the German announcer who pleaded with him, "Max, Max, get up, get up," but to no avail, of course. Herr Möbius, who, just as I, had been cheering for Joe Louis, was delighted. We broke out a couple of bottles of beer and celebrated Joe Louis's victory, which we considered a defeat of Adolf Hitler.

One evening, it was before I had my motorbike, I came back by train from a weekend visit to Berlin and saw to my surprise that Frau Möbius was at the railroad station waiting for me. She was visibly agitated and concerned. "Gerhard," she said, "you should not come home. The Gestapo, the secret police, has come to the house. They are looking for you. They surely will come back. No telling what they will do to you. What have you done?"

I told her that "I hadn't done anything, as far as I knew. I don't know where else to stay but with you. If they want to catch me, they'll catch me anyway, so I might as well face the music, whatever it is."

Sure enough, the next day a policeman came. He arrested me and took me to the local office of the Gestapo. It was very scary, of course. I had no idea what they wanted from me. The policeman asked me to sit down in a small Gestapo office, which did not really look too forbidding. Nobody else was in the room. Five minutes later a middle-aged man walked in. He did not look like the "classical," fear-inspiriting Gestapo man, or at least what I imaged a Gestapo man to look like. He was in his late 50's and had a bushy mustache, not the small toothbrush type that Adolf Hitler and many of his followers favored. Of course, I stood up when he came in and he told me to sit down. He looked through some papers and then, not entirely unfriendly, he said, "Hey, Gerhard – I may call you that, can't I?"

"Yes, sir, of course."

"Gerhard, do you know a girl by the name of Emma Schlopper?"

Did I know Emma? I had to think for a while until I remembered. She was the Czech-German girl that had come on to me in *Ober Klein Aupa*, the one who liked to touch and who taught me how to milk cows. It was not a good question. "Yes, I remember her. She was a farm girl that I met on one of my skiing vacations in the Sudetenland."

"Well, Gerhard," he said, "just between you and me, and it won't go any further, from man to man, you had sex with her, didn't you?"

Oh, oh, I thought. Here it comes. "No, sir, definitely not. I just met her and she taught me how to milk cows and we talked a little bit, but I didn't even touch her."

"Come on," he said, now quite a bit more sternly. "There is no use to lie about it. I have all these letters here."

"What letters?"

"The letters that she wrote you."

"Sir," I said, "I've never received a single letter from her. I didn't even know that she had my address."

At that, he opened a file that contained four or five letters, written in what looked like a childish hand. He turned the file around and let me read the top letter. It was an ardent declaration of love, how she missed me, how she would never forget what we had shared, that I was always in her dreams, and that she wanted to meet me in Berlin. Fortunately she did not say anything about sex; if she had, she would have been lying and would have had me in very, very, very big trouble.

Obviously, the Gestapo, having been informed by one of its countless spies, had gotten wind of our little "romance" and had intercepted Emma's letters to me. I had never seen them before. "Come on, these letters are very clear and there's no use of your further denying it. We can bring her in any time and she'll confess. You know what the penalties are for *Rassenschande*, the defiling of the purity of German blood."

Yes, I knew what the penalty was – if I was lucky, a very long sojourn in a concentration camp, but probably much worse.

"Sir, I have to categorically deny that I had any relations with that girl at all. As far as I can tell, she doesn't claim that in her letters either."

"You have to read between the lines. There is no doubt in my mind. I have to pass this on to Berlin. Next time you go to Berlin, which would have to be within the next two weeks, present yourself at the Gestapo headquarters at the *Alexanderplatz* for further investigation."

"Yes, sir," I said. I got up and left the room. I was very shaken.

Next week I went to Berlin. I told my father about Emma and the events with the Gestapo in Mittweida. He was terrified and so was my mother. They asked me the same thing as the Gestapo, namely to tell them "man to man" what had actually happened. I assured them of my innocence, that nothing had happened and they eventually believed me. What they didn't understand, I thought, was that ultimately it wouldn't make much difference what I had or had not done. If the Gestapo believed or chose to believe that I had done it, that would be more than sufficient.

The next day, a Monday, we went to the *Alexanderplatz*, where for decades the city's central police station was housed in an enormous red brick building. Now, the upper two floors had been cleared for the Gestapo. That's where we went. The first scary impression was of a cage in the middle of a big room in which about twenty-five people were held. They all looked beaten up and probably were, and seemed to be totally dejected, which was not at all surprising. Most of them, I am sure, were on their way to a concentration camp or worse. We waited for a couple of hours in that awful room. Then we were summoned to the presence of one of the Gestapo officers. He also was in civilian clothes but, contrary to the man in Mittweida, he looked his part, right out of central casting. The trademark black leather coat was hanging on a hook in the corner. We were standing in front of his desk because he hadn't invited us to sit down. He had my file, the same one as in Mittweida, with Emma's letters, in front of him. The file also contained what looked like a report from the man in Mittweida. Then he looked up and looked at me very sternly. He said, "We have investigated this matter thoroughly. There is nothing to it. You may go home but be very, very careful."

"Yes sir," I said. "Thank you very much." I was more than relieved. I almost peed in my pants. Up to that time it was the scariest experience I had every had.

Why did he let me go? It couldn't have been the "merit" of my case. That wouldn't play a role at all. I just assumed that he had bigger fish to fry that day and didn't want to waste his time with a seventeen-year-old boy.

In my day, in Germany, a driver's license could be obtained at the age of eighteen. In "special cases" and with a special exam, one could get the driver's license at the age of sixteen. I was told that the test was very tough and that Jews particularly were subjected to much chicanery, and that I should not attempt that. Still, I was determined to get a driver's license and went through the exacting procedure. No special license was needed for the motorbike, but I was determined to get a license to drive a car. I have no idea why. I certainly was in no position to buy a car, and there was absolutely no chance in the world that my father would buy one. But, I suppose it was a rite-of-passage that I wished to go through.

First, there was a written examination that lasted all morning and in which the most arcane questions about the most unusual things were asked – not just about traffic, but also about details of the functioning of an automobile and minutiae of the internal combustion engine. In the afternoon, I went to take a test in a "trainer," a simulator of an actual automobile. There was a movie screen in front, on which hair-raising traffic scenes took place. Babies were toddling across the road, lightning would strike, a tree would fall in front of where one was driving, a tire would blow out and other such calamities. Voice commands were given for sudden action – stop, sharp right turn, sound horn, flash light, etc., and an examiner took all of the responses down very carefully. If one passed those two parts satisfactorily, one would then be invited for an actual test drive the next morning. I didn't have a car, so one was provided for a fee. That test drive was not too different from what would be done in the United States. I passed the test, which was demanding and, I learned, had a high failure rate. I was very proud and pleased with myself. But there was one other serious complication. The Nazis, before they engaged in their murderous rampages, had already made things very difficult for Jews in Germany. I'll have more to say about it. But one of the meannesses in which they engaged was to give all Jews license plates for trucks, automobiles and motorcycles that started with the digits 100.   Thus, any policeman could delight himself to stop a Jew on some trumped-up traffic offense, which more than likely had no basis in fact and apply a heavy fine or worse. This "instant identification" and harassment of Jews was one of the reasons, though safety was the most important, I believe, that my father did not want me to have a motorcycle. Interestingly, I was never stopped by a policeman, which in itself was a minor triumph or miracle.

In the summer of 1938, I had arranged with Ulla and Mrs. Jespersen that I would again visit with them in Denmark. My parents demurred. They told me that I would eventually have to leave Germany, and that I should learn something that could immediately be applied and with which I could make a living. My father thought that I should learn metal working, working with lathes, drills, grinders, and welding tools. He had a friend, and a friend of that friend had a small metal-working factory, where he thought he could get me a job as an intern, meaning without pay, for the summer. I could learn something worthwhile.

We reached a compromise. The summer vacations were three months, so we agreed that I would go to Denmark for two weeks, then come back home to work in that factory. The little factory, Rosenberg & Sons, was in the outer reaches of Berlin. I had to get up very early to get there by two streetcars. I was very intrigued by what I saw. There were lathes, shapers, and other metal-working machines. They also had a shop for the winding of electrical motors. I thought that would be an interesting thing to learn and something I could apply in another country. I asked for permission, and I was assigned to that. In the ten weeks in which I was there, I really learned how to actually do it, especially since I had studied and learned the theory of it. In other words, I knew, for any given type of motor, what kind of wire to use, how many wires to each slot, and the pattern of winding. And I learned how to actually do it. It was very worthwhile and I really liked it. I thought it would be something with which I might be able to earn a living in a foreign country.

There was another boy in the factory, also an intern. His name was Günther Loewe. He was one year younger than I and a remote relative. He was the nephew of Aunt Nanny, Uncle Bernhard's wife. Günther worked in the metal-working part of the factory. One day, the boss led Günther to a big pile of metal scrap that was all mixed up, zinc and copper. He told Günther to separate this scrap and make two separate piles. Günther told him, "Mr. Eckert, I didn't come here to separate zinc from copper. I'm an intern. I don't get paid, but I came here to learn something. Separating scrap is not what I want to learn."

Mr. Eckert said, "Look here, Günther, you separate that scrap now or this is the end of your internship."

Günther told him, "That's just fine with me." He packed up his things and was not seen again.

Fast forward: Fifty years later Günther was living in Buenos Aires and eking out a meager living. He had learned that the Germans were going to pay some kind of compensation, some kind of monthly pension, to those among the refugees who had held jobs before they left. Of course, Günther hadn't held a job. He was an intern, worked for just about a month and, what's more, he had been fired. Günther needed a witness to testify that he had worked in that factory as a bona fide employee and that he had been fired because he was Jewish. It was a lie. I declined to make such a statement. My brother, also a resident of Buenos Aires and acquainted with Günther, wrote me a letter and asked me to make such a statement in a certificate. The Germans won't miss the money, he wrote, and Günther badly needed it. They owed him something anyway. So, I made out the certificate, had it notarized it and sent it to him. He got a little pension that helped him out for the rest of his life. I didn't feel all that good about it.

I went back to Mittweida to continue my schooling. That was in the month of October of 1938. In the last days of October, or it may have been the first week of November, something very scary happened. A young Polish Jewish man in Paris, I believe his name was Grynszpan, was admitted to the German embassy in Paris. He took out a gun that he had hidden and shot one of the Embassy deputies to death. His name was Ernst vom Rath. Grynszpan was enraged because his parents, residents of Germany since childhood, has been unceremoniously deported to Poland. That was done in one of the so-called *Abschubaktionen*, "push-out actions" in which the Germans deported all Jews that were not born in Germany, especially those from Poland.

The results of this deed were horrible. Or rather, this deed served as a pretext and gave "legitimacy" to what followed. The newspapers and the radio engaged in frenzies of hatred of Jews. Reichs Minister Göring – who later became the head of Germany's *Luftwaffe* and eventually was condemned to death at the Nuremberg trials (but escaped the noose by suicide), assessed the Jewish population of Germany a fine of one billion *marks*, which was apportioned on the basis of their latest income tax returns and which had to be paid immediately. It was a terrible burden, but much worse was to come.

With a heavy heart because of all of these events, I decided to leave Mittweida and took the train to Berlin on November 8, 1938. The train came from Chemnitz. Mittweida was the first station following Chemnitz. I entered the train compartment and a lone man, Jewish from his appearance, with torn clothes and with bruises and deep cuts – visibly beaten up, sat in the compartment. He was crying like a baby. "Excuse me, sir, what's the matter with you?"

He said, "Don't you know what has happened?"

No, what's happened?"

He said, "The Nazis are killing Jewish people on the streets and in their homes. They are clubbing them to death. I've seen it with my own eyes. They are burning the synagogues and are systematically destroying all Jewish businesses. I was beaten too, within an inch of my life, but I was lucky to get away. I'm going to Berlin. I don't know what for, because my business too was burned – I'm ruined."

I hadn't heard of that but I was greatly concerned, especially of course, about my own parents.

When we arrived in Berlin, and quite contrary to my usual habits and my mother's admonitions, I took a taxicab and went to my father's business on *Charlottenstrasse* #71. It was a ground-floor storefront. The window had been smashed, all of his merchandise was trampled and lying on the street and in the gutter, typewriters and equipment had been thrown out and were lying on the street. There was really nothing left. I learned later that most other Jewish businesses had been set on fire. I also found out later that, as a further "precaution", Mr. Göring had ordained that all insurance policies of Jewish businesses were invalidated. No compensation was to be paid to the Jews. Everyone was ruined.

I took another cab to our home and with great trepidation entered our apartment. My mother was sobbing and crying. My father sat in his usual black easy chair. He was stony-faced. He didn't say a word. After a while he said, "Gerhard, let me tell you about the business."

"Don't tell me, Dad. I was just there, I saw everything."

He said, "I'm ruined."

"I know, Dad, but horrible as it is, it doesn't make any difference. We have to leave Germany, and all of us have to start a new life."

He said, "I realize that we shall have to leave Germany, but, I am almost fifty-five years old. How am I going to start a new life again in a country where I don't speak the language and without a penny to my name?"

"Dad, let's worry about one thing at a time. We can just be glad that none of us has been hurt. Life for us will go on, you'll see."

Next day, it became clear what the damage actually was. It was just terrible. Many people had been killed, although not as many in Berlin as in the provincial cities. Virtually all synagogues in the country had been torched. Though somewhat attenuated, I was still in my religious period and I just could not understand why God would allow this to happen and why He did not send a terrible earthquake and lightning bolts to destroy those bastards. After all, as a lesson to Korah and his cohorts, as I had learned from the book of Leviticus, God had caused an earthquake to open up and swallow the whole blasphemous bunch. Why didn't He do it now? Why did He not destroy all of the Nazis, especially Hitler and that fat-ass Göring, with one mighty swoop? After all, were we not His chosen people? How could He allow these terrible things to happen to us and how could He allow the ultimate sacrilege, the destroying of His houses of worship to go unpunished? And I wondered later during the Holocaust why God did not intervene. I asked the rabbis and they told me, which is probably true, that God's ways are inscrutable. They are indeed.

Despite the unimaginably terrible things that had happened in the "Kristallnacht," the night of broken glass, even then, nobody could imagine what the Nazis had in mind and what the "final solution of the Jewish question" ultimately was going to be. But it became clear even to the most optimistic that all Jews had to

Ulla Hjalsted, the great love of my adolescent life. She was a
lovely girl but I did not realize how perturbed she really was.
She found a terrible end.

My "Danish family." I am in front with the family dog. Ulla is second from left, and Finn, the pesky kid brother, who is still one of my very best friends, is right behind me.

leave Germany. There was absolutely no future, none at all, and the present was slipping away beneath us as though we were standing in quicksand.

When I had come home from my vacation in Denmark, in the summer of that year, my parents informed me that my application to go to Palestine had not been approved by the British. I was very sorrowful about that, but I accepted it. Later, much later, after I had already lived many years in South American, I began to wonder about that. They had never shown me any documents, nothing at all. Were they telling me the truth or had they, in their worry about my involving myself in the "troubles" in Palestine, decided to lie to me so that I would embark on something else? In later years, I became inclined to believing that. Somehow or other, I never asked my parents about it. Even the very last time that I saw my mother and she made her final confessions about "family secrets" to me, I didn't ask about that. Mostly, it was no longer important and I was not sure that she, even then, would tell me the truth.

About two years earlier, in late 1936, my Uncle Bernhard, my father's younger brother, whom he had assisted and essentially supported virtually all of his life, had emigrated to Bolivia. Why Bolivia? Because it was, even then, one of the few countries to which one could go without too much red tape. Before emigrating to wherever, all people attempted to learn something with which to sustain themselves in their new country. Professional people, such as physicians and attorneys were in a bad position. It was clear that it would be very difficult and take a prolonged time to become accredited in the new country. Attorneys had no experience that could be applied abroad. What's more, attorneys were heavily dependent on language, and it would be more than difficult to conduct law in an unfamiliar language, even if it were otherwise possible. So, everyone tried to learn a trade. Some of the preferred categories were auto mechanics, shoemaking, locksmithing and, particularly for women, tailoring. My uncle and his wife, my Aunt Nanny, took a six-week crash course in shirt making, at the end of which they got cardboard patterns for all common sizes of men's shirts. My father paid for the course and my father also paid for the trip to Bolivia. After that, Uncle Bernard was on his own.

After my brother had finished his "studies" or rather his sojourn in Edinburgh, he and my parents attempted to get him into the United States. At that time, emigration to the United States worked by the so-called quota system, by which each country was allotted a yearly quota. The quota was meant to be representative and proportionate to the composition of the population of the United States. The German quota, the quota for people born in Germany, was one of the largest; so, at least in those years, it was relatively easy for a German-born person to get a quota number. But there was one another requirement, namely to get an "affidavit." It became almost a magic word. It was a guarantee by a solvent American citizen that the prospective immigrant whom he proposed to sponsor would not be a burden to the government, in other words, that he would not be a bum or a welfare recipient. If he/she became one, the issuer of the affidavit would be financially responsible. I don't know of a single case in which the issuer of such an affidavit ever had to pay a penny.

My mother had an uncle, Uncle Chaim, who she knew lived in California. He was my grandmother's brother. He had emigrated to the United States in the late 1890's and apparently had done very well. From what we understood, he owned a large lumber mill and much real estate. He was a somewhat mythical figure for all of us. He was the proverbial *"Onkel in Amerika."*

Once a year, for Chanukah, he would send to the whole family a large box containing nuts, almonds, dried fruit, raisins, chocolate and other delicacies – things that we really never got to see in Germany. It was a yearly event to which we all looked forward. My grandmother, Uncle Chaim's sister, divided everything up judiciously among the children. I mostly admired the splendid box itself, which was made of fresh pine and was lined with beautiful oil paper. I had never seen anything like that. And only once a year did I get to eat these wonderful things from far-away California, did I get to admire the box, which on one occasion I was allowed to keep, and which became the repository for my little treasures and important books and cards.

We never got to meet Uncle Chaim, but his wife Rose, came to visit once in Berlin. She did not speak a word of German and nobody in the family spoke a word of English – except me, who had a few years of English at the *Hohenzollern Gymnasium*, mostly under that crazy Herr Kuskopp. So I was pressed into service as an interpreter. I suppose I did reasonably well, but communication was difficult.

In any case, when my brother was ready to leave Germany, my mother wrote to Uncle Chaim asking him to please issue an affidavit for him. We considered the request to be essentially a formality. We had no reply for about two weeks. Then my mother wrote once more, with a little more urgency. About two weeks later, Uncle Chaim replied and told her that, much to his regret, he could not issue an affidavit because it would be too much of a responsibility for him. We were absolutely flabbergasted. This had never happened to anybody of our acquaintance. In fact, American Jews all over the country issued affidavits to people they didn't know, had never seen and to whom they were not related, in order to save them and to get them out of Nazi Germany. Entire congregations issued affidavits en masse. That was really a terrible thing that Uncle Chaim did. My mother never forgave him. She was right.

Many years later, when I was living in California, I met his children and grandchildren. They were, of course, innocent of Uncle Chaim's shabby action or rather inaction. I suppose they didn't even know about it, and we never discussed it with them, but always felt very cool and distant to that part of the family.

When it came my time to emigrate, therefore, we didn't even consider Uncle Chaim, because we knew that we would be getting the same negative response.

When I was still in Mittweida and knowing that I could not emigrate to Palestine, but that I had to leave sooner than later, I contacted MIT, the Massachusetts Institute of Technology, which I heard was the best engineering school in the world. That's where I wanted to go. I asked them to send me a catalog, conditions for entry, etc. To my pleasant surprise, they sent me that information by airmail and by return. I studied the hefty catalog with total attention, as though it were a holy book. I understood most of it, with the help of my trusty English-German dictionary. But there were two things that didn't make sense. The first was that "full and partial scholarships" were available. I focused on the word "scholarship," which is very similar to the German equivalent in that it means learning, knowledge or erudition. Its use as grant to a student was totally unclear to me.

The other statement, even more mysterious, was that "we have many Greek chapters on campus and we encourage our students to become Greeks." I wasn't at all sure what a campus was, but I let that go for the time being. But, why in the world would they want me to become a Greek. I was prepared to become an American, but had not planned on becoming a Greek. But, I thought, if in order to get into MIT I had to become a Greek, I was prepared even to do that. Sometime later I asked one of my Danish friends, who had spent time in the United States, what it all really meant. He explained to me the secondary meaning of scholarship and also told me that "Greeks" were members of fraternities, also a totally new concept to me.

Since I would not be able to take any money out of Germany, it was not clear how I would sustain myself if I got into the United States and were accepted by MIT. But, I was pretty sure that, because of my very good grades in Mittweida and because of my status as a fugitive from Nazi Germany, I would be granted one of those scholarships. As for living expenses, I expected that one of the Jewish help organizations would grant me a loan that would see me through the approximately two years I figured I would need to complete my engineering studies.

I was informed that there was such a thing as a student visa for which no affidavit was needed. Therefore, with some hope, I went to the U.S. Consulate in Berlin. That was in November of 1938. It was an almost indescribable scene. There were at least 2,000 people or more, all would-be immigrants to the United States, standing in line. There was no way, of course, that these people could be seen by a consular officer. A kindly consular employee came out, counted 200 people who he thought one of the consuls could see that day, and gave dates and numbers to all the others. I got a number, which invited me to come back the following week. I was pretty lucky.

On the appointed day, I went back to the consulate and stood in a special line for those who had appointments for that day. I waited for two hours outside and another hour in the holding area, which was a large room inside the consulate. Then my name was called. My English, of course, was not very good, but I had prepared a little speech to the effect that I wanted a student visa, that I wanted to go to MIT, that I expected to get a scholarship, etc., etc. When I entered the door to the inner office, I was quite taken aback. There were three desks facing me, and a consular officer sat behind each one of the desks. The chairs on which they sat were marvelous and of a kind that I had never seen before. They could lean back and forth and sideways and roll around, and these three men seemed to be doing all of that. The man in the middle, the one that beckoned to me had his feet on the desk. That was also something that I never in my life had seen before and certainly did not expect from a consular officer of a big country.

I got quite tongue-tied. I am sure that I didn't make a very good impression. The man was not entirely unfriendly, but obviously quite harassed. He probably talked to 200 people every day. He said to me, "Leave your information here, Mr. Joffe, and come back on the 12th of December. By that time we may have reached a decision in your case."

Well, that wasn't quite what I had hoped for, but it was at least something.

I came home and told my father what had happened. I told him that I thought things looked very good, and that I would in all likelihood be able to emigrate to the United States. "That is not certain at all," he said, "in fact, I rather doubt it. You know the old saying, 'Better a bird in the hand than two in the bush,' and the bird in the hand is that you are going to join your Uncle Bernhard in Bolivia. That's one place you can get to easily and quickly. I want you out of here as soon as possible."

As much as I hated it, I had to admit that he had a good point, but I had a fallback position. I had written Mrs. Jespersen about my situation and that I would like to go to the *Tekniske Højskole*, the technical university in Copenhagen, which was well reputed. In order to do that I would have to live with her and her family for the duration. She immediately replied and told me that, I would be welcome. I am not so sure how Mr. Jespersen felt about that. I told my parents about it and begged them to accept that solution which, of course, was most desirable to me because I would be with Ulla. I had decided by then that we would eventually get married.

My father, usually the most agreeable and mild-mannered of men, absolutely put his foot down and said, "You are not going to Denmark, you are not going to England, you are not going to France, and you are not going to any place in Europe. You have to get out of Europe, because Adolf Hitler is going to make war and that war is going to engulf all of Europe. During that time, or perhaps even before, he is going to kill all the Jews in Europe. You have to get out of here – now!"

Then he continued, "And what's more, your mother and I also are going to emigrate, but it might take us a little longer. We are going to join your brother in Argentina. I want you to go to Bolivia and stay there with Uncle Bernhard until we can pick you up. Then we'll all go to Argentina together and make our lives there – one way or another."

It sounded like a reasonable proposition. I made one request and insisted that it be granted. I wanted to make one more visit to Denmark and say goodbye and farewell to that wonderful family and, of course, to Ulla. My parents granted that request. Therefore, it must have been in the last days of November of 1938, I made one last trip to Copenhagen for the long goodbye – goodbye perhaps forever. It was a most nostalgic prospect.

An interesting thing happened on my way to Copenhagen. I traveled in what the Germans called a *D-Train* in which each car had a passageway from one end to the other with compartments off that passageway. I was standing in the passage smoking a cigarette (I was already a heavy smoker in those days), and I was joined by a young woman about five or six years older than I. I recognized her. Her name was Inge and she was a salesgirl in the shoe store (named "La Florida") that my Uncle Gustav and Aunt Martha had opened in the *Uhlandstrasse* in Berlin. Although she was obviously "forbidden fruit," I had always admired her good looks and sexiness and in fact made a point to visit my uncle and aunt in their store as often as possible, mostly to get a good look at her. Inge talked to me and asked me where I was going. Well, it was obvious where I was going, I was going to Copenhagen, just like she. "Whom are you going to see in Copenhagen? I asked her.

"Nobody," she said, "I'm just going to look around and see what's happening. What are you going to do, Gerhard?"

"Oh, I'm going to visit some friends because I hope to leave Germany very soon and I want to say goodbye to them."

She said, "I always liked you and I know you like me. I'm going to stay at the Astoria Hotel. Why don't you come and visit me there? I think we can have a very good time."

That was an offer that was very hard for me to resist. I said, "Inge, I cannot tell you how tempting this is to me, but I don't think we should do that. If they find us out they will send both of us to a concentration camp, or worse."

"Nonsense," she said, "those laws apply only to Germany. We are going to be in a foreign country. We are going to be in Denmark."

"No," I said, "I don't think so. The Gestapo (as I had already found out) have a long arm and have their spies every place. They are going to find out about it and it's going to be our perdition." So I had to decline the invitation of this very beautiful girl. Strangely, I did not find my obvious willingness to have sex with that temptress to be inconsistent with my professed love for Ulla. One was sex, the other was love (at least I thought it was.)

I only stayed a few days in Denmark and then went back to Berlin. The next order of the day was to get a Bolivian immigration visa. That turned out to be very simple. Bolivia did not have a regular consul in Berlin, but only a so-called honorary consul. It was somebody who had some business connection with Bolivia, but did not get paid by the Bolivian government for his consular duties and only profited by fees that he could collect for his services.

I looked the address up in the telephone book. The consulate was in the outer reaches of the Charlottenburg district. I took the #3 streetcar (called *Grosser Ring*), and got there after about forty minutes. The consul had a small import/export business, obviously very small potatoes, but while he probably had had no or only very little consular business for years, he suddenly had a chance of accumulating a fair amount of wealth. There were a lot of people in his anteroom, waiting with their passports to get a Bolivian visa. My German citizenship having been taken away from me, I had a gray stateless passport, which in contrast to the great pain it caused my mother, was not particularly annoying to me. As another act of chicanery, the Germans had given every male Jew the middle name of Israel and every female Jewish person the middle name of Sarah. If it hadn't been so incredibly mean and very sad it would almost have been funny.

Also, at the insistence of the nasty Swiss, and in order to be doubly sure that no Jewish refugees could accidentally enter their pristine country, the passports of all German Jews were "decorated" with a huge red "J" on the front page.

So here I was, Gerhard Israel Joffe, waiting for the Bolivian consul to give me a visa to go to a country where, as he told me, he himself had never been. A large Bolivian flag with gold tassels stood behind his desk. It was kind of impressive. He made me fill out a short form and made me raise my right hand to swear to something or other and then he put a visa stamp in my stateless passport. The charge was 100 *marks*, a quite large amount of money in those days, but certainly totally worth it. But that wasn't all. He said, "Mr. Joffe, there is one more step and that is to get a medical examination. Go to the consular doctor; he practices only three blocks from here." He gave me the doctor's card. I noticed that the doctor had the same last name as he did. He was obviously his brother.

I had no problem with that, I just noticed it.

I went to the doctor right from there, and, again, about twenty people were crowded into a small waiting room. But I noticed that the movement of people was quite quick. My turn came in less than an hour. I walked into the consultation room. The doctor, fairly impressive looking in his long white coat and with a stethoscope around his neck, had a great resemblance to the consul. That was not surprising, of course. The doctor was standing up and I was also standing up throughout the whole "examination." I did not have to shed any garment. He never touched me. He said, "You don't have any infectious diseases or anything like that, do you?"

"No."

"You look pretty healthy." Then he filled out the form confirming that he had thoroughly examined me and that he found me to be in perfect health and free of any disease or illness. The charge for that was 50 *marks*, another fairly large amount of money, and certainly not warranted by the "medical service" rendered. But, again, it was very much worthwhile, and I didn't begrudge him that any more than I had begrudged the consul to make a small fortune out of our plight.

Though getting the visa was a very important first step, it did not yet solve the problem. The problem was how to get out of Germany. There were no transatlantic airplane flights in those days. The only way to get out was by ship. My father and I went to a steamship agency in Berlin that had ships to all countries in the world. To our distress, but not too much to our surprise, everything was booked as much as a year or two in advance, certainly virtually all of them by Jews who wanted to get out of Germany. That was in a way pitiful, because we realized by then that no Jew could possibly survive another year or two in Germany. What to do?

It occurred to me that some steamship companies had their offices in the famous *Unter den Linden Avenue* in Berlin. But yet another problem came into play. In addition to the many terrible things that the Nazis had by then done to the Jews, there was much chicanery, many petty things, and more and more of them as time went by that made life miserable. For instance, Jews could not sit on park benches, except a very few designated ones that were painted yellow. There was one street in Berlin, the *Wilhelmstrasse*, that was lined mostly with government buildings. Jews were not allowed to walk in that street at all. For some bizarre reason Jews were allowed to walk only on the north side of *Unter den Linden*, but not on the south side. If they had any "legitimate business" on the south side of the street, they had to cross the street, and not at the corner, but at a right angle from the north side to where their business lay.

I walked with my father along the north side of that street and we did indeed visit two shipping agencies, an Italian and a French one, that were on that side of the street. They had no passages available at all.

Then I saw, on the south side of the street the office of *Hapag*, the Hamburg-America Line. I said, "Dad, let's cross the street here and see if they have anything for us."

My father said, "Don't waste your time. Everyone knows that the Hamburg-America Line only goes to North America. He was right. Everyone knew that, but we were pretty desperate, so I said, "Dad, we have nothing to lose. Let's try it anyway."

"All right," he said, so we went across the street (at a right angle) and went into the storefront office of the Hamburg-America Line. A nice young man attended us. We said that I wanted to go to South America, preferably the West Coast, and we knew that Hapag really didn't go there, but we'd thought we'd ask you, just in case.

He said, "Well, you're not correct. We do indeed have a freight service to the West Coast of South America. We don't advertise it at all. We have four ships that go there, two of them through the Panama Canal and two of them through the Strait of Magellan. Those are freighters that take twelve passengers, but I must tell you that we are sold out until March of 1940."

That was in early December of 1938. As we were about to leave he said, "You know, just in case, leave me your name and phone number. Every once in a while, very seldom, we get a cancellation. If we get such a cancellation, we'll call you."

We knew, of course, what a "cancellation" meant. It meant that somebody had been picked up and sent to a concentration camp, and we knew a call, should it come, would be at the last minute. Nobody, but nobody, would cancel a passage on a ship out of Germany. So, without much hope, we left him our name and address and phone number. We didn't know what else to do. That was on a Tuesday afternoon.

On the Saturday following, at about 1 p.m., I was home alone when the phone rang. It was that young man from the Hamburg-America Line. He said,

"Listen, Mr. Joffe, we had a sudden cancellation. The others waiting for passage are all couples; you are the only single on our long waiting list. I will be in the office until 6 o'clock. If you can bring me 450 *marks* by that time, I'll give you the ticket. The ship, the SS AMMON leaves from Hamburg on Sunday, December 18.

If you don't come by 6 o'clock with the money I'm going to have to give the ticket to somebody else."

Those were, of course, the days when people only dealt in cash. There were hardly any checks and certainly no credit cards. What to do? My parents had told me that they were to be at the *Romanisches Café* to meet with some friends. I knew exactly where it was; close to the Zoo. I took a cab (against my mother's strict rules, but this was certainly a valid exception), and found my parents. I told them what had happened and told them we had to get 450 *marks* together by 6 o'clock. We had about four hours.

My father and mother had about 100 *marks* between the two of them and we had no cash at home. The banks were closed. My father and I took a taxicab and we went to visit every friend and relative that we could think of to lend us some money over the weekend. Some people gave us 30 *marks*, others gave 50 *marks* and in one lucky case, a friend had 100 *marks* that he was able to lend us. To make a long story short, we had the 450 *marks* together by a little after 5 o'clock, at which time we took the cab back to the Hamburg-America Line office, where the nice young man was still working. "Oh, there you are, Mr. Joffe," he said. I was afraid you wouldn't be able to make it. I am so happy that you did."

We gave him the 450 *marks* and he gave me the ticket for my trip from Hamburg to Arica in Chile, through the Strait of Magellan, on the SS AMMON, leaving on Sunday, December 18.

My mother bought a lovely, large collection of clothing that, in the rough environment in which I was going to find myself, I would never be able to use. One of the more amusing and loving things she bought me was a tuxedo, which I did eventually use a couple of times in Bolivia, but that was eight years later. She also bought me a wind-up gramophone and about a dozen vinyl 78 rpm records, mostly of operatic tunes, with some admixture of South American music that she felt would be appropriate for the ambiance in which I was going to find myself. She was totally loving and devoted to me.

I have already described the interesting experiences I had in dispatching my two trunks so we can skip that.

On Friday, December 16, 1938, I left Berlin. My parents took me to the railroad station. I hugged my father who was composed and reserved. My mother sobbed bitterly and I had a hard time keeping my composure. Finally, the train left. Three hours later I arrived in Hamburg. Arrangements had been made for me to stay at an inexpensive hotel close to the port, so that's where I went. At the reception, I found a letter. It was from Mrs. Jespersen, who wished me God-speed and all the best and which contained a flimsy piece of paper with a picture of the Queen of England on it and the words *Pay to the Bearer 10 Pounds Sterling*. I didn't really know what it was. I thought it was some kind of a bond that I could redeem eventually. I didn't realize until I was halfway to the new world that it was actually a 10-pound note that she had given me. It would have been a crime to take money out of Germany, beyond the ten *marks* (about $2.50 at the time) allotted to each emigrant. If anybody would have caught me, I would have been in deep trouble. But since I didn't know what I had, I acted innocent and nobody searched me.

On the next morning, Saturday, the 17th, I went to the appointed pier of the Hamburg-America Line where I saw the SS AMMON at anchor. It was not exactly a rust bucket, but it was not too impressive or spiffy a vessel. Anyway, it was going to take me out of Germany and that was good enough for me.

There were twelve passengers. All of us stood in line until the officer of the passport control came. He made us cool our heels for about 45 minutes. I was number five in the line of twelve. The first person in line, a woman, approached him. The officer looked at her passport with the word "Sarah" and that big red "J" in it and he said, "You're a Jew, get to the back of the line." Exactly the same happened with number two, number three, and number four and, of course, with me, number five. I went to the back of the line. Number six turned out to be the only non-Jew among the twelve. He was a Hungarian, barely spoke any German and I still don't know what in the world he was doing on that ship and why he was going to the west coast of South America.

Eventually my turn came again and now, one of the most extraordinary and important things of my life happened. The passport control man looked at my passport and said, "You don't have an xxx stamp. You can't leave."

I wish I could tell you honestly at this point what the xxx stamp was. It was something totally idiotic, something I had never heard about before. It was either a stamp certifying that I had my dog vaccinated, that my bicycle was registered, or something equally stupid like that, which only could have originated in a German bureaucratic mind. But he was adamant, without it I could not leave Germany. It was the worst thing that had happened to me until then in all of my life. By then it was Saturday morning around 11 o'clock. I said to him, "Where can I get such a stamp?"

He said in a sarcastic and most unfriendly voice, "You can go to the *Rathaus*, the Municipal Building. They may give it to you if you are lucky. Unfortunately for you, they are closed today. And remember, you can't get out of Germany without that xxx stamp. Don't even try!"

I had no idea how the Hamburg municipal people could give me my dog vaccination stamp (or whatever) especially if all of the offices were closed. But I was desperate. I had absolutely no choice and nothing to lose. I took a cab to the Municipal Building. It was open, but clearly, nobody was working. At least, there was absolutely nobody on the ground floor.

Instead of a standard elevator, the building was equipped with a so-called *paternoster*. It was just like the one at the Schöneberg *Rathaus* that had played a role in one of the adventures of Horst Peck and myself. It was essentially a string of

Eigenhändige Namensunterschrift des Inhabers:

Gerhard Toffe

One of the last things I did before leaving Germany was to get a
German driver's license. It was quite a production. There was no
reason for getting it. We didn't have a car. It was a rite of passage.

On the SS AMMON, on my way to the new world.
That's me in front and my cabin mate Gerd Unger in back.

ever-moving boxes that one stepped into and was moved to the desired floor, up or down, at which time one would step out. It moved rather slowly.

I stepped out on the second floor and was confronted by a long hallway with perhaps twenty offices on each side. I tried three or four of the doorknobs, but everything was closed. I did the same thing on the third and on the fourth floors, but, not entirely unexpected, with the same unhappy results. The fifth floor was the top floor. Despite my disappointment on the other floors, I decided to try that one too. I got off the *paternoster*. At the very end of the hall I saw a man walking toward me. Since sunlight was shining into the window in back of him, I could really only see his outline. I noticed that he was rather tall. He was about 150 feet away from me. He walked towards me and I walked towards him. He was my last hope. When he was about 20 feet away from me, I saw to my horror that he was wearing a swastika button in his lapel, which showed him to be a certified member of the Nazi party. But what was much worse, the swastika button was surrounded by golden oak leaves, something I had heard of but had never seen. It meant that he was one of the one thousand *"alte Kämpfer"*, one of the first one thousand members of the Nazi party and obviously therefore one of the most vicious and virulent. It was the worst thing that could possibly have happened. "What do you want here?" he asked brusquely.

"Sir, I am Jewish," (which of course he realized immediately), "and I am emigrating to Bolivia. I have everything in order, except that I need the dog vaccination stamp" (or whatever it was). "I cannot leave without it."

"What do you want from me?" he asked.

"Sir, you look like someone in authority here and I thought that you could get it for me."

He looked at me for about ten seconds and didn't say a word. Then he said, "Come with me."

He walked ahead of me with long strides and I followed him. He stepped into the *paternoster*, with me after him, and we went down to the second floor. Obviously, knowing exactly what he was doing, he went to an office halfway down the hall. He took a big key ring out of his pocket, tried three or four keys and then opened the door. "Come with me," he said again. He went to one of the desks, apparently knowing exactly what to look for and where, and opened the drawer. There must have been thirty rubber stamps. He looked at several of them and then he thought he had found the right one. He put the stamp to a stamp pad and tried it on a piece of blank paper. I stood stock still. Sure enough, it was the right stamp, the dog vaccination stamp (or whatever it was). "Give me your passport," he said brusquely but not too unkindly. I gave him the passport and he put the coveted life-saving stamp into the passport. I put the passport back into my pocket. "Where did you say you were going?" he asked, not at all unfriendly.

"To Bolivia, sir," I said.

"I've never been there but I hear it's a tough country, very high altitude, and they live mostly by mining."

"Yes, sir, I think that is correct."

"Well," he said, "I wish you good luck." Then he added, "Remember me."

"Yes, sir, I'll do that," I said. He did not shake my hand. I turned 180 degrees and left.

I have thought about that encounter for many years and I still think of it now. Why did he do that? Why did he save my life? He didn't have to do anything. He could have just left me to my own devices which would have meant that I could not have left Germany and probably would have found a terrible end. I have several theories: Either he decided to play God – thumb up or thumb down, just like the Roman Caesars, and he decided arbitrarily to give it a thumb up.

Or, having done so many terrible deeds in his life, murdered or caused the deaths of no telling how many people, he decided to finally do something decent, just on a whim. My preferred theory, in my testosterone-saturated imagination, was that he had just had an exceptionally satisfying sexual experience, probably even on a desk in the office on the fifth floor from which he had emerged, and felt generous and in good humor. But whatever the reason, I was the beneficiary of it. Had it not been for that man I might have perished in Germany. He told me to remember him and I did. I wonder what happened to him? He probably died in the war – perhaps he was hanged for war crimes.

That I was very, very relieved is an understatement. Only fifteen minutes earlier everything had collapsed and I could see myself remaining in Germany, probably headed for a dreadful camp or worse, and all because of some stupid stamp, which perhaps wasn't even really needed, but which that nasty anti-Semite who sat at the toll gate required.

I went back to the ship. The same nasty guy was there. He gave me a baleful look, studied my passport with the new stamp as though it were an arcane document, and at the end, hesitating as he did so, put the final "Allowed for departure" stamp in my passport and let me go up the gangway.

By that time it was early in the afternoon and the ship was supposed to leave with the outgoing tide at 8 o'clock in the evening. Some snacks were available in the dining room of the ship so there was no problem with waiting. Punctually (of course, as everything in Germany) the ship left at 8 o'clock. I cast one last unsentimental look at the coastline and said to myself, "Goodbye Nazi Germany – and good riddance."

But not quite yet.

I met my cabin mate, Gerd Unger, a nice fellow about my age, who also was headed for Bolivia. We went to our cabin and tossed a coin for the bunk. He got the upper and I got the lower. The humming of the ship's engine, which would take us away from Germany, was most reassuring, and with that lullaby we went to sleep.

I woke early in the morning and noticed to my surprise and alarm that there was no sound, that the engine's were not moving. The ship was standing still. What had happened? Had Germany declared war? War was something that we had been fearing all along, and after all this trouble, weren't we going to be able to leave? I quickly got dressed and went up on deck. I talked to one of the deck hands. "What's happening?" I asked him.

"Why, nothing is happening," he answered. "We are at anchor."

"Yes, I can see that, but..." and then I looked. It really didn't look like Hamburg. "Where are we?" I asked him.

"We are in Bremen," he said. "Didn't they tell you that we are going to make a stopover in Bremen to take on some additional cargo? We're going to be here until the evening and then we're going to leave for good."

Wow, was I relieved! Nobody had told me about Bremen. What to do all day long? I had never been in Bremen before. I had heard that it was a very beautiful city. The main feature of Bremen, known in fable and song, was Roland the Giant, who was supposedly holding watch in front of the municipal building. I had heard about him all my life and so, since we had a whole day to kill and since I was now sure that nothing would keep us from leaving, Gerd and I decided to make a tour of the town. There would be no trouble getting back on the ship.

While we were in town it occurred to me that Spanish, of course, was the language of Bolivia and that I did not speak one single word of that language. I would have to do something about it, and do it quickly. It was clear that lack of language would be a distinct handicap in my new home. I had been so preoccupied with leaving that I hadn't paid any attention to that. So, I went to a bookstore on the main shopping street, but they didn't have any language books. The proprietor very kindly, however, gave me the address of a specialized store, which, he assured me, had textbooks in all languages. I went there. Sure enough, there was a large selection of books in all languages, including in Spanish. One book caught my eye. It was called (in German) *Spanish in Thirty Easy Lessons*. "Thirty easy lessons," I said to myself. "What a happy coincidence." The transatlantic trip from Bremen to Punta Arenas in Chile, our first landfall, was going to be exactly thirty days. So, if I studied one lesson a day, I could expect to have a reasonable knowledge of Spanish by the time I arrived. With that, I picked up another book called *Un Poco de Todo* – A Little of Everything. It was a neat soft-cover book in which, by the time the voyage was over, I really could read and understand everything: short stories, anecdotes, jokes, all very interesting and entertaining.

So at 8 o'clock that evening we weighed anchor once more and this time we really did leave. Once more I said goodbye (or rather, good riddance) to Nazi Germany and was happy to see the coast of that country fading and disappearing for a final time.

Part II

PUNCHING HOLES THROUGH THE ANDES

After all the unhappy experiences that we had in Germany, the worst of which was the *Kristallnacht* and the frightening event with that bastard at the final departure gate, the experience on the ship was just wonderful and quite surprising. It was a relatively small vessel, a freighter, and carried only twelve passengers. Apparently, under international maritime law, twelve passengers are the limit for a vessel still to be considered a freighter. Beyond that it becomes a passenger ship and all kinds of rules and requirements apply. One of them is that a passenger vessel has to have a doctor on board, whereas a freighter does not. Even so, we did have a doctor; I believe it was because it was such a long voyage.

There wasn't too much to do but walk around the deck and take in the wonderful meals, totally different from what we had in Germany. The crew and the officers were unfailingly courteous, including the captain. He was very reserved, but greeted each of us kindly and respectfully when he entered the dining room. That was actually the only times we saw him. The six officers ate at one table and we, the twelve passengers, ate at another.

Every morning, the purser, a heavy-set and very jovial man, distributed a news bulletin that had been received by telegraph overnight. It was always alarming. The voices of the Nazis got shriller and shriller, and Hitler's demands on his neighbors became more and more threatening and outrageous. Having annexed Austria and conquered Czechoslovakia, the next victim was obviously Poland. A stream of invectives and hatred against Poland was transmitted every day on the news bulletin.

All of us had one enormous worry, and that was that war would break out while we were at sea. In that case there was no question that we would immediately turn around and sail back to Germany. It was almost too awful to countenance. I firmly made up my mind that if that would happen anywhere we were in sight of land, no matter how far away, I would jump overboard and try to swim ashore. It was clear to me that I would most likely die in such an endeavor because of the cold, exhaustion, or being eating by a shark, but it did not deter me. I was absolutely determined not to go back to Germany and fully prepared to jump overboard and swim for it if necessary.

Every morning when I got up, I looked to where the rising sun was. Since our general direction was southwest, the morning sun had to be in the back of us. If,

heaven forbid, I saw the sun in front of us, I would know that we had turned around.
I had to be ready and I was ready to jump overboard if necessary.

Not having too much to do, except walk around the deck, I had no problem
in keeping to my resolution to study one lesson a day in my Spanish book. Each
lesson contained about thirty or forty new words, some grammar, some exercises,
and some reading material. I was almost compulsive about it. If, in my daily
review, I missed only one word or made only one mistake, I would start all over
again. I had to have it absolutely right before the next day, when I would go on to
the next lesson.

The first land we saw was after about twenty days at sea. It was a tiny island in
the middle of the Atlantic, called St. Paul's Rocks. I learned that it belonged to
Brazil – the first whiff of the new world. I would say that we passed to within two
miles of it. One of the fellow passengers had a pair of binoculars. He lent it to me. I
looked very carefully. I did see a couple of houses and a light tower, but no signs of
life. I knew (I was quite likely wrong) that if the ship would turn around now, that I
could swim to that island and be safe.

About five days later we came to another island, somewhat larger, which
also belonged to Brazil – Fernando de Oronha. Again, we passed within about two
miles and again I was determined to swim to that island if we would turn around
anywhere in the neighborhood

Then, about two days later, we came in view of the South American coast,
first Brazil and later Argentina. It seemed as though we were between two to ten
miles off the coast all the way and my determination to swim for it in case the vessel
would turn around became stronger than ever. And the likelihood that it would turn
around also became greater every day, because judging by those bellicose bulletins,
war in Europe seemed imminent.

Because we had passed the equator and since it was the first time for all of
the passengers, the officers gave us a little party and everything was as cordial as it
was unusual. It almost seemed as if the Germans were no longer Germans once they
were on the high seas.

Finally, on the thirtieth day we turned west and entered the beautiful Strait
of Magellan. The scenery on both sides, Patagonia on the right and Tierra del Fuego
on the left, the forest glades, the streams running into the Strait, the animals gazing at
us, all were just marvelous and totally new to me. Then about a half a day later, we
were in Punta Arenas, Chile, our first landfall. I had finished Lesson 30, the last
lesson, of my Spanish textbook the day before. I had a vocabulary of about a
thousand words and a good command of the grammar.

When I got off the ship, I knew that nothing could happen to make me
return to Germany. Even if war broke out right now, I would simply stay in Punta
Arenas and take it from there. If war broke out when, as planned, we went up the
west coast of South America, the ship would essentially be bottled up. It could only
return to Germany back through the Strait of Magellan or through the Panama Canal.
In either case, I figured that the ship would probably be impounded, but even if it

were not I didn't see any problem in getting off the ship at either of those two choke points.

Disembarking in Punta Arenas and finally feeling terra firma under my feet for the first time in thirty days, I saw some dock hands working, loading some cargo. I approached them and said, *"Discúlpeme señor, hay jardín zoológico en esta ciudad?"* (Is there a zoo in this city?)

It was not a sentence that had been in my textbook and it was not anything I had planned on saying. I just said it spontaneously. I don't really know why. I had no interest in a zoo at all. To my great pleasure and surprise, those burly men didn't laugh at me. They understood me very well. They told me, in Spanish of course, "Just go down this street until you come to the store of the *Austriaco* which is called *Blanco y Negro*. You can tell it because it has checkerboard squares on the wall. Then turn left one block, turn right again, and there's the zoo."

I was delighted. I had understood every word and knew exactly what to do. As I later learned, in that part of the world, at least in my days, all Europeans east of Vienna, and that included Hungary, Yugoslavia, Romania, Bulgaria, and Greece, were collectively called *Austriacos* – Austrians – a term left over, I suppose, from the Austro-Hungarian Empire. Those beyond, Turks, Arabs, Egyptians and all others were collectively called, *Turcos* – Turks. They made it that simple.

In any case, I followed the directions. I saw the checkerboard squares, turned left, then right, and half a block down there was indeed the so-called zoo. The zoo, however, had only two animals in it – two llamas. I had heard of those animals but had never seen one, not even in the Berlin Zoo, as well as I could remember. One of the llamas looked at me; I looked back. Suddenly the llama spit and hit me right in the face. Later, when I had a lot to do with llamas, when they were part of my work and of my life, I knew that they had a habit of doing that and I knew how to watch out for it.

The trip up the west coast of South America was uneventful. We unloaded freight in Puerto Montt, Valdivia, Talcahuano, Valparaiso, and finally reached our ultimate destiny, Arica. Arica is the northernmost point of Chili. It was wrested from Bolivia in one of their many wars, thus making Bolivia a land-locked country. As an act of generosity and international comity, the Chileans allowed Arica to be a free port for Bolivia. The final part of the trip was to be by railroad from Arica to La Paz, one of the two capitals of Bolivia.

I had imagined Arica to be a port somewhat similar to Hamburg, perhaps a little smaller, but it was quite different. There was no actual harbor. The water just wasn't deep enough, so our ship had to anchor about a mile off the coast, where the water was still deep enough, and a lot of flat-bottomed boats, called lighters, unloaded the cargo, baggage and ourselves. It was quite a procedure. It was about noon, the train was to leave that afternoon at 5:30 and we were told that, all going well, we would be in La Paz around noon the day following. Our luggage had been forwarded by the shipping company directly to the train.

We took our leave from the officers and from the crew with whom we had shared the vessel for over a month. We had become quite friendly with all of them. There was no hostility nor Nazism or anything of that sort. Even the captain shed his usual reserve, shook all of our hands and wished all of us good luck in our new country. It was a nice gesture and quite unexpected.

We assembled at the town square and took everything in. The first thing that caught my attention and engaged my unbelieving eyes were women on the square who were nursing their children, their breast sticking out for all the world to see. They were totally unselfconscious about that. All of us thought that was so unbelievable that, even without asking permission, we took pictures of what we thought was a unique scene. As we went along, we saw that every day and all day long, of course.

During the few hours in Arica, Gerd and I decided to have a look at the German consulate in this city. I don't really know why. So we asked and found it pretty quickly. It was not more than six blocks from the port. It was a fairly big, quite Prussian-looking building, with, of course, a huge Nazi flag with that damned swastika flying off a tall mast in the courtyard. There was a stone wall, perhaps eight feet high around the building. We were so angry, but also so totally relieved that these terrible and hateful people could never again insult us or threaten us. But there wasn't anything we could do to give vent to our anger. So, not being able to think of anything else, we both peed against that wall. It made us feel a little better.

The train did indeed leave at 5:30. Compared to German trains, it was a pretty clap-trap affair. But it served the purpose. We had to go from sea level to about 16,000 feet just within a fairly short distance, because the crest of the Andes Mountains, the continental divide, is very close to the Pacific coast. A group of young men in their early twenties, not much older than I, sat nearby and caught my attention. They were laughing and joking and singing, so I approached them and I introduced myself in my, by now, quite serviceable Spanish.

They told me that they were Chileans and that they were going to La Paz to visit relatives who had jobs there. One of the fellows played an instrument that looked very much like a mandolin and seemed to be played like one. The back of the instrument looked different, though. I inquired and found out that it was made of the shell of an armadillo. The instrument was called a *charango*. The fellows asked me to join them. I was very proud that I was so quickly accepted and that nobody took exception to my being younger and to my less than perfect Spanish. The tune that they sang was *La Cucaracha*, a tune with which I was familiar because it was also well known in Germany. After every verse they laughed raucously and slapped each other. Then another fellow would sing another stanza and they'd laugh again. I couldn't understand what they were singing because it was too fast for me. I asked them to sing it slowly so I could understand. I still remember two of the stanzas, both of them very naughty, the second more naughty than the first. The first of the stanzas went as follows:

Todas las mujeres tienen
En el pecho dos penachos
y dos cuartos mas abajo
La fábrica de muchachos

The translation means that all women have two plumes on their chests and two quarters below that the baby factory. They thought it was very funny and laughed uproariously.

The next stanza, as I said, was naughtier. It went as follows:

Una noche muy helada
Me tapé con la frazada,
La frazada tuve rota,
Me tapé con las pelotas.
Las pelotas tuve lejos,
Me tapé con los pendejos,
Los pendejos tuvieron vinagre,
Me tapé con la xxx de tu madre.

Translation: "One very cold night I covered myself with the blanket. The blanket had holes in it, so I covered myself with my testicles. The testicles were far away, so I covered myself with my pubic hair. The pubic hair had vinegar in it so I covered myself with your mother's xxx...," well you get the idea. They laughed, laughed, and sang that stanza over and over again.

During my sojourn in South America, I learned many songs in Spanish and in the Indian language Aymara. I remember some of them, but I never forgot those two stanzas of La Cucaracha, the very first things I learned in my new life in South America. There were other stanzas, equally naughty, but I don't remember them.

I had my first bout of altitude sickness, with a terrible headache and felt quite nauseous. La Paz, the commercial capital of Bolivia is located in a "hollow" of the Altiplano. The Altiplano is a vast plateau, approximately 14,500 feet high, between two ranges of the Andes. It occupies most of the western part of Bolivia. Most of the life of the country and virtually all of the mining is located there. The last railroad station before La Paz is called El Alto, which means "the high one." The train then descends, spirals down into the hollow about 1,500 feet below, where La Paz is located. We finally arrived, and Uncle Bernhard and Aunt Nanny were waiting for me, bundled me into a cab and took me to their home.

They had a pleasant groundfloor apartment consisting of three rooms: a large room which was the work room, the bedroom, and a small room that could be described as a living room. There were two large work tables in the front room and three women folding and pinning shirts and putting them in boxes ready to be sold and delivered. Two of the women were middle-aged and not particularly attractive. The third woman was about twenty years old and I thought she was gorgeous. Her name was Mercedes. Mercedes and I looked at each other and we knew that we were going to be an item. I liked Bolivia right away.

My uncle explained to me that the most important thing to remember was never to put toilet paper into the toilet. The La Paz plumbing and sewerage system simply was not designed for it. In even the finest homes in La Paz, at least in my day, there was a can beside the toilet in which the toilet paper was to be deposited. It was picked up once a week by a special service. In the finer homes, there was a cover on that can. The others did without. Uncle Bernard's can was open. I was sternly admonished about that and was told that if I put toilet paper into the toilet it would immediately stop up and flow over. A plumber would have to be called and a great mess and large expense would result. I learned the lesson and did it right from the very beginning.

Although my uncle had written my father that I could be a guest in his home for two weeks, I realized that that limitation was just a dumb thing and he really didn't mean it. He certainly wouldn't have tossed me out if I had overstayed the term. He was not the smartest man in the world, but essentially a nice guy. I knew that he would take care of me if I didn't find a job, but I decided not to test that and to find a job just as quickly as possible.

I rested up for about a day, mostly in order to get used to the altitude. It was clear to me that the only place that I could work was in one of the many small mines with which Bolivia was dotted. So, on the second day I started looking, climbing some of the steep hills in La Paz and learned that mining companies had an organization and that all mining companies, their owners, and the addresses were listed and available at the office of that organization. At that time, I also learned about the structure of the Bolivian mining industry, which was quite interesting. At the top there were three very large companies. The largest of them all was the Patiño organization, which owned five of the largest mines. The second was a group of mines owned by Mauricio Hochschild, a "lateral relation" of the American Hochschild family that owned and controlled American Climax, the huge U.S. mining company, and other important mining companies in the United States. Mr. Hochschild was a German Jew and, as I learned, a man with much political influence. He was probably very important in shaping Bolivia's relatively lenient policy regarding German-Jewish immigration.

Mr. Aramayo, a Bolivian just like Mr.Patiño, also had a large mining enterprise, but much smaller than those of Patiño and Hochschild. Still, he was one of the "Big Three."

I want to stop here a minute to tell you the amazing story of Antenor Patiño. It is really quite extraordinary.

Antenor, in his early twenties, married with two children, was a clerk in a grubstaker's store. A grubstaker's store is one that outfits miners, lends them some money and more often than not takes a "piece of the action" – a share in the property that the miner is working. It's a tough business, just as mining itself is a tough business.

One day, his boss looked at Antenor's books and noted to his horror that he had extended credit to a miner way beyond what he thought was prudent and what he had authorized. He got very angry and fired Antenor on the spot. He said, "You can have my share of the claim, but you pay me back the money that fellow owes me. I would never have authorized this line of credit."

Antenor, who really had no experience at all as a miner, and his wife left their children with the grandparents, took some provisions and rode out to the claim.

The mine owner was very discouraged. He said to Antenor, "Give me 500 pesos and I will give you the title to this mine."

"That won't work." Antenor said, "I don't have that much money, but I'll give you a promissory note."

"That's all right, too," the miner said. So they signed the paper and Antenor was the owner of the non-productive mine. Knowing next to nothing of what had to be done, he worked for two or three days and found nothing but rock. On the third day, he again drilled eight holes in the tunnel that the previous owner had started, loaded them with dynamite and lit the fuse. The tunnel advanced three feet. When he came back the next morning, to clean up the rubble and to face another day of disappointment, he saw the most amazing thing. There was a wall of sheer black, pure cassiterite, the mineral of tin. He had discovered the largest vein of tin, the mother lode, perhaps the greatest bonanza in the history of mining. Young and inexperienced as he was, he knew that something totally extraordinary had happened. He shut things down, told his wife to keep her mouth shut, and went down to Oruro, the mining center, where he had worked in the grubstaker's office, and told the man at the *Banco Minero*, the miners bank, what he had found. The banker could hardly believe his description. But he did send a man up and he verified what Antenor had told him.

Antenor then made a smart move. He immediately engaged an American mining company to take over the mine, to develop it and to make him enormously rich. They did exactly that. It is not known whether he ever again set foot in the mine or even in Bolivia. He retired to Paris, where he became the Bolivian ambassador to France. He built a palatial embassy with his own money. His daughters married French and Spanish counts. The American engineers discovered other very important mines besides the one that Antenor had found. But *Siglo XX*, Twentieth Century Mines, became the hugely profitable flagship property of the Patiño Mining Company.

I was told that one of the first things I had to do was to get a *cédula de identidad*, the I.D. document to be used and needed for many occasions. Even for sending a registered letter, for instance, it was necessary to present the identity card. I understood that the main reason for this requirement was to catch people who had evaded their obligatory military service. If it didn't say on the identity card that they had done their military service or that they were exempt, they could not possibly conduct any business, not even send a letter. Thus, on my document it said "exempted."

When I gave the official who handled these things my passport, it listed my name as Gerhard Ernst Israel Joffe, the Germans having maliciously given the additional middle name Israel to all male Jews and the name Sarah to all female Jews. It was just one of the many nasty chicaneries they engaged in before they got around to do their serious slaughtering.

The official said, "We'll have to change your name."

"Why?" I asked him.

"There is no such name as Gerhard in Spanish and all *cédulas* have to show Spanish names." He pulled out a list of equivalents of several hundred names of other languages. He looked under Gerhard and said, "Your name is Gerardo."

I thought for a second, but there wasn't anything I could do about it. But did I really care? Of course not! I was delighted to get rid of my German name, just as I wanted to get rid of any vestige of "Germanness" that still clung to me. "Yes," I said, "Gerardo is fine."

"What is Israel? It is a Spanish name, but is that necessary?"

"No," I said, "I don't want any middle name."

"*Muy bien*," he said. "Your name is Gerardo Joffe."

"Thank you," I said. It has been my name ever since.

From the list that I obtained from the Bolivian Miners' Association, I selected those that seemed to be most promising and plausible to me. One requirement for me was that they had to have their office in La Paz and that the mine would not be too far away, because I wanted to come back to La Paz occasionally. I also preferred that the mine shouldn't be too big, with not too many employees. I came up with a list of about twenty-five companies that fit my preferences and systematically visited them, one by one. I didn't have too much to offer. Obviously, I knew nothing about mining. But my general education was and would be considered desirable, and, of course, I had a fair amount of engineering knowledge. My first twelve interviews, which took me about three days, were unsuccessful. Nobody needed anybody with my qualifications or rather with my lack of them.

One company on my list was W.R. Grace & Co., an American company that owned a fairly good-size mine, Chojlla. That mine, in contrast to all others, was not located on the Altiplano but in the Yungas, the semi-tropical, fairly low-land area north of La Paz. As it turned out, W.R. Grace & Co. had a large office on one of the main commercial streets, in fact they occupied their own building. I was quite impressed. After a reasonable wait, I was asked to come to the office of Mr. Elsner, the head of W.R. Grace & Co. in Bolivia. After my first introductory sentences in my still somewhat deficient Spanish, Mr. Elsner interrupted me and said, "*Sie sprechen deutsch, nicht wahr?*"

What a relief! It turned out that Mr. Elsner was Swiss-German and so that made it a lot easier. He was an exceptionally nice man, but he explained to me, with what seemed like obvious regret, that they really couldn't use anybody like me in their Chojlla mine, but to leave my name and address. If anything came along, he would certainly be in touch with me. So it was another "no," but Mr. Elsner was very nice about it. I appreciated his courtesy and remembered him well.

Little did I ever dream that I would meet him again almost twenty years later – but that is another story.

So I kept trying. On the fourth day of my job search, I hit pay dirt. I was in the office of Sr. Raul Peró, who told me that he had a small mine called Chacaltaya, that he needed a manager for the mine and that I might just have the qualifications that he was looking for. I, the manager? I wondered whether he understood well about what I could and could not do. "Sir," I said, "I am very grateful for the job offer, but I am not sure that I can manage the mine."

"Look, I am going to come up about once a month and see how things are going. You just keep it running in the meantime," he replied. And then he explained my duties to me. It was mostly to visit the miners in their working places – actually there were about thirty of them – and to see that the ore would be delivered to the small mill, that the mill would be running properly, and, finally, that the ore was concentrated by the mill into the finished product, called the *barrilla*, (concentrate), and that it would be put into 100-pound sacks that he would pick up with his truck about once a month.

"Oh, yes, another thing," Sr. Peró said, "You will have to run the *pulpería*, but you won't find that to be a problem. And, of course, you will do the payroll every week."

"What is a *pulpería*, Sr. Peró," I asked.

"It is the company store. You will have it open two afternoons a week, sell the employees what they need, and keep account, so that you can deduct their purchases from their pay when you make up the payroll. And, of course, you will see what supplies you are short of, so that I can bring them up on my next trip. Two things you may never, and I mean never, run out of and that is coca leaves and carbide. The miners will not work without coca and they can't work without carbide because that is what fuels their miners' lamps."

Sight unseen, I knew that I could handle the payroll and the *pulpería*, but I wasn't so sure about supervising of the miners and the mill. He assured me, however, that there was a foreman who would look after all technical things, and not to worry about that. So I didn't worry. This was on a Thursday. He told me that he would pick me up from Uncle Bernhard's house on Monday morning and that we'd then go up to the mine. I was to get room and board and, I believe, the pay was 2,000 *pesos* a month which was equivalent to about $100. I had it made; I had a job, I was in business.

But first there was that unfinished business with Mercedes. She had given clear indication in word and deed that she liked me and that perhaps good things might be in the offing. Wouldn't that be wonderful, I thought – getting a job and losing my virginity all at the same time.

We arranged a tryst for Saturday night in a little park in La Paz. I was there first and she came about five minutes later. Somewhat simplistically I asked her, *"Mercedes, me quieres?* Do you love me."

Her answer floored me, not because of its significance, but because of the wonderful grammar she used. She said, *"Si no te hubiese querido no hubiera venido."* If I hadn't loved you I wouldn't have come." In that one sentence and without any effort she used the two future subjunctives, the most difficult Spanish verb forms, certainly for me. I was impressed.

We walked hand in hand. Without my asking her, she told me that she was a virgin. I believe she was. I told her that I was too and we decided to remedy that situation. Where to go? By that time it was about 10:30 in the evening. We finally found a nice grassy spot at the side of a tall building. While we were hugging and kissing, a window opened, a light went on, a man loosed a stream of curses and invectives, strongly expressing his disapproval of what we were doing or were about to do, and then threw a pot of cold water over us.

We both were sopping wet. Mercedes insisted on going home. I didn't blame her. I never saw her again.

Before I started on my job, and even though Sr. Peró had assured me that my lack of knowledge about mining would not be a real handicap, I did think that I should be somewhat informed. I went to a book store, poked around and found a book that was just right for me. It was called *Manual del Minero*, The Miner's Manual. It had been typewritten and reduced to book size, had many illustrations, had a nice black flexible binding, and explained in laymen's terms all – well, almost all – there was to know about mining. I read it over the weekend and became an "instant expert." The most important and surprising thing that I learned in that book was the concept of a "vein." I always heard that ore occurred in veins. It's the same in German as in Spanish and as in English. I thought, if I thought about it at all, of "veins" like those in the human body – tubular structures. What I found was that the reality was quite different. Metallic minerals usually occur in fissures within the rocks. Instead of tubular, they were essentially tabular deposits. That was a great insight and it made it clear to me what mining was all about. The book, while it certainly couldn't have been a text in any university course in mining, explained how things were done in a small mine in Bolivia, the tunneling, the making of the raises and shafts, the timbering, the use of explosives, and, equally important, how the ore was concentrated in the mill. I was no longer totally ignorant.

On Monday morning, just as agreed, Sr. Peró picked me up. We went to Chacaltaya, about three hours out of La Paz. Chacaltaya was also Bolivia's only ski resort – such as it was. It had one rope lift and ungroomed slopes. There was no lodge or anything of that kind. People drove up from La Paz, brought their lunch, did a day's skiing, and then went back to La Paz. It was all very primitive, but they seemed to have a lot of fun.

Sr. Peró had not told me anything about the accommodations that I would have at Chacaltaya. I was prepared for the worst. But it wasn't bad at all. I had a nice large room with an adjoining kitchen, connected by a pass-through window. It was better than I had expected. I looked for the toilet, but didn't find one. I asked Sr. Peró. He pointed me to the outhouse. Oh well, I thought, its something new, but I would be able to handle it.

I was introduced to my *cocinera*, the cook. Her name was Victoria Catacora. She was plump and sweet and about thirty-five years old. I realized right away that she was not going to be an object of my amorous attentions; my suspicion was confirmed when her husband, a burly fellow, picked her up that night.

Victoria was a *chola* and this may be a good time to talk about the social stratifications in Bolivian society, at least in my time. I understand that things haven't changed much to this day.

At the top of this social pyramid are the "*blancos*," the all-white people. They were, and to some degree still are, the ruling class. They dress just like Europeans. They speak Spanish, though all of them, without exception, also speak at least one of the two Indian languages. Quechua is the original Inca language and is spoken by almost all people (except perhaps those living right on the coast) from Ecuador all the way to northern Argentina). The area around La Paz and the Altiplano is Aymara speaking, a much less important language and an offshoot of Quechua. The blancos of the La Paz area speak Aymara with their employees, domestic and in business – and occasionally with family members.

The next level down in the social structure are the *cholos*, who are essentially *mestizos*, part white and part Indian. The men dress in the western way similar to the *blancos*, although their clothes are usually of much lesser cut and quality. Women, however, dress in their ethnic style. They wear *polleras*, skirts that form a perfect circle when laid down flat on the ground. They usually wear several layers of them – as many as four or five. They come in many colors and are made of wool or, for festive days, of silk. The Aymara *cholas* wear a bowler hat, exactly the same that a member of an English men's club would wear. The Quechua women, on the other hand, wear tall white cylindrical hats, lacquered for stiffness. The *cholos* speak the native language Quechua and Aymara, respectively, but most of them have a fair knowledge of Spanish.

On the bottom of the social structure are the Indians, the vast majority of the population of Bolivia. The men wear homespun trousers and shirts and *abarcas* on their feet. *Abarcas* are sandals made out of old automobile tires. The Indian women wear the same clothes as the *cholas*, only more homespun and less elaborately ornamented. Unless they can afford other shoes, Indian women also wear *abarcas*. Their language is almost exclusively Aymara or Quechua, although some, especially those working in the city or in the mines, do speak a little Spanish. There is hardly any mixing between these groups, with little upward or downward movement.

Sr. Peró showed me around. He introduced me to the foreman and explained the *pulpería* to me, shook my hand, and left me to my devices. I was the "manager" of a mine.

Victoria prepared her first meal for me. It was quite good, the kind of food that I would eat for the next five years. It was a lamb stew with vegetables, the most important constituent of which was a black item which tasted pretty good but which I could not identify. I found out from Victoria that it was *chuño*, which is a frozen and dehydrated potato. It seems that the Indians put the potatoes on the thatched roofs of their houses, they freeze them and then they also do something else to them. I don't know what it might be, but it turns out to be *chuño*. Some people never can acquire a taste for it. I liked it right away. Another thing I liked was that there obviously was no pork. That could have been a real problem for me. In fact, I can't remember seeing a single pig all the time that I was in Bolivia. I don't know why. All the meat was on the basis of mutton and occasionally some beef.

I quickly learned the ropes of what to do in Chacaltaya. I inspected faithfully all the work in the mine every day, even though, of course, I was not yet able to give instructions on what to do, without consulting with the foreman. I also kept track of the mill, collected the *barrilla*, had it put into sacks, had it weighed at 100 pounds per sack, and waited for Mr. Peró to come up once a month and pick it all up.

Twice a week I attended the *pulperia*, and once a week I made up the payroll and paid the workers. I liked the work, I was very comfortable, and made friends with the workers. There was not too much chance to practice my Spanish because, believe it or not, I was the best Spanish speaker in the mine. The language in the mine was Aymara.

All the time, of course, I was much concerned about my parents in Germany, particularly since the war cries of Adolf Hitler became shriller and shriller. The object of his current fury were the Poles who, according to him, had done terrible things to the Germans living in Poland or had even conducted cross-border raids into Germany, killing "innocent Germans." What nonsense! All of it was just pretext to start a war. The question on my mind was only, "When will it start?" I certainly hoped and prayed that my parents were going to be able to get out of Germany before the whole thing exploded.

When I had worked in Chacaltaya for about four months, Mr. Peró brought me a letter on one of his monthly visits. It was from my parents. They told me, to my great joy, that by some miracle they had been able to book passage on an Italian ship leaving from Genoa in the middle of June of 1939. They were going to travel to Arica through the Panama Canal and were going to be in La Paz on or about July 15. I was very happy about that, of course. The only pain it caused me was that I would have to give up my job, to which I had become used and the income of which I enjoyed, of course. Since I had no way of spending any money, I was able to save virtually all of my salary which, by the time my parents arrived, would be perhaps as much as the equivalent of $400. That was a fair amount of money in those days.

I told Sr. Peró about that and that I would have to quit at the end of July. He was not too happy because he thought that I was doing a good job and he liked me personally. But he understood. He made arrangements to pick me up at the end of July, which would be the end of my work for him.

Then, when at the end of July, Sr. Peró did pick me up, something happened that has worried me for many years. And, indeed, it still worries me more than over sixty years later. When we arrived in La Paz and were still at the outskirts of the city, we halted at a stoplight. To my unbelieving eyes, I saw my father on the other side of the street. He looked bedraggled and dejected, as he had every right to be. What I should have done, of course, was to tell Sr. Peró that this was my father, get out of the car, embrace him, and welcome him to Bolivia. I did not do that. Somehow I expected that some sentimental scene would develop, that my father would get overly emotional, and I didn't want Sr. Peró to see that. I didn't say a word. I had Mr. Peró drive me to Uncle Bernhard's house. Uncle Bernhard told me that my parents had arrived and they had rented a small apartment, I still remember the address, Calle Oruro #26. I took a cab and went there. Both my parents were there. It was a very emotional scene, not just because of their seeing me again, but the very fact of their having gotten alive out of Germany. Thankfully, my father had not only been able to arrange for passage for himself and for my mother, but also for his sister, my Aunt Selma, and her husband Salo. They also were in La Paz.

The only real purpose of my parents being in La Paz was to get their papers and documents in order for the final leg of their trip, namely to Buenos Aires, and to pick me up in the process. Although the ultimate outcome was not in doubt, there were all sorts of formalities and difficulties. My brother had to bring several guarantees, and the paperwork took time. They estimated that they would have to stay anywhere between two or three months in La Paz before they could finally leave for Buenos Aires.

Just as Uncle Bernhard had learned how to make shirts and as other people had become cobblers and mechanics, my mother had taken a course and had learned how to make candy. She hoped to make a living with that in the new country. Her main tool was an iron sheet about 18" square with the ends turned up on three sides and welded together to make a shallow pan with one open side. This box was heated by coils with 220 volts of electricity. It was a fairly primitive set-up but it worked. Her main ingredient was something called by the French word *couverture*, essentially big blocks of chocolate. Then there were all kinds of ingredients, nuts, cherries, almonds and what not, all of which she had brought from Germany. She had also brought about 80 pounds of *couverture*.

The first step in the process was to put the *couverture* in the iron pan and work it with a spatula until it was in some kind of viscous condition. It was then put in little forms that she had also brought. Then the filling was put in and the whole thing was covered again with chocolate and topped by an almond or other decoration. I must say that her candy was really excellent, more delicious than anything that one could buy in a store. She had also brought about 1,000 cartons that would hold 1/2 pound of candies (they were called by the French term *pralinés*) which then were to be sold. I was allowed to contribute $200 to the living expenses. I believe there was also a small loan from Uncle Bernhard, and my mother's sister, my Aunt Sarah, sent some money from Buenos Aires. But my mother was determined not to be dependent on the goodwill and charity of anybody. She started working the same day she unpacked her gear which was about two or three days after she arrived in La Paz.

Since I was the only Spanish speaker, I was assigned the job of selling the candy. I did it, but I hated it. I would go to stores and restaurants, offer a sample and then ask the proprietor to buy some candy from me. If I was lucky, he would buy three or four cartons. Most of the time I just distributed the free samples and had to go on to someplace else. I was reasonably successful, filled my "quota," but didn't like it at all. It was just not what I was wanting to do with my life. And I had the feeling that if I went to Buenos Aires with my parents, that was what I would be doing, unless I got a job in my brother's firm. I was quite sure that I would not like that either, especially not after the "freedom" I had experienced being the manager of the Chacaltaya mine.

Now I have to tell you about the piano. Although my mother never talked about it, I can understand how very difficult it must have been for her, how totally heartbreaking, to leave her home, her apartment, in which she had lived for over twenty-five years. I can understand how she would have felt when she walked out of that apartment leaving most of her possessions behind since she could not or was not allowed to take them with her. The very last thing she told me they did was to unscrew the *mezuzah* from the door and take it with them to South America, where they were going to (and eventually did) install it in their new home.

But, under the mad and inconsistent regulations of the Nazis, people were allowed to take a piano. So my mother decided to take her piano. She didn't play it and I didn't play, and the only reason, of course, they took it was that they might be able to sell it and get some badly needed money for it. It cost a lot to transport it from Germany to Bolivia, but that, of course, didn't matter. Money in Germany was worthless to them. Since they couldn't take it with them, they might as well spend it on whatever was desired or needed.

In Arica, as you may remember, there was no real harbor and things got unloaded into smaller boats called lighters. Well, what do you know, the piano didn't make it into the lighter and was clumsily dumped into the water. The workers picked it out of the shallow water and put it on the lighter, but it was soaked. By the time the piano arrived in La Paz, it was obviously totally useless. All the strings were either broken or corroded, the veneer off, the keys had come unglued – in short, nothing was left that resembled a working piano. My parents' apartment in La Paz had two rooms. The piano, or what was left of it, and the little stool were put into the second, smaller room. Nothing else was in that room. The landlord, a young man, whose first name was Mario, told my mother that he had a friend, a Sr. Andrade, who was a piano repairer and that he had no question that he could repair the piano. I doubted that anybody could and so did my mother. Still, she thought it was worth giving it a try. The man came. He was in his fifties, had "electric" hair like Albert Einstein and gave somewhat the impression of being a "mad artist." He said he would repair the piano, that it would be like new, and that he would do it for

2,000 pesos, the equivalent of about $100, and that during the time that he was working, my mother had to give him meals and that absolutely nobody could enter the room or molest or ask anything while he was working.

My mother sensed a scam and was afraid that she would have to pay him ahead of time. "When do you need to get paid, Sr. Andrade?" she asked him.

"When I'm finished," he said.

That was reassuring. So, every morning the man came, locked himself in the room and came only out for lunch to be handed him by my mother. Then he went back into the room. He left every evening at 5 or 6 o'clock. He had the key to the room and no one else.

After about two weeks of this, my mother became a little concerned and suspected that all the man wanted was to get a free lunch for as long as he could possibly get by with it. That day, she intercepted him when he left in the afternoon and said, "Sr. Andrade, if you can't fix that piano by the end of this week I think we should just forget about it."

"Don't worry, *señora*," he said, "I'm just about finished. It will be ready by day after tomorrow."

"O.K.," Mother said, "but that's all."

So next day Sr. Andrade worked again, but of course nothing happened. The day following, it was a Thursday, at 3 o'clock in the afternoon, we heard the sounds of the Blue Danube Waltz coming from the next room. We couldn't believe our ears. It was the piano and it sounded better than it had ever sounded before. All three of us rushed into his room, and there was Sr. Andrade, sitting on the little piano stool and continuing to play the Blue Danube Waltz. The piano was absolutely beautiful. Every string had been replaced, every key had been cleaned and put back into place, every veneer had been re-applied. The piano looked better than ever before and, of course, it sounded better. The man was an absolute genius in his art. My mother gave him the 2,000 pesos that she had promised him and even though she had very little money, she gave him a 200 pesos tip. I thought it was a wonderful gesture.

I'm getting a little ahead of myself at this point. Just before my parents left for Argentina, they had Mario put an ad in the paper for them, saying that the piano was for sale. On the very same day, a woman came by, looked at the piano, and she played a few (bawdy) tunes. She offered my parents 5,000 pesos (about $250 at that time). My parents thought they had won the lottery. They sold the piano to the lady. The next day she sent a truck and had it picked up. "Where are you going with it?" my mother asked.

"I'm taking it to Villazón."

"Where's Villazón?" she asked.

"Oh, it's the southernmost city in Bolivia. It's on the way to Argentina. The next place is La Quiaca in Argentina."

"And what are you going to do with the piano in Villazón?" my mother asked.

"I operate a – a business," she replied, "where I need to have a piano." And therewith she left. What she operated, as you may have guessed, was a house of ill repute and my mother realized it. My mother was scandalized that her piano, a wedding present from her parents, would wind up in a bordello, but 5,000 pesos was 5,000 pesos, and in any case she couldn't do anything about it.

I had in the meantime come to the firm conclusion that I was not going to go to Buenos Aires with my parents. While I realized that life in Bolivia was going to be hard and that it would probably be relatively "soft" in Buenos Aires, I thought that I would be best off if I stayed. I realized that if I went to Buenos Aires I would either have to sell chocolate or work in my brother's business, probably under his "tutelage," which did not sound attractive to me at all. Also, even then, I decided that I was not cut out to be a clerk in a large organization, or, in fact, not cut out to work for a large organization at all. I was most sympathetic to my mother's plight and her having to earn a living for my father and for herself by making chocolate and really greatly admired her for her energy and determination. But I did not wish to become involved in this business, perhaps as a salesman, or as a deliveryman, or in some other capacity. Finally, I realized that my parents were probably going to live in some very small apartment in Buenos Aires and that I would be sleeping on the couch in the living room. I would have no private life. I liked the freedom that I had enjoyed in Chacaltaya, thought that I would be able to find something similar, and perhaps even make a career of some kind in the mining industry.

So, about a week before our planned departure, I said, "Mom and Dad, I got to talk to you about something."

"What is it? my mother asked.

"Well, this is going to be a little difficult to say, but I have to tell you that I have decided not to go with you to Buenos Aires."

"What!" both called out in unison. "Are you crazy! What are you going to do here. this is a terrible country. You cannot accomplish anything here. You go with us to Buenos Aires and you will be with your family and we are all going to be well."

I said that I was sorry, but I couldn't agree with them. "I'm nineteen years old," I said, "and I need to develop my own life; therefore, I have decided to stay here."

My mother and my father exchanged meaningful glances. "You have a girlfriend, don't you?" she asked.

I wish I had, I thought and I told them that I didn't.

"You can tell me the truth," my father said, "Man to man, I could understand that, but you will see that these things pass and you might get yourself entangled in something that you might be very sorry about. Forget about that woman and come with us to Buenos Aires."

"Mom and Dad, really, there's no woman involved. I've just decided that I'm going to stay here. My mind is made up and you cannot change it."

Well, they did try to change it until the very last minute, but they were not successful.

Finally, the day for their departure came. I went with them to the railroad station and saw them off. My mother, once again, sobbed and cried and begged me to change my mind and to come with them. But I didn't. The train left. Because it had to go in serpentines up to El Alto, I could still see them and they could still see me for about 15 minutes after departure. My mother kept crying all the time. Even I was not entirely unmoved. The minute they were out of sight, I went into a bar and ordered a beer. That was the first time I had done that. I was now grown up and had to stand on my own feet. I was all alone in Bolivia.

The rent in the apartment in Calle Oruro had been paid until the end of the month, so I could stay there until that time. I could also have gone back to Uncle Bernhard and Aunt Nanny, but I decided against that. It would not be part of my "independence and growing up." I did, however, go to visit them the following day, partly, or mostly I suppose, to see Mercedes again. It turned out that Aunt Nanny had fired her. "Why did you do that?" I asked her.

"Well," she replied, "she didn't really work out. She wasn't quite right for what we wanted her to do." Aunt Nanny gave me a significant look. I thought I knew why she had fired her.

I had to find another job immediately, because having given virtually all of my savings to my parents, I had only very little left. My first thought was to go back to Mr. Peró to see whether that job in Chacaltaya was still open, but I decided against that. I thought I should start a new chapter.

I went back to my list of mining companies and visited the office of Eduardo A. L. de Romaña. It was a Peruvian mining company. They operated a pretty good-sized mine called Mercedes del Illampu, close to the little town of Sorata, and on the slopes of the Illampu mountain, one of the highest and most beautiful in Bolivia. Sr. de Romaña happened to be in the office. I told him about my experiences in Chacaltaya, what I could do and what I had learned. He said, "Well, if you come to work for us you will learn a whole lot more. You will really learn about mining and about milling and about assaying."

For some reason, I liked the part about assaying, namely making chemical analyses of the finished product, to determine how much metal it contained. Sr. de Romaña explained to me that, in contrast to Chacaltaya, which was a tin mine, his was a tungsten mine. Back then, tin was the most important mining product in Bolivia and tungsten ranked second. I had never heard of tungsten before. Sr. de Romaña explained to me that, while its most familiar use was for the filaments of lightbulbs, its greatest use and most important by far was as an additive to steel, in order to give it special hardness. The salary and room and board were the same as in Chacaltaya and I gladly accepted that. He told me that he had to go back to Lima on business but that his truck would take me to the mine on the following Monday and to be at the office punctually at 9 a.m.

I was there at the appointed hour. The driver invited me to sit with him in the cabin, which was a recognition of some distinction. There were about eight or ten workers standing on the platform of the truck and all kinds of supplies and equipment for the mine.

The trip took about five hours. At the destination, we got out of the truck and I found myself at the edge of a chasm, something like the Grand Canyon, though not quite that majestic. I looked across the chasm. On the other side was the mine – I saw the housing and the mill, all directly at the foot of the beautiful and imposing Illampu mountain. "How do we get across this chasm?" I asked the driver, innocently.

"In the bucket," he said.

"What do you mean, bucket?"

"Look over there," he said.

I did look. There was a large wheel, perhaps six or eight feet in diameter, with a steel cable of about one half-inch diameter wound around the wheel going across the chasm and, I supposed, around a similar wheel on the other side. There was a large bucket close to the wheel. I was invited to step into that bucket. A worker switched on a motor and the bucket started its slow journey across the chasm. I figured it was about 1,000 feet to the bottom. The thing swayed sideways and up and down and I was very scared. Halfway across the chasm, I was met by an identical bucket coming from the other side, but it was empty. Eventually I got to my destination on the other side. I was greatly relieved.

As Sr. de Romaña had instructed me, I presented myself to the *encargado*, the man in charge while Sr. de Romaña was absent. He showed me my room, which was small but very nice and clean, one of four such rooms in a strip, next to each other. I was then invited to have lunch which was, to my happy surprise, in Sr. de Romaña's private quarters. They were adjacent to the four rooms of the white-collar employees.

Sr. de Romaña arrived the next day, also in the bucket, of course, though I did not see that. He greeted me cordially and told me that he would start me out by working in the mill. I was assigned to the mill superintendent who explained to me how the ore coming from the mine was being processed. First, it went through jaw crushers, which broke it down into about fist-size chunks. From there, it went into the ball mill – cylindrical affairs, with their long axis parallel to the ground. These mills were lined with hard steel plates and loaded with steel balls. The mills revolved at a relatively slow speed and ground the rock to the desired size. It then had to pass through a sizing mesh; that which didn't pass was recirculated back into the mill. It all involved lots of water.

The material that passed the mill was then again divided by screens into coarser and finer particles. The coarser particles went into so called jigs which were chambers in which, by agitation of pistons, the heavier, metal-bearing particles went to the bottom and the lighter particles, the "gangue," the non-mineral bearing rock, stayed on the top and were thus separated. The finer particles went to so-called tables which were just that. They replicated mechanically what used to be done manually by miners' pans. They shook rhythmically and in so doing separated by gravity the ore particles from the rock particles. Constant vigilance was necessary to keep the divider between the two in the right place.

The ore, which, if milled properly, was supposed to have a fineness of at least 60% tungsten, was dried, weighed and sacked. The gangue rock was put on carts and thrown into that bottomless chasm.

It was pretty straightforward. Having read my trusty *Manuel del Minero*, I knew what to expect.

After about a week, I was put in charge of a shift, and had to see that everything ran smoothly. I really liked the work. Sr. de Romaña had a little chemical laboratory next to his living quarters. That was where he ran assays every day on the fineness, the metal content, of the ore coming out of the mine, and, of course, the refined product coming out of the mill.

Realizing that I was perhaps the only one in the mine that could properly understand the chemistry and the calculations that were required, he told me that within a month he would teach me the assaying and eventually turn it over to me. I was very pleased.

Another thing I liked about working there was that I made good friends with the other three or four white-collar employees, those who shared that row of living quarters with me. I was by far the youngest and they sort of adopted me and tried to show me the ropes in every respect. Also, the four or five of us ate with Sr. de Romaña, who had brought his cook from Lima. I found that I liked the Peruvian cuisine, particularly as prepared for Sr. de Romaña, even better than the Bolivian cuisine to which I had by now become accustomed, mostly through the ministrations of Victoria Catacora.

After about a month in the mine, my friend Umberto, who was the accountant/bookkeeper/payroll clerk and secretary, told me that he and the three other guys were going for the weekend to Sorata, the little town about three hours away by mule and about 3,000 feet below the mine. It sounded like a good idea, so they saddled a mule for me. I went on muleback on that long ride, down, down, down. I thought it was perilous because one misstep of the mule would have thrown us into that dreadful abyss that I had to traverse in that bucket on the day of my arrival to the mine. I was amazed and eventually assured as to how sure-footed those animals were. Even on the very narrow path, if they stepped on a stone that then fell down the chasm for 1,000 feet or more, they would immediately regain their footing and went on as though nothing had happened. They were wonderful animals. I was told that horses could never do that.

Unfortunately, as we arrived in Sorata, I fainted dead away, the first and only time that happened to me in all of my life. Apparently, the difference in altitude was just too much for me to handle. Well, eventually I was revived. I was put to bed, stayed there for the two days, while my friends were out carousing, and having a great time, I suppose. It went better on the way back. By then I had become accustomed to the altitude but had trouble in the "lowlands," at being at "only" 11,000 to 12,000 feet above sea level.

I remember my father, without any special training, having an uncanny facility with numbers. He could take a column of thirty, forty or fifty, five-digit numbers and add them up, going down the columns with his pencil, in no time at all. He never made a mistake. I have inherited that modest talent. When the first payday came around – miners were paid every two weeks in that mine, I told Umberto that I would help him. He had an adding machine. Each entry had to be keyed in, then there was a carriage that had to be moved, and finally a handle that had to be moved forward to print the final result. It was time consuming and there were quite a few errors because of erroneous entries. Everything had to be done at least twice. I said, "Umberto, I'm very good at numbers. Let me do it by hand."

"No." he said. "You can't possibly do it as quickly and accurately as the adding machine."

"Let me try," I said.

So he gave me a list of all the payments and, just like my father, I added them up very quickly and accurately. Umberto was amazed. My talent as a "mathematical wizard" was admiringly discussed; even Sr. de Romaña was much impressed.

Once a month, the Indians of the little village close to the mine had what could best be described as a court session. All those who had a complaint against a neighbor and the respective "defendants" would meet in a large room in the village elder's home. The elder, the headman, would sit in an elevated chair behind a desk and the assembled Indians sat on the floor in front of him. Umberto, despite his youth, was considered somewhat of a wise man; he sat at the side of the headman. On this occasion, being a visiting *gringo*, and with considerable ceremony, I was also invited to sit at the table, at the other side of the headman. All deliberations took place in Aymara of which I could not understand a single word.

Umberto would whisper to me from time to time, informing me what the procedure in progress was about. There was nothing very serious – one man had allegedly stolen a goat, someone claimed not to have been paid for some work that he had done, and at least one more serious case in which a young woman had been made pregnant by one of the local swains. The headman made decisions in each of the cases. In one of the cases, as a courtesy to me, the dispute, in this case, was about some blanket that had been sold by the defendant and for which the plaintiff claimed not to have been properly paid, the matter was translated into Spanish and submitted to me for adjudication. I made a good decision (I thought), "Pay the woman what you owe her."

All in all I had a very good time during my stay at Mercedes del Illampu, learned a lot, and was in good company. The weather was good, the food was good, and I enjoyed the work.

After about four or five months at the mine, Bolivia had one of its not in-frequent revolutions, a military *putsch*, and a new president, German Busch (honestly, that was his name, though he spelled it differently from our guys), assumed power. Mr. Busch was a colonel in the Bolivian Army. I don't know just what he did, but whatever it was caused the price of tungsten to drop by fifty per cent. Suddenly, Sr. de Romaña profitably little mine was deeply in the red. Mercedes del Illampu had to cut corners and, since I was the newest arrival, I was the first corner to be cut. Sr. de Romaña told me that he had to let me go by the end of the month. I was very sad about it and he truly, or so it seemed to me, was very sorry to have to do that. He told me to be sure to be in touch with him again once tungsten prices improved.

So, going back across that chasm on the same perilous journey, this time in the opposite direction, I boarded the truck and returned to La Paz. I needed another job and though I had saved money from my job at the Mercedes del Illampu mine, I thought I shouldn't lose too much time.

It occurred to me to go back again to Sr. Peró, my first employer, and I should try to work again at the Chacaltaya mine. Sr. Peró was really pleased to see me again but he told me that he could not help me because the job that I had held had been filled in the meantime by another man. "But I have an idea, Gerardo," he said. "My brother Juan is a much bigger wheel than I am. He is the owner and operator of Larramkota, a much larger mine. Tell him that I sent you and he'll probably give you a job."

Juan Peró's office was also in La Paz, not too far away from that of his brother's. But it was a somewhat more splendid affair. It was two or three times the size of Raul Peró's, there was some hustle and bustle, and girls working on typewriters. I told the office manager that Raul Peró had sent me and that I wanted a job. "What can you do?" the man asked me.

"I suppose almost anything that's needed around a mine."

"We don't need any generalist," he said. "Can you do anything specific – for instance, what we need is an *electricista*, an electrician."

"What would that involve?" I asked him.

"Mostly repairing motors that have burned out and that have to be rewound and put back into good condition."

That was exactly what I had learned at the Rosenberg factory in Berlin. I told the man that that was right up my alley and if that's what they wanted, I was their man.

He told me to come back in two days. "I'll talk with Sr. Peró and see what we can do."

I came back as he had told me. He gave me the job. Again, it was room and board, and a small salary, even a little more than I had made before.

I didn't really know where Larramkota was. So, he explained it to me. "Take the train," he said, "from La Paz to Oruro and get off at Eucalyptus, which is the third station before you come to Oruro." (I later learned that the two following stations were Silencio and Soledad (Silence and Solitude, respectively). It didn't sound like a very lively region. It wasn't.

"Then," he continued, "take any of the trucks that go from Eucalyptus to Quime and get off at Caxata, which is a crossroads and the last place before coming to the *Quimsa Cruz* (Three Crosses) Pass. There's a small inn in Caxata. Spend the night there. In the morning, one of our trucks will pick you up and take you to the mine."

So I did just that. I took the train to Eucalyptus. Then I took a truck to Caxata. I had to ride in the back, on the platform, the whole way, about three hours, together with Indians and cholos. I had no problem with that. But I learned something. Truck drivers in Bolivia occupied a special social niche: The place of honor, riding in the cabin with the driver, was always reserved for some young and possibly accessible *cholita*, whom the driver would sweet-talk during the trip. I could understand that. I probably would have done the same thing. But it was an interesting observation. Even though I was a gringo, which was something a little "special." I never got to ride in the cabin if a pretty *cholita* was available.

We finally got to Caxata. To say that it was a wide place in the road would be overstating it. There was just that little inn the office manager had told me about and not really anything else. It was, however, indeed a crossroads. I got off and the two women who ran the inn, who I found out were sisters, received me cordially and showed me to a spartan but acceptable and reasonably clean room. Then they told me that I could come and have dinner. There was a small dining room, furnished with a long table with benches on both sides. I was the only guest. They asked if I wanted a beer and I agreed. Then came the dinner, which was quite acceptable. It was a *caldo*, soup – again on the basis of vegetables and beans and *charqui*, the ever-present dried meat of mutton, what we would call jerky in the United States.

As I was finishing my *caldo*, sipping the last of my beer, another guest entered the dining room. He was a tall, rangy type, wearing a pair of high-laced boots and toting a holstered gun. He was obviously quite drunk. He sat down at the table, on the other bench, right across from me.

He looked at me balefully and said (all in Spanish, of course), "Who the hell are you?"

"I'm just a guy on my way to Larramkota, where I'm going to start working."

"I think you are one of those goddamn German Jews," he said, "who are overrunning our country and who are going to ruin it just like they tried to ruin Germany. But Hitler kept them from doing that and kicked their asses the hell out of there. Now you guys are coming here. We are not going to put up with that shit!"

I thought I hadn't heard right, but I had. Holy smokes, did I come to Bolivia to hear this kind of stuff? While I was ruminating about that, he pulled out his gun and pointed it right at my head. He was about two feet away from me. "I don't think I like you at all," he said. "I think I might shoot your fucking head off."

It was clear to me that he could do just that and that probably nothing much would happen if he did. Bolivia was not exactly a law-and-order country and certainly not in Caxata, which was pretty far from civilization. I knew I had to keep my cool.

"Look," I said. "I know you could shoot my head off, but it would make an awful mess. Inevitably the police would come and arrest you and chances are you would spend the rest of your life in prison if they don't hang you. Would that be worth your while?"

"I think you're full of shit," he said, but he holstered his gun.

I said, "goodnight," and left. I thought it was a close call.

A brief aside about Bolivian justice: Almost from the very first day I arrived in Bolivia, I made it a habit to read the daily paper, *El Diario* and found to my pleasant surprise that I understood everything. I was pleased with myself about that and congratulated myself for having bought that wonderful Spanish textbook.

On my third day in La Paz, I read a story that absolutely fascinated me, especially since it was accompanied by a very good picture. It seems that three men – I recall that they were Spaniards – had committed an armed robbery. In the course of that robbery, they had killed a man. The penalty was death by hanging. But under Bolivian law, which I believe was based on the Napoleonic Code, since there was only one death, there could only be one hanging, but it couldn't be discerned which of the three criminals had actually done the killing. Naturally, every one of them pointed to one of the two other guys. So, here's what the authorities did. They set up three gallows on a platform and put the noose around each of the three criminals' necks. A priest was standing by murmuring prayers. An executioner then walked up to the condemned men, only one of whom was going to die. He held a small black velvet bag in his hand. The bag contained three marbles – two white ones and a black one. Whoever drew the black marble was going to die, the other two were going to get a twenty-year prison sentence. The first man pulled a white marble, the noose was unceremoniously removed from his neck, and a policeman led him away to jail. Then the second man put his hand into the bag, very nervous for sure – he only had a 50/50 chance of survival – and perhaps trying to discern by the feel of his fingers which of the two remaining marbles was the white one. Eventually he made up his mind and pulled out a marble. It was the white one. As soon as he pulled out the white marble, it was obvious that the remaining one was the black one, the trap on the third man was sprung, and he was hanged. The second man was untied and he too was led away to jail. I thought it was an absolutely marvelous, though somewhat primitive, piece of justice. I kept that newspaper clipping for a long time.

Now back to Caxata and to the story: I double-bolted my door leading to the courtyard and pushed my bed right up against it. It thought that crazy man might have some second thoughts and might try to kick in the door to get me. Fortunately, nothing happened.

Next morning, after I ate a nice breakfast that the sisters had prepared, the truck from Larramkota showed up and took me to the mine, about 25 miles away. Sr. Peró was there. His greeting was very friendly. Then he showed me my workplace. It was a very primitive shop with a workbench. There were about 10 or 12 motors in various stages of disrepair which he asked me to put back into service. There was plenty of wire and cable and some primitive tools needed to take the motors apart to put the wires into the slots and to put everything back together.

I was not too certain about my competence, but fortunately, the first motor I repaired and which was put back into service in the mill, seemed to work properly and at least kept functioning during the time that I stayed in that mine.

The work was tedious, not nearly as interesting as what I had done in Mercedes del Illampu, but it was a job.

There was an interesting social stratification. Sr. Peró was the big boss, of course, *"el patrón,"* and then there were the bosses of the mill and of the mine, respectively. They were invariably married, with children, and had their own company houses. I had little contact with them. Then there were two Polish-Jewish men, about five or six years older than I, who were in charge of accounting and of the company store, the *pulpería*, respectively. They were single and lived in the same compound that I lived in. As for eating arrangements, the two Polish guys ate with Mr. Peró in his dining room. I, being a humble *electricista*, ate the same food, but I had to eat in the kitchen, rather than in the dining room. I didn't really care about that, as long as I was being well fed. That was the first time, by the way, that I received a regular paycheck. In my previous two employments, everything was handled by cash. I was impressed by the paycheck. It looked as though I had reached some kind of a milestone. I didn't quite know, however, what to do with it. I didn't have a bank account. One of the nice Polish guys cashed it for me.

Everything went well. I repaired several other motors and to my pleasant surprise, all of them seemed to stay working. One day, while I was working in my shop, the lights went out. I thought a fuse had blown and didn't give it too much thought. I prepared to go to the fuse box and change the bad fuse. At that moment, the mill boss rushed into my shop and said, "Gerardo, Gerardo, you must come immediately. The transformer has blown out. See what's wrong with it and repair it."

"Wait a minute, Alberto, what do you mean the transformer has blown out?"

"I mean just that," he said. "The transformer has burned out. See what's the matter with it. Hurry, repair it."

The transformer was one that transformed the 12,000 volt current that came through the overland power line to the 440 and 220 volt current used at the mine. While I knew, of course, the theory of how a transformer worked, I had never seen the insides of one, and I didn't think that this would be the time to get educated about it. I had a feeling that if I touched one wrong wire I would immediately be burned to a crisp. I actually visualized myself turning to coal. I was at an important crossroads. I could either go there and bluff my way through, hope not to get killed and, who knows, even repair the transformer and reap great glory. But I had the good sense to say, "Alberto, I'm very sorry, I don't know how to repair a transformer."

"What kind of electrician are you," he yelped, "if you don't know how to repair a transformer?"

"I'm the kind of electrician who can repair motors but I don't know how to fix a transformer."

"Well then you're no damn good for us in this mine," he said. "We need somebody in this mine who can repair and take care of anything electrical, and you, obviously, are not that man."

"I'm afraid you're right, Alberto," I said. "I'm not."

So Alberto went to Mr. Peró and told him about me. Sr. Peró came to the shop. He was very kind, but very determined. He said, "Gerardo, I'm afraid we cannot use you any more. We need somebody here who can take care of all of our electrical needs. You're not that man. Get your check and leave either today or tomorrow." He added, in such a kind tone that I thought, even then, that he would relent and allow me to stay. "I wish you lots of luck and I'm sorry that this didn't work out."

There was nothing else I could do. I told him that I understood, because I did. I thanked him very much for the opportunity to work there and wished him good luck with the transformer.

So, it was goodbye to Larramkota. I had kind of enjoyed working there and I was happy as long as it lasted. But I didn't think that I could risk my life for the job. I thought that I had at least a fifty per cent chance of dying in the attempt to fix that transformer. So, it was back to Caxata again. My nemesis, the man with gun, was no longer there. I never saw him again.

Once again, I was the only guest. I had my dinner and went to my room to go to sleep. There were two beds in the room.

I was already asleep when there was a knock at the door. I was surprised, got up and opened the door. Isabel, one of the two sisters who ran the inn, told me that there was a snow storm on the *Quimsa Cruz* Pass, about twenty miles ahead and that the truck from Eucalyptus could not get through. She had about fifty people there that needed accommodation. "Gerardo, would you mind sharing the room with somebody, just for tonight?"

"No, I don't think so," I said. "Who is going to be my roommate?"

"It's a nineteen year old girl, a German Jewish girl. I though she would be more comfortable with you than with anybody else."

Would I be comfortable? I thought I would be delighted! I thought this was a great stroke of good luck. Here was this German-Jewish girl, 6,000 miles from home, in a snowstorm all by herself, with all these strange people. How delighted she would be seeing me and talking with me in her native tongue, and what a comfort I was likely to be to her. Anything could happen. I was very excited. "Go right ahead, Isabel. Send her in. It will be fine."

"Well, I'm just going to feed them all. So it may take about an hour until she comes in. Don't lock the door."

No, I wasn't about to lock the door.

To my deep regret, however, I fell asleep before this lovely girl could arrive. When I woke up next morning, there was the other bed, unmade and empty. The lovely girl had been there but I never even got to see her. She had already left an hour earlier. The pass had been cleared and the truck took off as soon as it could. Another good opportunity lost.

I had to decide what to do next. Obviously I couldn't stay in Caxata. I had to go first to Eucalyptus and from there by train to either north to La Paz or south to Oruro. Oruro was much closer, so I decided on that.

I had enough money to be able to afford to go to the only hotel in the city. It was called Hotel Oruro (what else?). Then I went to a restaurant that had been recommended to me, and that was run by German-Jewish immigrants. They had a nice familiar menu. I ordered a *Wiener Schnitzel* and a bottle of beer. The beer arrived right away but the entrée took a long time. Finally it came. It was not *Wiener Schnitzel*. It looked like goulash. "Waiter," I said (in German), "I ordered the *Wiener Schnitzel*."

"That's what I ordered, too." the waiter said. "Look what they gave me." I thought I should not pursue that and ate the goulash. In fact, it was pretty good.

The next day, after a good night's sleep and a nice bath, I spent the day exploring. That evening I went to another restaurant. It was pretty full, and having asked permission, I sat down at a small table with a man who turned out to be an Englishman. His name, he told me, was Frank Thornton. I was delighted to meet an Englishman because I was always eager to practice and improve my English, which was quite halting at the time. All the "experience" I really had to speak English was what I had learned at the *Hohenzollern Gymnasium*. It was serviceable.

I struck up a conversation. I told him a little about who I was and what I was and where I had come from. Then he told me that he had been in Bolivia about twenty-five years, and that he was an employee of the railway. The Bolivian railroad had been built by the English, was owned by an English company, and its management was almost totally staffed by Englishmen. He told me that he was single and that he had never married. Although he never said so, he strongly implied that he was a homosexual. That, of course, was a closeted issue at the time, but I had no problem with it. I strained to understand what he said in English. One phrase he used continuously was "candidly speaking…" I didn't know what it meant. I only knew the word candy and thought that perhaps "candidly speaking" was the equivalent of "sweet talk." I never really understood it. It was his favorite expression.

Well, Mr. Thornton and I had a drink or two and then he told me that several years ago he had acquired, he didn't tell me how, an antimony mine off which he had never made any money. The mine didn't even have a name. Strictly speaking, it wasn't even a mine. It was a mining claim on which about twenty miners worked in independent tunnels. They delivered the ore to him and he paid them wages. He was being cheated right and left, he told me and I was pretty sure that he was right. After about another drink or two, he said to me, "Gerard," (that's what he always called me), "with all the experience you've had already, I want you to take on that mine."

"What do you mean?" I asked.

I could grubstake you. You go out there and make sure things are going right and we'll split the profits."

I didn't have much else to do. It was the first job offer I'd had. I wasn't totally sober, so we shook hands and I accepted that. He gave me a small amount of money in Bolivian pesos. It must have been the equivalent of around $300 or $400. Once again, I took the train to Eucalyptus, this time with a pass that Mr. Thornton had provided. Then I took the truck back to Caxata. Mr. Thornton explained to me where the mine was, about 15 miles out of Caxata. I had asked him where I would be living.

"Oh, we have a nice little house on the property. You will be very comfortable."

In Caxata, I engaged a *mulero*, a man who owns and drives mules. We took three mules, one for me to ride, one for him, and one for my gear and for the supplies I was taking. I had groceries and some medical supplies. I also had dynamite and detonators and a supply of coca and of carbide. I had asked Mr. Thornton about where the miners could buy their supplies and groceries. "You have a *pulpería*, I suppose, don't you?"

"We don't have that," he said.

"So what do the miners do?" I asked.

Once a week the miners tell the local *mulero* to pick up groceries and whatever else they need in Caxata and bring it back to the mine. The *mulero* makes a small profit on the transaction.

Mr. Thornton had also told me to get in touch with Rodolfo Mamani, who was the lead man of the miners and who would show me around.

The *mulero* and I arrived at our destination. We stopped in front of a structure that was built of rocks stacked on top of each other and which had a straw roof. The rocks were well fitted together, in an art that the Indians had brought forward from the age of the Incas, but there didn't seem to be any caulking between the rocks. I supposed that it would get pretty drafty. I was right. There was no door, only a burlap sack hanging from the small entry. The entire structure was about eight by ten feet. On the wall to the right after entering the "house," there was a platform of rocks about 3 feet off the ground extending the entire eight-foot length of the wall. That was the bed. I would have to say that the rocks were flat and pretty smooth, so that helped. The previous inhabitant, whoever he might have been, had left quite a bit of straw. I put that over the rocks and my bed was ready to go. I put the supplies on the other side of the room, paid off the *mulero* and was on my own.

One piece of equipment I had brought with me was a *Primus*, a kerosene stove. Since I had had fairly pleasant experiences in the other mines in which I had worked, I realized that this setup was going to be very desolate and more primitive than anything I had experienced up to that time. I was going to have to prepare my meals on that stove. As far as feeding myself was concerned, I had no knowledge at all of cooking, I only knew how to make one single "dish" namely, *supaypillas* which in Aymara means "blown by the devil" (I don't know why), and which is essentially a pancake made out of yellow corn flour. I had a copper pan without a handle in which I cooked my *supaypillas*. Light was supplied by a carbide lamp, which, in those days, was the only illumination in all mines. The lamp consisted of a container that was filled with carbide, into which drip water was admitted by a valve. The resulting gas went through a small orifice to the upper part of the lamp, pointing forward. It was then ignited. A circular mirror was behind the flame. It gave pretty good illumination.

There was one very important tool, both for the Primus and for the carbide lamp, and that was a so-called *chusiador*. It was a very thin wire attached to a sheet-metal handle. The orifices of both the Primus and the lamp had to be periodically cleaned with the *chusiador*. It was a vital tool. If you did not have the *chusiador*, you couldn't eat and you were left in the dark.

One morning, after about two weeks at the mine, I awoke, on my stone bed, and I could not move at all. That's not quite true. I could move my hands and fingers a little bit but the rest of my body, including my legs, was immobile. I was paralyzed. It would have been a deadly situation any place, but here, desolated and completely cut off, it was particularly perilous because I was so far from any help, and no one knew of my problem. I lay there for two or three hours, unable to move. I was getting more and more desperate. Suddenly I saw a shadow falling over my open doorway. I hollered. An old Indian woman came in. She didn't speak a word of Spanish. By that time I had picked up enough Aymara to explain, in rudimentary terms, what my problem was. The woman seemed to understand. Unlikely as it sounds, she seemed to be familiar with my symptoms, as though she had seen them before. I suppose it had something to do with the altitude, lack of proper food, or a combination of both. What happened next was right out of a grade-B movie: She took the blanket off me and took some evil smelling ointment out of her satchel. She began to rub my legs from the thighs down to the tips of my toes. Then she turned me around and did the same to the backs of my legs. After about 15 minutes of those ministrations, I was able to move my legs a little and was able to get out of bed and take some cautious steps. I had very little with which to compensate the good woman for the great service she had rendered me. I gave her 50 pesos, equivalent to, perhaps to $2 or $3, and she was quite pleased. I am sure she didn't do it for the money, she was just a nice person. She may have even saved my life. I still remember her fondly.

The first time I left the mine was two months after my arrival. During that entire time I only ate *supaypillas*, except for one day, when an emissary from Mr.

Thornton came. I had sent word that we were out of some vital supplies. I don't quite remember which – probably coca and carbide. That man came. He brought half a dried sheep (*charqui*), some oranges and some vegetables. I ate so much that night that I made myself quite sick.

There was no toilet, of course, and no plumbing of any kind. In front of my "house," a small pool had been dug by a predecessor, which held water that ran off the mountain. It was ice cold and more often than not, it was covered with a sheet of ice. I washed in it every morning and sometimes had to break the ice with a hammer before I got to the water. In sum, the accommodations were not very luxurious and quite a comedown from what I had enjoyed before. But I didn't feel sorry for myself. In fact, I never did feel sorry for myself during my entire sojourn in Bolivia, where, except for the last three years, I lived in the most primitive of circumstances.

The first day after I arrived at the mine, I went to look up Sr. Mamani, a nice man who spoke serviceable Spanish. He was the lead man of the miners in Mr. Thornton's mine. We agreed that I would deal only with him, that he would gather the ore from the miners, and that I would take it to Oruro every six weeks or so. Since Mr. Thornton had given me some money, I was able to give Sr. Mamani a small advance, for distribution to the other miners. There was no coordinated operation of any kind. Each miner had his own little tunnel from which he extracted the ore. There was no *pulpería*, but there was a smithy where the hand tools were sharpened every day.

The miners would work all day long and extract the metal-bearing rock. Then their women would take small hammers and break the rocks in order to separate the metallic ore, bright shiny silvery stibnite (the ore of antimony), from the gangue, the waste rock. Obviously, it was a laborious and inefficient operation.

All the ore was to be taken to the *Banco Minero* in Oruro, where it was weighed and assayed and where part prepayment, an estimated amount on account – was to be immediately made. The sacks in which we delivered the ore were provided by the bank.

After the agreed-upon six weeks, we had 200 sacks of ore ready for delivery to the bank. The women sewed the sacks up. I sent a man to Caxata to get the *llamero*. He came two days later with 100 llamas. Each llama would carry two sacks of ore – 100 pounds.

I preferred not to go with the llamas, so I left the night before for the 15-mile trip to Caxata. There was an almost-full moon. Between the mine and Caxata there was a mountain pass. But it wasn't as high as some of the other passes, perhaps only 16,000 feet high. I figured that since the mine was at about 15,000 feet, I had to climb about 1,000 feet on the serpentine road. At the top of the pass was a monument, if one could call it that, thousands of stones piled on top of each other. It was a custom of the Indians to leave a stone on the pass every time they went over it. It was for good luck and to appease *Pachamama*, the Earth Goddess. So, I put my stone on top of that also. I didn't much believe it in, but it couldn't do any harm. Of course, I did not wish to offend *Pachamama*, whoever and wherever she was. At that point, something dramatic happened.

I was totally tired and sat down at the top of the pass. I took off my shoes in order to rub my tired feet. To my horror, one of my shoes slipped out of my hands and started rolling down the mountain. Here I was, suddenly facing the unimaginably terrible prospect of having to walk down that road again, perhaps a couple of miles or more, either in my stocking feet, or with only one shoe, in order to find and retrieve that errant shoe. But to my great joy and relief, the shoe got hung up on a tiny brush about 100 feet down, that had managed to sprout in that inhospitable environment and at that altitude. I limped down, very carefully, retrieved the shoe, put it back on, and went back up. If the shoe had gone all the way, it could have been a real catastrophe. Chances are that I could have never found it. What would I have done? I couldn't have walked to Caxata with just one shoe. In any case, this worked out well. I then proceeded on my way to Caxata and waited for the *llamero*. He arrived late in the afternoon, with his 100 animals and with my 200 sacks of antimony ore.

I telephoned the dispatcher at the bank and told him that I had a truckload of ore to take to the railroad, hopefully the next day. The next day we trucked my production to Eucalyptus and from there by train to Oruro. There it was picked up by the truck of the *Banco Minero*, then taken to their warehouse to be weighed and assayed.

Stibnite, the ore of antimony has the chemical formula of Sb_2S_3, which means that the stibnite molecule has two atoms of antimony and three of sulfur. You can look it up in your old chemistry book, but the molecular weight of stibnite is therefore 339.50 of which the Sb, the antimony part, is 243.50. Thus, pure stibnite not accompanied by any impurity or any rock, will assay at approximately seventy-two per cent antimony. The bank would pay according to the weight and the antimony contained. For instance, if you delivery a 100 pound sack of ore and it was "pure" (which never happens) it would contain 72 pounds of antimony and you would get paid accordingly. If it was sixty per cent pure, you would get paid for sixty pounds of antimony, etc.

If it fell below sixty per cent, the bank would apply a penalty. For instance, if your ore contained only fifty-five per cent antimony you might get penalized five per cent and got paid for only fifty per cent. Well, you can see what I am leading up to. My ore contained only fifty-four per cent antimony and a substantial penalty was attached. The reason, of course, that my ore was so impure was the primitive method of concentrating it. We did not use any water – we didn't have any. All we did was have the women chip away the outer native gangue rock. It was inefficient and the bank payment showed it. I got very little money – less then I had expected.

I went back to the mine and showed the miners what I had received and distributed the money to them in accordance with their respective contributions by weight. I had to assume that the purity (or rather impurity), of all the lots was the same.

I got the miners together and told them what the problem was, that we had to make a bigger effort to increase both the quantity and purity. The miners promised to do their best, but I realized the limitations, based on the primitive conditions under which they worked. They only had hand tools. The tools limited their production. Further, they had no way at all of grinding the ore and no water with which to concentrate it.

So, we went through the same cycle again. I went on another trip, engaging the *llamero*, going to Caxata, across the pass on foot, leaving the rock for *Pachamama*, taking the production from Caxata to Eucalyptus to Oruro and hoped for the best. The miners had really tried. The quantity of production was higher than before and to my great surprise, the grade of the ore was also somewhat higher – fifty-eight per cent. But, of course, this still accrued a small penalty.

I was quite discouraged and decided to give up on that antimony mine, especially, of course, since I had worked for four months without any pay and was living in such dreadful conditions.

I told Mr. Thornton about my decision. He regretted it, but he agreed.

Once again, I returned to Caxata – which I am talking about so often that I make it sound like a minor world metropolis. Really it was absolutely nothing of a place – just a crossroads. I got in touch with the *mulero* who had taken me to the mine when I first arrived. I told him about my decision to quit, asked him to pick up my meager belongings and to give the money for distribution to the miners. Even though the *mulero* was an *hombre de confianza*, a man to be trusted, I asked him to bring me a receipt that the miners had indeed received the money. I also gave him the receipt of the bank, of course.

Once again, neither Mr. Thornton nor I got a penny.

I went back to Oruro flat broke. I had less than the equivalent of $10 left. I could not afford to stay in the Hotel Oruro. Instead, I stayed in a so-called *tambo*, which was essentially a flop house, in which the "rooms" were each about eight by eight feet, separated from each other, not by walls but by burlap bags that had been sewn together to make dividers. The tenants of the rooms, to my left and to my right, seemed to change periodically throughout the day and night, and all of them appeared to be engaged in noisy love making, which did not add to my peace of mind.

I parted from Mr. Thornton on the friendliest terms. He regretted, of course, just as much as I did, that we hadn't made any money in this mine, but that was nothing new to him. Apparently he had owned this mine for five or six years and it had never made a penny for him. I was still not really sure how he operated it, if that is the word, before I came along. He said, "Gerard, I really enjoyed meeting you and I am so sorry that we didn't have more luck with this project. I hope I will see you again. If you ever need a pass on the railroad, let me know and I'll get it for you."

I thanked him and prepared to leave. He said, "One minute. I have a room in La Paz, Calle Ayacucho #75. If you are ever in La Paz, you don't have to stay in a hotel. You may use the room because I am hardly ever there." He pulled out a key. "That's the key for the room. Use it any time."

"Thank you, Mr. Thornton," I said. I left. I didn't think I would ever use that key. As things developed, I did; and it turned out to be quite important.

Here I was, without any money, without a job, and without a safety net of any kind. I had to find a job very, very quickly or I wasn't going to eat.

I was aware that there was a large mine, San José, right outside of Oruro, owned by Mauricio Hochschild, of whom we've heard before. He was one of Bolivia's three big mining barons. I decided to try to get a job there. There was a bus running from the town square up to the mine, six or eight miles and about 1,000 above the town level. I didn't have money for the bus so I decided to walk. I started very early in the morning and got there about 10 o'clock. I went to the employment office. I asked for work. The personnel man looked at his list, flipped a few pages and said, "We need a draftsman in the geology department. Can you do that?"

"Oh yes, of course," I said, remembering my total frustration and failure at school in Mittwida where drawing was my nemesis. So he gave me a slip and told me to present myself to Sr. Trujillo, who was the head of the drafting department.

I went to where I was told, and gave my slip to Sr. Trujillo. There were about a dozen people working there, each one dressed in a white coat, I supposed so as not to dirty the drawings. Sr. Trujillo led me to a clothes hanger and gave me also one of those white coats, and told me to put it on. I did that. Then he led me to a drafting table. It was fortunately not a complicated geological drawing he wanted me to do. It was really only the tracing of a system of tunnels of one of the levels of the mine. I don't know to this day whether he actually needed it or whether he just wanted to see what I could do. I worked on it for about one hour and realized, not to my surprise, that what I had done was not very good.

At that time, Sr. Trujillo said, "Gerardo, you have to go to the infirmary now because a medical examination is mandatory for everyone before starting to work here. Come back when you get through."

"Yes, Sr. Trujillo." I did as I was told.

There were five or six people before me in the infirmary. Eventually I got called into what might be described as a consultation room. There was no doctor, only a nurse. She asked me some questions, listened to my heart and lungs, and pronounced me healthy. I wasn't surprised, but still, I was happy to hear it.

I returned to the drafting room, put on my white coat and went back to my table. To my dismay, somebody, I must assume Sr. Trujillo, had written the devastating words, "*no sirve*, (no good)" in black felt pen all over the drawing that I had started. While I was very unhappy, I had to recognize that the man was right. I philosophized that perhaps it was for the best, because even if I had passed this first day, I could never, never have bluffed my way through as a draftsman for any length of time. So I took off that white coat and, as much as I needed the money, didn't have the nerve to ask to be paid for the half day's "work," and walked back to Oruro.

The way down was easier than the way up, but my heart was heavier. I didn't know what to do.

Some miracle had to happen and had to happen very quickly. I went back to the *tambo*, paid my lodging and went to sleep, as best I could among all those libidinous neighbors. The next morning I got up and went to the market and bought a bottle of *papaya*, the national soft drink of Bolivia, on which I think not even Coca Cola could make inroads, and a *salteña*, a specialized, delicious meat pie. It was tasty and had to assuage my hunger for the rest of the day. Not having anything else to do, or rather not knowing what to do, I did something that, in view of my finances, was totally crazy and irresponsible. But it was something that became a turning point in my life. I can't imagine or reconstruct why, in my perilous financial situation it would have occurred to me, but I decided to have a haircut. I went to a barber shop. The barber, loquacious as most of his trade apparently all over the world, snipped away and engaged me in conversation. "Where are you from? What are you doing in Oruro? What kind of work do you do?" and so on.

I did not feel conversational. I responded curtly. In any case, he was able to extract elements of my story. "What's your name?" he asked.

I didn't think he needed to know, but I had no good reason not to tell him, so I said, "Gerardo Joffe."

"Gerardo," he said. "What a coincidence. You should try to go to work with Gerardo Sarmiento."

"Who is he?" I asked.

"Oh, he operates about ten small mines and I am pretty sure that he could always use a smart young fellow like you."

"Where does this Sr. Sarmiento live?" I asked.

He looked it up in the telephone book and gave me his address.

"It's about twelve blocks from here. You can't miss it."

I paid the barber and gave him a good tip. Perhaps this was my lucky day. I went to the address the barber had given me, rang the bell, and a *chola*, obviously the maid, opened the door. "I would like to talk with don Gerardo," I said.

"What about?" she asked.

"I'm looking for a job."

"Oh, I don't think don Gerardo is hiring anybody right now. There is no use disturbing him."

"Please, let me talk to him. I think I can be of much help to him in his work." Well, I must have been quite persuasive. She eventually let me in and knocked on the door of don Gerardo's office. He asked me to come in and I did.

Sr. Sarmiento, a stocky man – I figured about fifty years old and obviously a *cholo* – was extremely friendly. I always called him don Gerardo from then on out. He listened to my story, and asked me questions about what I could do. He was most interested in the experiences that I had gathered at the mill of *Mercedes del Illampu*. "Yes," he said, "I think I can use a man like you in my Poldi mine, which is close to the little town of Quime." I couldn't believe my good fortune and didn't dare ask how much he would pay me, but he volunteered. "There's going to be room and board and 3,000 pesos a month (approximately $150)." It was a small increase over my standard wage up to that time.

"Thank you very much, don Gerardo," I told him. "You will not be disappointed. I shall make a very good employee for you. When do I go up to the mine?"

"Let me see. Today is Thursday. I have a truck going up on Monday. You can go with it."

"Thank you, don Gerardo," I said. "But, I have a little problem. I wonder if you can help me?"

"What is it?" he said.

"I'm stone broke and I wonder if you could give me a small advance until Monday?"

He hesitated for only a second then he said, "Of course. How much do you want?"

"Would 500 pesos be all right?"

He pulled out his wallet and gave me 500 pesos. "Be there Monday morning. I'll see you when I come up to the mine. I want you to report to Bonifacio Zaconeta. I'm sending him a letter about you. He'll show you the ropes."

"Excuse me, don Gerardo. Who is Sr. Zaconeta?"

"Oh, Bonifacio has the general supervision over my properties in the area. But after he shows you the ropes, I want you to be in charge of Poldi. You will be reporting only to me."

I thought immediately that don Gerardo would be someone I would be happy to work for. My assessment was to prove correct.

So here I was, once back again, on my now well trodden road to Eucalyptus and to Caxata. But this time there was no pretty *cholita* around, and I was therefore allowed to ride in the cabin with the driver. We had to go beyond Caxata to get across the 17,000 feet high *Quimsa Cruz* Pass, before descending to the town of Quime. As is customary, we stopped at the crest of the pass for a rest stop, women to the right and men to the left. Since there is no vegetation at that altitude, large rocks, which fortunately abound, had to be sought for privacy. At the end of the pause, each of us left a rock for *Pachamama* on that centuries-old pile.

When the truck was ready to leave, we realized that two of the women were missing. We waited a little longer but they did not appear. Then the driver sent another of the women to search for them. She didn't come back either. So, he sent still another woman. About ten minutes later, all four women came back and, guess what, one of the women had a baby. She was one of the first two women who had left. Apparently, she had an easy labor because the whole procedure didn't take her more than fifteen minutes. She was wearing so many *polleras* (those voluminous skirts) that no one had noticed how pregnant she was. She seemed, amazingly, to be all right and the baby (a little boy, we were told) cried lustily. As an act of chivalry, I gave up my privileged seat in the cabin for the new mother and her baby.

What had just happened was something quite new for me; nobody else, however, seemed particularly impressed.

The truck stopped about twenty miles beyond the pass at the road that led up to the Poldi mine. Augustin Camacho, the *mulero*, was waiting for me. He had two animals. One for me and one for my gear. He himself preferred to walk on foot, the steep road, about 1,200 feet rise in elevation – I couldn't understand why, perhaps he rode mules so much that he wanted to locomote on his own feet for a while. I was pleasantly surprised about my accommodations at Poldi, especially of course after the disastrous living conditions at that primitive antimony mine. There were two actual rooms – one for my bedroom-living room, and another one for my office. There was a pass-through window to an adequately equipped kitchen and – wonder of wonders, there was inside plumbing, though of somewhat primitive design. But it was certainly light years ahead of what I had before. There was, however, no shower and no bathtub, but I had never had that before either, so for the whole time I stayed in Poldi I would put a bucket of hot water every Friday night in my bed-living room and took a sponge bath. It worked out O.K.

The *cocinera* was an old crone; her name was Esmeralda. She was no possible object of my constant state of sexual excitement. She was, however, a good cook and that was perhaps almost as important. I introduced myself to the foreman of the mine and the foreman of the mill and to the chief mechanic. The chief mechanic's name was Gerardo Parrado (another Gerardo!) and he and I became good friends, partly because we had the same first name, I suppose.

By now I had a pretty good knowledge of mining, both from what I'd seen and done and of course by the reading – not just the of the trusty *Manual del Minero*, but also of other books that I had bought in the meantime. The mine was fairly primitive in its layout and mode of operation. All the work was done by hand tools. The work consisted of making deep holes in the rock by hammering on long sharpened steel chisels, then filling the holes with dynamite, and then blowing it up. Then the rock would be shoveled up and put into a cart that ran on shaky old rails and rolled to outside the mine. There the rock would be hand sorted for that which was pure gangue, that was visually determined to have no mineral content at all; that which did show mineral content by visual inspection was sent down to the mill by a gravity-powered bucket line.

The people who made the holes in the rock did so by swinging 15-pound hammers against sharpened steel chisels of varying lengths; they were called *barreteros*. With each blow, the chisel was turned so that the cutting edge of the chisel could attack a slightly new face. It was long and exhausting work. The *barreteros* were the highest-paid workers and formed some kind of aristocracy in the mine. They were assisted by workers who held the steel steady while the *barretero* banged the hammer. And finally, there were boys who had to run back and forth with the chisels (called *barretas*) to take them to the smithy and have them resharpened. It was a constant process.

The people shoveling up the "muck" were somewhat lower in the social scale than the *barreteros* and got paid less. They were called *chasquiris*.

The mill was standard, about what I had run into in Mercedes del Illampu, though a little more primitive. But there were essentially the same kind of machines and the same principle of concentration. There was one added wrinkle, however. The ore in Poldi was heavily accompanied by iron pyrites, also called "fools' gold." It was called "fools' gold" because some of the early miners in California ran into those pyrites and thought they had found gold. Since pyrite is similar in gravity to cassiterite, the mineral of tin, it could not readily be separated from the tin ore by the standard gravity methods, which was the principle on which the mill worked. Therefore, the concentrated mineral had to be subjected to a final operation; it was called calcination. The mineral was put into very hot ovens, very similar to bakery ovens, in which the mineral was pushed back and forth by long iron rakes to assure even distribution. The intense heat drove the sulfur out of the mineral in form of sulfur dioxide (SO_2), which is a terribly stinging, smelly gas and very injurious to health, if inhaled. We didn't know how injurious it was, of course, and no precautions to breathing it were ever taken. There certainly were no masks or filters. I am glad that I was not subject to this dangerous gas for more than a couple of years and then only occasionally.

After the sulfur was driven off, what remained of the pyrite was iron. The mineral was then sent through a magnetic device that separated the iron from the tin ore. The iron was thrown away. It had no value as far as we were concerned. It certainly wouldn't pay for the transportation to a foundry. Sr. Sarmiento, a very smart man, had figured that out.

One of my jobs as manager was to keep the purity ("fineness") of the concentrate, the so-called *barrilla* to over sixty per cent. The chemical formula of cassiterite is SnO_2. If you remember your high school chemistry, you can figure out that pure cassiterite is seventy-nine per cent tin. So, I had some leeway to play with. I usually produced *barrilla* of a fineness of about sixty-five to sixty-eight per cent. One had to be careful, of course, because there's a trade-off: The higher the fineness of your concentrate, the more likely you are to discard mineral-bearing material.

I did a good job supervising the mine and the mill and got pats on the back from Sr. Sarmiento and a small but gratifying bonus for all the production above a certain quota. I beat that quota every month and I was proud of myself. I was very satisfied.

About once a month, I took the one-hour walk down to the road – I wouldn't call it a highway because it wasn't surfaced. I caught a truck to Quime, the small town – I'd say about 2,000 people – at the end of that road – about an hour away. Quime was much lower than the mine. It was at an elevation of about 13,000 feet. There wasn't much going on, but there were three German-Jewish people there, with whom I got acquainted and with whom I spent some time.

The first of these people was Walter Holzer. He wasn't really from Germany; he was from Austria, and he had a very pretty *cholita* companion. He had a small store selling odds and ends, and earned some kind of a living with it. He was a nice guy, though somewhat of a braggart and liar. He told me about his experiences as an officer in the Austrian army. I thought that virtually all of it was hot air and certainly unlikely for a Jewish officer. But he enjoyed telling those stories and I didn't mind listening to them – occasionally.

The other person was more interesting. She was a tall blond woman, Olga Blumenberg. She was a medical doctor, a general practitioner. She was employed by the Bolivian government and was the public health physician for the entire county. She was quite young, about eight years older than I, perhaps twenty-seven or twenty-eight years old. She was the most un-Jewish looking Jewish woman I'd every seen. I immediately lusted for her, of course, but considered her as somewhat of an unattainable object. She lived with her mother in a small, tidy apartment. They were from some town in Bavaria, I believe Augsburg, where her family had owned a quite important brewery, which had been in the family for generations. They had obviously been rich people, but like everyone else, they had left everything in Germany, of course. Olga and her mother liked for me to come visit for Friday night dinner which gave them opportunity to speak German with somebody they liked. They did seem to enjoy my company just as much as I enjoyed theirs. They were tired of Walter Holzer and his phony army stories. Also, Olga's mother strongly disapproved of his living with "that native woman."

After about six months in Poldi I decided to take a few days off to go to La Paz for "rest and recreation," and also perhaps to pay a small visit to Uncle Bernhard and Aunt Nanny. So I walked down the road to the "highway," and waited for the first truck going in the direction of Eucalyptus. I didn't have to wait more than 30 minutes. I got to Eucalyptus and took the train to La Paz. I arrived late in the evening, I'd say about 9:30 and was in the process of taking a cab to one of the hotels, though not necessarily one of the expensive tourist hotels, because I couldn't afford to do that. Then I remembered that Mr. Thornton had given me the key to his room in Calle Ayacucho #75. My mother had always taught me that "a penny saved is a penny earned," and "waste not want not" (yes, all these wise sayings also exist in German), so I thought I'd save the cost of the hotel and go to Mr. Thornton's room that he had so generously made available to me. I gave the taxi driver instructions and there I was. I entered the small building. I found myself in a rectangular courtyard, with a small fountain in the center and shrubs all around. The rooms were on all four sides, with three on each side. I remember that there was a big moon, though not a full moon. Mr. Thornton had told me that his room number was #11, so that's where I went. I put the key in the lock and opened the door. It was quite dark, but there was some light from the moon. I sensed that somebody else was in the room – in fact that someone was lying in the bed. I said, "Hello, is anybody here?"

The person in the bed said, "Who are you? What in the world are you doing here?" then leapt out of bed. It was a woman. She was stark naked. It was the most exciting sight I had ever seen. I almost fainted.

I said, "I'm a friend of Mr. Thornton's and he told me that I could use his room any time I came to La Paz. That's what I'm doing."

"Well," she said, "He told me the same thing. That's why I am here."

"What are we going to do?" I wondered out loud.

She told me that I might as well stay. "I think you and I are going to have a good time."

I couldn't believe my good fortune. I knew, of course, what was going to happen. I had worked so hard with Cilly Steinfeld and with Eva Siegler and quite a few others whom I had tried to "seduce," the latest, of course, being Mercedes, all without any success. Here, what I had been thinking of and dreaming of for years was suddenly handed to me on a silver platter and quite unexpectedly.

The girl, I would guess, was about twenty-five or twenty-six years old, tall for a Bolivian woman, with a beautiful body and long black hair. She was obviously very experienced. I got the beginners, the intermediate, and the advanced course in sex all in one night. In the morning I was very happy. I told her, "Let's get dressed and have some breakfast."

We did that and then I said, "I think I'm going to a hotel and take a bath. May I come back after that?"

"Yes."

I went to the hotel and paid my twenty pesos and took a bath. Then I went back to her and repeated some more exciting things. It was absolutely the greatest day in my life up to then. Sex was many times better than I had expected it to be, even in my most imaginative fantasies.

As I was leaving, about 3 o'clock in the afternoon, I said, "What's your name?"

She said, "Alicia."

"Alicia, I think you're wonderful. Thank you very much."

She said, "I had a very good time myself. That was your first time, wasn't it?" And then she added, "Don't forget me."

"No," I said, "I won't." And all these years later, I remember her as vividly as that Nazi with the golden-oak swastika in Hamburg, who saved my life. Both of them told me to remember them. I have.

I wondered what and who Alicia really was. For a while, I inclined to the belief that she was a lady of the night, who was so enchanted by my obvious eagerness and innocence that she didn't have the heart to tell me that. But on later reflection, I concluded that she was just a regular working girl, though sexually quite experienced. If she were a hooker, she wouldn't be lying in bed alone at 10 o'clock in the evening – she would be out hustling. Also, she was probably turned on by my innocence and inexperience and perhaps also by my heroic beginner's performance. I believe that she, too, had a very good time. It certainly must have been a new and different experience for her. If she is still alive – she would obviously be a very old lady by now – it is quite possible, though it was certainly not her first time, that she remembers me as well as I remember her.

What I never did find out was what her relationship to Mr. Thornton was and why she had a key to his room, just as I did. Even though I thought that he was a homosexual – what they call a *maricón* in Spanish – I might have been wrong. He could perhaps have been her lover. But, whatever he was, he certainly was not the sexiest guy in the world. And no question – he certainly had done me a big favor by giving me that key.

In any case, the long nightmare of my own virginity was finally over. I had been a boy and now I was a man. It had been a wonderful experience. I had a totally new outlook on the world.

One of my jobs in Poldi was to attend the *pulpería*, **the store where the miners** bought their supplies. Nobody paid cash, of course, and I kept track of what people bought and deducted the amount of their purchases from their weekly pay, which I also distributed – in cash.

Once a month, Sr. Sarmiento would either come to the mine himself or he would send an emissary, usually Augustin the *mulero*, to bring the money for the payroll. I had a wall safe in my office, where I kept the cash. Only I knew the combination.

There were about fifty workers in the mine. Most of them had families – I would say there were about 200 people altogether so I had to have *pulpería* hours three afternoons a week and people would stand in line to get served. I was by myself, with only one assistant, who mostly did lifting, bagging and such. I had to be very sure that all the "necessities" were available in the store. One of the most important items without which – if I wasn't stocked – everything would stop, and I mean really stop, was coca. I had already learned that in my very first job in the Chacaltaya mine. That's of course the famous plant from which cocaine is distilled, but, as far as I could tell, nobody in Bolivia used that drug.

People used only the coca leaves. They would stuff their mouths full of these leaves and then, apparently to bring the flavor out or whatever, they added a little piece of lye to it. It looked, awful and made a terrible mess. I tried it once. As far as I was concerned, it tasted awful. But the miners simply wouldn't work if they didn't have it. It was as necessary to them as air and water. So I made sure that coca was always available. It was not inexpensive, because the government taxed it highly. A good share of the miners' weekly wages went for coca. The second most important store item was carbide, which was needed for the miners' lamps. That was also an absolute necessity; I had already learned that in Chacaltaya. If there was no carbide, there was no light and they couldn't work. So those two products had to be always in ample supply.

Other important staples were *harina amarilla*, yellow corn flour. That's what those *supaypillas* were made of. Then there was dry corn on the cob. Another big item was lard, imported from Argentina because, as I said, I never saw any pigs in Bolivia. I don't really know why. I also sold *chuño* those freeze-dried potatoes, and *charqui* which is what we call jerky – obviously the same word, but all the *charqui* was from mutton, not from beef.

There were other items, some of less importance, such as candles, soap and cheap white cloth that came in rolls and which the women used to make towels and underwear.

You might wonder about bread. Once a week a *cholita* came up from Quime. She took the truck to the foot of the path leading up to the mine and carried her load of bread, usually 30 to 40 pounds, up the mountain to the mine. She spread her wares and people bought the bread. If it wasn't too late, she'd go back down, but usually she would spend the night with a friend in the mine. It was hard work with small rewards, but it was a living for these women.

One day, a new bread woman arrived. She looked different than all the other such women I had seen before. She was a *chola*, of course, and wore the traditional dress, including the bowler hat. She was about twenty-six years old, which means about six years older than I. She told me that her name was Zenobia. She was kind of pretty, very saucy and perky. She looked like lots of fun. In contrast to all the other native women, who had shiny hair, plaited into long braids, Zenobia's hair was curly and her braids were quite short. The people called her *churka* which means curly in Quechua. It wasn't until years later that I realized that Zenobia was perhaps as much as one-quarter black. This didn't dawn on me right away because I had never seen a black person, in Bolivia or anyplace else – except perhaps in the movies. Where would black people have come from? One of them would have been Zenobia's ancestor. Well, obviously from Brazil, which was at least 1,000 miles to the east, but in the course of human migration and for whatever reason, some of the black people there might have migrated to Bolivia. What they could have been looking for was not clear to me, other than exploration driven by curiosity, the way Europeans had been driven across the seas to distant lands.

I kind of liked Zenobia right away. We talked and I invited her to have dinner with me. We also had a couple of beers and a pretty good time. By that time it was getting late. "Oh my," Zenobia said, "it's late. Can you lend me a lantern to get home?"

"No, I don't have a lantern. But, why don't you stay here? You'll be comfortable."

She looked at me, thought for a few seconds, and said, "Yes, I think I will."

I thought she was a wonderful companion. In the morning, after having breakfast, I made her a proposal. I said, "Zenobia, you and I seem to get along really well with each other. Why don't you give up the bread business. There is not much money in it and it's very hard work. Come up here and be my *cocinera* and do my laundry and all that."

We both understood what "and all that" meant. She said, "Thank you for the offer, but that would be very difficult for me because I have two children. My sons are six and four years old. I don't think you would want them here, would you?"

I said, "No, Zenobia, definitely not. I really like you, but I don't think I would like to handle your children."

"Yes, I understand," she said. "So let's forget it."

Well, I did forget it, but really not quite. Next week, Zenobia came back again and it was pretty much the same routine. In the morning she said, "Gerardo, I talked to my mom and she said that I could stay here, that she would take care of the children. I would just need to go back to Quime about every other week or so."

Well, we made the agreement and Zenobia became my *cocinera* "and all that." She was a nice and accommodating girl. She was a good cook and it was a good arrangement.

I was doing a good job for Sr. Sarmiento. One day he came up to the mine and said, "Gerardo, I have a small tungsten mine on the other side of Quime. I would like you to consider taking over that mine as a *pirquiñero*.

"What is a *pirquiñero*?, don Gerardo."

"It means that you and I would work on halves. I stake you to all expenses and all of the materials. You send your production once a month to Quime, where I would have it picked up and then we split the profits."

Well, that was pretty much the arrangement I had with Mr. Thornton. It didn't work out at all for me. But, really, Mr. Thornton's antimony property wasn't a mine at all. It was just a few holes in the ground, very poor ore and no concentrating facilities. Sr. Sarmiento was obviously a much better operator and I could assume that this would be a better mine and a better deal. Also, of course, Sr. Sarmiento was solvent, whereas Mr. Thornton lived on a salary and had no money reserves at all.

"What kind of concentrating facilities are there, don Gerardo? Is there a mill?"

"No," he said, "there's no mill. But there are some manual concentrating facilities and there's lots of water. You will see."

"Don Gerardo," I said, "let me think about it for a week. I will send you a telegram to let you know."

"That's O.K.," he said. "*No hay apuro*" – there's no hurry.

I asked Zenobia what she thought about it. She liked it. She thought it was a good idea, mostly because it was closer to Quime and she would be able to see her children more often.

So I sent a telegram to Sr. Sarmiento. I told him that I would accept the offer. Bonifacio Zaconeta, who looked after Sr. Sarmiento's properties in the area, and I did not have the greatest relationship. That was about to be expected, because the hierarchy between us had not been clearly defined; also, I was quite sure that he was envious of me, my education, my youth – he was about fifty-five, and perhaps even my skin color. Even though we did not particularly like each other, we never had any real problems. He was going to take me to the mine, and I was going to operate it as a *pirquiñero*.

In any case, Zenobia and I moved to Quime, stayed overnight and then went up to the new mine, about a 45-minute walk, all uphill of course, from Quime. The name of the mine was *Juntuhuma*, which in Aymara means "hot water." It was really a quite beautiful place, fairly low in altitude – about 12,500 feet, with nice vegetation. There was a spring that produced thousands of gallons of hot water a minute. It had a slight sulfur odor, but not an unpleasant taste. I never had it analyzed. I always thought that if it were in a more accessible place, it could perhaps have become a second Marienbad, Vichy or Baden-Baden.

There was an adequate house consisting of three rooms – one was the *pulpería*, one was the livingroom/bedroom, and one was the kitchen. There was no flooring in any of the three rooms. It was all hard dirt. There were no bathroom facilities at all, but as I said, there was all this nice vegetation, so it worked out all right.

A deep gulch, a ravine, which started at the top of the mountain, about 1,000 feet above, ran all the way to the bottom, close to the town of Quime and right alongside the house. The gulch was perhaps 20 feet deep and 30 feet wide.

There were about twenty miners, each working in his own independent workplace. I was the *pirquiñero*, in other words, the contractor and they were the sub-contractors. We all made some money but nobody made a lot. There was no mill, but we had lots of water and we could do some concentrating of the ore by doing manually what would have been done in the mill by machines. The only problem, and it was a serious one, was to bring the ore down to proper size. We had no machinery with which to break it up. The miners' wives would work all day long hammering the rocks down to size. The name for them was *palliris*. It was hard and tedious work, but I always had the feeling that the women enjoyed it. It was an 8-hour day at least, with babies strapped to their backs and their other children scampering around and playing. But they had a chance to gossip and they seemed to do that endlessly.

Since the mine was so close to Quime, I went down every Friday afternoon, mostly to visit with Olga and her mother, who sort of expected me as their regular guest. At that time, I also became more "personally" interested in Olga, who obviously didn't have a boyfriend. There was nobody else with whom she could connect with in the little town. Also, she was a respected person of authority, as a physician for the entire district, and she had to be circumspect about her social life. So, inevitably, and even though she was quite a bit older than I, she focused on me. Quite frankly, I did a little focusing myself. One evening, after dinner, we went for a walk and I kind of suggested a "relationship" that we might find to be fulfilling for our weekends.

She said, "Gerardo, let me show you something." She took me by the hand and led me to her infirmary, which was a suite of two rooms in a street right off the town square. We went inside. The front room was the reception room and the back room was the consultation room. There was an examination table in the middle of that room. She said, "Do you see this table?"

"Yes, Olga, of course I see the table. What about it?"

She said, "Let me be quite frank. I haven't had any sex since I have been in Bolivia. I am with my mother all the time, and I really miss it. You and I could have it on this table every time you come down to Quime, but there is just one condition.

"What's the condition, Olga?"

"The condition is that you have to send Zenobia away. I cannot share you with her."

I said, "Olga, I would send Zenobia away immediately, but in that case you'd have to come up to the mine and cook for me and do the laundry. Would you like to do that?"

"Of course not," she said, "I'm a doctor. I have my duties here in Quime."

Well," I said, "I understand that, but please look at my problem. I'm up in that mine all by myself and I need somebody to take care of my most basic needs. You are not prepared to do that. Can we go ahead anyway without my getting rid of Zenobia?"

"No," she said. "That I can't do."

"Olga, I'm sorry but I cannot change that. Let's just stay friends."

"Yes," she said, "let's stay friends."

So that's how it was. Later on she got herself involved with an older man, who came to visit periodically from La Paz. He was about fifty or fifty-five. She called him Uncle Hermann. He was a crook and he soon took her money and all her mother's money in some crazy and fraudulent business deal that he had proposed to them.

One afternoon, after finishing my work, I began to develop a toothache. That toothache became worse. At about 8 o'clock it was unbearable. I didn't know what to do. I was in despair. There was no dentist, of course, within 100 miles. The pain was so bad I didn't see how I was going to get through the night. Then Zenobia informed me that a friend of hers had told her that in the next mine, about five miles away, there was a *gringo* part-time dentist and that he might be able to take care of me. I never had heard of that part-time dentist before, but I was desperate. With the unbearable toothache, in the dark and armed only with a lantern, I made that five mile hike to the next mine (I've forgotten its name). I asked around and was quickly able to find the *gringo*, the only *gringo* around. People were kind of vague about his being a dentist. I knocked at the door that I was told was his. The voice from inside said in English, "Who is it?"

So I told the man in my broken English that I understood he was a dentist and that I had a terrible toothache. "Just a minute," he said.

He opened the door and asked me in. He was a nice looking man, about forty years old. He introduced himself as Frank Livingston. He said he was from New Zealand.

I said, "Doctor Livingston,…"

"No, no," he said. "It's not Doctor, it's Mr. Livingston."

"O.K., Mr. Livingston, I understand you are a dentist."

"No, I'm not really a dentist. I am a missionary. I'm here to bring the true religion to these poor ignorant people who are besotted with Catholicism."

Beside myself with pain, I was still intrigued. "What is the true religion?" I asked him.

"The true religion is Seventh Day Adventism. It is my calling to bring it to these people. Have you accepted Christ as your savior?" he asked me.

"Well, not really," I said. "I'm Jewish and have not thought too much about Jesus Christ. Right now I have a terrible, terrible toothache and I was told that you could take care of it."

"I'm not a dentist but I do pull teeth. Your tooth sounds like it should be pulled."

Our conversation was half in English and half in Spanish. It turned out that Mr. Livingston spoke very little Spanish and I, of course, spoke very little English. Even in my pain I wondered how he was going to do missionary work if he didn't speak at least one of the Indian languages, either Aymara or Quechua, let alone not speaking Spanish too well. But, there was no time to worry about that. I thought he had the right diagnosis. The tooth had to be pulled, of course. There was no root canal work available in Quime; I would think it was not available in all of Bolivia, certainly not in those days.

"Do you have any dental instruments to pull the tooth with?" I asked him.

"Of course," he said. He opened his satchel, which was full of gleaming and dreadful looking tools.

"Let me have a look," he said. "Open your mouth."

I opened my mouth. He shone a flashlight into it and tapped what he believed to be the offending tooth. I screamed in pain. "Yes, the tooth must come out. I will pull it."

"O.K.," I said, "go ahead. How are you going to anesthetize me?"

"Oh, I can't anesthetize you. I'm not licensed to do that and I don't have the stuff to do it with. I have to pull the tooth without anesthesia."

"You've go to be kidding, Mr. Livingston. How are you going to pull the tooth without anesthesia?"

"I've done it a thousand times. It will be a little painful but you'll be all right."

Well, I had no choice. I opened my mouth and gripped the chair. "Doctor" Livingston selected the forceps that he thought would serve him best and – I have to give him credit for that – with one elegant swoop extracted the tooth. I thought I was going to faint, but I didn't. All I could do was think of those sailors on those old pirate ships who had their legs amputated without any anesthesia. Well, at least they got a drink – a half a bottle of rum – before the procedure.

Mr. Livingston put some cotton in my mouth and said, "Spend the night here with me. Go home in the morning. You can't walk right now."

So I went to bed. Livingston knelt by his bed, folded his hands, and engaged in a long, loud prayer session. It was a little embarrassing.

I went home the next morning and I was O.K.

I must have been the only person with whom Mr. Livingston had been able to talk more or less on his level in English or in any other language, so he came to visit me at least once a week. But those weren't just friendly visits. On each visit he made a really determined effort to convert me to Christianity. He was very clever.

He gave me citations from the Old Testament by which, according to him, the coming of Jesus as the son of God was predicted. While I thought of myself always as very "Jewish," I was not particularly, at least at that point in my life, imbued in "faith." I must confess that Livingston was so persuasive that had he been around for maybe another year, he might possibly have driven me to the baptismal font. I might well have become the first Jew for Jesus. Well, it didn't happen.

After about a year in Juntuhuma, we had a rainstorm that lasted for three days. Tons and tons of water came down from the skies. On the third day, the top of the mountain was soaked through and got dislodged by all that water. The gulch next to our house became a raging river of huge boulders, debris, and mud. It was like an express train racing by at 80 miles an hour. It was the scariest thing. One reads about these things in the newspapers, but to see this in person was unforgettable. Had our house been 50 feet closer to the gulch, it would without questions, have been swept away and crushed all of us in it. This lasted for the whole day. It was the most awesome natural spectacle I had ever seen.

Two of my miners were brothers, José and Carlos Camacho. José was the older, I would say twenty-five years old. Carlos was perhaps two years younger. José was married to a very pretty young *cholita*, perhaps twenty years old. One day, for a reason that I don't recall, José had to leave and go to Oruro. He was gone for about ten days. During his absence, Zenobia told me that some of the women gossips had told her that Carlos was "messing around" with José's wife. When José returned there was a very ugly confrontation between the brothers, in which blows were exchanged. José's wife sat by crying. We had to pull the two brothers apart but, obviously and understandably, there was very bad blood.

Next day Carlos did not show up for work. We all assumed that he had gone to Quime, probably to get drunk or to disappear from sight altogether. Two or three days later, one of the miners had some business in Quime and inquired about Carlos. Nobody had seen him. He came back up and told me about it. Then I really began to get concerned and, call it a hunch, I figured that something was very seriously wrong.

I took one of the miners with me and we went into the tunnel in which Carlos had been working. It was about 200 feet from the entrance to the working face. What we saw there was horrible. There was the body of Carlos without a head and without hands. The obvious conclusion was that he had committed suicide by putting a stick of dynamite in his mouth and exploding it. The brains, the hands and other parts were spread all over the face of the tunnel. We called two other miners, but not José. We picked up the corpse and took it down to Quime to the *alcalde*, the mayor of the little town. There was no inquest or anything like that. Things were quite informal. Anyway, we got Carlos buried and that was the end of it. José was stoic throughout the whole affair.

I had a contract with a butcher in Quime. Once a month he would walk a cow up from Quime to the mine. He led the beast by a halter. I don't see how the poor cow could make it all the way up. Those animals aren't made for climbing mountain paths. The cow probably lost ten pounds in doing so. Once the cow arrived, the butcher would tether it to a pole and would take a very sharp, pointed knife and in one swoop he would stick it between two vertebrae in the animal's neck. The cow would die instantly and fall down like a rock. It wouldn't even quiver. He then proceeded very skillfully to skin the cow and to butcher it. As the quasi-owner of the mine I had certain "feudal" rights, namely that I had first call on the skin, on the tongue, on the filets and on the liver. The Indians were skillful and made blankets and garments out of the skins. By the time I had two or three of those I had enough and I yielded my right to them. I really liked to eat tongue, but Zenobia hated it, so I decided to forgo that most of the time. I liked liver, so we took a few slices and Zenobia cooked them for me the way I liked it, with onions. In any case, I kept the filets, which made wonderful eating, of course. The miners bought the rest of it. Nothing went to waste. It was a good arrangement.

Zenobia had an old aunt. Well, she wasn't really that old, she was about sixty-five years old, but she looked like ninety. She didn't have a tooth in her mouth and could only eat mush. She didn't speak a word of Spanish. She had absolutely no income and would have starved without help. So, we took her in and put her in one of the little huts that we had for the miners. She had one great skill – she could make wonderful weavings. She set up a handloom in front of our house and would work all day long pushing that shuttle back and forth. She created wonderful blankets, shawls, ponchos, and whatever. All we had to do was supply the wool. She would even spin it herself and dye it. We couldn't use it all, of course, and we gave most of it away. Priscilla, my wife, is furious at me for having given all that good stuff away. But, in those days it didn't mean anything to me at all.

There were certain holidays (*fiestas***) when work stopped and great celebrations** took place. The most important was the *Seis de Agosto*, the Sixth of August, the Fourth of July of the Bolivians. In the province of La Paz, in which we lived, the other big holiday was the *16 de Julio* (July 16) which is the day of the *Virgen del Carmen*, who is the patron saint of the province of La Paz. There are other holidays, but those two are the most important. Unfortunately, they are quite close together. Many people got so carried away on July 16 that they celebrated all the way through August 6 and beyond. It slowed down mining production, of course.

The *fiestas* were punctuated by a great deal of drinking. There were really only two drinks, because beer was not much used in the mines and there was no wine at all. The two drinks were *chicha* which is a fermented drink of corn, about forty per cent alcohol, or 80 proof. The other drink, also very popular, was forty per cent straight alcohol, which came in rectangular cans. It was drunk by making two nail holes in the top of the can; then, just as I understand Chianti is drunk by the peasants in Italy, the can is held up and a stream of alcohol is directed into the mouth. This beverage has the picturesque name of *pussi tunka*. *Pussi* means 4 and *tunka* means 10 in Aymara. The name was a never-ending source of amusement for visiting Americans.

The entertainment was dancing. There are two principal native dances, namely the *cueca* and the *huayño*, which are danced by men and women waving handkerchiefs at each other. An expected, part of the festivities was for couples to stagger off into the bushes for their own purposes.

Music for these *fiestas* was provided by local musicians. The instruments were invariably the *quena*, a horizontal flute; the *zampoña*, the nose flute with many tubes; the *pinquillo*, a small flute, the equivalent of a piccolo, and perhaps the *bombo*, a big kettle drum to supply rhythm, and – not always, but in many cases – the *charango*, the mandolin-like instrument with a backing of an armadillo shell. I had encountered it on my very first day in South America, when I met those Chilean boys and listened to their naughty variations on *La Cucaracha*.

I was pleased to note that many of the women found me attractive. It had little to do with my personal charm or sexiness, but with the fact that I was quite different from any of the other men. Even though I was only 5'7", perhaps touching 5'8" at the time, I was considered tall and, of course, the light skin and also perhaps the fact that I was the boss made me attractive. In any case, when the women had enough *pussi tunka* in them, they would holler, *"Quiero al gringo"* – I want the gringo. Zenobia, however, kept me on a pretty short leash.

Usually, during these *fiestas*, a white llama would be sacrificed. It would be slaughtered under some age-old ritual of Inca ceremony and religion. Even though all of the miners and everyone else were nominally Catholics, there was still a lot of fallback to the ancient rituals. The priests didn't particularly object to that. I was always supposed to play some pagan ceremonial function in the sacrifice of the llama, which I fulfilled adequately, I thought. The llama was then eaten. I got the first plate. It was all right, I suppose, but I never really developed a great liking for it.

Another important feature of the *fiesta* was the shooting off of dynamite. I always realized that that was most dangerous and I was surprised that, at least in my presence, no serious accidents ever happened. We would take a piece of fuse, usually about two feet long, put the fuse into a detonator, and then crimp, fasten, the detonator on the fuse. That was always supposed to be done with a special crimping tool, pliers designed for just that purpose. But when the miners were drunk, they would do it with their teeth. If they didn't hit it right on the spot, if they bit in the wrong spot, the luckless celebrant would have his head blown off right then and there. The fuse/detonator assembly would then be put into a half stick of dynamite. The fuse would then be lit and the armed stick of dynamite would be thrown some distance away. The device would explode with a tremendous roar when it landed. I was always afraid that it might hit one of the loving couples that had retired into the bushes. It never did. Perhaps we were just very lucky.

I remember well the lyrics to some of the music to which we danced. Here is one:

En la punta de aquel cerro
Tengo una jaula de acero,
Donde cantan los jilgueros
La vida de los solteros.

The second stanza went like this:

Tarde de noche vengo,
Porque de día no puedo.
Yo no vengo por tus ovejas,
Yo vengo por tus amores.

Here is the English translation:

On the top of yonder hill
There is a cage of steel.
Where the finches sing
about the lives of the single men.

I come late at night
Because I can't come during the daytime.
I do not come for your sheep,
I come for your love.

There was much more of this, but you get the idea. It doesn't make a whole lot more sense in Spanish than it does in English, but everyone seemed to enjoy it. Of course, there were also many songs in Aymara, but I don't remember them at all.

We all made a little money, not a whole lot, to be sure – the Juntuhuma miners and I. With tin prices declining, and with only marginal profit for himself, Sr. Sarmiento decided to close the Juntuhuma mine, at least temporarily. Also, Bonifacio Zaconeta had gone on to other pastures, so don Gerardo decided to put me back in as manager of Poldi. That was all right with me. Even though Poldi was not a large mine, there were more comforts. So Zenobia and I packed up and went back to Poldi. Sr. Sarimento gave me a nice raise.

By that time, I was twenty-two years old, and while I was really having a very good time, I started thinking about the "future." It was clear to me that I had gone "native" to quite an extent, especially my living with Zenobia, with whom I had been by then for over two years. I had absolutely no desire at all to bring about a situation by which she would become my life companion, either by default or in some other way. But she was essentially a nice girl and very good to me. I didn't know how to handle the separation that I was planning, and I didn't do anything about it as I began to think through the change for my "future."

Eventually, I did talk to Zenobia and explained to her that we had been together a long time, that it was time for both of us to go on, that we should separate, and that I was going to give her some money to be sure that she would be all right. She did not take kindly to the suggestion. She screamed, she cried, she threw an unholy fit. I finally said that we didn't have to do this right away, let's just think about it a bit.

Then something happened. Once every month, if he didn't come himself, don Gerardo would send a messenger with cash in order to service the payroll. The messenger usually came on Monday or Tuesday, and payday was on Friday.

This week the messenger came also. He brought about 50,000 Bolivian *pesos* for which I gave him a receipt. I put the money into the wall safe in the office, of which only I (I thought) knew the combination. Just to be sure, I had put it down on a piece of paper, which I carried in my wallet. I made up the payroll on Thursday and opened the safe on Friday morning to put the right amount of money in each of the miners' pay envelopes. I turned the knob of the safe right and left to the proper combination and opened the door. To my horror, instead of the 50,000 pesos, there were only about 5,000 pesos. How could this have happened, I asked myself. I was the only one who knew the combination to the safe; what's more, nobody but Zenobia and I had access to the office. Nobody else ever came in there unless it was in my presence. Then it occurred to me that I had written the combination down, that Zenobia had looked in my wallet and knew what it was. She had stolen the money, most likely in preparation for my inevitable leaving and not being so sure how I would take care of her.

I was very upset and very angry. I confronted her and asked her point blank about it. She absolutely denied it. I grabbed her and shook her. She still denied it and she began to cry. Then I hit her, not too hard and only once. She said, "Yes, yes, I took it. Please don't hit me any more." She took me to our room where she had hidden the money under the bed.

I said, "Zenobia, this is the end of it. You cannot stay here anymore. Please get out right away because you have stolen from me and you have betrayed me. I can't have you around any more."

She packed up her meager belongings, crying and shouting colorful curses at me – in Spanish and Amarya. She left the mine. We had been together for over two years, but after that I never saw her again. Despite what she had done, I didn't think she was a bad person at all.

So, somewhat more dramatically than I had planned, one important chapter of my life had ended. But still, I was not satisfied. I promised myself that, staying in the Poldi mine, I would never again get involved with another native woman. Who knows, even Zenobia might come back. Then it would start all over again. And there was another point: Where was my professional future? I could have stayed in Poldi for another ten years and all I would have achieved was to have grown ten years older.

I was very friendly with many of the truck drivers that drove the route between Eucalyptus and Quime. One of them told me one day that the Colquiri mine, an American-operated large mine, not too far from where we were, might hire people like me. It would be worth my while to inquire. He also told me that he could drive me very close to it. He would show me how to get the rest of the way to the mine. I had heard of the Colquiri mine before. It was one of Bolivia's very largest mines and was owned by Mauricio Hochschild, one of the three "mining titans" of Bolivia. Also, I had met a couple of people in La Paz who I thought worked in that mine.

I thought about that and decided that I would look into it. In the meantime, I was leading a bachelor's life, to which I had become unaccustomed. I found a woman to cook for me, but that was all. I even started to think about Zenobia again.

About two weeks later, the weekly bread lady came up. She was a new one that I had not seen before. She was plump and very pretty and she told me that her name was Anastasia.

After she had sold her bread, I invited her to come into my office. Not surprisingly, and despite my good intentions, one thing led to another and since it was getting quite late, I persuaded her to spend the night. She readily accepted.

We went to bed. We hugged and kissed but then I noticed with horror that absolutely nothing was happening with me. I did, to coin a phrase, not rise to the occasion. Anastasia, of course, realized what was happening. Her most loving ministrations did not change the situation.

Here I was, twenty-two years old and I was IMPOTENT! My God, what had happened to me? Anastasia turned on the light, sat up in bed and said, "Gerardo, I know you are worried, but don't worry. I know exactly what's happening."

"What's happening?" I asked her in despair.

"It's Zenobia," she said.

"What about Zenobia, what does she have to do with it?"

"I'll tell you what she has to do with it," she said. "Zenobia took a pair of your socks and hung them in the belfry of the church in Quime. That's an old Indian trick. It makes the man who owns the socks impotent."

"That's the craziest thing I've ever heard," I told her. "It's pure superstition and it can't be."

"See for yourself, it's happening to you. Have you checked your socks?"

"No, I haven't checked my socks. I don't even know how many socks I own."

"Well," she said, "I assure you that's exactly what happened. I'm going to send my brother up to the belfry of the church and look for your socks. I'm sure they are there. When I come back you will see."

In the morning nothing having happened, I gave her a goodbye kiss and thought about the weird story. I didn't believe a word of it. I was very, very worried.

Two weeks later, Anastasia came back to sell her bread. After she had sold all her bread she came into my room. "Look what I found," she said. She pulled a pair of socks out of her pack. Sure enough, they were mine. "Now let's try it," she said.

By golly, she had been right. It worked. I could hardly believe it, but it had indeed been those socks. Well, live and learn.

I was getting restless and I decided to take up the advice of that truck driver and look for possible work in the Colquiri mine. I asked him if he would take me close to the Colquiri mine.

"O.K., I'll take you," he said. Be by the road next Monday morning around 10 o'clock. I'll take you to the place to where you have to go. By the way, do you have a compass?"

"No, I don't. But why do I need a compass?" I asked.

"Well," he said, "You have to walk exactly west from where I will drop you off, and I don't want you to get lost on the Altiplano.

"Don't worry," I said, "I'll manage going west without a compass. You just drop me off at the right place."

Next Monday, I went down to the road. He came by about fifteen minutes later. We went over the *Quimsa Cruz* Pass, then through Caxata. About 25 miles beyond that he stopped. "This is the place."

"What do you mean, this is the place? There is nothing here."

"That's the point. Go straight west and then you'll come to a big quarry. The quarry belongs to the Colquiri mine. From there it's about 15 miles to the mine itself and there are trucks going to the mine all day long."

I said, "O.K." I got out of the truck and started walking west. How did I know where west was? Well, it was 4 o'clock in the afternoon and it was close to sunset so I just followed the sun. He told me it was about six miles and sure enough after about an hour and a half there was the big quarry. I thought my trip was over. I didn't see any trucks, however. There was an old Indian man who didn't speak Spanish. In my broken Aymara I told him that I wanted to go to the Colquiri mine. I heard that trucks were leaving every hour and where were they?

Yes, he told me, trucks do indeed leave every hour, but the last truck leaves at 4 o'clock and now it's 5:30. Night was quickly falling. It was going to be cold. I had no place to sleep. "I don't think there is a hotel or anything like that around here, is there?" – an obviously silly question.

"No, there's no hotel."

"Well, where could I stay?" I asked him.

I'll let you stay with me," he answered.

It wasn't a great prospect, but I had no choice. I went into his room, which was lit by a carbide lamp. It was quite bare. There was a rudimentary bed, a table, and one chair. I realized that I would have to sleep in the same bed with him. Well, I wasn't squeamish, so I did just that. I went to sleep and woke up the next morning. The nice Indian man gave me some breakfast, which consisted of a cup of tea and some bread. I wanted to pay him for that but he refused. He told me that I was his guest and therefore he couldn't take any money from me. He told me to go down the road about 300 meters and I'd find the trucks to take me to Colquiri.

Zenobia Gonzalez sitting in front of our "home" in the Juntuhuma mine. She was a very sweet woman and I think she really loved me. Ultimately, however, we each had to go our own way.

This is Morales and I in front of the portal of Incalaya, the
main entry to the Colquiri mine. If it hadn't been for Morales,
I probably would have been fired the very first day of my
working there. He never knew how much he helped me.

I arrived in Colquiri about 10 o'clock in the morning and asked for the office of the manager. I went there. There was a young woman, obviously not a secretary, but some kind of a gatekeeper. I asked her whether the manager was in.

"No," she said. "Mr. Niedermeyer is in the mine."

"When will he return?" I asked her.

"Oh, I'd say in about an hour."

"May I wait here?"

"Yes, have a seat."

I waited for about an hour. Then Mr. Niedermeyer came in. He made an overwhelming impression on me. He was about 6'3" tall and weighed probably 300 pounds, all muscle, without an ounce of fat, as far as I could tell. He had on a hard hat which made him about 2" or 3" taller yet. He was physically the most impressive human being I had ever seen. Of course, I rose from my chair and stepped up to him. "Good morning, Mr. Niedermeyer," I said. The conversation, if one could call it that, that followed is as clearly engraved in my mind as though it happened yesterday. Here it is, word for word:

"I vant to vork here, Mr. Niedermeyer."

He mockingly replied, "You vant to vork, huh?"

"Yes sir, I vant to vork."

"What the hell can you do?"

"Mr. Niedermeyer, I can do most anyting in a mine."

"Oh yeah," he said. "Can you run a fucking transit?"

"I beg your pardon, sir. Can I do vat?"

He seemed impatient and made a quarter turn toward his inner office. "I asked you whether you can run a fucking transit," he repeated in a somewhat louder and more impatient voice.

A fucking transit, I thought. I didn't know what it was, but whatever it was – if he'd asked me if I could build a fucking rocket to go to the moon or if I could perform a fucking brain operation or make gold from fucking lead, I knew there was only one answer and that answer was YES. "Of course, Mr. Niedermeyer," I said, "I know how to run a fucking transit."

He made another quarter turn and took his first step toward his inner office. "Come back in three weeks," he said. He then went inside his office and closed the door. I stood there rooted to the floor like Lot's wife in the Bible, who was turned into a pillar of salt. What did these five American words mean, "Come back in three weeks?" Did he mean that I should come back to formally apply for a job? Did he want me back in three weeks to test me whether I knew how to run a fucking transit? Had he hired me? I stood there and wondered whether I should knock at the office door, walk into his office, and ask him what exactly he had meant. By that time, however, I had assessed Mr. Niedermeyer's personality and knew with near certainty that he would tell me to get the hell out of there and not to come back. That would be a one hundred per cent guarantee that I would not have a job. If I interpreted the five magic words to mean that I was hired, I thought that I would have at least a fifty per cent chance of having a job. Those were better odds. I turned around and left the office.

By that time, it was about 4 o'clock in the afternoon. I couldn't make that trek to the quarry that late in the day. What to do? I remembered that I had met a man by the name of Hirsekorn in La Paz. He was about six years older than I and I remembered that he had told me that he worked in the Colquiri mine. I went to the employment office and asked for Hirsekorn. Sure enough, he was an employee in the mill and I was told where he lived – about 2 miles down the road in the mill employees' singles quarters #11. Hirsekorn was not married. I went down there and Hirsekorn was in his room. I told him about my meeting with Mr. Niedermeyer and repeated word for word what had transpired. Hirsekorn just laughed. "He is a crazy guy," he said. "If you come back in three weeks he won't remember ever having talked to you. You won't be smart giving up the job that you have now."

"Well let me think about it. I believe I may take the chance."

"O.K.," he said. "It's your decision. What can I do for you?"

I said, "Hirsekorn, I have to spend the night here. Can I stay in your room?"

"No problem," he said. "I work the night shift from 12 midnight to 8 o'clock in the morning. I leave the room around 10 o'clock. You can stay here but please be out of the room by the time I come back around 8:30."

I told him how much I appreciated his kindness and that I was going to be sure to be out by 8 o'clock at the latest.

I got up at 7 o'clock, got dressed, bought a papaya and a *salteña* for breakfast and took the shuttle bus up to the main square of the mine. I learned that there was a much better way to get back to Poldi, namely taking a truck to Eucalyptus and then another truck to Quime. That, in review, is what I should have done in the first place, in reverse. I could have avoided that westward march across the Altiplano and the night I spent with my Indian host.

As usual, we stopped in Caxata. I went to the bathroom. I noticed something strange. I had a great deal of itching in the crotch area. I wanted to see what it was. What I saw horrified me. I was filled with lice. I had never seen those insects before. I had only heard about them. Where did I get those lice? Obviously, from the Indian that I had slept beside – nice as he was, he had infected me with lice. What worried me even more was that I probably left the lice in Hirsekorn's bed. Indeed I had. When I later met him, he told me about it. He didn't think it was funny at all.

What to do about the lice? I went back to Poldi and asked my friend Gerardo Parrado, the chief mechanic, what to do. Gerardo had answers for almost anything, certainly for lice.

He told me that it was very difficult to get rid of those lice, but that there were two sure-fire ways of doing it. "First, shave all of your pubic hair and wash thoroughly with black soap," (whatever that was). "The second way, you don't have to shave but you have to wash thoroughly with a combination of kerosene and lye. You have to do that twice a day for three days. By that time the lice will be gone."

I decided on route number two. It worked. I also burned the underwear that I had been wearing that day.

I sent a telegram to Sr. Sarmiento and told him that, for personal reasons, I would have to leave, that he should consider this my two weeks notice. I also told him how very much I had enjoyed working for him, how grateful I was for his having given me this opportunity, that I wished him all the luck in the world, personally and in his business, and that I hoped to see him again.

Indeed, fifteen years later, and in a quite new incarnation I went back to Bolivia and visited Sr. Sarmiento, who was then living in La Paz. It was one of my first orders of business. He was quite elderly by then and very happy to see me. He said that he didn't think that he'd ever see me again. I had not thought so either.

In the meantime, however, I had been thinking about that "fucking transit" that I had so boldly asserted I had no problem running. I decided I knew what it was. *Transito* in Spanish means traffic. It stood to reason that transit would mean the same thing in English. (I was not at all wrong, was I? There is such a thing as a transit authority that deals with urban traffic.) But I didn't know a thing about traffic in mines or anyplace else for that matter. I had to learn all about it in less than three weeks. I sent a telegram to my mother in Buenos Aires, in German of course, as follows:

> MOTHER, I URGENTLY AND IMMEDIATELY NEED A TEXTBOOK ABOUT TRAFFIC IN MINES (*TRANSITO EN MINAS*). IT'S VERY IMPORTANT. PLEASE GO TO A TECHNICAL BOOKSTORE AND GET IT TO ME IMMEDIATELY BY AIRMAIL. TO REPEAT, ITS VERY IMPORTANT AND VERY URGENT.
> LOVE, GERHARD

My mother, who did not know her way around Buenos Aires, hardly spoke any Spanish, who had never seen a technical bookstore, but had always come through for me, did just that in this case also. Within a week, I had the book "*Tránsito en Minas.*" It was exactly what I had asked for and what I needed. I was much relieved. The hardcover book, which I still have, had about 450 pages and discussed every conceivable aspect of traffic in mines. The locomotives, the cars, the rail systems, the signals, the schedules. It was complete. I read the book from cover to cover in two days; then I read it again and once again. By the time I had read the book for the third time, I was probably the greatest authority on traffic in mines in South America. I was prepared. Mr. Niedermeyer would not be able to scare me.

At the appointed time, three weeks after my first momentous meeting with Mr. Niedermeyer, I left Poldi and went to Colquiri. I thought it would be prudent to stay out of Mr. Niedermeyer's way and went directly to the employment office, the same one where I had asked about Hirsekorn. The man asked for my name, looked through a ring binder and after a minute or so looked up and said, "Oh yes, we are expecting you. Report to the engineering office."

I was totally relieved. That crazy Niedermeyer had indeed hired me and had told the employment office to expect me.

The man continued: "Before you go to the engineering office, go to the *Rancho Extranjeros* where the single foreigners live. You will find a Mrs. Ruud who will assign you to a room. All of this sounded pretty good. I went to the *Rancho Extranjeros*, which was a nice building, two stories high, with a large dining room and kitchen, twelve rooms on the first floor and twenty rooms on the second floor. Every two rooms shared a bathroom. It was the most luxurious thing I had seen since I had been in Bolivia.

Mrs. Ruud was a nice American lady. She and her husband were from South Dakota and were of Norwegian descent. She welcomed me warmly and asked me if I had had anything to eat. I told her that I hadn't.

"Go into the dining room and I shall tell the cook to make you some lunch."

The meal in the dining room, with a table with a tablecloth, with real china and real flatware, consisted of two courses. I don't remember the main course, but I will never forget the appetizer. It was pineapple chunks topped with mayonnaise. It was the weirdest thing I had ever seen or ever eaten, but in order not to offend Mrs. Ruud, I ate it. It didn't taste all that bad. But, having been used to the hearty Bolivian cuisine, I was a little concerned about what the food was going to be like in that *Rancho*. But my fears turned out to be ill-founded.

Having eaten and having put my gear in the second-floor room that Mrs. Ruud had assigned to me, I went to the engineering office and met my boss, whose name was Stan Dawidowich. He was an Austrian Jew.

I wondered why his name was Stan. There had never been a German or Austrian Jew, or German or Austrian gentile for that matter, whose name was Stanley. What might it have been before? I never asked him and I never found out. Stan was a nice guy, about two years older than I, and in the course of time we became good friends. He insisted on speaking only English with me during business hours. I thought it was strange. His English wasn't much better than mine. After work we spoke German, but during business hour it was only English. Well, he was the boss, so he set the tone. He said, "Gerardo, I understand that Mr. Niedermeyer hired you to run a transit. Is that right?"

"Yes, it is." But then I began to wonder about one thing. Both Niedermeyer had referred to it as "<u>a</u> fucking transit," and Stan referred to it as "<u>a</u> transit;" they never said "<u>the</u> transit." I wondered why "a" and not "the." It would be <u>the</u> traffic, and not <u>a</u> traffic, wouldn't it? Something was wrong. Did I have some kind of misconception? I began to worry about it. If I had misunderstood, then all of my work and study directing the traffic in that mine would have been in vain, and I still wouldn't know how to run a fucking transit.

Then Stan said to me, "You are going to work on the two upper levels. Their names are *San Antonio* and *Doble Ancho*. Morales here is going to be your assistant." He beckoned to one of the Bolivian men standing nearby. We introduced ourselves to each other. "I want you to go up with Morales to the *San Antonio* level and survey crosscut 25 West, between drifts 13 and 14 North."

"Say that again, please, Stan," I said.

"Of course," Stan said. "I want you to survey crosscut 25 West, between drifts 13 and 14 North."

"All right," I said, and turned around. The scales fell from my eyes. I suddenly and in a blinding flash realized what a transit, fucking or otherwise, was. A transit was what we in Spanish called a *teodolito*, an optical surveying instrument to measure horizontal and vertical angles. I knew what it was, of course, but I had never actually seen or operated one. Just like (in those days) a DC3 airplane – I knew what it was, I knew what it did, but I didn't know how to fly it.

Morales loaded the transit, the tripod, the steel tape measure, and everything else we needed on his shoulders. We walked up to the *San Antonio* level, about a 15-minute walk. I remembered the disaster at the San Jose mine, where I was effectively fired after three hours. I knew that the same thing was going to happen here unless I did something smart and I did it very quickly. I had an idea.

"Morales, how long have you been working here?", I asked him.

"Five years, *señor*," he replied.

"And what have you been doing in those five years?"

"Well, for the first three years I was a helper in the mine and then I got advanced. I became helper in the engineering department, which is a better and easier job. I always help the engineers in the surveying."

"Morales, I said, "have you learned anything in those years?"

"Oh yes, *señor*. I understand the transit very well. In fact, in an emergency, I think I could even do it myself."

"Oh come on, Morales," I said. "I don't believe that, but I tell you what; I'll give you a chance. If you do a good job for me, if you turn out to be a good assistant, I might eventually try to get you a promotion."

"Oh thank you very much, *señor*. I'll try my best."

We finally got to the *San Antonio* level. He led me to crosscut 25 where we were supposed to do our surveying between drifts 13 and 14 North. "Morales, what is the first thing you do?" I asked him.

"The first thing I do, *señor*, is to set up the tripod right under the last survey point. Then I put the transit itself on the tripod."

"That's right," I said. "Let me see if you can do that."

"*Sí, señor*," he replied.

He located our point of departure, which was marked by a hook in the roof of the crosscut. He planted the tripod, extended and tightened the legs, and positioned it under that point. Then he took the transit out of its box and carefully placed it on top of the tripod. He finished by fastening the transit on the tripod.

"Well, that isn't too bad," I said, "you seem to have really learned something. Now, what's the most important thing?"

"The most important thing, *señor*, is to put the plumb bob on the hook above us and see that it is centered right on the transit."

"Exactly, Morales," I said. "Now let me see if you can do that."

"*Sí, señor.*" He reached up, put the string of the plumb bob on the hook and managed to put it right on top in the center point mark on the transit.

I watched him like a hawk. "So far, so good, Morales. Now what is next?"

"Next thing, *señor*, I have to level the transit."

"Exactly, Morales, let me see you do that." I watched him work the four knurled knobs of the transit, with his eye on the tube levels. I saw that each pair of leveling knobs had to be turned in the opposite direction from each other. "All right, Morales, let me see if you've leveled the instrument properly."

"*Sí, señor*," he said. I looked at it. It was absolutely perfect.

I said, "Morales, I think you need to make a slight level adjustment in the east-west axis." He looked at it and, of course, it looked very good to him.

"I think you are right, *señor*," he said, and he gave it a slight adjustment that was not needed.

"I am really impressed, Morales. You seem to have learned a lot since you have been here. Now what do you do next?"

Well, I won't take you through the whole tedious story but he taught me how to do it. I concluded that it wasn't all that difficult. The final step was to measure, with a steel tape, the distance from point A to point B and to put all of the information, horizontal and vertical angles and the distance into our notebook.

I let Morales do two more points and then I took over. I now knew how to do it myself. Morales questioned me respectfully at one of the points. I told him that I was not used to this particular instrument, that I was used to more advanced equipment, and he bought the explanation. We had done a good morning's work. Morales picked everything up, put it on his shoulders and we went back to the office. Nobody had to show me the mathematics of the procedure. Those were clear to me. I found a mechanical calculator (one had to turn a crank), and a book with eight-decimal logarithms. I was able to plot the morning's work in no time at all. Stan asked me, "How did Morales work out?"

"I think he is a very good man. I had to teach him a few things, but I think in time he could eventually be an engineer himself."

Stan said, "Gerardo, they don't use Bolivians as engineers here, only Americans and, in some cases, Europeans. It is very difficult for Bolivians to get this kind of job."

"Well," I said, "Morales is really talented. I think he should do this kind of work eventually. I'll help him along."

I got used to the work and in fact did it very well. In about three months I was considered the top engineer and was entrusted with the most difficult projects. Stan took notice and so, though he never said anything, did Mr. Niedermeyer. By that time I had begun to understand the "social structure" of the mine. It wasn't that difficult.

On the top of the heap were the Americans who had all the top managerial jobs. The only exception was Stan, who had been working there a long time, was very smart, and probably got the job by default. Beneath the Americans came the Europeans, who were almost exclusively German or Austrian Jews. I would say that there were about ten or twelve of us in the company, and we had what could be called middle management jobs. Below that were the Bolivians who made up the workforce, but who also had some minor supervisory jobs, both in the mine and in the mill. It was a racist society, in which the Bolivians were totally discriminated against, even at the *Rancho Extranjeros*, which was reserved for Americans and Europeans. Single Bolivian men working on my approximate level lived in the *Rancho Bolivianos*, in which the living conditions were not comparable to ours. In later years, living in the American South, I often compared that with the schools of black children, which were supposedly "separate but equal." They were separate for sure, but they certainly were not equal.

Another most decisive social distinction was whether one was on the *Boliviano peso* or on the U.S. dollar payroll. I was on the *Boliviano peso* payroll. In fact, I had never seen a dollar bill in my life. My salary was 5,000 pesos, equivalent to about $250 a month. Out of that, I had to pay 1,500 pesos for room and board at the *Rancho*. I realized that in order to get anywhere I had to get on the dollar payroll, but I also understood that nobody was going to put me there unless I demanded it.

After about six months and having just completed a very important surveying project, I screwed up my courage and went to Mr. Niedermeyer's office. I knocked on the door. "Come in," he growled.

I walked in and said, "Mr. Niedermeyer, I'm doing a very good job here and I wish to be put on the dollar payroll."

"Why the hell would I put you on the dollar payroll," he snarled.

"Because that's what I want, and if you won't do it I'm afraid I'll have to leave." I almost peed in my pants. I hadn't meant to say that. It was the greatest bluff I had ever pulled in my life. What would I do if this wild man would take me up on that and let me go?

But he did something else. He got up from his chair, walked around his desk toward me, grabbed me by the lapels, shook me and lifted me up, and said: "Don't you ever come in here again and try to extort me. Now get the hell out and go back to work."

I did as he told me. I was very upset. My next paycheck was in dollars. It was $300. My bluff had worked. I was surprised.

I met Mr. Niedermeyer who, as you will see, continued to play an important role in my life, many years later when I was living in California. He came with Mildred, his wife, always a very nice lady. He was much subdued. Age obviously had mellowed him. Having attended the Harvard Graduate School of Business and having been imbued with their management principles, with emphasis on human relations, I thought about Mr. Niedermeyer, wondering how a man like him, with his brutal management methods, could possibly have functioned in a modern American corporation. But he did quite well in Bolivia. As we shall see, however, he did eventually overplay his hand, with almost fatal results.

About once every three months, don Mauricio Hochschild, who owned the mine, came to visit. That was the only time that I saw Mr. Niedermeyer being attentive, courteous and deferential. I never had occasion to be introduced to or to talk to don Mauricio. He was an almost God-like figure – ordinary mortals did not talk to him.

Mr. Niedermeyer, who was born in Bloomington, Illinois and who had his education at the School of Mines in Rolla., Missouri, probably had never met a Jew in his life before he was hired by don Mauricio. I often wondered whether the relatively large number of European Jews in the mine was at the direction of don Mauricio or whether we were hired because we were competent and because competent Bolivians with college education did not necessarily want to work in the mines. It was hard work and they knew that they were going to be subjected to the humiliating racism of the Americans.

At that time there was much political upheaval in Bolivia. The government was similar to that of Juan Perón a few years later in Argentina, headed by a colonel and by a military clique. The miners formed a union and became quite aggressive. Incredible though it may seem, all the "bosses," including myself, had armed ourselves while working in the mine. I always carried a holstered pistol. In retrospect, it seems unbelievable. Serious unrest was about to explode, and we all knew it. In our case, the spark that produced the general strike was that Niedermeyer, in his usual way of management by physical contact, had slapped one of the miners. It was about the dumbest thing that he could have done, but there it was. All the miners and the mill workers walked out. All the bosses, again including myself, were locked up in a small hall in the administration building. They caught Niedermeyer and beat him quite badly. It's a miracle that they didn't kill him.

While we were locked in that hall, a delegate of the miners' union walked in. He told us that he knew we were all armed and instructed us to hand over our weapons. He collected a gun from each of us and then he left. We were left sitting there for another couple of hours with nothing to eat or drink and not knowing what was going to happen to us. It was quite possible that all of us would be killed, either by being shot by the miners or by being blown up by dynamite. It was very gloomy.

Eventually, Ray Wood, the mine superintendent, produced a gun. "Where did you get that gun, Ray?" we asked him. "They collected all the guns."

He growled, "Do those greasers really believe a Texan would carry only one fucking gun!" In addition to his regular visible holster he also had an extra gun strapped to his leg. What a guy! We told him to put the gun away. We weren't going to be able to use it.

After being in that hall for the better part of the day, a government delegate, who had arrived from La Paz, came into the hall and told us that the miners were willing to settle the strike and go back to work if their demands were fulfilled. I don't remember what they were – I suppose an increase in wages of twenty per cent or something like that, certain holidays off with pay, etc. The big surprise was that they did not demand that Niedermeyer should leave the mine. They thought he was needed. They had beaten him up. That was good enough.

In any case, we all went back to work, and not too much damage had been done. I learned that it had been much worse in some of the other large mines.

Immediately following the strike, but in no way because of it, Mr. Niedermeyer approached me and asked me if I wanted to become a shift boss in the mine. The mine worked around the clock on three shifts. Each shift boss was in charge of two levels of the mine for an eight-hour period. I eagerly accepted, because being a mine shift boss was one level above being an engineer. Also, there was a $50 per month raise. Finally, I liked the staggered hours. I would be on the day shift one week, on the afternoon shift the next week, and on the night shift the week following. I thought it would add variety, and indeed it did. I eagerly accepted.

One of the most colorful people I met in Bolivia was a Welshman by the name of James Llewellyn. Llewellyn was born in 1855 in a small town in Wales. By the time I met him, he was almost ninety years old. He had a most amazing story.

Paraguay, a landlocked country southeast of Bolivia, had been embroiled in bloody wars almost since its liberation from Spain. The bloodiest and most disastrous of those was the War of the Triple Alliance, which Paraguay had provoked, and in which it fought against Brazil, Uruguay, and Argentina. The war, under the Paraguayan dictator Francisco Solano Lopez, lasted from 1864 to 1870. By the time it was over, virtually all males, except for very young boys and very old men, had been killed. It was a disaster on many levels. One of those was that the women of Paraguay had no men. It was clear that there would hardly be any more children – that the people of Paraguay would die out if something drastic was not done – and done quickly.

President Lopez had the idea of importing men for stud purposes to Paraguay. Being impelled by some racist notions and the desire to "upgrade" the racial stock of Paraguay, which was mostly Guarani Indians, he sent emissaries to various nations that he believed to hold the most desirable racial stock, namely Wales, Sweden, and northern Germany. Young men, not more than twenty-five years old, and who had passed the eugenic criteria of general Lopez's emissaries, were hired, with the enticement of an enlistment bonus, an attractive monthly salary, unlimited sex, and a bonus for every child they would sire.

The prospect of unlimited sex with Paraguayan maidens and, on top of that, getting paid for it was more than alluring to those young men. It was irresistible. The emissaries brought carefully selected and revealing pictures of prospective "partners." Those women looked much more attractive than the peasant girls with whom these young men were acquainted. There was no problem at all in enlisting the 1,000 men that General Lopez had requested. All of them went to Paraguay on one vessel and then were distributed throughout the country, where they were to assume their interesting duties.

Mr. Llewellyn was one of those who was selected and who signed up.

It sounded like a dream job. It seemed that all you had to do was to get fed well, have all the sex you could handle, and collect your salary and those performance bonuses. Mr. Llewellyn told us that the first five months were just marvelous. All these desirable girls and all that sex. But then it got difficult to keep those ravenous women away. He was assigned a horse-drawn trailer and stayed in a certain village until all eligible women had been properly serviced. Then he would have to go on to the next location. The enlisted men were expected to service a minimum of three women a day. The women to be serviced were selected by the old crones in each village, at that time during their menstrual cycle they believed to be the period of their greatest fertility. It worked pretty well. Llewellyn told us that he was certified for 6,500 offspring during his twenty years of this arduous work, and had received "performance" bonuses for them. After twenty years, he was then a little over forty years old, he asked for a vacation to go to Bolivia. He did not return, and he lived on his memories. What memories!

I should tell about my suite mate. I have described how each two rooms at the *Rancho Extranjeros* shared a bathroom. Together, the two rooms and the bathroom were considered a suite. My mate was Sergio Marinkovic. He was a Yugoslav and had been living in Bolivia since childhood. The story he told me was that his mother, who was a widow of a mining engineer who had worked in Chile, had returned pregnant to Yugoslavia, where he was born. She could not support him and therefore, when he was only ten years old, she sent him to live with an uncle in Bolivia. The uncle put him to work in the mines at a very early age. Sergio did not have much education but he was very experienced in mining. He also was a shift boss in the mine. He and I occupied a somewhat special position, because even though we both were Europeans and though Spanish was not the mother language of either of us, we both were perfect Spanish speakers and the only ones who used Spanish as our everyday language. We were fast friends. Once a month, on our days off, we would go to Oruro together and have a great time.

One evening around 10 o'clock, when most people who were not working had already gone to bed, we heard what sounded like pistol shots outside our suite. Both Sergio and I rushed outside and found a very drunk Bolivian army officer, I think he was a colonel. He was shooting his pistol in the air and he made several holes in the ceiling. Mrs. Ruud, who with her husband occupied a second floor suite,

My secretary, Malquiades Delgado, had a sideline as an artist.
He made this caricature of me, symbolizing, I suppose: hard
worker, party boy and heavy smoker.

I had advanced to shift boss in the Colquiri mine, an important job. The man next to me is Frank Bemis, one of the two mine foremen. He was my immediate boss.

rushed out of her room in a flimsy negligée. "Who's that ugly *gringa*," the Bolivian shouted and fired a couple more shots in the ceiling. Then he left.

Mrs. Ruud was totally shaken by the incident and told Niedermeyer the next day that she no longer wished to be the manager of the *Rancho*. Apparently it was not the pistol shots that did it to her – that she had witnessed before, but this man's referring to her as an "ugly *gringa*." She was very insulted.

By that time, in his rough and gruff manner, Niedermeyer had apparently taken a liking to me – I don't really know why, I didn't have too much contact with him. He called me to his office. "Gerardo," he said, "would you like to take over the management of the *Rancho*? Mrs. Ruud has had it, and I don't think I can put another woman in there.

Knowing Niedermeyer's mercurial temperament, I asked firmly but timidly, "Would I be compensated for this additional work?"

"You'll get an extra $50 and your room and your board free."

Wow! That was an $125 extra a month. It certainly was worth my while. I eagerly accepted.

I found that the role of manager of the Rancho was very easy. Once a week the cook presented me the menu for the following week, which I had to sign off on. There was not a single time that I took exception to what he proposed. We ate very well. The other duty was the supervision of the four girls who cleaned the rooms. That also was not too difficult. In fact, I became very friendly with Honorina, who was the lead girl of the crew. She was a very nice and accommodating person.

My English improved steadily because that was the language we spoke at work. Just as with Mr. Niedermeyer, when I had that memorable first interview with him, virtually ever sentence was punctuated with the "f" word. It just rolled off the tongue. We got American magazines, including *Time* and *The Reader's Digest*. I read every word of those two magazines, further improving my English.

I saw to it that we got a movie projector and once a week, every Friday evening, I showed a movie that I had ordered from Oruro. After every reel there was a five-minute intermission until the new reel was loaded. It was a welcome pause to get another drink. One movie that I ordered and that was a great success was Alfred Hitchcock's Saboteur, with Robert Cummings. In the last reel, the villain trying to escape, was hanging by one of the eyebrow on the Statue of Liberty. The hero, Robert Cummings, who is on the deck above him, tries to save him from certain death by holding on to his sleeve, trying to pull him up. In true Hitchcockian fashion, the camera focuses on the seam between the shoulder and the sleeve of the villain's coat. That seam slowly opens up and eventually separates. Cummings is left with the empty sleeve while the villain, giving a gruesome shriek, falls to his well-deserved doom. We saw that last reel four times. It was a great success.

Another source of entertainment was a bowling alley that I had installed in the basement of the Rancho building. Fortunately, it was long enough to accommodate it. I never got very good at it. My best score, more from luck than from skill, I'm sure, was 183.

In order to entertain the residents, I once brought in a group of Chilean performers. It was a father, a mother, and a very nubile daughter. They sang, played the piano, and the daughter performed some dances. It was certainly not a Broadway-type production. They gave two performances at the *Rancho*. One of my colleagues and friends was John McArdle. He was an Argentine, son of an American father and an Argentine mother. He also was a shift boss in the mine. He totally fell in love with the daughter, whose name was Elvira. "I want to marry Elvira," he said.

"You're crazy," we told him. "You've been without a woman too long. You surely don't want to marry Elvira whom you've only known for 48 hours. Why don't you go to Oruro and get laid, and get that nonsense out of your head."

"No," he said, "I'm in love and I know that Elvira loves me too."

Elvira and her parents left for other mines, where they had other shows scheduled. McArdle followed them. When he came back he told us that he and Elvira were engaged and that they had exchanged rings. He told us that he had bought a very nice ring with a small diamond at an Oruro jewelry store and that she had given him a simple gold band. The plan was for Elvira and her parents to come back within a month, supposedly after they had completed their *tournee* in Bolivia, and that they would get married at that time.

One day, McArdle said, "I don't know if Elvira really loves me, and I don't know whether the ring she gave me is gold or brass. If it's gold, she loves me. If it's brass, she is just playing with me. How can I find out?"

German Campusano, a Chilean, was the mine chemist. He was in charge of a group of about twenty people, because hundreds of assays had to be run every day. It was a fairly big operation. Campusano said, "McArdle, if you have any doubt about whether your ring is gold or not, it's easy for us to find out. Would you like for me to do it?"

"Please. Do that for me."

So all of us went down to the chemical lab. McArdle gave Campusano the ring. Campusano put it in a beaker and poured evil smelling fluids from two bottles into it. He put the beaker over a Bunsen burner, apparently to speed up whatever reaction he had in mind and took a glass stirrer to mix things up more quickly. In front of our eyes, the ring slowly disintegrated and then disappeared. "Congratulations," Campusano said, "she really does love you. This ring is pure gold."

"Oh, thank God," McArdle said, now give me the ring back."

"No, I can't give you the ring back," Campusano said, "I tested it and it dissolved in the *aqua regia*, which is a mixture of nitric and hydrochloric acid. It will dissolve gold and gold only, so now you can be sure that Elvira really loves you."

"Yes, but where the hell is my ring?" McArdle said. "I want it back."

"Don't worry," Campusano said, "Well get it back for you." He put another liquid, a base obviously, into the beaker so as to neutralize the acid. He let it stand a little while and perhaps did something else to it. In any case, in the end he poured the liquid into another beaker through a filter paper, and lo and behold there was gold dust on that filter paper.

"What do I do with the gold dust?" McArdle cried in despair.

"Keep it as a souvenir," Campusano said, "to remind you never to distrust your true love again."

As I later learned, Campusano was really playing a pretty dirty trick on poor McArdle. Aqua regia does not just dissolve gold – it dissolves all metals. So the purported "test" was really no test at all. It was just a prank he played on McArdle. Anything to get a little amusement in those tough surroundings.

Not to distrust his true love again might have been good advice, but McArdle now had a big problem, because Elvira was going to come for the wedding the following week. There was no way that he could now buy another gold ring. But we solved the problem. He went to the *pulpería*, which, this being a very large mine, was of course much better stocked than *pulperías* in other mines, and bought a brass wedding ring of the kind that the Indians wear. The wedding was next week. It was a pretty nice affair. He was never found out about the ring. I don't know whether McArdle ever replaced the ring with a gold one.

My boss, Stan, had big trouble with his wife. Even though there were two children, she had taken up with Tom Marvin, an American and the chief geologist of the mine. Marvin was an unusual character, certainly the most unusual of all the Americans who were working there, who, almost without exception were rough and tough mining types. Every night he would retire to his room, which was also in the *Rancho* and did what we would now call transcendental meditation, which was quite unknown in those days. Tom would also put on an Oriental garment and practice Chinese calligraphy. Most of the American macho guys who worked in that mine thought he was a homosexual, but he certainly was not. He had quite an intense relationship with Stan's wife. Eventually it blew up and Stan asked for a transfer to another of don Mauricio's mines, I believe in either Chile or Peru, so the job of chief engineer became suddenly vacant. There was really nobody else to take this job except me. Sure enough, Mr. Niedermeyer offered it to me in his brusque tone, but I could tell that he needed for me to accept, whether or not I wanted the job. "Yes, I think I'll do it, Mr. Niedermeyer, but how much of a raise will you give me?

"I told you once, don't ever try to extort me. I'll give you $50 more a month. Now shut up and get back to work."

"O.K., O.K.," I said, "I accept."

So there I was twenty-three years old and I was the chief engineer of what I think was the second-largest tin mine in the world. It was unusual to get such a job at my age and with really my lack of education and experience, but I took a realistic view of it. We were in the middle of a war and those were the days when twenty-two-year old boys were full colonels in the U.S. Air Force, flew B25's and were in command of a crew of perhaps eight or ten men.

We worked every day in the mine, Monday through Saturday, around the clock, but only had a skeleton shift on Sundays. The purpose of that shift was only to pull ore from the pass in the lowest level, which was San Juanillo. The electric train went out from San Juanillo directly to the mill. The single shift that worked on Sunday was the day shift. One of the shift bosses had that duty and it ran by rotation. That Sunday, I had the duty. There was not really very much to do. Essentially I would sit in my office, read the paper and went out every once in a while to see that things were going well. There was very little that could go wrong.

But suddenly something did go very wrong. A miner came running into my office and said *"Señor, señor,* one of the miners got hung up in the ore pass."

"What do you mean," I asked him, "he got 'hung up'?"

The man told me that the ore was not flowing, so someone decided to go up into the shaft with a steel rod trying to dislodge it. The man did dislodge it all right but he got caught and stuck in the shaft, surrounded by hundreds of tons of rock. He couldn't get out.

I couldn't believe my ears. The man must have been a complete idiot. How would anybody do something as stupid as that? That was the time he should have called for the boss, namely me. What I would have done would have been to put a very small explosive charge down that shaft from the level above to jar things loose. Only a fool would go up that shaft and try to pry the rock lose. I didn't know whether the man was already dead, crushed by hundreds of tons of rocks or whether he was "just" stuck.

All eyes were on me. I was the boss. I had to "do something."

I didn't feel good about this at all because I thought the miner (I never learned his name) either would be dead, or if he wasn't, he would immediately die if anything were dislodged. I also thought that if I went up there, I would die with him. But I had the responsibility. I walked up to the bottom of that shaft and I remembered the day in the Larramkota mine when I had been asked to fix that transformer. On that occasion, I decided that my better judgment was not to try to do that and to walk away from the job. Here I was confronted with a similar life-and-death decision. But this was different. In Larramkota I hadn't been the boss. Here I was the boss, at least for the time being, responsible and the ultimate authority. Everyone looked at me and everyone relied on me to resolve the situation. I asked for a ladder and carefully edged my way up the shaft. The trapped miner was about 15 feet up. He was alive, though he seemed to be badly shaken and I believed that several bones might have been broken. He was pinned at the shoulders by one large rock. If that rock were dislodged the whole thing would come tumbling down and would kill him and me – no question about it.

He screamed: *"Señor, ayúdeme, ayúdeme – no quiero morir!"* – help me, help me – I don't want to die! And then he cried.

I climbed all the way up to him and first of all tried to give him courage because he was obviously very, very scared, and then I said, "Listen, we are going to very carefully try to get you loose. Please don't make any hasty movement because if you do it will kill both of us. Let's just try our best, and why don't you say a little prayer for both of us."

With his free hand, the man crossed himself and said a prayer, half in Spanish and half in Aymara. Then I said, "Careful, very, very careful, lets try to get you loose." So I reached up behind his shoulder and very, very gingerly, very, very carefully pried him loose, making an enormous effort not to dislodge the big rock behind which he was wedged. It was probably the most scary moment of my life, and I am quite sure that he was equally scared. I got him loose and nothing moved except a few small rocks but the big one stayed in place.

When we got to the bottom, the man lay down and cried. He knew that he had been saved from what seemed to be certain death. We put him on top of the locomotive, and I uncoupled all the wagons and drove him out to the mill, the end of the line. We then got a stretcher and walked the miner to the hospital, a couple of hundred yards away. Dr. Córdoba, the physician in charge, told me that the man had broken his shoulder blade and probably a couple of ribs, but he was otherwise not seriously hurt. It was a miracle.

A report was made to Mr. Niedermeyer and to Ray Wood, the mine superintendent. Both invited me to their offices and told me that I had done a brave and wonderful thing. They even said they were very proud of me. Well, I was pretty proud of myself too, but I also thought that I might have been a little foolish. I put my life on the line for someone I didn't even know, but I thought that, just as in war, the officer is responsible for his men. I was responsible for that miner. The disappointing thing was that I never heard from the man. Neither he nor his wife called me or thanked me. Oh, well, virtue perhaps is its own reward.

One of the very few Bolivian engineers working in the mine was a single man by the name of Osvaldo Antequera. He was not a particularly nice guy. He seemed to always have a chip on his shoulder. I could see why. He was considered a second-class person by the Americans. One day, Antequera didn't come to work. We were all surprised because he had always been punctual and had never missed a day's work. But we didn't give it too much thought. But when Antequera did not appear for the second, third or fourth day we became a little concerned. They sent someone to his room at the *Rancho Bolivianos* and didn't find any evidence of his having left. All his possessions were there. It was somewhat of a mystery.

At the end of the week, I was the shift boss on the 100 level, the level 100 feet below *Incalacaya*, the main entry level into the mine. Some of my workers were pulling rock from the chute of the waste pass coming from the upper level. When we opened the chute, a human arm appeared. We opened the chute further and a whole human body emerged. It was that of Osvaldo Antequera. His skull had been smashed. We couldn't tell if the skull had been smashed intentionally or in his passage through the pass but there was no question that somebody had murdered him, because safety installations were such that nobody could accidentally fall down that shaft. It was a mystery and it was never cleared up. It could either have been a political matter or more likely a jealous husband who had taken his revenge.

Antequera had the reputation of being somewhat of a playboy. We left the body until the next day and then took it out of the mine. We didn't know any family to notify. He was buried at the local cemetery. No inquest was held.

During my sojourn in Bolivia, I had inevitably much contact with the Catholic Church because, after all, Catholicism was and is the state religion of Bolivia. I really never quite understood how the missionaries that came with the conquistadors were able to lure the Indians from their comfortable beliefs and into the Church, but they did. One of the secrets, I believe, was that the Church was able to adapt or combine the native Indian beliefs with the Catholic religion. Catholicism as it was practiced in Bolivia, certainly in the rural areas, always maintained many Indian customs and rituals.

Perhaps, as a consequence of that, priests did not take celibacy very seriously. The priest in Quime was a jovial Dutchman, Father Jann. He welcomed European company and I became his good friend. He had a "housekeeper" of many years who, even though she was half Indian and had never been married, had three beautiful tow-headed children.

One of the most important relationships in South American Indian society is that of *padrino* and *compadre*. If you are asked to be the *padrino*, the godfather, of a child, it is an honor and obligation that is bestowed on you. Your obligations are immediate and in the future. The immediate obligation is to provide a layette for the baby and to be present at its christening. The long-term obligation, or at least supposed obligation, is to be responsible for the child's spiritual education and, in case of the parents' death, to take the child on as though it were your own.

The parents of the child become your *compadre* and *comadre*, respectively. They have great moral obligation toward you and are supposed to do almost anything for you, for the honor you have done them in your having baptized their child. Also, it is a mortal sin for someone to have sexual relations with one's *compadre* or *comadre*. It is considered to be just as bad as incest. Therefore, I often felt that people preemptively selected somebody as *padrino* for their child who they believed could possibly have intention on his or her spouse.

I was quite startled when I was asked for the very first time to be the *padrino* of the child of one of my miners. I tried to explain patiently that I couldn't do that since I was not of the Catholic faith. They couldn't really understand that because they had never known anybody who was not Catholic. "Let me think about it and let me talk to Father Jann," I said.

Father Jann laughed and told me to go ahead and be the *padrino*. All they really want is that layette for the baptism; they can't afford to buy that for themselves. And, if you accept, you'll have a much better worker and a devoted friend for life.

"But, Father Jann, what about my obligation to be the spiritual guide to the child? I can't do that."

"Don't worry about that. I'll take care of the spiritual guidance."

By the time I left Bolivia I must have been the godfather to not fewer than eight or ten children. I couldn't count them. I wasn't flippant about it and I never felt quite right about my ambiguous role. But my *compadres* didn't seem to mind at all.

Here I was, still very young. Having made the decision to go to work in this important mine, had totally changed my living standard, career, and possibly my future. I was pleased with myself and so, apparently, was Mr. Niedermeyer, even though he was not forthcoming with much praise.

One day I proposed to him to make certain changes in the sampling routine at the work faces. I had given it much thought and had prepared a paper for his approval. He looked at it and said utterly dismissively: "Gerardo, you are full of shit like a fucking Christmas goose." I wasn't insulted. Though I thought he was wrong, I accepted his judgment. He was the boss. But I was totally fascinated by the analogy. "...full of shit like a Christmas goose." It was absolutely brilliant, I thought. How did the man come up with stuff like that? Those clever Americans!

One of my duties as manager of the *Rancho* was to organize occasional parties. There were about six such dates for those parties. The most important ones were of course, the Fourth of July and the Sixth of August, which was the Bolivian national holiday. Then there were Thanksgiving, Christmas, and one or two others. But, the Fourth of July and the Sixth of August were by far the most important.

No Bolivians were ever invited to those parties, not even to the Sixth of August, the Bolivian national holiday. I was, of course, aware of that, but I didn't think of it as a "rule," but rather as a custom.

The first party I gave was a Fourth of July party. It was a great success. It was the first opportunity to wear my tuxedo, which my mother had so lovingly packed for me many years earlier. The next party, of course, was the Sixth of August, for which I had even engaged an oompah band – that was the best I could come up with, and it was very well received. But I did one thing – not as an act of defiance, but because I thought it was the natural thing to do: I invited Ernesto Bustamante, who was the only Bolivian who, I would say as a token, had recently been advanced to shift boss in the mine. He was a very nice man, very competent, quite personable; his wife, a light-skinned woman, was exceptionally good looking. There were about 120 people at the party. Everyone was milling around, there was good food, much drinking, and everyone was having a good time. Suddenly Mr. Niedermeyer noticed Bustamante. He beckoned me to come over to him. "Why the fuck did you invite this greaser to the party? We don't socialize with Bolivians."

"Mr. Niedermeyer," I said, "I thought it would be the proper thing to do. After all, it's their national holiday, and he is a higher-level employee and very presentable."

"Don't give me that shit," Niedermeyer said in his usual refined way. "Get the son-of-a-bitch out of here. And you are just another guy with a hooked nose."

There it was: I was just another guy with a hooked nose. I knew what that was – a code word for a Jew. I wasn't really too surprised, but deep down Niedermeyer was just a rube from the heartland. I don't think that, besides Don

Mauricio, he had ever seen a Jew before. It was the only anti-Semitic remark he ever made, but I thought once was enough. I had his number.

I was so annoyed that I toyed with the idea of writing a letter to Mauricio Hochschild, but I decided against it. Don Mauricio would not have fired him, mostly because he needed him, and also because he had a contract. The contract, I was sure, did not specify that he could be fired for an anti-Semitic remark. I was the one who would be fired. So that was that.

The highest level of social accomplishment in the Colquiri mine was to be invited by Mr. Niedermeyer to participate in the poker games that he hosted every Friday night at his house. Only the top ten or twelve employees would be eligible for this honor, only eight or ten of them wanted to play poker. They were all Americans.

One day, I passed Mr. Niedermeyer in the hall and he growled at me, "You want to play poker?"

I hesitated for a few seconds because I didn't know how to play poker; I had never done it. I knew the principles of it and I didn't think of it as a difficult game like chess or bridge, but I did realize that here was a tremendous social opportunity and that if I declined I would never be asked again. "Of course, Mr. Niedermeyer, I would like to play poker. Would you like for me to join you at your game?"

"Yes," he growled. "Be there Friday night at 7:30 and don't be late. Put on a clean shirt."

"Yeah, thanks," I thought. I was planning to wear a dirty shirt, but I didn't say anything, of course.

That was on a Tuesday. On Wednesday I went to my friend Dave Davidson's room in the *Rancho* and told him about this "honor" that had been bestowed on me. He had been asked before to participate, but he had declined.

"Dave, I have this great "honor," but I don't know the first things about playing poker. Can you give me a few pointers?"

"Sure, sit down." He took a deck of cards and explained the rudiments to me. The value of the different hands, the difference between straight poker and stud poker, various wild games and never to draw to an inside straight, etc. He gave me about three one-hour lessons. When I arrived at Mr. Niedermeyer's house on Friday evening at 7:30 sharp (and with a clean shirt), his wife Mildred received me very cordially and passed hors d'oeuvres around. Hard liquor was consumed right away. We were seven of us and we sat down to play about thirty minutes later. At 10 o'clock, the game would end punctually, at which time a so-called consolation round was played, which would enable the losers to recoup some of their losses.

The first hands were pretty "normal," straight poker and stud, but as the evening progressed, the games (always dealer's choice) became wilder. Deuces wild, one-eyed jacks wild, split-beard kings wild, high-low, spit in the ocean – it was all left up to the dealer's imagination. There was steady drinking, of which, in order to be "one of the boys," I had to do my share. The initial evening cost me $23. That was a lot of money for me.

Next week, pretty much the same thing happened. And, again I lost over $20. This was a "great honor," but I didn't think I could afford to lose $100 a month playing poker with Mr. Niedermeyer and the other guys. So, again, I talked to Dave.

Dave said, "Listen, the main thing is to drink very little. You cannot say that you won't drink, because they won't have you any more, but you can pretend to be drinking a lot and you can drink very little. Also, since you serve yourself, you can pretend to be drinking gin and can actually be drinking water." Then he told me, "Watch for 'tells.' Study each player and you will find that he has certain mannerisms that become apparent. Particularly if he had something to drink, you will be able to see the 'tell' that indicates whether he has a good hand, a bad hand or whether he is bluffing." He took a book off his shelf. "Take this book. Read it carefully. Act accordingly and you will win."

It was a hardcover little blue book by Oswald Jacoby, who, I later learned, was a world-class bridge player. The name of the book was *Poker, How to Play a Winning Hand*. That was what I needed. I studied that book as though it was the Bible and the Talmud all rolled into one. By the time I joined "the boys" next Friday, I was prepared. I won $17. The next week I won $32. The biggest hand I ever won was a *mano a mano* against Frank Bemis, where I won a $42 pot. Frank had a "tell." He blinked very quickly with his eyes when he was bluffing. I had three 9's, he had two pairs. I kept track of my poker winnings. By the time I ultimately left the mine a year later, I had won just over $2,000. I couldn't have done what I was doing next had it not been for the poker winnings.

On the twelfth of April, 1945, President Franklin D. Roosevelt died. I was not aware of it until Niedermeyer stepped into my office. "Guess what," he said.

"What?" I asked.

"The son-of-a-bitch is dead."

I wondered which son-of-a-bitch he was talking about, Adolf Hitler, Mussolini, Emperor Hirohito. "Which son-of-a-bitch?" I asked.

"Roosevelt," he said and gave a big smile.

I was flabbergasted. Although my admiration for the man was perhaps not entirely deserved, Roosevelt was my hero. As far as I knew, or certainly as I hoped, he would be the man who would ultimately destroy the hated Nazis. That an American, regardless of his political persuasion, could refer to his president as a "son-of-a-bitch" and rejoice about his dying was totally incomprehensible to me.

"Who's going to be the president now, Mr. Niedermeyer?" I asked.

"A guy by the name of Truman. He's from Missouri, so he can't be all bad."

Well, poor Niedermeyer, he didn't know that Truman was going to out-Roosevelt Roosevelt by the time he got through.

I had the most ambivalent feelings about Niedermeyer. On the one hand, I really admired his management of the mine, but I was appalled by his methods, which as we have seen, involved much physical contact. But I also thought of his moral deficiencies, of which the remark about Roosevelt was one, and his remarks about that "greaser" Bustamante and my crooked nose were others. Those things really put me off.

One day he came into my office and sat down. He said, "Gerardo, I've been thinking about you. (He's been thinking about me? I thought, how strange!) You have this big job in this big mine and you are doing a pretty good job, but I can assure you that once the war is over and trained American engineers are available, you will not be able to hold this job. If you're lucky, you will be back in the in the mine working as a shift boss. It will be a big step down."

"Yes," I said, "I've been thinking about that myself. What do you think I should do?"

"I know exactly what you should do," he said. "You should quit and go to the United States and get a degree in mining engineering. You might be able to do it in three years because you told me that you already had some engineering training in Germany."

"Where would I go, Mr. Niedermeyer?" I said.

"I know where you'll go. You'll go to where I went. You'll go to the Missouri School of Mines in Rolla, Missouri, and, if you're interested, I'll see that you get in."

"That's very nice of you, Mr. Niedermeyer. Please let me think about it. I will be back to you."

It was clear to me that Niedermeyer was one of the "trophy alumni" of the Missouri School of Mines. He had a very big job and probably had been a big man on campus. So, I thought it might not be a bad idea. I had trouble, though, thinking about giving up a good job and the cozy life at the *Rancho*.

About a month later, Sergio and I took a brief one-week vacation and we went to Cochabamba. Cochabamba is the third largest city in Bolivia. It is much lower than La Paz or Oruro, perhaps 11,000 or 12,000 feet high, in a lush sub-tropical setting. I had been there briefly once before. So we went and stayed in a very nice hotel, fittingly named Hotel Cochabamba. It had nice public rooms, a beautifully appointed dining room, and all the guest rooms opened around a beautiful patio, with lush vegetation and a fountain in the center. It was clear that most of the guests were tourists from Europe and the United States.

The first evening, Sergio and I were sitting at a small dinner table, when my eye caught, halfway across the room, the eye of a beautiful, clearly American, girl. She looked to be about eighteen years old and she was there with what seemed to be her parents. We kind of looked at each other and I got the impression that she liked me too. She was, to put it crassly, the first "eligible white woman" that I had seen since I had arrived in Bolivia seven years earlier. We met after dinner, walked on the patio, held hands and told each other who we were, what we were, and what we were doing. My English at that time was already quite serviceable. She told me that her name was Norma Jean, that she was from Carbondale, Illinois, that her father was a civil engineer who had been working in Bolivia on a large construction job for the last year, and that she and her mother had accompanied him. She had missed a year of schooling and was preparing to go back to the United States to finish her senior year in high school. I though she was the most beautiful thing I had ever seen, but she probably was just another pretty girl and nothing special. But she was "very special" in the setting and under the circumstances.

As the days went by, we spent every waking moment together. One day we went to the movies and saw Orson Wells in "Citizen Kane." It had been very favorably reviewed. But I didn't get too much of the movie because there was a great deal of kissing and hugging in the intimacy of the theater. I was in love!

That evening, after Norma Jean retired to the room she shared with her parents, I told the concierge to get me two dozen roses, which he produced very quickly. Flowers in Cochabamba were easy to get. Then I gave (the equivalent of) $30 to the leader of the three-man dining-room band, and asked them to come out to the patio and play romantic songs in front of Norma Jean's room. My special request was "You Are Always In My Heart..." which Norma Jean and I had decided was "our song." Well, it was an enormous success. When the band started playing, Norma Jean came out and cried with emotion. The full moon shone through the flimsy fabric of her nightgown, which added to the excitement of this romantic moment. When the two dozen roses were delivered, she almost went to pieces. I think we could have consummated our love right then and there had it not been for her parents.

She left the next day, and I immediately decided to take Niedermeyer up on his suggestion to go to the United States and to get a degree in mining engineering. I looked at an atlas, saw that Missouri was a state adjoining Illinois, that it would probably just be a hop and a jump from Rolla to Carbondale and that I could possibly see Norma Jean every weekend. It was a great prospect.

Sergio thought that I was a little crazy, because he realized that studying mining engineering was a pretext and what I really wanted to do was to go after Norma Jean. Then he said, "If you are really determined to go to the United States, I don't want to stay here in this mine all by myself. I'll go with you."

"What are you going to do in the United States, Sergio?" I asked.

"What am I going to do? I'm going to do the same thing that you will be doing. I'm going to the University of Missouri in Rolla and get a degree in mining engineering."

Well, I thought that was a great idea because we were really such good friends. I knew that I was going to be more comfortable going to this new and different country with him coming along.

There was an immediate problem, however: While my English had become really fairly good in the years in Colquiri, building on what I had learned in the *Hohenzollern Gymanisum*, his English was virtually non-existent. All the English he knew was what he had learned in the mine and that was not very much and peppered heavily with the "f" word.

So we talked with Niedermeyer and told him that I was going to take him up on his suggestion and to see what he could do to facilitate my acceptance at the Missouri School of Mines. He was a little surprised that Sergio was also planning to go, but he didn't try to dissuade him. He wrote to the school and we both were accepted. It was as simple as that. He just had great pull.

The next step was the formality to get entry to the United States. That involved a U.S. visa – a student visa in the case of Sergio and myself. We couldn't both leave at the same time so I went first. I went to the U.S. Consulate in La Paz and told my story to a very pleasant vice consul, who caught my attention mostly for being about 6'4" tall and as thin as a reed. I told him what I wanted. He said, "Sure. That would not be a big problem. But, tell me, why do you want a student visa? Why don't you take an immigration visa?"

"I have no particular desire to stay permanently in the United States," I told him. "I want to get an engineering degree at the Missouri School of Mines and then come back to Bolivia and work in the mines."

"Mr. Joffe," he said, "believe me, once you are in Missouri you won't want to come back to Bolivia. And there's another thing: If you have a student visa, you can't work. You might want to work in order to get some additional money to stay in school. If you are an immigrant, you can do what you want."

"Isn't it very difficult to get an immigration visa to the United States?" I asked him. I remembered those long, long lines at the U.S. Consulate in Berlin.

"Oh not at all," he said. "You were born in Berlin weren't you? Being born in Berlin puts you in the German quota. We are at war with Germany; therefore, the German quota hasn't been filled for years. If you want an immigration visa you can get it almost immediately."

It sounded crazy, but "O.K.," I said, "I'll take it."

"Very good," he said, "let me see your birth certificate."

"My what?"

"Your birth certificate," he said. "You cannot enter the United States, either as a student or as an immigrant if you don't have a birth certificate."

"Sir," I said, "I don't have a birth certificate and since there's a war going on, there's no way in the world for me to get one."

"I'm awfully sorry. If you don't have a birth certificate, there's nothing really I can do. Why don't you try to find it and then come back."

I was desperate. Once again my carefully made plans were foiled. I had no birth certificate.

But then, of course, there was my mother. Hadn't she always come through? Didn't she find that book about traffic in mines. Perhaps she could do some magic and find my birth certificate. I sent a telegram right from La Paz. I said (in German):

> "MOTHER,   DESPERATELY   NEED   MY   BIRTH
> CERTIFICATE. PLEASE SEND IT IMMEDIATELY.
> LOVE, GERHARD."

Well, my mother came through once again. Immediately upon receipt of my telegram she sent me the birth certificate by registered airmail. Of the few things that she could salvage from Germany, my birth certificate was one thing she had taken. What a wonderful woman!

I returned to Colquiri and told Sergio what had happened. He would have no problem either with his Yugoslav passport. I specifically had asked the vice consul about that. "O.K., Sergio, we need your birth certificate."

"I don't have one. How the hell am I going to get it from Yugoslavia now? They are not only at war, they are in total collapse."

I had a hunch. "Sergio," I said, "let me see your passport."

"What do you want to see my passport for?" he asked.

"Just let me look at it," I said.

So he gave me his passport, which was in Serbian and in French. I couldn't read the Serbian, of course, but I could understand the French. On the line for place of birth it said Čile. "What is Čile?" I asked him.

"Čile is a small town in Yugoslavia where I was born."

"Sergio, are you sure it's a small town in Yugoslavia. Čile looks like the country of Chile. Didn't you tell me your father worked in Chile?"

"Yeah, he did, but I wasn't born there. I was born in Yugoslavia."

"Where did your father and mother live in Chile? In what town?'

"What difference does it make?" Sergio said. "They lived in Valdivia."

"Sergio," I said, "You were not born in Yugoslavia. You were born in Valdivia, in the Republic of Chile."

"Nonsense," he said. "Čhle is a small town in Yugoslavia, I'm telling you. It's close to Split, on the Adriatic Coast."

"Please help me with this," I said. "We are going to get your birth certificate."

So in Sergio's name, I wrote a letter to the *alcalde*, the mayor, of Valdivia (in Spanish, of course), as follows:

Dear Mr. Mayor:

I was born in your city on July 12, 1919. My
father was an engineer at the time. I need my birth
certificate for a certain important personal reason,
but I've lost it.

I include one-half of a $20 U.S. bill in prepayment.
As soon as I receive the birth certificate, I shall
send you the other half.

Sincerely yours,
Sergio Marinkovic

I took a $20 bill out of my pocket – part of the winnings of a recent poker evening. I cut the bill in half and scotch-taped it to the letter. "You must be crazy," Sergio said, "that is the dumbest thing I've ever seen."

"Sergio, I don't know where in the hell you were born, but wherever it was you'll get a birth certificate from Valdivia, I promise you."

I was right. About ten days later a letter arrived with a copy of Sergio's birth certificate properly signed and with all official seals. We sent the other half of the $20 bill.

Sergio went to La Paz and immediately got his U.S. immigration visa.

In those days, people didn't do much flying, certainly not over very long distances, so we decided to go to the U.S. by ship. The easy way would have been to go to one of the Chilean ports and from there to the States. But, of course, I could not leave South America without visiting my parents, whom I had not seen for eight years. For that reason we had to go south to Buenos Aires to visit with my parents and then we could leave from there. Sergio had no problem with that.

On one of my trips to La Paz I had been in the dining room of the Sucre Palace Hotel, the toniest place in La Paz, located on *El Prado*, the *Champs Élysées* of Bolivia. I had heard that there was a casino on the top floor. Since I had never seen anything like that, I went up to check it out. There was a roulette table, a couple of blackjack tables, and some private card games, I suppose poker, from which the house took its cut. I gambled a few dollars at the roulette table, betting either on black or on red, not knowing really what else to do. I lost consistently, but not very big. I think it cost me ten or twenty dollars. I then watched the blackjack action, but since I didn't really know what to do, I was a little scared of it, and didn't participate. I then strolled over to the poker game, which seemed to be for fairly high stakes. The table was covered with a green felt cloth. Suddenly, one of the participants, a Chilean as it later turned out, pulled a large knife out of his pocket and nailed the hand of another of the participants to the table. There was a terrible scream, of course, and blood stained the green felt. The Chilean had caught the other fellow with a card up his sleeve and that was his way of handling the situation. The screaming victim was carried out after the Chilean had removed the knife. It was most impressive. The green cover had to be changed, but then the game continued. I had seen enough action for one evening and left.

But I was intrigued by the roulette table. By the way, in all countries, except the United States, there is only one zero at the roulette wheel. There is a zero and a double zero in roulette wheels in the United States, which somewhat reduces the players' chances. But Sergio and I were intrigued and talked a lot about roulette. Then we figured out a system by which we couldn't lose, but were bound to make a lot of money. What we didn't realize was that the system, that we thought was totally original, had been invented a thousand years ago and was one on which casinos grew rich.

I believe the system is called "madrigal," at least in Spanish. It goes like this: You bet one unit (say $1). If you win, you put it away. If you lose, you double your bet, namely you bet $2. If you win, you're a dollar ahead, if you lose, you have lost $3. In that case, you double your bet and bet $4. If you win, you're a dollar ahead, if you lose, you're down $7, but you double your bet to $8, and so forth. You simply can't lose. We thought it was a stroke of genius to have "invented" this sure-fire system.

We found out that there was a big casino in Mar del Plata, a city about 300 miles south of Buenos Aires. We decided to go to Buenos Aires first, visit my parents, then take a train to Mar del Plata, work our system, hopefully break the bank, and then, much enriched, take a ship from Mar del Plata to the United States.

We engaged a travel agency in La Paz, which arranged railroad passage to Buenos Aires, from there to Mar del Plata, and then by sea to the United States. The mining staff, headed by Mr. Niedermeyer and Ray Wood, the mine superintendent, threw Sergio and me a nice farewell party, at which liquor flowed very freely. We left Colquiri on July 15, 1943. Honorina cried a little. It had been a most important and informative chapter in both of our lives. We went to La Paz and took the two-day train ride to Buenos Aires.

The last stop in Bolivia, the town on the border with Argentina, was Villazón. The train stopped there for a little over an hour for passport and customs control. I wanted to get off the train in order to visit the local whorehouse – not for any "action," but in order to cast a nostalgic last look at our family piano, which had found such an unglorious end in that locale. But Sergio persuaded me against it. He thought that I might get "distracted" and might not make it back to the train on time.

We arrived in Buenos Aires about 5 o'clock in the afternoon. My parents waited for me at the Retiro Station. I was quite afraid of an emotional scene at the reunion and, indeed, that is what it was. My mother sobbed and embraced me. My father, somewhat more restrained also cried. It took quite some while for them to compose themselves. While I was happy to see them again, I was more detached. I realized that they were much more involved with me than I was with them. It seems to be the way it works. Now that I have grown children of my own, I am not surprised that they are mostly interested in their own lives and in their children, and that I and their mother play quite a subordinate role. Well, that seems to be the way it is.

In any case, I hadn't seen my parents for eight year and they knew that I was only going to stay a few days; therefore, emotion was perhaps to be expected.

My parents had not expected that I would come with a companion, and it was clear that they didn't quite know how to position him. They exchanged meaningful glances with each other and the unasked question was whether we were a homosexual couple. It would have been quite impossible for them to bear. My mother told me that she wanted me to stay in their apartment, but I demurred. I preferred to stay with Sergio in a hotel instead. On the way to the hotel I told my mother some reassuring stories about girls, without going into much detail – just enough to put her at ease about her concern. I did not mention either Alicia nor Zenobia nor Honorina.

The next day, Sergio and I took a tour bus and saw the highlights of downtown Buenos Aires. My mother had arranged a small reception in the evening for our Buenos Aires relatives. We went to their apartment on *Calle Luis Saenz Peña*. I was shocked. Our apartment in Berlin had not been particularly fancy but it was acceptably middle class. The apartment where my parents lived now was just one step above a hovel. There was only one room in which my parents lived and slept and in which my mother made her candy. There was an outside tiny kitchen and an outside toilet that was also used by all the other people on the floor. It was really awful. I could tell that my father was not in good mental health, but my mother was sturdy as a rock. I had the greatest admiration for her, how, under these difficult circumstances, and how, at the age of fifty-five years, she was able to rebuild her life, earn a living, manage to keep my father's spirits up without ever, ever complaining. She was a wonderful woman.

The visitors for the reception were my brother and his new wife, Lieschen, whom I had not met before, my mother's sister Sarah and her husband Max and their three married children, my mother's sister Martha and her husband Gustav and their son Klaus. There were soft drinks, some wine, and a platter with cold cuts and cheeses and bread. I looked at the platter with cold cuts and recoiled in horror. It was all pork. I couldn't believe it. "Mother," I said, "what are you serving here? We don't eat pork."

She looked at me as though I was bereft of my senses. She said, "What's the matter with you, Gerhard, are you crazy? This is America."

I was stunned. Obviously, in order to live a new life, without the many restrictions she had imposed on herself while she was living in Germany, she construed that the laws of *kashrut*, that which is allowed and which is forbidden to eat, applied only to Europe. Apparently it worked for her. As for me, she had instilled in me such a deep aversion for pork, something she had always told me was an "abomination," that, following her admonitions and example, I still don't eat pork even today.

We stayed three days in Buenos Aires; then we took the train to Mar del Plata. Following the unbeatable roulette system that we had developed, we planned to make a small fortune before embarking for the United States.

The goodbye from my parents was really heartbreaking. They both cried and seemed to be disconsolate. They both said that they would never see me again. That was of course awful for them, being with me for only a few days, after eight years of absence. But their fears in this case were unfounded. I saw my father twice again and my mother several times, both in Buenos Aires and also in the United States.

Our ship, the SS GOLDEN EAGLE was lying at anchor at Mar del Plata. It was going to leave the next morning. We left our gear on board ship and planned to spend the night there; then we hotfooted it to the casino.

It was a splendid affair, much grander than we had imagined. Uniformed footmen stood at the staircases. Most men were in evening attire and women in elegant evening gowns. We definitely looked out of place.

But we were undeterred. We were going to use our system and really show them how to make money at the roulette table. We didn't actually expect to break the bank, but we were going to give them a little scare.

So as not to confuse ourselves, we decided to bet $1 per play and bet only on red. To our pleasant surprise red came up three times in a row and we had won $3. Then, unfortunately there were four blacks in a row, at which time, having followed our secret plan and having doubled on each losing bet, we were down $12. Our next bet was for $16 and the little ball landed on zero, another loss. We were down $28. We were getting a little discouraged but this was not the time to be faint-hearted. So, we followed our system and bet another $32. We lost and were down $60. We went into a huddle for consultation. This was not at all going according to plan. We only had $40 left of our stake and, to follow our system, our next bet would have to be for $64, which, if we won, would put us $4 ahead, but would put us $124 in the hole if we lost. While we were in consultation red came up three times in a row. We should have stayed. We decided to give it one last shot, added $24 to our stake, and put it on red one more time. The ball bounced back and forth then landed solidly on black. We were wiped out. We left the casino somewhat dispirited. It had not been a good evening.

The SS GOLDEN EAGLE was a freighter, with twelve passengers, exactly the same category of vessel that had brought me from Germany to South America. The accommodations were all right and the food was good, though it couldn't compare with that on the German vessel. We had no problem with it. The ship carried a cargo of nitrate fertilizer to the United States. The smell of the stuff was quite pervasive all over the ship.

I call attention to our accommodations because of the race situation in the United States, which separated the whites from the blacks on the ship. The below-deck crew was entirely black, with only the engineer being a white man. The above-deck crew, including the officers of course, was all white. There was no social interaction of any kind between the blacks and the whites. The blacks ate in their separate mess, which was of visibly lower quality than the mess for the white non-officer crew. The officers and passengers took their meals together in a pretty nice dining room, just as on the German ship, the SS AMMON, that had brought me to the western hemisphere, the officers at one table and the twelve passengers at the other.

The final destination of the ship was New Orleans. It was supposed to arrive there on April 10. It was cutting it a little close, because my visa expired on April 15. I didn't know what would happen if, for any reason at all, we would get there a little late, but I didn't worry much about it because it wasn't going to happen.

How could it? But after five days at sea, a terrible odor and smoke erupted from one of the holds. The cargo in that hold, those nitrates, had started a process of spontaneous combustion. In other words, the ship was on fire. There were flames and a terrible stench. The officers assured us that there was no danger in that the fire was in only one hold, was confined and was being kept under control. We could, however, not continue our trip to New Orleans as planned. We stopped at Port of Spain in Trinidad, about a day ahead of us. The harbor master came on board and when he saw the mess, the stench and the smoldering fire, ordered us out of port immediately and told us to dump the cargo, or at least the cargo in that hold, a minimum of twenty miles out at sea before returning to port.

So we went out to sea again, about 30 miles out, dumped the cargo from the affected hold and returned to port. The captain told us that we had to stay in Trinidad for about three days, until we got everything cleaned up and ready to travel again. We were put up at the finest hotel.

While that was most enjoyable, we now had a real problem. There was no longer any way that we could get to New Orleans by April 15. Sergio and I were really worried. We didn't know how picky the entry control people would be and whether, if we were two days late, they would send us back to Bolivia. We did not want to take that chance; therefore, we decided to fly from Port of Spain to New Orleans, then pick up our luggage when the ship arrived four or five days later.

We told the purser what we were going to do, but he advised us not to fly. Our first landfall, he told us, was going to be in Tampa, Florida and that was three days before New Orleans. "I can assure that it won't be later than April the 14th."

We had never heard of Tampa before, nobody had mentioned it to us and we didn't know where it was. The purser showed us a map. "We have to unload some cargo there, stay two days, then go on to New Orleans, our final destination."

Well, this would solve our problem. Indeed it did. We got off at Tampa on April 14 – just under the wire.

Part III

FROM THE OIL FIELDS OF ARKANSAS
TO THE IVIED HALLS OF HARVARD

How about **Norma Jean, the real purpose of my coming to the United** States? Since that last ardent goodbye kiss in Cochabamba, we wrote each other weekly, expressing our sentiments in florid and most steamy language. There was only one complication. About a month before, her father had been transferred from Carbondale, Illinois, to Atlanta, Georgia. That put an end to my dream of visiting her every weekend, because that certainly wouldn't be possible with her living in Atlanta. There was one small advantage, however: Atlanta was quite close to Tampa, so I would be able to see Norma Jean pretty much right away.

We went to the railroad station and learned that there was an overnight train to Atlanta that we could take. I had always heard about Pullman, which was a glamorous concept to me, so we bought two Pullman tickets to Atlanta, Georgia. We boarded the train and there were all those people sitting in their comfortable seats. A black porter noticed our bewilderment and said, "Follow me, gentlemen."

We did. He took us into a large room that contained four leather-covered black benches, obviously meant for sleeping, but surprisingly also four urinals and two toilet stalls. We had heard about the American obsession with plumbing, but even so, it seemed to us slightly excessive. The train started moving. We had had a long day and were very tired so we said goodnight to each other. Sergio lay down on one of the black benches and I on one of the others and we went to sleep. We were convinced that we were in the Pullman wagon, the overnight sleeper that we had heard so much about.

What must have been about an hour later, the porter waked us and told us that those were not our beds, it was the men's toilet for this particular wagon. We were quite embarrassed. He told us again to follow him and he led us to our respective sleeping cubicles. The seating car had been transformed by magic into a sleeping car. Those Americans!

I had Norma Jean's address, of course, and I wanted to go visit her right away after arrival in Atlanta. But Sergio's wise counsel was to get a day's rest, get acclimatized a little and then visit her the next day, at which time I would make a better impression. His argument was persuasive.

So we checked into an inexpensive hotel next to the railroad station and went out to breakfast to a small restaurant close by. We didn't quite know what to ask for so the waitress suggested that we take "the regular." We consented. What came appalled me. It was some ugly looking scrambled eggs, a large slice of ham, something which I later learned was red-eye gravy, and another awful looking thing which I later learned was called grits. I found the whole thing nauseating, but since I had to pay for it I ate some of it, except for the ham, of course. I just hoped that this was not an example of the cuisine in the United States. I knew that I couldn't get used to it.

We strolled through downtown Atlanta. Then it was lunchtime and we were hungry again. We saw a place called Morrison's Cafeteria. It looked pretty good and we walked in. If I had been disappointed with the breakfast, I was overwhelmed with enthusiasm when I saw the vast array of wonderful food at Morrison's Cafeteria. There were eight different salads, six different entrees, six different vegetables, and all those desserts and different breads. When I came to the end of the line my heart almost stopped. There was a big bowl with matzos. I hadn't seen matzos for eight years and they certainly would not have been displayed in Germany. Obviously it was Passover, a holiday I had not celebrated and never even thought of for all those years. And here, in this wonderful country, without any embarrassment, without any ado, there were matzos displayed for the Jewish clients or anybody else who would have them, and nobody paid any attention to it. I was delighted. I knew I was at home.

We took in a movie in the late afternoon, had some dinner and then went back to our hotel. By that time it was about 9 o'clock in the evening. We were lying on our beds, talking about a number of things, mostly our experiences in Colquiri, our trip to the United States and our future in Missouri. Suddenly there was a knock on the door. A very nice looking woman, perhaps twenty-five years old, walked in and said, "Hi, my name is Irma. Do either of you boys want to party?" She wasn't looking at me, she was looking at Sergio.

"What does she want," Sergio asked.

"Quiere saber si quieres hacer fiesta?," I told him.

"Tell her I don't want to go to a *fiesta*."

The woman understood some Spanish. "No, no," she said, "not *fiesta*, I mean sex."

Sergio understood that. "Tell her I don't want to go to any *fiesta* and I don't want any sex."

"O.K., boys," she said, "if you change your minds, I'm in room number 517."

I was astonished. First I had that great experience with the matzos at Morrison's Cafeteria and now this lovely person came and offered us sex. I was getting more and more impressed about the wonderful United States.

"Sergio," I said, "why don't you want sex. She's a nice girl."

"I don't want any. If you do, why don't you go to room number 517?"

I said, "I think I will." So I got up and went to room number 517, which was on the same floor. I knocked. She told me to come in. I said "Excuse me, you asked us whether we wanted sex. We said no, but I think I changed my mind."

"That's wonderful," she said, "let's go ahead." So we did. It was very good. I left and I felt quite elated. It was really an unusual experience. I don't quite know how I reconciled what I had just done with my great love for Norma Jean, whom I was going to see the next day, I hoped. It wasn't clear to me at all until much later that this nice and accommodating girl may have expected compensation for her loving ministrations. My kissing her good-bye, saying thank you and walking out without paying anything must have left her so astonished that she didn't find the words to protest. I was really acting in good faith. Well, the life of a working girl is not always fair and it isn't easy.

Next morning I shaved very carefully and dressed nicely. I inquired how to get there and took a streetcar to the address that Norma Jean had given me. It was nice neighborhood of detached homes. It was about 11 o'clock in the morning when I arrived at my destination, Norma Jean's house, I rang the bell. Nothing happened. I rang the bell again. I finally heard steps approaching inside the house. A lady opened the door carefully. It was Norma Jean's mother. She was in her bathrobe and looked somewhat disheveled. I think she'd had a couple of drinks, maybe three.

She recognized me immediately and said, "Come in, come in, Gerardo, what a wonderful surprise. Does Norma Jean know you're coming?"

I said, "No, I wanted it to be a surprise."

"Well," she said, make yourself comfortable. "She's in school and I expect her in about 45 minutes. Excuse me while I get dressed."

So I sat down and leafed through some magazines. Then the bell rang and, obviously, it was Norma Jean. Her mother motioned me to run up the stairs to the second floor, and then slowly walk down so as to give Norma Jean a real surprise. I did just that. Our eyes met. I expected that, just like Scarlett O'Hara of the same locale (but who had not yet been invented), she would run up the stairs and fall around my neck hugging and kissing me. But that did not take place. She looked at me and said, "Why you – of all people!"

It wasn't much of a greeting. Norma Jean's mother made us some lunch and after lunch we talked about Bolivia and about my going to the Missouri School of Mines and why her dad left Carbondale, etc. Then she asked me, "Would you and your friend like to double date tonight?"

"Excuse me Norma Jean, would I like to do what?"

"To double date, you know," she said.

I didn't know what a date was or perhaps I did know; it was a fruit, wasn't it? But I didn't know what a double date was. "Excuse me, Norma Jean, could you please explain what you mean."

Then she explained to me that since I had brought my friend Sergio, whom she had met in Bolivia, that she could also bring a friend and we could go together to the movies or something.

"That would be a swell idea," I said, using a term that I thought was very hip and even might have been in that day.

I left and we arranged that Sergio and I would come back around 6 o'clock and that we would be joined by a friend of hers (whose name I have forgotten), and that we would all go to the movies, after Norma Jean's mother would have served us a light supper.

So we did just that. Norma Jean's father was there. He remembered me well and was very cordial. After supper he said, "Gerardo, would you please come to my study with me. I would like to talk with you."

"Of course," I said. So we did.

"Please sit down. Do you smoke?"

"Yes, sir, I do."

He offered me a cigarette. "Gerardo, I want to tell you something about American girls. I know that you and Norma Jean hugged and kissed a lot in Cochabamba, and I know that you are here to see her. I think you may believe that you are in love with her, but quite frankly I don't think she is in love with you. American girls do a lot of hugging and kissing and necking..."

"Excuse me, sir, what is necking?"

"Well," he said, "it's about the same, hugging and kissing, you know. They do a lot of that but it really doesn't mean anything. I am very glad that you like my daughter. But you should really have no ideas that this is a special relationship, though. It really isn't."

I thought it was a very nice thing for him to explain that to me and I thanked him for that. We went to the movies and I said goodbye (there was no goodnight kiss). We went to the hotel and left the next morning for Rolla, Missouri, changing trains in St. Louis.

An extraordinary thing happened at the railroad station. Our train to St. Louis was leaving at noon. It was about 11 o'clock, so we decided to go to the waiting room and sit down until the train was ready to leave. We looked around and couldn't help noticing that there were only black people there. Some of them were in uniform and two or three were in wheelchairs, obviously having been wounded in the war. I saw at least one who had lost a leg. Both of us felt a little awkward for not having contributed anything to the war effort, except of course, by working in the tin mines.

While we were talking about this, a uniformed railroad employee, very short, very fat and with a very red face, approached us and, in a loud voice and in an accent that was barely understandable, shook his fist at us and berated us. He was obviously very enraged, but we barely understood a word. I finally got out of him that we had strayed into the wrong waiting room, namely the waiting room for blacks. He thought that it was an act of defiance on our part, and that he would have us arrested if we didn't get out immediately. He ordered us out of the waiting room.

He directed us to the white waiting room, which was across the hall. What a difference! In the black waiting room, there were wooden floors, wooden benches along the wall, a few rickety tables and chairs, and a snack-and-sandwich service. The white waiting room, beautifully carpeted, was a sea of tables with white tablecloths and beautiful china and silver on each table. White-coated black waiters flitted to and fro. We sat down and ordered a simple meal. We just felt awful about this. Here we were, on virtually the first day in our new country, for which we had done absolutely nothing. By virtue of our skin color only we were given preferential treatment. Those boys in the other waiting room had put their butts on the line for their country, some of them had been shot up badly, and many of their fellows had paid of course with their lives. They were relegated to second-class citizenship. It made a terrible impression on us. Naturally, we saw much more of it as we went along and, sad to say, we eventually became somewhat inured to it and, I'm afraid, almost even came to accept it as the natural order of things.

Sergio and I decided that, even though we were always going to remain best friends, that we should break up and not live in the same place. If we lived together we would only speak Spanish and we both were intent on improving our English, especially Sergio, whose English was very poor. In fact, I worried, rightly as it turned out, about how he was going to manage college with his scant knowledge of the language.

We went to the university and introduced ourselves to Mr. Hubbard, the Registrar. I was happy to learn that Mr. Hubbard, having reviewed my transcript from Mittwida with the faculty advisor, was allowing credit for all the courses in mathematics and physics that I had already taken. It was about 30 hours – a big help. That left about 126 hours, something that I thought I should try to manage in two years. The reason for some urgency was, of course, money. After paying the expenses for our trip and for tuition, I had about $2,300 left. Even in those days, when things were quite a bit less expensive, that wasn't too much money to get all the way to a B.S. in mining engineering. I realized that I would have to work during summer vacations in order to be able to make it all the way through. But I didn't think of that as a real problem. In fact, I was looking forward to working in American mines – as a miner, and not as an engineer.

Mr. Hubbard's office gave us a list of available rooms for rent. I found right away a quite adequate place on the second floor of a simple neighborhood house. The room was right under the uninsulated roof. I did not realize how unbearably hot it would be in the summer and how terribly cold it would get in the winter.

Sergio and I joined a loose fraternity of Latin American students, mostly Colombians and Peruvians, a smattering of Venezuelans, Mexicans and Argentines. They accepted us as "Bolivians," without any hesitation.

Almost immediately after the war was over and correspondence with Europe was possible, I wrote to Mrs. Jespersen, whose Copenhagen address I still had, to find out how they were and mostly how Ulla was. Inevitably, my love had abated over the years and in view of many experiences that I had had in the meantime. Still, of course, I had tender feelings for her and for her family. Mrs. Jespersen responded almost by return. She told me that Ulla had married a young law student by whom she had been made pregnant and had gone with him to Greenland, which was a Danish possession. He worked there as public defender or something like that. She had two more children and then committed suicide. It was a terrible shock to me and very sad, of course; I was quite devastated. As we go along with the story we will see that my connection with this family grew stronger and more significant as time went by.

Apart from getting a degree in mining engineering and, hopefully, establishing a "meaningful" relationship with Norma Jean, I worked toward three other goals that I wanted to accomplish in order to become a "real American."

One: In those magazines that I had read in Bolivia to improve my English, I became aware of Charles Atlas, the self-proclaimed "strongest man in the world," who had become that after he had been a "70-pound weakling." He had accomplished that feat, according to his advertisements, through a special exercise method that he had developed. He taught this method in a mail-order course. I was determined to subscribe to that course, and though I was not 70-pound weakling, but rather a 135-pound weakling, I wanted to look like Charles Atlas or a reasonable facsimile thereof.

Two: I wanted to buy life insurance. I had no idea why I wanted it, except that from reading of all those ads in the American magazines I had became convinced that ownership of life insurance was a necessary requisite to becoming a solid citizen and a "real American."

Three: I wanted to participate in the American stock market and buy shares in at least one U.S. corporation.

Let's start with number three: There was a Merrill Lynch office on Rolla's main street. I went in and told the man that I wanted to buy some shares of stock in a company that he could recommend and that he could assure me would go up in price. "I can't assure you of that," the man said, "but I shall be able to give you some advice. How much do you wish to invest?" I told him that I wanted to invest $50. "I'm afraid we can't do that," he said, "our minimum account would have to be $250."

I realized that I could not afford to speculate with $250 at that point in my financial career and excused myself. I decided to defer the stock purchase until later.

Now to #2: On that same street there was a storefront insurance broker. As I recall, the name was Long & Long. I walked in and told the man sitting behind his desk that I wanted to buy insurance. "What kind of insurance?" Mr. Long (I suppose) asked. "We have life insurance and we have casualty insurance. Which do you want?"

I had no idea what casualty insurance was, so I told him that I wanted to buy life insurance. The man was obviously perplexed. He had been in the life insurance business for many years; it was clear that his experience had taught him that insurance was something that got sold and not bought. I probably was the first person who ever walked into his store and asked to buy life insurance.

"How much insurance do you want to buy?" he asked.

"I don't know," I replied. "How much does it cost?"

"Well that depends on how old you are."

I told him I was twenty-six years old.

"Is $5 a month too much for you?", he asked.

I believe that was the amount but I'm not really sure. "No," I said, "I think I can handle that."

"All right, you just bought $4,000 worth of insurance from the New York Life Insurance Company. Who is the beneficiary?"

I didn't understand that concept and I hadn't thought about that. "What do you mean?" I said.

"Who will get the money if you die?"

I hadn't thought of that either. I didn't realize that I had to die to activate this thing. I couldn't think of anybody else, so I gave the names of my parents, even though I was pretty sure that they would die before I did. I still have the policy, but I changed beneficiaries quite a few years ago.

But really, #1, that Charles Atlas course, was the most important to me. I had cut the coupon from a magazine, had saved it and sent off for the course. The course cost $3.50 per month, for twelve months. I sent a check for $3.50, together with my coupon. About two weeks later I received a big envelope which contained Lesson One and a cover letter signed by Mr. Atlas himself. He assured me that if I followed his detailed instructions I would also become an awe-inspiring specimen with rippling muscles, just as he was. He also reiterated the promise, clearly stated in his ad, namely that I could cancel the course at any time and if I was not "100% satisfied," he would refund my money with five per cent interest. That was very reassuring to me.

I eagerly opened Lesson One, the first step to the perfect body. But I found the lesson a terrible letdown, a big disappointment. There were three things I had to do:

❖ Stop masturbating. I thought that was peculiar advice; in any case, I had abandoned that diversion a long time ago.

❖ I had to drink three glasses of milk a day, and not just drink the milk, but chew it. I had to put half a cup of milk in my mouth, keeping it there while moving my mandibles and then eventually swallow it. It was even worse advice than the first one. I hadn't drunk my mother's milk and I hadn't drunk a drop of milk since. The very smell of milk made me sick. So, I knew I couldn't do that at all – not drink the stuff, let alone chew it.

❖ The third was the essence of the system. It was called "dynamic tension." Essentially, it consisted of fitting my left hand into my

right hand and pushing one against the other. It sounded crazy
to me, I didn't like it at all, and didn't think that it would help me
to the perfect body that I had hoped to attain.

I decided to return the lesson and get my $3.50 back. I wrote a nice letter to
Mr. Atlas telling him about my dissatisfaction and would he please return my money.
"Thank you very much."

He did not reply, and two weeks later another lesson arrived. I felt honor-
bound not to open it and returned it, with postage applied by me. The same with
Lesson Three and with Lesson Four.

I wrote two more letters but the lessons kept coming and so came the
requests for more money. My letters to Mr. Atlas requesting return of my $3.50 plus
interest (as he had promised, in case of dissatisfaction) were ignored.

A few months later, having received the entire course in install-ments and
having returned every one of the twenty-four lessons, Mr. Atlas wrote me a nice
letter telling me that I owed him $38.50, the balance on the course; he hoped that I
would remit this balance immediately, and if I did so, he would send me an
autographed picture of himself, suitable for framing.

I was not interested in the picture. I wrote him again and told him that I
wanted my money back, with interest. He did not respond. A month later he sent
me another letter telling me that if I were to pay up now, he would send me not only
the autographed picture, but also a brass belt buckle with the words "Charles Atlas"
embossed on it. Again, I wrote him, telling him that I had no interest, that I wanted
my money back – with interest.

Another month went by and I received yet another letter from Mr. Atlas.
He told me that if I would finally pay up, he would send me not only the picture and
the belt buckle, but also the "Encyclopedia of Sex," which would contain
EVERYTHING that I might possibly want to know about the subject. Well, I wasn't
interested in that either; I also thought that anybody whose first advice to me was not
to masturbate could not be a very good guide on the subject.

But then, a month later, another letter arrived. On the left side of the
letterhead from top to bottom it had a picture of Charles Atlas, naked, except for a
strategically placed scanty leopard skin cover, displaying his muscles, with the
sentence underneath saying, "The strongest man in the world."

The letter read:

Dear Mr. Joffe:

You have not paid the money you owe me and I think
you are making a big mistake. You may know that I
am the strongest man in the world. I shall be in your
neighborhood within the next two weeks and I

propose to visit you and personally collect what you
owe me. You don't want that to happen. Be smart!

Sincerely yours,
Charles Atlas

I was really concerned. I really thought the guy might come by and beat the hell out
of me. What to do? I went to Mr. Long, my insurance agent and showed him the
letter. He just laughed. "Don't worry about it, Gerardo," he said. "This letter is the
bottom of the barrel." I hadn't heard that expression before, but I knew what he
meant. This was going to be his last attempt to collect money from me, and so it
was.

I never got those big muscles. While, I am no longer a 135-pound weakling
and I am many years older, I weigh 150 pounds and, even without Charles Atlas, I
am in pretty good physical shape. As to the $3.50, with interest? No, I never got
that back.

By the time I was about six months in Rolla, I got a letter from East Germany.
I was most surprised. Who could possibly have written me from East Germany? I
opened the letter. It was from Herr and Frau Möbius, the very nice people who had
been so kind and hospitable to me in Mittweida. I remembered especially Mrs.
Möbius coming to the railroad station, trying to warn me about the Gestapo. I
absolutely cannot imagine how, after all those years, they were able to locate me, but
somehow they did. It was a very sad letter, in which they told me about their
suffering, that they didn't have enough to eat, they didn't have any money, they didn't
know how they were going to survive. They begged me to send them some money,
whatever I could spare, to help them out. I read the letter several times and didn't
know what to do. Ultimately, I decided to not do anything, not to respond, not to
send them any money. I was so tightly budgeted – I just felt that I couldn't spare it.

There are two things in my life about which I feel very bad and that I wish I
had handled differently. The first one was the time that I ignored my father when I
drove into La Paz with Sr. Peró, wanting to avoid a scene. The second one was not
helping Herr and Frau Möbius in their time of need, people who had always been so
very kind to me. Many years later I went into counseling for a short time and those
were the two things that were on my mind and that I talked to my counselor about.

It was clear to me that, with the money I had available, in order to complete those
156 hours towards my degree, I would have to work during summer vacations so as
to earn some money. Also, of course, a job would help me get some experience in
the United States mining industry, which I figured might be somewhat different from
what we had practiced in South America. All those hours in just two years was
going to be a lot of work, more so since I was informed that labs – mostly in
chemistry and geology – would take three hours of time and were counted as only

one hour. But I decided to go ahead with the plan and proposed to make a really good record in college.

The most difficult part perhaps, but really the most enjoyable to me, was English. I took the required freshman English in my first year and the required sophomore English – English literature and American literature in my second year. I loved it. I made very good grades. One small incident surprised me. The English professor who taught in a large room that had blackboards all around called on eight students, me among them, to put the first stanza of the Star-Spangled Banner on the blackboard. It had to do with parsing, correct punctuation or something on that order. To my great surprise, I was the only one who knew all the words to the first stanza of the Star-Spangled Banner. That couldn't have happened in Germany, nor in Bolivia for that matter.

Chemistry, a difficult subject, was taught in a large room with amphitheater seating. There must have been 200 students in the freshman chemistry class. Our first big test was about six weeks into the semester. I worked very hard because I was determined to make a good grade. There was certainly no "grade inflation" in that university. Rather, there were many C's and a good sprinkling of D's and F's. A's were most unusual. I was determined to make an A.

The night before that exam, I had done my final studying for the test. It was about 9:30, I decided to turn in early and went to bed. I was awakened by a knock on the door. I looked at my clock. It was 1 o'clock in the morning. I was surprised and didn't know what to make of it. I opened the door and turned on the light. There was my Colombian colleague, Ernesto Ramirez, who was one of my buddies from that informal Latin-American fraternity.

"What's the matter, Ernesto?" I asked, "are you all right?"

"Yes, I'm all right. Please let me in. I have something important to talk to you about."

I couldn't imagine what it could be. He sat down and took four sheets of paper out of his coat pocket. "What is that?," I asked.

"It's tomorrow's chemistry test."

"Where in the hell did you get that?"

"Never mind how," he replied, "I know one of the girls who works in the duplicating office and she helped me get it. Let's you and me do this test right now. You seem to be pretty good at this stuff. Also, we have the textbook. We are bound to make a good grade – probably an A. Let's go to work."

I was very torn. I had no particular interest in helping Ernesto, but I knew that it would ruin my reputation with my Latin American "brothers" if I refused. I didn't want to cheat for myself because I didn't want to start my academic career and my life in the United States with committing a fraud. Also, I thought that I was sufficiently prepared and that I didn't need that.

"Ernesto, I am really pretty sleepy. I don't want to do that right now. Why don't you take the test home. Take the textbook and get the answers and you'll make a good grade tomorrow."

"*No sirve* – that doesn't work, said Ernesto. "I can't do this damn stuff, even with the textbook in front of me. You have to help me."

So I sat down with him for one hour. There were sixteen problems and we did all of them to perfection. Ernesto thanked me profusely and swore me to secrecy. I told him of course, and that I wouldn't mention this to anybody.

At the test next morning and with about 200 students in that big room and with monitors walking up and down the aisles to discourage cheating, the tests were distributed. It turned out that there was an *A* test and a *B* test which were distributed at random. By sheer chance, Ernesto and I both got the *A* test, the one that we had worked on the night before.

When the grades were posted, Ernesto and I both had straight *A*'s and there were perhaps another ten *A*'s throughout the class. There were about forty *B*'s including plus and minus, about one hundred *C*'s, thirty or forty *D*'s and *F*'s. I had a feeling that Ernesto would have preferred to have made a *B* or perhaps a *C*+ but he was stuck with that *A*. Ultimately he flunked the course; he never made better than a *D* on subsequent tests. I am pretty sure that the professor got wise to him. Fortunately, without cheating, I continued to make *A's* and *B's* and wound up with an *A* in that course.

One day, a month or so after arriving in Rolla, Ernesto, the same fellow who had wiggled that chemistry test, came to my room one evening and said, "*Gerardo, vamos.*"

"*Vamos?*" I asked. "*Adónde?*" "Where are we going?"

"We have a car. Sergio is here and two other guys. Let's go out to the Wick-Wack Club. It's 10 miles out of town on Highway 76."

"What happens at the Wick-Wack Club?" I asked.

"You'll see. There's music, dancing, but you have to 'brown bag' it."

"What does it mean 'brown bag' it?"

"You sound like a real greenhorn, Gerardo, but of course that is what you are. 'Brown bag' means that you have to go to a liquor store and buy a pint of whiskey and put it in a brown bag. Then we'll go to the club."

"This is crazy," I said. "Why don't we buy the liquor at the club?"

"*No, imposible, hombre.* Don't you realize that Missouri is a dry state. There can be no liquor served."

"Then what do I do with that brown bag?"

"You put it under the table and you ask for a 'set up.'"

"All right," I said. We went to a liquor store and I bought a half a pint of whiskey. I wasn't much of a drinker. We got to the Wick-Wack Club. It was a huge room, with about 500 people milling around. There were about a hundred tables around a large dance floor. An eight-man band, all blacks, was playing on the stage. One of them was the vocalist. There was a song called 'Hey Bah Ba Riba' which was about the weirdest thing I'd ever heard. I couldn't understand a word. Of course not, because there were no words. There were, however, plenty of girls and we all danced. But none of the girls wanted to leave with us.

The waiter came and we asked for a "set up." It consisted of a bucket of ice, a pitcher of water and a glass. It cost a dollar. The brown bag with the whiskey was under the table. Nobody supposedly saw it and nobody supposedly knew what was going on. I thought it was hilarious. I learned something new about America every day and every evening.

One evening I had a hankering for a hamburger and some fries and decided I would not eat at the school cafeteria. I went into a small place close by the campus. It was quite crowded and I sat down at a table where a woman was already sitting. She was short, somewhat overweight and had nice long black hair. I figured she was about thirty-five years old. Her name she told me was Lila Hines and that she worked for the U.S. Forest Service. "I'm going to the movies," she said, "would you like to go with me?" That wasn't really what I had planned, but I said why not, so we went.

We enjoyed the movie. I took her home and I stayed a long time. From then on out I saw Lila every Friday night, at least three times a month. Our routine was that I would buy a steak and take it to her home. She would cook it, we would enjoy it, we would go to the movies, and I would take her back home and linger for a while. It was a very good arrangement for both of us. I found that her mousy exterior was quite deceptive.

Sergio didn't get any credit for previous college work at all, of course. He had to start from the very beginning and do the more than 150 hours, hopefully in four years. It wasn't quite clear to him how he would manage financially, but I told him not to worry. I was likely to get a job when I graduated and would then be able to help him get through school. In those days, financial aid by the government or by the university system was not available – except for the GI Bill, of course, but that was not applicable to us.

We had health insurance through the school. That was a pleasant surprise. Fortunately I never got sick and didn't have to make use of it.

But, there was one small thing that bothered me. I had, for many years, a little growth on my uvula, a little piece hanging by a slender thread. It didn't hurt at all and obviously posed no danger to health, but it was somewhat uncomfortable because every time I swallowed the thing went down my throat and then somehow came up again spontaneously. It was a little weird. So having this insurance, I thought I might take advantage of it and have it taken care of.

I went to the campus medical office. Dr. Rasmusson was the attending physician. "What seems to be the trouble?" he said.

I told him.

"Well let me have a look." I opened my mouth. He shone a flashlight into it and says, "Oh that's something very simple. I see that quite frequently. I can take care of it in a second."

"O.K., that's good. Then let's do it."

"Now be sure to keep your mouth open."

He took a pair of scissors – actually, they looked like ordinary scissors to me but, they might have been surgical ones, shone that light in my mouth again, and simply cut the thing off. It hurt so much I thought I would faint. I almost did. Blood was gushing out of the wound.

"I could have given you some local anesthesia," he said, "but I didn't think it would have been worth your while." I was just barely recovering from the pain. He cauterized the wound and told me that I would be fine.

I was, but if that should ever happen to you or somebody you know, tell them that under no circumstances to have that cut off without anesthesia. That tiny little thread must have contained about a half a million nerves. At least that's the way it felt.

There was no dental insurance, however. One day I had a toothache, not really bad, but it was aching on both sides of my jaw. I went to the dentist recommended by the school, a Dr. Frank. He did a little probing but didn't take any x-rays. He said, "Your problem is that all of your wisdom teeth, all four of them, have to come out. They are badly impacted. They are going to get infected and they're going to give you a lot of trouble."

"Can you do that, Dr. Frank?" I asked.

"Yes, I could, but it would be quite expensive. I don't think you want to pay that."

"So what do I do?"

"I can get you an appointment at the dental school at Barnes Hospital in St. Louis. They'll do it for you and it won't cost you anything. Even if you need hospitalization which is quite likely, it will also be for free."

That sounded pretty good to me. I let him make the arrangements. On the appointed day I took the train to St. Louis, then took the bus to Barnes Hospital. They put me to bed and told me that the "procedure" was going to take place next morning at 10 o'clock. In the meantime I could have dinner in the dining room and could walk around the hospital and do whatever I wanted, but just be sure to go to bed not later than 9 o'clock, because "we want you to be fresh and alert in the morning."

The girl in charge of the floor was lively and quite pretty. She was about twenty-two years old, and she told me that her name was Harriett. This was very interesting. "Harriett," I asked after some chit-chat, "are you married?" I knew she wasn't because she didn't wear a wedding ring.

"No, I'm not," she said, "but I have a steady boyfriend."

She was telling me what I wanted to know, but she continued and volunteered, "I have a cousin, Bonnie McCabe, almost exactly my age. She's very pretty and I think you would like her."

"I think I would, Harriett, but I'm going to be here only for a few days and be laid up in the hospital. Then I'm going to go back to Rolla, so I don't think I'll every meet Bonnie. But, thank you for telling me about her."

"Not so fast," Harriett said. "Give me your address. Bonnie does a lot of traveling in her job, and it's quite possible that she might have some business in Rolla and then she could come by and look you up. Then you can decide whether you like each other or not."

That sounded like a reasonable idea. I gave Harriett my address. She had my name, of course.

I had a good nights sleep. The next morning, I was told to have a very light breakfast and then was led into the operating room and sat down in a very impressive-looking dental chair. After about ten minutes, a tall authoritative-looking man in a white coat came in. He was followed by phalanx of seven other men and one woman, also in white coats. The coat of Mr. Authoritative went half way down his calves; the coats of the "phalanx" were short ones. "I am Doctor Rambler," he said. "I'm going to perform this operation. These eight people are students and they will help me." He reeled up a tray with a great number of forbidding looking instruments.

"Are you going to use all of these instruments?" I asked fearfully.

Dr. Rambler said, "All of these, and you should see what we still have in the sink." It was meant to be a joke and his acolytes laughed heartily. I didn't think it was funny.

He made me open my mouth and held it open by clamps on both sides of my jaw. Then he began to explain to his attentive audience what he was going to do. This was essentially to drill holes to weaken the bone in each of the four quarters, then chisel the bone out and extract the respective teeth. He told his audience that he was going to show the procedure and then each of them could have a whack at me. That sounded pretty scary. I got the impression, and I believe I was right, that it was the first time that these people had worked on a live victim.

The first student got to drill three or four holes and his work found acceptance by Dr. Rambler. The second one did not do so well. Rambler hollered, "Stop, stop, stop. The way you're holding the drill, you're going to break the bit." He had hardly said it when the bit did indeed break. I had a piece of steel sticking out of my jaw. Fortunately, there was still enough of it sticking out so they could put some pliers on it and rotate it out. It was not a pleasant procedure. The chastised student went to the back of the line. Then the girl came. She did pretty well. Dr. Rambler gallantly praised her.

So it went. Then he demonstrated the operation of the hammer and the chisel. Again, the students attempted to emulate the master. They did pretty well, at least Dr. Rambler accepted what they were doing. Then came the turn of the poor guy who had broken off the bit. I was worried about him and so, apparently, was Dr. Rambler.

"Be very careful," he said, "because at this spot, if you slip you can very easily cut the third facial nerve and the patient's face will be paralyzed."

"Oh my God," I thought, "I should have gone in debt and let Dr. Frank do the procedure." The whole thing lasted about two hours and the anesthetic had to be refreshed twice. It was not a pleasant experience – but it was free. I stayed in the hospital for three days. Dr. Rambler came by every day. He assured me that I was making good progress. It still hurt very much but I was glad to be able to go home on the fourth day. I was very pleased that I had this behind me.

About a month later, at home in my room, boning up for a geology test the next day, the phone rang. Who could it be. "Hello."

"Hello, my name is Bonnie McCabe. My cousin Harriett told me about you. I am on my way to Kansas City and I'm coming through Rolla. I would like to meet you. Can we get together?"

Well, I had forgotten all about Harriett and had certainly forgotten all about Bonnie and I was very busy with that test on the next day. It was important to me, but I didn't want to be discourteous, so I said, "O.K., Bonnie. Where are you staying?"

"I'm at the Peachtree Motel," she said. "Why don't you come and pick me up?"

The Peachtree was in walking distance. "O.K., I'll be there in about half an hour."

Bonnie turned out to be a wonderful girl; everything that Harriett had told me and more. We became very good friends right away. She extended her time in Rolla to stay over the weekend. She managed to come through Rolla every other week or so. Once or twice we met in Jefferson City, the capital of Missouri, about 50 miles north of Rolla. It was a good arrangement. It also meant the end of my relationship with Lila Hines and the end of those delicious steak dinners.

One day, out of the blue, I got a letter from Norma Jean. She didn't have my address, of course, but she wrote in care of the school and they forwarded her letter to me. She told me that her father had lost his job in Atlanta and that they were moving back to Carbondale, Illinois. She told me that she loved me, that she missed me, and that she wanted to see me again. A lip imprint was planted on the bottom of the letter. I had never seen that before and I thought it was very romantic.

I replied to her. I told her that I loved her too, that I was very busy, that I didn't have any money for traveling, and what's more, I had to go to work in a mine as soon as the semester was over. I did tell her that I hoped we would see each other some time very soon, but not right now. I did not imprint a kiss to the bottom of my letter.

Through the employment office of the school, Sergio and I found summer jobs in one of the lead-zinc mines in the Tri-State area of Kansas-Missouri-Oklahoma. We were told to report to the company office in Miami, Oklahoma, about 20 miles west of Joplin, Missouri, on the Monday following the end of the semester.

We did just that, filled out a couple of forms and were driven to the mine. Since these lead-zinc deposits are horizontal beds, rather than the vertical veins that we were used to, this mine looked totally different from anything that we had ever seen. There was a headframe and a vertical shaft about 6 feet square. A steel cable with a hook at the end went over a bullwheel at the headframe. A cylindrical bucket, about 4 feet in diameter and about 5 feet deep was fastened to the hook. One had to stand at the edge of that vertical shaft, look down to the bottom, about 200 feet below, and pull that cable toward one and climb into the bucket. Then the man on the other side of the shaft would go through the same maneuver and would also climb in the bucket. One would then give a sign to the hoist man, who would drop the bucket, which fell like a rock down that vertical shaft. As if by miracle, the bucket would slow down about 20 feet above the bottom and came to rest with a soft landing. That was not automatic. There were no safety procedures. It all depended on the skill of the hoistman.

I worked there for almost three months and we had to do that every time we made that trip. At our lunch break, we had a choice to either have our meal down in the mine or be pulled outside and have it in the fresh air. I never did that. One trip a day down that shaft was more than enough for me. It was not the trip down so much that scared me, but pulling on that steel cable, the fear of missing the bucket and perhaps falling down all the way to the bottom; or, that the hoistman might make a mistake and, as I was trying to grab that cable, pull the bucket up and send me head-first 200 feet down to the bottom, or that he misjudged and didn't pull off that soft landing. I had nightmares about that.

The work in that mine was very hard on me. Mining was by the so-called room-and-pillar method, which is just about what it sounds like. The ore body was essentially horizontal. It would be mined out in "rooms," and pillars were being left for stability. Even so, the possibility of giving way and collapsing was always present, just as it was in the coal mining regions of the eastern United States, where similar mining methods were used. My job, for most of the time, was to shovel ore onto a conveyor belt or, worse, clean out the muck in the sump and put it on the conveyor belt. The sump was a pool into which all of the slurry and sludge of the mine would flow and settle. It was awfully hard to get the shovel in there and awfully hard to lift it up because of the water and because of the suction. It was no fun and I really didn't learn anything, except perhaps how to do hard work in an acceptable fashion. The foreman grumbled occasionally when he saw what I had done, but he never really chewed me out.

I made $2.25 per hour, which was pretty good wages in those days. Sergio and I lived frugally. We were able to save about $500 each.

About two months into this three-month stint, I got a phone cal from Norma Jean. I don't know how she tracked me down to that rooming house. She told me, again, that she loved me, that she wanted to see me, and that I should come to Carbondale. There was intimation that wonderful things would happen. So I decided to cut my work short by one week in order to visit her in Carbondale. I took that long bus ride all across Missouri to St. Louis, then took another bus from St. Louis to Carbondale. On that trip from St. Louis to Carbondale, I met a very nice girl from St. Louis, who was visiting her grandmother in Illinois. She said she was going to stay just overnight and then go back home. I didn't ask her, but she volunteered and gave me her St. Louis address.

The meeting with Norma Jean was another great dud. Nothing really happened. I didn't know why she had wanted me to come. I was pretty unhappy with her and with myself for having put so much time, effort, and emotional energy into that girl. I decided never to see her again and I never did. She wrote me another two or three letters, but I didn't reply.

But I decided not to make this trip a total loss if I could help it. So, when I got to St. Louis about 8 o'clock in the evening, I took a cab to the address that the girl on that bus had given me. She was happy and surprised to see me. She suggested that we take a cab and go across the bridge to a very nice nightclub that she knew in East St. Louis, which is in Illinois. I told her that I didn't want to go there.

"Why not?"

"I just don't want to," I told her. But I had a reason. I had been told about the so-called Mann Act, which supposedly imposed terrible penalties for taking a woman across state lines for "immoral purposes." I must confess that my purposes weren't "moral," so I decided to stay in Missouri. She turned out to be a very nice girl and we had a good time. When I left the next morning, it was clear that despite the disappointment with Norma Jean, this trip had not been a total loss.

One day, about two months later, I was walking across the campus in Rolla when a student stopped me. He introduced himself as Seymour Rosenbaum and asked me whether I was Jewish. I was startled. I was Jewish, of course, but nobody had ever asked me that.

"Yes, I am, Rosenbaum, but why do you want to know?"

"We are founding a chapter of a Jewish fraternity, Alpha Epsilon Pi, on campus, but we need twelve students to found the chapter. We only have eleven. If you join us we can do it."

Well I didn't have any desire to join a fraternity, even though many years earlier, MIT, to which I had applied for admission, had encouraged me to become a "Greek." By now I had heard about fraternities, and I had no desire to submit myself to the discipline of living in a fraternity house, the hazing, the duties, and all the rest that went with it. What's more, I was part of the Latin-American group and felt comfortable with them. "Rosenbaum, thank you for your offer, but I really don't think I want to do that;" I gave him my reasons.

"Listen," he said, "there will be no obligation for you to live in the fraternity house. As long as you are a member and allow us to count you in we can go ahead."

"O.K., count me in," I said. That's how I became a member of the Alpha Epsilon Pi fraternity, which I support financially even to this day. The fraternity was able to buy a nice house on Fraternity Row. I went to visit about twice a week and was glad to have joined them. They were a good bunch, we had a good time, and I made good friends.

Fast forward: Fifty years later, in 1998, I went to my fifty-year homecoming. It was a wonderful and very nostalgic affair. I met many of my old friends and their wives, and of course, we exchanged experiences, pictures, talked about our children, grandchildren, and, in at least two cases, great-grandchildren. Then I went to the AEPi house. It was a new one – much larger than the one in my day and much more comfortable. The guys were a really nice bunch, but there were two differences: First, only about sixty per cent of the boys were Jewish. It had changed from a Jewish fraternity to a "generic" fraternity, though the flavor was still heavily Jewish. The second difference, however, was more interesting. There were lots of girls around which, except for parties, would never have been permitted in my day. And, remarkably, many of the girls told me, without particular restraint, that they usually spent their nights there. Oh well, born fifty years too soon!

I took most of my meals – breakfast, lunch and dinner at the school cafeteria. The food was pretty decent, about the same level I had at the *Rancho* in Bolivia. The cafeteria was run by two young girls, a blond and a brunette. They were very popular on campus, of course. Since there were no women students they were the only two women among about 2,000 men. I dated the brunette a few times, which, given the setting, was quite a coup in itself, but nothing much came of it. I don't remember her name, but I do remember to this day that she was from a small town in Texas, with the unlikely name of Desdemona.

One morning I found myself at breakfast sitting next to a student whom I'd seen around – a big heavy-set fellow. He had ordered the same as I, namely two fried eggs on toast and hash-fried potatoes. I couldn't help noticing that he carefully cut the whites off the eggs and ate them. He pushed the yolks aside.
  "Excuse me," I said, "what are you doing? You don't like to eat the yolks?"
  "No," he said, I hate them; I only like the whites."
  That was a long time before cholesterol consciousness. "That's interesting," I said, "because I only like the yolks. Would you mind giving me your yolks next time and I'll give you my whites?"
  "Not at all," he said. "That sounds like a good arrangement."
  "How about our having breakfast again tomorrow?" I asked. "We'll do the same thing."
  We met again next morning. I ate his yolks and he ate my whites. After that, we became friendly. His name was A. Michael Deichmann. He was a big German-Catholic boy from St. Louis, who had just mustered out of the Merchant Marine. He was also a mining engineering student. We became fast friends. Neither of us was happy with our living accommodations, so we decided to find a better place, where we could live together. We were roommates for the rest of my student days. He is now retired in Phoenix. We still talk to each other on the telephone every other month or so. He is retired and has several children, and he always tells me about his Jewish son-in-law, whose name is Adler.

One of the fellows in my fraternity was from St. Louis. He had a car and once every two or three months he would drive to St. Louis for a weekend and take two or three of the fraternity brothers along for the ride. The first time I went with him, I remembered that one of my fellow passengers on the SS GOLDEN EAGLE had been a young man by the name if Erwin Vogel, who told me that he had a cousin in St. Louis and that I should look her up when I was there. "She's a nice girl," he had told me.

As I recall her last name was also Vogel; her first name was Ellie.

I didn't know many people, and I certainly didn't yet have what could be called a steady girlfriend, so the first time I went to St. Louis I called her up. I told her that her cousin Erwin had told me to call her, and here I was.

"How tall are you?" she asked me.

"What?" is all I could say.

"How tall are you?" she repeated.

"I really don't know," I answered truthfully. "I've never measured myself" – and I really didn't know.

"Do you think you are tall, medium or short?"

"I really never have thought in those terms," I said. "I guess you would consider me medium." As it turned out, I would be considered short in the United States, because I was and still am only five foot seven.

"Why do you need to know?" I asked.

"I need to know whether to wear heels or not," she replied.

I was totally intrigued. I didn't know what it meant to wear heels.

But the interview wasn't over. "What sign were you born under?" she asked.

"What sign?" I replied. "What do you mean?"

"I mean your zodiac sign."

"Listen, Ellie, I don't know what a zodiac is and I don't know what sign I'm born under. I've never heard of anything like that."

"What's your birthday?"

I told her June 22nd. "You are a Cancer." I got a little nervous. Was she making a diagnosis over the telephone?

"What do you mean, I'm a Cancer?"

"It means you were born under the sign of the Cancer."

"Is that good or bad?" I asked.

"It's neither good nor bad. I just needed to know your sign to find out whether you and I will be compatible."

"Are we going to be?" I asked.

"Yes, I think we'll be fine."

I picked her up, but there was nothing special. We were not as compatible as she thought we would be, according to the zodiac signs.

My second summer was rolling around. Again, I needed and wanted to go to work to earn money and to learn something. Under no circumstances, however was I going to go back to those lead- zinc mines in the Tri-State district. I wanted to try something totally different.

I went to the employment office to see what was available. I found that there was an opportunity in the Bunker Hill and Sullivan Mines in Kellogg, Idaho, way up in the panhandle. That sounded like something I wanted to do. One of my classmates was one Charlie Huffman who, I knew, was also looking for work. "Charlie, how about you and me going to work in the deep mines in the panhandle of Idaho. I think I can get us a job."

"Why not," he said. "You do the application work. If you can get us a job I'll go with you."

So I wrote to the employment office of the Bunker Hill mine and told them that we were looking for a summer job. A reply came back by return, telling us that summer work was available. So, Charlie and I took the bus to Kellogg, a very long trip. When we got there, we were assigned to the bunkhouse for single men. It was a spartan affair, but quite clean and was run by a motherly lady and her husband. Meals were taken down the street in a boarding house. I was fascinated by the boarding house. Both for breakfast and dinner, about 30 men were sitting around one long table. I had never seen so much variety and abundance of food as in that place. We all worked hard and were very hearty eaters. As to lunch, we would pack our own. There was a side room where about ten different types of wrapped sandwiches were available for the taking, also fruit, candy and juices. It was wonderful. As I recall, it cost $3 a day.

I was assigned to the personnel man at the mine, who asked me what I could and wanted to do. "I can do almost anything," I told him, not quite truthfully.

"You want to make money, don't you?" he asked.

"Yes, of course, that's the idea."

"Do you think you can be a raise miner?"

"Yes, I'm sure I could," I said. I was not all that sure of that myself. I had supervised and directed countless raises in Bolivia, but of course had never done it myself. A raise, by the way, is a vertical opening from one level of a mine to the next one above it. It is usually about 100 to 200 feet in length. It's just like a shaft, except that a shaft is opened downward, whereas a raise is opened upward. That is easier, because the "muck" falls down by itself. The end result is the same – a vertical opening between two levels of a mine.

"Give this slip to the foreman in the morning and he'll put you to work."

I got there in the morning, picked up my lamp and got on the train into the mine – a long ride, about two miles. Then I went on a so-called skip, which is a cart with benches that runs on rails down a steep incline. The skip was held by a steel cable and when everyone was seated, about 40 men, the skip was let go. I would say that the speed was about 30 to 40mph. It was scary but not nearly as scary as that vertical hole in Oklahoma had been.

I was assigned to the very lowest level of the mine. I was told that it was the deepest point in the United States. That was quite possibly the case. The heat was almost unbearable. The foreman took me to my place of work and marked the spot where I was expected to make that raise. He told me where to find my machine, a so-called stoper, where the water and air hoses were that had to be attached, where to find the timber that I would need to make the raise safe and to construct a daily platform for me to work on, and where to find all the other equipment and tools that I would need. I was a little shaky because, while I had supervised the construction of many raises, I had never done this myself. But, of course, I knew exactly what to do. Essentially, the work consisted of the drilling of eleven 5-foot holes in a pattern that the foreman described to me and with which I was familiar. Once I had the holes drilled, I would get the dynamite, the blasting caps and the lengths of wires, which I would reel out to a central location. At the end of the shift and, after everyone had left, the boss would detonate all the work done on his level.

After I had done my daily stint I could sit down, read a book, scratch my head or do whatever I wanted. My assigned job was to drill those rounds, load them with dynamite, and get them ready for the blast. The second and following days were more difficult, because, first thing in the morning, I had to build a wooden platform, which was an important and painstaking job. If the platform was not firm, and particularly considering the heavy equipment and the pressure against it by the holes that had to be drilled, everything would come crashing down and would surely hurt me very badly or possibly even kill me. So, I had to be very, very careful. It was not easy work, particularly as the raise proceeded to go up, because I did not just have to build that platform every morning, but had to climb up the ladder with that heavy equipment and the water and air hoses. It really was a man's job. I loved every minute of it.

While obviously a minor achievement, yet when I finished that raise, when I got it through to the next level and saw its lights, I was very proud of myself and had a great feeling of accomplishment. It was something I had never done before and had not really been sure that I could do.

In those days, just as many other young people, I had slightly leftish political inclinations and decided that I wanted to join the miners' union, called United Mine and Mill and Smelter Workers. It had a reputation as being radical and more than somewhat pinkish. It was just what I was looking for. I went to the union meetings and liked what I saw. It was somewhat thrilling to hear the speakers intone against the "bosses," against the "capitalists," and at that time mostly against, as they called it, the "Taft Hartley Slave Labor Act." I wasn't really sure what the Taft Hartley Act was all about, but it was clear that the union was vehemently opposed to it.

After I had attended my third meeting, I asked to join the union. I paid my initiation dues and was accepted. I had to swear an oath that I was never in my life going to cross a picket line. I knew what a picket fence was, but I didn't really know what a picket line was. In any case, I didn't think it would be a hardship for me not to cross it and I gave that oath. Eventually, of course, I found out what it was. I kept my promise; I have never yet crossed a picket line. Charlie Huffman did not join me in becoming a union member. He was very conservative, and that wasn't his cup of tea.

A man by the name of Steinmetz, one of the successful alumni of the Missouri School of Mines, had endowed the Steinmetz Prize for Technical Writing, which was to be awarded once a year to that person in the mining department who wrote the best technical paper. I was intrigued by that and thought how exciting it would be if I, to whom English was a third language, could win that prize. What I knew most about was the mining methods in Colquiri. So, I decided to give it a try and started a paper "Mining Methods at the Colquiri Tin Mine." I had been working on that paper before I went up to Idaho and took it with me to finish it there if I possibly could. I had even made some drawings which, considering my poor talent in that field, came out pretty well. I worked on it every evening after work and had it finished in about another three weeks. Now I had to get it typed. I didn't have a typewriter and, I didn't know how to type very well. The answer was obvious: I needed to find a girl – a girl that could type.

So I looked around and found one: Helen Johnson. Helen was six years older than I. She was a telephone operator and part-time secretary for the mine. She was, she told me, a top-notch typist. She was certainly that. But she was much more than that. I thought that she was absolutely the most beautiful woman I'd ever seen. She was the archetypal Swede, about 3" taller than I, a Scandinavian Venus of Milo and, as I later learned, the idea of anybody's trophy wife. By some masterful chemistry or by sheer good luck, she liked me. I took her out a couple of times. We became close friends very quickly, and I told her about my project. She agreed to type the whole thing up for me, about 40 pages. In those days, before computers and word processors and copy machines, it was quite a job. I needed six copies. Every time a typist would make a typographical mistake, the entire page had to be typed over again. She made few mistakes and typed the whole thing cheerfully and very competently. I repaid her only with my affection.

I am getting ahead of myself in my story, but to my immense satisfaction and for somebody who had only been in the United States for a little more than a year and to whom English was not his first but his third language, I did win the Steinmetz Prize of $100 for best technical writing. I thought it was just wonderful. Anyway, after her typing chores were finished, Helen and I became even better friends and spent all of our free time together.

Helen had a car and one of our pleasures was to drive to Wallace, Idaho, about twenty miles south of Kellogg and go to a honky-tonk. We did a little drinking and mostly danced the two-step. One song that the band frequently played, and that impressed me very much, had lines that I will never forget:

> I'm a-goin', I'm a-goin'.
> I leave you my fav'rite steer
> Because it looks like you, my dear…

What imaginative lyrics I thought.

By the time summer ended, Helen and I were very much in love, but I had to leave. We took tender farewell from each other.

I took a bus to Spokane, Washington, and then went back home to Missouri by train. I had not realized how vast and enormous this country was until I made that train ride. It seemed to take forever. Now that we mostly travel by plane, we don't realize its size so much, but this country is huge.

I was now entering the last semester of my college work. My grades were outstanding, and I was initiated into the Tau Beta Phi honor society, which is, I was told, the engineering students' equivalent to Phi Beta Kappa. I was very pleased. But the question was what to do after graduating summa cum laude. The idea of getting a master's degree intrigued me. Through the help of Dr. Forrester, the chairman of the Mining Department, and my own efforts, I was offered a one-year scholarship by the DuPont company, to conduct research on explosives in the school mine. I was prepared to accept that.

But then I looked at the class just behind me, the Class of 1949. It was much, much larger than our class, because all those fellows who had returned from the war and were going to school under the G.I. Bill of Rights were going to graduate a year after I did, at the same time that I hoped to get my master's degree. I came to the conclusion that getting a good job would be much tougher in the year hence and I therefore decided to abandon the master's degree project and try to find a job instead.

I interviewed with several mining companies and got a couple of interesting offers. While I was thinking of those one evening, Michael, my roommate, said, "Gerardo, there's an interviewer on campus from the Schlumberger Well Surveying Company. They are looking for people to work in petroleum engineering. I understand that the salary is outstanding. They pay $350 a month, and there are all kinds of bonuses associated with it."

I said, "Michael, thanks for the suggestion but I'm a hard-rock miner and I have no experience of working in the oil fields and really no interest in it."

"Gerardo, have a look at the guy. What do you have to lose?"

"All right, I'll go have a look at him."

So I made an appointment with the interviewer whose name was Rolla (really, he was named after the town), T. Wade. He was a division manager of the company, headquartered in Shreveport, Louisiana. We sat at a table across from each other in the interview room. He had a spreadsheet in front of him, which I could read upside down. It had columns labeled "Attitude," "Appearance," "Ability with Words," and two or three others. All the time that we were talking to each other, he made check marks on his sheet. The rows were "Excellent," "Good," "Adequate," and "Poor." I thought it was the funniest thing I had ever seen. In any case, I made good marks in all of his categories and I was pretty sure that I was going to get a job offer. The salary, he told me, was $350 a month, which to me and at that time was a small fortune. In addition, once I got beyond the trial period, I was going to get a $50 per month raise and be paid $6 for every "job" done. A "job" was a service performed in the oil fields. Sometimes there was only one job and sometimes there were two or even three jobs. I also was going to be paid mileage for my car, and for the meals taken in the field. It sounded marvelous as far as compensation was concerned. Still, I felt as though I was somewhat of a "traitor." I had, by then, dedicated ten years of my life to hard-rock mining. Was I going to change now just for a little more money and go into the oil fields? I had to make up my mind.

One thing that I didn't understand during the interview was that Mr. Wade quite obviously did not realize that I was Jewish. The Gerardo and the Spanish accent threw him off. It didn't occur to him and, of course, it didn't occur to me, but the fact was that I wound up to be the only Jew among about 10,000 people who were employees of the Schlumberger Well Surveying Company in the United States. Even then, the Arab influence and the Arab hatred of the Jews were such that no oil company or any company connected with the oil business would hire a Jew. They made a mistake with me, but it worked out all right. Of course, Schlumberger is a good old Alsatian Jewish name. But that was not particularly stressed and certainly would not have been an advantage in the petroleum industry.

In March of 1948, it was more than a month before my graduation, I received a telegram:

> DEAR MR. JOFFE: WE ARE PLEASED TO INFORM YOU THAT YOU WILL BE EMPLOYED WITH SCHLUMBERGER AS AN ENGINEER. PLEASE REPORT TO OUR ABILENE OFFICE ON MONDAY, MAY 17.
> ROLLA T. WADE.

I was very pleased. Even though I had to leave my field of hard-rock mining, I thought it might be a good change for me to learn something totally new and to get into petroleum engineering. It was time for a change – but Abilene? Where in the heck was Abilene? So I went to the library and looked at the gazetteer of an atlas. There were two Abilenes, one in Kansas and one in Texas, both of them in oil country. Texas, however, seemed to be the more likely. I thought it would sound a little stupid if I called Schlumberger and asked which Abilene they had in mind, so I called information for Schlumberger in Abilene, Kansas and found out that there was no such office. Then I called Texas and, sure enough, there it was.

I graduated with highest honors, as number six in a class of over 400. The dean shook my hand, congratulated me, and told me that I had a great future in engineering.

But I knew that he was wrong. I had a dirty little secret, which I knew would keep me from ever being a really good engineer, much less a great engineer. What was that secret? It was that I could not and still cannot today visualize anything in three dimension. I can look at a blueprint and all I see is full lines, dashed lines and dotted lines, but I cannot see the object itself in three dimensions. In intelligence tests that I had to take on occasion, I always flunked the entire section that dealt with spatial relationship, where objects were rotated and you had to tell how many planes or angles are on the other side, etc. I just can't do it. And that is a fatal flaw for an engineer. My brother-in-law, Hugh Cunningham, who is a dentist, told me that they used to have that same problem in dental school. Some students take all the pre-dental work and do very well; then, when it comes for the first time that they have to look into a patient's mouth and work upside down and with a mirror they are totally lost. It isn't quite as important in engineering as in dentistry, but the inability to visualize things from blueprints in three dimensions would be totally unhelpful. Of course, my lack of talent as a draftsman was also a handicap.

Before I reported to Abilene, there was one more thing I had to do. That was to "give closure" to my relationship with Helen Johnson. We wrote each other every week and it was getting pretty steamy. Even though I was totally enamored of her, I was obviously not prepared to make any kind of a "commitment." Also, in more sober moments, I was concerned about the difference in our ages – she was six years older than I. I had a feeling that she had the same idea but still, we were going to meet one more time. So, we arranged to meet in Salt Lake City. It was a beautiful, romantic occasion. The next day, when we kissed goodbye, we both knew that we would never see each other again. We didn't.

I arrived in Abilene, Texas (not Kansas!) as instructed, on Monday, May 17. The boss was a Mr. Wilson who told me that for the first couple of months I was going to work as a junior engineer, being assigned to a senior man who would instruct me and teach me the ropes. "Gerardo," he said, "first of all, find a place to live. Here's today's paper. I'm sure that many places are advertised. If you find something, come back tomorrow morning. If not, don't worry about it and come back on Wednesday."

I took the paper, circled a few likely looking places, took a cab and went to the first one. I rang the bell. An attractive woman in her late 40's or early 50's opened the door. I told her that I wished to look at the room that she had advertised.

"Oh yes," she said, "Come with me, please." We went across a small patio and there was what we would call a mother-in-law suite. In fact, the lady who introduced herself as Mrs. McGregor told me that's what it had been until her mother-in-law had died, not too long ago. The room was nice and large and clean and had a nice bathroom, really just what I'd hoped for.

While I was still inspecting the room, a young woman, perhaps twenty-eight or thirty years old came into the room. A four-year old boy was with her. "Oh, Mr. Joffe," Mrs. McGregor said, "This is my daughter Ellen and my little grandson, Bobbie McGregor."

"This is a very nice room, Mrs. McGregor. But I have some others I want to look at, so let me think about it." At that moment, the telephone in the house rang.

"Excuse me," Mrs. McGregor said, "I'll be right back."

The minute she left, Ellen McGregor (apparently she hadn't changed her name, or maybe she never had another name), turned to me and said, "Don't look at anything else. I want you to take this room. I promise you that you'll like it here." She looked me deep in the eyes. There was an understanding.

The moment Mrs. McGregor came back she said, "All right, look at those other places and stop back in if you like this. Let me know. We'll be glad to have you."

But I thought I should give Ellen the benefit of the doubt. Perhaps she'd really make my life in Abilene very pleasant. I said, "Mrs. McGregor, this is a very nice room and there's no reason for me to look at anything else. So I'll take it."

I was not mistaken about Ellen McGregor and about her meaning. She brightened my otherwise most unpleasant stay in Abilene

I reported to work the next day and was assigned to an engineer whose name I have forgotten but who was from Corpus Christi, Texas, a city I had never heard of before and which I found to be a most unusual name.

I went on my first job with him. The work consisted of lowering an electronic probe called a "sonde" into the drill hole of the prospective oil well. The "sonde" was lowered on a steel cable, which was mounted on a very large drum on the back of a truck. The electric leads inside the cable were connected to electronic equipment in the rear cabin of the truck, which also contained a recorder on which the electrical characteristics of the bore hole were displayed as the sonde descended to the bottom of the hole. On the way up, a record of the characteristics was taken on a film called the electric log. We developed the film right in the field and we were able to interpret the geological formations that had been traversed and where fluids, often salt water, but, hopefully oil, would be found. I though it was intriguing and quite interesting. We also offered other services. The most frequent one was the so-called side-wall coring. For that, we lowered a different tool into the hole and, at the appropriate depths, as located from the original electric log, we would shoot hollow bullets into the formations, bullets powered by explosives that had been loaded into the tool. Those bullets were retrieved on the surface and the contents removed. The geologists would then compare the samples with the electric log and draw their conclusions. Each operation was called a "job," and the engineer received a bonus of $6 for each job performed. I figured that with my $350 base salary, with my $50 promised raise, and performing two jobs a day, I could easily make $500-$600 a month. It was a very substantial pay in those days.

But then trouble started. I observed that, except for the supervisor, all employees in the shop – those who cleaned the trucks, who loaded the guns, who got the equipment ready for the next job, were all blacks, and that all those in the field – the engineers and the so-called helpers (two for each truck) were white. I thought that it was unfair. I remembered Morales in Bolivia, who had helped me so much when I first got to Colquiri, and who had been held back, just because of his skin color. I decided to do something about it now. I complained to Mr. Wilson how unfair I thought it was that the blacks didn't get any of the good jobs and were not given a chance. Mr. Wilson told me – he advised me very strongly – not to meddle in the social structure of Schlumberger's business, that of Abilene, or that of Texas for that matter, and just to do my job and forget about it.

I realized that I couldn't stem the tide and I decided to follow his advice. But in the meantime word had spread and the term "nigger lover" was attached to me. It was about the worst thing that could happen to me. People stopped talking to me, or if they talked to me at all, it was in order to insult me.

I have told you about my little secret, namely that it was impossible for me to visualize things in three dimension or to interpret a blueprint. I had another secret, one that nobody suspected: I couldn't drive. Sure, I had obtained that driver's license in Germany, but that was twelve years ago. I'd never really driven a car. Even in those days, it was expected and taken for granted that every American sixteen years or older could drive a car. One day we were out in the field on a very big job, in which not just the man from Corpus Christi and I, but six other people were involved. All of them were my seniors and my superiors. One of them told me to move a Dodge Power Wagon to another location about 100 feet away. I couldn't drive, but yes, I could do that. I could move it that far in low gear for a short distance. So, I went there and attempted to do that. I turned the key in the ignition, the engine started and…the car burst into flames. I don't know what they had done to it but it was a very nasty prank. I didn't think that I personally was in danger because I would not have had any difficulty getting out of the Power Wagon, but I knew that the vehicle would burn up and that I would be blamed for it. I would lose my job.

Everyone stood around laughing. It was the funniest thing they apparently had ever seen. Ultimately, the Corpus Christi man, who had become somewhat of a friend, came with a fire extinguisher and put the flames out. It was a terrible day. Everyone obviously hated me and they wanted to get rid of me. Frankly, I wanted to get out of there myself. I didn't have to worry. Within two days the "big boss," the division manager from Dallas, came to Abilene and in an almost comically French accent, told me that I just didn't fit into this organization, that in Rome one does as the Romans do, and other such clap-trap. Then he told me that I was fired, that I would be paid to the end of the month, but to leave right away.

Well, I thought that would be the end of my career with Schlumberger, and I wasn't all that unhappy about it. It just didn't work out for me. But then, Mr. Wade, the man who had hired me in Rolla and who was the division manger in Shreveport, heard of my having been fired. He was not too happy about that, not that he had developed any particular affection for me, but it was clear that if anybody got fired whom he had selected and hired, it would be a bad mark against him. So, he called me from Shreveport, Louisiana, and told me that he would give me "one more chance," that I should come to Shreveport just as soon as possible, and that he would reassign me. He repeated to me, "This is your one last chance. You screwed up in Abilene. If you screw up here, you are through."

I said, "Yes sir, I shall keep that very much in mind." I packed up my things, kissed Ellen goodbye, and took the bus to Shreveport.

In Shreveport, Mr. Wade once again repeated his admonition about "one last chance." He told me that he was in charge of four districts, namely Shreveport, Louisiana; Monroe, Louisiana; Tyler, Texas; and Magnolia, Arkansas. I was to be sent to Magnolia, Arkansas to finish my training and that it would be my location after that. He also told me that, since I was going to be the only bachelor engineer in the entire division, he would feel free to send me, as needed, to the other three locations, though I would remain stationed in Magnolia. It didn't sound like a glamorous spot, but I didn't have much choice. Of course, in the long run, because that's where I ultimately met my wife Priscilla, it turned out to be the most wonderful place of all.

I went to Magnolia and was well received by the district manager, Bob Alger, and by all my future colleagues and by all of the employees. The people made a much better impression on me than that racist bunch in Abilene. But I also decided that I would keep my sociological observations to myself. I couldn't change the world.

After about three months, Mr. Alger deemed me to be "ready" and I was sent to the Houston headquarters of Schlumberger to take my engineer's examination. I passed without difficulty, got the promised increase in salary and went back to Magnolia to assume my own crew of four men (two of whom would always be on call). I was told to buy a car in order to be able to drive to the locations when needed. But there was that problem – I couldn't drive. While I was still in Missouri, I had bought a driver's license in a drugstore. It cost fifty cents. No other formalities were required, but still, I couldn't drive. It was a real problem. I understood that the Missouri driver's license would still be valid in Arkansas for one year from date of issue. I had a few months left to go.

On my first free day, I took the bus to Shreveport and went to a second-hand car place that had been recommended to me. New cars were almost unavailable at that time. I bought a Ford Coupe for $1,300. I was very proud of this, my first car. The only problem was that I did not know how to drive it. I told the salesman (who had a nameplate "Call me Vance" on his chest), "Vance," I said, "I'm not familiar with the traffic in Shreveport. Would you drive me across the Red River Bridge toward Bossier City?" It was an unusual request. That bridge was about three miles away and Vance wanted to sell another car and not drive me around. It never occurred to him that I couldn't drive.

"I can't do that, Gerardo," he said, "but I'll drive you out of the lot. Good luck."

So here I was. I had a car, I had to drive it through city traffic, across a bridge, through another city, and then about 80 miles north to Magnolia. I was very concerned. The car was stick shift, of course. It took me the better part of the day to drive to Magnolia. I stopped every couple of miles or so but I didn't have an accident. By the time I got to Magnolia I pretty much had the hang of it, though my shifting was still not too smooth.

I worked hard and did well. The work was quite demanding because we had to be on call 24 hours a day, every day of the month, except for four days a month that we got off. There were no cell phones at the time, of course, and being on call interfered very much with social life, such as it was. I dated a few local girls, but nothing very serious. Romance was invariably interrupted because I had the obligation to call my dispatcher every thirty minutes to see if I had to go on a job. My boss, the clients and the oil operators, seemed to be satisfied with my work and in many cases they insisted that I, rather than another engineer, do the job for them. That was flattering but, even though I liked the extra money, I also felt that I needed some time for myself. And one of the people I did several jobs for and who was always requesting me, was a drilling contractor and oil operator by the name of Jack Kern. He thought that I was great and I felt the same about him. Neither of us thought that the relationship would deepen and become a quite a different one as time went by.

Bob Alger, the district manager, was, just as I, and our boss, Rolla T. Wade, a graduate of the Missouri School of Mines. As a fellow alumnus, I had somewhat of a leg up with him. I liked him very much. He was a religious man, a deacon of the Methodist Church and a member of its choir. He had a very nice baritone voice. After about two months in Magnolia, he asked me to come to lunch after church, around 1 o'clock. I gladly accepted and presented myself punctually at 1 o'clock at his house.

I took some flowers for Mrs. Alger, and they were well received. There were two children, a boy about twelve and a girl about ten. They were a very clean-cut, "all-American" family.

There was some conversation, then Mrs. Alger ("call me Louise"), called us to the luncheon table. There was a nice tablecloth, good china and flatware. There were no wine glasses.

Mr. Alger offered a prayer in which Jesus Christ was prominently and repeatedly mentioned, and that made me somewhat uncomfortable. I wondered why he could not have modified his prayer for the occasion, addressing himself only to the Father and leaving the Son and the Holy Ghost for another time. It didn't occur to him. He meant no harm. The appetizer was lettuce leaf with pineapple chunks covered with mayonnaise. It was exactly like the first dish Mrs. Ruud had served me at my first meal at The *Rancho Exteranjeros* in Colquiri five years earlier. By this time, I had become accustomed, of course, to American cuisine and I liked it fine.

Louise went out to the kitchen and came back with an oval platter that carried a medium sized steak, about the size that I would have for lunch or dinner in Bolivia. She put the platter in front of me and said, "Help yourself, Gerardo."

I said, "Thank you," and put the steak on my plate.

After an awkward silence lasting about ten seconds, Louise said, "Gerardo, the steak is not for you. The steak is for all of us. Please cut off the piece that you want."

I was so embarrassed, I thought I would sink into the ground. What a terrible social blunder. So I cut off a little less than one-fifth of the steak and then passed the platter on which I had re-deposited the steak to my left, for the children and for Mr. and Mrs. Alger to help themselves.

The little incident colored the remainder of my visit. I took my leave early and did not think of this visit as a social success. Much later, I told Priscilla about this incident and asked her how she would have handled it if she had been Mrs. Alger.

"That's so simple," she said. "I certainly wouldn't have embarrassed you that way. I would have let you have the steak and then I would have cast a quick glance around the table and would have said, "You will excuse me, Gerardo, the steak is for you. This is the fifth Sunday (or whatever) after Easter, and we are not allowed to eat any meat." Then I would have gone out into the kitchen and scrambled up eight eggs for my husband, for myself and for the children.

That's very smart, I thought. That would have made me feel good. "How come you would have thought of that so quickly?"

"I learned these things from my mother and from my grandmother," she said. "In those small towns, occasionally the preacher would unexpectedly drop in after church, and, of course, if he was a single man, he would be urged to stay for lunch. Then there were two possibilities: either there was enough food to accommodate the guest or there was not. In the first case, my mother would cast a reassuring glance around the table and whisper the letters 'MIK.' It was understood, 'Don't worry, there's More In the Kitchen.' But if there wasn't enough, she would cast a stern glance around the table and would softly say the letters 'FHB', which meant 'Family Hold Back.' Everyone would then act accordingly. I thought it was awfully clever and wished that Mrs. Alger had done something like that.

One problem of working in the oil fields were the roads. As soon as one got off the paved highways, one would drive on dirt roads that had been bulldozed by the people drilling the well. During rainy weather, those roads could turn to rivers of mud in which a truck and certainly a car could almost disappear and would have to be hauled out by winches and with great difficulty. Late one night, I had the bad fortune of being on one of those roads. I was all by myself, my truck and my crew had left about an hour earlier. I was stuck in the mud. There was no way that I could get out. It was raining buckets at the time. I saw the lights of the derrick about a mile away. They were waiting for me and I couldn't be too late. Downtime on a drilling rig can cost thousands of dollars an hour because men and equipment are tied up standing idle. I got out of the car and started walking toward the lights of the derrick. I had no flashlight with which to illuminate my way. I went through bushes and brambles and my clothes were torn to pieces. I was sopping wet and my clothes were heavy with water and caked with mud. I sat down, threw all my clothes away except my undershorts and T-shirt. I kept my briefcase. I kept my rubber boots on and my hardhat. I walked the rest of the way and I finally got there. People had gotten worried about me, but when they finally saw me – a pitiful figure in his underwear, with boots and a hardhat – they thought it was very funny. I did my job, but I wasn't in great shape. I was scratched and bruised all over my body.

We finished the job, went back to my car in someone else's car, got my crew, and, with their winch, pulled out my car. It was a rough night.

The next day I needed medical assistance for the cuts and bruises that I had suffered in this accident. The nurse made out a report. One of the questions was: "How could this accident have been prevented?" The answer was: "By keeping his pants on." That, of course, caused great hilarity in the office. It was posted on the bulletin board, and underneath were handwritten scribbled bawdy suggestions as to what other "accidents" could be prevented by keeping one's pants on. It was really awkward.

One day, as I was sitting in my office, I got a call from the Missouri School of Mines. I was surprised. What could they possibly want? "Just a minute, Mr. Joffe, Mr. Hubbard, the Registrar, wants to talk to you." Mr. Hubbard came on the line and he said, "Gerardo, I have very bad news. Your friend Sergio has been in a serious car accident. He is between life and death and he might possibly lose an arm. He is in very bad shape and we thought you should know about it. He's been asking for you."

"Thank you," I said. I was very perturbed. I asked Bob Alger, my boss, for time off and drove to Rolla. It was about 400 miles away. Sergio was in the hospital. He was still alive. He had lost his left arm. He was in terrible shape. I felt just awful for him and realized that nothing I could possibly say would be of great help. I said, "Sergio, I know this is awful. There is really nothing I can do to make this right, but I want you to know that whatever you need, I will be available for you." He nodded. I stayed with him for four days. Then I went back home to Magnolia. I was very depressed. We stayed in contact. Between the two of us, we decided that he should shift from mining engineering to mining geology because he could not work in a mine with his handicap, but he could work in an office as a geologist. He thought it was a good idea and he proceeded to do just that. I was able to offer some financial help to him and he finished with his class.

There was one small "bonus" in this sad affair. On my way back to Rolla, I had to go through St. Louis. I arrived there about 4 o'clock in the afternoon. Not having anything else to do I decided to call Ellen Vogel, the one who had wanted to know how tall I was and what sign I was born under. It turned out that she had been right after all. We were indeed quite compatible. Her interpretation of our Zodiac signs had been correct. We spent a long and delightful evening. It was a ray of light in that otherwise very sad journey.

Work in the oil fields, I found out very soon, involves a whole lot of down-time. Understandably, the drilling rig operators don't want to pull the drillstem out of the borehole until the surveying truck arrives at the scene. Time is just too important and too expensive and, of course, they don't worry about the time that <u>we</u> would lose waiting for <u>them</u>. So, more often than not, I might arrive at a location and might have to wait an hour or two until things were ready for me to start my work. After some time, it occurred to me that I could apply that down-time more usefully than by just reading papers, books or magazines. I thought that I might perhaps make a good attorney and thus still fulfill my father's insistent wish. So I decided to enroll in the correspondence law program of the LaSalle Extension University in Chicago. I found it to be an excellent course and very stimulating. They told me that it would take about three years to get through it, and I was prepared to do that. With every lesson I had to turn in an essay about the material covered and answer between 20 and 30 examination questions. I did very well.

Within a year of my studies, my courtship with Priscilla, and eventually being a young husband, did however slow things down considerably. I did graduate from LaSalle about a year after we were married and could have taken the Arkansas bar examination at that time. But I didn't do that because by then I had other plans. I am very pleased, however, having taken that course, because it gave me a good legal education that has been helpful to me throughout my business life.

I was told that I would have to go to Tyler, Texas, for about six months. That was welcome news. I did like it in Magnolia, but it was somewhat of a dead place, nothing much really going on. Tyler, I understood, was a much larger city, I would say that even in those days it had a population of about 100,000. So I drove to Tyler and went ahead doing the same work that I had done in Magnolia, which by now was easy and to which I had become much accustomed. I had no problem, of course, in performing any of the many downhole services that we performed.

Also, I was able to make many new friends. I am still in touch today with some of them, more than fifty years later.

One morning I drove back to Tyler, dead-tired after having pulled an all-nighter in the Rusk County part of the East Texas oilfield. I was tired and I was famished, so I went to one of my favorite restaurants, the one that was popular with all the oilfield people. It was called "The Oil Patch." They had an unusual breakfast menu. The most elaborate and most expensive was called "Superintendent." That was followed by the "Tool Pusher." That was followed by the "Driller." Then, in descending order, the "Derrick Man," and finally the "Roughneck." The "Superintendent" (those were the good old days) cost $1.35 and consisted of a tall glass of orange juice, three pancakes, three scrambled eggs, hashbrown potatoes, a rasher of bacon, a portion of cheese, toast, marmalade and coffee.

I was so hungry that I ordered it. I told the waitress, "Cut the bacon, I don't eat it."

After a while, she brought the whole thing, the pancakes, the juice, the eggs, the potatoes, the toast – everything except the bacon that I had declined. I gobbled it all up, I was so hungry. I asked for the check. She brought it. It was $2.55.

"$2.55," I wondered. I called the waitress. "Miss, there must be an error. It says that the "Superintendent's Breakfast" is $1.35, and you charged me $2.55."

"Yes, but you told me to cut the bacon which makes it *à la carte*. So I have to charge you for each individual item."

"You've got to be kidding. You mean because I didn't get the bacon you would charge me more?"

"Yes," she said, "it's *à la carte*."

I couldn't believe it. She was dead serious. "I'll tell you what." I said, "Bring me the bacon."

"O.K.," she said. She brought me the bacon, which, of course, I didn't eat, and she changed the check to $1.35." She never smiled and was totally matter-of-fact about it. It was really one of the weirdest things that ever happened to me.

Many years later I saw a movie with Jack Nicholson. It was called "Six Easy Pieces"; almost exactly the same thing happened to him. Unbelievable isn't it?

There was a hierarchy in the field personnel at Schlumberger. At the top were the graduate engineers, such as myself, who, among other things, were responsible for and in charge of the equipment trucks that performed the electronic down-hole services in the oil fields. The second category were those who were not graduate engineers, but who had worked their way up to a more qualified level and were allowed to perform only one service, namely that of "shooting." After the casing pipe was set on the well, Schlumberger would bring in equipment that would lower a gun down the cased hole. At a point predetermined by the electrical logging that the engineers had performed, the "shooters," controlling it from the above-ground equipment, would literally shoot holes into the steel casing pipe, allowing the oil (hopefully) to flow into the pipe and come to the surface, either by itself or by pumping. These shooters were supposed to be and actually were less skilled than the graduate engineers and drew less pay. Having, however, worked themselves up from what one might call the ranks, they were usually older than the engineers and in most cases somewhat resentful of those "young upstarts," who were supposed to be so smart and got more money and more respect than they deserved.

The third level of hierarchy were the so-called "helpers" on the trucks, who were, in fact, the crew under the control of each engineer. There were mostly what could be classified as "good old boys."

I had a crew of four helpers, two of whom came with me on every job. One day, late in the evening, we were sitting on a location, waiting for the drillpipe to be pulled out of the hole, so that we could begin our work. We had time on our hands and talked about this and that – mostly about women. A new engineer had been hired. The two men started discussing him. They weren't impressed by him and, quite frankly, I myself thought that he was somewhat of a horse's ass, but I couldn't say that, of course. "How do you like Gilroy? (that was his name)," they asked me.

I didn't quite know what to say so I said, "Oh, I think he is all right, perhaps a little supercilious."

"What?" they asked. "What is super-whatever?"

I tried to explain as best I could. They listened. "Oh," one of them, "you mean chicken shit."

He was serious. I just nodded; it was really a pretty good definition of supercilious.

But there was one level still below them: those were the shop personnel, those who took care of the trucks, repaired the equipment, loaded the guns, and did all the other work required to get the trucks ready and cleaned them for service. Except for the foreman, they were exclusively blacks, and their "social status" was practically zero. One of the most dreadful and annoying things as far as I was concerned, was that we had a Christmas party every year at the Magnolia Inn, the "fine" hotel in Magnolia. It was always a splendid affair, with great food, a little bootleg wine (Magnolia is in dry Columbia County), and even some entertainment. The black employees were not invited. They got $10 each and were asked to buy their own dinner. I thought it was awful. But after my bitter experiences in Abilene, I decided to and managed to keep my mouth shut.

While I was working in Tyler, one of the shooters was one Millard Larsen. He was a crude, somewhat boorish fellow, but otherwise he was O.K. I didn't have too much to do with him. Millard had a health problem, something really bad with his back – a crushed disk, or whatever. He had to have surgery. Even though Tyler had a pretty good hospital, it was decided that this surgery would have to be performed by a back specialist in Dallas. Mr. Thiess, the manager, called us all together and told us that Millard needed several pints of blood, which was not covered by insurance; therefore, he and his family would be very grateful to anybody who would go to Dallas and would put a pint of blood in the blood bank, for which Millard would be credited.

I had days off coming and even through Millard was no particular friend of mine, I decided to be "Mr. Good Guy" and to give a pint of blood for him. So I drove to Dallas, about 150 miles away, and went to the blood bank. I gave my pint and asked that it be credited it to the account of Millard Larsen. After that, I went to the hospital to see how he was doing and to tell him that I'd given a pint of blood for him. He was lying in bed moaning and groaning, with his wife by his bedside holding his hand. "Hi, Millard," I said. "How's it going?"

"Moan and groan," he replied.

I sat there for a few minutes. Then I turned to Mrs. Millard and said, "I think Millard is doing much better." I couldn't see that, but I thought that was the right thing to say.

"Yes, Millard is coming along all right. He'll need several pints of blood."

"Mrs. Larsen," I said, "I've just come from the blood bank and I've given a pint of blood for Millard."

"God bless you. That's really wonderful," she said. "Thank you very much." Then she paused, looked thoughtfully and said. "Isn't that funny, nobody will ever know that he's getting that Jew blood."

"I guess you're right," I said. "Nobody will ever know. Goodbye, Mrs. Larsen. I hope Millard gets better very quickly."

Since I had left Germany in late 1938, and through my years in Bolivia and here in the United States, with the exception perhaps of my membership in the Alpha Epsilon Pi (Jewish) fraternity in Rolla, I had not really had any contact with Jewish people or with Jewish institutions. I thought I should be able to remedy that in Tyler. The first thing I learned was that they had two synagogues, an orthodox one and a reform one. That was an interesting and somewhat new concept to me. I decided that I might be more comfortable being affiliated with the reform congregation. So, at the first occasion, I went there and introduced myself to the rabbi, who seemed happy to see me. He asked me about my background and experience in Jewish life and Jewish education. When he learned that, even after the hiatus of so many years, I was still reasonably competent in Hebrew and had good knowledge of scriptures, he asked me to consider teaching religious school – once a week on Sunday, for three hours – on a pro bono basis, of course. He put a little pressure on me and told me that he really needed a teacher and would be very grateful if I accepted. I told him about my work and that I was on-call 24/7, but that I would look into it to see whether it was possible.

The next day I talked with the district manager, Mr. Thiess, and asked him whether he could work around me on Sunday mornings, because I had to teach Sunday school. He was a religious man and he was quite impressed. "Yes," he said, "we'll arrange that." I don't think he realized that I was Jewish. I certainly didn't mean to keep it from him, but it didn't occur to me to explain it to him.

Teaching Sunday School was really a most satisfying experience for me. I had never planned on doing it, but I did well and enjoyed it. What's more, my pupils, mostly twelve to fourteen year olds, seemed to enjoy my teaching them.

Through my work as a Sunday School teacher, I became involved in the Jewish community of Tyler. I realized that as an eligible single man – and there were quite a few girls of marriageable age around – I was a welcome addition to the community. I had many dinner invitations and met nice and interesting people, also some nice girls.

The girl that eventually became my "steady" was one Doris Gruber. She was, unfortunately, not very pretty and also flat-chested which, being eternally a "breast man," I found (and still find) unattractive. But she was very smart and very entertaining and also a good artist. So, almost by default, we dated almost every evening that I was not working. We became good friends, but any more intimate relationship with her seemed to be unattainable. She told me what nobody (except Mercedes, way back in La Paz) had told me before, namely that she was a virgin and that she wanted to "save myself for my husband." That was that, and I had to accept it. I didn't give her too much argument about it, mostly, I suppose, because I wasn't all that turned on to her.

What became uncomfortable was that she made very strong moves that she wanted to marry me and that I should do something about it. I was noncommittal. Her parents had a nice store on the main square and they told me in private but quite clearly that Doris was their only child and that she would "inherit everything" and that I should keep that in mind. I was not tempted.

There was a play in Dallas that she wanted to see and for which she had tickets, and she asked me to go with her. It was one of my days off and I agreed. So we drove to Dallas which is about 150 miles west of Tyler. About 20 miles out of town she began telling me how much she loved me, that she didn't want to live without me, and that we ought to get married. I said, "Doris, how could we possibly get married if we never had sex with each other? We might be totally incompatible and then regret getting married for the rest of our lives." I was quite proud of myself. I thought it was a very original line. By the time we mulled that argument back and forth, we were in Terrell, Texas, about halfway to Dallas. I stopped in front of a motel. It was 9 o'clock in the evening. I said, "Doris, let's go in here and do it. Then we will know whether we are suited for each other or not."

"Do you promise to marry me if we do it?" she asked.

I thought about that. I had absolutely no intention of marrying here. It was the furthest thing from my mind. But, really, even though she was not the most attractive girl in the world, I had been dating her for so long that by then that I really had, inevitably perhaps, become somewhat sexually interested in her. I felt the relationship's longevity itself should somehow automatically lead to intimacy. But could I lie to that virgin? I decided I couldn't. "No, Doris, I cannot promise that to you but I don't think you should make it a condition."

She started crying. "I just can't do it unless you promise to marry me and I really, really mean it."

"Maybe we should forget it," I said, "and just go on." I started the car and we went to Dallas. I left her at her aunt's and went to a hotel. We saw the show the next day – it was a matinee, and went back to Tyler. We did not discuss the incident, but I did not date her anymore and never saw her again.

Fortunately, my stint in Tyler was over and I was told to report for another extended period in Shreveport, Louisiana. I understand that Doris eventually got married, had two children, had a job as editor of a company magazine for a large oil company, and eventually drank herself to death. She was a nice girl.

I was glad that I was the "bachelor swing man" for the whole district because it gave me occasion to work in different places, meet different people, and, of course, learn more about the geology of the area.

While I was quite involved with the Jewish community in Tyler, I had no such contact at all in Shreveport. There was no reason for it; it just didn't happen. One reason, perhaps, was that I made a big mistake right off the bat. I did something which I had promised myself never to do: I got myself involved with a girl in the office. I always thought that was a bad idea, and I was right. Myrtle was a very beautiful woman, much taller than I, divorced, with a five-year old boy. She and her son lived with her mother. She, too, wanted to marry me and I had a hard time evading it. She did not at all have the same sexual hang-ups that Doris had. One day, I was at the Woolworth store to buy an item that I needed and I saw a counter with brass wedding rings. The rings were the kind that my Colquiri buddy McArdle had bought after the real thing had been dissolved in acid. On the way out I bought one of them, I think it cost $1. I went back to the office where Myrtle was working. I said, "Myrtle, I have a present for you." I took the wedding ring out and gave it to her. I thought it was a good joke. She didn't think it was a joke. She started crying, put her arms around my neck and kissed me. All of the other girls in the office started hugging me and congratulating her. I said, "Myrtle, please wait. This is just a brass ring. It's just a joke." She got very mad, as she had every right to be. She pushed me. She threw the ring on the floor and stomped out of the office. It was certainly the dumbest thing I'd ever done until that day. I actually can't think of anything dumber that I've done since.

I realize that I am talking a lot about women because with the work I was doing, having very little time to myself, always being on call, women had begun to play an important role in my life. Of course, I was about the right age – I was twenty-nine years old and the juices were flowing overtime.

So you can count on more such stories.

I was told to go back to Magnolia and I did, hoping to stay there for the foreseeable future. It was a small town but I knew many people by then, had quite a few friends, and I was quite happy there. I had to look for a new place to live. I found one with Ms. Matt Monroe. It was a nice large room with its own bathroom, a separate entry from the backyard, but also with a connecting door to the main part of the house where Ms. Monroe lived. Ms. Monroe was a widow and the sister of a prominent Arkansas industrialist. She was impressed by her lineage and liked to talk about it. I would say that she was about fifty years old – an old lady as far as I was concerned and totally uninteresting, of course.

One day, after living there for about two months, she knocked on my door in the morning, came in and gave me breakfast. I had not planned on that. That developed into a routine so that every day that I was home in the mornings, she would have breakfast ready for me.

Some time later, she asked me if I would like to have lunch and dinner with her, but I demurred. I thought it was getting a little bit too close, particularly since she made quite clear, that with only the least urging, other services would also be available. I thought about it. Even though she was in her 50's, she was very nice looking and in very sound physical condition. And even though Benjamin Franklin, in Poor Richard's Almanac, gave several reasons why one should take up with older women, I thought it wouldn't do for me to have "everything" under one roof. I declined all beyond breakfast.

But then something really important in my life happened. The MacNaughton Fuel Company, the largest oil company in town, had hired a woman geologist – in itself a rather unusual thing in those days. The woman's name was Betty Rawling. Since the MacNaughton Fuel Company had their offices in the same building as Schlumberger, it wasn't too long until I met her. She was a very good-looking woman, of medium height, a wonderful body and a great smile. She was about my age, maybe a year or two younger. The first time I talked with her, I realized that she was somebody that I could be seriously interested in. There was really nobody else in town, as far as I could tell, that could be my steady woman friend, to whom I could relate, not just physically, but also intellectually. The same was true for her. I was, as far as I (and she) could tell, the only eligible guy for a girl like her.

We became fast friends, saw each other every evening and, since we worked in the same building, several times during the day. She was witty and we were spiritually and intellectually definitely on the same wavelength. Since she was obviously a "nice girl," I took my time before putting even the mildest sexual pressure on her. But when it came to that, I was astonished. She was absolutely and adamantly opposed to any physical contact – not even a kiss. It was a "first" in my, by that time reasonably extensive experience. I kept up the pressure but it was to no avail. It was very frustrating.

One day, Betty gave me a book, *The Well of Loneliness* by Radclyffe Hall. "Please read the book," she said.

"Why do you want me to read that book?"

"If you read the book, you'll understand me a little better."

So I read the book. It was about the experiences of a lesbian girl. I didn't find it particularly interesting. I still didn't understand why she had given it to me. "Did you learn anything?" she asked when I returned the book to her.

"No," I said, "I didn't. I don't think it's a very good book." She didn't say anything.

One day Betty and I decided to go to Little Rock which was her hometown and where her parents lived. For some reason she wanted me to meet her parents – in retrospect, I really don't know why. On a previous date, we had been to a fancy restaurant in Little Rock and we had decided to go there again and have a really good dinner, after seeing her parents. We went to Betty's home and I met her parents, who were nice people. Her father was apparently a fairly high-ranking officer of a major Arkansas bank. After some conversation we said, "We want to go now, we are going out to dinner to a nice restaurant that we have been to before."

"No way," Mrs. Rawling said. "I have prepared a special dinner for you two. Please don't go. Stay here for dinner."

Betty gave me a questioning look, and I said, "Sure, that would be wonderful. Let's have dinner here."

So we sat down at the table and Mrs. Rawling brought in a big ham. There was no way I could eat that ham. It was an utter abomination to me. Betty knew that. She opened her mouth to tell her mother that I would not eat that. I thought it would be somewhat of a scene and I didn't want to embarrass anybody, certainly not Betty's parents. I gave Betty a look, which meant for her to shut up. As the guest of honor, Mrs. Rawling gave me a thick juicy slice of that ham. Not knowing what else to do, I ate it in big gulps. I thought the faster the better. I was the first to finish, but I was about to be sick – I thought I was going to throw up. "Did you enjoy your ham, Gerardo?" Mrs. Rawling asked me.

"Oh yes, Mrs. Rawling, it was just delicious."

"Let me give you another slice," she said. Before I could protest, another thick slice of that dreadful ham landed on my plate. I ate it too in the same way. Then I excused myself. I went to the bathroom and did get sick.

One day we went to Shreveport, about 80 miles south of Magnolia, to see a show. It was very late when we returned. Halfway home she said, "Pull over and stop the car." So I did that. As soon as we stopped the car she put her arms around me and kissed me in the most passionate way. It was very intense and I thought surely that this was the overture of much better things to come. But, it wasn't. "O.K., let's go," she said.

"Wait a minute," I asked her. "What's this all about."

"I just want you to know that I could do it if I wanted to," she said. "Please, let's go."

So I did, but by that time, also because of its being an apparently un-reachable goal, I had become totally obsessed with her. I screwed up my courage and one evening I said, "Betty, let's get married." I actually did say it.

She looked at me and said gently, "Gerardo, you are the best friend I ever had and I am having more fun with you than with anybody I can think of. But I can't marry you."

"Betty, why? Why can't you marry me. I love you and I know you love me."

"I can't marry you, Gerardo, because, believe me, it would never work. You just don't understand." That was that.

I was pretty sure it was because of my being Jewish. There was nothing I could do about that. Despite my being pretty "experienced," I was obviously quite naive in believing that to be the "problem."

Within a few months Betty quit her job and went to Stanford University in California for a master's degree. I ran into her by coincidence once more in my life. After that, I never saw her again.

Ever since I had left home, first when I was sixteen years old, my mother wrote me every week without fail. Even though nothing much happened in her life, she always managed to write four full pages in her small handwriting and on that transparent airmail paper that makes it very difficult to read because the writing from one side shows through to the other. For the last few years, she'd made some very broad hints that she wanted me to find the proverbial "nice Jewish girl and settle down," whatever that meant. After the disappointing experience with Betty I thought that she might have a point. But how to go about finding those "nice Jewish girls?" There weren't any in Magnolia, and I had explored the available pool in Tyler and did not find anybody that I would be really interested in. Even though I was almost totally uninvolved with the Jewish community, it never occurred to me that I would marry a non-Jewish woman. But where to find that "nice Jewish girl?"

So, I started my first direct-mail campaign. The three cities closest to Magnolia that could be expected to have Jewish communities of any size were Texarkana (the closest but also the smallest), Shreveport, and Little Rock. So, I wrote identical letters to the presidents of the sisterhoods of the three congregations, only changing the names, of course.

> Dear Madam:
>
> I am a twenty-nine-year-old engineer working for the
> Schlumberger Well Surveying Corporation in Magnolia,
> Arkansas. This being a very small town, I have no
> occasion to meet Jewish girls.
>
> I am quite sure that there must be eligible girls in your
> community and I would like to meet them if it were
> possible. Could you arrange such a meeting? I would be
> really grateful.
>
> Thank you very much for your courtesy. I am looking
> forward to hearing from you.
>
> Sincerely yours,
> Gerardo Joffe

It was a great success. The first woman who answered was the lady from Texarkana. She told me that they had a very small congregation, that they only had one girl that would fit my specifications, but that, unfortunately, she was away at the University of Texas in Austin – also, she was engaged. So, that was a blank. But the sisterhood ladies from Shreveport and Little Rock told me that they were happy to hear from me, that indeed there were several eligible girls in their community, and that they were sure that they would like to meet me. They invited me to their forthcoming Chanukah party, to be the guest of the congregation. Both letters were almost identical in style and wording and it was difficult for me to make a decision.

Shreveport, of course was in Louisiana and Little Rock was in Arkansas. But Shreveport was much closer and I had worked in Shreveport and had been there countless times. I only had been three or four times in Little Rock in all the years that I had been living in Arkansas.

So, I decided to try my luck in Little Rock. I wrote the lady in Shreveport and expressed my regrets that I wouldn't be able to come and accepted the invitation of the lady in Little Rock.

I went there at the appointed time. I was quite impressed with their beautiful temple, which I thought was remarkable for what couldn't have been a very large congregation. The people were very nice and I got the impression that the congregation was quite affluent. That was all right with me too. If I was going to marry a nice Jewish girl, I might as well marry a rich nice Jewish girl.

The sisterhood lady, I regret that I don't remember her name, introduced me to four girls at the Chanukah party, all of them within a year or two of twenty-five. They were all attractive and I liked every one of them.

I had arranged for a long weekend, a month before, for four days off. I arranged dates with each of those four girls in those four days. I really liked them all.

The first date was with a girl who ultimately wound up marrying a prominent colleague of mine in the mail-order business. To make chitchat, I told her that I knew Betty Rawling who was about the same age and had gone to high school in Little Rock. I told her that I had been friendly with her and asked whether she knew her. "You were _what_ with her," she asked me, "friendly?"

"Yes," I said. She gave me the most peculiar look and changed the subject. I couldn't understand it. In any case, I didn't think it would be a good idea to bring up the subject with the other girls. It was kind of a difficult decision, but I decided to settle on #3, whose name was Faye. She was not a raving beauty, but sort of attractive, funny and obviously a very good sport.

Although it was quite a way, I made it a point to visit her in Little Rock at least every other week. The longer I knew her, the better I liked her. She introduced me to her parents whom I liked right away. They appeared to be the kind of family with which I would be happy to be connected.

Naturally, our courtship was kind of long because I could see her at the most only every other week or so, and she declined visiting in Magnolia. But eventually, without being "committed," we had a "quasi understanding" that we were in what one might call the "pre-engagement state." I don't know that I was madly in love with her, but I decided that if nothing interfered that I was going to marry her. As my mother said, "It was time to settle down," and she was the quintessential "nice Jewish girl."

But then something cataclysmic happened. Magnolia had the usual service clubs, of course, such as Rotary and Lions. But they also had one I had never heard of before, namely the Optimist Club. It happened that one night the Optimist Club was giving a benefit for the Heart Fund and one of my colleagues urged me to go with him to see that show. I had absolutely no interest in that, but he insisted – he didn't "want to go by myself, blah, blah," so finally I thought it would be the path of least resistance to accede and go see that show. It cost $3, which was a pretty good ticket price for those times and for that kind of show.

We had very good seats right close to the front. At first there was a little music, then a girl appeared on the stage who sang a song _Tea for two and two for tea,_ *me for you, and you for me…*and she was dancing to that song. She was absolutely the most exciting, the most beautiful, the most wonderful woman, the sexiest I had ever seen in my life. It was what they call "love at first sight" in novels. I was a little jaded by then and I didn't think that love at first sight really existed, but that is what it was.

What to do? How could I bring myself to her attention, a woman so gorgeous, who obviously had scores of admirers and suitors, even in a small town like Magnolia. Then I remembered the great success I had had in Cochabamba with all those roses to Norma Jean, and I figured that women were pretty much the same all over the world and that what had worked in Cochabamba might very well work in Magnolia also. I knew the woman who ran the local flower shop. Hoping against hope, I called the number, but the shop was closed, of course. So I called her at home. "Rose," (honestly, that was her name) I said, "I need to ask you a favor."

"Anything," she said. "What can I do?"

I said, "Rose, go to the store right away and get me two dozen red roses and deliver them to the girl who is performing in the auditorium at the high school."

"Gerardo," she said, "it's 9 o'clock at night. I don't want to go to the store now. I don't even know if I have roses."

"Please, I've never asked you for a favor before. Do this for me. It's very important."

"O.K."

At the end of the performance, a messenger walked up the aisle and delivered two dozen roses to the performer who had so much impressed me. Quite obviously, she was surprised and quite pleased. It was an unusual thing in Magnolia, to say the least. Naturally, I had added an appropriate card to the flowers.

I was so excited I couldn't sleep well that night. I tossed and turned thinking about that girl whose name I had found out was Priscilla Kern. I knew that my search had ended and that I was going to marry her.

The next day I wrote a letter to Faye, the kind of letter that during the war had acquired the name of "Dear John" letter. It went like this:

Dear Faye,

You and I have been friends for many months and we like each other very much.

But something has happened: I have fallen love with a girl here in Magnolia and I have decided to marry her.
Therefore, I'm afraid that we cannot see each other any more.

You have been a wonderful friend and I shall always fondly remember you and the good times we had together.

I very much hope that you have the same sentiments for me.

Warmest regards,
Gerardo Joffe

I went over the letter several times, changing a word here and a comma there, but that's what I ultimately wound up with. I mailed it. Faye never replied.

So the next day I called Priscilla, introduced myself, and asked when I might come and visit her in her home. She gave me a date for the next day, which was a Thursday at 4 o'clock in the afternoon. They lived on East Parkway.

I spruced myself up appropriately. I went to East Parkway the next day, rang the bell, and the door opened.

In front of me, in the middle of a couch, sat a woman, about forty years old (I later learned that she was forty-two), who was absolutely beautiful, obviously the mother. She had on a red dress, closed at the neck in what I believe is called a mandarin collar. She had black hair, fastened in a bun. She had high cheekbones which gave her face somewhat of an Asian cast. I later learned that she was one-eighth Choctaw Indian, which explains that. She said, in a very nice voice, "You must be Gerardo. Come on in. Priscilla will be here in a minute."

I thought, "Oh my gosh, I'm going to marry this girl, and in middle age she's going to look like that. That's wonderful."

Before Priscilla made her appearance, her little sister came in. Her name was Diane. She was fourteen years old. I though that she was beautiful and well developed. I liked the family.

Then Priscilla came in. I thought she was even more gorgeous than she had appeared on the stage. Things were a little awkward. There were light refreshments and then Priscilla and I left.

Magnolia, of course, is a pretty dead town. One of the hot spots was the Dew Drop Inn, which I thought was a clever name, but it wasn't much of a place. "How about driving to Eldorado?" I proposed.

"That's fine by me," she said.

Eldorado is a somewhat larger town, I'd say 30- or 40,000 people, about 30 miles east of Magnolia, on Highway 79. So, we decided to do that. As usual on first dates, we tried to find out about each other. I gave her my edited life story and she told me about herself. She was born in a very, very small place in Oklahoma; then, as a baby, her family moved to New London in East Texas; she had gone to high school there, then to Texas State College for Women in Denton, Texas, and finally wound up and graduated from the University of Texas in Austin.

"What are you and your family doing in Magnolia?" I asked her.

"Oh, my dad is in the oil business and I'm out of school and I'm helping him in his office until I decide what to do."

Well, I thought to myself, I know what you are going to do. You are going to marry me. But the thing about the oil business intrigued me. It became clear to me that her father, Jack Kern, was one of my Schlumberger clients. For years he had known me very well and I knew him. Fortunately, he had always been satisfied with my work; and I always had a good relationship with him. In fact, he usually insisted that I be the engineer in charge on any of his jobs.

After having explored each other's background, Priscilla started telling me about her work at the University of Texas and offered the concepts of "kinesthesia" and "kinesthetic response," two terms that were totally alien to me and that I had never heard about. I though, oh my gosh, not only is she such a great beauty, but an extraordinary brain. I shall have a hard time keeping up with her." I was right on both counts.

I tried to arrange my work so as to have as many evenings free as I could. We dated almost every evening. My love for her deepened and I began to have the impression that my feelings were being reciprocated.

There was, of course, the matter of which both of us were aware. I was "different." I was foreign, I wasn't even an American citizen yet and, most important, I was Jewish. I quite understood that it was a novelty for Priscilla, and it was certainly a novelty or much more than that to her parents. I was by now a fairly frequent visitor in their home. It was pretty clear that they liked me all right, but I didn't believe that they were overjoyed at the thought of their daughter marrying a Jew and having a Jewish son-in-law.

In those nineteenth century novels, the young girl who was involved with somebody whom her parents believed to be inappropriate, was usually sent on the grand tour to Europe, in hopes that time and new impressions would clear the air and clear her head. My future father-in-law had apparently something similar in mind. After we were dating for about four weeks, he packed up the family, his wife and the two girls, for an automobile trip west, all the way to California and then back again. It was going to take six weeks and while I wasn't told that, the expectation, quite clearly, was that under the influence of new impressions and of the Golden State; Priscilla would overcome that "foolishness" about me.

But, being a meticulous businessman, he had left his day-to-day itinerary with his office so that they could get in touch with him if they had any need. Priscilla, of course, had a copy of that itinerary and she gave it to me. I wrote her every day, by general delivery of the post offices in each town in which they would be scheduled to stay overnight. She told me later that she had a very hard time reading my handwriting, but she did respond every day and to every letter I wrote.

I have told how my mother, for all the years that I had been away from home – and by that time it was almost fifteen years – wrote me a four-page letter every week. I always marveled about what she had to write about and how she could fill those four pages. Her life was uneventful, but that did not deter her. She gave me her observations about events and about things that were quite interesting. I thought she had the spirit of a fine poet or that of an accomplished prose writer.

Regrettably, I was a poor correspondent. I would, perhaps write every two or three weeks and then never more than a page or so. I would tell her about my work, that I had gone to Dallas and that I had met a nice girl or had gone to Shreveport and gone out with a girl there, and so forth. She never particularly commented on that.

I also told her about Faye, the "nice Jewish girl." She was enthusiastic about that, because that "nice Jewish girl" was right down her alley. But she did not comment excessively. She obviously tried to be cool. After I met Priscilla and after our first date, I mentioned, as I thought casually and in one sentence, that I had met this nice girl in Magnolia, that her name was Priscilla, and that I was going out with her. That's all I said.

My mother fired a letter back immediately. Instead of her usual four pages it was only half a page and it dealt with only one topic. After a perfunctory introduction she said as follows: "This shiksa that you plan on marrying, please keep in mind that your father has a bad heart and is not the strongest man in the world. Any serious upset could be very dangerous to him. Love, Mother."

I didn't know what to think of that. First of all, of course, I marveled about my mother's discerning ear, immediately intuiting my intention to marry Priscilla. When she said she was a "shiksa" she took that for granted, because all I had said was that I had met a girl and didn't add the reassuring phrase of "nice Jewish". And then her trying to dissuade me, with what she obviously thought was great subtlety, by citing my father's state of health, which wasn't all that good, but his heart wasn't his principal problem. Of course, this correspondence did not change the course of events.

I waited two days after Priscilla left on the trip with her parents. I asked myself, "Was I really in love? Did I really want to marry this woman or was it just a temporary infatuation?" I thought I should give myself 48 hours to find out. Then I decided that no, this was indeed the real thing. This was the woman with whom I wished to spend the rest of my life. So, I decided to get this thing done, to buy an engagement ring. The easy way to do that would have been to go to Jerome's Jewelers on Magnolia's town square and buy that ring. But even in my excited and love-besotted state, I was able to combine passion with prudence and I decided to drive to Hot Springs, Arkansas, and to buy a diamond ring at one of their famous auction houses.

Hot Springs is the "sin spot" of otherwise quite straitlaced Arkansas. Almost anything goes. One of the great attractions of Hot Springs is its main street, with its row of bath houses on one side and, across from them, fine restaurants and stores, and a great number of auction houses. I had been to Hot Springs several times before, but I wasn't too familiar with the scene. So I went there, got a room in a nice hotel and the next morning, after a massage and mud bath, and other treatments in one of the bathhouses, went to one of those auction places. It was great fun to see the auctioneers in action, warming up their audiences by giving things away and selling others at ridiculously low prices, all in order to get them ready, to warm them up for the "real stuff." The real stuff was jewelry.

I was (I thought) very cool and waited for my chance. I was going to buy a ring anywhere between .75 and 1.25 karats , and it would have to be of top-notch quality. Finally, after all kinds of jewelry, watches and artwork had been sold, a diamond ring came up. It was .82 karats. I asked the auctioneer, "Excuse me, if I bid on this ring, will I get a certificate with it?"

The auctioneer was not prepared for this question. It was out of the ordinary. He was flustered. "Of course you will, but will you now please sit down."

I sat down. The bidding started at $300 and, in increments of $50, it went up to $600. It slowly went up to $700 and then $750. I prevailed at $875. It was a fair piece of change in those days. I bought the ring. "What about my certificate?" I asked the auctioneer. "It should certify that the stone was .82 karats and that it was a first class color, clarity and cut." That's what I wanted. "This is most unusual," the man said, but he did it. I made out my check for $875 and wanted to take my ring.

The auctioneer said, "Just a minute, please." He went to the back room and called the First National Bank in Magnolia, which confirmed that the check was good. He put the ring in a little box and gave it to me. "Good luck to you, he said."

I said, "Thank you." I climbed in my car and went back home.

Priscilla came back after her six-week trip to the western United States. We had been in touch every day by mail. Again, we dated every night and my certainty that I wanted to marry her became clearer and clearer. I had that ring in my pocket all the time, but never mentioned it to her. One evening, about two weeks after she had returned, we were out on a date. It was about 9 o'clock. I called my office and was told that I had to be in Smackover, about 20 miles east of Eldorado, by 11 o'clock. I had about 30 minutes before I had to leave. It seemed like good timing. The ring was right there in my pocket. I said, "Priscilla, would you like to marry me?"

She said, "Yes, I would love to."

That's wonderful. I have a ring here for you. Would you take it?"

"Yes, I will." She put her arms around my neck and kissed me.

I told her that I was very sorry, but that I had to go on a job and would see her tomorrow. I thought it was the best way to do it – sweet, but no great scenes.

The next day I called her and asked her if I could visit her parents. I wanted to tell them myself about our impending marriage and wanted their blessing or approval or whatever one calls that. So I did just that. I went there the next day. Mr. Kern shook my hand and wished me well. Mrs. Kern hugged my neck and shed a tear or two. Diane, the little sister, seemed to be the most enthusiastic of the bunch. I knew that there were reservations on the part of her parents, but I could not help that. The real test was still to come.

All this happened in the middle of September of 1951, so now we had to decide when to get married. Always thrifty and with an eye on the tax man, I suggested that we should get married before the end of the year. Priscilla, like most women, had her own schedule and decided that Friday, December 28, would be the right day. That was fine by me.

Now came the hard part. "Priscilla, there is one important thing."

"What is it?" she said.

"I have to ask you to convert and become Jewish." I had decided not to talk about that before I had asked her to marry me. It could have been construed as a condition. But I don't know what I would have done if she had declined. Would I have gone ahead with this marriage? I've often asked myself that. But I believe that I wouldn't have. Her becoming Jewish and eventually having a Jewish family was most important to me. My request came as no surprise to her.

She said, "I knew it was going to come up and I don't have any real problem with it. Frankly, you are only the second Jewish person I've met in my life; the first one was Professor Sofer – he taught scene design at the University of Texas. I liked him very much." And then she continued, "I am not too connected with the Christian religion, and I believe that if we're going to have a family, it would be best if all of us had the same religion. How do I go about becoming Jewish?"

"You have to take instructions," I said, "from a rabbi. The closest rabbi is in Texarkana so that is where we should go."

"One thing," she said, "I'll do that, but you have to do something for me."

"What's that?" I asked.

"You have to become an American citizen. I would not want to marry you without it."

Well, that was no real problem or "sacrifice" at all; I had, of course, planned on doing that all along. In fact, I had been studying for that for the last month or so. I promised her I would do that – no problem at all.

So about three days later, my having made an appointment by telephone, we went to Texarkana and met with the rabbi of that small congregation. He was elderly, had a short beard and seemed to be a very nice man, but he told us that he would not do the conversion. "Why not, Rabbi?" I asked him.

"I cannot be convinced of this young woman's sincerity of truly becoming Jewish and joining the Jewish people. I think it is very likely that she wants to become Jewish only in order to marry and I don't want any part of that. I wish you lots of luck but I don't wish to do that."

It was a grave disappointment to me and it certainly was a turnoff for Priscilla.

"What should we do now?" she asked.

"Let's go to Shreveport and try our luck there."

We did just that. Rabbi Lefkowitz was a young man who seemed to be very much "with it." He was also the chaplain of the Louisiana chapter of the Veterans of Foreign Wars. He immediately accepted the task. He gave literature to Priscilla, told her to study, and to return within two weeks for personal instruction. He told her that it would take about six or eight weeks. He asked her to give her full attention, to be fully instructed, and to be able to become a convert in sincerity and in good faith. Priscilla accepted that.

So she studied for about two weeks. I helped her all I could. Then, I drove her back to Shreveport, for about one hour of instruction from Rabbi Lefkowitz, and we repeated that three times. On the third time, he conducted a small ceremony with her, by which he accepted her into the Jewish faith. Priscilla seemed to be quite sincere about it. I was very happy and greatly relieved. I realized that this could not have been entirely easy for her and for her parents. I suppose it wasn't.

I had promised Priscilla that I would become an American citizen. That was not a real sacrifice, of course, because I had planned to do that all along. I had applied for citizenship to the Federal Court in Texarkana and they sent me ample study material to prepare myself for my citizenship examination. I notice that today, several thousand people, most of them not speaking any English and not having the foggiest notion about American institutions, get sworn in as citizens en masse. In those days it was entirely different.

Priscilla and I went to Texarkana, a town lying half in Texas and half in Arkansas, at the appointed day and time and, per my instructions, I presented myself in Room 302 at the Federal Courthouse for my examination. There were two men, and they grilled me in turn. Here are some of the questions they asked me, taking turns with each other:

- What is the Bill of Rights and how did it come about?
- Explain the Third Amendment to the Constitution.
- Explain the three branches of government and their respective functions.
- What were the origins of the War between the States (that's what they called the Civil War in the South)?
- What are the Federalist Papers?
- Who was James Madison and what did he accomplish?

There were about ten more questions like that and I was expected to give detailed answers to all of them. I did very well.

Then came what turned out to be the last question. "What is your view on fornication?"

"I beg your pardon," I asked.

"What is your view on fornication?" the questioner repeated.

"Excuse me, sir, what is fornication?"

They looked at each other. "Fornication is the act of sexual relations between unmarried people. What do you think of that?"

"Could that be a trick question," I asked myself. But obviously not, the man was serious. "Fornication," I replied with righteous indignation, "I think it's terrible. It should be outlawed."

"It is," my interrogator helpfully said. "It is illegal both in Arkansas and in Texas."

I realized that I had passed the test.

"Please wait in the anteroom and we will be with you in a few minutes."

I was not concerned. After a few minutes, both men came out, shook my hand, and congratulated me. They led me into the judge's chamber who swore me in as an American citizen. I was very proud. The judge told me that my naturalization papers would be mailed to me within two weeks.

I told Priscilla that I was now an American citizen. She was overjoyed because deep down inside she wasn't really quite happy about getting married to a "foreigner."

We had a very short engagement, less than three months, which was about the minimum time needed for Priscilla and her mother to get every-thing ready for the wedding. It does seem unusual in retrospect, considering that today the practice seems to be for people to live together for five or ten years before they decide whether or not they should get married.

One evening, about a month after we got engaged, Priscilla called me. She was crying and she told me that she needed to see me immediately. She had to make a confession and she would not blame me at all if I were to cancel the engagement. "Please come over right away," she told me, "this just cannot wait."

"What could that possibly be?" I thought. It could only be one of two possibilities: Either she had been married before or she had a baby that was stashed away somewhere – perhaps both. I decided that neither would be a problem and, in fact, if there was a baby, I would welcome it because I felt that being a father to her child would cement our relationship right away. In any case, I was prepared for whatever it might be.

I got to her house in about five minutes. There she was in tears. "What is it, sweetheart?" I asked her, "you can tell me anything and there will be no problem."

The big confession was that she was three courses short from graduating from the University of Texas. Nobody knew it. I was the first person to whom she had confessed. Her parents were under the illusion that she had graduated. Of course, I was vastly relieved. I thought it was kind of funny that she would make such a big issue of it. She thought I might not wish to marry someone who was not a college graduate. I had a hard time keeping a straight face. "What are the courses you are missing?" I asked her.

"French, Anthropology and Twentieth Century European History."

"I'll tell you what," I said, "I am sure that the University of Texas, just like any other university, would let you take these three missing courses by correspondence, and then you can graduate. Let me suggest that you take Spanish instead of French, because I can be a real help to you with that. We will get it done, no problem at all."

She hugged me and was greatly relieved that I had not taken it as a setback. Of course, it really didn't matter to me at all.

She completed the courses within the year and received her diploma attesting that she had obtained her B.A. in Fine Arts from the University of Texas.

She hung her diploma on our living room wall. Just in case her parents may have had any doubts, they could now see that she had indeed graduated.

So we had less than two months for getting married and everything and everyone was focused on that, of course. I spent much time with my new family and a couple of minor mishaps occurred, which were a little embarrassing to me, but they really didn't change the relationship.

The Kern's had a white piano in their living room, which was pretty old. It played fairly well, but there was one thing wrong with it. The middle E stuck and wasn't operative. One would have to avoid several major and minor keys in order to work around it. It made playing quite awkward. So, very valiantly, but ill-advisedly, I offered to fix the piano and to unstick that key. I thought that my musical insight and my mechanical dexterity would impress both my bride and her family. Unfortunately, in my attempt to make this repair, all the innards of the piano, which were utterly fragile, fell apart. By the time I got through, nothing at all worked, and the piano was useful only as a somewhat dubious piece of home decoration. Whatever faith that Priscilla and her mother had in my mechanical ability was gone.

The other thing had to do with marzipan, which is a German delicacy, particularly popular around the Christmas holiday, but of which nobody in Magnolia had ever heard. So I asked my mother for the recipe and also for the recipe of Aunt Jenny's chocolate fish. She sent both.

The chocolate fish was a great success, just as good as I remembered it from Aunt Jenny, but the marzipan was a total disaster. One of the ingredients of marzipan is rose oil which is, of course, not readily available in stores, certainly not in Magnolia. So, I went to the Wilson-Bearden Pharmacy on the main square and asked for rose oil. Mr. Wilson looked it up in his big pharmacology book and told me that, yes, he could get it from his wholesaler in St. Louis, but it was dreadfully expensive – $250 (in those days!) for one ounce, the minimum quantity one could buy.

"$250?" I asked. "Why is it so expensive.

He called his wholesaler in St. Louis and the explanation was that it was only produced in Bulgaria or someplace like that and that it took something like an acre of roses to make one ounce of the stuff.

I told him that I could not afford that and I was about to leave. He called me back. "Gerardo, I see here that we can also buy synthetic rose oil which, it says here, is just as good as the real thing. It is much less expensive, only $2.50 for four ounces, the minimum quantity." So we ordered that.

The main ingredient of marzipan is blanched almonds. So we worked on that. We ground the almonds to a paste. Then the recipe called for adding four drops of rose oil per pound of almond paste. We decided to enhance the taste somewhat and put in one-quarter cup of the precious ingredient. Not only was the resulting mess impossible to eat, but the whole house smelled of roses for two weeks and had to be aired with fans both day and night. It was a minor disaster.

I learned quite a few things in the two-month period between our engagement and our wedding, things that I had never known about. First of all, my future mother-in-law "commanded" us to see Dr. Weber; in order to learn about "matrimonial relations," also that Priscilla should have a "pelvic examination," which sounded very mysterious and which, apparently, she had never had before. After the examination, which she passed with flying colors, Dr. Weber took us into his private office and explained about "marital relations." What he tried to explain was how to have sex without having a baby. That was long before the pill, of course, and there was only one reasonable way of how to avoid having a baby. I knew that, of course. It was somewhat of a yawner, but I listened with feigned attention as Dr. Weber explained patiently what a condom was and how to apply it.

Another thing I learned and which I found quite intriguing was about brides "registering" their preferences for silver, china, and crystal. Priscilla registered with Jerome's Jewelers on the main square of Magnolia, and I remember her choice of silver. It was Contour by Towle. People gave her a teaspoon, a knife or a fork, some real sports gave two or three pieces, some others a full setting. The grandest present came from Faye, the one that I had ditched for Priscilla. She gave us a full salad serving set, which was the most expensive item on the roster of pieces. I thought it was very cool, even extremely generous. I had invited her to the wedding, but she declined and decided not to come. I think it was too painful for her and it would have been somewhat awkward for both of us. The only person that was really unhappy about my getting married was Matt Monroe, my landlady. Even though she was twenty or thirty years older than I, she firmly seemed to expect that I would become her lover and establish some permanent relationship with her. My getting married spoiled that altogether. She pouted, didn't give us a present and did not come to the wedding, even though she was invited, of course.

Three days before the wedding, I met an old family friend, a contemporary of my future father-in-law, Bill Stewart. He owned the big trucking company in town. He congratulated me on getting married and that I was getting such a "fine girl." He asked me where we were going to get married and who was going to marry us. I told him that we were going to go to Shreveport and be married by Rabbi Lefkowitz. He was somewhat taken aback because he had never heard of anybody being married by a rabbi. I'm not sure that he quite knew what it was. He wanted to say something nice. "Rabbi Lefkowitz?" he asked. "Yes, I've heard of him. I understand that he is a very fine Christian gentleman." It was the highest compliment he could bestow. Then he said, "You have your Louisiana marriage license don't you?"

"My what?" I asked, "my marriage license?"

"Yes, you can't get married without a marriage license."

"Where do I get that?"

"Well you can't get it here if you're going to get married in Louisiana. You'll have to go to Louisiana to get it."

So, having only two days left, I jumped in my car and drove south to Homer, Louisiana, the closest Louisiana county seat and got that license. It was quick and only cost a dollar. A very good buy and certainly a great investment! Wow, I almost blew that one.

I asked Sergio to be my best man. As bad as he felt, he came down from Rolla to stand up for me. He looked very pitiful. He was such a tall and handsome man, but his left sleeve was empty and tucked into his coat pocket. He handled it very well, better than I perhaps could have handled it.

Priscilla had a friend from the office, JimmyLee Bean, as her maid-of-honor, so we all went down to Shreveport in two cars. Sergio and I and Diane, Priscilla's sister, in one car, and my future in-laws, Priscilla and JimmyLee in the other.

Rabbi Lefkowitz was what I thought of as very "attuned." He obviously was experienced in these kinds of interfaith marriages and understood that it wasn't easy for the non-Jewish parents. The rabbi conducted a fairly brief but quite beautiful ceremony. I stomped on the glass and we were married.

Mr. Kern took us all to a famous Shreveport fish restaurant. I remember all of us having a flounder dinner. Then he asked me, "Gerardo, will you do me a big favor?"

"Of course, Mr. Kern, what is it?"

"I want us to go back to Magnolia and I want you to be remarried or have your marriage blessed and reconfirmed by the minister of the Methodist Church. I would be grateful to you for doing that."

I though for only two seconds. It was not at all what I wanted to do, but then I realized how important it was for my in-laws and that I really owed them that. They had been loving and understanding about the whole thing. So we went to the Methodist Church in Magnolia. The pastor, Brother Holzendorf, was equally "sensitive" to my needs; he blessed our marriage, but Jesus Christ played no role in the proceedings.

There was a nice reception at the Magnolia Inn, the local hotel. Then we were off or our "honeymoon" in Hot Springs, Arkansas. I put the word "honeymoon" in quotation marks, because, since I only had four days off a month, two of which I had already taken, we only had two days, probably one of the shortest honeymoons on record.

Hot Springs is about 100 miles north of Magnolia. By the time we were about mid-way, I asked Priscilla, "Sweetheart, how much money do you have?"

She said, "Let me see." She looked in her purse and told me she had $3.75.

I asked her, "Priscilla, didn't your father give you any money to start your married life?"

"No, he didn't give me anything at all."

I thought that was kind of strange but, I thought, other people, other customs. So I took out my wallet and gave her a hundred-dollar bill, which I had set aside just for that purpose. "Oh, you don't have to do that," she said, "I don't need it."

"Priscilla, you have to realize that we are now married. My money is your money. We're just putting it into another pocket – yours instead of mine."

She thought about that and said, "You're right, we're married. I have to get used to it." Then she told me "I don't want to have any children for at least the first year because I want to enjoy married life unencumbered by pregnancy, so you know what to do to avoid that." I thought it was a somewhat unusual request – was she perhaps just trying to check me out for a year before being totally "committed?" I couldn't really blame her. Obviously, she had been thinking about that. And yes, I knew what to do to avoid that.

The honeymoon, brief as it was, was wonderful and unforgettable. No question, I had married the right woman.

On the day following the wedding, I took her to the auction house where I had bought the engagement ring. "This is something you have never seen before," I told her, "but be careful. These are wonderful sales people and they are going to try to sell you something. Don't open your mouth."

"O.K.," she said.

So we went in and the man immediately recognized me from my previous purchase and made a big deal to the entire audience about newlyweds. He made us take a seat in the first row.

He went through his usual spiel, selling crystal, silverware, power tools and all kinds of things at bargain prices. Then he came to the jewelry. He said to the crowd of about 100 people: "You see these newlyweds sitting in the first row?" Then he posed a rhetorical question: "What is it that those folks least need?" And he answered the question himself: "The one thing they don't need is an engagement ring, do they? Now watch me, I'm going to sell them one." To make a long story short, he did just that. With our limited resources we bought, or rather were sold, another diamond ring. The man was a real artist.

That evening we went to a semi-kosher, in any case Jewish, restaurant and had a delicious meal of things that Priscilla had never eaten before – typical New York-type Jewish dishes. We topped the meal off with a tasty cheesecake. Priscilla was delighted with it; it was a novelty to her. The owner's wife was at the cash register. Priscilla asked her, "That cheesecake was so delicious, what kind of cheese do you use in it?" The woman gave her a baleful stare and said, "It took me twenty years to perfect the recipe for this cheesecake. Do you think I'm going to give it away to somebody just by her asking for it?"

Priscilla was appalled and so was I. I was very embarrassed. It was the first Jewish person besides myself and that professor at the University of Texas that Priscilla had ever met. I thought that it reflected badly on the people she had just joined. It was not a good experience.

Priscilla, even though born in a tiny place in Oklahoma and brought up in almost as tiny a place in East Texas, spoke English without any discernible regional accent, without any of the twang that is so typical of that part of the country. Nobody else I knew in Arkansas or in Texas spoke as she did. The reason she spoke so well was that she had taken a course in diction at Texas State College for Women,

Cutting the wedding cake with Priscilla. It was the happiest day of my life, and to marry Priscilla was the most wonderful and smartest decision I ever made.

Members of our wedding party in Rabbi Lefkowitz's study. My best man and best friend, Sergio Marinkovic, is on the left. He had lost his left arm. Next to him is my sister-in-law Diane, then the happy couple, and Priscilla's mother Vera Kern.

and all those diphthongs, "caow" for cow, and other such things were absent from her speech. I loved to hear her talk. She made a real effort, not perhaps entirely successful, to iron out my own speech, which was, of course, affected by both German and Spanish accents. She taught me that "awry" is not pronounced to rhyme with "hoary." She taught me that the word "series," has only two syllables, not three. And, she taught me that the word "character" is accented on the first, and not on the second syllable. We drilled such sentences as *The color of the caller's collar is colored*, which had all sounded pretty much the same to me before she took me in hand. While I still don't sound as though I was born in San Francisco, I would sound much worse were it not for Priscilla's tutelage.

By that time I had become somewhat dissatisfied with my job. There was nothing really wrong with it and the pay was pretty good, but I couldn't see it leading anyplace. There was no "career path." I had finished my law course with LaSalle and had graduated. Perhaps I could do something with that – take the bar exam and become an attorney.

Also, having to be on call at all times was disruptive to the family life that we were trying to establish. Even when we were at the theater to see a movie, suddenly, in the middle of the show, a flash would appear on the screen, "Gerardo, call your office immediately." My office had called and I had to go out on a job right away.

Without telling Priscilla about it, I wrote to the Colorado School of Mines and applied for a scholarship to get a master's degree either in mining engineering or in electrical engineering. When I told Priscilla about my application, she asked, "Why do you want to do that? How will getting a master's degree in engineering change things? Do you want your boss's job, because that's what you might be getting if you get a master's degree?"

What a clever question, I thought. No, I definitely didn't want my boss's job, so getting a master's degree in engineering was not the answer to what had begun to be a somewhat nagging problem for me.

By that time, a year of marriage had passed. It was wonderful. I had never been so happy in all my life. I was so delighted that I had done the right thing and I had the feeling, and Priscilla confirmed it, that she felt the same way.

Schlumberger had a neat rule. If you took your vacation in the summer, you got two weeks. But, if you took your vacation in the winter time, which nobody wanted, you got three weeks. So I chose that, and almost exactly one year after we got married, we drove to Aspen, Colorado, for our "real" three-week honeymoon.

We booked lodging at the Prince Albert Hotel, which was one level down from the top and where "young professionals" like ourselves congregated. Priscilla learned to ski and seemed to enjoy it. I relearned my skiing because, what I had learned in Germany was totally useless with the modern equipment. The ski school in Aspen taught the Austrian so-called Arlberg system of skiing, which was in vogue at that time. The principle was that, in order to make a turn, you had to throw your shoulders in the direction of the turn. I can still hear our teacher, Friedl, calling "Shoulders, shoulders, shoulders" when he felt we hadn't given a turn enough emphasis. Both Priscilla and I earned the coveted Two-Bell pin, which was awarded for skiing Ajax Mountain from top to bottom all the way down, without falling and in what the instructor considered good form. We were inordinately proud of our pins.

One day at lunch, we met a couple about five years older than we, Bob and Ellen. They lived in a fancy suburb of Chicago. He had what sounded like an exciting job at an investment banking house. He hinted at making a very good salary. He then told us that he was a graduate of the Harvard Business School. I was a little envious. That sounded so exciting – to work in an investment banking house, instead of sloshing around in the oil fields, never to get muddy, not to have to get up in the middle of the night, and to make a nice salary besides. I had heard of the Harvard Business School, but he personified it for me. After lunch, I said to Bob, "Let's go back for another few runs."

"Maybe later," Bob said, "We're now going to have our noonie."

"Your what?" I asked.

"Our noonie," he said.

"What is a noonie?"

"Don't you know what a noonie is? Where have you been? A noonie is making love at mid-day."

We had never made love at mid-day. It sounded terribly exciting to me and I believe also to Priscilla. I too wanted a job where I could have noonies. Schlumberger wasn't it. The Harvard Business School began to be much on my mind.

Of the many people that I knew in Magnolia there were a few that I admired and one or two after whom I wished to pattern myself. One of those was Bill Lisman. He was an independent geologist and consulted with oil companies in the area. He apparently got "a piece of the action" as part of his fee in every deal on which he worked. He was about ten years older than I, somewhat of a role model. His wife Marian was an educated, elegant and most attractive woman. They had no children. About four or five months after we got married, Marian called Priscilla and asked her to come to dinner next Friday night. Priscilla said she would consult her calendar (a joke!); then she called back and told her that we were available and would love to come.

On the appointed evening, we went to their very beautiful home, impressive in every respect and something that we hoped we could one day emulate. Marian served a very nice dinner – an interesting spicy soup, a filet garnished with what I later found out was Bernaisse sauce, and a high-class dessert involving exotic fruit (kiwi, as I learned later) and chocolate chips. There was also a bottle of very nice wine – a novelty for us. I was impressed by the sophistication of everything. After dinner was served, she picked up the dishes and took them to the kitchen. Priscilla helped her. I, wishing to be the great American husband, also got up and took some plates into the kitchen. She said, "Gerardo, please do not come into the kitchen. You see Bill sitting there in that easy chair? There's another chair next to his. Why don't you sit there and talk to him. When we come out of the kitchen, I'll tell you why I want you to do that."

So the two women did the kitchen chores and when they came back, Marian said, "Gerardo, I want to tell you why I didn't want you to come into the kitchen. When Bill and I got married, about ten years ago, he wanted to help me in the kitchen and I told him, 'Bill, I don't want you to help me in the kitchen. I want you to sit in that easy chair and I want you to think how you can get me out of the kitchen, rather than helping me with the dishes.' He took my advice and he has done that and has done it successfully. I go into the kitchen only on weekends, when the maid isn't here. You should do the same thing. Let Priscilla do the kitchen work and you think about how to get her out of that."

I thought that was an absolutely brilliant idea and wonderful advice, and I have patterned my life accordingly. I never went into the kitchen to help. I sat in my chair and thought about how to get Priscilla out of the kitchen. It worked. She goes into the kitchen only on weekends when the maid isn't there.

Priscilla told me, about fifteen months of marriage having passed, that she now wanted to have a baby. With what must have been an astronomical sperm count and excess of testosterone, I succeeded to make her pregnant at the very first try. My concerns about Dr. Leider's "last ditch" treatment of the eczema on my buttocks – the repeated zapping of my testicles with x-rays – fearing that it would make me sterile – were utterly unfounded. We were both very happy and so were Priscilla's parents. My parents were happy too, I suppose, but they were far away in Argentina and, sad as it was, they didn't play a big role in my life any longer.

In those days, of course, there was no way of predicting whether the baby was going to be a boy or a girl. It was always a surprise. Who knows, maybe it was better that way. My mother-in-law, who, my being "foreign," was always afraid that I might do something very strange, asked me, quite tentatively, what we would call the baby if it were a boy. "Anastacio," I said, without hesitation. I have no idea why I thought of that name. It just popped into my mind. I knew it would appall her. I must have thought of General Somoza, the dictator of Nicaragua, who was the only Anastacio I had ever heard of – and of President Roosevelt when told that Somoza was a son-of-a-bitch, was reported to have said, "Yes, he is a son-of-a-bitch, but he's our son-of-a-bitch."

"Anastacio," she said, with only thinly disguised apprehension. "What kind of a name is that?"

"It's a proud Spanish name," I told her in mock seriousness "and that's what I'm going to call my son."

"But what are you going to call him when you talk to him?" she asked. "You can't call him Anastacio."

"I'm going to call him Tacho," I said.

"I see," my mother-in-law said with barely hidden dismay. Hoping that I would think of something more acceptable if the baby were a girl, she asked me what I would do in that case.

"I'd call her Anastacia."

"Anastacia?" she said. "For heavens sake, what are you going to call her when you talk to her?"

"Tacha," I said.

She was very, very concerned that her first grandchild was going to have such a name. She fretted about that continuously, but she refrained from arguing about it with me.

Doctor Sizemore, who had by now supplanted Dr. Weber as the family physician, determined that the baby was going to born on Christmas Day, December 25. By the time Priscilla was eight months pregnant, she was so big that I thought it was a miracle that she could move at all and that she didn't pop open like a overripe melon. Her mother had given me an ointment called "Mother's Helper" with which I had to massage her tummy, which was as tight as a drum and as shiny as a mirror. I did that every evening before going to sleep. I thought she would burst. I had never seen anything like it.

Christmas came around and there was no baby. The 26th and the 27th came and went and still no baby. The 28th was our wedding day, and still no baby. I was somewhat concerned because I fully expected and planned on this baby being a tax deduction, by being born before the end of the year. On December 30, I called Dr. Sizemore and asked him to please "do something" to make sure the baby would be born before the end of the year. "Don't worry, Gerardo," he told me, "I'll do something."

On December 31, 1953, the baby not yet having been born, I had to leave early on a job in Miller County, about 60 miles west of Magnolia. I came back at about 4 o'clock in the afternoon, hoping to be a father, but I was not. Priscilla was still very visibly pregnant. "Did Dr. Sizemore give you something to make the baby come?"

"Yes," she said, "he sent me to the Wilson-Bearden Pharmacy to pick up something to induce labor."

"Did you pick it up?"

"Yes, I did and I took the medication" (which I believe was quinine or something like that).

"How long did he say it would take before you will have the baby?"

"Twelve hours after taking the medication," he said, "without fail."

"What time did you take the medication?"

"At 2 o'clock in the afternoon."

"Priscilla," I said, "we won't have the baby this year. The baby will be born in the new year about 2 o'clock in the morning. We are losing the tax deduction."

"Who cares," she says, "we're going to have a baby and that will be wonderful."

I conceded that she was right.

We went to the hospital at 3 o'clock in the afternoon. She got a private room, which I clearly remember cost $9 per day. I thought it was a little steep, but what the heck, it was an important occasion. I took off from work for the rest of the day and walked up and down the hallway most of the time. I must have smoked two packs of cigarette during that time. There were twelve patient rooms off that hallway, six to the left and six to the right. Two of them were open; patients were lying in oxygen tents in both of them. I asked the nurse, who was a friend of the family, who those people were. One of them was a forty-year-old woman from Stephens, Arkansas, about 30 miles away. I didn't know her. The other was a man from Magnolia, thirty-five years old, whom I knew fairly well. Both of them were dying of lung cancer. "Lung cancer," I thought, "my God, and here I am smoking like a chimney." As those thoughts went through my mind, I heard the crying of a baby. It was my son. I took a last long drag off my cigarette, threw it on the floor, ground it out, and said to myself, "This is the last cigarette I shall ever smoke in my life. I am not going to have my son see his daddy have such an ugly vice." I haven't smoked a cigarette since. That was almost fifty years ago.

The baby was born at 2 o'clock in the morning on January 1, 1954, just as I had figured. I went home and I was exhausted. I crawled into bed and slept. I woke up about 10:30 in the morning. I made myself a cup of coffee and went outside to pick up the paper, the *Magnolia Banner News*. There was: "Michael Kern Joffe, first baby of the year in Columbia County." My mother-in-law, the dear lady, being fearful that I would carry out my threat of naming the baby Anastacio, had preempted the situation and had named the baby herself. It was an unusual thing for her to do, but it was a good choice, and both Priscilla and I were quite happy that she had preempted us and had picked that name.

A big ado was being made of our having the first baby of the year in the county. The bank gave Michael a $50 savings bond, we got a year's free diaper service, we got a set of dishes, all kinds of baby gifts and, of course, mention in the local press. It was worth losing the tax advantage and also, who wanted to be born on December 31? January 1, to be a New Year's baby, was much better, wasn't it? Everyone was very happy.

But now that I was a "family man," the Harvard Business School (and quite frankly, also those noonies) stuck in my mind. I decided to write to the Business School and seek admission. As it turned out, even in those days, before affirmative action, Harvard was somewhat interested in "diversifying" its student body – but, apparently, not too radically. Having somebody with a first name of Gerardo and from Magnolia, Arkansas, sounded like a twofer – Hispanic and Southern. Having reviewed my college transcript and my work record, they informed me that I would be accepted, subject to an assessment and interview with one Robert Miller, an alumnus and graduate of the Class of '48. He was the president of a lumber company and of a small railroad in Crossett, a town about 60 miles east of Magnolia.

I, and (it was emphasized) my wife had to meet with Mr. Miller in Crossett on Monday, September 13 in 1954. Mr. Miller was a nice man. It wasn't much of an "examination." He invited us to lunch and I had the feeling that he approved of our table manners. But mostly I thought he wanted to make sure that we were of the "Caucasian" race, or something very close to it, because in those unenlightened days, there were no blacks at the Harvard Business School, except for one man from Ethiopia who was, we were told, a nephew of Emperor Haile Selassi.

Within a week of our visit to Mr. Miller, we got a letter from the Harvard Business School that I had been accepted to the Middle Management MBA Program and that classes on the Boston campus would start on Monday, January 3, 1955. My life was about to change.

The Middle Management MBA Program of the Harvard Business School was an experimental program that had been suggested by the Westinghouse Corporation. It was designed for people who had between five and ten years of actual business experience. The first year of this two-year program started in January of the year instead of in September of the preceding year, when the regular program began. Unlike those in the "regular" program, we did not get a long summer vacation, but only a one-week break, between the first and second years. So, after the end of the first year, we were caught up with the "regular" students and were part of the general student population in the second year.

Each student in the Middle Management Program had to be sponsored by a company. I was sponsored by my father-in-law's company the Kern-Trimble Drilling Company. It was a nominal thing. I got no financial help.

Money, of course, was a big issue. Priscilla and I had some savings – not very much, I believe $2,000 and then I would receive my vested profit sharing in Schlumberger which was perhaps another $4,000. So we had about $6,000 altogether. The tuition, as I recall was in the neighborhood of $3,000 for the two years. That left between $3,000 and $4,000 for about eighteen months of living. Things were certainly much less expensive then than they are today, but still, especially with having a baby and Priscilla therefore being unable to work, it didn't quite compute. We hoped for the best.

But then, about two months before leaving, an opportunity arose that could perhaps solidify our finances. Mr. Kern, my father-in-law, called me to his office and said, "Gerardo, we are putting together a syndicate to drill a well in Miller County, in the area with which you are so familiar. If you wish to participate, I can deal you in for a one-sixteenth – for $800. Quite frankly, I was a little disappointed. I would have hoped that my father-in-law would have given us a present of that one-sixteenth participation, but he was strictly business. I asked him how much time I had to think about it and he said, "You have to make a decision by day after tomorrow. We are under time pressure here."

So I went to my office and studied all of the electrical logs that I and my colleagues had taken in that particular area and I decided that we had a very good chance of producing oil in that spot, in an established deposit, at a depth of about 3,200 feet. I talked to Priscilla and she told me to go ahead, make that investment and take that chance. So I wrote a check for $800, and gave it to my father-in-law. It was a big chunk of our small fortune, but I thought it was a pretty good gamble.

But things never quite turn out the way one hopes and plans. At 2,900 feet we hit a fault which displaced in a lateral direction the oil-bearing sand that we had expected to hit at 3,200 feet. There was no oil. It was a dry hole. Eight hundred dollars down the drain. So, as they say, we went back to the old drawing board.

We understood the geology and what that fault would have accomplished. We were pretty sure that by moving our location 400 feet north we would hit that oil-bearing stratum that had eluded us in the first hole. My father-in-law said, "Gerardo, I know that's a lot of money for you. You don't have to do it, but if you wish you can participate in our second attempt; but you'll have to pony up another $800." Now this was quite serious. We figured that we would somehow be able to absorb the loss of that first $800, but $1,600 was going to make much more than just a crimp in our plans. Priscilla and I sharpened our pencils over and over again and still didn't quite see how we could get through those two school years if we lost another $800. But, once more, studying the geology and the electrical logs that I had taken of adjoining wells in the Miller County area, I was pretty sure, let's say, better than eighty per cent sure, that we would be successful. So we decided to go ahead and invest the additional $800. Also, we would have felt like complete fools if they would have hit oil, as we quite firmly expected, and if we had not participated. I couldn't help thinking of my grandfather and Abe the shoemaker and the lost opportunity to win big in that Prussian state lottery.

I won't bore you with the geologic details, but something else happened with that second well. We hit that oil-bearing stratum all right, but it was what is called a "pinch-out," in which the stratum, which is expected to be essentially uniform in thickness, narrowed to a degree that made it unproductive. Another $800 (literally) down the hole.

It was now a week before my leaving for Boston. We had decided that I would go by myself and that Priscilla and one-year-old little Michael would follow once I had myself established. I bought a big second-hand car, an '88 Oldsmobile, and rented a U-Haul trailer into which I put all of our belongings.

Before I left, the investor group had one more meeting, to decide whether or not a third hole should be drilled. The consulting geologist and participants in the deal was Bill Lisman (the one whom his wife had told to sit in that easy chair and to think of how he could get her out of the kitchen). He and I studied and restudied the geology of the small area, including the information that we had gathered from the two dry holes that we had drilled. I was the expert in the interpretation of electrical logs of surrounding holes, productive and unproductive ones, and the two dry holes that we had drilled.

Lisman and I triangulated a point about 500 feet away from the two dry holes, where we were "absolutely sure" oil would be found. The participants, of course, had the right of first refusal to put up another $800 or to bow out. Four of the sixteen people had enough and bowed out. After an agonizing discussion that lasted for hours, Priscilla and I decided that we could not afford to participate, but we could also not afford not to participate in this "sure thing." So, we decided to ante once more with $800, which we could not really afford at all. Somewhat to my disappointment, and knowing that we would have no further income for almost two years, my father-in-law once again did not offer to pay our share. I thought it was a little strange; I wrote another check.

Drilling on the new site began immediately, because it was a simple matter to move the drilling rig just a few hundred feet.

I said goodbye to all of my friends and colleagues, kissed Priscilla and the baby goodbye and went on my way to Boston, 2,000 miles away.

I had no trouble driving the big car with that U-Haul trailer, but I learned very quickly that I was unable to back it up. Every time I tried it would jack-knife on me. I simply couldn't get the hang of it. I admitted to myself that it would be impossible for me to stay overnight at a motel because it would involve my having to back up. Therefore, I decided to drive three or four hundred miles and then, when I got sleepy, I would pull off the road and catch a few winks. Then I would start driving again. It took me five days to get to Boston.

Part IV

CIGARETTE FILTERS, CONTRACEPTIVE COMPUTERS, THE SHAVER THAT WENT TO THE MOON, AND MUCH MORE

The first thing when I arrived in Boston was to call Priscilla. I said, "Darling, I made it. I'm here, and I'm going to find a place for us to live."

She said, "You won't believe this. Something wonderful has happened. The well has come in and it's much more productive than anybody had expected."

What a great surprise! I had expected this "sure thing" to be a success, but now that it actually had happened we were most elated, of course. But there was one more thing: The well had to be "completed." That meant steel pipe had to be set, pumping equipment installed, and all the other things that have to be done to make a hole in the ground a producing oil well. Our cost of participating in the completion was another $800. Even on this totally "sure thing," we simply did not have an additional $800 in our budget. So Priscilla finally put her foot down and told her dad that she expected at least one act of generosity from him and for him to pay our share of the completion. He mumbled a few things about being "grown up, and being independent," but then he put up the $800.

This well gave us an income of approximately $300 per month for two years. Then it went down to $200, then to $100 a month for another year, then we had a "work-over" which cost $800 per participant and that, of course, included us. Then, over the course of the next two years, it gave us $100 to $150 a month, until it finally had to be shut down. Altogether, over the course of five years, having made $6,000-$7,000 out of that investment, it gave us peace of mind and even allowed us a few luxuries and even some traveling that otherwise would not have been available to us.

I found a reasonable little apartment, a small house in fact, in Watertown, Massachusetts, about five miles away from the Business School. With the assistance of a fellow I hired to help me unload my trailer, I arranged what little furniture we had as attractively as possible. I knew that Priscilla, when she arrived, would rearrange everything. I was correct.

Business School was a total revelation for me. My class had about forty students, most of them employees of Westinghouse. And as required, all of them had about five to ten years working experience. I had been out of school for eight years but even so, the intellectual climate in which I now found myself involved was something utterly new to me. The amount of work that was piled on us was more than I thought I could handle.

My budding post-graduate career was almost nipped in the bud because I came down with mononucleosis, the second day of classes. I had to stay out for a whole week, and I managed to get by only because my new-found friends brought me the cases (all work at HBS is by the case method) to our home and summarized the lectures that had been given. I don't think I could have made it if I had been out for another four or five days. As it was, I was just getting along by the skin of my teeth.

The first-year courses in which I was most interested and in which I did best were marketing, finance and control. Harvard also put a lot of emphasis on human relations, but I found that somewhat boring. There were no textbooks and no lectures in the ordinary sense of the term. Everything was taught by the case method, in which actual business situations were discussed and analyzed. We quickly learned that many business situations had no clean-cut "solutions," but had to be managed, improvised and nurtured as one went along.

One of the abilities that the school expected its students to have, and which it made an effort to foster and improve, was the ability to express oneself well in writing. Most of the students in my section were engineers and had little experience in written expression. One of the courses was called WAC, which stood for Written Analysis of Cases.

An especially knotty and difficult case would be presented and we had to present a written (typed, of course) analysis of the case, usually in not fewer than 1,000 words. That analysis was to be deposited in a special mail chute on campus, not later than 10 p.m. on Friday night. It was kind of funny to see grown men racing through the campus to deliver their written case analysis to the chute exactly on time. If you were one minute late, the chute closed automatically, and you got a failing grade.

One day in a post-mortem analysis of one of these cases, Professor Raymond, who taught this course, asked one of my colleagues whether a certain situation in the case was indeed factual. His answer: "So at least it would seem to the casual observer."

"To the casual observer?" Professor Raymond answered. "Let me tell you a story. A few weeks ago, I did a little slumming in Charlestown (the tough part of Boston). I saw two fellows in a terrific fight. I recognized one of the combatants to be one of my students. He was in terrible shape. His clothes were torn, his face was bloody, one eye was swollen almost shut, and it looked as though one of his ears had been partially ripped off. The other fellow had left. 'You poor fellow,' I said. 'You seem to have gotten the worst of this fight.' Through bloody lips and with one or two of his teeth seemingly missing, he said, 'Professor Raymond, thus it would seem to the casual observer. 'But,' he said, as he opened his hand, 'pray, whose testicles do you think are these?'"

In all likelihood it was an apocryphal story, but the point was well made. In business situations, the perceptions of a "casual observer" are mostly quite useless.

Toward the end of the second year, I began to look for a job and interviewed with several companies on campus. I was most intrigued by W.R.Grace & Co., who, at that time, in addition to being a substantial chemical company in the United States, had commercial and mining interests in several countries of South America. They also owned a shipping line and one-half of an airline. I thought that, because of my knowledge of South America, my fluency in Spanish, and my extensive background in mining engineering, I would be the right person for a job with them. The recruiters agreed and I was hired at a salary of $1,000 per month, beginning immediately after graduation.

I graduated from Harvard with cum laude, pretty much at the top of my class. I did not reach the exalted level of Baker Scholar, which was the upper five per cent of the class. It bothered me a little; I thought that I should have accomplished that.

It was fortunate that I found a job right away, because, even with the shot in the arm from the oil well, we were about out of money and could not, without having to ask my father-in-law for a loan, have made it for another couple of months. Of course, I wanted to avoid having to ask him for a loan if at all possible.

I looked up the cost of living index in 1956 when I graduated from Harvard. Money was worth almost eight times as much then as it is now, so that $1,000 monthly salary translated to about $100,000 a year of today. It wasn't that bad for a starting salary.

We sold or gave away most of our furniture, climbed into the trusty Oldsmobile, strapped in little Michael, and drove to New York, where we had only been as visitors once or twice before. First order of the day was to find a place to live. People had told us that we should try to find an apartment in Queens, preferably in Forest Hills, so that's where we went. We found a very nice apartment in a brand-new building. We bought some furniture and proceeded to settle in.

On Monday of the following week, I presented myself at the offices of W.R. Grace & Co. Even though I was already hired, I had to be interviewed by five or six vice-presidents. It was an old-fashioned kind of place. There was one huge room, and perhaps as many as twenty vice-presidents sat in this large hall, each by his own elaborate roll-top desk. Next to each desk was a smaller desk, with the man's secretary. A room like that, I learned, was called a "partners room." Apparently it was the way things were handled in the steamship business. W.R. Grace & Co. owned the Grace Line. There were five passenger ships, with names that all started with the word "Santa," and several freighters.

That business didn't last. The passenger business was taken over by huge cruise liners. Grace also had a fifty-fifty partnership with Pan American Airways in the ownership of the Panagra Airline that serviced primarily the West Coast of South America.   It was not a happy arrangement; the Grace people were always at loggerheads with the Pan Am people.   The board was 50/50, and nothing constructive was ever accomplished. Both the steamship company and the airline were eventually jettisoned.

I seemed to have passed muster with the vice-presidents. I was then sent to see Mr. Felix Larkin, who was then the personnel manager and who eventually became the president of the company. Mr. Larkin explained to me about my salary, where I was going to work (the South American Division, of course), who my boss was going to be, where my office was going to be, etc., etc. I got up to leave and he said, "Just a minute, Gerardo. I want you to know that I'm very impressed by you." Of course, I was happy to hear that, but I didn't quite know what was so impressive about me.

"Thank you, Mr. Larkin," I said. "Why do I impress you so well?"

"All the people I've interviewed day after day want to know about fringe benefits. You are the first person in a very long time who didn't ask me about anything like that. You know – health benefits, vacations, bonuses, and that kind of thing. That means that you are our kind of guy."

Well, of course, at that point I wasn't interested in any benefits. I needed a job in the worst possible way and that thousand dollars a month – benefits or no, looked mighty good to me – for me, for my wife and for our child. But I was happy to hear, of course, that I was their kind of guy. I had made a good first impression.

As I looked around, I realized that Grace was an old-fashioned company and that the "partners," whom I had just met in that big room, were perhaps indicative of its style. The "big boss," major stockholder and the grandson of the founder, was Peter Grace, who was about forty years old at that time. He was determined to totally restructure the company and to modernize it. It was really a very fuddy-duddy kind of place, and the "partners" whom I had just met and their work habits were reflective of it. Also, what was peculiar for a place like New York, even in those days, virtually without exception, all jobs, from lower management up, were filled by Irish Catholics. Peter Grace made the remark, "We've got to spice this place up. Let's get some smart Jewish boys in here." And that was one of the reasons I was chosen. It was quite in contrast to Schlumberger, of course, who even though they got me by mistake, made it a point not to hire any Jews, at least not knowingly.

Peter Drucker, who even today, almost fifty years later, is still considered one of the country's outstanding management gurus, was the main consultant to Grace and entrusted with the task of suggesting and devising how to restructure the company. The Planning and Policy Committee was formed, of which he was the chairman and to which four or five key executives were assigned who worked on the committee on a part-time basis.

Two other men and I were permanent members of the Committee. We worked on the restructuring plan for a full year, prepared an extensive report in which we surveyed and analyzed all sections of the company. We came up with the following key decisions:

- Jettison the steamship line
- Jettison the airline
- Jettison all of the Latin American business
- Concentrate on and expand the domestic chemical business

All of those suggestions were adopted rather quickly and, for better or for worse, Grace became essentially a domestic chemical company.

In the meantime, however, we did much work in South America, and another quaint Grace habit came into play. On my first trip to South American for Grace, I went with my boss Pete Harris, who was the head of the South American division, his deputy Jack Duncan, and another two men. The odd thing as far as I was concerned was that both Harris and Duncan traveled with their own private secretaries. I thought it was a weird arrangement, especially since these trips had a tendency to last for up to six weeks, all the men were married and the secretaries were nubile and very attractive, and became more attractive as the weeks went by. On this first trip, we were mostly concerned with Grace's Peruvian business, primarily their vast sugar cane plantations and the connected bagasse processing and manufacturing facilities. (Bagasse is the pulp that remains after the juice has been squeezed out of the sugar cane.) We were freshly ensconced at the Crillon Hotel in Lima and had a fair amount of time on our hands. One of the traveling secretaries came on to me quite strongly and made it clear that all kinds of entertainment would be available at the slightest suggestion. I had by then been gone from home a long time and New York was far away. I was quite young, the juices flowed freely and urgently. The decision to turn this only thinly veiled offer down was not an easy one. But I decided that if I took the road to adultery I would continue down that path and inevitably ruin my marriage. Perhaps as important was that I was and still am such a poor liar. I knew that Priscilla would know immediately that I had been playing around, the minute I stepped off the airplane. I couldn't risk it, so I thanked the young woman as kindly as I could so as not to hurt her feelings and forwent the pleasures she had to offer. It was a difficult decision, but I am still sure that it was the right one.

Priscilla picked me up at the airport and she looked at me. Yes, I was right. She would have known immediately if I had done anything wrong. But she said that she had something to tell me. "Tell me," I said.

"No, let's wait till we get home.

We drove home. Little Michael was asleep in his bed. "What is it you want to tell me?" I asked her.

"I've decided that I want another baby," she said.

"Oh, is that what it is? I think I can oblige you." I did right away.

Just as the first time, it took on the first try. Rachel, an absolutely darling little girl, was born on May 15, 1957. She was the first baby to be born in the new Salvation Army Hospital. What intrigued me was that they had a special circumcision room. Having a girl, we didn't need it, of course....But only in America (and probably only in New York)!

I didn't get to stay home very long. I had to go on another trip, this time to Bolivia, by myself, and without those traveling secretaries to tempt my virtue and steadfastness.

My assignment was to review, report and make proposals on the Chojlla Mine that Grace owned in Bolivia and also on a gold placer prospect. I have mentioned the Chojlla mine before. It was where I hoped I could get a job when I first came to Bolivia, almost twenty years earlier. To the best of my knowledge, it was the only mine of any size that was in the subtropical Yungas region, north of La Paz, rather than on the frigid Altiplano. When I got to El Alto, La Paz's airport, I was picked up by limousine and by Mr. Elsner, the manager of Grace's office in Bolivia. He was the same man to whom, eighteen years earlier, I had applied for a job and who had told me very kindly that he had nothing available for me. I had good memories of him. Of course, I recognized him right away. I don't recall whether we spoke in English or in Spanish, but we didn't speak in German. He said, "Have you been in Bolivia before, Mr. Joffe?"

"Yes, I have been in Bolivia."

"You look familiar. Have we met before?"

I thought for a minute and said, "No, I don't think so Mr. Elsner. I can't recall." I thought it was the best way to handle it. I was now one of the fairly big shots from headquarters in New York. It would have been somewhat awkward to make him realize how things had changed.

I was driven to the mine about three hours out of La Paz and stayed at the house of the manager, Joe George, a very competent mining engineer from San Jose, California. Joe and I became very good friends.

One evening, after a day's work, I sat in Joe's living room and picked a magazine up from the side table. It was *Time*. I leafed through it and found an interesting story about a San Francisco entrepreneur by the name of Joe Carney, who had purchased an enormous tract of land in the province of Mendoza, Argentina, a tract that he planned to develop into a large agricultural enterprise, with mining and petroleum production and, in the upper reaches, a ski resort. I was fascinated by the story and thought that it was exactly the kind of thing that, with my training and background, I could do very well. But I didn't give it much more thought.

Priscilla was not happy in New York. What mostly bothered her, I suppose, was that, with help only one afternoon a week, she was pretty much confined to our small apartment in Queens, with those two little children. There was some babysitting switching with neighbors, but she wasn't happy.

One evening we had been able to arrange for a night out, a nice dinner and a movie. The movie that had been recommended to us was *Vertigo*, with Jimmy Stewart and Kim Novak. It was a psycho-thriller and we both enjoyed it. "What city is that?" Priscilla asked.

"Didn't you see the Golden Gate Bridge?" I replied. "It's San Francisco."

"It's beautiful" she said. "Let's get out of New York and let's go live in San Francisco."

"The scenery looks pretty attractive," I agreed, "but I have a job here with a good company. I'm beginning to make a career and we just can't go off to San Francisco with those two children and with little money and try our luck in California."

"Well, why don't you find a job in San Francisco?"

"O.K.," I replied, laughingly. "I'll try."

But then I remembered Mr. Carney, the San Francisco man who had bought that enormous tract of land in Argentina, and about whom I had read in *Time*. I would get in touch with him, I thought. Who knows, he might need a man like me and would give me a job.

I went to the library and asked for last year's bound issues of *Time*. I went through the whole year of issues, but couldn't find the story. I sent a cable to Joe George in Chojlla and asked him whether he still had that magazine in which I had seen that story. (I had discussed the story with Joe at the time.) He replied that he had thrown away the magazine "a long time ago."

Then I called the research department of *Time* and told them what I was looking for. They went through their index and couldn't find it either. Could I have been mistaken? Could it have been *Newsweek*? I didn't think so, because I was really quite sure that I had read it in *Time*. But even so, I went through the same process with *Newsweek*. Still no luck. I went back to *Time*. The research assistant was a very nice woman. She really tried to find the article. Then she asked, "Where did you see this?"

I told her that I had seen it in Bolivia. No wonder, she told me that I couldn't find it. "You must have seen it in an issue of Time's South American edition. That's something quite different," she told me. "They have an expanded South American section that features articles of special interest down there." She found the article and sent me a copy.

The rest was easy. I called Mr. Carney in San Francisco, introduced myself, and told him that I had read his story and I would like to go to work for him. He was noncommittal. He told me that he would be in New York within the next sixty day and that he would give me a call when he got there.

Sure enough, about six weeks later, Mr. Carney called me one evening and told me that he was staying at the Waldorf Astoria Hotel and would I come visit him at his hotel the next afternoon at 4 p.m.

I did that. He was a big man, smoking a big cigar. He was about sixty-five years old. He told me about the Argentine property and about other projects that he had handled in California, all of which were quite impressive. He also was president of a small steamship company and apparently had made a lot of money during the war.

"How much do you need to earn?" he asked me.

"Twenty thousand dollars," I told him, having by then received an increase at Grace to $1,400 per month, $16,800 a year.

He didn't blink or twitch.

"Let me think about it," he said. "I'll be back in New York in two weeks. I'll call you again and then we'll firm this thing up. I think you are what I need."

That was good news, so I decided to proceed as though I had already landed the job. Next day I told my boss, Pete Harris, that I had found another job and was going to move to California.

"Don't be so hasty," he said. "You have a great future here at Grace. Let's have lunch and talk about it."

He took me to Delmonicos, a very nice place, and I told him about the job offer which, perhaps not entirely honestly, I proclaimed as firm. I told him that my salary was going to be $20,000.

"We'll match that," Pete said without hesitation. "No problem – you can stay here."

I thought that was kind of funny, though I wasn't really amused. Why would I be making only $16,800 and be offered $20,000 now that somebody else was willing to pay that?

"There's one more thing, I said to Pete: "In order to stay I would have to become an assistant vice-president of the South American Division. "I can give you the money," Pete replied, "but I can't decide about the assistant vice presidency. Only Mr. Grace can do that. He's in Brazil right now."

In retrospect, it was an act of considerable chutzpah, but I said, "Pete, if you want to keep me, I have to be an assistant vice-president. Therefore, I must ask you to please cable Mr. Grace and ask him whether he would do that."

Pete was uncomfortable with that, but he said, "O.K., I'll do it."

Mr. Grace cabled right back. "Tell Joffe not to push too hard. I'll have to think about that and won't make a decision on the run. I'll let him know when I return next week."

But then I had an important insight, namely that in the long run, and even though the Harvard Business School had trained me and in a way "destined" me to "big business," that I was not really cut out for the big corporate life. I didn't like the jockeying, the infighting and the political game-playing, that I had already observed. I also thought that, somewhere down the line, I might pick up a rival or an enemy who might block my career. Finally, and even though Mr. Grace had the inspired idea of getting a "few smart Jewish boys" into the company, corporate success, entry into the highest levels of management was very difficult for Jews in those days. It happened rarely. I thought that however well I might be doing, I would probably ultimately get stuck in some upper middle-management level. That would not make me happy. Working for a small company, such as that of Mr. Carney, and perhaps ultimately working for myself, sounded much more attractive. It seemed the way to go.

Mr. Carney came back in two weeks, offered me the job and told me to come to San Francisco just as soon as possible. A new chapter of my life had begun.

Having lived in New York for two years and having had a reasonably well-paying job, we now had a regular household that we had to transfer to San Francisco. A moving company was hired and we told them to keep our things in storage if, as was quite likely, the moving truck would arrive in San Francisco before we did or before we would know where we would live. We went to Magnolia, deposited the children with their grandparents, and then flew to San Francisco.

The first order of business, of course, was for us to find a place to live. A friend in New York had told us that "there are only two places," to live in San Francisco, namely in the Pacific Heights area of San Francisco itself or across the Golden Gate Bridge in Sausalito. In retrospect, that was somewhat weird advice. We installed ourselves at the Sheraton Palace Hotel. We then went to visit Pacific Heights. We realized that the advice that we had been given was useless. Those were all old patrician homes, all beyond anything that we could even consider. And, obviously, those were not rental units. So, realizing that this had been bum advice, we crossed the Golden Gate Bridge to Sausalito. After some looking around we found the absolutely ideal home, a beautiful structure of redwood and glass with a fantastic view of San Francisco Bay, three large bedrooms and a nice yard. It wasn't actually in Sausalito, but a little beyond and on the Tiburon peninsula. The house had never been lived in. The owner, who had planned to move in, was a single man, a petroleum engineer, and had accepted a 3-year contract in Saudi Arabia. Rental was about ten per cent more than we had planned and had decided to be our maximum. Priscilla wanted to take it right away, but I advised caution. "Let's go back to the hotel," I said, "we can decide then."

The rental agent's office was right across the street. As we drove off, another car drove up and a tall, blonde woman stepped out of the car. "Stop," Priscilla said.

"Why?" I asked.

"That bitch is going to get our house."

It was an unusually harsh statement for her. "Let's go back and nail this thing down," she said.

"No," I said, "she's not going to get our house. Let's go back to the hotel, just as we had agreed, and think about it on the way."

By the time we got back to the hotel, we had decided that we would take the house. A message was waiting for us at the front desk. It was from the rental agent. "So sorry, someone took a three-year lease on the house." Priscilla, with fine feminine intuition, had obviously properly assessed the "bitch."

Ultimately we found a very nice place, one-half of a duplex in the Anza Vista area of San Francisco. It was a good arrangement.

Next morning I presented myself to Mr. Carney. His office was in a corner building at California and Battery. The name of the company was Hillcarn Steamship Company. The reason for the name was that the company had owned two steamships, which long-since had been sold. Hillcarn was a combination of the two owners' names. Mr. Carney greeted me warmly and assigned a very nice office to me.

Mr. Carney suggested, this being my first day, that we have lunch. He offered to take me to his club – The Merchants Exchange Club, which was a couple of blocks down on California Street. There was going to be another man, John Lawler, an American who was his resident manager on the Argentine property.

We met at 12 o'clock at the club. John Lawler was already waiting. We sat down at a small table and ordered lunch. In the middle of the table there was a medium-sized pitcher filled to the rim with what I assumed to be water. I poured a glass and started drinking it. Yuck, it was gin. I wasn't able to drink it, of course, certainly not at lunch. But I looked around; there was a pitcher like that on every table and most people, parties of two, three or four seemed to have no trouble emptying it, and in some cases ordering a refill.

After we were halfway through our lunch, Mr. Carney took his plate and his silverware and said, "I hope you'll excuse me, fellows, I'm going to go play dominoes."

"Dominoes?" I thought. I had never seen a grown-up person play dominoes. That was a children's game, and how was it possible that he'd invite us to lunch and then leave us alone to go play a game with other people! But, that was the kind of person he obviously was.

The company occupied about half a floor and employed six or seven people; none of them, as far as I could tell right away, had very much to do. The reason for that became quite clear: The company existed mostly on past glory and the recent Argentine project, in which Mr. Carney had invested about $350,000 by that time. The most important employee was a Ms. Dressler, about 45 years old. She was a CPA and the controller/accountant of the company. It became clear to me that she also had a close personal relationship with Mr. Carney.

One of the employees was a translator. He had to take all documents that came from Argentina and translate them into English for Mr. Carney. It was a totally useless undertaking, especially with me on board, but I didn't say anything because I did not want that good fellow to lose his job.

I immersed myself immediately in the Argentine project, with what little material was available. I asked Mr. Carney whether he had prepared at least a preliminary budget and he waved that aside with "Oh, we'll need about a million and a half dollars."

"Excuse me, do you have that million and a half dollars available or are you planning on raising it?"

"I'm going to sell fifteen share of the Argentine company at $100,000 each. I talked to my good friends and they are all going to come in on this, every one of them. What we have to do is to prepare a complete operating plan and a budget, and that's what you're going to do."

That was fine by me. That's what I had expected to do. That's what I was trained to do and what I was very good at. But I wanted to come back to the money question. "Those fifteen people who are going to put up the $1.5 million, what share of the company are they going to own?"

"They're going to own forty-nine per cent and I'm going to own fifty-one per cent, so I can keep control."

"Mr. Carney..."

"Call me Joe," he said.

"Joe," I said, "I may be getting ahead of ourselves, but you've invested $350,000 and they're going to invest a million and a half. They're not going to be satisfied with 49 per cent."

"I don't give a damn what they're satisfied with," he said. "If they don't want to come in on my terms, they don't come in. I'm not going to give up control."

I was going to tell him that there were other ways of maintaining "control," but I decided to let the topic drop for the time being.

Ms. Dressler explained the system of payroll payment to me. It was different from anything I'd seen before, but I thought it was a pretty good way of doing it. My $20,000 per year salary worked out to $1,667 per month. I would be paid forty per cent of that, $667, on the fifteenth of the month or, if that date fell on a Saturday or a Sunday, on the Friday preceding. It was to be considered an "advance." Then, at the end of the month, the balance would be paid less the appropriate deductions. The first fifteenth rolled around and I got my $667. The end of the month rolled around and I got $750, which was the balance, less the deductions. The same thing happened the next month. I thought it was a neat system.

The fifteenth of the following month fell on a Saturday, so in accordance with our agreement, I expected to be paid on Friday the fourteenth. But I wasn't. Nobody said anything, and I didn't either. I thought that I had perhaps misunderstood and that I would be paid on Monday, which would be the seventeenth. But again, nothing happened. I was a little surprised, but I didn't say anything. I didn't even mention it to Priscilla. The end of the month came and there was no payday. The following fifteenth came and, again, there was no payday either. I had been working for large companies for over ten years and one thing, of course, that one always takes for granted and expects is that payday is as sure as the rising and the setting of the sun.

After I had missed my third payday, and although I found it to be most embarrassing, I approached Ms. Dressler. I said, "Frances, this is a little embarrassing, but I seem to have been overlooked for the last three paydays. Can you please look into it?"

"Did nobody talk to you?" she replied.

It was a loaded questions because she would have been the only one to talk to me about my pay. "No," I said, "What's there to talk about?"

"Oh, Mr. Carney is a little short on cash right now.   That happens sometime. Don't worry, he'll pay you eventually. He always does."

I was somewhat staggered. That was a totally new experience for me. I told Priscilla about it and she, too, could hardly believe it. As it eventually turned out, I and all other employees worked for six full months without pay. The others, the old hands, seemed to be used to this kind of thing and nobody complained. I certainly didn't hear anything. I suppose they were just glad to have a job.

In the end, Mr. Carney was able to sell an old gold dredge that he owned and which was a remnant from one of his previous businesses. His employees were paid off, every penny. Fortunately, Priscilla and I had about $10,000 in savings at the start of this "no-pay situation," and were able to survive the drought. We could not have made it for more than another month or so.

Despite the shortage of cash, or at least not enough cash available to pay the employees, Mr. Carney decided that we should make a trip to Argentina to visit the property and for me to get additional material for my report on the project, which would be the basis for financing.

The traveling group consisted of Mr. Carney, myself, Ms. Dressler and Mr. Carney's wife (referred to as "The Mama"). I had the feeling that the Mama insisted on coming along, in order to keep an eye on her husband and Ms. Dressler. There was another person in the party, namely Homer Capehart, a staunch Republican and former senator from Indiana, who had been chairman of the Senate Foreign Relations Committee. Somehow or other, he had met Mr. Carney and had persuaded him that he could use his supposedly substantial influence with the Argentine government, which was already making ugly noises and mentioning the words "expropriation" and "Yankee imperialism," in connection with Mr. Carney's huge property.

We traveled first class and ensconced ourselves in a suite of rooms in the Plaza Hotel, the finest of Buenos Aires, with Mr. Carney and his wife occupying a magnificent corner suite. I had no idea where the money was coming from. I still, at that time, hadn't been paid. Apparently, Mr. Carney had his own set of priorities. The Argentine company, of which Mr. Carney at that point was the only stockholder, had three local directors. As far as I could tell, they did not do anything, but were reasonably well paid.   Mr. Carney thought that he needed them as his "local presence." He may have been right in that. There were meetings every day with the directors and with the commercial consul of the U.S. Embassy, and some functionaries of the Argentine government. We decided that the following Monday, three of us, Mr. Carney, I and Jorge Mayer (one of the Argentine directors) would fly out to the property in the province of Mendoza in a private plane that had been chartered for the occasion.

Two interesting things happened. The ritual was that every morning at 8 o'clock, Senator Capehart, Ms. Dressler and I would gather in the Carney suite. Breakfast would be ordered. Since I was the only Spanish speaker it was my duty to transmit the orders to room service. One morning, Senator Capehart had not arrived at the appointed hour. We waited fifteen minutes. Then Mr. Carney said to me, "Gerardo, please go to Senator Capehart's room and wake him up if necessary."

So I went to his room and knocked on his door. "Just a minute," a voice growled. The door opened. There was Senator Capehart, absolutely stark naked. "Come in, my boy," he said. He really did say "my boy." I wondered what he wanted. It was an unusual situation and I felt a little uneasy. Keeping my distance, I said, "What can I do for you, Senator?"

"Come into the bedroom with me," he said.

It began to sound ominous, but I thought I would have to follow his instructions; after all, he was an ex-Senator. He was a tall man, about 6'2" and weighed at least 350 pounds. He had the biggest belly I had ever seen on a naked human being. "You see that girdle over there?" he said. Indeed, there was a girdle lying there. "I can't get it on myself. Will you help me."

"Yes, of course, Senator," I said.

He slipped the girdle over his head and across his belly, braced himself against the bedpost, and I, after having taken off my shoes, put one of my feet in his back and tightly laced the girdle. Apparently, I did a satisfactory job.

As I exited his room, I told him: "Please hurry up, Senator, they are all waiting for you."

He was able to finish the rest of his wardrobe himself because he joined us in Mr. Carney's suite a short time later. That was the only time I had to do this particular chore. He must have worked out another system or perhaps he engaged room service for other such occasions.

Here is another anecdote about Senator Capehart: One day, just he and I were having lunch in the Jockey Club, in the basement of the Plaza Hotel. It was the fanciest room in the fanciest hotel in Argentina. After the second martini, the Senator said to me, "Gerardo, I really like Argentina."

"Yes, I do too, Senator," I said.

"I'm glad you feel like that. Just look around you," he said. "People are just like us – you know what I mean?"

I looked around and, sure enough, not unexpectedly, this was the cream of the cream of Argentine society; they were as totally unrepresentative of the people of Argentina as they could possibly be.

Senator Capehart, who had been chairman of the Senate Foreign Relations Committee had, in all likelihood, never been any other place but the American Embassy and Foreign Ministry of the country he was visiting. He always stayed in the fanciest hotel in the capital, and he formed his views of each country in this manner – by surveying people in fancy restaurants. I thought it was a little funny, but also kind of sad.

The other peculiar and significant thing that happened one breakfast was this: After I had ordered breakfast, the waiter would arrive about fifteen minutes later with the food on a rolling cart. He would then present the check to Mr. Carney, who would initial it. The waiter would make a bow, turn and leave. One day, when the waiter arrived, Mr. Carney was on the telephone talking long distance to the United States. It appeared to be a long call. The waiter stood with the check, and after waiting for about five minutes, he asked me if somebody else could perhaps sign the check. No problem, I thought. I signed the check. Eventually Mr. Carney got off the phone and we ate our breakfast and began our day.

For the rest of the day and the two days following I found that Mr. Carney was noticeably cool toward me. When we were alone I asked him, "Joe, is anything wrong?"

"Yes," he said, "sit down. Something is indeed wrong and I need to talk to you." He continued: "How could it possibly occur to you to sign that check? I paid for the breakfast and it was my privilege to sign it. You had no right to do that."

I thought I might have misunderstood him. It was the weirdest thing I had ever heard, but before I could say anything, he said, "Let me tell you a story and explain to you how I feel about these things. Dr. Gordon is one of my best friends. About six months ago, we had a party at our house. There were quite a few people and The Mama (his wife) had a beautiful roast beef in the middle of the table. I was called away to the phone. When I got back, I saw that Dr. Gordon had sliced the roast beef. He had no right to do that. It was my house and only I had the right to slice the roast beef. I told him to get the hell out of my house and he did. I've never talked to him again. You did just about the same thing by signing that check. You had no right to do that."

I thought he was insane. What a totally weird thing. But it was a clue to his personality. From then on out, for all the years that I continued working for him, I always asked him in case of any doubt, "Joe, is this your roast beef or mine?" and he would say "it's mine" if he decided it was his or, if he felt it was mine, he would say, "It's yours – go ahead and slice it." What a weird person!

When Fidel Castro came to power in Cuba in 1959, one of the first things he did was to expropriate all American companies. That put the kibosh on all foreign investment and especially, of course, Latin American investment. All those great friends that Mr. Carney had – and he really had them, withdrew their support for the Argentine project, one by one. At the end, only one remained, a Mr. McCaw from Seattle, Washington, whose son later became the head of the great communication empire that carries his name. Mr. McCaw put $100,000 in escrow, to be released if the fourteen other scheduled investors would put up their shares within six months. It didn't happen. The project collapsed and I lost my job. I stayed with Mr. Carney for another year in a consulting capacity, but he was out of money. There were no investors and the project disappeared.

But I also thought, and had told Mr. Carney from the very beginning, that his terms were too harsh, too unfavorable for the investors. These were all seasoned business people, and especially in a risky project such as this, wouldn't put up over eighty per cent of the equity for less than one-half of the ownership. I told Mr. Carney that there were other ways to maintain that "control," that he was so keen about, but he was inflexible about this.

Eventually, the Argentine government took the whole thing over and paid only nominal compensation to Mr. Carney.

Apart from the peculiarity of the roast beef and some other quirks, Mr. Carney had unfortunately a serious defect. He was a racist and an anti-Semite. He loved to tell "nigger" jokes until I told him one time that I felt uncomfortable with that. After that, he didn't do it in my presence. As for anti-Semitism, it was what I would call of the "country club" variety: nasty jokes, and, of course, he wouldn't associate with any Jews. You might wonder why he would have hired me. I was quite simply his proverbial "smart Jew" to help him with his projects. And, of course, he told me that I was "different."

One day he told me this story: "The Mama" and he had taken a cruise around the Mediterranean. There was some trouble with the ship's engines and they had to make an emergency stop in Haifa, a port that was not on the itinerary. They had about two or three days available and they decided to make a side trip to Jerusalem. A Mr. and Mrs. Sugarman (Jewish, of course), distant acquaintances from San Francisco, were also on board, and the whole cruise party went together to Jerusalem. When they came to the Western Wall, often called the Wailing Wall, Mr. Carney told me that he saw Mr. Sugarman crying. "'Why are you crying, Mr. Sugarman?' I asked him." And according to Carney, Sugarman said, "I'm crying with joy because I don't have to stay here and can go back to San Francisco."

That story really pissed me off. I said, "Joe, this is a nasty story and it isn't true."

"What do you mean it isn't true?"

"I mean it isn't true because nobody, and certainly no Jew, could have gone to the Western Wall which was in possession of the Jordanians."

"What are you saying? Are you calling me a liar?"

"No I'm not calling you a liar. I think you are just mistaken."

"I am not mistaken," he said.

"Just a minute." I stopped him. I picked up the phone and called the Israeli consulate. "I have a man here who says that he could have gone from Haifa to Jerusalem and to the Western Wall. Is that possible?"

"Impossible," the consular employee said. "Just a minute. Please tell my friend that." I gave the phone to Carney and the consular official repeated the message. Carney slammed down the phone.

"What the hell difference does it make. So I made a mistake."

He had other anti-Semitic anecdotes like that and he told them without apparent malice, totally insensitive to the fact that they would be hurtful and annoying to me.

Mr. Carney liked to talk about his lineage – his noble ancestors. He told me, in all seriousness, that he was descended from General Lee on his mother's side and from a line of Polish kings on his father's side. I listened respectfully, but I had more than grave doubts about this story, on which he loved to elaborate. He didn't look like a Polish king, and he certainly did not resemble General Lee in the least. Also, I found it most unlikely that such discordant strands could have come together in one family. But it was important to him. It made him happy strutting his fantasy ancestry. I had no problem listening to it.

But he wanted to make absolutely sure and he wanted to document it.

One of his employees was a Mr. Gilbert, an old retainer, who had been with him for thirty years or so and who, at that time, had really nothing much to do. He entrusted Mr. Gilbert with tracing his ancestry, to spare no expense, and to go where he had to go in order to study old records and documents. Mr. Gilbert accepted the task. He came back after about a month and no official report was made of his findings.

A few months later, after work, I took Gilbert out to have a drink. He really wasn't one of my intimate friends, but we always got along well. He was quite a bit older than I. I was curious as to how his investigation into Mr. Carney's ancestry had turned out. After the second martini, I said, "Gilbert, tell me about your research for Mr. Carney. What did you find?"

"Well," he cackled, "it was quite interesting. My search first took me to New Orleans, from there to Natchitoches" (which, by the way, is pronounced Nac-a-tosch, a nice little town on the Red River downstream from Shreveport. I had been there many times, while I was stationed in Shreveport, working for Schlumberger).

"What did you find in Natchitoches, Gilbert?" I asked him.

Well, he laughed. "It's interesting. I went through the records and found that Mr. Carney's ancestor was one Kaufmann Abraham Cohen."

"That was the name?" I asked.

"Yeah, that was it and it's right there in the civil register, for everyone to see."

I didn't want to correct Gilbert but, of course, the man's name was Abraham Cohen, and not Kaufmann Abraham Cohen. *Kaufmann* in German merely means "merchant," and that, being obviously an immigrant from Germany or some German-speaking part of Europe, was how he described himself.

"So what did you do next, Gilbert?" I asked him.

"I sent Mr. Carney a telegram and told him what I had found."

"And then what happened?" I asked him.

"Mr. Carney telegraphed back: 'End your search...return immediately.' Would you like to see that telegram?"

"Yes, I wouldn't mind."

"I just happen to have it in my pocket. I keep it as a souvenir."

He showed it to me. He thought it was very funny. I did too.

Mr. Carney, a nice and talented man, with delusions of aristocracy, turned out to be the great-grandson of a German-Jewish peddler. I thought it was hilarious. He didn't know that I knew and we never talked about it. But he never talked about General Lee and about those Polish kings again. Also, he no longer told any anti-Semitic jokes.

The children were growing up. Rachel was a sweet little girl of three. She had only one problem. She was very allergic and had respiratory problems. Priscilla was referred to a pediatric allergist, a nice and very impressive old lady, who came to the house and told us that, from an allergy point of view, the heating system made the house impossible for us. We would have to move. So we moved to an upper flat in the Marina district, owned by a nice Italian lady. We threw all mattresses away and substituted foam rubber pads instead. All carpets had to go also and all curtains. Rachel got much better.

Michael was a different problem. He threw fits and was a problem in school. I didn't know how to handle him and neither did Priscilla. We spanked him a lot, which was, of course, a bad mistake. We still often blame ourselves for having done that, but it probably made no difference in the end. We also discussed putting him under the care of a child psychologist, but we never got around to doing that. What really happened, I think, was that we thought of it as somewhat shameful to have a child that wasn't entirely "normal." So we didn't do it. Would it have changed the ultimate outcome? I doubt it, but we shall never know.

Since I no longer had a job, I had a problem of making a living. My "nut," the minimum amount I had to have was $1,500 per month. Somehow I had to piece it together. One of Mr. Carney's friends was Tom Slick, a rich Texan from San Antonio, whose father was one of the developers of the fabulous Spindletop Dome oil field out of Beaumont. Tom was a nice man but totally eccentric. He had weird religious beliefs and was, to put it quite bluntly, a sucker for con men of many sorts. One project in which he invested tens of thousands of dollars was to find Bigfoot, the legendary ape man, whom the Indians called Sasquatch, who was supposed to be roaming in the mountains of California's Humboldt County. He had a man on a large monthly retainer, who kept stringing him along on this project with bogus information. Tom hired me at a retainer of $500 per month to check out various projects that he had – some of them related to petroleum and mining, in which I was knowledgeable. Unfortunately, none of his projects made much sense.

One day he called me and told me that he had acquired the right of first refusal on an enormous gold-bearing placer out of El Paso, Texas. He asked me to go down there immediately, to meet with two men, and to do exactly as I was told, however strange it might seem to me.

I flew down to El Paso and met with those two men. They did not make a good impression on me at all. In fact, they looked and smelled like con men to me. They told me that they would take me to the placer, but that in order to maintain complete secrecy I would have to be blindfolded. That was even more weird than I had thought, but since I had been told to play along I accepted that. We drove for about an hour. Then we stopped. They took off the blindfold. We were in the middle of a barren landscape, somehow reminiscent of Bolivia's Altiplano. "This is the place," one of the men said. "We are now going to take some samples in your presence and then we are going back to our lab and in your presence assay the samples for gold."

"Just a minute," I said, "if there are any samples to be taken and if I am expected to make a report to Mr. Slick, I am the one who is going to take the samples."

"No you're not. We take the samples ourselves, but you can watch us."

So I watched, but totally without interest. The art of "salting" samples, especially for gold, is as old as the world. The matter had no interest at all. But they insisted. They had twelve sample bags, which I, of course, was not allowed even to inspect. They walked around in a perimeter of about 500 feet and took what looked like random samples of soil, filled the bags and then tagged every one of them.

The blindfold was put back on me and we returned to their office, in which they had their own assaying lab. They proceeded to assay the samples for gold. I said, "Fellows, this is totally useless. First of all, the samples are without value because I have not inspected the bags in which you took them, nor the places from which you took them. And, of course, to have any validity, you can't possibly assay your own samples."

"Well you stay here until we finish. You can then take the results to Mr. Slick, who will be very pleasantly surprised."

Well you can imagine, those samples were wonderful. If this had been for real, it would have been without question the greatest gold discovery in the world ever, by far surpassing the Yukon or California, or anything else. Tom was enthusiastic when he got the results. It took much effort to dissuade him not to invest even a dime in this project. I told him that I would go back out there again and would even allow myself to be blindfolded, but that I would take my own sampling bags, do my own sampling, and pick my own laboratory in which to assay for gold.

Tom demurred for a while, but in the end he accepted my advice. My modest request was not acceptable to the two "gold men" and nothing more was heard about tremendous gold finds in Texas.

It came to my attention that Congress has passed legislation to assist small businesses – the Small Business Investment Act. Under that Act, one could form an SBIC (Small Business Investment Company), a corporation with a minimal capitalization of $150,000. The government, or more precisely the Small Business Administration, would match that and, after certain conditions were fulfilled, would match it again. In other words, the $150,000 equity of the investors would be supplemented by a $300,000 loan (on very favorable terms) by the government. There was no personal liability for the loan on the part of the investors. That interested me greatly. With the help of Tom Slick, I formed such a corporation. I invested $5,000 of my own meager resources. Tom Slick invested $10,000, and other friends of Tom's invested money, and I found a number of investors on my own. We had no problem at all getting our $150,000 together.

I learned that if one had one or two good "names" in an investment, other people would follow. The problem was to get the first investors, and we had them.

Tom Slick himself was one; another was Ben Swig, a big *macher* in the San Francisco Jewish community, and owner of the San Francisco's Fairmont Hotel.

I paid myself a salary of $500 a month, so, with Tom's retainer and the $500 a month I still got from Mr. Carney for my consulting services for him, I had the $1,500 a month I needed to meet my expenses and to keep the family together.

My SBIC investors demanded "action." So, I worked ceaselessly trying to find investment opportunities. I found quite a few. I regret to say that my experience with the SBIC was the worst I ever had. Ordered by my board of directors and with their approval, I made twelve investments, almost the entire $450,000, excepting only small office expenses, which included my own very modest salary. With the exception of one, all of them failed in short order. The one that worked is still in operation, more than forty years later. It is a plastic molding company.

Virtually all of the SBIC's failed and the government abandoned this program that they had started with such high hopes. The only ones that survived, as far as I can tell, were those that did not invest in "small businesses," but that invested in real estate. While the SBIC Act did not specifically prohibit investment in real estate, it was not at all what it had intended, what the government had wanted to achieve. But that's the way it worked out. For years, I felt bad about this one real failure in my business life. Even though I had not done anything wrong I felt ashamed and I did not wish to meet or confront any of my investors, who had lost all of their stakes in this venture, of course. I remember one time, when I saw one of them a block away coming down the street toward me, that I crossed the street so I would not have to confront him and talk to him. It took me a long time to get over this failure.

There was one investment, or rather an investment opportunity, which if I had completed it would have made my stockholders and me very rich. Here's what happened.

One day a young man came into the my office, unannounced, and told me that he had an interesting item to show me, which he hoped our investment company would consider for funding. He needed $60,000. $60,000 was the limit that the government allowed us to invest in any one venture. Therefore, if it was of sufficient interest, we could handle it. He opened his briefcase and pulled out a pair of earphones, to one side of which a slender tube was attached. The tube curved so as to end close to the user's mouth. "What is it?" I asked.

"This is my and my partner's invention. We have the patent on it. It is something totally new on the market," he said. "It will be of great use, mostly for airline pilots but it will have many other applications. It's a combination of earphones and microphone, all in one piece, and operation is hands free."

It didn't mean very much to me, because I had no knowledge of aviation and nothing to compare it with. I said: "Could you leave it with me for a couple of days? I have two men on my board of directors who might be able to assess this much better than I can." One of my directors was, indeed, an aviation consultant. Another was a private pilot, so surely, between the two of them, they could determine very quickly whether this was something that had merit.

The young man, whose full name I can't remember – I believe his first name was John – reluctantly agreed to leave the prototype with me. I took it to my director who was the aviation consultant. He said, "Gerardo, this is an absolutely wonderful invention. It's invaluable for aviation and will have many, many other applications in other industries. It is the first really good thing you have brought up. We should definitely invest in it."

I was very pleased, because while I had looked at scores of prospects and had wasted much time, I had come to realize that good investment opportunities are very hard to find, and that others, more experienced than I, were always on the prowl to pick the raisins out of the investment cake. Perhaps this man's coming to me was a true opportunity. The strange thing was, as he had told me, that he had presented this to at least ten venture capital firms, most of them in the Palo Alto "investment gulch," all of them much larger and much more experienced than we were, and that all of them had declined to make an investment in this project. He told me that I was his last chance and if we were not going to invest in it, he was going to give up on the project and find a job.

I called him that evening in Santa Cruz, where he lived. I told him that we were prepared to deal and to meet me with us the next morning at 9 o'clock for a working breakfast in the dining room of the Sir Francis Drake Hotel.

He was there the next morning, with his partner. On our side, there was I, the aviation consultant, and one Forrest Tanzer, who was also a director of the SBIC. The deal was very quick and very clean. We were going to invest $60,000 in the company for which we would receive one-third of the company's stock. Our share in the company could not be diluted without our written consent. We would have to approve executive salaries. There was no haggling. Everything was very quick and very straight. I had a yellow pad with me, wrote a one-page Memorandum of Understanding, put down what we had agreed to and that we would formalize our understanding as quickly as possible. We signed, shook hands all around, made a copy of the Memo on the hotel copier, and our prospective partners took off for their homes in Santa Cruz.

I got a call from John the next morning. "Gerardo," he said, "let me tell you what happened. On my way home, I stopped in Palo Alto and met with a potential investor who had previously declined to participate. I told him that you guys had committed to invest $60,000 for a third of the company and that sparked his interest. Now he, too, wishes to invest $60,000, but of course, we cannot give each of you one-third of the company. With this man's additional investment, it will be a much stronger company. What do you think if we give each of you twenty per cent?"

I was pretty stunned and thought for just a few seconds. I said, "John, I don't really care if our share ultimately is thirty-three per cent or twenty per cent or whatever, but I just cannot accept that you would consider such an arrangement, changing our deal after we had a firm written understanding of what we were going to do. I no longer wish to participate in this venture."

"Please," he said, "don't be hasty. I assure you that it's now a much better deal for all concerned because we now have much better financing and have a better chance for success."

"No, I don't think I wish to do it," I said. "But let me talk to my directors." I polled them by phone. I told them what happened and they agreed with my decision. "If he is going to play these kinds of games with us now, what will he do once we get going with this business." So I called John back and told him that we were out. So that was that.

Plantronics, which was the name of this nascent company, is now one of America's important high-tech companies. Sales are on the order of $211 million per year and profits are $36 million. Obviously, in the course of time our original one-third share, or twenty per cent share, would have been greatly diluted, but still, had we accepted the modified deal, initially one-fifth of the company, all of us would have made a very great deal of money. I don't think about this very often, but I do feel a little foolish for having let "principle" prevail; and yet, by accepting this small change, this small deception, we could have been very successful. Well, no use crying over spilt milk, and who knows, John might have bushwhacked us again down the road. He was in control – we were not. I wish I could have learned something from this incident or could have drawn different conclusions, but I haven't and I couldn't.

Tom Slick who was the largest investor in the SBIC did not really care about the SBIC at all. The $10,000 that he had invested was literally chump change for him. My good relationship with him continued and I worked on several of his projects – not many of them, unfortunately, made a great deal of sense. He was a dreamer, and perhaps the greatest service I could render him was to keep him from being taken by the many unscrupulous people who were only after his money. The "gold placer" was one of several such examples. I never did succeed, however, to get him to abandon the Bigfoot project, on which he continued to squander large amounts of money.

One day I was sitting in his home in San Antonio. He was divorced and living by himself, with only a servant. He asked me what I thought about smoking. I told him how I had given up smoking the day my son was born. "I'm glad you did," he told me. "I think it's one of the greatest health hazards in the United States and of course all over the world. " And then he pulled open a drawer and pulled out a gadget.

"What is it?" I asked.

"It's the TarGard, a cigarette filter. It was invented by the chief tool engineer of United Airlines and I bought the patent and own it. It's a boon to those who can't give up smoking, because it eliminates the heavy tars from the smoke stream, and the heavy tars are what causes lung cancer."

He took the gadget apart and showed me how it worked. The smoke went through a tube that became narrower, and a baffle plate was behind it. He explained to me, and I understood that right away of course, that according to Bernoulli's theorem, the speed of a stream – liquid or gaseous – varied inversely to the square of the diameter of the orifice. In the TarGard the smoke stream was therefore greatly accelerated by being forced through the narrow orifice. It then impinged on the baffle plate behind it, and the heavy tar particles in the smoke stream were deposited on it, keeping that nasty stuff out of what the smoker inhaled. He couldn't demonstrate it because he didn't smoke either.

He said, "Gerardo, I've been trying to get this important item into production and circulation, but I have not been successful. I have no interest in the money. I only want to bring this to the American people and benefit them. Let me make you a proposition: I'll give you eighteen months. If within those eighteen months you can generate one million dollars of advertising support for this item, and start bona fide production and marketing of it, I'll give you the patent. You can do with it what you want. But if you don't accomplish this in eighteen months – and not a day longer – the patent reverts to me. Do you accept that?"

I didn't have to think very long. I had no idea where and how I was going to get a million dollars of advertising support, but obviously it was a proposition in which I could not lose – except for the time and effort I would have to put into it.

"Thank you very much, Tom," I said. "I'll do my best. Would you mind giving me this in writing?

"Not at all. You'll have a letter from my attorney by the time you're back in San Francisco."

One of my investors and a member of my SBIC board was one Forrest Tanzer. He was a difficult man, not easy to deal with, but I remembered his telling me that he had a close connection with the McFadden Publishing Company, the publishers who owned ten or twelve women's and movie magazines, with very large circulation. What if Forrest and I could give part of the ownership of the patent to the majority stockholders, owners of McFadden, who were Forrest's personal friends, so that we could fulfill that one million dollar advertising requirement.

First thing when I got back to San Francisco was to propose that to Forrest. He thought it was a great idea. We drafted a proposal by which, in return for one million dollars in advertising, the owners (or rather the principal stock holders) of McFadden would receive fifty per cent of the patent and Forrest and I would split the balance – twenty-five per cent each.

At that time, a million dollars in advertising seemed to be an almost unimaginable sum to me, but it was pretty easy. McFadden had so many magazines and each of the magazines usually had a couple of "holes" into which, if no paying advertiser came up to the plate, public service announcements (what we call "Smokey the Bear" announcements) would be placed. So why not put TarGard ads in Smokey the Bear spots. Also, there's a difference (usually a substantial one) between the "rate-card rate," which is the official rate that a publisher puts out, and what people actually pay. Naturally, in order to fulfill that million dollar advertising requirement, the "official" higher rate-card rate would be used.

I wrote some good full-page and fractional-page ads for TarGard, which were, in effect, primarily public service messages, with the TarGard logo, about the evils of smoking, because we had nothing else to sell at the time.

Within a little more than a year, the one-million-dollar advertising commitment was fulfilled. We owned the patent – well, almost. A few weeks later, while our advertising was still running, Forrest Tanzer received a phone call from the principal stockholder of McFadden Publications, the head of the family that had the majority interest in the company. He told him that a stockholders' suit had been filed against them, alleging that they were using the publications for their own personal purposes, and not in the best interest of the minority stockholders. He told Forrest that, on advice of counsel, he would have to abandon the TarGard project. "Never mind the million dollars in advertising that we've put into this," he said, "we are sorry we cannot continue with this project. We are giving our rights back to you. You own the patent; it's all yours. Thank you very much."

So Forrest Tanzer and I were the owners of the TarGard patent, but, in accordance with my agreement with Tom Slick, we had one more important hurdle to overcome: We had to form a company to produce and to market the item. We didn't have too much time left. That was going to be my next big effort.

At a marketing conference, I had met a man by the name of Bob Dailey. Bob called himself a "marketing man." He had been working for many years for a major consumer products company. Now he was out of a job. At that time, I had a small one-room office in the Balfour Building on California Street, and Bob came to visit me almost every day. You may say that he latched on to me. Even though I had no connections at all, except that to Joe Carney – and he was a falling star – and to Tom Slick, Bob somehow felt that I could help him get back on his feet. He got electrified when I told him about the TarGard project, what I had done so far, and that I now needed to get manufacturing and marketing for the product, in order to keep the franchise that Tom Slick had conditionally granted me.

"If I find somebody to finance this project, will you deal me in?"

"Of course, Bob," I said. "Whom could you find?"

"Let me worry about that," he said. "I think I have an idea."

He came back two days later and told me that he had approached George Long, who, until just a few months earlier, had been the president of Ampex, the pioneer Peninsula company that manufactured the first magnetic tape dictating and recording equipment. George was looking for "something to do" and he had lots of money, Bob told me.

"How much do you think we would need, Gerardo?" he asked me.

I had worked out a rough manufacturing/marketing budget and told him that we would need a commitment of $200,000 – not all of it would have to be contributed immediately.

"I think he'll go for it," he said.

Bob called me the next day and told me that he had set up a meeting at the offices of one of San Francisco's major law firms for 10 a.m. the following day. He told me to be there and to be prepared to sign a contract.

I was delighted, of course. I called my attorney to accompany me; I was not going to get into the arena with one of the experienced captains of American industry all by myself. It also occurred to me that in case of any conflict, Bob Dailey would side with George Long, and not with me. His bread was obviously buttered on the other side.

We met at 10 o'clock the next morning. George Long turned out to be an amiable fellow, with whom I would have no trouble getting along. There was a little horse trading, but we quickly agreed on the basics. George would immediately contribute $100,000 and commit to contribute another $100,000 in six months, or earlier if needed. There was some arm wrestling about the respective ownership shares but that too went quickly. Bob Dailey was going to receive five per cent as a finders fee, and Forrest Tanzer and I were going to receive twelve and one-half per cent (1/8th) each, of the company – provided we each put $5,000 into the corporate kitty. It wasn't quite clear to me why George wanted or needed that, but he was quite insistent on it – apparently he considered it a necessary showing of good faith.

"Mr. Long,…." I said

"Call me George."

"George," I said, "I have no real problem with contributing $5,000, but I don't have $5,000." It was the truth.

"No problem," George said. "I'll lend you the $5,000 and you give me a promissory note to repay it without interest within a year."

"O.K.," I said, "I'll do it."

"How about Mr. Tanzer?" he asked.

"No problem, I'll call him and he'll agree."

I called Forrest, told him that I had negotiated the one-eighth participation in the company for him, but that he would be required to make a $5,000 contribution to the project. "I'm not going to contribute a goddamn penny," he shouted over the telephone. "Tell this guy, that I want my share, but I'm not going to pay anything." He hung up.

I toned it down a bit, but I told George that Tanzer was not willing to contribute any money. "O.K.," he said, "if that's the only way he wants to play, he doesn't have to pay anything, but I'll cut him down to five per cent. Call him and find out if he will go along with that."

So I called Tanzer back and told him that if he didn't want to contribute $5,000, he'd be cut down to five per cent. If he didn't accept that, there would be no deal. Then I said, "Forrest, don't be foolish. If you believe in this project at all – and you told me that you did – don't you think that the seven and one-half per cent of this company that you would be losing, would be worth at least $5,000?"

"Never mind what I think," he said, "I'm not going to give this guy a goddamn penny. Five per cent is O.K. with me."

So I went back to the meeting room and we made a deal. George was going to own seventy-seven and one-half per cent of the company, I was going to own twelve and one-half per cent and Dailey and Tanzer were going to get five per cent each.

But there were two things that were bothering me, one of which only my attorney and I knew. The first, that only my attorney and I knew, was that this was the very last day of the franchise that Tom Slick had given me. This was the day that the eighteen months that he had allowed me were up. If I didn't make a deal today, everything would revert to him. Obviously, nobody was supposed to know that, because it would have fatally damaged my bargaining position.

The second thing that bothered me was this: This was going to be a very small company, with George Long, the majority stockholder, having absolute control. He could draw whatever funds he wanted from the company. He could milk it dry, without my ever seeing a penny. So I said, "George, we have a deal, but I have one condition."

"Sure," he said, "what is it?"

"Do you plan to draw any salary out of this company?" I asked him.

"No, of course not. I don't need it."

"That's good," I said, "but, I want you to make an agreement with me that if you should decide to draw any salary, regardless of whatever work I do or don't do, I'll get one-half of that salary."

"Why in the world would I pay you one-half of my salary if you only own one-eighth of the company?"

"It's just a technicality," I said. "I need to protect myself. Since you don't plan on drawing a salary at all, it makes no difference."

What I didn't tell him was that we had had a case at the Harvard Business School that was almost analogous to what we had here. It was a small company, which did very well and made a lot of money. The majority stockholder, who owned only fifty-one per cent of the company, drained the company's cash with a big salary, fancy travel, entertainment, and all kinds of perks for himself. The minority stockholders were left holding the bag. I was afraid that might happen to me if I didn't protect myself by such an agreement.

He wouldn't agree to it. He was adamant. He and his attorney left the room several times for fifteen minutes at a time and came back and made counter-proposals that were not acceptable to me. Of course, they didn't realize that I was bluffing. I had no way not to accept any deal at all, especially since my time was running out within a few hours.

At 4 o'clock in the afternoon, he finally accepted my condition. We signed the contract and shook hands. The atmosphere was somewhat more chilly than it had been earlier in the day.

It was agreed that I would not work for the company but that Bob Dailey would, as vice president of marketing. That was all right with me. Although I would have welcomed some cash flow, of course, I had no real problem, since I would get one-half of whatever monies George Long would draw out of the company.

Within a week something really wonderful happened. The Surgeon General of the United States came out with his report titled "Smoking and Health." Despite the assertions of the tobacco companies that cigarette smoking was a healthy habit, particularly beneficial to what they called the "T-zone," most people were aware that smoking was deleterious to one's health. That's why, ever since I can remember, people called cigarettes "coffin nails" and other such descriptive names. But the Surgeon General's report went way beyond anything the public had suspected. He connected smoking directly with various kinds of cancer, mostly of mouth, larynx and lung, and with emphysema – and he declared that the biggest culprits were the heavy tars in the tobacco smoke. He didn't actually say that if the heavy tars were eliminated, smoking would be beneficial, but he made it quite clear that if the heavy tars could be eliminated, smoking would be much less dangerous.

Heavy tars? Well, that was exactly what TarGard eliminated. It pulled the smoke through that tube and smashed it against the baffle plate where all the heavy tars remained. It was an awful-looking, smelly gook. Most people, when they saw it for the first time shuddered, realizing that such nasty junk could have gone into their system.

We contracted for the manufacturing, assembly and packing for the product and had a substantial inventory available within a month. Our manufacturing and packaging cost per unit was minimal, our profit per unit was very large. Under the guidance of Rod Farrow, an experienced executive in a major San Francisco advertising agency, we launched an advertising campaign in major print media and on radio, quoted from the Surgeon General's report and played up how our product eliminated that component of the smoke that the report had described as being so dangerous. Sales took off like a rocket. Having worked all my life for wages and for consulting fees, I hadn't realized and was astonished about how much money could be made in such a short time and with so little effort. Trouble was, I didn't see any of that money. It all accumulated in the company's coffers and, thanks to my cautionary agreement, George could not pull any money out of the company without giving half of it to me. He didn't like that.

After a year of ever-increasing sales, we had about $200,000 in the bank – just lying there. George felt that he could not afford to pull it out.

But, apparently, George Long had received some advice from his accountants, to the effect that there was a tax problem letting money cumulate in the company without distributing a reasonable portion of it, either as salaries, as dividends or both. George, understandably, didn't like dividends because it wouldn't be an expense to the company and therefore not tax-deductible; and he didn't like paying himself a salary which, even though it would be an expense, would benefit me disproportionately. So, after about a year, he called me to his office and said, "Gerardo, how would you like for me to buy out your share of the company, and buy Mr. Tanzer out also while I'm at it?"

"I hadn't thought of it," I lied. What do you have in mind?"

"I'll give you $25,000," he said.

"You must be kidding, George. One-eighth of what we have in the bank alone is worth $25,000 and then, of course, there are future earnings. This is a very valuable company."

"O.K., he says, "I'll give you $50,000 but that's my limit and I'll forgive you the $5,000 that you owe me. But, I won't give you a penny more."

I had a feeling that he meant it. I figured that one-eighth of the company was worth at least $100,000 and probably more, but I really wanted that $50,000 very badly so I could go on with my life and on to something else. In fact, there was something that I had already planned, that I knew would put TarGard in the shade. "O.K., George," I said, "I'll take the $50,000."

George opened his drawer and pulled out a contract that his attorney had already prepared. He just filled in a number – $50,000. I signed the agreement and he immediately gave me a check for $50,000. We shook hands, we wished each other good luck and we parted as friends.

Tanzer also signed; he got $20,000 for his five per cent share. He wasn't all that happy about my having gotten so much more, but there wasn't very much he could do about it.

I had never seen that much money in my life and I never thought I'd own that much. I was almost giddy with excitement. I went home and told Priscilla what had happened and how happy we could be having that much money. "What are we going to do with the money?" she asked. "What are we going to invest it in?"

"We're not going to invest it," I said. I have a fantastic business plan and we are going to be very, very rich."

"What is your plan?" she asked me, sounding not as enthusiastic as I had hoped. In fact, she sounded somewhat skeptical and concerned.

"I can't tell you now, sweetheart, it's still a secret, but you'll be very pleased and very impressed when I tell you about it."

Tom Slick had turned all of his rights in TarGard over to me and I had fulfilled his requirements. He was very happy that TarGard was in circulation, that it was helping people, and that it was so successful and so well received. That had been his desire all along. He felt as though he was rendering a service to the American people by reducing the danger of smoking. The money involved was of little interest to him. He was very rich, and any profits that he might have obtained from TarGard would have only been a small blip on his financial statement.

I tried to call him in San Antonio, but I was told that he was in Oregon on one of his Bigfoot expeditions. I reached him there and I told him what had happened. He congratulated me. He told me that he was traveling in a private plane and with a pilot and that he would come the next day to San Francisco to talk about new projects and to have dinner with me and Priscilla. To my deep sorrow, his plane crashed on its way to San Francisco, and both he and the pilot were instantly killed. He was an eccentric, but a great guy and a wonderful friend. Quite apart from the money, I was much enriched by having been associated with him. I count his death as a great loss.

My parents and I seemed to be so far apart – they lived in Argentina and I in the United States, and having not lived with my parents for so long – I left home when I was sixteen years old – my feelings toward my parents were probably different than they would have been had we not been living away from each other for such a long time. My feelings were perhaps more those of a dutiful son than those of a deeply loving son. I often felt and still feel guilty about it, but that cannot be helped; it's just the way it turned out. I was so intent on my own life and on surviving and getting ahead that I really paid little attention to them. I only wanted them to stay well and not to have so many heartaches nor financial concerns. Neither, unfortunately was the case.

My mother was in pretty good health until the end of her life. My father, however, was (understandably) deeply depressed, was overweight, and suffered from diabetes and its complications. One of the consequences of diabetes was that by the time he was seventy years old, one of his eyes had to be surgically removed and a glass eye substituted. It was very traumatic for him and I felt infinite pity when I learned about it. There wasn't anything I could do. As to their economic condition, it was dreadful. I have described the awful hovel in which they lived in Buenos Aires and how my poor mother kept herself and my father together and made their living by manufacturing chocolate candy, under almost intolerable conditions. It was awful.

The economic hardships, however, ended abruptly when the German government, wishing to atone, to the degree that it could be atoned for at all, for the terrible things that they had done to their Jewish fellow citizens during the war, decided to pay *"Wiedergutmachung,"* literally "again good making," as compensation to their Jewish victims of persecution. As I recall the numbers, my parents received a lump sum settlement of, I believe, 25,000 *marks*, which, like everything else, was worth a whole lot more than it is now, and a monthly pension of, I believe, 850 *marks*. That amount was adjusted for inflation from time to time. With that, their situation suddenly and dramatically changed for the better. Their daily preoccupation with survival, with their only safety anchors being my brother and I, was suddenly removed. On one of my trips to Argentina, while I was still working with Mr. Carney, and after they had already received the money from the German government, I talked to my father.

"Dad," I said, "Why don't you move out of this hovel, buy a nice apartment and make life pleasant for yourself and for Mother? You can afford it now."

"No," he said, "I can't spend that money. That is for a rainy day."

"Dad," I replied, "the rainy day is here. What's more, the war is over. You're going to get a pension from the German government every month, for the rest of your and Mother's life. As for money, you have nothing else to worry about."

"Don't tell me what the German government will provide. I've seen too much of them. There's no telling whether they might not make another law six months from now and decide to cancel the whole thing."

He died six months later at the age of 74. I was not there. Like most of the German-Jewish people of his generation, he had a very hard life. Fortunately, both my mother and he and of course my brother and I, were spared the ultimate, namely extermination in Auschwitz, or some other such accursed place.

Within not more than a month of my father's death, my mother, five years younger than he and also a much brighter and more positive spirit, bought herself a beautiful apartment in the Belgrano district of Buenos Aires, close to where my brother and his wife Lieschen lived. She was content with her life. Of course, she did not work anymore and was now able to live off her pension. She went to the movies and visited with her friends and relatives and with my brother. Her only sorrow, which she confessed to me, was that my brother Heinz and his wife did not have children. She didn't think it was "his fault." I thought that was a peculiar statement.

Both physically and financially, she was able to travel and visited us in San Francisco about every two or three years. Her Spanish was flawed and she did not speak one word of English, so communication with Priscilla, who was essentially in charge of her all day long, was very difficult and impossible with the children. Everyone waited until I came home at night so that I could be the interpreter. It was not easy.

My mother totally admired everything about San Francisco and about the United States. The air was better than anything she'd ever breathed, the water tasted better, the bread, the vegetables, and everything else. My mother had a love affair with the United States. The most wonderful thing of all, however, was the love that she felt for Priscilla – the *shiksa* about whom she had cautioned me since childhood and intimating that my marrying her might well endanger my father's health and life. While she had occasional questions and doubts about me, there was absolutely nothing that Priscilla could ever do wrong. She was a princess, as far as my mother was concerned. And, of course, she was right.

One day, during one of her visits, she and Priscilla were going out on a pretty cold day. Both women were wearing overcoats. "Priscilla," she said, "why don't you wear your good coat?"

"*Grossmutti*, this is my good coat."

"What do you mean, don't you have a fur coat?"

"No, *Grossmutti*, I don't have a fur coat."

My mother summoned me. "What's the matter with you, Gerdchen, that you don't buy your wife a fur coat."

"Mom, she doesn't need a fur coat. It doesn't get very cold in San Francisco. She does not want a fur coat."

"Every woman has to have a fur coat," she commanded.

Nothing would do, so next day she and Priscilla marched to a furrier salon on Post Street and Priscilla bought a beautiful spotted cat coat. It looked fabulous on her – and still does. Regrettably, wearing furs does not seem to be politically correct any longer, so the beautiful coat is languishing in the closet. Every once in a while Priscilla models it for me, but then hangs it back into the closet.

At the time, we were still living in the Marina District of San Francisco, in the flat owned by that Italian lady. My mother loved to take a magazine or a book and walk to the Marina Green, about two blocks away, and spend the afternoon there. Priscilla had cautioned to her to be very careful when she crossed Marina Boulevard where, particularly in commute hours, traffic was heavy and quite fast. She told her to cross the street only at intersections and to walk between the white lines that were clearly marked for pedestrians.

One day, my mother did just that, but even so was hit a glancing blow by a car. She was an old lady and it was potentially serious. An ambulance came and took her to Mt. Zion Hospital. She was able to give them my telephone number and I was called to the hospital. I was very alarmed, of course. It turned out that she had only a broken ankle, which could easily be patched up. We were told that she should be up and running in a couple of weeks. The doctors, however, were concerned about her high blood pressure.

My mother said incessantly (in German, of course), "It's my fault, it's my fault."

I said, "Mother, please be quiet. This is an insurance matter and your telling everyone that it's your fault doesn't help at all. Please be quiet."

So, we took her home. She was able to rest peacefully and to recover. But even at home, she said over and over again that it was her fault. She was afraid that we would blame her for her carelessness and for the "trouble" that she was causing.

The driver's insurance carrier contacted us. The agent, who sounded like a pretty nice guy, asked whether he could come by and talk to my mother and discuss possible settlement. I thought that I should lay some psychological groundwork. I told him that my mother was very weakened from the terrible accident and that we must do everything possible to avoid upsetting her. But I told him to come by the next afternoon at 3 o'clock, but to be very careful. The concept of insurance and that somebody would get paid for being hit by a car was an utterly a new one to my mother. In Argentina, apparently, if somebody runs over you, you're lucky if he pushes you into the gutter so that you won't be hit by another car. Nobody expects to be paid any compensation.

She had a hard time internalizing the concept. The next day, a young man, the agent – he was indeed nice – came at the appointed hour and introduced himself as Albert Hoffinger. I had to caution my mother, once again, not to say anything at all and to let me handle everything. Hoffinger came right out and said, "It was our insured's fault and we want to compensate your mother, of course, and make a quick settlement. How does $2,000 sound to you?"

I said, "It sounds awful to me and I wouldn't even suggest it to my mother. She is an old lady and, because of this accident, in an even more fragile condition. The annoyance of hearing such a low-ball offer could kill her, and then we really would be in trouble, wouldn't we." My mother tried to understand what was going on. By that time, she had learned a little English, but not enough to follow this conversation.

"All right, all right," said Hoffinger, "I can give you $3,000 but that's my limit."

"Mr. Hoffinger, if that's your limit, you might as well go home now because I refuse to submit this unfair offer to my mother."

Hoffinger got up. Then he sat down again. "All right," he says, "I'll tell you what my absolute, and I mean absolute, limit is. It's $4,000. Ask your mother, please, to take it. If not, we'll have to go to trial on this."

I said, "Mr. Hoffinger, did you bring a checkbook?"

"Yes, I did."

"Are you authorized to write the check for $4,000?"

"Yes, I am."

"Well, hold it a minute, I'll talk (in German, of course) to my mother. This may upset her a little, but I'll try." I approached her bed. I said, "Mom, I don't know whether you understood what we were talking about, but the man is offering you $4,000. Do you wish to take it?"

She looked at me as though I was demented. *"Bist du verrückt*? (Are you crazy?) *Nimm es, natürlich!* (Take it, of course!)"

I turned to Hoffinger and said, "I don't know whether you understand any German, but my mother is highly indignant about your minimal offer. Still, I advised her, that in order to avoid long complications and because she wants to go back home to Argentina, she will reluctantly accept your low offer of $4,000."

"Wonderful!" Hoffinger said. He pulled out a checkbook, wrote out a check for $4,000, handed me a release for my mother and me to sign, shook hands and left. My mother's conviction that America was a wonderful country, in which one could be paid $4,000 for just a broken ankle, was confirmed.

My mother, having recovered from her accident and having received that totally unexpected $4,000, felt now much more frisky. About two weeks before the date that she planned on leaving, she said to Priscilla, "Priscilla, I have a great idea. Why don't you let Rachel go with me to Buenos Aires. She can stay with Heinz and Lieschen and she can go to an American school in Buenos Aires. That school would be half in English and half in Spanish. It would be a totally new experience for her, she would get to know her family better, and, of course, she would turn out to be a perfect Spanish speaker. It would be helpful to her in later life.

Priscilla was nonplused. That had never occurred to her. Rachel was just twelve years old. How could she possibly let her go to a foreign country, even in the company of her grandmother and living with an aunt and uncle. Priscilla didn't know quite what to do so she consulted me. "Let her go," I said. "My mother and my brother and our sister-in-law will take very good care of her and it will indeed be a wonderful experience for her."

So, we decided to let her go. Rachel cried a bit, but she was excited about the prospect of this adventure, something that none of her peers had had. She went and indeed spent a school year in Buenos Aires. It was a great experience for her. Priscilla's mother, the other grandmother, also thought that it was a pretty good idea. She insisted on buying her a training bra, just in case she would need it while in Argentina. It turned out that she didn't need it. I suppose that had the need arisen, such a garment would also have been available in Buenos Aires. But it was a thoughtful gesture. Rachel still feels very connected to her uncle and aunt and, of course, she became a perfect Spanish speaker. Will Rachel allow her daughter, Rebecca, to do something like that? I am not so sure.

There was this great idea for my new business in which I would invest the $50,000 I had received from TarGard and which I was certain I would multiply to great riches.

Here's what happened:

One day I had been in Los Angeles on business, working with a company, Abacus, in which we (the SBIC) had an investment, an investment that ultimately was lost. It was about 9 o'clock in the evening and I was driving to the airport. To the left of the highway, there were thousands of acres of suburbs, dotted with small one-family homes. Most of them were lit, but then, in one after the other, the lights went out. "The lights are going out," I told myself. "What are they doing now." The answer came to me in a flash. They were having sex. It occurred to me that if we had been able to make so much money out of smoking, how much more money couldn't I make out of sex, if I could just find the proper approach. I was bemused by the thought, because I realized that even more people had sex than those who smoked. Surely, there must be some money to be made with that. I thought that condoms were a great idea but, of course, they had already been invented a long, long time ago. Then the great insight came to me. Being a married man, I was aware, of course, of women's menstrual cycle. I vaguely realized that conception, or rather the likelihood of conception, was somehow governed by that cycle, and that, if I could invent a device, a computer, that women could program to their menstrual cycles and could determine when they could or could not conceive, it would be bound to be a great success.

In the meantime, the nice Italian lady who owned the building in which we occupied the upper flat was getting restless and told us that she would prefer for us to leave. She had two reasons: In the first place she wanted her daughter and her family to move into the flat, but mostly she was increasingly annoyed by our active children running back and forth through the apartment, which, because of their allergies, had no carpets. So we obliged her, and rented, with an option to buy, a very nice house close to, but not within, the fashionable Sea Cliff district of San Francisco. Having that $50,000 from TarGard gave us a sense of confidence. Also, ever since the sale of my TarGard share, we had been able to have a full-time live-in maid which made life very much easier and more pleasant, especially for Priscilla.

I now spent many of my evenings in the medical section of the San Francisco Public Library studying up on women's menstrual cycle. There is, of course, a great deal of literature on that. By the time I got through with my study, I probably knew as much about it as some of the medical resident in gynecology. I was particularly intrigued by a scientific paper written by two doctors, a German and a Japanese, Dr. Knauss and Dr. Ogino. The paper stipulated that a woman's fertile days could be "pinpointed" by averaging, over the last twelve months, the lengths between the monthly onset of her menses and the "variance," namely the spread between the longest and the shortest such cycles within the last twelve months. This "discovery" was to be my golden key to great success.

I put the Knauss-Ogino discovery into a mathematical formula, an algorithm, and proceeded to design the concept of a hand-held computer. It had three concentric moving parts in which a woman could program her personal data and then – unerringly, I was quite sure – determine when she could and could not conceive.

I elaborated on my idea, wrote it up, made appropriate drawings and presented it to a patent attorney. He thought it was a very good idea and intimated that he might be willing to take a "piece of the action" in lieu of his fee. I thanked him, but I declined. I had heard of many people who had given away part of their equity just to save a few dollars in attorney's fees. I was not going to make that mistake. In due course, I received a U.S. patent for what the patent office called a Catamenial Computer. I was in business – well, almost.

So far, the idea existed only on paper. Now it had to be designed and manufactured.

I scouted around. I found an excellent industrial designer; his name was Gene Tepper. Gene took my idea and designed it into a truly attractive device. It was palm-sized, shaped like a flying saucer, gray with red and white accents. It was a thing of beauty. "You have to give it a name," Gene said. "What do you want to call it?"

I thought about that. "Let's call it Rodell-7."

"Why Rodell-7" he asked.

"I don't know," I said. "It just sounds good. Rodell gives the impression of things going around and around which, of course, is the case of both the menstrual cycle and of the device itself. And 7 is just a good number; it appears over and over in mythology."

"Rodell-7 it is," he agreed. "And, I'll design a beautiful logo for you, which will be embossed on top of the item."

I was so taken with the name and the logo that I used it and applied it to other merchandise until the end of my marketing career, long after the little fertility computer was no longer on my horizon.

What with the attorney and the designer, with the new house and the full-time maid, I had now spent a fair chunk of that $50,000. It wasn't quite a much money as I had thought. But the real expenses were to still come. Gene put me in touch with a plastic manufacturer, who, based on his detailed drawings, produced the molds to manufacture the item. It was quite expensive because there were more pieces involved than I had anticipated. Making the metal molds, the "tool," was the expensive part. The actual production and assembly of the items was not. I ordered a first run of two thousand units. The $50,000 was greatly reduced – we were down to four digits.

Sparing no expense and no effort, I then produced excellent packaging for the product, including a beautiful orange flannel pouch in which the customer could carry the device in her purse (for quick ascertainment as to whether she was fertile at the time or not) and a booklet explaining the theory and the function of the device, medical testimonials, etc. On the last page was a picture of Priscilla who was the "Director of Women's Services" and who invited customers to direct any "confidential" questions to her. My war chest, which not too long before had seemed to be almost inexhaustible, was getting very quickly depleted.

Now, how to sell the Rodell-7? I didn't have the money to set up a sales organization, as we had done with TarGard. Also, I doubted that, in those somewhat more squeamish days, it would be an easy item to sell over the counter in drugstores. So it occurred to me that the way to sell the Rodell-7 would be by advertising it in media. Without being aware of it or so intending it, I had started on my mail-order career.

I placed one-third-page black/white ads in several media. The media that I selected were romance and movie magazines, like those of the McFadden group, where we had "spent" that million dollars for TarGard. I thought that those magazines would be read mostly by blue-collar women of an age when they would be most likely to be sexually active. I also put advertisements in Catholic magazines, for women whose faith prohibited them from using contraceptives; and *Parent Magazine*, in the conviction that a woman who had just had a baby and was therefore likely to be a reader of *Parent Magazine*, would not want to become pregnant right over again.

From my new two-room office on the eighth floor in the Merchants Exchange Building, also on California Street, and with the help of one secretary, I conducted this business with fair success. By success I mean that each of our ads made some money. Some made a little more, some a little less, but we always made money. I was beginning to replenish that war chest.

This old-fashioned office building had men's and ladies' rooms on alternate floors – men's rooms on the odd-numbered and women's rooms on the even numbered floors. The men's room on the seventh floor served that floor and the eighth floor. It was a place where one met many people. Two people I met were Cliff Wilton and Samm Coombs, an art director and a copywriter, respectively, for a large ad agency on the seventh floor. We became best friends, especially after I found out that Cliff and Priscilla were attending the same art seminar at the San Francisco Art Institute.

I told Cliff and Samm about the Rodell-7. They were fascinated by it, and thought that it was a really great idea, with great marketing potential. They offered their help and totally redesigned my ads, both in appearance and with punchy copy. Sales improved substantially.

Priscilla, though impressed by my inventiveness and energy in producing and distributing such a novel item, was never quite as convinced of its infallibility as I was. Naturally, since we were sure that we had our family formed by then, with a boy ten years and a girl seven years old, we definitely wanted no more children and used contraceptives routinely. After the invention of the Rodell-7, and being the proud president of the Rodell Manufacturing Company, I insisted that we do away with all that old-fashioned stuff and use the Rodell-7 and, with pinpoint accuracy, put our own family planning into the modern age.

One of my great pleasures was to get correspondence from my customers which was directed to the Director of Women's Services (Priscilla), telling her how pleased they were with the device, how it made their love life happier, and so forth. After a few months, however, I got one perturbing letter, as follows:

> Dear Madam:
>
> I am thirty-five years old and I have had regular sex
> since I was sixteen years old. I've never been
> pregnant. Then I started using the Rodell-7. Now
> I'm knocked up. I'm not happy at all.
>
> Sincerely yours, …

Well I wasn't happy either, but even in the most perfect product there could be one failure rate in a thousand, and, who knows, she probably didn't read the instructions properly.

But perhaps I should have paid more attention to that letter and should have considered it as somewhat of a warning sign.

Priscilla was very skeptical, but eventually she gave in and we had "unprotected" sex, only guided by the Rodell-7. It worked very well for a month or two, and we were both pleased that we could make love more "spontaneously," and without romance-destroying paraphernalia. Then – suddenly – I got a call in the office one day. Priscilla sounded very concerned. She said, "Guess what? I believe I'm pregnant."

"That's impossible," I said with entire conviction. "The Rodell-7 is infallible. It's impossible." But I was perhaps not quite as convinced as I sounded. When Priscilla went to see a doctor – and of course she knew what she was talking about – she was indeed pregnant. Her statement to me was, "You and your x@#\x@!!$ inventions!"

I must confess that I was very unhappy about the news. Our family was formed and we surely did not need another child, seven years younger than Rachel. Once more I was struggling with a new business and simply did not want any additional responsibility. I suggested to Priscilla that she should have an abortion. It was very difficult in those days in the Untied States, but one could go to Japan or to

Scandinavia, or perhaps even just across the border to Mexico to get it done in a discreet and competent way. She absolutely rejected the possibility. She would not hear of it. "It's my responsibility that I got pregnant," she said, "I shouldn't have relied on your great invention. What you don't realize (and what I indeed didn't realize) is that a woman's body is not a machine. It's not a computer and it cannot be governed by a computer. But now I'm pregnant and I'm going to deal with it. The only thing that worries me is that I'm thirty-eight years old. I'm very fearful and hope and pray that I'll have a normal child."

Fortunately, the pregnancy was normal and quite uneventful. Everything was going well, but still, we were quite worried, though we didn't talk about it.

About a week before the projected delivery, my mother-in-law came, in order to take care of the house and the children and to assist Priscilla after she came back home, following the hoped-for normal delivery and with the hoped-for normal baby – boy or girl.

One day, while Priscilla was in the hospital, in the first stages of labor, without anything having triggered it, and out of a clear-blue sky, my mother-in-law said to me:

"How did you decide to put another child in the world, after having done such a poor job with Michael?"

I was stunned. It was an unkind question, though she was right in her assessment that we had done a poor job with Michael.

Why would she say or ask anything like that, I wondered, especially at a time like this? I thought that she was overwrought with anxiety about her daughter, and I decided to just let it go. But, though I didn't tell her that, I also remembered an old German song:

> *Wenn Du eine Schwiegermutter hast,*
> *So betrachte sie als süsse Last.*
> *Denn wo kämen all die schönen Mädchen her,*
> *Gäb es keine Schwiegermütter, Schwiegermütter mehr.*

Which means:

> If you have a mother-in-law,
> Consider her a sweet burden.
> Because where would all those beautiful girls come from,
> If there were no mothers-in-law.

It's true – a fine piece of Teutonic wisdom!

Well, little Joe was born at the appropriate time. He was perfectly normal and he continues to be that to this day. Priscilla's not yielding to my blandishments about abortion was the best decision she ever made. Our son Joe has given us infinite joy, especially in view of what happened later to his older brother Michael.

One quick fast forward: Joe is now married himself and has child of his own, little Sammy. The Rodell-7, the invention responsible for his being here on this planet, has been beautifully encased in a plastic box and hangs on the wall of his living room. He delights in telling people about how it all happened and why he is here.

So, we had to deal with this new baby and with the new struggling business for which I had invented a whole mail-order apparatus – all those forms and all that methodology. There was no precedent, nobody to advise me, nothing that I could refer to. I had to start from scratch.

Things went along pretty well when two bad things – bad for the business – happened at almost the same time. The first was the Pill. The Pill, of course, had been invented quite a few years earlier, but sales were slow because there was little acceptance of it. Most women were deadly afraid of it; they had heard reports about its use causing all kinds of serious problems – mostly an increased tendency to breast and ovarian cancer. Then a report came out, widely publicized in media, to the effect that the same formulation of the Pill, but with smaller dosages of the hormones involved, made the Pill totally safe and equally effective and that women could use it without fear of any danger to their health. That made a big and immediate dent into the Rodell-7 business.

The other problem came from the Catholic Church. It became clear that young Catholic couples, against the doctrines of the Church, which considered it a mortal sin, were beginning to use contraceptives, just like almost everyone else. The Church apparently realized that it was losing adherents, so the Pope called a consistory, a congregation of cardinals, to decide whether contraception was still to be considered a mortal sin or whether it should be allowed. It was clear to most that the Church was trying to find a way to climb off that particular limb, which was alienating many of the faithful. Everyone believed that this consistory would take about three years and that, at the end of the day, the cardinals would have decided that contraception was no longer a mortal sin. Ultimately that didn't happen. It turned out to still be a mortal sin. But more and more young Catholic couples, firmly expecting that the ban on contraception would be repealed, began to use conventional methods of birth control, cutting sharply into the sales of Rodell-7. Thus, the double whammy of the Pill and the Pope quickly and sharply reduced sales of Rodell-7. The ads that I placed in media and which had always been profitable suddenly no longer worked. I was losing money with every ad. I realized that Rodell-7 had lived a beautiful but short life. Its days were over. In order to keep my head above water and to feed my family, which had now increased, I had to do something different, and I had to do it quickly.

So, I had to do something – but what? I took stock of myself and realized that I had spent most of the $50,000 from TarGard, that I had a large inventory of Rodell-7's, which I probably was going to be unable to sell and – what else? Oh yes. I had created a mail-order apparatus and methodology of how to sell things by mail, including forms, procedures – everything needed. I had created all of it from scratch. There were no precedents. I realized that this new-found knowledge was my best business asset and that in order to succeed I had to do something with it. I also realized that I had good business knowledge. My training at the Harvard Business School was really meant to prepare me for a career in a major American corporation – not to run a small business. Still, it would be very helpful. Furthermore, I had a knack for words and was a good writer. I had knowledge of languages and was very good with numbers. I concluded that I could use these talents by importing and then trying to sell by mail consumer merchandise from Europe and from Asia, merchandise that was not yet known and that was not readily available in the United States.

Where to find such merchandise? I went to the library of the World Trade Center in San Francisco and studied (and I mean studied) import and trade magazines from Europe and from Asia. In those days, Asia, for that purpose, meant primarily Japan. I decided to pick one item that I thought would find a market, order a moderate quantity, write an advertisement for it, place it in a proper publication, and see what would happen. As my first item, I decided on a table cigarette lighter from Japan. Why in the world I would have picked a cigarette lighter as my first item, not being a smoker myself any more and after having "crusaded" and having made a fair amount of money with that "anti-smoking" device, isn't clear to me today. In retrospect, it was somewhat of a weird choice.

This lighter had the shape of a truncated cone and came in two colors: red or black. I wanted to order 100 to get my feet wet and not to take too big a risk. The lighters cost $2.75 each at the factory and had a landed cost of about $3.25. So, I couldn't be hurt too much with a purchase of 100 units. Although I had some experience with the Rodell-7, I didn't entirely realize yet that the real cost in this business was not in the merchandise, but in the advertising. That revelation was to come later.

To my disappointment, the Japanese manufacturing company would not accept my order for 100 units. They told me, and they were adamant about it, that the minimum order would have to be for 250 units. Two hundred-fifty units was over $800, including freight and duty, and that was already a little more serious. But after some reflection, I decided to take the plunge. I ordered 125 in the black and 125 in the red execution. I had no credit arrangements, so I prepaid for the order. It would take about 60 days before the lighters arrived here in San Francisco.

I arranged a small working dinner for our friends Cliff and Samm, restroom acquaintances and by now advertising friends from the Merchants Exchange Building. We decided that our first order of business would be to find a new name for the company. Rodell Manufacturing Company, the flag under which we had sold the Rodell-7, would no longer do.

After a couple of glasses of good Napa Valley Chardonnay and lying on the carpet in our living room, Cliff, who was English, said, "You know, the most euphonious, the most sweet-sounding names for American ears are city and town names from the south of England. I thought it was a weird association, but we decided to bring out the atlas and scour the map of the south of England, looking for a town with a name that we could put on our new company. We looked at about twenty possibilities but did not find anything that suited us. Then Priscilla said, "If you can't find it in the south of England, how about New England in the United States? Let's look at that."

It made about as much sense to me as the south of England, but why not try that. So, having affinity for and good memories of Massachusetts, we looked at the map of that state and found three names that looked good to us. They were Barnstable, Concord, and Haverhill. Priscilla said, "I don't like Concord."

"Why not?" we asked her.

"Reminds me of Manischewitz wine. I don't think that is the right connotation."

It was a somewhat crazy point, but it was a point.

"How about Barnstable?" we asked each other.

"No," I said, "I don't like Barnstable. My very first case at the Business School was the Barnstable case. It dealt with a calendar company going broke. I didn't like it and I think it would be a bad omen."

"Well," they said, "if Priscilla doesn't like Concord and you don't like Barnstable, that leaves us with Haverhill, doesn't it?"

"I guess it does," I said. "So let's call it that. Let's add an apostrophe and an 's.' That's what Macy's does and quite a few others and I think it looks cool." So we had another glass of that Chardonnay, shook hands and decided that our company was going to be called Harverhill's. That was in 1967 and it's still called that. The only change is that we have dropped the apostrophe. We didn't think that it was any longer all that cool.

"There is one other thing," Cliff said, "you want to have distinctive artwork to show your products, not just plain old photography, but illustrations that POP OUT, that jump the beholder in the face."

"What would that be?" I asked.

"Go with scratchboard; it's a British specialty and it's marvelous. I know just the source for it."

It turns out that scratchboard is a technique (now done by computer) that was, in those days, laboriously done by hand. A picture is created on a tablet with a white chalk surface over a black chalk surface (or vice versa), in which, with a sharp knife, lines are meticulously graven into the upper surface so as to make the lower surface show through. For instance, if the upper layer is white and the lower black, a line cut through the white will show a black line. It sounds a little complicated and I suppose it is, but the effect is stunning. Cliff put us in touch with an English firm that did this kind of work. As a first assignment, we sent them a photograph of the lighter and they produced a scratchboard rendering of it. It was very expensive. It cost $350, when in those days an equivalent photograph would cost $25. In fact, we used a $25 photograph as a pattern for the scratchboard rendering.

From then on out we did all of our illustrations by that method. It became our "trademark" and we became famous for it. The initial high cost ultimately didn't make any difference, because our advertisements ran hundreds of times and in millions and millions of circulation.

But now I had to find where to advertise my new product – that cigarette lighter on which the hopes of my newly created business rested. I decided to concentrate on what was called the "executive" market. It was somewhat ill defined. I thought I should advertise the lighter in *The Wall Street Journal* because, surely, if "executives" were reading anything at all, they would be reading *The Wall Street Journal*. So I called the advertising office of the *Journal* in San Francisco and was connected to a fellow by the name of Al Moss, who was the local advertising manager. I asked him to come and see me, that I wished to place some advertising. He came the next day. Al was a nice guy, about my own age, and he told me that I should try an ad in the Western Edition of *The Wall Street Journal,* rather than in the full run of the paper. In the size in which I had designed my ad – two columns by five inches – it would cost $750. That was a lot of money. I figured that the landed cost of the lighters was going to be $3.25 each, and I planned on selling them for $12.95. Thus, I had to sell about 80 lighters to break even on the ad. That, of course would not pay for any overhead, let alone any profit – it would be just the breakeven quantity.

For no good reason, I called this item Maruden Lighter. The name clicked.

"Al," I said, "I don't know whether I can afford to do that. It sounds like a lot of money and that I'll have to sell quite a lot of merchandise to break even."

"Wait a minute," Al said. "I've got an idea. Why don't you advertise under our retail rate? The retail rate is about one-third of the so-called national rate. In other words you can get the same ad for $225 if you qualify as a retail store."

"Well, that's wonderful," I said. "It means that I would have to sell only about thirty of these lighters to break even. But, Al, how can I possibly qualify as a retail store here on the eighth floor of the Merchants Exchange Building?"

"Just a minute," Al said. "Let me look at the rules." He opened up a booklet and read from it. "Listen to this," he said. "To qualify as a retail store you have to have display shelves and you have to have a cash register. I'm afraid you don't have either. You don't qualify."

"Just a minute, Al, would you please read that again. I need shelves and a cash register?"

"Yes, that's what it says."

"Al, come back next week and you'll see the shelving and you'll see the cash register."

"O.K.," he said, and left.

I talked to the engineer of the Merchants Exchange Building and told him to put six shelves into my office. He did it on his own time and charged me $50. Then I went to a second-hand store and bought a non-functioning cash register. It cost $35. I put it on my desk. I called Al Moss. "Al, come back. I think I qualify for the retail rate in *The Wall Street Journal*."

Al came, looked at the shelves and looked at the cash register, winked at me and said, "You qualify. Place your ad." He then pulled a document out of his briefcase. It was a one-year advertising contract at the retail rate. We both signed it.

I reserved space for my two columns by five inches ad – essentially a square – in the Western Edition of *The Wall Street Journal* and gave Al my order. It cost me $225.

I told Cliff and Samm. They had the scratchboard rendering. Samm wrote some good copy and I sent the ad to Al Moss. It ran in the June 6, 1967 Western Edition issue of *The Wall Street Journal*. I sold 57 lighters with the ad, 38 in red and 19 in black. Since I had a gross margin of about $9.50 in each lighter, that worked out to about $540 in gross profit. Subtracting the $225 that the ad had cost me, I had profited over $300 from this one ad. I projected that to the full edition of *The Wall Street Journal* and realized that I was going to make close to $2,000, under the not unreasonable assumption that sales in the other section of the country would be pretty much the same as on the West Coast. I had latched on to the "golden formula." My fortune was made.

Of course, I realized that I could only do so much with just one item, just that one cigarette lighter. So, based on the study of merchandise that I had done, I ordered two other items, in addition to reordering 1,000 cigarette lighters. I ordered 250 units of a Japanese telescope, which came both with a handgrip and with a table tripod. I thought it was a very neat item. I called it, for no good reason, the Bicky Telescope and had that brand name silk-screened on the item. In addition, I ordered another item from Germany, the Emoskop Vest Pocket Optional System, for which Samm Coombs wrote some marvelous copy. I was able to use that same copy for over thirty years. Things were going much, much better than I had hoped.

We were now in September of 1967. The holiday period was coming up and I projected how much money I was going to make with only the three products that I had by then and the quite a few others that I had earmarked and for which I was prepared to place orders.

Things were going swimmingly at the office, but we had a little problem at home, because with Joe, the new baby, things had become very tight – in fact, we really had no room for Joe. For the first year of his life and a little beyond, he slept on the landing between the first and second floors of the house. Everyone who came by coochee-cooed him. We still think even today that he has such a pleasant nature and sweet personality because when he was a baby, all pampered and caressed him when they came by, walking up and down the stairs.

So we decided that we had to find another place. Even if we didn't have very much money at the moment, we obviously had fantastic prospects, and we thought we should "improve" ourselves, as far as housing was concerned. We needed to find something bigger.

Priscilla spent weeks roaming the "nice" sections of the city, but she could not find anything that she thought would be suitable. One Sunday, I was picking up the older children from Hebrew School in Temple Emanu El. In talking to them I missed my turn onto 27th Avenue where we lived and had to turn on 28th Avenue instead. We were in the "fashionable" Sea Cliff section of the city. There was a house with a "For Sale" sign on the front lawn. I told the children, "Let's go in there and look at it. Mom said we need another place to live."

"No, Dad," they said, "we're hungry. Let's go home and have lunch."

"It will just take a minute," I told them. "Let's go have a look." They grudgingly agreed. We went inside. There was a woman showing the house. The house had three floors. It looked exactly like what Priscilla had told me we needed. So we went home for lunch. I said, "Priscilla, there's a place on 28th Avenue that looks just exactly like what you told me we needed."

"That's impossible," Priscilla said. "I have looked at all the houses in Sea Cliff. That's the first thing I did. There's not a single house that has enough room for us. They all are only two stories high and don't have enough bedrooms."

"Priscilla," I said, "I assure you that this house has three floors and all the bedrooms that we need."

"That's impossible," she replied. "I've looked at all of them."

But still, she grudgingly consented to look at the house after lunch. It was just around the corner. Well, of course, it turned out that it was exactly what she had wanted. She felt a little sheepish about having run all over the city looking for a house, when what she wanted and needed and in a neighborhood she liked was just around the corner. "Around the corner" was in Sea Cliff, and that was in one of the two or three "most exclusive" neighborhoods of San Francisco. That helped. The asking price for the house was $69,500. We made an offer of $68,000; our offer was immediately accepted.

There was a little problem, however. A down payment of $17,000 was required. That so impressive $50,000 that I had received from my sale of TarGard was now reduced to a small remnant, and I felt that it was the minimum I needed to run my business. We could come up with $5,000 without hurting too much. My mother, always a thrifty woman, had accumulated a little stash in savings from her pension money, and she was able to lend us $7,000. The lady who sold us the house, a dentist's wife with five children, whose husband had absconded with the hygienist, agreed to take back a $5,000 purchase money mortgage, and with that we were able to close the transaction. We took out a 25-year mortgage for the principal. We had a beautiful new home. It was the first home we had ever owned.

Because of the miracle of inflation and also because of the miracle of the California, and especially the San Francisco, real estate market, this home is now appraised at about $3 million dollars. We have, however, over the years, put about $600,000 into sprucing it up and expanding it.

You may remember that uncle in America, Uncle Heyman Chaim, whose family would not give my brother an affidavit to get into the United States. Obviously, I had no interest in those people and never made any attempt to find them. My mother, on the other hand, was very interested. Every time she visited, she spurred me on to find them. Without much enthusiasm, I tried as best I could to satisfy her, but I was never successful. She had some vague idea that the uncle had lived in Marysville, California. I tried Marysville telephone information, but, as expected, without success.

One of our new neighbors in Sea Cliff, was a Mrs. Osterman, whom we knew casually. Her husband was a doctor. They were a couple about our age and they had a son, William, a classmate and almost exactly the same age as our son Joe. When Joe was still a baby and my mother came to visit, she often had Priscilla call Mrs. Osterman and told her that she wanted to take Joe to China Beach in his pram and would Mrs. Osterman and William like to come along. Despite the difference in age and the difficulty with language, the two women always enjoyed each other's company and had a good time together.

One day, many months later, we were invited to another neighbor's dinner party. It happened that I was seated next to Mrs. Osterman. For some reason she said, "My grandfather Heyman always used to say "......."

I said, "Wait a minute! Your grandfather Heyman? What was his last name?" and she said "it was Chaim." I said, "Susan, you won't believe this, but you're my second cousin twice removed." I didn't know if that was exactly the right degree of relationship, but it sounded good. So I explained to her how we were connected, but of course never mentioned the refusal of the affidavit. That was water over the dam. I immediately called my mother in Buenos Aires. "Mom," I told her, "your search is over. I found your uncle's family." She was so excited that I had located the family and even more surprised and excited when she learned that Susan Osterman, whom she knew well and liked very much, was a granddaughter of Uncle Heyman. She really wanted to meet all of those people. She was going to make a special trip to the United States, just for that.

Well, she came. We had a big family reunion. There were exchanges of reminiscences and, again, nothing was said about that denied affidavit. My mother was such a sweet and forgiving lady that she may even have erased that from her memory.

We are still reasonably friendly with the Osterman's. They are nice people.

On that occasion, my mother sensed, and she turned out to have been right, that it would be the last time that she would see me. She felt that she had to clear the air, be totally truthful, and she decided to make three confessions to me.

The first was about my Aunt Martha and her son Klaus, who I knew all along could not possibly be Uncle Gustav's son. She told me about the affair that my aunt had had with that ship's doctor, how she confessed what she had done to her husband, and that Uncle Gustav accepted Klaus as his own son, and that Klaus himself never had any doubt about his parentage. Frankly, I never had too high an opinion of Uncle Gustav, but I was most impressed by how he handled this difficult, most important matter in his life. It overshadowed all the less impressive qualities that I had ascribed to him. Of course, my mother's disclosure was no revelation and no big surprise to me.

The second "confession" related to her brother, whose name was also Gustav. She had always told me that he had been gassed or shell shocked during the war, and therefore had to be institutionalized. I never met him. I knew that that, too, was a fishy story. It had been concocted by the family in order to avoid the taint of mental illness in the family. It might have been difficult for any of the five sisters to find husbands, with that "blemish on the family," since people were convinced that mental illness was hereditary. The reality, of course, was that Uncle Gustav was a schizophrenic. By the time she told me about it, he had long since died. That, too, was no revelation and no real surprise to me.

The third "confession" was something entirely different. I was rather touched by it. She told me how much she regretted and how wrong she had been in her haughtiness and disdain of the *Ostjuden* – the Jews from the East – from Russia and Poland – that were not "pure Germans." That disdain, that haughtiness extended even to my father's family. She realized that, certainly for the Nazis, such distinctions did not exist at all. Even more important, when my parents and so many others came to Argentina, the existing Jewish community – about 250,000 strong at that time, was virtually in its entirety composed of *Ostjuden*. They created institutions and set up organizations to help the new immigrants from Germany, who, almost without exception, thought of themselves as "superior' to those who assisted them in their need. My mother thought that she had been foolish and that she regretted her arrogant thoughts and especially how she had treated the members of my father's family, including his parents. All of them fell into the category of *Ostjuden*, even though, except for my grandmother, all of them were born in Berlin. I thought that it was very handsome of her to have thought about it and to tell me about it. I must say that I loved her more for that than for many other things that she had said or done.

Things were going pretty well. We had a beautiful home, I had what I thought was a promising business, and a nice family. There was one fly in the ointment. It was our son Michael.

Michael, by that time, was about fourteen years old. He had really been a problem since a very early age. He was disruptive in school, and Priscilla and I were invited to frequent unpleasant conferences with his teachers and with the principals. In two cases, it was strongly suggested that he change schools, and we did that. But nothing seemed to really help. He had friends that we disapproved of, he stayed out late at night on mysterious errands, and he exhibited erratic behavior. In addition, our home was permeated by a constant sweetish odor that we could not identify until one of our guests one day told us bluntly that our home smelled like a marijuana den, because that's what it was. We were total innocents. There was a fairly unpleasant scene, and marijuana smoking, at least in the house (and at least when we were not traveling), ceased. It was a very small victory and it did not address the main problem, of which we were still totally unaware.

But things went well at the office. That Maruden Cigarette Lighter, which I had by now reordered several times, continued to sell well in all editions of *The Wall Street Journal*. We now had also received our shipments of the Bicky Telescope and of the Emoskop Vest Pocket Optical System. They also sold very well, far beyond what we needed to pay for the ads – at the retail rate – in *The Wall* Street Journal. I had discovered the road to quick riches – or so I thought.

One morning in early November, a Mr. Paradise appeared un-announced in my office. He caught my attention because he was exceptionally short, I would say not over 5' 1" tall. He was very serious, all business, and introduced himself as the Assistant Advertising Manager of *The Wall Street Journal*. What could it be, I wondered.

"Have a seat, Mr. Paradise. How can I help you."

"I'm here to tell you," he said unsmilingly, "that your retail advertising contract with *The Wall Street Journal* is canceled as of immediately. If you wish to advertise with us, you may do so at the general rate."

"Wait a minute, Mr. Paradise," I said, "I have a specific agreement with Mr. Moss about how to get classified as a retail establishment. He read it to me from the rule book. All I had to do was to have shelves and to have a cash register. Here are my shelves and here is my cash register. What else do you need? In fact, I have a one-year contract allowing me to advertise at the retail rate."

"This is all a scam," he said. "You know that you're not a retail store and I know that you're not a retail store. Therefore, you're not entitled to the retail rate. And I don't give a damn what the rule book says. You will be billed at the retail rate for the ads that are running now. Any new ads that you may wish to place will be at the regular rate, which, as you know, is about three times as high as what you are paying now."

"Wait a minute," I said. "You can't do that. I have a contract."

"This is a fraudulent contract," he said. "That's what I am going to do. Goodbye." He turned his tiny body around and left without another word.

Wow! The little so-and-so had destroyed my dream of an unending stream of cash with one blow. There was no way that I could make any money at the regular rate. I didn't know what I could do now. Here I had all this merchandise coming in, with Christmas, the peak selling season, on the horizon, and this disgusting little guy had cut me off by the knees. To say that I was very perturbed is greatly understating it. I called Al Moss. "Al, what's the matter! I've been told by this guy Paradise that I can no longer advertise at the retail rate."

"Yes," he said. "I know. Mr. Paradise has been here. He's my boss. There's nothing I can do."

"Al," I said, "you're my friend, but if your boss on *The Wall Street Journal* will insist on that, I'll have to sue them."

"I'm sorry to hear that, Gerardo," he says, "but there's nothing I can do. They made their decision in New York, and I'm helpless. This whole thing isn't doing anything for my career either."

So I went to one of San Francisco's fine law firms, Feldman, Waldman and Klein, who had previously done some work for me. I told them my story and showed them my contract. FW&K thought that I had a good case and they sued *The Wall Street Journal* for $6 million in damages on my behalf. Six million dollars?

Yes! First they computed what my actual and potential damages were as the result of breach of contract. They took the results of sales and profits to date on the contract, projected it out for one year, assuming that I took full advantage of every opportunity, and came up with the (what I thought was the substantially "generous") amount of $2 million in projected profits. Then they decided that this was an anti-trust or restraint-of-trade action, in which triple damages were applicable. That's how they came up with $6 million. I liked the number and I admired their handiwork.

At first, the attorneys for *The Wall Street Journal* acted as though this was funny. In the conferences that we had, they totally denied and belittled the claim. But my guys insisted on the $6 million. They didn't budge and they weren't smiling. Obviously, there were conferences between the big boys of Dow Jones (*The Wall Street Journal's* parent company) in New York and their attorneys in San Francisco. Somebody must have got the idea that we might go through with this suit and that some crazy jury, feeling that a powerful publishing enterprise was abusing a small businessman, might indeed come up with a verdict in my favor of $6 million or at least a substantial fraction of it. Also, of course, an important precedent would have been created.

A few days later I got a call from my attorney. "Gerardo," my attorney Murray Waldman said, "they want to settle with us."

"How do they want to settle?" I asked.

"They want to give you the right to advertise at the retail rate."

"For one year only?" I asked.

"No," he said, "without limitation. But they have a condition, which I think is really only a face-saver, and I would suggest you accept that."

"What is that?" I asked.

"They want you to form a separate corporation, called Haverhills Retail or something like that."

"No," I said, "I'm not going to do that. That's not in my business plan. But what I can do is to form a division within the same corporation, and that will be my retail division."

"Let me go back to them," he said, "and see if that is agreeable. There's one more thing Murray said, but not a condition. It would be much better if you would indeed open a bona fide retail store. It would keep them from having the same difficulties with other advertisers."

"All right," I said, "as long as it's not a condition, I'll try to do that."

I thought that opening a retail store wasn't a bad idea at all and that I should perhaps do so eventually anyway. But I also realized that I couldn't open a retail store with just two or three articles of merchandise. So, I decided to go full bore, add perhaps 40 or 50 new pieces of merchandise and instead of just advertising in *The Wall Street Journal* and some other media that I had pinpointed by that time, that I should publish a catalog. It would be a catalog that I would send to my customers and, if I could get their names, to others who might be interested in our kind of merchandise. All these things sound very simple and are indeed commonplace today. There are many catalogs. In fact, most people claim that they get more catalogs than they wish to receive, but in those days it was a novelty. Nothing quite like that really existed to any extent or in any organized way.

My friends Cliff Wilson and Samm Coombs quit their jobs with the major agency for which they had worked for many years, and decided to open their own agency, with me as their first client. Of course, even though I was beginning to make quite a few waves, I was surely a very small account, so they had to hustle and get some other business. I certainly could not even begin to support them. They were very talented and attracted clients who were much more substantial than I was. They did so well in fact that, not too many years later, they merged with a major national agency and made themselves quite rich. But that was still in the future.

One day, Cliff called me and said, "Gerardo, you know that girl Cayla Werner working here, who works on your catalog?"

"Yes, of course, I know her. She seems to be a very talented woman. What about her?"

"She is very pregnant and we don't feel comfortable with that. Would you give her a job?" Even in those unenlightened days, it sounded like a weird reason to get rid of an employee. Today, of course, this would be impossible.

"Yes, send her by. I think I would like for her to do the catalog in-house. It might save some money and be more productive."

So, Cayla came over. I had known her only fleetingly. She wasn't all that pregnant – maybe three months. She barely showed. I hired her, and her work was quite sensational. She was one of the most difficult people I had ever worked with, but she was so productive and so talented that it made it all worthwhile. She took over the entire artistic direction of my fledgling company and set the tone, the concept, and the "image" of the business for many years to come. In addition, though no one had really asked her to do that, she took over as the merchandise manager and, subject to my approval, selected all of the merchandise for our first catalog and for our new store, about one hundred unique items altogether.

At this time, most consumer merchandise suitable for our business came from Europe, primarily Germany and some of it from Italy. In order to conduct our German business, we hired an agent in Germany, a Mr. Albrecht, a very knowledgeable merchandiser, who served us on a retainer basis for many years. He led us to many good sources and did a great job. But I had great misgivings about my dealings with Germany. This may be a good time for some reflection.

From the very beginning, I was conscious that I was Jewish. It was an important matter to me, but not really anything to which I gave much thought or to which I paid much attention. It was what I was, just as I was a boy, that I had white skin, that I had brown hair – and that I was German. I didn't give any of these things much thought. They were all part of me. There was absolutely no conflict as far as I could tell between being German and being Jewish.

During my entire stay in Germany, and that includes the Nazi period, I personally was not subjected to a single anti-Semitic incident, much less even an outrage. Yet, even though there was not much talk about it, I became aware at an early age of the "difference," some of it imposed and some of it self-imposed, between "us" and "them."

My parents, relatives and acquaintances would often talk about anti-Semitism, what they called *rishiss*, which, apparently in the days before the Nazis came to power, manifested itself only in subtleties and in discriminations that were understood and accepted, and which, as far as I could tell, did not bother anybody very much. I learned at an early age – nobody really told me, I just became aware of it – that, with very few exceptions, Jews would not serve in the military or in the civil service, and certainly were not welcomed in the upper echelons of management or in the board rooms of major corporations. Thus, inevitably, most Jews were either in the professions, primarily law and medicine, or in the arts; the great majority were owners or employees of small businesses.

I also could not help noticing that, without exception, all of my parents' friends were Jewish. I don't recall, apart from a live-in maid, that a gentile person ever visited in our home, nor that we ever visited in the homes of gentiles. Although those things existed, we did not know anybody in a mixed marriage. My parents would probably not have associated with a couple in such a marriage. It was not that they "disapproved." But, they just wouldn't have been comfortable.

My first four years in school were only with Jewish children; then, in the *Hohenzollern Gymanisum*, we were together with gentile boys. We never had any trouble with them, but we kept mostly to ourselves. Rarely would we visit the home of one of our gentile fellow students, and the same was true the other way around.

My sense of Jewishness, which later, under the Nazis, morphed into fervent Zionism, was heightened by enthusiastic participation in the Jewish Boy Scouts.

I received a thorough and meticulous education in the German *Gymanisum* and am totally imbued with German lore, German songs, German poems, German history, and German culture. All of that I considered my own, just as I considered my Jewishness my own. I found no conflict and no problem.

All of that changed when the Nazis took power in Germany in 1933, and made the demeaning, the vilification, and the debasement of the Jews, though not yet the violent persecution (at least not in Berlin), the main plank of their program. I developed a feeling of loathing and disdain for Germans and for Germany that I kept for a very long time.

After I arrived in Bolivia, I had little opportunity and sought no opportunity to speak German and avoided it if at all possible. When the Bolivian authorities issued my *cédula de identidad*, my identity card and decreed that my name "Gerhard" had to be hispanisized to "Gerardo," I did not protest at all. I welcomed that. I wanted to get rid of any vestige of Germany that was attached to me.

When the naturalization people in Texarkana asked me whether I wanted to revert to Gerhard in my naturalization document, I declined. I wanted to stay Gerardo and I have been identified as Gerardo ever since.

I followed the war, of course, with the greatest attention. I celebrated every Allied victory and mourned every Allied setback. I knew that if the Nazis won the war, any normal life for me, wherever in the world I might be, would have ended. My rejoicing was almost boundless when Germany was finally defeated. I savored and read and reread the reports of the hangings of the Nuremburg criminals and of the suicide death of Adolf Hitler, his wife of two days, and of Joseph Goebbels, his wife and his children. My only regret was that they had not fallen alive into the hands of the Jews. They would have known how to take care of them, even better than the Soviets would have.

My views changed somewhat, to almost ambivalent feelings, when the Germans, being engaged and preoccupied with their own social and economic recovery, decided to do all they could to compensate the Jewish victims of Nazi persecution. Obviously, nobody could bring the six million dead back to life nor assuage the horrors that the Nazis had perpetrated on those that survived the extermination camps. The only thing they could do was to dispense money and they did that with little questioning and with generosity. It seems that they gave all claimants every benefit of the doubt. To the degree that they could, they atoned for the crimes that, not necessarily they, but their parents, had committed. They made themselves responsible. It was a generous gesture and I had to recognize it and be grateful for it.

I was particularly impressed by the fact that my parents' life had so dramatically changed from utter misery to relative well-being. The Germans made it possible for them to have no further financial worries.

I, too, was entitled to compensation under these new German laws. My claim was for "interruption of education." I did not wish to apply for any compensation. I felt that it would have made me feel beholden. I didn't want to be that. But my mother insisted and insisted. Finally, I gave in, just to keep her satisfied and received a small compensation, I believe it was $1,000. Since I had gone to both university and graduate school, I was informed that I was entitled to an additional, somewhat larger compensation. Despite the urgings of my mother, I decided not to pursue that at all. In fact, for a long time I felt "guilty" for having accepted this small compensation of $1,000.

Quite a few years later, the Berlin government invited Priscilla and me to a two-week first-class all-expenses-paid trip to Berlin, a gesture of atonement, friendship, and compensation by the City of Berlin. I did realize the good will in which it was offered, but I just couldn't bring myself to accept it, so I declined. I learned that many other cities in Germany did the same thing for their Jewish former fellow citizens.

Despite the benefits given to my parents, for which I was truly grateful, I just could not bring myself to use any German product, not even a Mont Blanc pen. I remember that, when I was at the Harvard Business School, I needed to buy a manual typewriter to do those written analyses. The typewriter that I had was no longer serviceable, so I went to a small typewriter store on Harvard Square. The proprietor turned out to be Jewish. He said "Gerardo, the best typewriter by far for the money is the German-made Adler typewriter. That's the one you should buy."

I said, "Mr. Lipschitz, I just can't use a German product. I would feel uncomfortable."

He replied, "Gerardo, the war is over and has been over for a long time. I know how you feel, but today's Germans are really good people and they make fine products. We have to understand the new reality. Buy this typewriter and be happy with it."

So I did buy that Adler typewriter. I got over my hangups and used it for many years. Still, even today, I can't make myself drive a German car, especially not a Mercedes because Adolf Hitler drove one and, of course, I could never drive a Volkswagen, which was the "people's car" that the *Führer* promised the German people ("a Volkswagen in every garage"), which, perhaps somewhat cynically, had been revived after the war and which became, of course, a very great success.

My daughter Rachel and her husband, who do not share my hangups and perhaps don't even understand them, drive Mercedes cars. I keep my mouth shut about it, of course – it's their business, but I have somewhat of a hard time with it.

This whole matter of Germany and my relationship to it, though I have mostly come to terms with it, is so important and so perturbing to me that I will talk about it once more at the end of this chronicle.

Even though I had some money, which was left from the sale of my stake in the TarGard Company, I was sure that in order to run my new Haverhill's business properly, I would need additional money. I had no credit and I knew that the media, especially those of Time Inc., would wish to be paid in advance until they were convinced that my credit was solid. Also, I had to have a bank line of credit in order to write the letters of credit necessary to import merchandise.

I made the rounds of San Francisco banks, all the way down the newest and smallest, the San Francisco National Bank. There is another small corollary to this story: A friend of mine, a Harvard Business School colleague, was in the brokerage business. He hit on me to buy some stock from him. I really didn't want to buy anything, because I didn't have any money to spare for that purpose. But he persuaded me to buy 100 shares of the stock of the San Francisco National Bank. It was $3 a share. So, really against my better judgment and desire, but since it was a small amount of money, I gave him $300 plus his commission, and told him to buy 100 shares for my account. He came back three days later and gave me a stock certificate for 100 shares. "Ed," I said, "I have no place to put this certificate. Why don't you put it in your safe for me?"

"No problem, I'll do that."

I forgot all about those shares. About a year later I read something about the San Francisco National Bank in the *San Francisco Chronicle*. It was good news. I remembered the shares and since I still needed money – it seems that in those days I always did – I asked Ed to sell them for me at the market. "What is the quotation, now?" I asked him.

He punched a few keys on his computer and said $38.50. "Wait a minute," I said, "you mean that my $300 investment is now worth $3,850?"

Yes, that was what it was worth. "Please sell it immediately. I certainly need that money." This is fantastic."

So he sold it the next day. That was the absolute high the stock ever reached. Within four or five months it was down to less than $1, then, not much later, down to nothing. I told that story one evening at a dinner party. A man across the table from me, a person I had never seen before, said to me in what I hoped was mock anger, "You son-of-a-gun, I'm the guy that bought those hundred shares from you at $38.50 and sold them for zilch. Thanks a lot."

Well, that's the way of the stock market. Some people win and some people lose. Anyway, some people were made happy by the rise and fall of the San Francisco National Bank, but quite a few others were made quite unhappy.

So I made the rounds of San Francisco banks and told my story to a number of flint-eyed and stone-hearted loan officers; they listened to me, but all of them were reluctant to make a commitment. I finally went to the San Francisco National Bank, in which at the time I still owned those 100 shares of stock. The bank was the creation and practically the personal fiefdom of one Don Silverthorne. Mr. Silverthorne was a man of enormous physical proportions, a bon vivant, a pillar of the San Francisco social scene, and the virtual monarch of the San Francisco National Bank.

I told my story and made formal application to the loan officer of the San Francisco National Bank. He looked over the information of what I wanted to do, what income I had from my various activities, what insurance, what assets, what liabilities, etc. He told me that there would be no question that this loan (I had requested $10,000) would be approved and that it was simply a matter of "formalities" to be completed. "Please come back tomorrow," he said. "Your loan will be approved by then."

I was pleased that I had finally solved my financial problem and counted quite firmly on those funds. When I returned the next day, the loan officer, somewhat sheepishly, handed my application back to me. It had been defaced by the word DISAPPROVED in enormous block letters stamped diagonally across it. I was angry and surprised and asked the loan officer why, after having just yesterday informally approved this application, he was now rejecting it. He looked around furtively, lowered his voice to a whisper and said: "Look, Mr. Joffe, in this bank only Mr. Silverthorne makes the decisions. He didn't like this application, he didn't explain why, and just told me to reject it. I am not about to ask him for his reasons." I was really outraged and wrote a scathing and indignant letter to Mr. Silverthorne, complaining about the high-handed way in which he ran his bank and treated would-be customers, including stockholders. This was the good-bye kiss to the San Francisco National Bank, as far as I was concerned. I was simply letting off some steam.

Imagine my surprise when, two days later, Mr. Silverthorne's secretary called me, told me that there must have been some misunderstanding and invited me for the following day to an interview with the great man himself. I went and found

Mr. Silverthorne in a palatial office, surrounded by walnut, leather and jade, an environment befitting the last of the Borgias, rather than the president of a small bank.   I must confess that I was impressed and somewhat awed.   He cut a magnificent figure and he talked to me in a kind but rather condescending manner for about two or three minutes. My loan application was on his desk, in front of him. He didn't look at it once. Suddenly he said, "My boy, I like the cut of your jib." (I was over forty years old, but, honestly, those were his words. I had read them once in Captain Hornblower, but I had never actually heard anybody utter them.)

"How much money do you want?" he asked. I hesitated for one second and said "$10,000." He immediately made a 180 degree swivel turn in his chair, opened a drawer, took out a standard form and wrote out an order to his cashier to open a credit of $10,000 for me. I opened and closed my mouth two or three times and cursed myself for not having said $20,000, instead of $10,000, because I had the distinct feeling that he would have approved that also. After all, he liked the cut of my jib. I debated with myself for a few seconds whether I should reopen the subject, but then prudence won out and I decided to leave well enough alone.

Just about one month later – in the meantime, I had fortunately sold my 100 shares of stock – Mr. Silverthorne's bank went into bankruptcy. He was indicted and convicted of all kinds of dreadful crimes against the banking laws, for self-dealing and whatnot. Deposits in the bank were, of course, protected by FDIC – up to $10,000 at the time – so I did not lose any money. I transferred the Haverhill's account to another bank and came unscathed out of the whole affair. But I always remembered Mr. Silverthorne fondly for recognizing quickly that I was a good credit risk, that my business plans made sense and had potential, and that I was going to turn into a good customer for his bank. I understand that I was the only person who wrote a kind letter to Mr. Silverthorne while he was in prison. I told him how grateful I was to him, how I appreciated that he had extended credit to me when I needed it, and that my thoughts were with him in his present misfortune.

So now I was in this new business and it became clear to me that I really couldn't be in it and do what I was doing if I were to deny myself German merchandise. At that time, Germany was the main source for the kind of consumer merchandise that I wanted to feature in my business.   I had to overcome my misgivings. Within a year of having started Haverhill's, we had close to 100 items of merchandise of which not fewer than 70 or 80 came from Germany. Our efficient agent, Mr. Albrecht, brought us new merchandise ideas almost every week and virtually all of them were good ones.

By that time, and in line with my quasi promise to *The Wall Street Journal*, we had moved to a nice ground-floor location on Washington Street in San Francisco, opposite to what now is the famous Pyramid Building, San Francisco's most beautiful landmark. The space lent itself and we chose it for that reason, namely to have a store in front, with offices in the back and warehouse and shipping facilities in the basement. It was an ideal location.

We engaged a topnotch store designer and spared no expense. We wound up having a beautiful store that immediately became popular, productive, and very profitable.

We had a wonderful Salvadoran mature woman, Laura, as our live-in housekeeper. We felt that Priscilla was not needed full time at home, and that she should help in the business, particularly with the store and also with merchandising. That became somewhat of a necessity because Cayla, who until then had been the sole source for art direction and merchandising, was pregnant again and could be expected to be out for at least six months. So Priscilla became a full-time employee of Haverhill's and, among other duties, permanently "manned" the new store.

While that was a good and profitable decision for the business, it turned out to be a disaster on a personal level. Our son Michael, who by that time was about sixteen years old, was beginning to act more and more strange, stayed out late at night, and began to have his first brushes with the law. But innocent as we were, we thought of it as a "stage" that he would outgrow. While it did of course, concern us, we didn't realize how serious it really was.

Mr. Albrecht suggested to us that, in order to be truly successful, it would be desirable or perhaps even mandatory to attend the important European yearly merchandise shows – mostly and at least the yearly Hanover Messe, the Milan Fair, and perhaps also the Basel, Switzerland, Watch and Clock Show. One advantage was that all of these shows were pretty much at the same time so that they could be attended consecutively, on one trip.

So we decided to do just that. We took off on our first European merchandising trip. We flew to London, mostly for the purpose of buying an MGB car, a little number that Priscilla had coveted for a long time. We had ordered it in the States and we picked it up from British Motors in London. We were immediately enamored of it. It was dark green. We nicknamed it "Greenie." We loved that little car.

We were somewhat intimidated by the traffic in London, with which we were unfamiliar, especially since the British drive on "the wrong side" of the road and since Greenie had American (left-hand) steering. In order to get out of London, I hired a cab and gave the driver ten pounds. I told him to please drive in the direction of Dover and we would follow him. I told him to stop when the meter reached nine pounds and to keep the tenth pound as his tip. That's how we got out of London. I don't think we could have otherwise done it.

We got to Dover, crossed the channel on the ferry, "did" Paris, then drove on to Strasbourg, which, of course, used to be the German Strassburg. We parked by the left bank of the Rhine River. It was easy to see the German town of Kehl on the other side. As for over a century, a bridge connected the two cities, one in France and the other in Germany.

Priscilla and I stayed in Strasbourg for two full days. I just could not give myself the push to step on German soil, after over thirty years. The very thought made me almost ill. While I had not experienced it myself, I remembered the many stories of Jewish people who crossed or tried to cross from Germany into France, who were subjected to painful interrogations that could last for hours, to the complete tearing apart of their poor possessions and, if they were unlucky, and for any pretext or none at all, could be arrested and put into a concentration camp, or worse. I had all of that in mind when I looked at Germany, which appeared so sunny and so peaceful on the other side of the Rhine river.

Eventually, however, we could no longer delay. We either did what we had come to do or we didn't So, we did the deed. We climbed into Greenie and went eastward across that bridge. In the middle of that bridge stood a uniformed German – it could have been a soldier, a customs person or whatever, who looked the total antithesis of those dreadful and ferocious SS men who used to guard that border. He was perhaps eighteen or twenty years old and, unimaginable in the "old" German army, sported long sideburns and a stringy goatee. His stance and general appearance were far from martial and could in fact be described as somewhat casual, probably even as sloppy. I felt reassured and was favorably impressed. We were prepared to stop, show our passports and subject ourselves to interrogation, but he just smiled and waved us on. We never stopped. We were in Germany.

My experience with Germany, with German suppliers, and with the German people at large were always most pleasant. As soon as people realized who and what I was – and that was usually very fast because my German, of course, was that of a native speaker, they would almost fall all over themselves to do whatever they could to show me their good will. It was sort of touching. Somewhat embarrassingly, almost without exception, and certainly without my questioning them, they told us that they had been against the Nazis all along, but that they were helpless to do anything against the "excesses" (what a euphemism!) that the Nazis had committed. It might all have been true. None of the people that I dealt with looked or acted like somebody who could have deliberately have sliced open pregnant women, could have buried people alive, or would have driven entire communities into synagogues and then burned them down.

But the thing that haunts me to this day is what happened to those who actually did these terrible things. The people that were hanged at Nuremberg or condemned to long prison sentences were certainly guilty, and so were the few hundred smaller fry who also got caught in the "de-Nazification," but all those were obviously only the tip of a very large iceberg. What happened to the many tens of thousands or hundreds of thousands of others who indeed were "Hitler's willing executioners?" Nobody seemed to know and they never surfaced. It is clear that virtually all of them, except perhaps for those bigwigs, who, with the money that they had stashed with the willing Swiss, escaped to South America, simply blended into German society and continued life as before the war, and in many cases occupied important positions in industry, in commerce and even in the government. Their fellow citizens, their neighbors, knew who they were, but all of them kept their mouths shut. There was a great conspiracy of silence.

Some of our German suppliers eventually became personal friends, though in the back of my mind I always wondered what they had been doing during the war.

haverhill's, the direct-marketing firm that I had started was going gangbusters. Here I am with Cayla Werner at a catalog press run. She was a great help in getting the business off the ground and in making it successful.

This is during one of my mother's visits from Argentina (the year was 1965), Rachel was five years old and Michael – still happy and unencumbered – was twelve years old. Joseph was still in his mother's tummy.

One of those friends was Arthur Seibert, somewhat of an optical genius from the "optical town" of Wetzlar, the inventor and manufacturer of the Emoskop. I ultimately sold far over 100,000 of these wonderful products. When Mr. Seibert retired from his business and therefore discontinued production, I had the same item manufactured in Japan, and renamed it Episcope. I sold more than another 100,000 units.

Another of my friends was Klaus Meuter and his wife Ingrid. They manufactured a mechanical manual calculator, the kind that was operated with a crank. Its name was Multator IV. We were able to sell it for $99, a wonderful price at the time. We sold thousands and thousands of these beautiful machines. That business ended virtually from one day to the next, but that is another story.

Our most important item in Europe, however, was not manufactured in Germany but, of all places, in the small principality of Monaco.

Here's what happened: I had read in one of the consumer trade magazines about a wind-up shaver – something that neither I nor anybody else had ever seen before. I thought it was a great item and something that would fit into our lineup of merchandise. The factory was in Monaco. I wrote to the factory, sent some money and asked them to send me a sample. No reply. A month later I wrote to the factory again, reminded them of my previous letter and of the check I had sent them – still no reply.

Knowing that Monaco was and is still essentially a dependency of France, I then wrote to the commercial attaché of the French Consulate in San Francisco, sent him copies of my previous letters to that Monaco factory and told him how disappointed I was that this factory, with which we were trying to do some business, did not respond.

He, or somebody in Paris, apparently put a needle in those Monacans because ten days later we had a nice letter and a sample of the shaver. They called it the Riviera Shaver. I thought it was a great item. I immediately placed a sample order of 500 units, advertised it, and was happy to find that it was a substantial success. We made money with every ad we placed. What's more – and that is the greatest measure of success in this business – people reordered for themselves and for their friends. We had a winner!

But one day I got a certified letter from a law firm in New York advising me sternly that "Riviera" was a trademark owned by that firm's client. If I did not cease and desist immediately, they would do all kinds of terrible things to me. I decided not to fight that, although I might probably have prevailed because, as my attorney explained to me, the other party's Riviera mark was not applied to an item that could possibly be confused with the shaver. But I made the very wise decision – a decision that, regrettably, I did not always follow later in my business life – not to fight it and not to get involved with attorneys and with lawsuits. I dropped the Riviera name. We re-dubbed the shaver "Monaco" and created a trademark that ultimately turned out to be extremely valuable. Of course, I checked it out. Nobody else was using that name on any product.

The "Monaco Shaver," under its new name, continued to be a great success. Within a few months, I was the most important importer of Monaco merchandise in the United States – more than just an asterisk and a footnote in the budget of the Principality of Monaco. But of course, that did not mean a whole lot, because Monaco is not what you would call an industrialized power. Still, it was an important item for the Principality, which existed and still does exist almost exclusively on tourism and on gambling. Mme. Rollet, the manager and owner of the factory, told me that Prince Rainier had taken notice and had one of his courtiers write her a letter of appreciation. He did, however, not invite me to an audience. Oh, well!

So we now had a number of winners: The Maruden Cigarette Lighter, which gave me my start, had now begun to peter out somewhat. Also, not being a smoker, I didn't really have my heart in the item. But the Bicky Telescope from Japan, the Emoskop Vest Pocket Optical System and the Multator IV from Germany, and now the Monaco Shaver (from where else? – Monaco) were real money makers. My main medium was still *The Wall Street Journal* with its advantageous retail advertising rate, for which I had fought so hard. But now I had expanded into other national media. I was on a roll.

One day, one of the girls that opened the mail and who was, therefore, the first link in the order-filling process, told me that somebody in Washington, DC had placed an order for twelve Monaco shavers. That was a substantial order; we never had had anything like that before. But what most surprised me was that this party did not ask for a discount or any other freebies. Usually, people who buy multiples or wholesale quantities want to get a little something extra or certainly a quantity discount, and usually we would accede to it. But the party that ordered the twelve shavers just sent a check for the full amount and didn't ask for anything else. While I was a little surprised, pleasantly of course, I didn't give the matter of the twelve shavers any more thought.

About six months later, I got a call from a representative of NASA. He introduced himself as Francis Mullins. He said, "Mr. Joffe, I have an interesting piece of information for you. Your Monaco shaver went to the moon."

"What do you mean?" I asked him.

"Yes," he said. "We put the shaver on our Apollo 14 spacecraft, for the use of the astronauts."

"Oh, that's wonderful," I said. "Did they like it?"

"Oh yes, they liked it very much."

Then I said, "Excuse me, do you think I could mention this in my advertising and use the NASA Apollo 14 emblem with it?"

"Oh, no," he said. "That's quite out of the question. We don't ever allow the commercializing of NASA and of the space program."

"Mr. Mullins, it would be very important to me," I told him. "It would mean a whole lot. Could you not perhaps talk to your supervisor and get permission?"

"Well, I'll try that, but I don't think there is much purpose in it. In any case, I want to thank you for making this excellent shaver available to us. The astronauts enjoyed it very much. In fact, I'm using one myself. It's a great item."

Naturally, I was elated about this news, but it didn't help me a lot if I could not use this important information for my advertising campaign. But a couple of weeks later, the same man, Mr. Mullins, called back.

"Mr. Joffe, you're obviously very persuasive, and this could be your lucky day. I talked to my supervisor. You will be allowed to use the Apollo 14 emblem in your advertising, provided, however, that we approve the copy. We are sending you a facsimile of the emblem today."

Wow, that was a terrific breakthrough – one of those pieces of good luck that don't happen too often. So, immediately, we re-dubbed the shaver "Monaco – the shaver that went to the moon," and put it on all of our advertising. There was no problem getting approval of our copy from NASA.

Sales went (excuse the expression) through the stratosphere, until the time that Mme. Rollet died, about five years later, and the factory closed. By that time, we must have sold over 100,000 of those shavers. Until I sold Haverhills, more than thirty years later, I still had inquiries about the shaver but I couldn't help anybody with it, of course. More painful, and perhaps even a little embarrassing, was that we gave all buyers a lifetime guarantee on the shaver. It could be returned for replacement or for repair at any time. When the factory went out of business, we stopped advertising, of course, and by that time we had a small inventory left, perhaps 200 units. We used those for warranty purposes only. Even until two years ago, when I still owned Haverhills, I would get the (fortunately, very rare) request for replacement under the lifetime guarantee. Of course, I could no longer deliver on the guarantee, but I sent every one of those people a $50 certificate for any other merchandise. Everyone was happy.

I had the telephone number of Francis Mullins, the man from NASA, with whom I had been dealing. One thing puzzled me, and it was this: The shaver was really quite heavy because it was powered by a large steel spring. It weighed much, much more than an ordinary shaver. I was aware that one of the great concerns in space travel was weight. The keen desire was to avoid any excess ounce of weight. Then, why would they wish to have a shaver that weighed over a pound when a regular plastic disposable shaver would weigh no more than half an ounce? It really puzzled me. So one day I picked up the phone and I got Francis Mullins on the line.

"Mr. Mullins, I'm so happy that Monaco is the shaver that NASA chose for the Apollo 14 space flight. But why would you take such a heavy item when a regular shaver weighs less than half an ounce?"

He hemmed and hawed and said, "I'm afraid, Mr. Joffe, I cannot really talk about that."

How very peculiar I thought. But, I insisted – apparently, I am, indeed, not just "quite persuasive," but also quite persevering. "Mr. Mullins, I really would like to know and I think you owe it to me to tell me." Obviously that was somewhat of a stretch. He didn't owe me anything.

Then Mullins said, "O.K., I'll tell you. One of the great fears we have in space travel is that something goes wrong and I don't mean a sudden explosion. We could somehow handle that. What we most worry about is the possibility of the spacecraft getting out of orbit or missing that "keyhole" for re-entry and that it could not be directed back to earth. In that case, the astronauts would know that they were condemned to a slow death and an excursion into the infinity of space. We are very afraid of possible suicide of the astronauts in such as a case and the possibly fatal public relations impact of such an event. Therefore, we don't have any razors, anything with a sharp cutting edge at all on board because it could be used for just such a purpose. The Monaco shaver cannot be so used."

Well, that was an interesting reason. I was impressed. Though, obviously I would have preferred it if he had told me that the shaver was so superior that it was worth the added weight.

One of my "Bibles" to find good items to import was a publication called *Made in Europe*. It came out once a month and had a complete smorgasbord of consumer items, many of which I believed would be suitable for my budding business.

One very small ad in that publication caught my attention. It was about "Miracle Gloves." It was a pair of gloves that would clean vegetables – potatoes, carrots and anything else without having to peel them. Though I am not much interested in what goes on in the kitchen (I always remembered Marian Lisman's admonition to stay out of the kitchen), those gloves intrigued me. They were manufactured in Hamburg, Germany. So I sent a check for $20 and asked the maker to send me three or four pairs. They promptly arrived.

I thought they were absolutely wonderful and Priscilla agreed with me. They were sturdy kitchen gloves, but instead of being slick, they had tiny, very hard ceramic crystals embedded in the palms. You could take a potato, hold it under running water and, by rubbing it in your gloved hands, the skin would quickly come off, without taking any of the meat of the potato away. It was very fast and very clean. The same with a carrot. You could hold a carrot in one hand and pull it through your other gloved hand and the carrot was ready to eat or ready to cook. It was a marvelous product.

But how to sell it. It occurred to me that this was a product that had to be demonstrated. The place to demonstrate, I decided, was Woolworth, which, in those days, had a very large and popular store on Market Street in San Francisco. I went to Woolworth and asked to see the manager. He was busy, of course. The receptionist asked me what I wanted. I told her that I wanted to demonstrate a product that would astonish the manager and that would be a great success for Woolworth.

"I'm sorry," she said, "we don't buy anything in this store. You have to go through Central Purchasing," which was somewhere in the middle of the country – Topeka or Omaha or something like that.

I pulled out one pair of my gloves and explained their function to her. "They are my present to you." I said. "It will make your homework a whole lot easier. It's a marvelous product." She looked at the gloves, visualized what they would do, agreed that it was a great product and thanked me for the gift.

I had softened her up with my small present. "Let me have a look," she said. "Maybe I can get him to give you a minute." She came back a few seconds later, winked at me and said, "Come on in. He'll talk to you."

I don't remember the man's name. Let's call him Smith for this purpose. "Mr. Smith," I said, "I'm going to show you this marvelous product. Please ask your secretary to bring us a pan of water." He was a little surprised. I went to the half-open door and said, "Miss, please bring us a pan of water." She was now my friend, of course. She brought the pan of water. There was no running water in the office. I demonstrated what the product would do with one of the potatoes and one of the carrots that I had thoughtfully brought along. He was impressed.

"Yes," he said, "this is indeed a marvelous product for demonstration. Would you want to demonstrate this yourself?"

I was tempted. I'm somewhat of a ham. But I didn't think it would be quite the right thing. I thought I might be more useful as a shill. "Oh no," I said, "I'll get somebody more suitable. When can we demonstrate it?"

How soon can you do it?"

"Well," I said, I'll first have to restock my inventory. They are moving so fast (I exaggerated slightly) that I can't keep them in stock."

"What do they sell for?"

"We sell them for $4.95, the pair," I improvised.

"That sounds like a good price," he said. "How about giving Woolworths $1.50 for each pair you sell?"

"That sounds like a fair deal to me," I said. And I thought it was. We agreed that I (or my surrogate) would demonstrate the item in the store on the Saturday after next.

I went back to the office, called my man in Hamburg and asked if he could send me two gross of the gloves right away by air freight. I would immediately pay him by wire transfer. He agreed, and a few days later I had the gloves in my office. I looked around and found a woman to demonstrate the gloves. She happened to be German. When she saw the gloves and tried them out, she said, "Ach, those Chermans are so clever!" I thought she was right. I guaranteed her a minimum wage, plus a commission of 50 cents per pair of gloves that she sold. We shook hands on it. It seemed like a good deal all around.

On the Friday before the demonstration, Lisa (that was her name) and I went to Woolworth, where Mr. Smith had installed, at a very strategic corner location, a counter with a sink. A hose which looked about an inch in outside diameter was installed as the drain and was connected to the sewer. It was a neat arrangement. The only thing that worried me was the small diameter of the hose.

On Saturday morning, Lisa was punctually at her post with about five pounds of potatoes and quite a few carrots. The water was running. People were looking. I arrived at about 9:30 and, as I had planned, proceeded to be the shill – the person who made the first purchase. She began demonstrating, peeling about ten or twelve potatoes and as many carrots with those miracle gloves in no time at all. People were impressed. But nobody had yet bought anything. I was standing in the back and said, "Those gloves are marvelous. Give me three pairs." She gave me three pairs. Then other people began to buy. By the time we had sold about twenty-five pairs, I would say in the first fifteen minutes, something went wrong. All those peelings had clogged up the hose. With water flowing freely, things quickly overflowed and messed up the entire area around the counter with water and with vegetable peelings. Then, in response to the pressure that had built up, the hose jumped out of the sewer and water spewed all over the floor. It was a minor disaster. Mr. Smith was alerted, ran out of his office and shouted, "Stop it, stop it immediately." Then he said to me, "This demonstration is over. Take your damn gloves and get out of here."

Well, that's what I had to do. I owed Mr. Smith $37.50 for the twenty-five sets of gloves that we had sold, but neither he nor I stuck around long enough to consummate that part of the transaction. Lisa was hurling German curses, which I hoped only I understood. It was clear that she did not come from a refined background. I gave her $25 for her services which she thought was very generous. "*Danke schön*," she said, and we shook hands. We didn't see each other again.

That was the end of my career as a demonstration salesman and as a shill. I am happy to say, however, that the gloves continued to sell very well in mail order, though the price of $4.95 a pair was really too low to make them a truly attractive item for me.

One day, a tall, clean-cut young man appeared in the office. He spoke good English but had a very heavy German accent. He was obviously German. "Mr. Joffe," he said, "I heard about your business and I'm interested in it. I wonder if you can give me work? I'm from Pforzheim, Germany. I'm trying to learn about the Untied States, about American business methods, and to perfect my English. My name is Gerd Schneider. Can you give me something to do?"

"I really don't have a job for you, Gerd," I told him, "but I can give you a few days' work. Come with me." I took him out to our warehouse, which was really a big garage that I had pressed into service for this purpose. It was a mess, it was a shambles. "Gerd," I say, "why don't you straighten out this warehouse. Put everything in its proper place and clean up the mess, and then come back. It will keep you busy for some time." I thought of it as a two-day job for somebody who really applied himself.

At the end of the day when, quite frankly, I'd forgotten all about Gerd, he came back into the office and said, "I did the best I could. Why don't you come and have a look."

I was stunned. It was absolutely marvelous. Everything was in its proper place. Things had been tagged and inventoried. The floor was clean. Everything was straightened out. It had never looked like that before. I said, "Gerd, I don't know exactly what you're going to do, but you're hired. I need a guy like you."

Well, Gerd became my trusted right hand, and as the business grew he became totally indispensable.

One evening, at the end of the day, we were endorsing the checks we had received during the day by mail and in the store and also the cash. Suddenly, Gerd turned to me and said, "Mr. Joffe, I found a $20 bill, but there's supposed to be an American flag flying over the White House, isn't there?"

"I don't know, Gerd, I never looked." But in any case it was not a good question. I told him so.

"Why is that a bad question?" he asked.

"Because I'm quite sure that you have a counterfeit bill in your hands and now I have to turn it over to the bank. I'm out twenty dollars."

"No!" he replied. "In the first place, we can't be sure that it's counterfeit, and even if we were why should you have to know. I count the money, I make the deposit slip, and I deposit it."

"We can't do that, Gerd. It's against the law. You know about it and what is more important is that I know about it. We can't do it."

He gave me the $20 bill. Sure enough, there was no U.S. flag over the White House. We looked at five or six other $20 bills, and not at all to my surprise, every one had Old Glory flying over the White House. So we made our deposit, put the flagless $20 bill aside and turned it over to the bank as counterfeit money. They gave us a receipt for that. Well, it wasn't a big deal; I was out twenty dollars, but I was proud to have done my duty as a citizen and to have that receipt.

About three months later, when I had totally forgotten all about that $20 bill, I got a letter from the bank, telling me that the $20 bill that I had turned over to them was, indeed, legal tender. It was a bill that had been issued by the Bank of Virginia shortly after the Civil War. Because they were still chafing under their loss against the hated Yankees, they didn't want to put the Stars and Stripes over the White House. The bank assured me that the bill was very valuable, a collectors item, and, as I later found out, worth several hundred dollars. The bank did not return my bill. But they did credit my account with $20. Honesty was not necessarily rewarded!

By that time, three or four years out of the starting gate, we had created a solid, successful, and profitable business. When I look back on those years, I am astonished at the great deal of creativity that went into everything we did. Advertising in media, direct mail pieces, catalogs, everything was first class, and everything was successful. I personally wrote every word of copy for this business – all media ads, all direct mail pieces, and all catalogs. We established a reputation for unique and excellent merchandise, for creativity, and for clever copy. Still, it was a fairly small business with sales not over a million dollars per year and profits of not much more than $100,000 a year.

Not a big deal, but being in the mail-order business or, as it is often called, the direct-marketing business, one makes inevitably a lot of noise, creates a great deal of attention, more than the size of the business would seem to warrant. There are millions of advertising impressions in the national media, catalogs are being sent out several times a year, and so are direct-mail pieces, and much more. One, or rather one's business, comes to the attention of many people.

Interesting people would appear in my office unannounced. One day, it must have been in 1969, Priscilla, who was working in the store, came to my office and said, "Gerardo, there is a man out here who says he's from CBS. He wants to see you."

"From CBS," I wondered. What might he want? "O.K., send him in."

The man's name was Jack Opper. He came in and gave me his business card. He was the vice president of development for CBS. I was a little puzzled.

"What can I do for you, Mr. Opper?" I asked him, not imagining what he could possibly want.

"Mr. Joffe, your business, Haverhill's, has come to our attention. We are trying to expand beyond the broadcasting area and we believe that a national mail-order business such as yours might be a good fit. What do you think?"

I told him that the thought of selling the business or that a major national company would take any interest in it had never occurred to me. But of course, I was interested. I was intrigued. "I really had never thought of that, Mr. Opper," I told him truthfully, "but it sounds like an interesting possibility. What would you like for me to do?"

"We have been following your advertising and your merchandising," Opper said, "and you seem to be doing a very good job. What I would need is three years of financial statements, which I would like to take to New York. I am going to leave in the morning."

"Mr. Opper," I said, "we have no problem with the statements. Are you already registered in a hotel?"

"No, he said, "I've just come in. I think I'll go to the St. Francis Hotel."

"Mr. Opper, why don't you come home with us. We have a wonderful guest room and we'll take you out to a nice restaurant. It'll give us an opportunity to talk a little more about CBS, about Haverhill's, and how the two of us might fit together."

Mr. Opper thought this over for a few seconds, then said, "O.K., I accept your invitation. It sounds like a good idea."

So we took him home and had a good chance to talk to him. It turned out that CBS wanted to break into areas other than broadcasting, and that he, Opper, had been entrusted to lead the way to this diversification. He thought, and the "big boys" seemed to agree, that the excursion into the direct-marketing field would be a promising direction, particularly, of course, because of the almost unlimited advertising facilities that CBS, through its broadcast and its other media, could make available to such an acquisition. It sounded like a perfect match, a perfect case of symbiosis.

Haverhill's, he told us, had particularly caught their attention because of the good taste, the excellent advertising, the creativeness, the inventiveness, and the selection of interesting merchandise that we brought to bear. After a couple of drinks, I said, "Mr. Opper, how much would this business be worth to CBS?"

"We'll it's a little bit early to talk about that, but if we go ahead, and from the numbers I've seen so far and the impressions I have, I think it will be around a million dollars."

I thought to myself, "A million dollars! Wow! That would be the fulfillment of the Great American Dream." In my last deal with TarGard, I had made $50,000 and now I am on the verge of making a million. I knew that that was the magic figure. If you attained that, if you were a millionaire, you had achieved success and unquestioned accomplishment.

We had a great visit with Mr. Opper, and I took him to the airport the next day. "We will be in touch," he promised.

And so he was. We talked on the phone once or twice a week. He asked for additional information, all of which I was able to provide and all of which seemed to satisfy him. One afternoon, he called me. "Gerardo," he said, "the deal is pretty much set. There is a directors meeting tomorrow. I'll make my presentation, which I have already made informally to the individual directors; there's no question that the deal will go through. We'll work out the details with you later, but, just as I told you, you can count on a million dollars in cash or in stock, or a combination of both. It's going to be your choice. I'll talk to you after the meeting."

Well, that sounded pretty good. Naturally, I was quite happy. That was on a Thursday and I firmly expected to hear from him on Friday, most likely before noon, especially in view of the difference in time between the coasts. But I didn't hear from him – all day long. I suppose I could have called him, but I didn't want to seem too eager.

He called me on Monday afternoon. He sounded very crestfallen. "Gerardo," he said, "the deal didn't go through. They rejected it."

"Why is that?" I asked.

"Well," Opper said, "all of the directors were in favor of it, but Mr. Paley, the chairman, opposed it. Anything that Mr. Paley opposes can't go ahead."

"What was Mr. Paley's reason?" I asked. "He was the one who sent you on this errand in the first place, wasn't he?"

"Yes, he was, but you know, Mr. Paley doesn't give any reason for his decisions and I wasn't about to ask him. I'm very sorry for all the work I've caused you."

I put a brave face on it. "It makes no difference, Jack," I said. "I made your acquaintance, you're my friend, and that's worth a lot to me." I was sincere in that. I really had come to like him very much, but, of course, I would have liked it even better if CBS had bought Haverhill's for that million dollars.

But Jack Opper wasn't the only interesting visitor. One day a Mr. Frank Murphy announced himself. He was a vice president of the Bowmar Corporation of Acton, Massachusetts. I had never heard of the Bowmar company, nor did I know where Acton, Massachusetts was. "How can I help you, Mr. Murphy?" I asked.

Murphy sat down, acted somewhat furtively, and said, "Mr. Joffe, can I count on your entire discretion?"

I didn't know what he was talking about. "Of course," I said. "What is this about?"

"I'm going to show you the most amazing thing you've ever seen."

"O.K., show me. I'm ready."

He opened his briefcase and pulled out a small black box, about three inches wide, five inches high, and about an inch thick. The box had keys on its front and a narrow window on top. A black strip, with the digits one through zero in red was pasted on the window.

"What is it?" I asked.

"It's something totally new. It's an electronic calculator."

"What" I asked, "is an electronic calculator? What does it do – how does it work?"

"It's amazing," he said. "I'll show you. Give me any kind of a problem."

"O.K.," I said. "3 plus 5."

"No, no," he said, "nothing like that. Give me a multiplication."

"O.K., how about 5 times 6?"

"No," he said, "give me something more complicated. Let's multiply, say, a three digit number with a four digit number."

"O.K.," I said, "357 times 4,489."

"All right," he said, "you do it," and he handed me the "electronic calculator." "Punch in 357." I did that. "Now punch the "x" key, which signifies multiplication." I did that. "Now punch in 4,489." I did that. "Now punch in the equal sign." I did that. "Voilá," Mr. Murphy said, "that's what an electronic calculator does."

"Wait a minute, Mr. Murphy. Where's the result? It still says 1, 2, 3, 4, 5, 6, 7, 8, 9, 0 in the window."

"Oh," Murphy said nonchalantly, "this is just a prototype. But, when we are ready, and we'll be ready in not more than thirty days, the result of this multiplication will appear in this window, and not just multiplication. It will also do division and, it goes without saying, addition and subtraction."

"Are you sure?" I asked him. "Or are you pulling my leg?"

"I'm not pulling your leg. This is one of the greatest inventions ever. We are impressed with your advertising and your promotional savvy. We want to give you the exclusive mail-order right to this calculator for the upcoming Christmas season, provided you place an order for 250 units and proceed to feature it prominently in your upcoming Christmas catalog."

"A scam," I thought. How stupid does he think I am.

"Just a minute," Murphy said, "I know what you're thinking. You don't have to pay us anything now. You pay us thirty days after we deliver the merchandise."

That sounded a lot better to me. "What is this gadget going to sell for?" I asked him.

"$240," he said. "You buy it for $120."

Two hundred and forty dollar in 1970 was a great deal of money. It was equivalent to what is about $1,000 today. That seems almost incredible now, since electronic calculators, with many more features, now sell for less than $10. But I was very intrigued and I decided to go ahead with this deal.

That was in August. Our Christmas catalog was almost finished, so in order to accommodate this pie-in-the-sky electronic calculator I would have to take two or three already scheduled items out instead. Obviously, this breakthrough gadget would have to be the lead item and would deserve ample premium space in the catalog. So I went ahead, totally on faith. I was taking a big risk. I was either crazy or I was a genius.

September and October rolled around, but no Bowmar calculators. I was getting a little nervous. I called Murphy. He told me to be calm and to have confidence. He promised to have the calculators ready in ample time for Christmas. "They'll be there. Don't worry about it."

Well, I couldn't help worrying about it. But, sure enough, the first week of November, almost too late for comfort, 250 Bowmar calculators, beautifully packaged, arrived. I tried one of them immediately, of course. It worked splendidly. I had never seen anything like it before and nobody else had either. I was totally impressed. Quite apart from what it meant to me, I knew that the world had entered a new phase of technology, one that was truly "revolutionary."

We sold those 250 calculators at $240 each within the first two weeks the catalog was out. It was a sensation. We couldn't reorder them fast enough. We were among the very first who sold electronic calculators in the United States, and the very first-mail order company to do so.

There was one small sad side to it, however. It was clear that the Multator IV, the hand-cranked mechanical calculator that we sold for $99, which was one of our main items, and which had been the only means of support for my friend Klaus Meuter in Hamburg, was suddenly becoming utterly obsolete – literally from one day to the next. Who would want to buy a 5-pound clunker, turn the crank and move the carriage back and forth if he could buy a 3 oz. electronic item that he could carry in his pocket that would do the job ten times as fast. Sure, it cost more than twice as much as Klaus's calculator, but people didn't seem to care. We had about 100 of the Multator IV's left in stock. Nobody wanted to buy them – at any price. We finally gave them away to the Salvation Army and got a small tax write-off.

One day my secretary called me on the intercom and said, "Mr. Joffe, there's a man from Time Inc. on the phone. He wants to talk to you."

"Tell him I have no interest," I told her. I knew that he was trying to sell me advertising and I just had no additional room for that in my budget.

But a week later she buzzed me again. "Mr. Joffe, that man from Time Inc. is on the phone again. He really wants to talk to you – he is very insistent."

Again I told her, "Please tell him that I don't have any interest in talking to him. We don't wish to advertise in his media."

She came back. "He doesn't want to talk to you about advertising. He wants to talk to you about something entirely different."

"Something entirely different?" I thought. "What could that possibly be?" I said, "O.K., put him on."

The man introduced himself. His name was Ralph Gallagher and he was the man for "new developments" at Time Inc. "Hummm," I thought, "the same thing as Opper at CBS."

He said, "Mr. Joffe, we have been watching your advertising and your merchandising for over a year. We think it would be a good move for Time Inc. possibly to get into the mail-order business, and we wondered if you would be interested in joining forces with Time Inc.?"

Of course I was interested, but I was not prepared to go through the same thing as I had with CBS. "Would you mind coming to New York so we could talk about it?"

"No," I said, "I am afraid I won't be able to do that. Why don't you come to San Francisco and talk to me?"

"That isn't possible for me right now," Gallagher said, "but I really want to talk to you. How about Chicago? That's right in the middle."

Chicago sounded all right to me because Priscilla and I were in any case going there within two weeks for the electronics show. So I made a date with Gallagher to meet with him at a private conference room in one of the big hotels in Chicago.

Gallagher turned out to be a very nice guy – a big burly Irishman, roughly my age. We had a good meeting with him and he made an interesting proposal. He told us how interested Time Inc. was in Haverhill's, even though they were also looking at a number of other mail-order companies. But he and his management were most impressed by Haverhill's because, just like CBS, they liked our style, our merchandise, the quality of our copy and illustrations, and everything else about us. They thought that we would be a good fit with them. But they preferred not to make an immediate commitment. He said, "Can I propose a 'trial marriage' to you?"

"A 'trial marriage.' What's that?"

"What we propose is to let Haverhill's advertise in Time Inc. media for six months, for which we'd sell you all the space you want at thirty per cent of our rate card. For instance, you would pay only $300 for an ad that would ordinarily cost $1,000. For an ad that would ordinarily cost $5,000, you'd only pay $1,500. You can't lose. We'll monitor the response to the ads and if the response is satisfactory, if things work out, we'll 'get married' after the trial period."

That sounded very good to me. It was a great proposition. Here I had the opportunity to advertise in media with large circulation, at a sharply discounted cost that would not be available to any other advertiser. Even if we didn't get "married," I would stand to make a good deal of money by that seventy per cent discounted rate. I agreed, we shook hands, and we were in our "trial marriage."

At that time, Time's only media were *Time* and *Life*. I took full advantage of both, but mostly of *Time*, which I rightly assumed to be a better medium for our purposes. At the seventy per cent discount from regular rates, or "rate card" as it was called, I couldn't help but make a lot of money. It was just wonderful.

Time Inc. watched each of our ads and their response like those proverbial hawks. After running the numbers, they came to the conclusion that it was a perfect fit. Long before the six-month "trial period" was over, indeed, after only three months, they called me and said they would like to come out to San Francisco and arrange to buy the company. Ralph Gallagher came together with one Nick Nicholas, who later became the CEO of what was by then Time-Warner. They had already done their due diligence, and we were able to make a quick deal.

Just like CBS, they offered me essentially the same, namely a million dollars in cash or stock or any combination of both – my choice. At that point, I believe I made the smartest decision of my business life. I decided to take it all in stock. Not only were there no taxes to pay, but the stock, of course, increased more than tenfold in value over the years.

But before we closed the deal, I did something else which, with the wisdom of hindsight, I don't know whether it was really very smart. I gave ten per cent of my stock of Haverhill's to each of our three children. So they each got ten per cent of Time Inc. stock or each $100,000 worth. It too, of course, has increased in value manifold over the years.

It worked out very well for Joe and for Rachel. It gave them a really good leg up in life. It did very poorly for Michael, much as everything else would. But that was something I could not have foreseen at the time.

So now I was part of a big company, Time Inc. I realized that my life would change, that I would no longer be my own boss, that I would have to be responsive and responsible to other people, and that my performance would be closely watched – and judged. I also realized that Time Inc. would be interested in growth, but that they would be able and available to finance that growth.

I prepared a business plan. As a small part of it, we would move out of our downtown San Francisco premises to a 40,000 square foot facility in South San Francisco, which would accommodate the growth that I knew and was told was expected. About a week later, I had a phone call from a woman, who introduced herself as Jean Hadley. She told me that she was the manager and president of the division of which Haverhills was to be part. She was my boss. Ms. Hadley told me that she was going to be in San Francisco by the end of the week and that she wished to discuss business plans with me.

That was perfectly reasonable and I could not take exception to it. Still, I had a slight feeling of unease because having had to respond only to myself until now, I now had to prepare a presentation for another person and had to have my plans scrutinized and approved.

Ms. Hadley did indeed come to San Francisco. Maybe I had the wrong attitude, but the first thing I noticed about her was that she had an extraordinarily big behind. She also had a habit of scratching it whenever she got the least bit agitated. She said, "Gerardo, I want us to be totally clear. We did not buy this business for it to stay at its present size. Sales now are about a million dollars and profits are about $100,000 per year. I want you to bring the sales to at least ten million dollars within two years, with commensurate profits. Those are your marching orders."

Oh my, I thought, here are my "marching orders." I'm not going to like this. The woman filled me with immediate antipathy. I wondered right then, and I even wonder today: Was it because she was my boss that I had a hard time subjecting myself? Nobody before in my life had imposed goals on me, certainly not any goals that I thought would be impossible to reach, and nobody had given me any "marching orders." But it is also possible that I had a hard time accepting a woman as my boss. That may have been a good part of it.

I said, "Jean, I'll do the best I can, but I think that your goals are a little ambitious. Why don't I try the best I can and let's see to where we get?"

"No, that won't be good enough," she quickly cut me off. "You heard me: Ten million dollars in sales in two years and commensurate profits. Nothing else will be satisfactory."

Then she cooled down a bit, and continued in a more mellow tone. "There's something else, Gerardo: My husband represents a firm of catalog printers. I would appreciate it if you would give your catalog printing business to him. He'll do a good job for you."

I thought of it as a somewhat unusual request under the circumstances. I said, "Yes, Jean, I'll consider it, but I'll have to get the best price, of course. Don't you agree?"

"Yes, of course, I agree," she said, "but he'll give you the best price."

I met the husband a few days later. He was a big fellow and seemed to be a pretty nice guy, but he certainly was no match for that wife of his. "Gerardo," he said, "my wife said that you'll probably print a million catalogs or something like that, four times a year. I certainly would appreciate your business."

"Bob, give me the best price and you'll get the business."

"No problem at all."

Well, as we usually did, we put the catalog up for bids and he came in third. I didn't give him the business. I don't think his wife ever forgave me. It was not a good start.

Part V

LIFE WITH TIME, NOT EASY TO BE A FATHER, PHILANTHROPY, AND SOME REFLECTIONS

I had been interested in and concerned with Israel since my early teens. In those days, Israel as such did not exist. There was only the *yishuv*, the Jewish population in what was then Palestine. It had been my desire and my firm intention to leave Germany for Palestine. To the best of my knowledge, although later some doubts assailed me, it was the British and their infamous White Paper that prevented me from doing so. During my long stay in Bolivia, though always conscious of my Jewishness, I gave little thought to Palestine, mostly I suppose, because I heard very little about it. I read few newspapers and they didn't give it much play in any case. Then later, like all American Jews, I was happy and thrilled when the State of Israel was founded in 1948. I suffered with it during the wars that were infamously imposed on it, and I rejoiced and was greatly relieved after Israel's stunning victory in the 1967 war, the Six-Day War, which gave the world a totally different view of what Jews were and what they could do. After that, the heroic view of Israel was enhanced by the Entebbe raid, a most daring and unprecedented rescue action that freed over two hundred hostages on a plane that had been hijacked by Muslim terrorists.

I became concerned and alarmed when I noticed a barrage of Arab-Muslim anti-Israel propaganda in American newspapers. One series of ads by the oddly named Arab-American Anti-Discrimination Committee featured such inane juxtapositions as **American Midwest Farmers Suffer a Second Year of Drought While Israeli Jews Travel All over the World**.

There was other crazy stuff like that, but most of it much more vicious.

Why does the Israeli Government, and the Jews supposedly being "so smart," not do something about that, I wondered? Why do they not hire one of the large public relations agencies to tell their story and to create favorable opinion with the American public? I talked to some people at the San Francisco Israeli Consulate General. They just shrugged their shoulders. "We just don't do this kind of thing. We let the facts speak for themselves."

I thought about that. It was a strange response and totally inadequate under the circumstances.

So I decided to do something myself. I had the ability to write cogent copy, I had an art department that could set type for me, and I was willing to spend time and money on the project. I gave myself a budget of $20,000, and I decided that I would try my very best and that the money would hopefully last for a year. If after that time the project would not be self-supporting I would reluctantly and sorrowfully have to give it up.

But what was the organizational structure in which I could do that? It was clear that it would have to be a non-profit philanthropy, which, in tax terms, means a 501(c)(3) organization, an organization that was tax-exempt and to which people could make contributions that were tax-deductible.

I talked to my attorney. He told me that the IRS was understandably wary of people wishing to establish such 501(c)(3) organizations, since many, if not most, were attempted to be established for self-seeking purposes. I was told that the IRS would take a long, hard, and a very slow look at such proposed organizations and that, as likely as not, it could be ultimately declined; last not least, it would cost a lot of money in attorneys fees. I didn't want to wait that long, and I didn't want to spend a big chunk of my $20,000 budget on attorneys either. What to do?

So I called AIPAC in Washington, the American Israel Public Affairs Committee. Fortunately, after being shifted to two or three different people, I found the right person. My thought was to put my nascent organization under the aegis of AIPAC, thus solving my 501(c)(3) problem.

"Mr. Joffe," the man said, "you've come to the right person, because I think I can help you. But you've come to the wrong organization."

"Why the wrong organization?" I asked.

"Because AIPAC is not itself a 501(c)(3) organization. We are a lobbying organization and therefore do not qualify for tax exemption." I didn't know that.

He continued, "But, I have an idea. There's a woman in this town, her name if Win Meiselman. She runs a very small organization, literally off her kitchen table; she calls it CAMERA."

"What does CAMERA stand for?" I asked him.

"I don't really know, he said, but get in touch with Ms. Meiselman. She'll tell you that and she might be willing to accommodate you under her tax-exempt umbrella. That would solve your 501(c)(3) problem." He gave me Ms. Meiselman's telephone number in Washington.

I called Ms. Meiselman on the phone. She sounded like a nice lady and very enthusiastic. I told her in principle what I had in mind. She seemed to like the idea. "Why don't you come to Washington, Gerardo, and let's talk about it."

"O.K.," I said, "I'll be there next Monday."

And that's just what we did. Priscilla and I flew to Washington, met with her and were impressed by her energy and enthusiasm. "Win (we got on a first-name basis right away) what does CAMERA stand for?"

"It stands for *Committee for Accuracy on Middle East Reporting in America.*" I thought it was pretty clever.

"What do you do and how much of a budget do you have?"

"Frankly," she said, "all I really do is write letters to *The Washington Post*, which is very hostile to Israel. "As to budget," she said, it's really non-existent. I get some contributions from friends every once in a while, but we have virtually no money and, as you can see, no office."

I had already written three messages but had not yet published them. The first was "The PLO – Is it a force for peace in the Middle East?", the second was "Aid to Israel – Is the U.S. getting its money's worth?", and the third was "Those Palestinian Refugees" – Who are they and what is the real story?" Win read all three and liked them very much. "What do you plan on doing, Gerardo?"

"Here's what I propose, Win. I'll write these messages and publish them under CAMERA's name in major national media. I have a minimal budget of $20,000 of my own money, but I am very hopeful that I can raise money after these ads appear, with an acquisition mailing that I plan on sending out."

"What is an "acquisition mailing?" She asked.

"It's a term of trade for letters soliciting money." I explained to her, and to recruit new "members," hopefully future contributors to one's project. Then I continued: "Here's the cooperation between us that I propose:

- I have complete liberty in writing what I want, but I shall always keep in mind the reality that I am technically part of another organization, namely CAMERA, and I shall do nothing to embarrass CAMERA and to hurt its good name.
- I will be totally responsible for expenses incurred by such advertising and shall keep all funds collected.
- I shall keep all the names of my donors and shall not have to share them with anybody.

Win interrupted me: "Just a second, Gerardo," she said, "all this sounds very good for you but, to put it bluntly, what's in it for me and for CAMERA?"

"Win," I asked her, "how many people know you and how many people know CAMERA?"

"All my friends know me and many of them are helping me with what I am doing."

"Yes, I am sure they do, Win, but how many people outside your circle of friends know you? How many people outside of Washington, D.C. know you?"

"Not really anybody."

"Win, within the next three months, the CAMERA name will have appeared in a dozen publications or more. I shall have created millions of advertising impressions for you in no time at all. CAMERA, of which now virtually nobody is aware, will be a 'brand name.' All over the United States people will know what CAMERA is and what CAMERA believes in and what CAMERA does. Does that sound like a fair trade-off?"

"You're right," she said, "that's what will happen. This sounds very attractive to me. Let's go ahead and do it."

There was no formal document or anything. We just shook hands, went out to dinner with her and her husband, a college professor of economics, and had an agreement.

I placed my first three ads, "The PLO," "Aid to Israel" and "Those 'Palestinian Refugees.'" I committed for three insertions in *The New Republic*, *Harpers*, and *The Atlantic*. I spent a good portion of my wad with this one triple shot. I decided to use much of the rest in a direct mail campaign, in an acquisition mailing.

I engaged a mailing-list broker, who specialized in Jewish lists and rented, for one-time use, 50,000 names, 5,000 each from ten Jewish organizations that appeared to address related concerns. I wrote a four-page letter soliciting support and included copies of the three ads that I had written, a transmittal card, and a reply envelope. If this wouldn't work, I was out of business.

But it did work. The ads, each of which in those days carried a coupon with an invitation to contribute, had good response, but most of the money came from my acquisition letter. With a response of about three per cent, the 50,000 letters produced about 1,500 supporters for CAMERA, with an average donation of $25. I was in business, because I knew from my direct-mail experience, that while I could, perhaps, count on two to three per cent response from "blind" mailings, I could count on ten to fifteen per cent response on any follow-up mailings to the group that had already contributed once.

Being now pretty sure of success, I immediately expanded my advertising to other national magazines and contracted with a newspaper agency in New York, to place advertising for CAMERA in major metropolitan newspapers.

In the course of just a few months, and just as I had predicted, CAMERA became a household word and a well recognized Jewish-American organization. On the strength of this advertising, Win Meiselman, always energetic, was able to spread out and to establish CAMERA branches in Boston, Seattle, Philadelphia, and Ft. Lauderdale. It turned out, just as I had told her, to be a wonderful example of symbiosis – everyone profited and everybody was happy.

But as often happens with young love, that happiness did not last forever. After we had worked together for about a year and both of us having been very successful, each in our own way, Win called me one afternoon, Gerardo, she said, "I don't really quite agree with your ad on *The Arabs In Israel*. I would like for you to make a few changes."

That was something unexpected, unwelcome, and totally new. It was not what we had agreed upon. "Win," I said, "our agreement is quite clear. I have absolute independence and editorial discretion. You cannot change what I am writing."

"Yes, I understand, but you are using the name of CAMERA, and everything you say affects me and my organization."

"I'm afraid that's too bad. I try not to say anything that would offend anybody but you don't necessarily have to agree with everything I say."

"All right." she said, "But let me come out to San Francisco and let's talk about it."

So she and her husband came. We put them up at our house and had a good time – until we started talking about what she had come for. Then she laid down the law. "Gerardo," she said, "there are three things that we have to agree upon. One: I must have the right of censorship of your ads. Two: I need for you to give me the names of all of your contributors. Three: You have to share with me the funds received and that you will continue to receive."

"Win, I can't accept any of these, because it goes against what we had specifically agreed upon. It just won't work for me."

Well, we were both adamant and argued back and forth. Though no voices were raised, it was clear that we had a problem and could not continue. I thought about it and talked with Priscilla and we decided that it would be best if we had a friendly divorce. I told Win so and we parted as friends. I started FLAME (Facts and Logic About the Middle East), but that's another story about which I'll talk later. In the meantime, however, CAMERA became an important Jewish American organization. Win, the founder, retired and turned the scepter over to a young woman in Boston, who is doing an excellent job.

I had now severed my relationship with CAMERA, but I wanted and needed to continue on the same path. Also, I had made a commitment with media and I could not suddenly pull out. But that was secondary. The main thing was that I wanted to continue this work. So the first thing, and as quickly as possible, I had to found another tax-exempt 501(c)(3) organization in order to do this work. Since the CAMERA name was no longer available to me, I had to come up with another name. The name that occurred to me was AFLAME. I thought that it expressed the fervor that I felt about the subject. It was a case of having the acronym first and then finding words to fit it. Now I had to find an attorney who would do this work for me very quickly and hopefully inexpensively – perhaps even, who knows, for free.

So I looked at the roster of my donors, who by then were about 3,500. About five hundred of them were California residents. Looking through my database, I found two attorneys. One was living in Los Angeles and the other in San Ramon in the East Bay, about 40 miles from San Francisco. The man's name was Wilbur Duberstein. So I wrote a letter to Mr. Duberstein, asking him if he would do this work for me.

He called me right back. After a few preliminary words he asked me, "Gerardo, (we were on a first name basis right away), have you filed declaration XXX (I forgot the number of the form) with the California Secretary of State?"

"No I haven't. Should I do it?"

He answered, "*Frug keine sheiles.*"

"I beg your pardon," I said.

He repeated: "*Frug keine sheiles*

"What does it mean?"

"Don't you speak Yiddish?" he asked.

"No I don't," I said. "I speak German and I believe that I can pretty much understand what you're saying. It means 'ask no *sheiles.*' But, what are *sheiles?*

"*Sheiles* are questions," he said.

I didn't know the word, but then I remembered from my Hebrew that *sh'elot* means questions in Hebrew, so it was about the same word.

"What do you mean by that?" I asked him.

"Just leave well enough alone. If you didn't submit that in the very beginning when you started CAMERA, don't do it now with CAMERA, but let's do it with this new organization."

But I was intrigued. "Wilbur, where did you get that expression?"

"It is from my grandmother," he replied. "Back in the old country, every Friday, she prepared a chicken for Shabbat dinner. She would open up the chicken and inspect its innards to see if it was kosher. If any organ was not quite in the right position, if anything at all was out of order, the chicken was not kosher, could not be eaten, and had to be discarded. One day, she opened the chicken as usual and found that something was not in order. The liver was on the wrong side or the gallbladder was in the wrong position or something like that. She said to her husband, Wilbur's grandfather, "I don't think the chicken is kosher. I'm going to see the rabbi and ask him." Wilbur's grandfather said, *Frug keine sheiles*, cook the chicken."

I thought it was very good advice and had many applications. In other words, ask no unnecessary questions, to which you might get unfavorable answers, especially to "authorities." I've since tried to adapt that piece of wisdom to my own needs.

In any case, Wilbur Duberstein remained my closest friend until his untimely death, not too long ago. He created a 501(c)(3) corporation for me, not in the six months that the previous attorney had told me it would take, but in about four weeks. He knew which strings to pull and which buttons to push. He got things done.

"Gerardo," he said, "I don't' feel that your proposed organization should be named AFLAME. It sounds, well, you know, too inflammatory. You don't want to sound like that."

"What do you think I should call it instead?"

"Why don't you just call it FLAME?"

"I think you're right. It sounds better. AFLAME is indeed a bit inflammatory. But now that we have the acronym, we need the words to fit it."

"I have the words," he said. "It's Facts and Logic About the Middle East, and FLAME is its acronym."

I thought it was splendid. So we called it FLAME. It has, in its way, been a great success and has now close to 30,000 contributors and more than 25,000 affiliates. It is now considered to be one of the major Jewish organizations in the United States.

One morning, just having fed my fish and getting ready for a day's work, two tough-looking hombres appeared unannounced in my office. Without further ado, they introduced themselves as representatives of Local 10 of the Longshoremen's Union. That was Harry Bridges's union, a waterfront-toughened outfit. I knew they weren't there to buy any shavers or anything else.

"What can I do for you, gentlemen?" I asked.

"It's very simple," they said, "you can save yourself a lot of trouble and a lot of money by meeting our demands or you can do it the hard way. Our demands are to unionize your shop."

"What makes you think I will agree to that?

"We have a petition from some of your employees, a sufficient number under the rules of the Labor Relations Act. You can either accede or we can engage you in a long drawn-out campaign."

I thought about that. Not too many years earlier, I had sworn loyalty to the United Mine and Mill and Smelter Workers Union, an even tougher outfit than the Longshoremen, and I had sworn never to cross a picket line. Now I found myself on the other side of the union, on the other side of that picket line. I was a "boss," and the idea of having a union in my business was utterly distasteful to me. It was distasteful mostly because I knew who the man was who had started the organizing drive. I knew that he was going to be the shop steward and that he was going to give me a very hard time and be a constant pain in the ass by being in my office every day with grievances and other headaches.

I thought for a minute, then I told them, "I think I'll go for the fight."

"O.K.," they said. "it's your choice. We've been in this business for a long time and we've never been defeated. You'll regret your decision. Thank you and goodbye."

By that time we had about fifty employees, half men and half women. I knew of a few who I was quite sure would go with the union and I know of some others who I was very sure would stick with me. There were about one-third of them that I wasn't really sure about. I understood right away that in those organizing battles, one had to tread very carefully, because if you made only one bad step, anything that could be construed to be in violation of the Labor Relations Act, the union could ask for automatic certification and the battle would be over.

In order to avoid such a mistake, I hired a consultant, Frank Vetterlein. He was very knowledgeable because he had been a union official for many years. He then decided that he would have more of a future playing on the other side. His role, as far as I was concerned, was mostly to keep me out of trouble, to avoid my making any fatal mistakes.

The first thing I did was to hire ten more people, mostly personal friends and relatives of employees who I thought would be totally loyal to me. Then I issued weekly bulletins included in the pay envelopes explaining what a wonderful company we were, especially being associated with such an outfit as Time Inc. I was generous with bonuses, time-off, and many other small courtesies, pushing the envelope of what was allowable under the Act, but never bursting it.

For election day, I organized a big party with wonderful refreshments and live music from a small combo. Then I called the employees together and told them that, regardless of the outcome, we were all one big happy family and that nothing would change, even if the union were elected to represent the employees. Finally, I had three prizes. The first one, a complete sound system, the second, a beautiful luggage set, and the third, a dinner certificate for two in a fancy San Francisco restaurant. Those prizes were for those who came closest to foreseeing the result of the election – regardless of who won, the company or the union.

All of these things were allowed, though barely, under the National Labor Relations Act.

I won the election by a landslide. I had put a great deal of work, effort and imagination into it. It probably was worthwhile. I don't think I would have been happy having both a demanding dragon lady from New York and that union shop steward breathing down my neck every day.

The end of our first year with Time Inc. rolled around. We had doubled sales from the previous year but profits had increased by only about 30-40%, not sufficient to satisfy "headquarters." The principal reason for not meeting the profit goals was that we had put substantial infrastructure – warehousing, etc. into place to meet future goals. That infrastructure, that overhead was a drag on profits. The people in New York were not satisfied. And they really had a point. Time Inc., even in those days, was about a $6 billion company. We were so small that, literally, we didn't even merit a footnote in the annual report. I saw no way that we would ever reach sufficient size to satisfy the expectations and requirements of Time Inc. It did not make me happy.

One day I got a call from Jean telling me that she thought I needed an assistant and she was going to send somebody from headquarters to help me.

I said, "Jean, I don't need any help. And, if I do need help, I'm going to hire my own assistant. I don't need for you to send anybody from New York."

She insisted. Frank Lester came out the following week. They paid half of his salary and I was expected to pay the other half of it.

I really didn't go around the company compiling ethnic statistics, but it was clear to me that of the thousands of people employed by Time Inc. at the time, only Lester, I and one other man, Jim Diamond, an attorney, were the only Jews in that company. There simply were no others, as far as I could tell. At that time, Time Inc. was still totally under the sway of Henry Luce, the founder of the company, who had died a few years before. While I have no reason to believe that Mr. Luce was an anti-Semite, he certainly had no truck with Jews at all. He was the son of missionaries in China, the number one champion of Chang Kai-Shek and his wife, and the greatest influence on the China policy of the United States. I was the "Jew that came with Haverhill's." Mr. Diamond was there because apparently they thought they needed a "smart Jew attorney;" I don't know why they would have hired Frank Lester. It was never clear to me, and I am sure it was a mistake.

An interesting sequel – a "fast forward," actually: One of Mr. Luce's successors, CEO of the by then much enlarged company – AOL Time Warner – was a Jew, Gerald Levin. And to make things even more astonishing, Mr. Levin's successor as CEO and chairman of the Board is a black man – Richard Parsons. What was the world coming to? Surely, Mr. Luce must be spinning in his grave.

If I didn't like Jean, I liked Frank Lester even less. His only job apparently, was to make daily reports on me to Jean. How did I know? I saw the telephone bills. There was a long distance call, usually fifteen minutes or more, every afternoon to Jean's private number.

One day I was told to come to New York for "consultation." I did that and found myself in a somewhat tense meeting, at which nothing of real consequence was transacted or decided. After the meeting was over, Jean asked me to go and see Mr. Diamond, the attorney, in his office right away.

I went to see Mr. Diamond. He closed the door. He said, "Sit down, Gerardo. I just want you to know that we're on to you."

"You are on to what?" I asked him.

"We know of your thefts. We may not yet know of all of it, but we know enough."

Whatever gloves there were, had come off very quickly.

"Are you out of your fucking mind, you asshole! What thefts are you talking about?"

"Please watch your language," he says. "The specific theft I'm talking about is that you're skimming ten per cent in commissions off all of your imports. And that's probably not all. That's all we know so far. It's probably just the tip of a much larger iceberg."

Our imports at that time were on the order of about one million dollars per year.

"But there's more," he said. "You think you're pretty clever, but I know your kind of people."

'Your kind of people?' I asked myself. What in the hell is this bastard talking about? Is he referring to Jews? He was one himself. And so was the guy who had "discovered" my so-called thefts.

"Jim," I said, keeping my (relative) cool, "this is an interesting accusation. I think you should either give it to me in writing or bring in your secretary and repeat it in front of her, preferably both."

"You would like that, you tricky bastard." he said, "But, I'm not going to do that."

"Well, if you won't do that, go fuck yourself and go to hell," I said, as I walked out of his office. It had not been a good meeting.

Not only had I of course not done what I was being accused of, it never had even occurred to me. My only concern – under my own ownership and that of Time Inc. – was always and exclusively to increase sales and profits.

Things didn't get any better. Although we made what I thought of as good money, it was never quite sufficient for Jean and I suppose for the other people at Time Inc. Our relations became increasingly tense, especially between her and me. Diamond, of course, was beyond the pale. I never saw him again.

After about two years of being part of Time Inc., I was told that the San Francisco location was not convenient for them – it was too far from New York and that in order to be in the mail-order business one could be located any place in the country. They were right about that, of course. Fortunately, however, I had insisted on a clause in my contract to the effect that I could not be forced to move from San Francisco and that they would have to buy out my contract if they wanted to move. Buying out the contract was no problem, because it was only for three years, and two of those years had already passed. I did, however, believe that the plan to move Haverhill's was foolish. We had good and experienced employees; we also had two profitable retail stores in the Northern California area. I thought it was a shame to give all of that up. Their number crunchers, however, had decided overhead could be reduced and that Haverhill's would be better off and more profitable moving to Chicago, where they had ample space available in a downtown building that they owned. Well, it had to be without me, but perhaps they were not too concerned about that.

They did indeed move Haverhill's to Chicago where it gave up its ghost about six months later. I mulled the experience over, and even today I think about it from time to time. My suspicion or conviction that I was not cut out for the corporate life had been correct. It was one of the reasons, the main reason really, why I had left W.R. Grace & Co. in New York. Somebody more pliable, more adaptable might have been able to smooth out some of the rough spots. The strange idea that I was a thief, however, was really too much; beyond that, I did not find the "climate" at Time Inc. too congenial. The shadow, the myth, and the spirit of the late Mr. Luce hovered above everything. It was not a spirit that was in tune with me.

We parted on relatively friendly terms though the farewell from Jean was a cool one. I did not say goodbye to Jim Diamond. I had permission to do whatever I wanted. My no-compete clause was rescinded. I was at liberty to go back into the same kind of business if I wished.

Throughout our sojourn with Time Inc., Priscilla and I continued to make our yearly trips to Europe to visit the European trade fairs. Asia, and especially Hong Kong and Taiwan, were beginning to emerge as important sources of supply, but they still could not rival Europe for our kind of merchandise. The big trade fairs were still Hanover, followed by Milan and, occasionally, also Frankfurt, which was particularly important for leather goods. All of these played a big role in our merchandise lineup. We usually bought a car while in Europe, drove it and then had it shipped home. On one of these trips we bought a yellow Opel which, in memory perhaps of Greenie, we called Gelbchen. It was a reliable car. In 1970, we decided to make a side trip to Copenhagen to visit Mrs. Jespersen, Ulla's mother, who by then was quite old and had lost much of her eyesight. I had been corresponding with her through the years. She was obviously still very fond of me, feelings that I reciprocated. She had been more of an influence in my life than she probably knew.

While in Copenhagen, I decided to renew acquaintance with Ulla's little brother, Finn, who by then was in his middle forties and was married to Lene, a very nice lady. They had three teenage children, two girls and a boy. Finn was a prominent attorney, specializing in admiralty and aviation law. The friendship with Finn and Lene turned out to be a most important one for us. It endures and has strengthened to this day.

Usually, those trips lasted about three weeks. We were pretty sure that things were going well at home, and that everything was cool and under control. Our housekeeper, Laura, a middle-aged Salvadoran woman, who had been with us for many years, was "in control of the situation," or so we supposed. In reality, as we eventually found out, she was not in control at all. Our son Michael, who was then seventeen years old, took over as soon as we left. He threatened Laura and forced her and also his little sister and little brother to silence. There were, as we found out, nightly orgies in which liquor, sex, but mostly illegal drugs played the major roles. But these revelations did not come until later. We still did not know what was going on.

The first indication that something was seriously out of whack was that things began to disappear. I routinely left my wallet lying around the house. I never knew quite how much money I had in it, but it caught my attention that after I might have picked up $100 from the ATM, I had only $15 left in my wallet the next day. The same thing happened to Priscilla. The money never disappeared in its entirety. There was always some left, but most of it would be gone. The immediate suspicion fell on Laura, who was really an unlikely suspect. She had been with us for many years and she had our full confidence. We were simply too innocent to realize what was really happening. Then Priscilla's jewelry began to disappear, then the pictures off the walls, and finally one expensive beautiful mirror that had an antique frame covered in heavy gold leaf. Eventually, the suspicion fell on Michael, but he stoutly and with seeming sincerity protested his total innocence. Why would he steal anything? He had everything he needed. Nothing was denied him. Inexperienced as we were, we believed him.

One time, it was the week before Easter, he confronted both of us. "Mom and Dad, the police are after me. I and my friend have broken into a house and they know it was us. They're going to be here any minute. The reason I did it is that I have a heroin habit, which I have to feed. I have to steal. I've been doing it for quite some time."

We were absolutely horrified. It was an utter, total shock to us. Priscilla broke into tears. I was beyond stunned. It was the worst thing that had ever happened to us. We were numb. We were so dumb, so inexperienced and innocent that, even though all the symptoms were there, we had not suspected anything like that at all. We said, "Michael, this is terrible. Why did you not tell us? Maybe we could have helped you."

The only thing to do was to hospitalize him immediately. He did not resist.

We took him right then and there to St. Mary's Hospital and committed him to a special ward for juvenile drug addicts. He lasted three days and then he escaped. We took him back and he escaped again. It was a problem that was going to haunt us for the next twenty-five years.

But life had to go on. I had to somehow get back into business. I couldn't rest on my laurels and there were the other two children to take care of. Rachel, by then, sixteen years old, had developed into a lovely young teenager. She went to private school, had many friends, and did very well, both in school and socially. One thing that particularly impressed me about her was that, even as a teenager, and without really having any real need for it, she always insisted on working. She wanted to earn her own money, mostly, I suppose, in order to buy her own clothes, without tutelage and permission of her mother. She kept up this working habit all through college and for years into her marriage. I greatly admire her for that.

Joe was eight years old. In contrast to Michael, who, though loving and sweet, was always difficult, Joe was always pleasant and easy to get along with. I made it a point and was able to spend more time with him than I had ever spent with Michael. We joined the Sierra Club and went on many hikes. What he liked to do most was to go swimming with me at the Press Club of San Francisco, where I was a member and which had a good-size swimming pool in the basement. It was for men only, and only nude swimming was allowed.

But what about business? It was obvious what to do. I certainly wasn't going to go back into mining or into the petroleum industry. I had been successful in the mail-order business, had pioneered in merchandising and advertising and I had quite a few imitators, some of them more successful than I was.

I decided to go back into the same business and start from scratch. What to call the new business? We decided on Henniker's. The name was somewhat reminiscent of Haverhill's, but it had something else in common. By that time I had developed a preference for New England names and I found Henniker in New Hampshire, not more than fifty miles away from Haverhill. I thought it would be a good omen.

But talking about Haverhill's, I remember something funny that happened about a year or two after I had started in business. Haverhill, in the very northern part of Massachusetts, is a fairly good-size town, about 40,000 people. They have a newspaper, the name of which I can't remember. It was something like the *Haverhill Observer*. One day I got a letter from the features editor of the *Haverhill Observer*. He wanted to know how I had come up with the Haverhill's name for my business. I told him that I was reluctant to tell him, but that I would do so if he promised not to reveal my name. He promised. So I made up a story and told him that I had been a student at Harvard "several years ago," (I was vague about the time). I had met and had been in love with this beautiful girl from Haverhill, that we had consummated our love, but that cruel fate had torn us asunder. "I cannot mention her name for your newspaper column, but she will know who she is when she reads these lines," I told him. Would you believe that I had letters from four women in the town of Haverhill; each of whom believed that she was the one who had consummated her love with the unnamed president of Haverhill's?

Before I tell you about my next business venture, Henniker's, in order to keep track you should know how old I was at that time. It was 1973, I was fifty-three years old. I am writing this journal, the story of my voyage through life in 2002, being over eighty years old, just about thirty years later. From a chronicler's point of view, the first thirty or forty years of my life were perhaps the most interesting and the most adventurous, especially, of course my experiences in Germany and then my experiences in Bolivia. Once I got married and started a family, even though they were the happiest years of my life, fewer things "happened" and five or ten years can be summarized in just a few pages. So, that's what I am doing.

Talking about my happiness: The happiness of having married Priscilla, that happiness was only interrupted by two events: One a very big and tragic one, namely the descending of Michael into drug addition, and about the awful end that he took.

And there was one other incident in our marital happiness, which at the time appeared to be earth-shaking, but which, in retrospect was only a small blip on the happy curve of life. I'll talk about that in a minute. But I often reflect about the almost incredible stroke of luck of having found a woman like Priscilla in such an unlikely place as Magnolia, Arkansas.

In those days, engagements were of short duration. I met Priscilla in July of 1951, and we got married in December. Most of that time she was traveling with her parents. We were engaged for only two months. In those days, when premarital cohabitation, certainly in a small town like Magnolia, was out of the questions, sex was not available, or only rarely, furtively and accompanied by much anxiety. In reality, people married mostly to find sexual fulfillment. It was called love. I believe that, to some degree, that may also have been the case with us. It certainly was with me. We were of such different backgrounds, ethnically, religiously, country of origin, big city versus small town, in almost every respect. That we have been able to accommodate ourselves to each other and still love each other more than fifty years later as much as we did when we first got married, is really a miracle. Another miracle, of course, is to have found a girl like Priscilla in Magnolia. The analogy that often comes to my mind is that, even today, one can go to the Tuolemne River or to the American River in California with a pan, and with some effort, still find some flecks of gold. It's much work, but it can be done. But to dip that pan into the Arkansas River and to come up with a "nugget" like Priscilla is a miracle worthy of Ripley's *Believe It or Not*. I think of that often and how very fortunate I am – really just by dumb luck.

But back to business. I rented space in a nice office building at the southern edge of San Francisco and started Henniker's about at the same level as I had left Haverhill's before I sold it to Time Inc. I knew what to do. I had all the sources and I had the working capital to finance it. Things went very well. I always believed that a retail store was a proper adjunct to a mail-order business. Therefore, after a couple of years, we moved to a location in San Francisco just at the edge of downtown. It was exactly what we needed. We had a very good-looking retail store, ample office and art department space behind it, and a basement for warehousing and shipping, with direct access to the outside. It was an ideal location. In addition, we opened an attractive boutique in downtown San Francisco, another store at the San Francisco airport and showcases in both Bay Area airports and in most major hotels. We were once again on a roll.

One thing occurred during those years that was of little consequence, but which was, and still is a mystery, and which at the time concerned me greatly. It has never been cleared up. Here's what happened: We were banking with a downtown San Francisco bank. Each week, they gave us a series of zippered bags that came supplied with a padlock. Only I and the bank had the keys for the padlock. We would put each day's deposit, checks and cash into one of those bags and label it with the day of the week. We kept the bags in the office safe. At the end of the week, on Friday night, one of our employees would take the five bags and put them into the night deposit chute of the bank. That worked very well for a couple of years. There was no hitch at all.

The person who did this was a young woman who had been with us for about two years; we trusted her fully. She put the deposit together every night, made up the deposit slip, and closed the bag. Her name was Donna. She was a big girl and was from Arkansas, not too far from Magnolia. Priscilla, especially, took sort of a motherly interest in her. Donna was about twenty-two years old, single and lived with her sister in an apartment in Oakland. She had to cross the Bay Bridge every morning to drive to work and cross it again every evening to go home.

One Monday afternoon, I got a call from the president of the bank. He said, "Mr. Joffe, we would like for you to come to the bank right away. There's something wrong with your deposit."

I didn't like it. Nothing could be good about a "wrong deposit."

"What's wrong," I said. "Is the money there?"

"Well, we don't know," the man said. "You'd better come down here right away."

The deposit in question, five days of receipts, was a little over $20,000, a fairly large sum for a small business like ours. I raced down to the bank, took the copies of the deposit slips with me and was invited to come to the president's private office. The five bags were lying on the president's desk. Each one of them had been slit open, presumably with a razor. All the money and all the checks were there. Everything was clearly in apple-pie order, just as it had been bundled. Not a penny was missing.

"What happened," I asked him.

"It's a most amazing story," he said. "I had a call from an attorney (he gave me the attorney's name) who said that he had received a telephone call asking him to open his office door and that he would find some money bags in front of his office door, that he should call the bank and tell them that he had the bags and that he could deliver them by messenger to the bank or have the bank pick them up."

What a strange story. I said to the president, "Do you believe that?"

"No," he said, "I don't believe that at all. But Mr. Jones (let's call him that) is a reputable attorney and is well known to us. If he 'shaded the truth' he had good reason. I am just very surprised and very happy that all the money is here."

I was happy too, but I really wanted to know what had happened. I told Donna about it and she feigned complete ignorance and innocence. "Donna," I said, "this is so important to me. I have full confidence in you, of course, but would you be prepared to take a lie detector test?"

"Of course, not at all. I would be happy to do that."

So we made an arrangement with a polygraph firm. Priscilla went with her, and Donna took the test. The result? Absolutely nothing. Whatever the polygraphist asked her or told her, she showed no response and no emotion at all. We got the printout of the questions and got a look at the graph. The curve was flat in response to the most provocative questions. At the end, in order to get some response at all, the polygrapher had the bad taste of asking Donna some racially loaded questions (Donna was black). Even then, there was a straight line, no emotion at all.

"I can't tell you anything at all about this girl," he said. She is a complete stoic. I conduct about five or six tests a day and I see one of those every three or four years. It is very rare. But, the polygraph is totally inconclusive. I can't tell you anything about her."

There was no loss of money, but I was totally intrigued.

I did a little sleuthing of my own and here is what I pieced together: Donna had a boyfriend and that boyfriend was a bad apple. He had a record. The attorney who advised the bank about the bags was the one who had been appointed by the court to defend him in his last caper. Apparently, Donna and her sister had a party on Friday night. Donna had forgotten to drop the bags in the night chute. So she took them home and put them in her closet, intending to deposit them sometime over the weekend or on Monday morning. The boyfriend, who was at the party, found the bags, slit them open and took the money. When Donna retired to go to bed she opened her closet and found the money bags all slit open and with all the cash gone. She knew what had happened. She jumped in her car, raced over to her boyfriend's, probably beat him up (she was big enough to do so), and told him to return the money immediately or she herself would take him to the police. So the fellow returned the money, and Donna, with the deposit slips in hand, reconstituted the five deposits, just as she had originally arranged them. But what to do with the bags? She herself took them to her boyfriend's attorney on Monday morning and told him what had happened. The attorney concocted the story about the mystery phone call and finding the money in front of his office door. I am quite sure that was how it happened. In any case, we had our money back.

Donna stayed for about another six months and then she left. I've never heard from her again.

We were doing well at Henniker's. We had beautiful merchandise, beautiful catalogs, great ads in media and a nice list of customers. Profits were good. I was happy with my second chapter in the mail-order business. But I was intrigued about that million dollars that Time had been willing to pay for my first business, Haverhill's. I had an obvious talent for building such a business. It was now clear to me that a mail-order business, even a relatively small one, was an interesting potential acquisition for a large corporation. The reason was the large national exposure and the well-known name that such a business inevitably had. It was a business that, in the right environment and with a partner that had access to lots of inexpensive advertising, could easily and quickly be expanded. I wanted, if possible, to repeat the coup. I thought I should put out some feelers. It was at this point more interesting to me to create and sell such a business than to run it.

Our business, Henniker's, was by then quite substantial; so, in order to produce the large amount of printed material and media that we put out, we needed our own art department, staffed by a director and two assistants and our own typesetting equipment in-house. That, of course, was before the advent of computers, which made all such typesetting equipment – big clunkers that looked like pianos, but were essentially sophisticated typewriters – obsolete. But having this equipment in-house and not keeping it busy full time, it occurred to me that I should put it to additional use. I decided to write a book. I would write a book about what I knew best, the mail-order business. So, I went to work on that.

I made a rough outline of the book that I planned to write. I decided that it would be approximately 400 pages with perhaps 100 pages of exhibits and illustrations. This would mean 300 pages of copy. I figured that there would be about 400 words per page, a total of about 120,000 words. No problem. I had so much information that I would have had no problem writing a million words about this business. I decided that once I got it started, I wanted to finish the book in not more than one year. I should not be too difficult for me because I didn't have to do any research – I knew exactly what I was going to write about.

Also, I had and still have the facility of dictating seamless copy, copy that would only need minimum editing. So I decided to go to work and I kept right to my schedule. Every morning, my secretary would print out the copy that I had dictated the previous day. I would then edit the typewritten draft and give it to the woman who operated the typesetting equipment. She had the galleys (as they are called) ready by that evening. I then took them home, gave them a final edit, then gave them to the typesetter to make the final galley.

As it turned out, it didn't take me a year. It took me only about nine months to write the book. After the final go-through, I noticed to my dismay that the book had been set in sans-serif type, the type that has letters without those little wiggles. It makes long copy a little less readable. I had been so intent on the copy itself that I had never really consciously noticed the typeface. Well, now it couldn't be changed. It would have been a tremendous job to do it all over. Today, of course, with computers and word processing programs, it would be very simple and fast, literally three keystrokes to change the typeface or the size of the type and almost anything else for the whole book. But, it was impossible to do that in those days. If I didn't like the typeface and couldn't accept it, we would have to do it all over.

I decided that the book was of sufficient importance to bring it out in hard cover and I also decided to self-publish it. I contacted a number of printers and asked for a quotation on 5,000 books, which I decided was going to be my first printing. The best bid I got was $2.18 per book, just over $10,000 altogether. I thought it was a risk worth taking, and went ahead.

I had no immediate interest in placing the book in bookstores; since it was a book about mail order, I thought I should sell it by mail order. And so I did. I advertised it in my usual media, with emphasis on business media such as *The Wall Street Journal, Business Week*, but also in such media as *Entrepreneur Magazine*. Things went well. I was now a successful published author. I quickly made a good dent in that first printing of 5,000 books.

I liked the publishing business and I was looking forward to writing and publishing other books that I had in mind. I was interested even in perhaps publishing books written by others. So I decided to form a publishing division, Advance Books. The name of my corporation was Jomira formed from the first syllables of my children's names – Joseph, Michael, Rachel – not in proper sequence but my Mirajo would not have sounded well. So I now changed the name of the corporation to Jomira/Advance in honor of the new division. It has been my corporate name ever since.

We have seen that interesting people came to my office from time to time. Here was another such case. The man who came to my office, unannounced, was a Mr. Bennett. He gave me his card and introduced himself as a Vice President of Harper & Row, at least in those days, one of the country's largest publishers. He told me that he had seen and read my book, that he thought it was excellent and that it had great possibilities. He did not think that I exploited these possibilities fully by selling the book only by mail order. I had to agree with him.

"Why don't you let us publish the book for you. We'll pay you a nice royalty – twenty per cent, and you can leave production of the book, sales and all other headaches to us."

"I don't think I would be too interested in such an arrangement," I told him. I wasn't quite telling the truth. I was really very interested. "But could we not possibly make a deal where I, or rather my firm, continued to be the publisher of the book and Harper & Row would distribute it for us?"

"That would be a most unusual arrangement," he said. "We've never done anything like that, but let me come back to you."

He came back a week later and said, "I think we can make the kind of arrangement with you that you suggest."

"How would it work? I asked him. "How would revenue be distributed?"

At that time, the book business was much simpler than it is now. There were no super chains, and by and large books were sold at the cover price printed on the inside flap. My book sold initially for $19.95; when I got through with it, the last three printings, it sold for $29.95.

"Here's how we do it: We sell it to the book stores at forty per cent off list, which (at the initial retail price of $19.95) would be $12. They make $8 profit per book. You would get seventy-five per cent of the $12, and we would get twenty-five per cent. In other words, you would get $9 per book and we get $3."

It sounded almost too good to be true.

"What else would I have to do?" I asked him.

"We would expect you to put a one-page ad at least once a quarter in *Publishers Weekly*, promoting the book." That was going to cost about $400. It wouldn't be a problem at all. So I readily accepted his proposal.

If I had accepted the 20 per cent royalty agreement I would have gotten $4 per book. With this deal, I would get $9 and my profit per book would be that, less the cost of printing – in other words I'd make approximately $7 profit per book sold. That sounded like a very good arrangement.

And it was. The book went through eight printings in about eight years – about 30,000 copies sold altogether. At the end, under the same formula, with the book selling for $29.95, and with printing costs not having increased a whole lot, I made between $10 to $11 profit per book. It was really a very sweet deal.

But that was not all. Not long after Mr. Bennett's appearance, I had a call from Canada, from a publisher that specialized in so-called self-help books. He'd seen the book and wanted to publish it in Canada. I looked at my contract with Harper & Row. They had the exclusive right to the book for the United States only. So I made a deal with the Canadian firm, who published the book in soft cover and paid me a $2 royalty per book sold. It wasn't quite as good a deal as with Harper & Row but it was pretty good.

I really liked publishing. It seemed to be an even better business than the mail-order business, and I thought that I had finally found my true calling.

A few weeks later, Bennett appeared in the office again. "Guess what, Gerardo," he said.

"What?"

"I've quit Harper & Row and I'm going to open my own publishing company. I think I already have one good author. Would you like to join me?"

"Well," I said, "I would be interested in principle, but I don't want to be part of your publishing company. You want me to join forces with you? Then lets publish any books under both of our imprints. What's the name of your publishing company?"

"Harbor Publishing," he said.

"Sounds good. What book are you going to publish?

"A book about money. It's called *Your Money Matters*."

"That's a good title," I said. "It's kind of clever."

"Yes, and the author is a great guy. He is a banker and a bishop in the Mormon Church."

"Sounds like a great combination to me. Can I see the book?"

"Yes," he said, "I'll show you the manuscript."

I read the manuscript. It looked pretty good. I thought the book would be a success. So Bennett and I ordered our first printing, 5,000 books. The publisher was Harbor Publishing/Advance Books. We were in business – big time – or so I thought.

The book sold very poorly. In fact we never did sell more than one-third of the first printing and had to "remainder" the rest of it. We suffered a fairly substantial loss. What was the reason? It was a good book. It became clear to me that we could not have sold *Gone With the Wind* or the *Harry Potter* books the way we were doing it. We just didn't have any distribution. Bennett should have known that, of course. After all, he had much experience in the publishing business. But I didn't understand that yet. That became clear to me later, but not soon enough to do me any good in this case.

I continued in business, of course, including the publishing business, but Harbor Publishing was out of sight after just this one trial.

One of my closest friends was Karl Bach. Karl was about five years older than I. We had a lot in common. He was born in a small town in southern Germany, the son of a butcher. His was the only Jewish family in town. They were not kosher butchers, of course. They butchered everything, including pork. From what I understood, they had a very nice business. And of course, just like all other Jews, they were driven out of Germany with barely their clothes on their backs. The Jews in small towns, where no restraint for public relation reason was necessary, suffered much more and much sooner than we did in Berlin.

Karl was about nineteen years old when he came to the United States. He went to work in a butcher shop in New York, but he really didn't like it. That was not, he thought, what he had come to the United States for. He had relatives in southern California. He wrote them and asked to let him come to California to see whether he could find a job there. They didn't reply. He wrote again, and again they didn't reply. So, he went to California anyway. He had no money, no education, and he spoke very little English. There was one more thing. He had a physical defect. As a result of childhood polio, one leg was shorter than the other. When he walked it sounded like kla-plonk, kla-plonk, kla-plonk.

Not knowing what else to do, he got a job as a Fuller Brush salesman, working only on commissions. Within a couple of months, he was the most successful salesman that Fuller had ever had. The company was so intrigued by him that they sent an executive vice president from headquarters in Rhode Island to find out what his secret was. They wanted him to teach it to the other salesmen in the Fuller Brush organization.

"I have no secrets," Karl told him. "I just sell those brushes and do the best I can."

But he told _me_ his "secret." "When I come to a house or an apartment," he said, "I would ring the doorbell and then I would walk back just as far as I could.

The lady of the house would look through the peephole and see me about twenty feet away. She didn't feel threatened. All other salesmen stood right by the door. So, not feeling threatened, she would open the door and from twenty feet away I would talk to her and tell her about the brushes. Usually she would invite me to come closer. When she saw my physical problem, my limping, she felt at ease, unthreatened, and very confident and would usually invite me to come in. Once I was in, I would sell those brushes."

So it occurred to Karl that, being so successful in selling brushes, he could probably sell anything else. An acquaintance advised him to go into the life insurance business. So he did just that.. Within a year, he was the most successful life insurance salesman his company had ever had and had become a member of the Million Dollar Roundtable. He wrote a book, *How I Sell 25 Million Dollars of Life Insurance or More, Year after Year*. He said, Gerardo, "Do you want this book? I'll let you publish it and you pay me a small royalty."

"I'll do it, Karl," I said. And I went ahead. I printed and published it and it sold well. "Do you have any other books like that?" I asked him.

"Well, not right now," he said, "but I'm writing one."

"What's the name?"

"The name is *Selling is Simple...if You Don't Make it Complicated.*"

I published it too. It was very successful. In fact, now, more than twenty years later, I have republished it. It sells just as well as the first time around. It is one of those timeless books that, just like Dale Carnegie's "How to Win Friends and Influence People," is as relevant and valid today as when it was first written.

Karl was so successful that he stopped selling full time and proceeded to found the San Francisco Life Insurance Company, which he later merged into the Philadelphia Life Insurance Company. Unfortunately he died when he was only about sixty-five years old. He was one of San Francisco's foremost philanthropists, especially for Jewish causes. He left a wife, from whom he had been separated for many years, seven children and a couple of girlfriends. All of them became very rich. Apart from being a wonderful friend and a great salesman, he also had a keen eye for the ladies. He was one of the most unprepossessing-looking men. But women loved him – and not just for the money.

Even though I was one of his closest and oldest friends, he never ceased trying to sell life insurance wherever he went and whomever he was dealing with, and that included me. He told me that one of the greatest opportunities for selling life insurance was at gravesides. People were conscious of death and therefore receptive to buying life insurance.

I had lunch with him three or four times a year, always in the Garden Court of the Palace Hotel. It was his favorite place. He would never fail to try selling me life insurance. He would frequently succeed. His technique was interesting. The scenario was pretty much always the same. I'd say, "Karl, you look upset today. What's the matter?"

"Oh I don't want to talk about it. It's just too sad." he would say.

"Go ahead and tell me," I would reply.

Well," he would say, "I just came from Mrs. Robinson. She is the widow of Dr. Earl Robinson. He was only forty-two years old and he suddenly keeled over and dropped dead, just like that. I had made a presentation to him about two weeks ago to buy $3 million worth of life insurance, which I thought he needed for the welfare of his family. He told me that he would think about it, but he never got around to it, he never did anything. Now, his widow with their two little children is left without any money at all. It's a real tragedy, a terrible story."

This story had a variant, which was that Dr. Robinson had indeed purchased those $3 million life insurance just two weeks before and that now, thank goodness, because of that policy his widow and those little children were well taken care of. He was the greatest salesman I had ever known.

The last time we had lunch, he told me to my shock and consternation, that he had been diagnosed with colon cancer that had spread to his lungs and that he only had a few months to live. He was composed and cheerful. He told me that the doctors had advised him that he could perhaps prolong his life by a few months if he switched to a fully macrobiotic diet. He thought it was a good idea and he hired a German cook, just for that purpose. He told me that he had tried it for a couple of weeks, but that it tasted so awful that he decided to discontinue it. "What difference does it make if I live a couple of months longer or not? I've had a great life and I am not going to make the last months that I have left miserable by eating that awful stuff."

He died two months after our last meeting. He was a great guy, a wonderful friend, and I still miss him.

The relationship with my in-laws wasn't the greatest. They ultimately accepted me, but there was really little warmth. I am quite sure that the reason for the coolness was my Jewishness, my being a "foreigner," and my general "otherness." My father-in-law, Jack Kern, and I had really very little in common, except that both of us were or had been in the oil business, and we both loved Priscilla, of course. I think he liked me better as an engineer than as a son-in-law. And, of course, I had those notions of "Jewish family life," a certain warmth that I did not find in that family at all. For example, I was somewhat disappointed and surprised when he made the participation in those oil wells on an arm's length basis with me, and treated me just as he did any other investor. I didn't think that a Jewish father-in-law would have done that.

When we were in Business School, the principal purpose of which of course was to take myself and therefore my family (his daughter and his grandchildren) to a different level of accomplishment and income, he never once told me how he admired my moxie, and never encouraged my doing that. He certainly never offered to subsidize our living expenses in any way. I will say, however, that I am quite sure that, if needed, he would have helped us out.

But then he did something generous and very interesting. Quite a few years down the road, I urgently needed some money for the business, $50,000, which I couldn't get from the bank or any other source. Of course, we had that Time Inc.

stock that was in the brokerage account, but I was not too eager to sell any of it. My father-in-law would be the logical source of any loan. Priscilla and I agonized endlessly as to whether or not we should ask him for a loan, but finally I did. I wrote him about it. I labored over my letter, to be sure to say exactly the right thing and to explain my needs as carefully as I could and how I would repay the loan.

He answered right back.

> Dear Gerardo,
>
> I understand your need for money and being in business myself I know how these needs can arise. But I don't want to lend you any money. I don't want you to be my debtor and I certainly don't want to have to dun you for payment. It would not be good for our relationship. Therefore, I have arranged with the First National Bank of Magnolia Arkansas, for a loan to you in the amount of $50,000. They will send you a loan agreement and you will pay them as agreed.

I was very grateful for his handling of this, and I told him so. But more than that, I thought that it was marvelous solution. He had facilitated the money for me, but I would not have to deal with him at all. He was a guarantor. If I didn't pay, the bank would eventually come after him. So I would have to avoid that and, of course, I did. It was the nicest thing he had ever done for me. I was very grateful to him.

But then something happened that very much changed our relationship. My in-laws were coming for a short visit, arriving on a Friday and preparing to leave again on Monday. I don't know why that visit would have been so short. We didn't see them all that often, but that's the way they wanted it. My father-in-law (Jack) was, I thought, in a somewhat combative mood when he arrived. For no reason at all he engaged me in a discussion about taxes. Even though I don't think of myself as an expert in that field at all, I was quite sure that he made a statement about it that was not correct. I should not have argued with him, but I did. There was tension in the air. We then went out to dinner. Instead of letting us pick a restaurant, he had made up his mind where he wanted to go. He wanted to go to Emilio's, one of San Francisco's finest and most expensive restaurants. He had heard about that restaurant from one of his friends in Magnolia, who claimed that his son-in-law owned it. It turned out that the son-in-law was not the owner, but the bartender. Since my father-in-law was very thrifty and since dining out in Magnolia consisted of going to the Chatterbox, where the main attraction was chicken-fried steak with mashed potatoes, for $1.95, I tried to talk him out of it. I thought that he might be somewhat awed by the prices in that restaurant. But he insisted, and so we went there. When he got the bill, he almost fainted. He'd never seen anything like that before in his life. He couldn't believe it, but there it was. He did pay it, of course, but it didn't put him in a good humor at all.

We got back home and we all had a couple of drinks. He then engaged me in another argument, this time, I believe, about politics. Priscilla and I were, and still are, Democrats – she much more so than I. She is what we used to call a "yellow-dog Democrat," who is one who would vote for a Democrat even though he were a yellow dog. Jack was a staunch Republican. He also had been a Democrat, but he shifted gears as soon as he got some money. But that was not unusual. Many people go through that mutation. In any case, he engaged us in an argument about politics and I don't remember at all what I said, but his riposte was "That's just like a Jew to think that way."

I thought I hadn't heard right. He finally said what he meant and he told me how he really felt about me. He blanched. He knew that he had said the wrong thing. My mother-in-law (Vera) started to cry immediately. She knew something awful had happened. Jack stood up. He knew he had committed a bad blunder. Priscilla sat there petrified.

But what did I do. If I had had any good sense and any real desire of avoiding a family feud, I would have laughed the whole thing off, ignored it or made a joke about it. Instead, my immediate feeling was one of "gotcha!", and I knew that I now had something on him that would take him a long time to erase. I could have defused the situation, but I didn't. It would have been the right and generous thing to do. After they both left the next morning, I was not proud of myself at all. Sure, he had made a big blooper, but I could have smoothed the whole thing over, and I hadn't. Ultimately that was my fault and my mistake. It took some years before things were straightened out between us, and it wasn't until shortly before he died that he really made me feel like family. I'll talk about that later.

By that time we had about twenty employees and Priscilla decided that it **would** be a good idea if we gave them a Christmas party. I agreed. We sent out fairly formal invitations and invited all employees to a buffet dinner at our house and, of course, to bring their spouses, boyfriends or girlfriends. They all came, about 40 people altogether. We had them all in our home and it was a little crowded. But the food, as always when Priscilla was in charge, was excellent and though we didn't have any hard liquor, there was plenty of wine and beer. Some people got a little tipsy.

One of our employees was a fellow by the name of Andy, who was one of the workers in the warehouse. He wasn't too bright, but he was a good worker and a good guy. He was, by appearance, a full-blooded American Indian. Most of us were sitting around on the floor and Andy began to expound about the nobility of native Americans. Everyone agreed with him.

Priscilla, always sociable, stepped up and said, "I'm from Oklahoma. I'm an Indian too, one-sixteenth."

Andy asked her, "You're one-sixteenth Indian? What tribe?"

"Choctaw," Priscilla said brightly.

Andy, without a word, uncoiled his 6 foot 2 inch frame. "You're what?" he asked in what sounded like a menacing tone.

"Choctaw," Priscilla said, somewhat more meekly and slightly intimidated.

"I'm a Blackfoot," he said. "We are the eternal enemies of the Choctaw and I'm eating food in the home of a fucking Choctaw squaw." He spat on the floor. "Fuck you," he said, and he left the room and the house. His wife started crying, offered apologies and left after him.

It was not a good social moment, but we all had another glass of wine or another beer and got over it.

But, after what had happened, it seemed pretty clear that Andy could no longer work with us. He didn't come to work the next morning or the morning after that. On the third day he called me. "Mr. Joffe," he said, "I'm truly sorry about what happened, but that's how I really feel about the Choctaw. They are the hereditary enemies of the Blackfoot Indians."

"Well, I'm sorry to hear that, Andy," I said. "I hadn't known that, but you obviously can't work here anymore."

"Yes, I understand that. But I have no ill will to you and I hope you don't either. Would you like to help me out?"

"How can I help you out, Andy?" I asked, somewhat surprised about the request.

"Since I can't work for you anymore, and since I have to feed my family, I've decided to go into the janitorial business. But I have no money to buy the equipment I need . I want you to lend it to me."

"How much money are you talking about, Andy?"

"I would need $2,500 and I would really be glad if you would lend it to me."

I thought that he really wasn't a bad guy, just a damn fool, and I wanted to help him. But I didn't want to get involved in any money situation with him. Then I remembered what my father-in-law had done for me. I said, "Andy, I won't lend you any money directly, but I'm going to guarantee a $2,500 loan for you at the Wells Fargo Bank. You go to the bank and they'll give you the money. They'll tell you how you should pay it back. I suggest you be very meticulous about paying that debt."

"Be what?" he asked.

"Meticulous," I said, "you know, do what they tell you to do."

"Thank you very much. I'll do just that."

The bank gave him the $2,500 loan, repayable, if I recall correctly, in twenty-four installments, of around $130 each. Two weeks after the first payment came due, the bank called me and said, "Mr. Joffe, Andy did not pay his first installment. We are going to have to ask you to do that."

"I would have no trouble doing it," I replied, but I think we should make an extra effort to see that he pays it himself. It think it's important. So, I called him. "Andy," I said, "it's most important that you make that payment. If you don't, you will ruin your credit rating forever, and you cannot stay in this janitorial business and you can never get into another one."

"I just don't have the money," he said.

"Well, you must get it from somewhere, because if you don't pay it it's very bad. Your credit rating will be ruined forever.

Three weeks later he paid the installment. I went through exactly the same song and dance with him with every payment – always late and always the bank asking me to pay for him and my finally always talking him into paying – until the final twenty-fourth payment came around. The same thing happened. He just wouldn't pay. After he was four weeks overdue, and after listening to my little speech, he said, "You know, Gerardo, you fired me and you owe me something. You go ahead and pay that fucking installment. I don't have the money and I don't feel like paying it. Goodbye."

So I did go ahead and paid the last installment to the bank. I never heard from Andy again, I don't think that he really got very far in business. I had been right – he was a fool.

Things continued to go well with Henniker's. We did exactly the same thing that we had done with Haverhill's. We put ads in media, sent out beautiful direct mail to our customers, and catalogs four times a year to our own customers and to others; anywhere between 500,000 and one million in each round. It was really a very major effort and was accomplished with very few people. Sometime I look back on the work that Priscilla and I did in those days. It was really impressive.

Feeling good and very confident, we opened a fashionable store on Rodeo Drive in Beverly Hills, the ritziest shopping district in California or perhaps in the United States. We spent a lot of time, effort and money on that store.

We did find, however, that it was not too successful. It is possible that our merchandise, which was mostly "gadgety" and utilitarian, was not quite right for that tony shopping district. Also, the sales personnel that we had was not adequate. They needed supervision that we did not or could not provide. And finally, there was too much additional overhead connected with that store. Priscilla or I or both of us had to fly to Los Angeles and visit that store at least every other week. With airfare, hotel costs, and what not, it added up to quite a bit of money. Ultimately, in order to effect at least some economies, we rented an apartment in Beverly Hills, close to the store.

We tried it for about a year, but we weren't making any real money, certainly not commensurate with the financial investment and the personal effort that we continually had to put into it. We finally gave it up. It was our first, last, and only business "failure."

But the stores in San Francisco did well. We ultimately opened two more stores – one in the principal medical building in downtown San Francisco, and another one close to our offices, which we used as on outlet store for merchandise that we had either discontinued or on which we were overstocked. We called it

"Honest Anne's Store" because the manager was Anne Finnegan. She became a minor San Francisco legend and did a great job.

Once a year, usually just before the Christmas season, we would rent a large loft space and have a blow-out sale of all discontinued and overstocked merchandise. We advertised that sale heavily in the San Francisco newspapers and, by direct mail, to our Northern California customers. It always drew big crowds. People were standing around the block before the sale doors opened. We would reduce prices by five per cent every day. We made money and had lots of fun.

But still, one thought kept gnawing on me. I remembered fondly that million dollars that Time Inc. had paid me for my Haverhill's business. Could it be that I had a talent for creating businesses that people wanted to buy? I was itching to try it again. In fact, the last chapter in my mail-order book was "How to Make the Big Score." It dealt with how to prepare a mail-order business to make it attractive for purchase by a large, preferably publicly-held, company.

So I kept my eyes and ears open to try it again and dropped a word here and there that I would be amenable to sell Henniker's if the right suitor came along.

One day, I had a call from an old friend, Walter Karl, who was the "dean" of list brokers. What are list brokers? They are the people who facilitate the use of names, mostly for direct marketing and philanthropy purposes, by other firms. For instance, if Henniker's needed to send out a catalog, we would send it to our own house list, which for Henniker's was about 250,000 names at the time. Then we would rent, for one-time use, names of "compatible" firms, usually our competitors. Why would our competitors rent names to us, and vice versa? Or, most usually, exchange them with us? Because competitors in all likelihood would have customers who would buy the kind of merchandise we had to sell. You really couldn't do without it. The list broker would get a pretty good commission for his "match making" services.

In any case, Walter Karl called me and said, "Gerardo, I've heard rumors that you would be willing to sell Henniker's. Is that true?"

"Well," I said, "I don't know where you got those rumors, but yes, of course, I would be interested if the right offer came along."

"Gerardo, I have exactly the buyer for you. It is the Franklin McGregor Company of Ashton, North Carolina. They're looking for acquisitions in the mail-order field."

"What do they do?" I asked.

"They are in the mail-order shoe business. Having big warehousing and all mail-order facilities, they want to apply that overhead and increase their business without too much additional cost."

"Well," I said, "It sounds pretty good to me. Have the owner call me. What is his name?"

"His name is Carlton Firestone," Walter said. "He is a little peculiar, but a fine old Southern gentleman. You and he will get along very well."

"O.K., have that fine old Southern gentleman call me and I'll be happy to talk to him."

Sure enough two days later, Carlton called me. We had a pretty good visit on the phone. We agreed that he would send his "right-hand man" to come and visit with us, to review the financials, and to look at the operation in general.

The man arrived three days later. He was a short, dumpy fellow, an ex-seminarian who had decided that he did not have the vocation and perhaps too much testosterone in his system to become a priest; he had therefore dedicated himself to business. He had an MBA degree. He was a nice guy.

Bradley – that was his name, stayed with us at our house for three or four days. He was good company. He liked what we were doing and he liked the numbers. He told us that he was going to give Carlton a very good report about us. He said he would recommend a purchase offer.

Carlton called me two days later and told me that he was very interested in buying this business. Following Bradley's very good report, he invited Priscilla and me to come to Ashton so that we could discuss a deal.

We followed his invitation and went to Ashton. We were quite impressed with Carlton and his business. He was, as Walter Karl had told me, indeed, a "fine old Southern gentlemen," or he certainly looked the part; in fact, he looked like something out of central casting. He was tall, silver-haired and favored string bow ties. He had a beautiful home filled with exquisite African art. To top it all off, he had, in addition to the obligatory swimming pool, an indoor tennis court attached to his home. Though Priscilla and I were not yet tennis players, we were most impressed.

The deal at which we eventually arrived was much leaner than the Time Inc. deal had been, but it had an apparently very good "rear end." There was a relatively small down payment, but an attractive participation in profits. Since there would be no additional overhead, the profits could be expected to be quite a bit larger than they had been under our independent operation. Additionally, I was to continue with the company as president and would receive a pretty good salary. I would stay in San Francisco doing only purchasing and advertising. It was not a great deal but it was a good deal.

Matter of fact, this fine old Southern gentleman turned out to be much more cagey than he looked, than I had thought and had given him credit for. He certainly ultimately outsmarted me. I had a bad attorney and a badly written contract. After six months of doing pretty well, the fine old Southern gentleman decided to sell the Haverhill's division to a large company in Minnesota. He got a pretty penny for it, certainly a lot more than he had paid me. Unbelievably, my contract had made no provision for such a contingency. I was out of luck. My attorney – the one who had vetted and approved that foolish contract, advised me to sue, but I decided against it. "Forget it," I told myself. "I know how to do this business and I'll start over again. To hell with North Carolina." And perhaps my attorney was the one who should have been sued for writing or approving such a dumb contract.

So I started over again. I still had the lease on the same San Francisco premises, the same store, and the same personnel. The only thing I couldn't do was use the Henniker's name.

I had been friends for many years with Rama Russell. She was a lovely lady from India. She had a small letter shop and even when technology had utterly superseded her, I gave her much of my work. I was greatly fond of her. She was improbably married to a big Irishman by the name of Mike Russell. He absolutely adored her.

I told Rama what had happened and that I was going to start all over again in business. "What would you think if I called my business Russell's in your honor?"

She said she would be delighted and she gave me a big hug. So we started over again as Russell's. We did exactly as we had done before. The fine old Southern gentleman had taken all of our inventory, including everything that was obsolete and overstocked. That gave us a chance to start all over again, and with fresh merchandise. Even though I hadn't made a very good deal, we had ample working capital from retained earnings and from the aborted merger with that North Carolina shoe company.

It was now 1977. Our older son Michael was twenty-three years old. Rachel was twenty, and Joseph, our little afterthought (or, perhaps more accurately, our little accident) was twelve years old. Michael was a serious problem. He had become a heroin addict. Nothing that we tried could really "cure" him of his addiction. We rented a small apartment for him, but it became clear that we could not entrust him with any money. Every penny we gave him would go right into his arm. It was awful to see him that way. For a number of years, we made arrangements with various restaurants in San Francisco to feed him anything he wanted and to bill us or charge our credit cards for it. We would give him a very small amount of pocket money, just enough to buy cigarettes, to which he was also addicted, bus fare and so on. We would not even give him enough money to buy clothes because it was clear that it would be used for drugs. Priscilla would buy his clothes. It was a bad situation.

One of our friends, whose daughter had a problem similar to Michael's, recommended a psychiatrist to us, a Doctor Aramini who was reputed to have had much success with addicted teenagers and those in their twenties. We arranged to meet with him. He insisted that the whole family participate in the sessions. Dr. Aramini had a very nice office near the University of California Medical Center on Parnassus in San Francisco. He was of Iranian background and struck me right away as somewhat of a pompous person. He would arrange the five of us in uncomfortable chairs around his consulting room. He would sit in the middle of the room, in a beautifully upholstered swivel chair that could move up and down, around, and in all directions.

I took somewhat of an instant dislike to him, but that was probably my fault. I just "didn't believe" in psychiatry, thought of it as "psychobabble" and didn't really think that it could help our son. Ultimately, I was right, of course,

In the middle of one of these sessions, Dr. Aramini was called to the phone for some emergency. He left the room for about five minutes. I decided to change chairs and to sit on Dr. Aramini's throne, as I called it. When he came back he said, "Mr. Joffe, can I have my chair back."

I said, "Dr. Aramini, surely you don't need this comfortable chair to conduct your therapy. Why don't you sit in one of the other chairs. It shouldn't make any difference. I think I would feel more comfortable in this chair."

Dr. Aramini said, "Please give me my chair back or we have to end the session."

Priscilla interrupted, somewhat agitated, "Gerardo, give him his chair. We have come here to get help for Michael. We haven't come here to pick a fight with Dr. Aramini."

So I yielded the chair. It may have been a pretty dumb thing on my part, but I wondered why he had to sit on his throne in order to conduct his therapy.

When we left, he said to me, "Would you like to have your dagger back?" I thought it was a strange remark, but the therapy, which cost a lot of money, was utterly useless, just as I had believed it would be.

Rachel was now twenty years old. She had graduated from Sarah Dix Hamlin School which was for girls only for the first eight years, then had some token boys – very few really – for the last four years of high school. She was now at the University of California in Santa Barbara and was doing well. She was very beautiful I thought, and people shared my opinion. She was sweet and pliable and never gave us any trouble. Being a girl, I didn't interact with her as much I would have wanted to. I now regret that very much.

The addiction of Michael would have been a tragedy in any case, especially since it became evident that it would be very difficult, if not impossible, to "cure" him. It had now been going on for seven years and there was no relief and none in sight. He went on methadone maintenance. He was sweet, he was loving, and he was funny. In addition to that, he shared many of my ideals and purposes. He was the most "un-Jewish" looking of our children, but he, just like I, was very interested in Judaism, in the State of Israel, and most especially in its air force.

My delight was Joe, our little latecomer. He was then about twelve years old. Even though I was working very hard – I invariably took work home every night, writing copy, laying out new mail pieces, checking catalogs, and much else – I still made it a point to make time for him. Almost every Saturday we went to the San Francisco Press Club to swim and then go out to lunch – usually for burgers and fries. He loved that.

On many Sundays, we would go on Sierra Club hikes in Marin County and other areas close to San Francisco.

One day, we were walking side-by-side on a narrow trail in Marin County. He told me that his backpack was too heavy. "Dad, I just can't carry it any more. It's too heavy."

"I'll carry it for you, Joe," I said, "but you must make me a promise."

"Whatever it is, Dad, I'll promise it."

You know, Joe, eventually you'll get married and you'll have children. Will you promise me to call your first-born son Gerardo, Junior?"

He didn't give it thought. He might have thought it was a great idea or he wanted to get rid of that backpack.

"I promise that, Dad."

He has regretted that promise ever since and has tried to wiggle out of it. I certainly was not serious, but I always threatened to hold him to it. Of course, I wouldn't because, under Jewish custom, one cannot name a child after a living relative. It just isn't done. And of course, I hoped that he would have his first son while I was still alive.

The closest I ever came to Rachel on a father-daughter basis was in 1970. As we had done in previous years, Priscilla and I had planned to spend our winter vacation, the ten days or so between Christmas and right after the New Year, on the North Shore of Lake Tahoe. We usually rented a cabin with two bedrooms in the little town of Incline Village. When we were ready to leave for Lake Tahoe that year, Joseph fell ill with the flu and could not travel. Priscilla, of course, had to stay with him. What do to? We decided that Rachel and I would go by ourselves. It was the first time that we had been alone together. She was thirteen years old.

When we arrived at our destination, she assumed immediately the role that her mother would otherwise have played. She commandeered the food, told me what we were going to eat, told me what my duties in the house were going to be, and so on. I was quite surprised, found it very charming, and I did exactly as she told me. She and I went skiing every day at what was then called "Ski Incline," right at the edge of the little town. We realized that we weren't very good at it and that we should take some lessons to bring us up to speed. So, we did just that.

The private teacher that we engaged took us to the top of a gentle hill, skied down to the bottom in beautiful and graceful turns, and then motioned us to come down, one at a time, and make at least three or four turns. Rachel apparently did passably well. The teacher, Brent, told her that with three or four lessons he would be able to bring her up to standard. Then he motioned for me to come down the hill. I did what I'd learned many years earlier in Aspen, as taught by Friedl Pfeiffer, under whose guidance Priscilla and I had earned the coveted Two Bells pin, the mark of Alpine accomplishment.

"Stop, stop," he hollered," after only my second turn. "Where in the world," he asked, "did you learn this? "I've never seen anybody ski like this for at least twenty years."

"This is the Arlberg method," I told him. "That's what I learned in Aspen."

"Forget everything," he said. "Modern American skiing is totally different; in fact, it's the exact opposite. Do not under any circumstances throw your shoulders around as you have learned. You ski with your legs."

"What do I do with my body," I asked.

"Here's the secret," he said. "Always look downhill; always look down to the parking lot. If you do that, you'll become a good skier."

I followed his advice. I looked down to the parking lot and skied with my legs only. He was right. I turned out to be a pretty fair skier, have enjoyed it for many years and still do.

On our way back from that trip with Rachel, she insisted that I put on chains to get over the Donner Pass. I didn't really think that we needed them, but she was so insistent that I thought it would be preferable to appease her. When we were about five miles beyond the pass, it was time to take off the chains. I was not at all experienced in that; in fact I had never done it before. So I unhooked both chains on the outside and attempted to drive out of them. It seemed to be the easiest and least messy way to do it. I didn't get very far – only about six feet and then the car stopped with a jerk.

"What happened?" Rachel asked.

"I don't know. Let me have a look.

It turned out, as I noticed to my dismay, that the chains on both wheels were inextricably tangled around the rear axle on both sides. The only way to get them off was to jack up the car, take off one wheel at a time, take off the chain, put the wheel back on, then jack up the other wheel and do it again. Rachel, who went to a girls school and who had lived a pretty sheltered life, told me that in the fifteen minutes or so that it took me to perform this maneuver she learned more foul language and bad words than she'd ever heard before or since. She thought it was very funny. In any case, even with that mishap, that was a wonderful time for both of us – my first and in a way my last time of being really close and alone with my daughter.

By that time, I had been in business for almost twelve years. There had been much hard work, a great deal of creativity, contact, mostly pleasant, with many suppliers, associates, and employees, the drama and excitement of selling the business twice (and as we'll see, it wasn't the last time), and the interactions pertaining to that. Essentially, as far as business was concerned, I did in all those years essentially the same thing as when I stared in 1967 – naturally, updating as I went along – until I finally hung it up for good in 2001, thirty-four years later after I had started.

We were doing well with Russell's. Nothing had changed. It was really the same business that I had dreamed up in 1967. But there was a shift in emphasis. Now virtually all of our merchandise came from Asia, mostly Hong Kong and some of it from Taiwan. Japan, which, after Europe, had originally been the main source of merchandise, was being nosed out. Costs were too high. Europe, as far as our merchandise was concerned, was out of the running altogether, except for the few important specialties such as the Monaco Shaver (the one that went to the moon), until the very day that Mme. Rollet, the owner of the factory died. The Emoskop, the brainchild of Arthur Seibert of Wetzler, Germany, was such a wonderful product that, when he finally died, we had it manufactured in Japan, under the name of Episcope. When the Japanese became too expensive, we had it manufactured in Hong Kong. Their production was just as good at it as that of the Japanese and as that of the Germans. But, there was an important difference: The "Made-in-Hong-

Kong" item cost half as much as the "Made-in-Japan" item, which, in turn, cost half as much as the original German-made item. Since the sales price of the item had been established over many years of advertising, there was no need to change it and our gross margin multiplied. That was wonderful, of course.

Still, Priscilla and I made our yearly "pilgrimages" to the European fairs, partly, I suppose, to buy a new car while we were there, and to take a little vacation while we were at it. On one of those trips, we went to the Milan fair (*Fiera di Milano*) and saw two items that greatly intrigued us. They ultimately became best sellers with us. One was a telephone that looked as if it were sculpted and came in five different colors. It was what is called a "fun item." It was a total contrast to the austere MaBell issue, which in those days, came only in one somber color, namely black. We took it on and called it the BoBo Phone. The BoBo Phone became a huge success. There was only one thing wrong with it. It had a rotary dial. When keyboard dialing was introduced, the BoBo Phone quickly fell by the wayside.

Another item we found on this trip was LaBisquera. It was a big square earthenware pan with a hinged bottom and a lid, in which almost anything – vegetables, fish, but mostly meat – could be cooked without grease and which, as we advertised, would make round steak taste like T-bone. It avoided calories, cholesterol – and big grocery bills. The manufacturer in Cremona, Italy, prepared food for tasting right in his LaBisquera stall at the fair. It was really delicious. We were enchanted with the item. We placed a small sample order of 250 pieces. Mr. Saminelli, the owner and company representative, gratefully accepted the order, told us that he would start working on it as soon as the fair was finished, and that he would be able to ship within eight weeks.

We were a little surprised that he would need so much time for such a small order but we didn't give it much thought.

It was a great item. As soon as we arrived back in San Francisco, I started writing advertising copy and, though that was really against one of my "rules," I also immediately designed a direct-mail piece on this item to be mailed to our customers and to outside lists. I was very enthusiastic and had great hopes for LaBisquera.

The shipment finally arrived. It was a terrible disappointment. About two of every three pieces were broken and had to be thrown away. It was a great calamity. We wrote Mr. Saminelli and told him about it. He did not seem to be too surprised. "It's a fragile item," he said. "There's nothing that we can do about that. I'll have to replace the broken items. That's the only honest thing to do. Please send me just the handles of the broken LaBisqueras and I'll replace every one of them."

Well, that was very nice of him, but it didn't really solve the problem. But we knew just what to do. We designed a new Styrofoam nest and an outsized padded box. The LaBisqueras were now perfectly cushioned and could no longer break. We sent him the nest and the box. He had it replicated in Italy and that problem was solved. LaBisquera was one of our most popular and most profitable items. We handled it for years.

The experience with LaBisquera taught us the importance of packaging and that one should not give up on a good thing if there was a way to remedy what appeared at first glance to be an insurmountable obstacle.

I don't know of too many men who worked in their business with their wives. Naturally, there are many "mom and pop" stores but that's a different story. Until then, I had never seen it in any size of business such as we had. Priscilla went to work at Haverhill's in 1969, first working in the store and then taking over merchandising and the artistic direction and catalog preparation. She did an outstanding job. We never, never could have attained the success that we did had it not been for her. But how did it help or hinder our marriage?

It worked out wonderfully. I think it strengthened our marriage, sharing interests, not just in the family, but also in business. One thing may have helped: We drove to work together every morning, then each went to our own office. We usually didn't see each other all morning long. Then, we'd get together for lunch; sometimes we brown-bagged it, and sometimes we went out. It was a good time for us to be together. The same thing happened in the afternoon. She worked in her office and I worked in mine. We might interact once or twice during the day, but not very much. Then we drove home together and talked and thought of our family and of our children.

Priscilla has often reproached herself for working every day and for so many years. She thinks that, perhaps, if she had been around home more, she could have nipped Michael's problem in the bud and things would have turned out differently with him. I doubt it. He made his own destiny, and as it turned out, nothing and nobody could stop him.

One year, the pressure of business was such that I did not think it was possible for me to make the yearly trip to Europe. Priscilla did not want to go by herself so she asked Rachel to go with her. It didn't take much persuasion. One of the main stops of that trip was to be Cremona, Italy, to visit Mr. Saminelli's factory, where the LaBisqueras were produced. Priscilla and Rachel went by train from Milan. Mr. Saminelli and his wife picked them up from the station, immediately took them to a hotel, then to a very nice restaurant.

"I would really like to see the factory," Priscilla said.

"*Domani, Domani,*" Mr. Saminelli said. "Tomorrow, tomorrow. there's no hurry."

Next day, Mr. Saminelli picked them up from the hotel. "Let's go to the factory," Priscilla said.

"Yes, yes, but first let's see Cremona. It's such a beautiful city. They spent all day sightseeing. At the end of the day Priscilla said, "Please, Mr. Saminelli, my husband told me to be sure to see the factory, because LaBisquera is so important to us."

"*Domani, Domani,*" Mr. Saminelli said.

Priscilla was a little surprised, but she agreed. Next morning, Mr. Saminelli came again. "Let's see the factory," Priscilla said.

"There is no hurry," Mr. Saminelli said.

"Yes, there is a hurry, because we're going to have to leave this afternoon."

Mr. Saminelli said, *"Beni, Beni* – O.K., O.K., let's go see the factory."

It turned out that "the factory" was in the back yard of Mr. Saminelli's home. It consisted of three workers kneading the clay and putting it into forms and then putting the forms into a small kiln that also was in the backyard. It was the most primitive operation Priscilla or anybody else had ever seen. But they were able to turn out about 50 LaBisqueras a day. We were their largest customer by far.

On one of our trips to Europe, Priscilla and I decided to make a side trip to Denmark. I had not been to Denmark since I had left Europe. I had sweet and bitter memories of Denmark. Sweet because of my puppy love for Ulla, and bitter because of her suicide. But I was interested in seeing Mrs. Jespersen, Ingrid, again. She had been so good and loving to me when I was a teenage boy. She was such a large influence on my life, had opened her home to me while I spent my summers in Denmark courting her daughter, had offered me her home while I would be attending the technical university in Copenhagen (but of course, ultimately didn't'), and had sent me ten British pounds as my farewell present from Europe. I realized, of course, that she would be a very old lady by now.

We called her from Germany and told her that we would be visiting with her in two days. She was very happy to hear from us.

Quite in contrast to the previous grand style of her life, she now lived in a very small apartment, mostly the beneficiary of the expansive Danish welfare state and of her son, Finn – Ulla's pesky little brother – who was by now a prominent attorney in Copenhagen.

It was a wonderful, touching and nostalgic visit, marred only by the fact that her eyesight was almost gone. She was virtually blind. She told us that after Ulla had "disappeared," she sat by the telephone for six months hoping that she would call her. It was strange because Ulla's body had been found, but Mrs. Jespersen was apparently in full denial about that.

Then we went to visit Finn, who had a beautiful home, a lovely wife, and three children: two girls and a boy, ranging in age from sixteen to twelve. It was a wonderful family and we realized, even though we had re-found each other so late in life, that we would be good and best friends or the rest of our lives. It turned out to be just that way.

One of our good friends, were and still are, Al and Betty Black, a couple perhaps only a few years younger than we. We shared interests and had much in common. They had two adopted children, but seemed to have much trouble with them. Betty had one very special talent. She could "fix up" houses. They would buy a small house in San Francisco or in one of the suburbs for, say, $50,000 or $60,000, work on it for a few months and put, say, $20,000 into it. They would then sell it for perhaps $90,000 or $100,000 and make $20,000 or $30,000 profit on their money and time and effort invested. It was a pretty good deal for them but it was all relatively small potatoes. One day they came to us with a proposition. They had spotted an apartment building on Lake Street in San Francisco, right in our immediate neighborhood, with six units, that could be bought for $400,000. It needed a $100,000 down payment and they could not swing that by themselves. They wanted us to go in with them and contribute $50,000 to the down payment. Betty was confident, and we believed her, that within six months and with an investment of about $100,000 for improvements, she could make the property worth at least $750,000, but probably more. We were to advance or guarantee the $100,000 improvement loan and she would give her time and expertise. Then we would be 50-50 partners. It sounded like a good deal and especially attractive to us, because we did not own any real estate at all, except for our own home that we had just purchased.

I said, "Al, this sounds like a pretty good deal, but let me talk to the seller."

"What for?" Al said.

"I think I would really like to negotiate the price."

Don't do it," Al said, "it isn't worth your while. Even if you could knock it down $25,000 – and I don't think that you can – it wouldn't make much of a difference in the long run, and I think the property is fairly priced. Somebody else will come along and pay the full $400,000. It's what it's worth. We'd lose a very attractive deal."

"Al," I said, "believe me, I'm an experienced negotiator."

"O.K.," Al sighed, "if you insist, go and talk to the owner. I still don't think it's a good idea."

"Trust me," I said.

I met with the seller two days later and made an offer for $375,000.

The seller told me the price was $400,000. He said he wouldn't come down from that.

"I am prepared to write a check for the down payment right away," I said, as I pulled out my checkbook with a flourish.

"I'll think about it," he said.

He did think about it. He sold the house the next day for $400,000 to a man from Hong Kong, who had instructed his San Francisco agent to look for desirable rental properties. We were very unhappy about it. Al and Betty, who quite rightly thought of this as a great opportunity lost, also were not happy at all. The house is now worth about four or five million dollars. Every time Al sees me, he asks, mockingly, "Gerardo, do you still have any other great negotiating ideas."

"I am sorry, Al, I said, "I screwed up. I meant well, but I screwed up."

"Oh well," Al said, "another opportunity will come along" – but nothing like that ever did, or at least it was never brought to my attention. But I did learn one lesson from that: If you see something that you really like and you think the price is fair, don't mess around by trying to knock off a few dollars. It won't make any difference in the long run. It certainly didn't for the buyer who is now the owner of this beautiful and very valuable apartment building.

Things were going well, the children were growing up, and business was good. Finally, we had a little money and thought of how we could improve our life.

One of the things that we liked to do was to go skiing at Tahoe during the week or ten days around Christmas/New Year. Rachel and Joe by this time were teenagers and they liked to ski. Michael did not participate. He had other pursuits. We had always rented a cabin, which was quite expensive but worked out pretty well.   But we never felt entirely "at home" in the rented cabin or entirely comfortable. So, when the winter of 1978 approached, Priscilla said, "You know, we like to go up to Tahoe so much and the children like it and we have some money. Why don't we buy a place of our own?"

It was a totally new idea for me, but I thought it was a good one. So we packed the two younger children in the car and drove to Tahoe. We went to the South Shore first but we didn't really like it. Even though the skiing at Heavenly Valley is one of the best in the area, or perhaps in the entire country, we were not too keen about the gaudiness and hullabaloo of all of the casinos on the South Shore. So, we drove north along the east side of the Lake. We came to the little Nevada town of Incline Village, where, of course, we had been many times before. We walked into a real estate office and were received with open arms. The woman assessed our family and made discreet inquiries about how much money we had available, and then said, "I think I know exactly what you need and I happen to have it available."

Well, we would have been surprised if she hadn't had something available, but that was all right. She took us to a development, Mountain Shadows, which looked well maintained and had about two hundred individual "cabins," usually four to a block, which came in all sizes, from one bedroom to four bedrooms. We liked No. 19. It was two stories, with three bedrooms and two baths on the lower floor and a large living area, kitchen, bathroom, and storeroom on the upper floor. It also had a beautiful deck which, unfortunately, opened to the woods, and not to the Lake. We were not alert to that difference and might have looked at something else. But, it was just fine.

"What is the asking price for this place?" I asked the agent.

"$80,000," she said. I was a little surprised. Only twelve years earlier, we had bought our beautiful three-story home in San Francisco for just $68,000 and now they were asking $80,000 for this cabin in the woods. It didn't sound right.

"It sounds a little expensive," I said to the agent. "Is this negotiable?"

"Not at all," she said. "These cabins are in great demand. If you want it, you'll have to pay the full asking price of $80,000. There will be no negotiating."

I remembered my unhappy real estate experience with the apartment building in San Francisco and decided not to attempt any negotiation. Either we'd buy it or we wouldn't. I said to the agent: "Why don't you please go back to your office. My wife and I will discuss it and we'll be with you in about fifteen minutes – one way or another."

So Priscilla and I talked about it, which wasn't quite easy because the children were jumping up and down. "Buy it, buy it," they hollered.

"Will you please be quiet; your mother and I want to talk about this and it's a really serious decision for us."

"Buy it, buy it," they repeated.

We decided that we could easily afford the down payment of $16,000. We were sure that we and the children would enjoy the place very much. Priscilla thought that she could do many wonderful things in decorating the place. The only decoration that it had when we bought it was a line of empty beer cans on top of the mantel.

Within three days of our return to San Francisco, I had a call from a Chinese man. He introduced himself as Mr. Wong. He said, "Mr. Joffe, I heard that you have just bought unit #19 in Mountain Shadows in Include Village for $80,000. Would you consider selling it to me for $85,000?"

:No, I am afraid I wouldn't," I told him. My children just wouldn't forgive me if I did. But thank you very much for the offer." I was really glad that I had learned my lesson and that I hadn't attempted to "negotiate" (and in all likelihood lose) this deal, just as I had done so disastrously with that apartment building in San Francisco.

We also remembered that house in Marin County when we first came to San Francisco, that we were going to think about leasing, with an option to buy, that we were going to think about on our way back to the Sheraton Palace Hotel and which "that bitch" that Priscilla had spotted, had closed on in the meantime.

We still have that Tahoe place. It's our home away from home. Priscilla has done truly marvelous things in decorating and transforming it. It is a work of art. In the early years, winter or summer, we used to go up there at least every other week. Then, as the children grew older, they lost interest. Now only Priscilla and I go up there – every other month, if that often. But we never fail to spend the last week or ten days of the year in our Tahoe condo.

I am still a reasonably good skier, but Priscilla gave it up several years ago. That's a little sad because it is not that much fun skiing by oneself. "Why don't you want to ski anymore?" I asked her.

"I have my reasons," she said.

"Tell me your reasons," I insisted.

"Well," she said, "if you really need to know, it's just such a hassle to go to the bathroom, with all those clothes. And there's something else."

"What's that?" I asked.

"I'm kind of scared of hurting myself and hurting my tennis game." (I'll talk about tennis later.)

My mail-order book kept selling. Harper & Row did a wonderful job in distributing it and, there can be few things as satisfying as receiving a quarterly

Rachel, about twenty years old, and I. What a lovely girl!
I only regret that I did not spend enough time with her.

Michael and Marybeth look to be a happy couple. But Michael
was already in deep trouble and he had a tragic and bad end,
not too much later.

royalty check. There was a pretty good-sized one every time from Harper & Row and a somewhat smaller one from my Canadian paperback publisher. It was just wonderful —almost like an oil well, money that came in without having to do any work.

People were obviously interested in the mail-order business. So I thought I would give it another, bigger whack. I proceeded to write a mail-order course, which consisted of seven volumes. I titled it "How to Build a Great Fortune in Mail Order." Taking my lead out of the playbook of the Book-of-the-Month Club, I organized it as a "negative option plan." What that meant was that the buyer, having purchased the first volume, would automatically get subsequent volumes, approximately six weeks apart, unless he canceled. It worked quite well, but it wasn't as successful as the mail-order book. That was a blockbuster and a real moneymaker, partly because of the very favorable deal I had negotiated with Harper & Row and in which I came out much better than if I had been paid royalties, instead of being the publisher.

I was perhaps getting a little tired of the mail-order business. I'd been doing essentially the same thing for the last thirteen years, and Priscilla and I had been doing most of it ourselves. Even though I had gone to Harvard, which was considered the finest business school in the country, I had not properly learned the art of delegating. I felt that nothing was truly well done unless I did it myself. That unwillingness or inability to delegate severely limited the attainments and growth of my companies. Some of my students, following the principles and methodology that I had established and which I had taught them, were able to build much more substantial companies. The most prominent among them is The Sharper Image, founded by Richard Thalheimer. In an article in *Newsweek*, he was gracious enough to acknowledge that "I owe it all" to Gerardo Joffe and his mail-order course. He was exaggerating, of course, but I am sure that I had helped him a good deal in building his large, publicly held and very profitable business.

While I just didn't seem to have the desire or, who knows, the ability to build a really large business, I was comfortable with the size and performance of what was now Russell's, where I was in control of everything.

I was now on my third company – first Haverhill's, then Henniker's, and now Russell's. But I felt much nostalgia for Haverhill's and regretted that Time Inc. had let it lapse. I decided that I wanted the name back. I didn't really know what I could do with it, but I suppose I was mostly concerned that it wouldn't fall into anybody else's hands.

One of the vice presidents at Time Inc., with whom I had and had maintained good relations over the years, was one William Baer, so I called him one day. I said, "Bill, what would you guys think of selling the Haverhill's name back to me?"

"That shouldn't be any real problem, Gerardo. Let me talk to the legal people and I'll get back to you." He did indeed call me the next day. "Gerardo, we can't really sell you the Haverhill's name because we don't own it any more."

"What do you mean, you don't own it any more?" I asked. "I sold it to you."

"Yes, you did, but we haven't used the name for over seven years; therefore, our ownership in it has lapsed. You can have it if you want. It's all yours. We can't sell it to you."

"Bill," I said, "that's interesting news, but I wouldn't really feel good about having the name and not paying you for it even if, legally, you didn't own it."

"Gerardo, you can't pay us for it, but if you wish and if it would make you feel better, you could make a charitable contribution in our name."

"That sounds like a good idea, Bill" I said. "I'll do it. How does $5,000 sound to you?"

"That sounds like a very generous offer. If you do that, we'll send you a quit claim document."

I asked him what he meant by "quit claim."

"What it means is that whatever rights we may have in the name, we'll give to you. Then we definitely won't have any more rights."

"Well, that's fine. O.K.," I said.

"I'll send you a list of the approved charities of Time Inc. and you can pick the one you want."

I thought about that. I didn't think that any of the philanthropies that Time Inc. had on the list would be anything that I would choose. The list had probably been put together by Mr. Luce, whose "philosophy" in virtually all matters would seem to have been quite different from mine. So I decided to preempt. I made a check for $5,000 to the Jewish Community Federation of San Francisco, telling them that this gift was on behalf of Time Inc. and that Time Inc. should be given credit for it. I sent the check and the cover letter to Bill Baer by overnight mail.

Bill called me the next day. "Gerardo, didn't you get the list of our approved philanthropies?"

"No, Bill, I haven't received that list yet, so I decided that I would go ahead and make out the check to a charity of my choice, namely to the Jewish Community Federation of San Francisco. That surely should be acceptable to you."

"No, I'm afraid not," he said. "The Jewish Community Federation of San Francisco is definitively not a philanthropy that Mr. Luce has established and approved." Well, I wasn't really surprised. Bill continued: "Mr. Luce's favorite charity was the Olava Foundation. (I make the name up here, because I simply can't remember it. It was something very much like it.)

"The Olava Foundation? What is that?"

"It's a philanthropy that Mr. Luce has personally established. It trains Chinese girls for secretarial work in the United States. He was very partial to this and gave a lot of money to it. That would be an acceptable philanthropy for your $5,000 gift."

"Bill," I said, the Jewish Community Federation of San Francisco is my favorite philanthropy, but the Olava Foundation is a close second, so let's go with that."

I made out a new check to the Olava Foundation and three days later I had my notarized quit claim deed for the Haverhill's name. I had no plan for using it. It was an act of nostalgia for which I was willing to invest $5,000. Little did I suspect that it would once again play an important role in my life.

There was a change in Priscilla. I couldn't put my finger on it, but there it was. She had taken up art. I was amazed by and proud of her originality, imagination, and artistic competence. She produced beautiful paintings, which adorned and still adorn our home and our place in Tahoe. But there was something else – there was a noticeable estrangement. I couldn't really understand it. Was I right? And what and why could it possibly be? But then she told me. I learned that she had decided that we were really not suited for each other, that we had made a big mistake, that I was not really the man with whom she could spend the rest of her life. Then she told me that she did not love me any longer and that she was in love with a man by the name of Edwin Ferguson, her sweetheart in high school, whom she had met again when she went to her thirty-fifth high school reunion and who was really her "soul mate."

Apparently they had not met since that reunion, but there were now continuous correspondence and almost daily telephone calls. We had sex and she cried. Could it be that she had the feeling she was cheapening herself making love with a man whom she no longer loved and to whom she was bound only by marriage? Was it just "fulfilling a duty," while she was in love with someone else?

All that was very hard on me. I suppose it wasn't easy for Priscilla either.

She decided to take a trip to Texas, ostensibly to exhibit some of her artwork, but it was clear to me that she wanted to see and be with Edwin and perhaps to decide how she would structure her future.

She did one very smart thing. She took Michael along, partly, I suppose, as a chaperon, but also probably in order to prevent her from doing something really stupid. Michael was twenty-two years old. He watched her like a hawk and reported to me daily. He was totally devoted to the family and to me, and thought that his mother, whom he dearly loved, had (temporarily, he hoped) lost her mind.

Michael told me later that Edwin drove a white Cadillac with steer horns on the hood, that, of course, he always wore cowboy boots and a cowboy hat, and that he kept a keg of beer in the back seat of his car. Priscilla told me later that the steer horns were Michael's invention. Despite my pain, I found it somewhat amusing. I could not see how in the world Priscilla could have related to me, the exact opposite, for so many years, and then take up with a man like Edwin.

After sojourning in Texas for about a week, always under the careful scrutiny and watchful eye of Michael, they went on to Magnolia to visit with her parents and, I suppose, for Priscilla to break the news that she was going to divorce me and marry her childhood sweetheart. There was no contact with me at that time.

I was quite desperate. I loved Priscilla so much, had always imagined that she was happy with me, and never, never dreamed of the possibility of divorce. It was the worst and most unexpected surprise that I could imagine. When I could almost bear it no longer, I called Magnolia. My mother-in-law answered the phone. "What do you want?" she asked in a harsh voice.

"I want to talk to Priscilla," I said, "my wife."

"This marriage is over," she hissed at me. "Don't call here again. Jack (my father-in-law) wants to sleep. Don't wake him up." It was 8 o'clock p.m. their time.

Priscilla and Michael came back a week later. Michael was very perturbed. I decided that the divorce was now inevitable, and I planned and hoped that we could arrange it in a friendly way, and, if at all possible, with only minimum intervention of attorneys.

I wrote a four-page letter telling Priscilla how much I loved her, how hurt and surprised I was about her having entered into a relationship, on whatever level, with another man, and that despite all that had happened I would love to have her back and promised to love her for the rest of my life. In the eventuality, however, that things could not be put together and that she would insist on a divorce, I had also prepared a document proposing how to split our community property. Then I prepared an ad, to be published in the *Jewish Bulletin of Northern California*, that read as follows:

Abandoned

> After over twenty years of happy marriage and three wonderful children, my wife suddenly left me and ran off with a cowboy (honestly, his name is "Tex"). I am heartbroken, feel very lonely and am seeking new companionship. I am looking for a woman (non-smoker) between about forty and forty-five. She should be good-looking, slender, educated, productive, informed, skier, opera lover, bright, and socially adept – with potential for tenderness and love. My children (quite a few others, and even my former wife) think that I am a very nice and entertaining man. I own a business, a beautiful home, a condo in Tahoe, have substantial education, a wide range of interests and am loving and affectionate. Even after the financial ravages of divorce, I am still quite well to do. If you think that we may be able to fill the voids in each other's lives, please do write to me, and perhaps send me a picture. I promise to return it, and to respect your confidence. Box YY.

After sending in the ad, I called the paper. Please hold it for the time being. I am not yet quite ready to run it. I thought, I hoped against hope, that we might still work things out.

So we arranged a family dinner – Priscilla, I and the three children. Feelings were quite tense. The children made it totally clear to Priscilla how much they disapproved of what she was doing and what she seemed to be about to do. They made it clear, Joseph included, that under no circumstances were they going to go to Texas, but that they were going to stay in San Francisco and, in the case of Joseph, would stay with me. It was up to her to make up her mind.

"Let me think about it," she said. Two days later she said, "Gerardo, I've made up my mind. I must have been crazy. I don't know what happened to me. I think the reason for all this is that I am so concerned and so undone about Michael's drug habit. But what I did and what I was going to do was obviously the wrong thing. I don't know what possessed me. I love you and I'll stay with you for the rest of my life." She gave me a big kiss. We made love. She didn't cry.

It took me a little while, however, to reconcile myself to my mother-in-law who so gleefully had told me that "this marriage is over." What was the matter with that woman? I'd never done her any harm. I had treated her daughter well through all these years and, to the best of my ability, had been a good father to her grandchildren. But I did eventually get over her unfounded animosity against me and was able to feel and show affection to her in the last years of her life. My father-in-law, while he may have had his opinions and might have given advice if requested, stayed out of this matter, as far as I could tell. The one who was steadfast, stuck with me and advised her sister about giving up on her craziness, was my sister-in-law Diane, a girl/woman whom I have known since she was thirteen years old and of whom I always thought of as my own sister. I know she felt and feels the same way about me. It makes me feel very good.

This dreadful episode – the black cloud on the sunny sky of our bliss, happened in 1980, over twenty years ago. Priscilla tells me, and I have absolutely no reason to doubt her, that she had never had any further contact with Edwin. She has been the most loving wife that anybody could ask for and a wonderful helpmate and a person that I totally admire. The matter of Edwin never comes up. We overcame this hurdle. Who knows, just as some people who have had a heart attack are healthier because they are more conscious and take better care of themselves, so may our marriage have been strengthened by this dreadful event. We may be more thoughtful, more considerate of each other than we otherwise might have been.

Having finally and happily settled our marital problem, Priscilla said that we all should get some counseling. I was not really in favor of it because I didn't think that I needed help, but Priscilla insisted. Michael was pretty busy with his own problems, so it was decided that Priscilla and I and Rachel and Joe should see a psychologist. The man that we selected was a family friend, Charles Ellison. We learned later and it became clear that that was not a good choice. He was a good man, but he should not have taken us on; he should have alerted us to the fact that a psychologist and counselor should not be anyone who is a friend of the family. I don't know what he did with Priscilla and with the children, but I don't think that he helped me at all. The first time I went to see him I talked about my father and about problems I thought I had with him – not too many. The second session I talked to him about my mother and the problems I thought I had with her. Also, not too many, but more than with my father. I also talked about the Möbius family, who had asked me for help and to whom I had not responded. It was still very much on my mind. I had done that wrong. I was really worried about what to talk about the next time. I didn't have anything else that was bothering me, so I said, "Charles, I don't know what else we could talk about because I've told you everything that's on my mind . There is really nothing else."

"Well," he said, "if you feel that way, let's just consider that the counseling is over."

I told him, "Thank you very much," and left. All members of my family, Priscilla and the children and their spouses have been in counseling off and on. I never have again. If it makes them happy, and if they believe that it makes them feel better and become spiritually healthier, that's fine with me. I just don't feel that I need it, and don't really quite believe in it.

As we have seen, interesting things seem to happen when people unexpectedly come to my office. Here was another case: One day, I believe it was in 1984, two men came to my office; one was fairly tall and athletic looking, the other was much shorter, slightly built and blond. They introduced themselves as Ed Gordon and Frank Johnson, respectively. Gordon was director of development for Frontier Airlines; Johnson was a CPA and the airline's assistant controller. They told me that they had watched Russell's for some time. They were impressed with our advertising and with our merchandise.

"Thank you very much, gentlemen, what can I do for you?"

"We've been thinking that we could generate additional revenue for Frontier Airlines if we put your catalogs in the seatbacks of our planes. Also, we own space at the Denver Airport and have options on space in other airports, which would allow us to open stores. We have been following your advertising and we have seen your stores here in San Francisco and we are impressed. Would you consider selling this business to us and merge with Frontier Airlines?"

Of course I was interested and I wanted to hear more. I had made such a good deal with Time Inc., and I was willing to overlook the somewhat lesser deal I had made with that fine old Southern gentleman of the shoe company. "Yes, I would be interested. I hadn't thought about it, of course, but I would be interested. What do you have in mind?"

"If we go ahead and do the deal," Gordon said, "we'll do something that would be totally satisfactory with you. But, we would like to have your permission for Johnson to stay a week with you, to look around, to examine the financials, to check the inventory, and to get acquainted with the company."

"No problem," I said. "Would Mr. Johnson like to stay at our house. We have a big place and we'd like to have him?"

"No." Gordon said, "Thank you, but that won't be necessary. We have leased space at the Hilton Hotel for our crews and Johnson can stay there."

That was on a Friday afternoon. Johnson stayed in San Francisco for a little over a week. He watched our procedures, thoroughly checked the financials, assessed the inventory and everything else that would have to be done for due diligence. I also had to give him my bio (resume) which, of course, included my educational history. At the end he said, "Gerardo, I talked to Ed, and I have recommend that we buy Russell's. Ed will be here early next week. He'll make you a formal proposal." He then left for Denver.

But Ed didn't come, and neither he nor Johnson even called. The same thing the next week and the week after that. I just couldn't understand it. By I decided not to call them. If they had changed their minds, that was all right with me. I just wondered about the way they handled it. I thought that they should at least let me know that they had changed their minds and why.

Three weeks later I got a call from Ed Gordon. "Gerardo, we're prepared to go ahead with the deal but we need for you to come to Denver first and talk to our president, Mr. X (I've forgotten his name). You'll fly Frontier Airlines, of course, as a guest of the company."

"Ed," I said, "I will be happy to talk with Mr. X, but before I go, what is the deal?"

"We wish to give you a lump sum down payment and participation on profits."

Well, I had that before with the fine old Southern gentlemen so I was a little concerned. "What is the down payment?" I asked him.

He gave me a number which was quite acceptable to me. "What is the participation in profits?" He gave me a percentage. That was also acceptable to me. It sounded pretty good. But I was still a little wary. I could not get out of my mind the experience with the fine old Southern gentleman, who sold Henniker's six months after he had bought it and left me holding the bag. "Ed, I said, "this all sounds pretty good, but suppose somewhere down the road you decide to sell the company. What happens then?"

"No problem at all," he said. "In the unlikely case that we do that, you would get the same percentage of the proceeds that you will be getting on profits."

That sounded good.

So, the next day I went to Denver on Frontier Airlines and was picked up at the airport by limousine. I was impressed. The president, Mr. X, turned out to be a nice man. He asked me to tell him about my plans for the future, beyond the seatback program and possibly the stores at the airports. I did just that. Then I met some of the other executives of Frontier, who impressed me well. Then, finally, the deal was made, the check was written, and hands were shaken in the general counsel's office. Russell's was part of Frontier Airlines.

But there was one thing that bugged me, that I was still curious about. Over drinks with Ed and Frank, following our little ceremony, I asked: "Ed, tell me how come I didn't hear from you for three weeks, after Frank told me that I would hear from you the following day?"

He hemmed and hawed and wanted to change the topic. But I insisted. In the end, he said: "Here's what happened. We had to verify your bio. We checked with the University of Missouri, and they confirmed that you had indeed graduated there with a B.S. degree in mining engineering. Then we talked with the Harvard

Business School. They looked and informed us that they couldn't find you. They told us that they would check further and would get back to us if they had any further news. They called back and told us that, no, you had never attended the Business School. That was bad news, because we knew that you had lied to us, that you had inflated your credentials. We do find that quite often in resumes. When we do find it, it is the end of the applicant."

"I understand," I said. "But how come we are here now and have made this deal?"

"Last Wednesday" Ed continued, "we got a call from the Harvard Business School. They told us how embarrassed they were about their error. They didn't realize that you got your MBA in the Middle Management Program, and they didn't check there. When they found you, they called us back and informed us. We then felt free to go ahead with you."

I thought it was an interesting story, but, though I didn't tell them, I didn't think they had handled it too well. They should have called me and confronted me with the discrepancy. We would have cleared it up right away and they could have determined that I was not a liar. Had it not been for that person at the Business School to call Frontier back two weeks later, the deal would have died – perhaps under some pretext – and I would never have known the reason.

In order to accommodate the growth of our business, we immediately moved into a larger and more suitable office and warehouse building. We had about forty employees.

Our new offices were just great. We had plenty of space and wonderful accommodations for our "executives." (I put this in quotations marks because there were really only I, Priscilla, my secretary, Priscilla's assistant, and the two or three people in the art department, who could possibly be described as part of the executive corps.) We had plenty of room for our warehouse and for shipping. There was only one thing missing. We couldn't find a nice place nearby for lunch. We had fallen into the habit of going to the Press Club almost every day, but that was now on the other side of town, much too far. There was a small Mexican restaurant in the neighborhood, but who wants to eat burritos every day? Then, somebody suggested to us that we should take out a luncheon membership at the San Francisco Tennis Club, which was only a block away. "A luncheon membership?" we asked. Do they have things like that? Yes, one doesn't have to play tennis. The luncheon membership is relatively inexpensive and the food is really quite good.

So we went to the Tennis Club and introduced ourselves to the membership director, a women by the name of Hilda. She said, "Sure, a luncheon membership is a good idea. It cost $500 for the two of you, plus, of course, the meals that you consume. But why don't you take out a tennis membership? It doesn't cost that much more and then you can play tennis and use all of our athletic equipment and all of our other facilities."

We weren't really interested in tennis, we told her. We just wanted to have a place to eat lunch.

Priscilla and her sister Diane sitting in front of their mother's portrait. When I first saw my future mother-in-law, on my first date with Priscilla, I thought that she was the most beautiful woman I had ever seen.

Joseph and I, not too many years ago. He prescribed the identical
costumes that we were going to wear for this portrait.

She was a good saleswoman. "Let me show you around," she said. She
took us to the balcony and we saw those happy people whacking their tennis balls
back and forth. It didn't look too bad to us. Then she took us to the gym room and
to the weight room, and showed us all the other facilities. It really looked very good.

"I'll tell you what," she said. "You can take out a 'Silver Tennis
Membership' which is only $1,000 for the two of you, or you can take out a 'Gold
Tennis Membership' which costs $1,500."

"What's the difference between the two?" we asked.

"With a Silver Membership you can only play tennis in the non-preference
hours. With Gold you can play at all times."

"If we wanted to, could we eventually upgrade the Silver to a Gold
Membership?"

"Of course," she said. "Any time."

The non-preference hours looked good to us. So, we took out the Silver
membership and started taking tennis lessons. Our teacher was Matthew Donaldson,
a wonderful athlete. We learned all the basics from him, though for the
"refinements," the fine points, the nuances of spins and slices, the (hopefully) killer
serves and all that, we later took some specialized instruction. In any case, we
became pretty acceptable tennis players, after only a short while. It has become part
of our way of life. Even today, almost twenty years later, we play two or three times
a week, mostly doubles, and have lots of fun. Priscilla turned out to be a much better
"natural athlete" than I would ever be, and she is a much better tennis player than I
am. I have learned to accept that. In fact, she and her team (the "Piranhas") won the
national USTA championship in her age group. I, and many others, were much
impressed.

Not much later, the Tennis Club quietly gave up the differentiation between
the Silver and Gold memberships; so now, of course, we can play any time we want.

Although I understood little or nothing about the commercial aviation business,
it was clear to me that Frontier, one of the smaller airlines, was vulnerable and pretty
much at the mercy of the routes that the "Big Five" would let them have, and the fare
pricing that they could impose. I also suspected that the big carriers, should they so
decide, could crush a small airline like Frontier at any time. While it concerned me,
of course, it was not my immediate worry. My immediate worry was to make
Russell's grow, in line with the business plan that I had given the management of
Frontier.

There was one immediate and wonderful benefit of being part of an airline.
Just as when we were part of Time Inc., all employees got free distribution of the
company's magazines, we now had something much better, a much more attractive
benefit: All employees got almost free travel on the airline, although there were
certain restrictions. They and their immediate families could travel, I believe it was
five times per year, and pay only $25 per trip. Even though Frontier had a somewhat
limited reach, at least at first, it was a wonderful benefit. The employees loved it. I
and my immediate family fell into a much higher benefit category. We could travel

any time, as often as we wanted and without any payment. If we wanted to go someplace where Frontier did not go, arrangements could be made with another airline to get us there – first class, of course.

There were times when I told my son Joe, "Joe, how about the two of us going to Jackson Hole in Wyoming for a day's skiing tomorrow?"

"All right, Dad," he would say, and we'd go to the airport at 7 o'clock in the morning, were on the slopes by 10, and back home before dinner. It was great.

Also, we could buy tickets, at $50 a pop, for travel for our extended family. That was most welcome, of course, to my in-laws, their children and the children's spouses in Georgia. Uncle Gerardo's and Aunt Priscilla's popularity soared. Those were good times.

But then things went wrong. I never quite understood what happened, but it had to do with the deregulation of the airline industry which, apparently, put small carriers such as Frontier at great disadvantage and under financial pressure that threatened their survival. Within less then a year, after much struggle and attempts to reorganize and attempts to shed unessential businesses, Russell's among them, the airline collapsed. Frontier was in bankruptcy. Everything, all the planes, all the property – and Russell's – were liquidated.

It was quite a blow, but I was determined to stay in business and not to let this deter me. There was about $200,000 of inventory. We (Frontier) engaged a San Francisco auction house to sell it off – at about ten cents on the dollar. Nothing impeded me to bid in that auction. I purchased about $50,000 worth of inventory, the most desirable portion, for about $5,000. It was the basis for going on in the same business, even though under a different name.

Shortly before the collapse of Frontier, a young man came into the my office one morning, unannounced. He was tall, blond, about forty years old, and his name was Charles Weibert. He had good references, had much experience in the direct-marketing business, seemed to be knowledgeable of merchandise, and was looking for a job. He was just the kind of person this business needed. He could free me and Priscilla of much of the work that we had been doing. "Charles," I told him, "you are just the kind of person we need. Unfortunately, I can see the handwriting on the wall for Frontier. I am afraid that it's going to go belly-up and there won't be a job for you. Why don't you try to find something else here in San Francisco, but let's stay in touch. If the worst indeed happens, I'm going to start back in business. And if and when I do, I'll want you to be my vice president of marketing. You seem to have just what I need. I have a little secret with which I am going to get this new business off to a rousing start."

"What is that?" he asked.

"Charles, can you keep a secret? I asked him.

"Of course."

I opened my drawer and pulled out a watch. "You see this watch?" I said. "It does everything that men want: It's digital, it's analog, it has a built-in stop-watch, date, alarm, timing bezel, and a steel band. I can buy it for $12 and sell it for $50, and I'll sell at least 100,000 of them."

Charles was skeptical. "What makes you think you can sell that many watches?"

"I just have a nose for merchandise," I told him, "and I know how to promote it. This watch is going to be a very big winner."

I wasn't out of business for more than a month. I took the inventory that I had bought at the auction and ordered 1,000 Navigator Watches – that was the name I'd given them, half in black and half in silver. I was right back in business. As a matter of nostalgia, I put the Rodell-7 logo – the mark on my "catemanial" computer that started me in business – on the dials of these watches. I hired Charles to be my vice-president of marketing, expecting that it would ease the load on me. That turned out to be indeed the case. He was a competent man and a hard worker.

What to call this new business? It was clear: Haverhill's, of course, the name I had reacquired by making that $5,000 donation to the Olava Foundation in the name of Time Inc. I made only one change. The "old" Haverhill's was with an apostrophe and the new Haverhills was without apostrophe. That was the only difference, and, of course, I registered the name, something which, almost inexcusably, I had not previously done.

We made a lot of money in the first two years, mostly because of the fantastic sales of the Navigator Watch, which even exceeded my optimistic expectations. My hunch had been right: That watch was a sensation. It sold well in all media, including television. In fact, we made so much money that I had to find some legal way of deferring earnings so as to reduce income taxes. What legal way? In the mail-order business, that is relatively easy. If you want to defer, say, $100,000 in earnings until the following year, all you have to do is write, on December 25, a check to the US Postal Service for $100,000, as prepayment of postage. Presto, your earnings for the year are reduced by that amount. Among other things, we mailed about one million catalogs every quarter, with postage, at that time, of about $150,000. So, that was a most convenient way to handle things – and to defer taxes. Yes, I do know that from a strictly accounting point of view that would be a prepaid expense. But that isn't quite the way it works in "real life."

Michael wasn't doing well at all. He was on methadone maintenance, but we always thought of that as only a stopgap solution. And that is what it really was. He was totally addicted, and that was all there was to it. He never really had a job. He lived only by our allowing him to draw a small monthly amount from his trust fund. We tried to avoid his handling any cash. We paid his rent, bought his clothes, and made arrangements in restaurants in which he could eat. It was a bad situation.

But then some hope appeared. A friend of ours, Alan Muster, had a windshield repair business and seemed to be doing quite well. He suggested that Michael could work for him, that he would keep an eye on him, and that he would keep him very busy. We accepted that and so did Michael. Things seemed to be working out all right. Alan, his boss, was happy with him and he made some real honest money. But it was all on the surface. Underneath was still the constant craving for drugs, on which virtually all the money he earned was spent. We were pretty desperate.

Eventually we heard about a sport figure in Houston, who was said to have attained unusual success in dealing with drug-addicted men and women, especially young people. We called him and he sounded good and positive. He told us that he could almost assure us, if we entrusted Michael to him for six weeks, that he would be cured. We felt good about it. It was not inexpensive. It cost $10,000. We sent him a check. We thought it was a good investment. So Michael was bundled off to Houston and our hopes and prayers went with him.

Rachel went to the University of California at Santa Barbara. She was lovely and lively, a beautiful reflection of her mother. She did well at the university and roomed with another girl whom we also liked very much. She had a steady boyfriend, whom we met. He was a really nice guy, and they seemed to be pretty "serious." His father worked for the government, for the Voice of America. They lived mostly abroad but had a home in Southern California. We invited them for dinner. They seemed to be nice people. If this young man were to have been her choice, it would have been acceptable to us. Still, we did not think that he was entirely "right" for her. But, of course, it would have to be her choice and her decision. My hope, however, was that she would eventually marry a Jewish man and would raise a Jewish family.

All along she had wanted to be able to go to the University of California at Berkeley, but had so far been unable to gain admission. She tried again and was accepted for her junior year. We were happy about that, naturally, also because, even though she did not plan to live at home anymore, she would be living right across the Bay and we would be close to her. We liked that.

One of the electives she chose at Berkeley was Jewish Studies. That pleased me, of course, while at the same time it surprised me. I didn't think that she had that much interest in Jewish matters. Well, as a parent you can always get surprised, and this was one of those happy surprises. Then something interesting happened. She met a young man in the Jewish Studies course whom she liked very much. Apparently, the attraction was mutual. His name was Derek Benham. We met him and, right away, we also liked him very much. We did not know how this relationship with Rachel was going to develop, but we thought that he looked more like the "right one" than the other one.

We got a thumbnail sketch about Derek's background. He was from Bakersfield, California and, as we understood it, his father headed a large agricultural-industrial organization, of which he was part owner. We met him. He was a large and very nice man, an athlete and a crackerjack tennis player. We liked him right away. His mother, Phyllis was a small woman, very lively, and very much the outdoor type. She was a licensed pilot and flew her own plane. They were an interesting couple, a couple that we knew we could feel most comfortable with.

Even more interesting, at least to me, was that Phyllis was one hundred per cent Jewish, at least ethnically. She did not like to talk about it at all, and certainly did not think of herself as being Jewish. She was brought up by a mother who, of all things, had converted to Christian Science. But, interestingly enough, Derek was technically "more Jewish" than Rachel, because he was the son of a "born" Jewish mother, whereas Rachel was born of a mother who was a Jew by choice. One is not quite as kosher as the other, but at least until much later, Derek never thought of himself either as being Jewish.

We liked Derek right away. He was tall, very good looking (a good gene pool for babies!) and he seemed to have a lot of "go" power. He seemed to be what my father-in-law would admiringly have called a "going Jesse." He came from a big and stable family. There were six children, four boys and two girls. He was the fifth child. There was a younger brother to whom he was very close, and who wound up playing an important role in his life.

Rachel was living in Berkeley with a very nice girl, Trisha. Trisha was the daughter of a well-known, you might say "prominent," San Francisco Jewish family. It was a good arrangement. But, one day, pretty much out of a clear-blue sky Rachel informed us that she was "moving in" with Derek. While we were aware of such arrangements and knew that they were by then fairly common, it did shock us somewhat. We had not visualized and had a hard time thinking of our own daughter in such a relationship. We simply weren't used to it. We had a bit of a hard time accepting that our daughter would be living "in sin," even though we had grown very fond of her partner. But what can a parent do? Just smile and do nothing.

To get ahead a bit in my story, they stayed in that arrangement for seven years before they finally got married. I thought of that and still do think of it as somewhat of a shame and a waste because if they had decided to marry earlier, they could have had their children much earlier and could have enjoyed them that much longer.

How about Joe? Joe went to Town School for Boys, a San Francisco boys school K through 8. He made good grades but didn't like the school at all. It was too organized, too structured for him. He was very much of a free spirit. But he soldiered on and he soldiered through. I kind of liked the school. Even though it was only a pale reflection of it, it did remind me of the discipline and structure of the *Hohenzollern Gymnasium*, which I had attended. Then he went on for his last four years to Urban High School, a very "advanced" school, with an unusual and with what I came to consider a somewhat "unstructured" curriculum. To my taste, the school was a little too "loose," but that was, perhaps, not too important. He seemed to thrive in that environment, learned a lot, made good grades, and lifelong friends.

While still a very young teen, he discovered his interest in music. So, following his request, we let him take piano lessons. He liked the instrument, but he didn't like the teacher. He quit.

"I want to learn the saxophone," he said.

"The what?" I said.

"The saxophone," he said.

Then I thought of my own father and was determined not to make the same mistake that he had made. According to my father's world picture, the older son of a

German Jewish family had to learn the piano and the second son the violin, just as the first son had to become a doctor and the second an attorney, regardless of individual preferences. The saxophone would very definitely not have fit in my father's scheme of things. "Why do you want to learn the saxophone?" I tried to temporize.

"I just like the look and the sound of it, and that's what I want to learn."

He seemed to be preparing for an argument, but he didn't get it. "The saxophone?" I said. "Sure. Let's find a good teacher for you and you learn just that."

He found a good teacher. He learned to play the saxophone, became very proficient, and ultimately even made money with it by playing in a small combo. His main interest was in jazz. Much later, in his thirties, he grew tired of it, virtually from one day to the next, and started up with the piano again.

He enrolled as a freshman at the University of California at Santa Cruz. Though he liked it in Santa Cruz and seemed to be quite happy, he had heard that the best jazz school in the United Stated was, of all places, at North Texas State College in Denton, Texas. He asked that we let him go there. We did. Denton was most successful for him – on every level. He became a wonderful musician, learned to direct a band, wrote his own compositions, and, best of all, met his future wife, Stephany, an absolutely wonderful girl and just right for him.

The new Haverhills prospered. I seem to have a touch for this business, the merchandise selection, the promotion, and the copy writing. After Charles Weibert came on board, he took over virtually all of the merchandise selection and the direction of the catalog – subject only to my veto. I never vetoed anything that he had decided.

I told you about all these people who came into my office or called me and things happened. There was that man from Bowmar, who showed me the first electronic calculator. Then there was Fred Opper of CBS, and, of course, the very important call by Ralph Gallagher of Time Inc., the visit from Gordon and Johnson of Frontier Airlines, and others. I always remembered the quotation that my English teacher at the *Hohenzollern Gymnasium*, Mr. Kuskopp, had put in my album, the one from Julius Caesar about the tide in the affairs of men. I tried to keep my eyes open and tried not to let opportunities get away. Here came another one.

Fred Manchester was the representative of the Kyocera Company of Japan. Kyocera is a huge company, manufacturing and dealing in ceramic industrial products. One of their small sidelines – I never could really quite understand why they would go into such a relatively tiny business – was to produce ballpoint pens, the writing points of which were ceramic, rather than metallic balls. It actually made for much smoother writing. Also, the pens were beautifully styled and exquisitely finished. Mr. Manchester told me that he had been impressed by our advertising and that he wanted to introduce this pen in the United States. If we would agree to give it a level of advertising support, a minimum of $100,000 per year, we could have the exclusive representation of the pen in the United States.

My brother Heinz (Enrique) and his wife Lieschen, shortly
after their wedding, in Bariloche, Argentina.

Monaco, "the Shaver that went to the Moon," and the Emoskop Vestpocket Optical System were two of the most successful items that I developed at Haverhills. They are what we call "evergreens" in the trade. They go on and on.

Of course, $100,000 advertising was no problem at all. I thought the pen was a winner, almost as good perhaps as the Navigator watch. We could buy the pen for $9.50 and I thought that we would have no problem selling it for $39.95. It was definitely a premium price at the time, when other ballpoint pens could be bought for perhaps as little as $1.95. But it was a luxury item, very elegant, very efficient, and beautifully styled. I figured that people would be willing to pay that. After all, people pay $60,000-$80,000 for a car, even though they could get "wheels" for less than $10,000. And, just as with razors and razor blades, I could see a substantial follow-up business in selling those replacement cartridges.

I said, "Mr. Manchester, I think I'll do that. About how many pens do you expect me to sell?

"Oh," he said, "do you think you could sell 1,000 per month?"

"I think I'll have no trouble doing that. But let me propose something else. I would like for you to give my wife and me a first-class trip to Japan, a stay of two weeks, and lodging in 4-star hotels, after I've sold 100,000 of these pens."

He laughed. "Let's see you sell 100,000 of these pens and there will be no problem," he said. "You can have the trip."

"Why, thank you, Mr. Manchester. But I would very much prefer to have that in writing."

"You don't need that in writing," he said. "My word is good enough."

"Yes, of course, Fred, but I don't know whether you are going to be in the same job a couple or three years from now and I would just prefer to have it in writing."

"O.K., if you insist," he said, "It's not really necessary, but I'll send you a letter to that effect."

Sure enough, about a week later I had a letter from him promising me exactly what I had requested: a deluxe trip for two, a two week stay in Japan, after I had sold 100,000 of those pens.

What to call the pen? Names are always important. I had named so many things successfully, the Monaco shaver, LaBisquera, the Emoskop, the Navigator Watch, and so many others. What to call this pen in order to launch it on its goal toward the sale of 100,000 units. I decided on Mount Fuji. I thought it sounded cool, and it hinted at its Japanese origin. That was quite important, because by that time, mostly because of Japanese automobiles, Japanese merchandise had acquired a deluxe cachet. And, of course, it was vaguely allusive to the Mont Blanc pens, which were the standard of luxury in writing instruments. So Mount Fuji was a great name, a good idea – but, as it turned out, not quite good enough.

About one month into my advertising campaign, for the Mount Fuji Pen, I received a certified letter from a fancy law firm in New York. It had been my experience, not too surprisingly, that certified letters from attorneys never, never contain good news. There was one exception to this rule of experience of which I shall talk later.

Sure enough, this was a very sternly-worded letter from the attorneys of Mont Blanc that told me that by naming my pen Mount Fuji I was encroaching on the good name of their client and threatened all kinds of dreadful legal things unless I immediately ceased and desisted using the Mount Fuji name and confirmed that I would not again use it nor any name that had the word Mount, Mont or Mountain in it.

I didn't see how anybody could confuse Mount Fuji with Mont Blanc, but I was not prepared to engage in a legal battle with a large firm. Even if I could have won – and I believe that I might have prevailed, the legal expenses would have been exorbitant. Obviously it wasn't worth my while and my money, so I signed that document, and having had "Mount Fuji" knocked out from under me, had to think of something else.

It came to me in a flash: If they didn't like Mount Fuji, how about calling the pen Fujiyama? That is, of course, exactly what Mount Fuji is in Japanese, but which could not at all be confused with Mont Blanc, even by those most determined to do so. So it has been Fujiyama ever since. Now, almost twenty years later, and having sold Haverhills, it is still a best seller. It is simply a wonderful pen. It's worth every penny.

I didn't give that Japanese trip a great deal of thought, because it really had been agreed to somewhat in jest, and perhaps deep down inside I may have doubted that I would be able to sell 100,000 pens or more.

Fast forward to eight years later. Fred Manchester was no longer with the company. His successor wrote me and told me that the cost of the pen would be increased by $3 to $12.50. I thought that was totally unwarranted and protested strenuously. He did not budge. I was very unhappy. Then I remembered the letter that Fred Manchester had given me and which I still had in my file. We had kept copies of all the purchase orders of the Fujiyama pens that we had issued since inception; I found to my joy, but not too much to my surprise, that by that time we had purchased over 115,000 pens. We had handily exceeded the 100,000 hurdle that I had set myself. I sent a copy of the letter to Mr. Manchester's successor (I believe his name was Roloff, but I am not entirely sure), and told him that my wife and I would like to take that deluxe trip to Japan just as soon as possible.

He wrote back and told me that he could not honor Manchester's offer, that he was no longer with the company, and what's more, that he had had no right to make such a promise in the first place. "Oh yes," I thought, "wait until my attorney writes you a letter about this."

Well, of course, Mr. Roloff collapsed right away and he offered to settle with me for $3,250 in cash. I called him. "Mr. Roloff, $3,250? Where do you get that amount?"

He began to explain that we could get a discount round-trip tourist class fare to Japan for $650 each, that we could say in a 2-star hotel in the suburbs of Tokyo for $50 a night, and that if we were "prudent," meals for the two of us would not cost more than $20 a day – and that would leave "a tidy sum for extras and sightseeing."

"Mr. Roloff, you didn't read the letter carefully enough. Please note that on the third line it mentions "first class." First-class means first-class round-trip air fare, first-class hotels, first class entertainment, and first-class meals. We don't want any money, we want to take the trip."

He wiggled and woggled and squirmed back and forth. Frankly, I didn't really want to go to Japan at that point. I just didn't have the time. I finally settled with him for $10,000 in cash. I think he got a bargain. He made a wonderful deal.

But what about the pens and the increase in price to $12.50? He would not budge on that. Then I looked into this a little more closely. There was no design patent on the pen. The only thing that Kyocera really owned was that silicon ball cartridge. It wasn't that big a deal. I surveyed pen manufactures in Taiwan and found a reliable firm, which, against my commitment to take at least 10,000 pieces, was willing to make tools and molds for the exact same pen that I had purchased for $9.50 from Kyocera and which was going to be raised to $12.50. The Taiwanese pen was to be equipped with a German cartridge, not made of silicon, but equivalent in quality or perhaps even superior to the Japanese original. Total cost? I couldn't believe it: $3.50. Wow! There was no reason to reduce the price of the Fujiyama pen from $39.95 to anything less, because that price had been established for years and by millions and millions of advertising impressions. Our profit margin on the pen was now fantastic. We proceeded to sell another 50,000 pens, until I finally sold the business. It's still going strong with my successor.

This brings up my "philosophy" on pricing. (I say this tongue in cheek – I know it sounds somewhat pompous), but I firmly believe that in this kind of business, contrary to, say, selling food or medication, things that people really need and can't do without, one should charge as much as the traffic would bear for such optional or luxury items, and should not feel guilty about it. One should experiment or intuit how one can maximize one's profit, and that is to find a price and thus profit per unit that would produce that number of unit sales that would make the greatest overall profit. Think about it a minute. Selling 100 units at $1 profit per unit is more profitable than selling 200 units at $.30 profit per unit or 50 units at $1.50 profit per unit. It is a straightforward concept, though many, even experienced merchandisers in my business, still don't seem to have quite grasped it.

My secretary at the time was man. His name was Brett Neff. He was a sweet person, very competent – and a homosexual. He got afflicted with AIDS and died very quickly. It was a great personal loss because I had really come to love that man and to treasure his fine work. Brett was a lover of fine music and had a good selection of classical cassette tapes. Knowing that I also loved classical music and that I took those long trips to Tahoe, he made up cassettes for me that he called "Music for Driving." They contained selections of the best of classical music and movements of symphonies.

About three weeks after Brett died, a woman appeared in my office. She carried a large grocery bag. She introduced herself as Brett's sister, and told me that in his will and out of his very meager possessions, he had bequeathed his entire tape collection to me. I was very touched. I must have been a good boss to a very good and special person, who was my friend as well as my employee.

But on a more practical level, Brett's death left a gap that had to be filled very quickly. With all those different things that I was doing I couldn't be without a permanent and very competent secretary for any length of time.

In the Tennis Club, we had met and become very friendly with a woman by the name of Lori Bunting. She was an African-American, good tennis player, and mother of four. I would say that Lori was in her middle forties. She had been working as an aide to one of our Bay Area congressmen, but she quit because she was preparing to go to law school. She was a crackerjack secretary. She knew I needed help urgently.

"Gerardo," she said, "I'll work for you until you can find somebody permanent, but I can't do it for any longer than maybe six weeks, because that's when law school starts." That was fine by me. So she came to work for me and did a great job. I put an ad in the *San Francisco Chronicle*, interviewed several applicants and finally settled on a young man by the name of Chester. I gave him a test and was not too impressed. But I had to have somebody permanent, so I hired him. I was quite sure that he, too, was a homosexual (which is not too unusual in San Francisco). That did not bother me. What bothered me was that he just couldn't do the work. We tried and tried, but it didn't quite work out.

I called Lori. I told her, "Lori, the thing with Chester doesn't work out. Can you possibly come back and work for me again?"

"No way, Gerardo. I'm starting school next week, but I think I have somebody who can do the work for you. Her name is Peaches. She is a friend of mine. She works for a secretarial service and mostly handles the work of attorneys."

"Please send her by. She sounds pretty good."

Peaches came by the next day. It was a Wednesday. She was a black woman, exceptionally good looking, and seemed to be about twenty years old. I gave her a standard intelligence and general knowledge test that I had created. She did fantastic. She didn't miss a thing. Then I gave her a typing test and she did very well on that also. I had found exactly what I wanted. I hired her on the spot; I asked her to come to work the following Monday.

The next day, Thursday, I had a call by a woman who introduced herself as Marjorie. She told me that she was a friend of Lori's. She was an attorney and Peaches was doing all of her work at the secretarial service. She had heard that I had hired her and she told me that I was doing her a disfavor and great damage because her pending work would not be finished if Peaches came to work for me.

"Marjorie," I said, "I certainly don't want to damage you at all. I have never heard about you, but I wish to cooperate with you. Why don't I let Peaches come to work for me a week later and she can finish up your work in the meantime. Would that suit you?"

"No, that wouldn't suit me at all," Marjorie said. "I shall need her permanently."

"Marjorie," I said, "you cannot lay claim to that woman permanently. She has her own life to live, and she wants to find a permanent job. She cannot be bound in part-time employment to you."

"I can't accept that," she said, and slammed down the phone.

I didn't feel too good about it, but I knew that I hadn't done anything wrong. The fact that Lori was involved made it even more awkward. Then I had a brilliant idea. I said, "Chester, you know that I won't be able to use you any longer, but I know this attorney who is looking for a good secretary. You might just fill the bill."

"O.K.," Chester said, and he went to see Marjorie. Marjorie hired him right away. She liked him. Now here comes the most remarkable part of this delightful tale. Chester wound up marrying Marjorie. He really did. I couldn't imagine how this could work. The last I heard they were still married. There are no children.

But there's more. About a month later, on a Sunday, I was at the San Francisco Tennis Club, getting ready for a doubles match, when I saw our friend Lori talking to another woman, a white woman. I approached them and Lori introduced her as Marjorie.

"Oh, Marjorie, how are you? I've talked to you but I've never met you."

Marjorie looked at me and said, "So you're the son-of-a-bitch who stole Peaches away from me?" In so saying she threw a full glass of wine in my face. I stood there, I was aghast and I was soaked. I didn't know what to do. I called the manager who threw her out. Before she left, she took the wine bottle and broke it on the marble top of the table. It was totally weird. She was not invited back to the Tennis Club.

Back to Peaches. She was the most marvelous employee I've ever had. She was exceedingly smart, totally discreet, and had exquisite skills. She had to be told things only once, and she would never forget to do them right. She stayed with me for seven years, through thick and thin. I saw her through two romantic disappointments until she finally found the man that she eventually married.

She spent her honeymoon at our place in Tahoe. About a year later, she had a little boy who was born two months prematurely. It was nip and tuck but everyone pulled through. I thought of her, and still think of her, as if she were my own daughter. She is a marvelous person.

Getting ahead of myself, but finishing the story of Peaches: One day, about seven years after she first came to me, she said, "Gerardo, I am so happy here with you and working for you but I think I should look for a more promising career. I think I should work for a larger firm."

I said, "Peaches, you are right. Go ahead and do it," and she did. She found a very responsible position with one of San Francisco's large construction firms and is doing exceedingly well.

I enjoy writing, seeing my name on book covers, having people discuss my books, and, of course, getting those royalty checks. My first book, *How You Too Can Make at Least a Million Dollars (But Probably Much More) In the Mail-Order*

Business had been a heady experience. The seven-volume course was also doing pretty well. What else could I do now?

I had always been interested in words and I thought up a puzzle that I called "Anagraphics." The principle was to take five- or six-letter words that could be scrambled ("anagrammized") to form another word. For instance, SHELF/FLESH, PLEAD/PEDAL, or LADIES/IDEALS – you get the idea. It's a little difficult to explain but somewhere in this book, I'll show you an example.

I had to find a good cartoonist to illustrate these puzzles. I found him. He was an Englishman by the name of Napier Dunn. He was a wonderful French horn player, a member of the London Philharmonic Orchestra, and a cartoonist on the side. He was just what I needed.

So we worked together and brought out our book *Anagraphics I*.

How much I would like to tell you that the book was a smash success, that we hoped would be followed by *Anagraphics II*, etc., but that was not the case. We never even managed to sell out our first issue of 2,500 books. Was the world not ready for us? We had some moderate success in placing the puzzles in magazines. But that was more of a labor of love than anything else. We had a lot of fun with "Anagraphics I," lost a little money, but I think of it as one of my better intellectual achievements. Not everything succeeds financially.

Charles Weibert did an excellent job as vice president of marketing. He was full of good ideas for merchandising and directed the catalog production. He relieved me of a great deal of work. He was a young man who really understood this business and it seemed likely that he could eventually take it over. The problem was that he did not have any money. He was in no position to buy it. We didn't talk much about it, but I knew that it was very much on his mind.

I signed off on all merchandise that he scheduled for the catalog. It was actually only a perfunctory action because I had so much confidence in his good sense and good taste that I didn't do a lot of checking. I had my questions about some of the merchandise, but I never vetoed anything. Nothing that he ever picked for the catalog was really over the top. He experimented and that was fine with me. Some things worked and others didn't. That was the way it had always been.

One day I received a certified letter (return receipt requested) from the Federal Trade Commission – the federal government. What could they possibly want from me? It could not possibly be any good news. It turned out that the contents of that letter were the worst news I'd ever had in my business career. If I had known how things were subsequently to develop I would certainly have handled it quite differently.

And what could possibly be in that envelope? Nothing good, of course. I opened it up. It was about ten pages of tightly packed legalese, the gist of which was not quite clear at first reading. I read it again. Here it was: The Federal Trade Commission had found two items in our catalog that they did not believe were acceptable, which made claims that could not be proven and that were dangerous to the public health. The two items were: First, a gadget that was to be put into the fuel line of one's car and that supposedly improved gasoline mileage by twenty per cent. I didn't really know that it was in the catalog. I thought it was a stupid item and I wished that Charles hadn't put it in. But nobody is perfect. It would be no problem not to feature it in the next catalog.

The second item the FCC took exception to was a tanning device. It was a coffin-looking item. It had fluorescent tubes on the bottom and in the lid. One lay down on it, closed the lid, and was radiated by sun-like rays. The printed instructions and explanations that we received from the manufacturer made it clear that there was no danger to the user and that all of the harmful rays, whatever they were, were being filtered out. Charles set up a beautiful illustration for the item. One of our employees, a lovely girl from Sardinia, Italy, was the model. She wore a most sexy bikini. Unfortunately, she was not wearing any protective goggles, which she should have, of course, and to which the Federal Trade Commission particularly took exception.

The last page of this ponderous document contained an understanding that I was supposed to sign, to the effect that I was prepared to sign a cease-and-desist agreement, agreeing that I (my firm) was never going to feature these two items again. I signed immediately. That was much easier than I had thought. Of course, I told Charles about it and told him that we must discontinue these two items immediately, because the one thing we definitely did not need was to get in trouble or involved in any disagreement, feud, or any other entanglement with the federal government.

I thought that that was the end of it, but it wasn't. About two weeks later another letter arrived, again by registered mail and even fatter than the previous one. It contained the complete cease-and-desist agreement that I had promised to sign. I read it, and it was clear that it was a little more intense than what I had expected; not only must I agree not to feature those two items any more or anything like them, but I also would agree not to feature any merchandise on which I would make health and safety claims that I could not prove. That was a little more difficult because this was a business in which some "puffery" was always used. Things were "safe," things were "the best," things were "good for you," etc. It would be easy to run afoul of that commitment. Still, I didn't feel that I had much choice and after discussing it with Charles who, quite innocently of course, had been the cause of all this trouble, I went ahead, signed it and sent it back to the Federal Trade Commission. I thought that was the end of that story. I never even discussed it with my attorney. I didn't think that it was all that important.

But, as you will see, it turned out to be a very big deal indeed.

Priscilla and I went to Magnolia to visit her parents at least once a year. The unhappy anti-Semitic remark that my father-in-law had made years ago, was, if not entirely forgotten, put way into the back of consciousness. So was my mother-in-law's gleeful statement that our marriage was over.

Every time we visited in Magnolia, I always liked to drive to Taylor, a very small town nearby. What interested me was that they had a goldfish hatchery, from which they shipped goldfish all over the United States. There were two kinds of fish: Little ones that were used as feed, mostly for bigger fish, and big ones, fancy show fish. I was interested in those. They cost at least $20 or $30 a piece in San Francisco, but I could buy them in Taylor for $3 or $4 each. Fish were and still are, my hobby. I've always had a couple of tanks at home and another big tank at the office. Every time I went to Magnolia, I made a side trip to Taylor and would buy a dozen fish or so to be shipped by air to San Francisco to restock my tanks.

One day, it was in 1985, Jack, my father-in-law was retired and was in very poor physical condition. He was seventy-eight years old. About twelve years earlier he had sold his drilling and oil exploration business to a company in Shreveport, Louisiana. He told me, and he worded it carefully, that a Jewish group had paid him a very hefty price for the company. He told me that he had "bested" them. It made him feel particularly good because everyone knew how smart the Jews were and he had been able to outsmart them. But he hadn't. It was at the cusp of the great oil boom. The people, those "smart Jews" that he had supposedly outfoxed, made more money out of the business than he had ever thought possible. It made him kind of thoughtful, but he did not dwell too much on it, at least not with me.

He was retired. Apart from his ailments and hurts, he was reasonably happy. He had cumulated the million dollars that he had always dreamed of as his financial goal, and he led a quiet and good life in Magnolia, mostly reading, going for walks, talking to his old cronies and other good things.

He had, however, acquired a terrible habit, namely chewing tobacco. It was the most disgusting thing I had ever seen. He always had a paper cup in his hand into which he spit that nasty juice that he had to dispose of every so often. It was just awful. My mother-in-law absolutely hated it, but there was not a thing that she could do about it.

There is a very dangerous intersection in Magnolia, Highway 79 and Highway 82, going east-west and north-south respectively. They cross at right angles on the eastern edge of town. It's a four-way stop. One day in about 1980, Jack, who was never a very good or careful driver, came to the intersection and stopped. He opened the car door to pour out the disgusting juice from the chewing tobacco, but having done that, and without looking left and right, he started the car and drove through the intersection. He was hit broadside by an 18-wheeler. He broke every conceivable bone in his body, was given up for dead, stayed in the hospital for two weeks, and came out very badly damaged and in pain for the rest of his life. So that's where he was in 1985, when we came to visit.

"Mr. Kern," I said (I never called him Jack and he never invited me to), "may I borrow the car? I want to go to Taylor to buy some fish."

"Go right ahead," he said, "but let me come with you."

I was surprised. He had never suggested that before. "Of course," I said, "let's go." So we went to Taylor, about fifteen minutes out of town. I bought some of those fancy fish and had them shipped to San Francisco. All the time he was chewing his tobacco and spitting that disgusting juice into his cup. On the way home he said, "Gerardo, stop a minute." So I pulled over and stopped. He opened the door and poured out the juice. I was going to re-start the car. "Wait a minute," he said. "I want to ask you something. Tell me, do Priscilla and you go to the same church?" "Yes, I said, "it's not a church exactly. We belong to a Jewish congregation and go to a synagogue."

"Well, that's what I mean," he said, and he spit out another big glob. "You did the right thing, Gerardo," he said. "A family has to go to the same church in order to stay together. I agree with what you're doing. Let's go."

That's all that was said. We had been married for over thirty years. It was the first time that he had expressed approval that Priscilla had become a Jew by choice and that the children were being brought up as Jewish. It was a very important statement for him and a very important statement for me. He finally, informally, had accepted me. It made me very happy, but it was about time.

He died about two months later. He had put all of his affairs in order. He left an estate of $1,150,000, all in cash, all in CD's, in ten different banks. Of course he owned his home. He left $25,000 to Cleo, a woman who had for twenty-five years attended him and my mother-in-law, ("the finest nigger woman I have ever seen," were his unselfconscious words of praise), and left the rest in trust, one half for his wife and the other half to be divided equally between Priscilla and her sister Diane. I had been told that I was going to be the executor of the estate, which was really the proper choice. I was the older of the sons-in-law, also the older "in service," and what's more, I was a businessman, and my brother-in-law, Hugh Cunningham, though very smart and very delightful, was a dentist. So whatever the small duties as executor would be, it could be assumed that I might be more qualified and would have better office facilities. But then Priscilla informed me one day – about a year before his death – that, without having been told, I had been replaced by Hugh as the executor. Priscilla knew about it, but she kept it from me for a long time. She told me that her father had done it because he was afraid that I would give all the money to Israel. It was a little sad and a little funny. But I didn't really care.

We have seen how Jack described Cleo. He used the "n" word, which, according to Johnny Cochran is "the most hateful word in the English language," freely and, as far as I could tell, totally without any malice. He did not associate with any black people, except in their capacity as servants or low-level employees. That was the way things were. I never heard him say anything hateful or anything demeaning about black people. He loved Nat King Cole and he called him the "singin'est nigger I've ever heard." He meant it as a great compliment.

We, or rather Priscilla, received the $250,000 check, of her share of the inheritance, within two weeks of his death. "That was very thoughtful of your father to leave us this inheritance," I said. Even though we were by that time pretty well fixed financially, that quarter of a million wouldn't hurt at all, of course.

"Gerardo," Priscilla said, "we did not inherit anything. I inherited the $250,000."

"What's the difference?" I asked.   "The point is that California is a community property state. Whatever I own, you own, and what you own, I own. It's all the same."

"No it's not," she said. "Inheritances are excepted from the community property." She was right, of course, but how did she know that? Where did she get that legal education?   Well, I suppose that women have a way of informing themselves of things that either are important to them or that they believe might become important to them. But of course it was all pretty much in jest. "All right, Priscilla, it's your money, what are you going to do with it? You are going to put it into our brokerage account, aren't you?"

"No," she said, "I'm not going to put it into any account. I'm going to remodel our house."

"Are you out of your mind?" I said. "Why would you want to put $250,000 into this house?"

"Trust me," she said, "I know what I'm doing."

That's all I could do, of course – trust her. And, I have to admit that the trust was not misplaced. She superintended a marvelous, total restructuring of the lower floor of our home. New bathroom, sunroom and family room, all glass bricks on rounded corners, skylights, fancy fixtures, granite countertops – the works. It became a showplace of the neighborhood. I grumbled a bit, but ultimately, though somewhat reluctantly, had to agree that the money was well employed. Naturally, having an extra $250,000 in the bank wouldn't have hurt either. But, looking back, she did the right thing.

There was one black cloud in our otherwise bright sky: It was Michael. He had gone through his treatment center and was now in a halfway house. From what the director told us, he was "cured." We tried to believe it, but we were still somewhat skeptical. We had had too many unhappy experiences in the past.

One bright spot was that he had acquired a steady girlfriend – Marybeth. She was a divorced woman with two children. We went to Houston to meet her. She was indeed a nice and attractive person and there was some hope that she could stabilize Michael. The worrisome part was that she herself was a "cured" addict – her poison was alcohol. The man she had divorced, the father of her two children, was also an alcoholic. But in any case, Michael was now in what seemed to be a stable situation. We had high hopes.

The one thing that was bothersome to me, but that I tried to disregard as much as I could, was his constant need for money. Just as the other two children, he had quite a bit of money available because the $100,000 in stock that we had put into his trust fund when we merged with Time Inc. had by now already grown substantially.

He came to visit us in San Francisco. He looked quite good and very healthy. "Dad," he said, "I'm going into the computer business and I need $35,000."

"$35,000, Michael?" I said. "Why in the world would you need that much money."

He gave me a detailed list of equipment that he needed and he made it add up to $35,000 including $10,000 of "working capital" that he insisted he needed to start his business.

"What's your business going to be?" I asked him.

"I'm going to do computer graphics," he said.

"Who are your clients?"

"I don't know yet, but I'm going to get them."

"Michael, I can get you this equipment for much, much less and I don't think that you need $10,000 in working capital right away. But here's what we'll do. I'm going to give you all my computer graphic business and that's going to be at least $3,000 a month and maybe more. You'll have a very good start. But let me buy that equipment for you."

He threw a fit, an absolute tantrum. He accused me of always cutting him short and putting him at a disadvantage – that he was trying to start a new life and that I was preventing that and frustrating him. So, just as I did many times later, and had done so many times before, I released $35,000 from his trust account. I could do that because, his being a certified drug addict, I had the court appoint me his conservator. As it turned out, I didn't do a very good job in that capacity.

But there was undiluted joy with the other children. Joseph was by now a freshman at the University of California in Santa Cruz, totally dedicated to music and to his instrument – the saxophone. While a career in music was something quite new to me and quite unexpected, I was totally accepting of it. Priscilla, the artist of the family, was enthusiastic. She had not totally been able to dedicate her life to the arts, but now her son, though in an entirely different field, might be able to do it.

As to Rachel and Derek: After living together for seven years – an almost biblical time – they finally decided to tie the knot. Here is how I heard the story – it gets embellished in the repeat retelling: One day Derek gave her a little box that contained a diamond ring. While the significance of the gift would have been apparent to all, he made it a point to say that it was not an engagement ring, but a "friendship ring."

Rachel, in the presence of her future father-in-law and other assorted future relatives took the ring off her finger and hurled it away (being careful to determine that it would not fall into some kind of grating or otherwise be lost from sight). "I don't need your @!x%=%$#@ friendship ring. Take it back to where you bought it."

Well, Derek had to make one thousand excuses and amends. He told her it was an engagement ring, that he loved her, that he wanted to marry her, etc, etc. Hugs and kisses ensued and the wedding date was set.

Priscilla and I decided to go on a survey and buying trip to Hong Kong. Rachel decided that she would like to go with us in order to buy several things – exotic fabrics, I suppose, and fancy shoes that she thought she might need for her wedding. We accepted her proposal, of course.

In Hong Kong, we rented a large room in one of the deluxe hotels, with a double bed for Priscilla and me, and a roll-away for Rachel. On the first day of our exploring the annual Hong Kong Watch and Clock Show, we had about ten samples of watches, four of which emitted a tiny beep on the hour. But, just as all electronic watches, they were otherwise completely silent. Obviously they didn't tick. "Dad," Rachel told me, "I need to have a room for myself."

"Why is that, Rachel?"

"The watches with their eternal beeping keep me awake all night long."

I realized that I had a "princess on the pea" on my hands. As an indulgent father I acquiesced to her wish and gave her a separate room. What's another $200 a day for your favorite daughter? I just hoped that her husband-to-be would be sufficiently affluent to accommodate her unusual wishes. He indeed turned out to be just that – in spades!

As is well known, the role of the father of the bride is not an enviable one; it's one of endless requests and expenditures. It was not any different in my case. "Dad, I have decided (yes, that's the word she used) to have the wedding at the Mark Hopkins Hotel."

I would have preferred a less expensive venue but, of course, I didn't say a thing. "How many people do you plan on having?"

"I think a minimum of 250," she said, "but I think we should count on about 300."

"Three hundred?" I temporized. "How much is that per setting?"

"About $40, I think."

It didn't take me long to figure out that that part alone would be about $12,000. When she saw the frown on my face, she added brightly, "But Dad, Derek is in the wine business and we'll get a very good deal on the wine – wholesale, you know."

"Well, that's good news," I said. "Anything else?"

"Yes, Dad, I'm going to have to make a down payment on the dresses of my bridesmaids and..."

"Rachel," I said, "how much do you think this whole production is going to cost?"

"Oh, I thought maybe $25,000," she said, looking at me searchingly.

"Twenty-five thousand dollars?" I said. "O.K., here's what I'll do. I'll open a special checking account and I'll put $30,000 into it. Only you and your mother will have signing privileges on that account. That makes it much easier for me. I get it done all at one time and we won't exasperate each other over money. Anything that you spend less than the $30,000 is yours to keep."

She thought it was a splendid idea. I thought so too. It worked out very well.

Rabbi Kirschner, the senior rabbi (he was only thirty-five years old) of Temple Emanu El was to officiate at the wedding. On the day of the wedding, he set a little room aside at the Mark Hopkins Hotel and talked to several people to give instructions and to ask if there were any questions. He sent for me. "What a wonderful day for you and your family, Gerardo," he said. "Your daughter looks lovely and I am really impressed by your future son-in-law. May I have the marriage license, please?"

"The what?" I asked him, although I knew exactly what he was talking about.

"The marriage license," he said, somewhat more sternly.

"Rabbi, I don't have a marriage license. Nobody has told me about it."

"Well you know, Gerardo, I cannot perform a wedding without the license."

"So what do we do, Rabbi?"

"Well," he said, "the only thing we can do without a license is to see that your guests have a good time. I can give a little speech, bless the future bride and groom and all that, but I cannot perform a wedding."

I was stunned. This day that we all had looked forward to so much was going to be the second worst day of my life. The first bad day of course was my first day of school when I had to stand in the corner. I staggered out of the room and looked for my daughter who was ensconced with her maid of honor and her bridesmaids. "Rachel," I said (as I was later told, white as a sheet), "we cannot proceed with the wedding."

She thought I'd gone out of my mind. "Why not, Dad?" she said.

"Rachel, I hate to tell you this, but I don't have a marriage license."

"Dad, don't worry about that. Of course we have a wedding license. Trish has the license. As the maid of honor that is her responsibility. Trish, give him the license."

I took the license, and with shaky knees went back to Rabbi Kirschner and said, "Rabbi, here is the license."

"Oh good," he said nonchalantly, "I can proceed."

"Wait just a minute," I said, "I want to have a large brandy before we do anything else." I did just that. My nerves were partly restored.

Well, everything was cool. We could now go ahead – but not just yet. The expensive organist whom Rachel had engaged under her generous budget started a piece to put the company of about 300 people in the right mood. In proper sequence, people entered. The bridegroom's mother and father, and Priscilla on the arm of our son Joseph. Rachel and I were standing, my arm linked in hers, behind the closed door of the aisle leading to the *chupah* under which the marriage was to be performed. The organist broke into the first chords of the traditional Lohengrin Wedding March and the maid of honor was about to open the door. "Stop," Rachel screamed, "we can't go ahead."

"What's a matter with you," Trish asked.

"I can't go in," Rachel said, "my period just started. Does anybody have a tampon?"

Of the seven girls involved, only one, Pam – her future sister-in-law, opened her purse and gave her a tampon.

Trish said, "Rachel, you're crazy. Your period started two weeks ago."

I thought, "Do women keep track of stuff like that?" But, in that case perhaps yes. Trish was, after all, her roommate. (And, since time immemorial, did not women plan their wedding date to avoid just that contingency?)

"Yes, you're right," Rachel said, and returned the tampon to Pam.

But I, being of such disposition, and because of my previous involvement in the menstrual cycle business, the mathematical implications of the situation immediately fascinated me. I posed myself the following problem: Suppose you have seven women, all of appropriate age, and assume that each woman's period lasts exactly six days, and that her cycles last exactly thirty days. What is the probability that at least one woman will have her period on any given day and what is the probability that none of them will have her period on any given day? I wish I could tell you that I solved the problem right then and there, but I didn't It occupied me for a long time – until I finally solved it. It's not easy. Try it yourself.

Well, anyway, the doors opened. All of the hurdles – the missing marriage license and the false period – having been overcome, we approached the *chupah* to the rousing strains of Wagner's music – though Wagner, Adolf Hitler's great inspiration, hadn't exactly been my choice. I kissed my daughter and turned her over to the rabbi and to her husband-to-be.

The wedding, if I say so myself, was a quite splendid affair. It was certainly the most lavish party that I had ever attended. All the appropriate people made appropriate speeches. Mine was based on the Ogden Nash poem "Song to be Sung by the Father of Infant Female Children," the first stanza of which goes as follows:

My heart leaps up when I behold
A rainbow in the sky;
Contrariwise, my blood runs cold
When little boys go by.
For little boys as little boys,
No special hate I carry,
But now and then they grow to men,
And when they do, they marry.
No matter how they tarry,
Eventually they marry.
And, swine among the pearls,
They marry little girls.

It was warmly received. The whole thing was a great success. Rachel, having had to manage her own money, told me later that she had been able to make certain economies and that she was able to stash away a nice portion of that $30,000. More power to her – I had done that right!

Business was doing very well. Sales were increasing every year and so were profits. I have to give credit to my #2 man, Charles Weibert. While I was getting a

Rachel and Derek on their wedding day. The beautiful
chupah under which they were married is right behind them.

Again, Rachel and Derek on their wedding day, flanked by
Priscilla and by me.

little tired of the whole thing, he was unflagging with enthusiasm, did most of the merchandising and catalog preparation, and took over more and more responsibilities.

One thing Charles did and which gave the business a great boost was to introduce us to so-called "syndication." From previous jobs, he had connections with firms that specialized in inserting promotional material for merchandise in the billing statements of oil companies. Many millions of mailings are involved every year, and if one has a hit, it can be quite profitable.

We had several such hits. One of them was the Antenna Multiplier, which had already been very successful in our media advertising. It was a device that one connected to the terminals of one's television set. It makes incoming signals stronger and clearer and pulls in even stations that otherwise wouldn't be available.

Another great success in syndication, also just as it had been in other media, was the PowerVox IV which, though we did not sell it as a hearing aid, amplified the sound and was a great help, even to those with quite normal hearing. We sold tens of thousands of those devices through syndication and other media. It was most profitable.

So one day over lunch Charles said, "Gerardo, you're getting on in years (thank you for reminding me!). Have you considered selling this business?"

Of course, I had considered it. I had now sold it three times: First to Time Inc., then to the "fine old Southern gentleman," and finally to Frontier Airlines. I was, by that time pushing 70, and was increasingly interested in my philanthropy – CAMERA, by now renamed FLAME – and in my writing. I had done the direct-mail business for almost twenty-five years, day after day and month after month. I was getting a little bored and the thing was taking its toll on me. Also, I was financially well fixed, didn't need the money, and, to quote Priscilla, "should really smell the flowers a bit."

So I told him: "Well, Charles, it's not really a bad idea but it is not going to be easy to find a buyer for this kind of business." That wasn't entirely true because, indeed, a direct-mail business, by virtue of millions of nation-wide advertising impressions, if it is well known as a brand name, can easily be expanded if associated with the right partner, one with national advertising reach, such as, for instance, CBS and Time Inc.

"How about selling it to me?" Charles asked.

"That would be a great idea," I told him. "You understand the business and could run it as well as I can, perhaps even better. But, you don't have any money."

"Give me a chance," he said. "I think I can drum up something."

I told him to go ahead to see what he could come up with.

Charles was fired up by the prospect of buying Haverhills. With his typical energy and with his wide acquaintances in trade circles, he did indeed come up with two groups of prospective investors/buyers and brought them to me.

About the same short conversation ensued with both groups. After the preliminaries and small talk, I told them, "Gentlemen, I'm willing to sell this company. Here are the financial statements for the last three years. I wish to retire and I am not going to drive a hard bargain. I want Charles Weibert to have a substantial equity in this business. My price, and it is not negotiable, is … (I gave them a number in the moderate seven digits). Now, please show me your financial statements and tell me how you are going to finance this purchase."

They hemmed and hawed and told me about bank loans, about other partners (those proverbial "money men") that they were going to bring in, etc. The upshot was that they didn't have any money at all, certainly not enough to even finance a modest down payment. They planned to (hopefully) finance it and pay me out of the profits of the business. I thanked them courteously, invited them to a nice lunch at the San Francisco Tennis Club, and told them that I would not be interested.

But on the third try, Charles came up with a live one, a Mr. Hadenberg who, together with his son and a silent partner, owned one of Lake Tahoe's major ski resorts and had additional substantial assets. He was solid, certainly as far as money was concerned. Hadenberg was about seventy-five years old, he was tall and gaunt and, unfortunately, reminded me, both in his appearance and in his mannerisms, of the "fine old Southern gentleman," with whom I had had such unhappy experiences. He did, however, not wear a string bow tie. That was one point in his favor. Still, naturally, I was somewhat cautious.

There was a little haggling, but not too much of that. He agreed in principle to the very reasonable price that I was demanding.

Things acquired a momentum of their own. "Charles," I said, "this looks pretty solid. But Hadenberg is not going to help you run the business. He is strictly a money man. Whom do you have to help you to run this business? You can't do it by yourself."

"You're quite right, Gerardo" he said. "I have thought about that myself. But I think I found the right guy. His name is Michael Donovan. He used to work for one of the large clothing retailers and he recently quit. He wants to join this venture."

"What does Hadenberg think of that?" I asked him.

"It's fine with Hadenberg, but he insists that both of us make a token investment in the company."

It reminded me of George Long and his token investment that he had demanded from me and (unsuccessfully) from Forrest Tanzer.

"What is the token investment?" I asked him.

"Fifty thousand dollars each," Charles said.

"Do you and does Michael have that kind of money?"

"No we don't," he said, "but we are both prepared to put a second mortgage on our homes to come up with that money."

"Charles, I know you well and I have met Hadenberg only once and I have not met his son at all. I have some questions about them, quite frankly, and I don't know Michael, your prospective partner, at all. What do you think about the three of us, you, Michael, and I, going on a one-week ski trip together. We'll all stay in the same room and we'll get to know each other much better."

"It sounds like a great idea," he said. "Where do you want to go?"

"Well, I usually go to Tahoe. In fact, you know, we have a place there. But why don't we go someplace entirely different. How about Taos, New Mexico?"

"Sounds good," Charles said. I'll make the arrangements.

So we went to Taos, New Mexico, had a great week of skiing, and did indeed get to know each other better. I had my questions about Michael. He seemed to be a weak Nelly, somewhat shifty, and he did not impress me with his smarts and with his ability. But I thought that he might be O.K. as a second banana for Charles, in whom I had much confidence.

You might wonder why I would be interested in the quality of these people at all. It's a good question, but there were two good reasons. The first was that the deal I was going to make would involve a payout over a three-year period. Even though the bulk of it was guaranteed by Wells Fargo Bank, I would not feel comfortable with people that might possibly get into trouble or give me trouble down the road.

Second, it was agreed that my "major talent," if any, in this business, lay in writing great media advertising, selecting merchandise for such advertising, and negotiating good medial deals. Therefore, part of the deal was that I would stay with the company in a "consulting" capacity for three years, earning a percentage of the profits made in the media advertising, which I was going to direct.

I overcame my hesitation about Hadenberg and about Michael; and I had no doubt about and no problem at all with Charles. So, after just a little soul searching and after discussing it with Priscilla, we decided to go ahead with the deal.

My attorney at the time was one Frank Ruster, partner in one of San Francisco's major law firms. I told him about the deal and asked him to write up a contract incorporating all the things that the Hadenberg group, which by that time had named itself the "Rainbow Group," and I had agreed upon.

I called to his attention the fact that we were under a Federal Trade Commission cease-and-desist order. While I didn't think it had any significance at all, I thought it would be important to mention it in the contract. Frank agreed with that.

On the designated day, we met at the attorney's office, read the final version of the contract, made no objections, signed it, and I received a check for $200,000, the immediate down payment on the deal. I was quite happy. Though it was nice and profitable company, it was a great responsibility and a lot of work. I didn't know what would happen if (as they say in the life insurance business) "something should happen to me." I was over seventy years old. So, it was a prudent move.

Priscilla, who knew, of course, what was going on, was waiting for me at the Tennis Club. I joined her. We went out for a celebratory dinner.

The next day, I began as a consultant to what until the day before had been my life and my business. I think I handled it pretty well, but it was not an altogether easy transition for me.

I had always been somewhat cautious with "expansion" of the business, perhaps too much so, which may be the reason that Haverhills never exceeded a certain size. The very day the new group started, they had grandiose plans on how to grow the business. Their business plan called for increasing sales three-fold within the first two years and profits, of course, correspondingly.

It sounded incautious to me and unattainable. But, I was simply no longer the owner and at the helm, so I kept my opinions to myself. And, who knows, those young people could indeed be more "aggressive" and therefore more successful.

The first thing they did, in line with their business plan, was to move from the totally adequate and quite attractive premises we occupied into some grandiose space. They spent a very large amount of money on embellishing and refurbishing it. I thought they were a little incautious. But, I kept my thoughts to myself.

But what was revealing and really quite annoying to me, was an immediate and total change in attitude toward me personally, both on the part of Michael and on the part of the employees. My relationship with Charles was always cordial and continued to be so.

As I found out later through disclosure of court documents (yes, court documents, because we came to that), was that Michael had requested that the key employees make detailed written reports to him of every meeting and every interaction they had with me. Some employees, in order to curry favor with the new bosses, wrote absolutely terrible things about me. I was very disappointed. I really had treated every one of them well, and had thought of them, not just as employees, but also as friends.

One day, as I was leaving the office, Michael stopped me. "Gerardo," he said, "I want you to make me a report of proposed media advertising for the next six months, complete listing of items, costs and media, and projected sales and profits. I shall need that the day after tomorrow, and I expect you to have it on my desk in triplicate."

"Michael," I said, "you don't understand. I'm not your employee. I'm a consultant here. I'm not going to make any reports in triplicate or in any other way by day after tomorrow or by any other time, unless I feel like doing it."

"Oh yes you are," he said, "and if I tell you to make ten copies, you're going to do that too. Don't defy me on that." He slammed the door in my face. I thought the guy had gone bananas and, of course, I didn't make any such report. But I now understood what kind of person he was. The gauntlet had been thrown down. He was not my friend and neither, I was sure, was Hadenberg. I felt for Charles. He was caught in the middle. Poor guy!

Things didn't get any better. In fact, they deteriorated steadily, both as far as their business was concerned and then as to our personal relationship. I suppose the two went hand in hand. They did all kinds of grandiose things, all of which lost money. Even the syndication business, which had been so profitable, became a source of deep red ink. They just didn't put the right merchandise into it. The only thing that consistently made money was the media advertising, which was under my guidance and for which I was responsible. Under my contract, I not only got a consulting fee, but also a percentage of the profits on that advertising. It was a good deal for me. They hated it.

In my capacity as media consultant, I was authorized to and responsible for the placement of advertising in major media such as *Time, Newsweek, US News &World Report*, and many others. I had, of course, splendid relationships with all these media. I had done business with them for years. And, of course, I had always punctually paid my bills. About six months after the sale, a nice lady from *US News & World Report* called me and said, "Gerardo, I'm very sorry but we can no longer accept your advertising."

"You can't, Doris? Why?"

"You haven't paid your bills for six months. You owe us $63,000."

"What!," I exclaimed incredulously. "We haven't paid the bills? There must be some error. Let me look into it."

I went to see the "controller," an incompetent jerk they had hired. He had pretended that he was a CPA (it was a lie). I asked him about the alleged indebtedness to *US News & World Report*. "What's the matter, Joe, how come these bills are unpaid?"

"I'm not allowed to talk about that," he answered.

"What? You're not allowed to talk about it? Why not?"

"Talk to Michael or to Charles."

This began to sound ominous, so I talked to Charles. "Charles, how come I can't place any more advertising? What's the matter? How come these bills are unpaid?"

"Gerardo, we are having a cash crunch right now. You know, with the expansion and everything, and all these new programs, but our projections show that we are going to be solidly in the black within two or three months. Right now, however, things are a little tight. Don't worry about it."

"It's not that I worry about it, Charles, but I can't place any more advertising. It's likely the other media haven't been paid either, have they?"

"Yes, that's right. Nobody has been paid for the last four months."

Well, I thought, this is just awful, mostly because they hadn't told me. Fortunately, just before selling the business, I had written to all of the media, by certified mail, telling them about the pending sale, expressed my hope that they would continue to do business with my successors, but that I would no longer be responsible for any payments, and that credit to the successors had to be granted at the media's discretion, and without any recourse to me.

When I ran all the numbers, I found, to my horror, that there were more than a quarter of a million dollars in unpaid media bills. I didn't see how they could possibly make up for it. They didn't.

I knew that the end was near. I was still owed quite a bit of money, but fortunately I had had the foresight of having made a good part of the payment guaranteed by Wells Fargo Bank. When one installment was unpaid, and it remained unpaid even after very pointed reminders to Charles and Michael, I called Mr.

Hadenberg and told him that if I didn't get paid within forty-eight hours I would take recourse to the bank guarantee.

He got very upset with me, called me a number of nasty names, and then told me, totally to my surprise, that I had defrauded him, and "you'll hear from our attorney."

How could I have possibly defrauded this guy? I thought. In the first place, even though he was the money man, the actual purchaser was Charles Weibert, and he knew the business as well as I did. There was nothing hidden from him. Also, and quite properly, Hadenberg had engaged a firm of CPA's and a platoon of three men and one women who were in the office for about two weeks preceding the sale, going with a fine-tooth comb over all the accounts, all documents, all creditors and debtors for verification. In other words they did what is called due diligence. And I thought they did a very good and a thorough job.

I got my money from the bank, but Hadenberg was very unhappy with me. Tension grew against me at the office. Of course, I didn't have much left to do because since media had not been paid, I could not place any more media advertising. It was a shame because the advertising that I had placed was the only thing that consistently made money for the firm.

Of all the old key employees Peaches, my secretary, was the only one whom they could not induce to report badly against me.

One day, Peaches came to me and said, "Gerardo, Michael wants to see our Federal Trade Commission (FTC) file. Shall I give it to him?"

I was surprised and wondered why in the world he would want to see that file, and if he did, why he wouldn't have asked me. "Give me the file," I said. I looked through the file. It contained the correspondence that I had with the FTC about the cease-and-desist order. Though I didn't have any obligation to give them any of my files, I saw no reason why not. So, I gave it to Michael and I said, "Michael, here's the file you have requested. But, please, if you want anything else, don't ask Peaches, ask me." He mumbled something unfriendly.

By that time, all possible moneys had to be scraped together to meet payroll. Then people were beginning to be laid off. When I had sold the business about ten months earlier, we had about forty employees. They bulked it up to about sixty. I never knew what for. Of those sixty, about fifty were laid off. Only a skeleton staff remained. It was clear that the end was very near now.

They declared bankruptcy almost exactly a year after they had bought the business from me. I couldn't understand it. I had operated this business for twenty-five years and had always been successful and profitable, had established the Haverhills brand that was well known, well liked, and respected by customers and by suppliers; now, those stupid people had run this wonderful and long-established business into the ground in just under one year. It was distressing and unbelievable.

As for me personally, I came out quite well, having had the foresight to have most of the money guaranteed by the bank. I came out almost whole. But many suppliers, mostly media, were hit very hard. Then, of course, there were those many customers who had sent their money and didn't receive their merchandise, and many others who had returned merchandise and didn't get their refunds. What a mess!

While things were in the process of winding down, a young man came into the office one morning and said, "Are you Mr. Joffe?"

"Yes, I am. What can I do for you?"

"I have some papers for you, sir, would you please sign here."

Papers, I wondered, what could they possibly be. So I signed for what appeared to be an ominously official looking document. What was it? Well, you guessed it. The sons-of-bitches had sued me for having defrauded then in selling them the business. That was so ridiculous, it was so utterly preposterous that I could hardly believe it. Charles knew the business intimately and they had done the most meticulous due diligence. How could they possibly construe fraud? I read the complaint. It was about thirty pages long. The gist was that I had not properly disclosed that the business was under an FTC cease-and-desist order, which prohibited me from making any health or safety claims for any of the products that I advertised, unless I could actually prove such claims. I had never considered that as any hindrance to the business, but in any case it was a ridiculous claim. The actual buyer was Charles who was, of course, fully aware of our entanglement with the FTC. What's more, the cease-and-desist order was mentioned in the contract that the buyers had signed. It didn't make any sense. I did note, however, that Charles was not one of the plaintiffs. He had refused to participate in the complaint. It made me feel a little better.

I decided that Frank Ruster, my attorney for many years and the attorney who had written the contract, was not the right man for litigation. He was, at least in my opinion, what the British would call a "solicitor" and not a "barrister" – an office attorney and not a courthouse "junk yard dog."

While I didn't think this silly matter would ever come to trial, I thought I would be best served if I got a barracuda type of attorney, one who would demolish the opposition right away and, in the unlikely case that it indeed came to trial, would be able to overwhelm the jury with his arguments and with his courtroom presence.

I talked to some of my friends. The consensus was that I should engage Bob Lichtfield, partner in a large litigation-type firm. He was supposed to be the "barracuda" I was looking for.

I called him, briefly summarized the situation and made an appointment to see him a few days later. In the meantime, I faxed him the complaint so that he would be fully apprised of what was involved.

At the appointed day, I went to his office, which was on a very high floor (the higher the floor, the higher the rent), in one of San Francisco's top office buildings. I was impressed by the walnut, mahogany, and marble of the reception area, the beautiful plants, the secretaries and receptionists that looked like models – exquisitely dressed and coifed, and the panoramic view of the Golden Gate Bridge.

After about ten minutes, an absolutely gorgeous young woman appeared and told me that she was Mr. Lichtfield's secretary and that I should follow her. I did. Mr. Lichtfield was an impressive man. His office reflected the lavish reception area. This is going to be expensive, I thought. As it turned out, I was more than right.

"Have a seat, Mr. Joffe," he said. I have read the complaint. I don't think that we'll have any trouble at all handling this. I think I'm going to ask for a dismissal. The case has no merit at all. Before we proceed, however, I shall have to ask you for a retainer of $10,000. Here's a schedule of our rates."

He handed me a list in which the partners' were listed at $150/hr. Remember – that was quite a few years ago. Today, it would be considered a bargain. Then it listed the costs of junior attorneys, of paralegals, the cost for the secretaries, all the way down to the hourly rate of the copy machine operators which, as I recall, was $40. A footnote added that all services were charged at a minimum of a one-quarter hour basis. Oh my, I thought, the girl that runs the copy machine could make one copy for me and it would cost $10 right away. I didn't particularly like it. So I said, "Mr. Lichtfield,…"

"Call me Bob," he interrupted.

"O.K, Bob, I have no trouble with the retainer, but if I possibly could, I would like to avoid litigation altogether. Why don't we try to reach a settlement with the plaintiffs."

"That would be a foolish thing to do," he replied. "I don't recommend it. This is an easy case to win, and we'll win it. You should not give them a penny."

"All right," I agreed. It was a decision that I was to regret.

Mr. Lichtfield filed an impressive brief. My opponents, the plaintiffs, had an attorney who worked by himself, was not a member of a large law firm, was not intimidated, and filed an equally impressive brief right back. "What do we do now?" I asked Bob.

"Easy," he said. "We simply file a demurrer."

"A demurrer?" I asked. "What in the world is that?"

"It is a brief to the court in which we allege that the opponents' brief has a defect, either in substance or in form."

"And what's the purpose and the effect of that?"

"Well, if the court agrees with us, he either has to file another brief or be thrown out."

Oh my, I thought, this can go back and forth many times. I was so right. I think there must have been a total of eight demurrers going back and forth. Each one cost me a minimum of $10,000. I began to get the impression that Lichtfield, though probably a very good attorney and certainly concerned about my welfare, was more interested, or perhaps even fascinated, by the legal process rather than by the result.

This went on for about a year by which time I had spent approximately $150,000 in attorney's fees and I had absolutely nothing to show for, except a lot of work. Because for the entire period that this litigation was unresolved, all I did was to work on that lawsuit.

After about a year, I got to be very concerned about both the outcome of this lawsuit, which had seemed so clear and easy in the beginning, but also about the ruinous attorney's fees – never less than $10,000 a month. I talked to my friend Wilbur Duberstein, a retired attorney and co-founder of FLAME. He reviewed the documents and called me. "Gerardo," he said, "you need a different attorney altogether. This Lichtfield is not the right guy for you. Just dismiss him. I think I have the right man for you. His name is Bob Kantor. He's just the guy you need. With your permission, I'm going to give him the material that you sent me and let him review it."

Kantor called me two days later. "Mr. Joffe, I have reviewed your material. You have a serious problem, I think. Let's set up a meeting and I'll explain it to you. Maybe we can settle this case but I'm afraid it's going to be much more expensive now."

We made an appointment in my office for the following day. "Bob," I said (his name was Bob also) "what is the problem?

He said, "Read this paragraph which is in your contract."

I read it. It said:

> 9.07   Seller has complied with, and is not in violation of applicable
>   federal, state or local statutes, laws or regulations affecting the
>   business or its operation, except as set forth in Schedule 9.07.
>   Seller is not subject to any federal or state cease and desist
>   order or any other injunction or consent decree.

I was speechless for a moment. I couldn't believe my eyes. Here it said in black and white that I had not been under a cease-and-desist order and, of course, I was. I couldn't believe it. "Hold a minute, Bob," I said. "Let me look something up." I went to my file and pulled out the original draft of the contract. It had been given to me by Frank Ruster.

It read:

> 9.07   Seller has complied with, and is not in violation of applicable
>   federal, state or local statutes, laws or regulations affecting the
>   business or its operation. Except as set forth in Schedule 9.07,
>   seller is not subject to any federal or state cease and desist
>   order or any other injunction or consent decree.

What had obviously happened was that a careless secretary had mixed up a comma with a period. There should, of course, have been a period before the word "Except," and a comma following 9.07. to convey the intended meaning, namely that except for the disclosure in the appendix, we were under no cease and desist order. Now, by making the period after Schedule 9.07, and following with the statement:

'Seller is under no cease-and-desist order,' I had obviously given my opponents a hook to hang myself with.

I engaged Kantor right away and gave him a somewhat more modest retainer than I had given Lichtfield – $2,500. He said: "The first thing I believe I'll do is talk to plaintiffs' attorney and feel them out as to whether that is indeed the hook. I am quite sure it is."

He reported back. "Yes, that is indeed the hook, and there is something else. They believe that the cease-and-desist order, although it was mentioned in Schedule 9.07, should have been attached to the contract, rather than just mentioned. I'm not quite sure that they are correct in that," he said, "but it certainly would have been the proper thing to do and would have been very helpful to you." Regrettably and almost unforgivably, Ruster had not caught this crucial punctuation mistake in transcription, and neither had Bob Lichtfield. And, of course, Ruster had not considered appending the cease-and-desist order, which, as a careful attorney, he should have done.

Bob said, "With your approval, I think we'll enter settlement negotiations right away. But I don't think it's going to be inexpensive."

"What do you think they are going to ask for?"

He named a figure that was about forty per cent of the purchase price. "I don't think I'm going to do that," I said. "I believe I'll take my chances in going to trial and put my faith in a jury."

"Gerardo," he said, "let me tell you about juries. They are composed of retired bus drivers, old ladies who may not hear clearly, have not more than a high school education, if that, and certainly nobody in the jury is going to understand what this is all about. But they will see you, however, and their attorney will tell the jury about your being a Harvard Business School graduate and a very experienced businessman, and will make it plausible that you did indeed attempt to defraud the buyer."

"This is nonsense, Bob," I said, "the fact that they went bankrupt had absolutely nothing to do with the FTC cease-and-desist order."

That's true, but I don't think it makes that much difference with a jury. If the attorney can convince them that you tried to defraud them, even if their bankruptcy was not the result of this alleged fraud, you are in big trouble. And you know what, he is going to ask you not just for the alleged damages, but he will also ask for punitive damages. And, the jury, especially if there is even a whiff of anti-Semitism – the "smart Jew" scenario – you are sunk. Don't doubt it, they surely will be hinting at that if they believe the jury to be receptive to it at all."

Priscilla was present at the meeting. "I want to settle it at whatever cost," she said. "This guy (referring to the opposing attorney) will try to totally clean us out, and I think he may even be successful. I do not want to take my chances with a jury. Please settle it!"

What did bother me more than somewhat, was that Bob Lichtfield, the mahogany-walnut-marble attorney, whom by then I had paid more than $150,000 had not noticed the dangerous flaw in the contract that Frank Ruster had drawn.

So I told Bob to go ahead and try to settle it. He did better than I had feared. We settled for about one-quarter of the sale price – still a very substantial lick and more painful since it was totally undeserved. Well, no use crying over spilt milk. I could not dwell on that. I had to go on with my life, so I wrote a check for this very large amount of money. The case on which I had spent almost two years, and about $250,000 in attorneys' fees was finally over.

$250,000 in attorneys' fees: I thought about that. If my attorney would have been a little more attentive, and would not have allowed that stupid mistake in punctuation to go through, there would not have been any case at all, and I would not only have saved the substantial settlement amount, but also most of the attorneys' fees. "Bob," I said to Kantor, "can we sue Frank Ruster for malpractice and can we succeed?"

"Yes, we can sue him." he said, "And I think we can succeed. Let me handle it for you. So we went ahead and sued the Ruster firm for $400,000. Kantor agreed to take the case on a "semi-contingency" basis. That meant that I would pay him a minimum of $20,000 or thirty per cent of any recovery, whichever was more, but not more than $50,000.

Kantor was very good. He was the barracuda that I had been looking for all along. They realized very quickly, of course, that they had made a tremendous and fatal mistake, and that that mistake had cost me a lot of money. They certainly did not want to go to trial on this. I had a very good case, and also, juries are not terribly friendly to attorneys. We finally settled for $250,000 of which Kantor, of course, got $50,000. He hadn't done too much work on it, but it was well deserved. He had reduced my damages by $200,000. It was not a happy affair. I had not made many friends. Several years later, I met Ruster on the street. He was walking with his wife and a dog. There was eye contact and he gave me a dim smile.

By that time I was seventy-two years old, much too early of course to retire to the golden pastures. Also, I was deeply involved with FLAME, which took at least ten to twenty hours a week of my time. I did almost everything myself, mostly, of course, I wrote all of the *hasbarah* (educational and clarifying) messages/ advertisements which I continued to publish in major national media. By that time FLAME had about 25,000 supporters. It was a fairly substantial operation.

But I wouldn't be happy doing just non-profit work. Even though I didn't "need" to work – I still had enough money despite that unhappy litigation – I knew that I had to do "something." The first thing that came to my mind was to purchase the Haverhills assets – essentially only the customer list, from bankruptcy court. I did just that and started back up in business again.

At first, I didn't think it was too smart a decision. Even though the company (Haverhills) went through liquidation and bankruptcy, people now came after me – suppliers and media that had not been paid – quite a bit over one million dollars – and many customers who had not received their merchandise or who had returned merchandise and had not gotten a refund. I couldn't do anything for the media and for the suppliers, of course, but I tried to satisfy good Haverhills customers by giving them credit for new merchandise.

Priscilla thought I was a little crazy, and she was also concerned that I would make large investments in this new/old business. I told her that I would not. I promised not to do the most expensive thing, namely to issue catalogs. Business was to be based only on advertising in media, something that I knew how to do very well and had always done successfully.

Our son Michael was an ongoing, never-ending concern for us. Yes, we had been assured that he was "cured," and we very much wanted to believe that – and actually did. He was living with Marybeth and her two children, and his life seemed to be somewhat regularized. He didn't have a job. The last and only job he'd ever had was the one with our friend Alan Muster, in the windshield repair business, but that was a long time ago.

He was really a wonderful person, big and loving and boisterous and quite different in appearance and demeanor from the other two children. He shared with me the passion for the Jewish people and for the State of Israel, especially after his visit to the country. He crisscrossed it from east to west and from north to south in a rented car. I wanted him to learn Hebrew, but he never got around to that. He was totally taken with Israel's military prowess and with its military, particularly its air force. He knew every plane in the Israeli air force and could describe every detail of every battle they had fought. He had a copious library on the Israeli military. He took great interest in my work with FLAME and made good suggestions on topics that I should write about.

But something wasn't right. He needed to have a steady occupation – a job. He needed to have something to do. So I called him and said, "Michael, you have that fancy computer equipment. I'm starting back in business. Why don't you become my art department. You can do all the ads for FLAME and all the ads for the new Haverhills." He accepted it right away and enthusiastically. We established a dedicated telephone line between my office and his and talked to each other – about business and also about everything else – several times a day. We had a good relationship.

There was, however, always the clamor for money and for more money. Many things seemed to go wrong, for which he always needed money right away and usually in fairly substantial amounts. And he usually pleaded that it be sent by overnight mail. It often had to do with his car, such as the transmission had fallen out or he had a small accident and body work had to be done, which was not covered by insurance, etc., etc. I got a little concerned about it because it was a possible symptom of drug use. I talked to Priscilla about it.

"Let's go for a visit and see what they are doing," she said, "If they are on drugs, they can't hide it from me. I'm very perceptive about these things."

So we went to Houston. They picked us up from the airport. They seemed to be a loving and very compatible couple. In fact, Priscilla and I began to hope, even though Marybeth was somewhat older than Michael, that they would eventually get married and that this would bring stability and happiness to his life. We went out to dinner at a Chinese restaurant that they had chosen and where they seemed to be regulars. Everything was smooth, everything was happy, our worries about drug use had been unwarranted. We were just too suspicious.

I worked well with Michael. He did really good work for Haverhills and also for FLAME. The only thing was that he was quite a bit more expensive than what it would have cost with a local service. But what the heck, he was my son and the few hundred dollars a month more did not make any big difference. But there was always the clamor of being paid right away. "Michael," I told him, "this is a business you are in with me. We pay our bills within thirty days. We cannot make an exception for you."

"Please, Dad," he would say, "our water bill is due and they threatened us with cutting it off if we don't pay it right away. Please send me the money by overnight mail."

"O.K.," I agreed, but I was always uneasy about that.

Rachel and Derek bought a lovely home, way up in the Oakland Hills. It had a wonderful view of the Bay, the estuary, and of San Francisco. Derek had to be away on business in Los Angeles, and Rachel felt uneasy to be by herself. She was eight months pregnant. She asked her brother Joe to come and stay with her for the duration. Joe did that. The afternoon of the next day, a huge fire broke out in the Oakland Hills, on which they lived. It had been a very dry season and the wooden growth that covered those hills burned like tinder.

Rachel and Joe, seeing the fire approaching, put a few precious and special things into her car and escaped down the choked road. Nothing happened to them. It was a miracle.

The fire raced down the hill, destroying hundreds of beautiful homes in its wake. Damage was estimated in the hundreds of millions of dollars. It was all very fast and many people died, in their homes or on the road trying to flee the fire. So, even though Derek and Rachel lost almost everything, Rachel and Joe and the unborn baby were able to escape alive. What a relief. We were so grateful.

About a week later, after everything had cooled down, Derek and Joe went back to where the house had stood. Everything was gone. Only a chimney remained standing. Joe's car, which he had to leave behind in their escape, was reduced to a lump of molten iron. There was absolutely nothing else left beyond heaps and heaps of gray ashes and a few globs of molten and hardened glass.

But wait, what was that lying there? They looked. It was a page of a book. What book? It was the textbook of their Jewish studies course at the University. The page was singed but fully readable. It described the history of the Jews of Argentina. It was the only item that had survived. It was a miracle. A piece of paper; how could it possibly have survived this inferno? They had it framed, and it now hangs in their home.

We have a big home – all the chickens had flown the coop, so we invited Derek and Rachel to stay with us – for as long as needed, of course.

Rachel, eight months pregnant, was sitting on her bed in her old room, in the lotus position, crying like a baby. "Why are you crying, sweetheart?" I asked her.

"Dad, we are totally ruined and what we have lost can never be replaced."

"Rachel," I told her, "Here with us you can, of course, stay as long as you want and you have a very competent husband who I know will doggedly insist that you be made whole. And you know what I believe? I believe that you'll come out much better than you were before. You'll come out smelling like a rose."

"I hope so, Dad," she said.

Because Derek and Rachel were able to stay with us for unlimited time, they were able to drive the hardest possible bargain with their insurance company. Derek, who conducted those negotiations, was relentless. His and Rachel's were one of the very last claims that was finally settled. Too much time had elapsed and the open and unpaid claims of this disaster were beginning to be a public scandal. The California Insurance Commissioner gave notice that those companies that did not settle all claims within sixty days might be precluded from doing any further business in California. So they all settled. Derek's doggedness and perseverance prevailed and had paid off.

Rachel and Derek did indeed come out smelling like roses – and then some.

I told you, and perhaps your own experience bears it out, that a letter from a law firm – especially if it is "Certified Mail – Return Receipt Requested" is always bad news. But I had one notable exception:

One of the donors for FLAME was one Monroe Guttmann. He wasn't a big donor, but he gave us about $100 year after year. One day he came to San Francisco and, quite unexpected and uninvited, came to my office. He turned out to be a man of about seventy years – very pleasant and very interested in FLAME and in what I was doing.

I took Mr. Guttmann out to a nice lunch. Also, that afternoon, the Israeli Consulate General was giving its annual *Yom Ha'atzmaut* reception, the anniversary of Israel's Independence Day. I was invited and, having Mr. Guttmann with me, I requested and got permission to bring him along. He enjoyed the occasion.

Then, Priscilla and I took Mr. Guttmann out to dinner because he appeared to be somewhat at loose ends.

Over dinner, he told us that he was a widower – his wife had died the year before – and that he felt very sad and very lonely. He had a home in Pittsburgh and another home in Florida. He seemed to be fairly well off, but he was totally unassuming.

Both Priscilla and I took a personal liking to him and urged him to come back to San Francisco as often as he could, and when he did, not to stay in a hotel, but to stay with us.

For the next two years or so, Mr. Guttmann upped his yearly contribution to FLAME from $100 to $500. He was obviously lonely and he talked to me on the phone once every month or so.

But then I didn't hear from him for a long time, and I became concerned about him. I tried to call his homes both in Florida and in Pittsburgh, but the lines had been disconnected. It didn't sound good. I didn't quite know what to do. Then, about a month later, I got a letter from a law firm in Pittsburgh. Yes, it was "Certified – Return Receipt Requested."

To make a long story short, Mr. Guttmann had died and had left a large estate, in excess of ten million dollars. He had left minor bequests to some nephews and nieces and all the rest of it to philanthropy. There were twelve beneficiaries, about half of them Jewish and the other half general – such as the Red Cross, the Salvation Army, the Cousteau Society and some others. But, guess what – FLAME was one of the six Jewish philanthropies he had selected. Naturally, it put FLAME on a financially secure basis for the foreseeable future. It was totally unexpected; certainly, our kindnesses to Mr. Guttmann were rendered without any expectation and without having anything like that in mind. I had never given any thought to his net worth. I certainly had no idea that he was that rich and never dreamed that we would be beneficiaries under his will.

While Priscilla and I were most saddened by the death of this very nice man, it was, to repeat, the only time in my entire business career that a letter from a law firm, "Certified – Return Receipt Requested" contained at least some good news.

Derek and Rachel had their first baby, Max Zadok, born in 1992. I was very pleased with the name. Max had been my father's name and I was happy that it would be perpetuated in his great-grandson. What about Zadok? Zadok was the name of one of the principal protagonists in James A. Michener's "The Source." It means "righteous one" in Hebrew. It thought it was a lovely name. I was happy that the tradition of Biblical names that we had established with our own children – Michael, Rachel, and Joseph – would be perpetuated.

Derek seemed to be quite unhappy with his job as representative of a winery. He intensely disliked his boss. But he was successful in his work and seemed to be well compensated. It was clear that he and Rachel had all the money they needed for a happy and pleasant life.

One day, I remember it was very the day that Time Inc. merged with Warner – all of us were substantial stockholders, so it was of much interest to us – we took Derek and Rachel out to dinner. We dropped the women off at the restaurant and Derek and I parked about three blocks away. On the way to the restaurant, Derek said, "Gerardo, I've decided to quit my job and to go into business for myself."

"You are?" I said, "I have much confidence in you, whatever you decide to do. What is it you have in mind?"

"I'll be a *negociant*," he said.

"A *negociant*?" I asked him. "What is that?"

Rachel's and Derek's children – Rebecca, Zaddy, and Jake.
What a wonderful family! How lucky we are.

Priscilla and I in 1996, at the fortieth reunion of my Harvard Business School class.

"It's a term in the wine trade," Derek said. "It's a person who coordinates the process from buying the grapes to having them pressed and the wine made, applying a brand, all the way to a person's table – the consumer. In other words, from vine to table."

"That sounds interesting. I wish you lots of luck and I know you will be successful."

It's not just me," he said. It's going to be me and my brother Courtney."

I hesitated. Should I give my opinion on that? I did. "Derek," I said, "You are about to make a big mistake. Business is one thing, and family is something quite different. I've seen controversy between you and your younger brother – back and forth."

"Oh," he said, "that's just talk between brothers. It doesn't mean anything."

"Maybe it didn't mean anything, but once you are in business and you have altercations, it may become difficult. I would strongly advise against it. Of course, ultimately you'll have to do what you feel you have to do. What percentage of the business would you give your brother?"

"We're going to go in on a 50-50 basis."

"Derek," I told him, "your first mistake is to take your brother into the business. I think it is a serious mistake. But giving him fifty per cent of the business is possibly fatal. Even if you don't have great controversies, somebody has to be in charge and somebody has to be able to make ultimate decisions when that becomes necessary." I told him the story about the airline Panagra, which was jointly owned – 50/50 – by PanAmerican and by W.R. Grace and Company, when I was working for Grace. They never could agree on anything. The five directors of PanAm and the five directors of the W.R. Grace just sat there glowering at each other across the table and never accomplished anything. Even in the burgeoning East Coast and West Coast South American markets, which they could have dominated, they eventually failed through haggling and for lack of decision-making. Derek was not impressed.

"I just owe it to my brother," he said. "I could not do it any other way."

"O.K.," I said, "I warned you, but I hope it will turn out fine. What are you going to do for working capital?" I asked him.

"I really don't have any and I kind of hoped that you would set me up with that – with a working capital loan to get started."

"Of course, I will. How much do you need?"

"My business plan calls for $50,000," he said. I think I can repay it within a year or perhaps sooner."

"No problem, Derek," I'll give you the $50,000, but I think you also should ask your father. If it is possible for him, I think he might also like to participate. At least you should ask him."

That evening both Derek and I made serious business mistakes. His mistake was not to accept my advice not to take his brother into the business, or, if he insisted in doing so, that he should not give him fifty per cent of the voting stock of the company. I also thought that if we had perhaps parked the car two blocks farther away, I could have talked him into that. But maybe not.

My mistake (and also his father's because, yes, he did participate with a $25,000 loan), was not to insist that we should be co-owners in this new business rather than lenders. Instead of a 50-50 standoff, in case of any disagreement that could not be resolved, we would be able to break any deadlocks. Also, as things turned out, both of us would have made a great deal of money, and I mean really a great deal of money, had we been stockholders of only five per cent each in this new company, rather than lenders.

Derek seemed to be doing very well with his new business. He would call me at least once a week and give me progress reports and tell me what problems he was having along the way, fortunately all of them minor ones. The main burr under his saddle were two Jewish-Argentine brothers, who were the buyers for one of his major accounts and who put the screws on him in every conceivable way. I often wondered whether Derek consulted with me about them because I was his father-in-law and because what he believed to be my business savvy, or because he ascribed to me special knowledge of the psyche of Argentine Jews.

Eventually, Derek ceased to call me altogether or ever even to talk to me about his business. He and his brother engaged their father to act as a consultant and also as an arbiter of the differences that seemed to develop and which seemed to open a cleavage between Derek and his brother Courtney – a cleavage that eventually widened into an unbridgeable chasm.

But there was more good news from the Benham household. Rachel was expecting again and in due course gave birth to a darling little girl – Rebecca, our only granddaughter thus far, became the apple of our eye.

I had worked in the mail-order business for eighteen years with the loving and competent assistance of Priscilla. She did all the merchandising, all art direction, especially catalog preparation. Whatever success we attained is largely due to her. I am forever grateful for her loving help and for her wonderful merchandise and marketing sense.

Finally, after the collapse of Frontier Airlines, she said, "Gerardo, I've done this now for eighteen years and in a way I may have neglected our children in order to help with this business. I feel sort of bad about it, because I think the troubles with Michael might perhaps have been avoided if I had stayed at home all along. So now I am going to retire from this business. If you want to continue in this business, which you don't have to, you have my blessing and my support, but I no longer wish to do that. I've done my share." She was right.

"What are you going to do now?

"Well, I'm going to tend to my home and to Joseph, who still needs my attention. Also, I think I'm going to study painting."

"Painting?" I asked her. "What for? You have never shown any interest in that. Do you know whether you have any talent for it?"

"I don't know if I have talent or not, but I'll find out."

The rest is history. From a standing start, she became a wonderful artist. Her work has been exhibited in several solo shows. Priscilla's oils, collages, water colors, decorated furniture, sculptures, and more adorn our homes, in San Francisco and in Tahoe, the homes of our children, and the homes of those to whom she has given or who have purchased her art. Eventually, she got hooked up with a most interesting lady by the name of Margie Boyd, who ran the travel program for the San Francisco Museum of Modern Art. Margie arranged monthly art tours in the Northern California area, and she made several trips a year to foreign countries, in some of which Priscilla participated. I was always asked to come along, but I never had the time. Quite frankly, I also never really had the interest for doing that.

They made a couple of trips to Oaxaca in Mexico, a trip to Morocco, and a trip to Germany to the so-called Documenta, which is a European once-every-five-years major art event. On that particular trip, they went to Dresden, the major art city in Germany. There they looked at the work of one Hubertus Giebe, an up-and-coming major artist of the German Expressionist School. Priscilla bought a couple of his pieces and was enthusiastic about his work and about him and his wife Marlies, who was and still is the restorer for the famous major museums of Dresden. Being always more than somewhat effusive, she said to them, "Listen you guys, if you ever come to the United States, by all means visit us in San Francisco." She added, "*Mi casa es su casa*," somewhat in the conviction that Spanish is the language that all those who do not speak English would understand. In this case, she was right; they did understand that.

I'm getting a little ahead of myself, but about six months later, we suddenly got a phone call from Germany. I was on the phone and the person on the other side was speaking in German. He said, "My name is Hubertus Giebe. Your wife invited us to come to the United States and stay with you. Did she really mean that?"

I was a little flummoxed about this because I had never heard about it. But I rose pretty well to the occasion. "Of course, she meant it. She means everything she says. Tell us when you will be here and you will be most welcome, of course."

They came and they stayed with us for about ten days. We found them to be wonderful people and you might say that we "fell in love" with them. Priscilla organized a big party for them at our house – about forty people. It was a success. Even though they are much younger than we are, just a little older than our children, we think of them as close friends. He is a very talented artist and they, as also their son Casper, are wonderful people. We phone and correspond and visit each other as often as we can.

Later in this story, I shall have some further reflections about Germany and then I'll talk some more about Hubertus and Marlies.

Joe had an easy puberty – at least as far as we were concerned. Who knows what kind of turmoil he went through. He was fortunate (or was he?) to have two girls in the neighborhood, one about two years younger and one about three years older who, we found out later, initiated him into the secrets of amour to quite an unusual degree. But I think that it served him well, because he did not seem to be engaged in the teenage angst and in the fruitless explorations that I went through at that stage of my life.

He was easy to get along with. The only sign of what could possibly be considered rebellion was that he let his hair grow to his shoulders. Only once or twice, when I ventured into the Haight Ashbury district of San Francisco, the turf of the hippies and of the "peace generation," did I see other people with hair that long. I was amazed that Joe's hair would have that kind of vitality or whatever it was.

All along I had the feeling that he expected us – Priscilla and me – to say something about his hair or to insist that he cut it. But we didn't In the first place, we really didn't care. If he wanted to wear his hair that way, that was his business. But we also knew that he might have waited for such a parental demand, because it would have given him the opportunity to assert his budding manhood and his independence. We did not give him the opening.

Joe, just like his brother Michael before him, was bar mitzvahed and then, a year later, confirmed. Frankly, I don't think "confirmation" is much of a Jewish custom and I believe it's only practiced by Reform congregations. I think it is an adaptation or emulation of Protestantism, which, with the small but significant exception of the role of Jesus Christ and the Holy Ghost, Reform Judaism somewhat resembles. In any case, it was a custom in our congregation, Emanu-El, to organize a trip to Israel for all the confirmands – boys and girls. That part of it was a very good custom. To acquaint American Jewish children with the State of Israel and hopefully to develop affectionate concern for it was certainly a worthy goal, very much a step in the right direction.

About a week before the trip, we found that Joseph was becoming increasingly fidgety. We asked him what was troubling him. "Nothing, nothing," he said. "What makes you think that something's troubling me?"

"Well, you're fidgeting and seem to be concerned about something. What is it?"

He came out with it. "Mom and Dad," he said, "I've decided to have my hair cut. I want you to take me to the best barbershop, which is in the Fairmont Hotel, and have them cut it."

That was the most expensive barbershop in San Francisco, but we thought it would be worth the money. In any case it wasn't worth arguing about it. So he went, had about two pounds of hair cut off and emerged with a beautiful face and with a great haircut. We were pleased but quite surprised. We asked him, "Joe, what made you suddenly decide to have your hair cut?"

"Well, Mom and Dad, I have to be truthful. I've been told that when you arrive at Ben Gurion Airport in Israel, there's a bunch of tough-looking Israeli soldiers roaming the halls. If they see anybody with long hair like mine was, they immediately pick him up and put him in a military barbershop and give him a military haircut. Some kids say that they also press him right away into the Israeli army, but I don't really believe that. So since I do want to go to Israel and I'd prefer not to have an Israeli military haircut, I thought I'd better get it done at the Fairmont Hotel. It doesn't look all that bad, does it?"

But for the two days preceding his trip to Israel, he stayed in seclusion at home. He did not emerge until we drove him to the airport where his peers barely recognized him and, after they did, mercilessly teased him. That hair thing was really the only very small act of rebellion, if you want to call it that, on the part of Joe. He was an easy person to get along with – and still is.

Michael, on the other hand, was a different story. The poor boy had really been nothing but trouble to himself and to us from early childhood. He was a constant preoccupation. We thought, and we were of course happy about it, that he had licked his overriding problem, namely his drug addiction. He now lived with Marybeth in Houston. I was very close to him and we communicated with each other over our special dedicated phone line at least twice or three times a day. He did all the graphic work for Haverhills and for FLAME. He did a very good job.

One day he called me: "Dad, I am afraid I have bad news." My heart sank. There was never any really good news from him, and what could it be now. "Dad," he said, "I was feeling bad and all kinds of nasty things happened to me, so I went to a doctor and found out that I have diabetes. What should I do now?"

"Michael," I said, "you'll have to get immediate treatment. You are a member of the Kaiser-Permanente Health Plan, but I'm afraid they don't have a facility in Houston. But they do have one in Dallas, so please drive up there right away and put yourself in the hands of a doctor there. They'll take very good care of you."

"O.K., Dad."

Why would he have diabetes, I wondered. I asked myself whether it could be connected with his drug use. Probably not, but more likely, the fact that he was considerably overweight and led a totally sedentary life contributed to it. In any case, that's what it was and we had to face it.

Even though I talked to him at least twice a day and nagged him every time, he didn't go to Dallas until about six weeks later. I suppose that his symptoms, whatever they were – he did not discuss them with me – got worse and he decided that he had to do something.

"What did the doctor tell you?" I asked him.

"He gave me a kit so I would prick my finger several times a day, take a drop of blood and determine my blood sugar."

"Are you doing that, Michael?"

"Well, not yet, but I'm going to start next week."

"Why not yet?" I asked him. "You have a serious health problem and you should follow your doctor's instructions meticulously."

"Yes, I'm going to do it, but not just yet."

"What else did he tell you?"

"He told me to lose some weight. He gave me a diet that I should follow and foods that I can and can't eat."

"Are you following those instructions?" I asked him.

"Not yet. You know, Marybeth has the children and so it's very difficult for her to cook different meals for me."

"Michael, I don't care how many children she has, but you have to lose weight. You're at least twenty pounds overweight. You must follow your doctor's instructions regarding diet for adult-onset of diabetes, which is what you have. Following your doctor's diet and instructions is the best way to treat it."

"Yes, Dad," he said, "I'm going to do that. Just give me a little time."

It was exasperating.

About a week later, Marybeth called me. "Gerardo," she said, "there has been a small accident and I had to take Michael to the hospital."

"Oh my God," I thought. "What kind of an accident?"

"He fell on the street and he scraped his hand. It didn't heal and got worse instead. Then he started running a very high fever. I think it's all because of his diabetes, so I took him to the hospital and they tell me that he's in very serious condition. It might be best if you or Priscilla came to Houston."

So Priscilla took the first plane. When she got there, she called me and told me that he seemed to be indeed in very serious condition. I went to Houston the next day. He had a single room in the Methodist Hospital, which is one of the finest in the United States. Dr. DeBakey, the heart transplant guru, made it famous.

Michael didn't seem to be conscious. He looked terrible. I sat by his bedside for the better part of two days and talked to him. He never acknowledged my presence or even opened his eyes. It was awful. One thing that I saw badly surprised me: His poor arm was full of needle tracks. He was still a junkie, just as he'd always been.

It made me terribly sad and also quite angry – angry at myself, that I had allowed myself to be fooled, to be hoodwinked for such a long time. I suddenly understood where all the money had gone over the years. And I was also angry at Marybeth, who obviously would have known what was going on and who had never informed us about it. Was she a "co-dependent" or was she scared that if she revealed the truth to us, he might either leave her or hit her! I don't know and I have never found out.

The doctor gave us information that stunned us. As a result of the infection that the wound in his hand had caused, he had developed an ulcer on his heart, which had to be surgically removed. So we agreed to that. It was a very major operation. Priscilla stayed with him all along, but I went back to San Francisco after the operation, which was declared a success.

But things didn't get better. About two days after the supposedly successful operation, Priscilla was told by the doctors that the procedure (as they called it) had not been successful after all. There was another ulcer and they had to operate again. I was on the phone every hour to keep abreast of what was happening. At about 7 o'clock that evening, Priscilla was on the phone crying. "Gerardo," she said, "he's in a coma. I don't think he's going to survive. You've got to come right away."

So I raced to the airport. There was a 1 A.M. flight to Houston, which I booked. It was about midnight and I was roaming the halls, 2,000 miles away, and my son, Michael, my oldest and the one I loved so much, was in Houston lying in a coma and possibly at the threshold of death. Suddenly a voice came over the loudspeaker. "Mr. Joffe, urgently to the white courtesy phone, please."

"Oh my God," I thought, "this can't be good news." It wasn't. It was my son Joe on the other line.

"Dad, I have terrible news. Michael just died."

I arrived in Houston early in the morning. Houston is two hours ahead of us in time. I took a cab to the hospital. Both Priscilla and Marybeth were in tears. So was Diane, my sister-in-law, who had come to stay with Priscilla.

"I want to see Michael," I said.

"You can't see him," the nurse told me. "He is in the morgue."

"I want to go down to the morgue and see him," I said.

"No, I'm afraid nobody is allowed in the morgue."

"Let me talk to the head nurse," I said, "or somebody in authority."

"What do you wish to do?" she asked.

"I need to see my son," I said.

"Mr. Joffe, you can't go to the morgue, but let me see what I can do."

She came back in about ten minutes and said, "Mr. Joffe, you can go to the third floor to room 314C and they are going to bring Michael up for you to see for the last time."

So I went to that room. It was a very small one that was quite empty, except for one chair. I waited and waited. After about fifteen minutes there was a knock on the door. A gurney came in, with a body covered by a sheet. "Here's your son," the attendant said.

"Thank you," I said, and he left. I pulled the sheet back. It was Michael, of course. He looked calm and peaceful. I touched him. He was a block of ice. I sat there for five minutes. I cried and communed with him. There was nothing else I could do. I rang the bell for the attendant and then left. It was the worst day of my life.

But there were practical issues to attend, namely to arrange embalming and transportation of the body from Houston to San Francisco. Embalming is frowned upon or forbidden in the Jewish religion, but the airlines won't transport a body without it, so I had to do that. Then I had to contact the Sinai Memorial Chapel in San Francisco to handle the funeral arrangement. Then I called my friend Cantor Martin Feldman of Congregation Sherit Israel in San Francisco to arrange for a small – family only – funeral service at Home of Peace, one of the Jewish cemeteries in San Francisco, or rather in near-by Colma, San Francisco's "cemetery city." All of that was very painful.

Then came the hospital bill. It faded into insignificance in view of the terrible blow of Michael's death. But it was enormous. It was just a shade under $250,000 – for two weeks in the hospital and the "procedures" that had to be performed.

I thought that the bill was my moral responsibility, even though I was quite sure that I had no legal obligation. After all, Michael was certainly grown and he had admitted himself into the hospital as an emergency case and as a Kaiser patient. On the other hand, I had authorized the expensive operations that were performed. In any case, I thought I had a moral obligation to pay that enormous bill if it actually came to that. But should it come to that? Michael, was a member of the Kaiser Permanente Health Plan and had been paying (or rather I had been paying) his premiums for the last fifteen years. Kaiser at first balked at paying this bill. They claimed, with some justification perhaps, that, even though his premiums had been paid in full all these years, that he was not a "bona fide employee" of my firm, since he was not a full-time resident in San Francisco. Also, the fine print of the contract stipulated that, except for emergencies while an employee might be temporarily out of town, all medical services had to be performed by a Kaiser facility. It was somewhat of a tentative rearguard action on the part of Kaiser. But after only very little argument about it, they paid the whole bill. I thought highly of them for that.

As planned, we had a very private interment – only the family present and Marybeth and her children. Cantor Feldman did the rituals. As a surprise – somewhat of a shocker really – the cantor performed the Frank Sinatra song "Doing It My Way." He meant well, of course, but "my way," in the case of Michael, was totally the wrong way. It was the doper's way, the junkie's way, which ultimately brought him to his death, at just 42 years old. Rachel put a Beach Boys disc on his casket. That was really more appropriate. The Beach Boys had been his favorite group. He would listen to them for hours.

We had planned on a memorial service for him at Temple Emanu El about three weeks after his death. We had reserved the chapel, which holds about one hundred and twenty people. But there was such an overflow, such an outpouring of sorrow and sympathy, that the service had to be transferred to the main sanctuary. There were about two hundred and fifty people. I was surprised and very touched.

I was the main eulogist for the occasion – a very sad assignment. I decided that the eulogy should be anchored on a Shakespearean passage. I considered several, but nothing really quite seemed to fit. Then it occurred to me that I could be well served if I consulted an expert.

I had heard that my alma mater – the Missouri School of Mines, now redubbed the University of Missouri at Rolla – had a renowned Shakespearean scholar as head of its Humanities department. His name was Nicholas Knight. I called him and he immediately agreed to help me in my sad task. He proposed several passages. All of them were good and appropriate, but none of them quite "clicked." But then he offered Juliet's lament from "Romeo and Juliet."

> Come, gentle night,
> Come, loving, black-brow'd night,
> Give me my Romeo; and when he shall die,
> Take him and cut him out in little stars,

> And he will make the face of heaven so fine,
> That all the world will be in love with night.

I thought it was perfect, just what I needed and what reflected my sentiments. The audience seemed to be as touched by it as I was.

Nick Knight and his artist wife Diane both of whom we got to know in person when we revisited Rolla on the occasion of my fiftieth (golden) homecoming, turned out to be very best friends – friends for life – just as Finn and Lene Hjalsted and Hubertus and Marlies Giebe.

My new Haverhills business, the one that I had resuscitated from the ashes of the bankruptcy, did very well. Just as I had promised Priscilla, I issued no catalogs; I only advertised in media. For the first three years I kept my promise not to publish any catalogs. In the fourth year, I broke my promise. I brought out a small – only 16 pages, catalog for the holiday season. Just as I had expected, that catalog was a great success. So, without ever "confessing" to Priscilla, I did that holiday catalog every year until I finally (and, honestly, for the last time) sold the business.

As on previous such occasions when I sold the business, this time, again, I did not look for buyers. They just came to me. The buyer in this case was a young man, about thirty-eight years old. He was from Minneapolis. I had already established an interesting business relationship with him. He was what we call a media broker. Those are people who establish connections with media, magazines and newspapers – perhaps even broadcast media – to buy space or time at reduced rates, or, most desirable, on a "per inquiry" basis. "Per inquiry" is somewhat of a misnomer, but that is what it is called. Under that plan, sometimes coupled with a minimum guarantee, the medium in question, say a magazine, sells space and charges a percentage of sales made through the ad in this particular publication. That has to be strictly on an honor basis, because the advertiser tells the medium what has been sold. If there is any suspicion at all, any cheating or not reporting sales properly, there is no more business, of course. Word spreads in the trade that one is a cheater and should not be trusted. No one else will touch him.

In any case, the young man from Minneapolis was a live wire and brought us lots of good media. One day he said, "Gerardo, you are getting on in years." (Had I heard that before? Thanks for telling me, I thought. But he was right.) "Don't you want to sell this business?"

"Paul," I said, "do you have any money?"

"No, I don't, but I can come up with some. I can put a mortgage on my home and I can have my bank guarantee part of the balance."

"O.K.," I told him, "let's try and make a deal."

To quote the Godfather, I made him a deal that was so wonderful that he could not possibly refuse it. I was really getting a little tired. By then, I had done the same thing for over thirty years. That's why I made him such a wonderful proposition. I wrote the contract, this time without an attorney. I wanted to be sure that it was right. We signed it, we shook hands, put all of the inventory in one huge truck and shipped it to Minneapolis. He is doing very well and I am very happy because, naturally, having been the founder of Haverhills, and having worked with it for so many years. I still think of it as "my baby." I want the person who follows me also to be a great success.

I kept a small interest in the business, just to keep track of what is going on.

Joe is our remaining son and the result of that fortunate failure of the "Rodell-7" contraceptive computer: He graduated from North Texas State University in Denton, Texas, and turned out to be a wonderful musician. He played the saxophone, composed music and directed. He put together a small combo and played in various clubs. Ultimately, he got tired of it. In fact, he also got tired of the saxophone and he switched to something quite different, but also in the music field. He formed a small company and composed advertising jingles, mostly for car dealerships. I thought they were marvelous. He is very talented. It turned out, however, to be a tough business, and in spite of having done some excellent work in that field, he eventually gave it up and moved on.

Next, he formed a company to do computer graphics for trial lawyers, showing complicated architectural relationships, crime scenes, defective merchandise, etc. In that field, too, he did outstanding work. Again, it just didn't take off as quickly as he had hoped and he decided to ditch that also. I thought he might have given up a little too quickly, but I suppose that he knew what he was doing. He now has settled down in the real estate field and is doing well. I am very proud of him. But he really did need to settle down because he got married. They now have their first child. That of course has a way of maturing one. He married a wonderful girl that he had met in Denton. Her name is Stephany. We love her dearly.

There was one slight complication. She is Catholic. I don't know whether or not Joe suggested to her to become a Jew by choice, just as his mother had. I never talked to him about it, and he didn't volunteer to talk to me about it either. Naturally, it would have pleased me very much. It worked out so well for his mother and for me. I am quite sure it would have worked well for them also. But perhaps it was not in the cards. The wedding, which took place in a beautiful setting in Marin County, north of San Francisco, was conducted jointly by a rabbi and by a priest. That was something totally new and unusual for me and it took me some effort to get my mind around that one, but eventually I did. And how about Stephany's parents? Surely, it couldn't exactly have been what they had planned. But they were most gracious and accepting of what must have been an unusual ritual for them as well. And finally, how about my own in-laws? They uncomplainingly coped with something quite unexpected and probably not entirely welcome, namely a Jewish wedding, a Jewish son-in-law and a daughter who had converted to Judaism. It was certainly even more unusual then than it is now – especially in an environment such as southwest Arkansas.

Stephany Morrow, the future Mrs. Joseph Joffe. What a
wonderful girl, what a wonderful addition to the family!

Stephany and Joe on their wedding day. Aren't they a great couple?

Stephany and Joe's wedding was officiated by both a rabbi
and by a priest. It was something quite new to me and as
I am sure it was also to her parents. It all worked out
wonderfully well for all concerned.

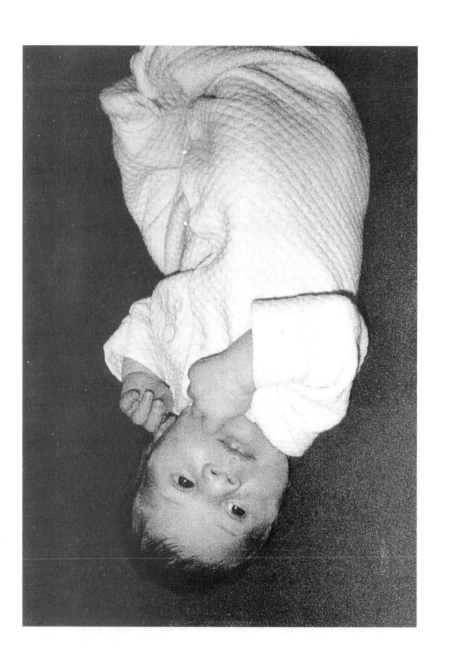

Samuel Kern Morrow Joffe – "Sammy," of course, for short.
He is the newest addition to the family and the apple of
everybody's eye.

They did so in good spirit, and I could not do anything less. But whatever – Jewish or not Jewish – Joseph could not possibly have married anybody tuned better to him and to our family then Stephany. She is an absolutely wonderful person. We are so happy!

I am coming pretty much to the end of my story. When I look back and think about it, the first thirty years were perhaps the most "exciting" – and the most "interesting." The last fifty years were perhaps less "exciting" and less "interesting," but they were certainly the happiest. I found a wonderful wife and have a wonderful family, marred only by the death of our beloved son Michael.

I created an interesting and nationally well-known business and was able to make quite a bit of money in the process. So there are absolutely no complaints. And I created and am president of a major Jewish philanthropy, which I believe – and many share my opinion – is playing a substantial role in telling Israel's story to an often uninformed and misinformed American public.

I'll now just wrap up a few odds and ends and then I'll close this memoir with a few reflections.

Priscilla and I try to make it to Buenos Aires at least every other year or so. It is a very long trip. It is made more burdensome by my refusal to fly anything but tourist class, especially on long trips. "Will I ever be able to fly at least in business class?" Priscilla asked me?

"Yes, perhaps, darling," I said. "with your next husband, but not with me."

"Why not? We can afford it."

"Yes, we can afford it," I said, "but you know, when I land at Ezeiza Airport in Buenos Aires and realize that I have just saved $3,000 by forgoing a little leg room, and a 'deluxe dinner,' I feel awfully good." It still is a point of minor contention with us – not a big one. But it does come up every once in a while.

On one of those trips, we took Rachel with us. She had been to school in Buenos Aires for one year and she speaks the language quite well. Of course, she is very fond of her Uncle Heinz and her Aunt Lieschen, who stood in *loco parentis* while she was living there. The next time, we took Diane, Priscilla's sister. At that time, I was working on a book – I'll talk about it in a minute – and had the first 60 pages, still handwritten, in my briefcase. I was going to work on the book while I was in Buenos Aires, but that was, of course, a silly idea to begin with. I wouldn't have had the time for it. In any case, when we arrived, we loaded our luggage onto one of those carts with my briefcase in a little compartment in front of it. We went through customs and were waved right through. We just don't look like your average drug bandit or smuggler. Those customs people have a nose for that.

Lieschen, our sister-in-law, was waiting for us right outside of customs. I let go of my cart, turned and gave her a hug. It wasn't more than ten seconds. When I turned back to the cart, my briefcase was gone. I was devastated. I didn't care about the case (a quite expensive one), and another leather portfolio inside the briefcase, my spare pair of glasses, my medication, a couple of books I had brought, or anything else, just that manuscript, the first 60 pages of my book.

We went to the airport police, though I knew it was probably totally useless. There was no way that the police would recover that briefcase or would even try. I went to downtown Buenos Aires and had a printer make up twelve large self-adhesive labels, each about 6 x 4 inches. In very large type it read:

RECOMPENSA

Se perdió un portafolio negro en el aeropuerto. Se ofrece una recompensa de $250 a quien lo devuelva al Hotel Claridge. No se harán preguntas.

In English:

REWARD

Black briefcase lost at the airport. Reward of $250 is offered to the person who delivers it to the Claridge Hotel. No questions will be asked.

I pasted those twelve labels surreptitiously all over the Ezeiza Airport. I am quite sure that was against the law, but I was pretty desperate. Even though I had offered $250 to get my briefcase back, there were no takers. The thieves, not finding any money or anything else of value to them, probably had thrown the whole thing away.

About that book: For many years I was a member of the San Francisco Press Club, which was close to my office. Priscilla, who was still working with me at the time, and I would go there to lunch almost every day. They had a bountiful buffet and we enjoyed the food, the setting, and the company. After lunch, I would always go for a swim in their basement pool, despite my mother having impressed on me never to go into the water on a full stomach. I would swim laps – 30 laps, about half a mile.

Anybody who has ever swum laps knows that it's very boring.

I had been diagnosed or classified as "hyperlexic," which describes a person unduly, perhaps even obsessively, interested in both words and in numbers. It's a relatively rare combination. Quite a few people are interested in words and others in numbers, but only the hyperlexics, people like myself, are interested in both. So while doing those laps, I thought of numbers and I developed a system – I call it the 16-level paradigm – of 52 different ways of how to multiply two 2-digit numbers with each other. I know it sounds a little strange, and it's difficult to explain in a few words, but, at least in my opinion, it does for the mind what lifting weights does for the body. So I decided to write a book about it. It was really quite an effort. It runs 460 fascinating pages, and I gave it the explanatory title "How You Too Can Develop a Razor-Sharp Mind and a Steel-Trap Memory." There was even a subtitle, which quite frankly, but not altogether, was somewhat tongue in cheek: "...And Perhaps Even Improve Your Sex Life and Extend Your Days." Why do I say it's not altogether tongue in cheek? Because the proven reality is that smart people have better sex than those who are not so smart. Dumb ones may do a lot of grunting and groaning and sweating, but they don't have good sex. Smart people have good sex.

The extra bonus is that – again a "scientifically proven fact, " – that people who have better sex live longer. Voilá! That was my book – you can get smarter, have better sex, and live longer – what a bargain for $29.95!

The book in now in its fifth printing. While it is not quite "Gone With the Wind" or "Harry Potter," it is doing very well. I am quite happy with it – and so seem my readers to be.

The name of my firm, the family corporation, was and is Jomira/Advance. Haverhills, the mail order business was one of its divisions and the other one was Advance Books. But for the last many years, only Haverhills was truly active. When I sold it, I was left with Advance Books.

So that is what I am doing now. I lease a small office, in the South of Market district of San Francisco, pretty close to downtown. In addition to my "Brain" book, I also sell a new and updated edition of my seven-volume mail-order course "How to Build a Great Fortune in Mail Order," and a book by my late friend Karl Bach called "Selling is Simple…If You Don't Make It Complicated," for which he had given me the copyright many years ago, just before his untimely death. It all moves pretty well. And finally, I sell "remainder" books on self-help, books that are out of print and of which I buy the remaining copies and sell them through my mail-order book catalog.

My main interest, however, is in my philanthropies, primarily FLAME which has become a fairly large factor on the American Jewish scene. We have about 30,000 supporters and more than 25,000 "affiliates," prospective supporters, who have been suggested to us by those who are already on our roster. It is really a major effort, and I am quite proud that I handle virtually the whole thing by myself – something that might involve at least four or five employees if it were done by someone else. I just have somebody come in once a week to help with the incoming mail and there is a part-time bookkeeper, of course, who does the numbers. I do all of my philanthropies on a pro bono basis, don't draw any salary, and I've done it that way for over fifteen years.

Until not too long ago, I was the president of another substantial Jewish philanthropy, Friends of the Danish Jewish Museum. Here is how it happened.

You will remember Ulla, my first love, that little girl in Denmark who, during the War, married another man and who ultimately committed suicide. I have always stayed friendly with the family and especially with her mother, who got to be almost one hundred years old, and with her brother Finn, his wife Lene, and with their family.

Finn is about six years younger than I. Over the years, we and our extended families have become very close friends. By extended families I mean his and Lene's children and grandchildren, but also Ulla's children and grandchildren, most of whom live in Copenhagen. We try to get to Copenhagen at least once every other year, if possible, more often. The whole gang gets together for festive dinners, for remembering old times, and for singing old Danish songs.

Finn is half Jewish, of course, and as far as the Nazis were concerned, he was a Jew. Like virtually all other Danish Jews, his mother and he – his sister Ulla was already married and was with her husband and child – prepared to get smuggled to Sweden, across the Sound. The Sound is the stretch of water that separates Sweden and Denmark. Something went wrong. It seems that someone betrayed them. They and all the others with them were captured by the Nazis and put into a German concentration camp in Denmark, preparatory to deportation to an extermination camp, probably in Poland.

Then something extraordinary happened. Someone in authority, obviously with good connections to the Germans, argued that Finn was not really Jewish, that he had a Danish name (Hjalsted) and, somewhat incongruously, that he was not circumcised. In any case, Finn and his mother were released. It was most unusual. They were allowed to go back to Copenhagen. But, the situation for the Jews in Denmark became more and more ominous. In fact, the German naval attaché, horrified by what was going to happen, secretly informed the chief rabbi to alert the community that, on that very weekend, the Nazis were going to round up all Jews still remaining and that they would ship them to an extermination camp. So, they made another attempt at escape, to be smuggled to Sweden. On the second attempt, they succeeded.

After Denmark's liberation from the Germans, Finn studied law and ultimately became one of the most prominent attorneys in Denmark, specializing in aviation and admiralty law, a senior partner in a large law firm. As far as I could tell, he never thought of himself as being Jewish and still does not. But his consciousness was raised. He felt somehow connected to the Danish-Jewish community. It is a tiny community, not more than perhaps 3,000 families at this time.

It occurred to some activists in that small community that they should build a Danish-Jewish museum in Copenhagen. It would document their existence in Denmark, which dates back to the seventeenth century, and would highlight their contributions to the Danish nation. It would also express their gratitude to their Danish compatriots, who, uniquely among the nations occupied by the Germans, not only did not turn on their Jews, but actively protected them by smuggling virtually all of them to Sweden.

So, since Finn is such a well-known, well connected person, they approached him and asked him to be on the board of directors of this museum project. He accepted. The Danish government and the Queen made a contribution of approximately one million dollars to this project and made space available for it in the central government building complex. But much money remained to be raised. The obvious place was, of course, the United States.

They made some false starts with that and then – mostly out of friendship to Finn, but also because of my enthusiasm for this project – I was instrumental in the creation of the Friends of the Danish Jewish Museum, which is, in effect, the fiscal agent for this project in the United States.

Using the techniques that have stood me in such good stead with FLAME over so many years, I organized a successful fund-raising campaign. I continue to be really quite successful in that; now, however, I do have a problem. After the initial enthusiasm for this project among wide circles of American Jews, there is now some hesitation in contributing money to it. The reason is that anti-Semitism, the age-old scourge of Europe, which so many thought had been buried for good, has emerged again, just like a malignant virus that science thought had been expunged and which then suddenly erupts again, perhaps even in a more malignant variant. Regrettably and surprisingly, this anti-Semitism has found its most vocal expression in the Scandinavian countries, especially in Norway and in Denmark.

The purported reasons for this anti-Semitism, which is mostly disguised as the socially more acceptable anti-Israelism or anti-Zionism, are the upheavals in Israel in which, perversely, many if not most Europeans side with the Arabs. That is very painful to me and to many others and almost incomprehensible, but it is a sad fact.

In any case, the sale of my books and writing additional books (such as this one), and my philanthropies keep me very busy.

Most of you who are reading this are probably much younger than I am now. I can strongly recommend to my male readers, never to "retire," but always to keep working, even though on a possibly somewhat reduced scale. I promise you that that will keep you young and active and make you live a longer, more interesting, and more productive life.

There are two more grandchildren as of this writing. At the age of forty or forty-one, our daughter Rachel got it into her head to have another child. She already had a lovely family of a boy and a girl. We couldn't understand why she wanted another one, at her age and with the well-know odds for possible problems, but she was determined. Why would that have been? Could she have wanted to "compete" with her mother, who had three children, or with one of her sisters-in-law, one of whom had four children, another had three children, and the third sister was working on her third child? Whatever it was, she succeeded in her effort. At the age of forty-two, she gave us little Jake, another apple of his grandfather's eye. And, of course, there is Samuel, Joe and Stephany's little baby boy – dear Sammy.

There's one more thing I want to talk about: It's Derek's business. His father and I got him started, each with a loan of $25,000. He paid that back very quickly. He took flight much faster than anybody could have expected. In the beginning he consulted me frequently but, quite frankly, somewhat to my disappointment, that ceased very soon. His father became his business confidant and that was, of course, quite proper since the business – Codera Wine Group (I had coined the name) – was owned fifty-fifty by him and by his brother Courtney.

Things went fabulously well. They developed a number of wine labels that were leaders in their category and big sellers all over the country. To make a long story short, about eight years out of the starting gate, they sold the business for a huge amount of money. By huge, I mean in the nine digits. I have been in business for many years and I have had my share of modest successes, but I have never seen

Timely and professional attention
in the listing or purchase of your home.

Joe Joffe
510 387-2236 *direct*
510 428-0900 *office*
510 433-7168 *voicemail*

Joseph tried a couple of things before he settled down to real estate, which seems to be his calling. Do you want to buy or sell some real estate in our area? Please call any of the numbers shown above.

Priscilla and I as we are today – after over fifty years of marriage. She is a gold nugget from the Arkansas River. How lucky can a guy get!

or never even thought possible anything like that. It was incredible. But, unfortunately, there is a downside to this great success story.

Somewhere down the line, the problems between the brothers, the disagreement that I had predicted and that I had warned Derek against, came to pass. I was not in the loop and I don't quite know the details and how it came about.

His brother and he, who – and that's the way Derek had wanted it – were equal partners had developed an enmity to each other of almost biblical proportions. Cain and Abel, and Jacob and Esau come to mind. The rift seems to be unhealable and involves the respective families. Their parents are is in a terrible quandary. Even though they may have their views as to who is "right" and who is "wrong" in this feud, they do not venture their opinion or even attempt to mediate the enmity, lest they destroy their relationship with one of their sons or the other. And both Derek's father and I, I believe, made our big mistake by lending money to the fledging company, rather than getting at least small shares in it. Both he and I would have been able to vote our shares, which would have been decisive, and we could have influenced the course of events. We could, quite possibly, have been able to deflect the fraternal enmity and, if the two brothers would have been in harness together, rather than working against each other, could probably have negotiated an even better deal. What a shame that this almost unbelievable success story, this enormous amount of money, would have been marred by such a dreadful family rift. How remarkable it really is. One could understand that two brothers, partners in business, could turn against each other if they were a failure – if the business had gone into bankruptcy – one might blame the other. But how such enmity could come about in obtaining such tremendous success is almost inconceivable. I have never understood it, and I don't think I ever will.

I want to close this story with some reflections.

REFLECTIONS ON MY FAMILY

My joy in my family and my happiness are unflawed, except, of course, for the terrible tragedy that we suffered in the death of Michael. The tragedy of his death is made even heavier because, even after all these years, both Priscilla and I think endlessly on what we might possibly have done to prevent it. Could we have done it by having been more alert to the signals of his addiction? Could Priscilla have prevented it by staying home instead of working in the business? Who knows? Doctor Amanini (the psychiatrist who wanted his chair back) told us that we could not have changed the ultimate outcome, even if we had dedicated every minute of our lives to Michael's welfare. We try to console ourselves by thinking that he was right.

There were a few signals along the road that we did not see. In retrospect, we now realize that, even as a baby, he exhibited symptoms that pointed to a chemical imbalance, to something being wrong, but nobody in Magnolia, Arkansas, was smart enough to realize that. Then, when he exhibited strange and obstreperous behavior in his early school years and all along the way, we might have taken him to a child psychologist. Who knows? Whatever it was that could have helped, we did not do it.

I am delighted with our two surviving children. Rachel is a wonderful woman and a wonderful mother and, it is quite clear, a wonderful wife to Derek. She was able to attract an exceptional man as her husband. It just couldn't be any better.

Joseph took a little while to find himself, but now it seems that he has. He also was "settled down" by Stephany, the wonderful girl that he married. Without question, he will be further anchored by having become a father.

But the most important thing is Priscilla. We have now been married for over fifty years, and the love and affection that we feel for each other seems to become stronger as the years go by. At least, by observation, I don't see many couples, married as long as we, who seem to be as loving and as committed to each other as we are.

And what a miracle it really is. We got married after "dating" for only four months, for almost two of which she was traveling, and really without knowing each other too well, or well at all. Then there were the differences in backgrounds. I was European and had a further overlay by my experiences in South America. She was essentially a small-town Oklahoma/Texas girl. Unsophisticated would be the term that could describe her. And, most important of course, there was that difference in religion. She told me that, before me, she had only met one Jew in her life, one of her professors at the University of Texas, so she had no personal acquaintance at all with Judaism and with Jewish people. "Jew" was a new concept for her. I was and still am eternally grateful to her for her accepting my request of converting to Judaism, becoming a Jew by choice.

In later years I often wondered what I would have done if she had not acceded to that. Would I still have gone ahead with this marriage or not? I am quite convinced now that I wouldn't have. It would have been very hurtful, but I wouldn't have done it.

As in all other things, she lived up, in full measure, to what I expected of her in that respect. She did what she could to bring up the children as Jewish and, to the best of her ability, to create a Jewish home. Our children are indeed Jewish. They have no question about their identity. I am forever grateful to her for that.

With all of our "differences," it seems that we would have been prime candidates for divorce. We never had any problem. There was that thing with Edwin, of course, but it was just a bump in the road. It is long forgotten and far behind us. And I've already told you that when I think about finding such a treasure in such an unexpected place, I come up with the analogy of trying to pan for gold in the Arkansas River. It is impossible because there is no gold. You can pan for a whole year and never find a single fleck, but I dipped my pan into the Arkansas River and I came up, not with just a fleck, but with a big gold nugget. It is the real thing.

And then there is the extended family. My older brother Heinz (or Enrique) lives in Buenos Aires. He is not well at all, mostly burdened by near blindness and near deafness. I always felt a little sorry for him. He did not lead as full of a life as I have. I could have been in his position, working for a large company in Buenos Aires if I had not made the most important and crucial decision in my life, namely to stay in Bolivia, and not go to Argentina with my parents. Also, he has no children; he told me, not to my surprise, that that was his greatest regret.

When we both were children in Germany, I really had little contact with him. He was six years older and he had his own pursuits. We were always quite different. Now that we are both much older, and his being my only living close relative, I've come to love him and to admire him. I am sorry for all the years that we lost in not being together.

Then there are my in-laws, Diane and Hugh Cunningham. I have known Diane since she was fourteen years old. I really love her like a sister, and in all these years she has always been true blue and totally supportive. When Priscilla went through her crazy period, Diane was the one who always stuck with me and who told her sister to straighten out her head, to forget about this nonsense, and to try to be happy in our marriage.

I have a really good relationship with my brother-in-law Hugh, though we are different in almost every respect. He's a hunter and very politically conservative. He is what he is: a man from Southwest Georgia. He always seems to be somewhat reserved with me, but that's all right. We are good friends.

And I am good friends with and a good uncle to all of Diane's and Hugh's children, and I think they love me too. They always tell me that "Uncle Gerardo" is their favorite. I think they mean it. I believe it.

REFLECTIONS ON MY PARENTS

How about my parents? That is a quite different story. In fact, I have been carrying a great deal of guilt about them for many years. I still have not quite resolved that. I believe that I have been a somewhat indifferent and negligent son. The worst incident, and what causes me the greatest burden, was what happened many, many years ago when I came down from the Chacaltaya Mine with Mr. Peró. I saw my father, walking on the other side of the street. I should have asked Mr. Peró to stop the car immediately so I could embrace my father, whom I hadn't seen for over six months. But I did not do that. I was afraid of some kind of an emotional scene on his part, perhaps even on mine. I did not want Mr. Peró to be a witness to that.

Also, when my mother came to visit in San Francisco, I was often impatient with her and with her "old-world" ways, which I had long since shed (and probably never had), and the necessity of always having to be the interpreter, English-Spanish-German between Priscilla and her. But she was very patient with me and always forgiving. One "excuse" perhaps was that I had left home when I was sixteen years old and was really somewhat estranged from her and from my father. My determination not to move with them from Bolivia to Argentina – the most important and most fundamental decision of my life, I believe – was mostly based on my wish to distance myself from them and to start life on my own, in whatever difficult environment and unforgiving conditions it might be. It was that important to me.

Until they received restitution from Germany, they lived in the most primitive and virtually destitute conditions. There was not too much I could do about that. I was struggling myself. One time, when apparently they saw no other way out, they asked me for some money – I believe it was $300. I remitted that immediately, of course, and I don't know how they managed it, but they did repay me, even though I certainly didn't ask for that. But that was the way they wanted it. It took them some time.

Now, having children and even grandchildren myself, I know how bad I would feel if my children would show me the relative indifference that I believe I showed my parents. It would be very hard for me. Perhaps it was hard for my parents. If it was, they never let me know.

If I could redo one thing in my life, it would be to have been more attentive and more loving to my parents.

REFLECTIONS ON GERMANY

I have talked about this before, but it is such a troublesome and important matter in my life, so close to my self-identity, that I have to address it again.

I never, never think of myself as German. I despise not only the Nazis, but really all Germans of my generation, for the fact that they had allowed themselves to be seduced by that scoundrel Adolf Hitler and by the entire Nazi apparatus. And, with very few exceptions, they succumbed very willingly. I know – I was there.

In contrast to what happened to many others, the Nazis were not able to break my spirit. I thought they were vicious and ridiculous (what a combination!), trying to classify me and others like me as *Untermenschen*, or sub-human beings. I knew they were crazy. They were the ones who were sub-humans. I was a Jew, a member of the oldest surviving and most successful group the world had ever seen. What did those stupid Nazis know!

For the very longest time, surely for the first twenty-five years or so after leaving Germany, I would under no circumstances buy a German product, read a German book or even a German newspaper, or have any truck with any Germans. I would try to avoid speaking German if I possibly could. I told you about my first person-to-person contact with Germans, when I was sojourning in Strasbourg and was looking across the Rhine. When I started to do business with Germany I did actually acquire a number of good business acquaintances and even friends, such as Klaus Meuter and his wife Ingrid, and Arthur Seibert. But I was always wary. At that time, most of the German people I knew and dealt with were about my age or just a little older. Even so, without being asked, everyone hastened to assure me that they had never been Nazis, and in fact had tried to help their Jewish neighbors, etc. I never quite believed it. I could never find a single Nazi in post-War Germany. And I know that almost all of them, even the most dedicated murderers, were able to meld into the German populace after the War – disappear without a trace. Their neighbors, many of them being guilty of awful crimes themselves, gave them cover.

But now, another twenty-five years later, most of the people who could have been Nazis or in any way active against the Jews, are either dead or very, very old. I don't deal with them. Slowly, slowly my attitude toward Germany has changed.

Really, the most significant change in my thinking came about when, under the chancellorship of Konrad Adenauer, the Germans, themselves just recovering from the destruction and ruin they had suffered and brought upon themselves during the War, made it an obligation of honor to compensate, to the degree that it could be done with money, the Jews that they, or rather their parents, had driven out of their country, deprived of their property, and in many cases killed. As far as I could tell, they gave the Jews every reasonable benefit of the doubt, in the awareness that nothing really, no amount of money, could ever fully compensate for the insults, the suffering, the destruction, and the countless murders that they had caused. I have to give them enormous credit for making such an honest and successful attempt to "make good" – in fact the German word they used for these actions was *Wiedergutmachung*; it means "making good again." And that's what it was.

My own parents, who had been living in abject misery in Buenos Aires received a fairly substantial lump amount and a very adequate monthly pension. I was so happy for them to be able to spend the evening of their lives in relative comfort.

The German government, or rather the Berlin municipal government, invited me and Priscilla to an all-expense-paid trip to Berlin, as a demonstration of good will and atonement for injustices suffered. I did appreciate that gesture but could not make myself accept it. It just would not have felt right for me. I wrote them a nice letter, thanking them for the kind thought, but told them that "for personal reasons" I had to decline.

As time went by, however, I became friendly, really friendly with a number of Germans. Among them was their remarkable Consul General in San Francisco, Ruprecht Hanatsch, and his wife Veronika. They made it a point to invite us to some of their personal parties and to all of the "official" ones, of course. It felt quite awkward at first, but then I became used to it.

The greatest change in my thinking about Germany, however, came about in our establishing friendship with Hubertus Giebe, the artist, and Marlies, his art-restorer wife, from Dresden. They are much younger than we. In fact, they are not that much older than our children, but we have become very close friends. We really love them, their son Casper, and Marlies's mother, Gitta. I know that they love us too. We try to go to Germany and visit them as often as we can. We have come to think of them as part of our extended family. And I am very glad about that, because it is the final step in my reconciliation with Germany.

And I am most appreciative and grateful to the German government and to the German people for their real and honest effort to make amends – beyond the money – for the crimes that they (or their parents) had committed. There are the splendid institutions – the beautiful synagogues in big and small cities, Holocaust memorials, and the spectacular and magnificent Jewish Museum in Berlin.

There are two matters that remain.

First: Even today, I cannot make myself drive a German car, and certainly not a Mercedes (the "*Führer's* car") or a Volkswagen, (the "people's car"), the car that Hitler had destined for the "Aryan" German masses.

Second: I cannot understand how, after what has happened, and even though it's now over fifty years ago, Jews would want to live in Germany. How can they possibly feel comfortable in a country that carries so many terrible and indelible memories? Still, Germany now has a fairly good-sized Jewish population, about 100,000 people, the great majority of whom are not natives, but mostly immigrants from Russia. I have a certain feeling of mild contempt for them. Why, for perceived or real material advantages, would they wish to live in this place of terrible memories and bring their children up there? The Biblical flesh pots of Egypt come to mind.

But apart from that, I am reconciled with Germany, even have managed to develop some affection for it. I am happy that I have been able to resolve that conflict in myself, at least most of it.

Quite in contrast to my parents, especially my mother, who was devastated when their German citizenship was taken away from them, I really didn't give a damn about that. I was totally indifferent to it. I did feel very sorry for my parents, of course, not just because of their citizenship being taken away, but for the entire terrible impact that the Nazi regime had on them. They lost virtually everything they owned, and being more than fifty years old, had to leave their country and their home and go, without any money, to an alien and indifferent place where, essentially without any employable skills and having to deal with a foreign language, they had to try to start a new life. So, for them, I did not just disdain the Nazis, I totally hated them. I did not want to have anything to do with Germany if I could help it. I made an effort not to speak German even with native German Jewish speakers, such as myself, if I could possibly avoid it. When the Bolivians gave me a Spanish name – Gerardo instead of Gerhard – I eagerly accepted that. When I became an American citizen and the judge asked me what name I wished to choose, I rejected Gerhard, dropped my German middle name (Ernst) and continued to be known as Gerardo. And, of course, I have been that ever since.

But there is another side to this story – and that is what makes it difficult. I am the product of an absolutely first-class German humanistic education, went to a top-notch German school and am totally imbued with German history, German literature, German lore, German poetry, and German songs. Even the Jewish Boy Scouts, though totally involved with Jewishness and with Zionism, sang mostly German songs, and played German games, really just quite like the Hitler Youth, except, of course, for the specific Nazi content. Naturally, there were Hebrew songs also, but German always predominated. Even today, I know scores of German songs and German poetry. My German friends, all much younger than I and of a different generation, take delight in hearing me recite and sing songs and recite poetry that they had never heard before.

REFLECTIONS ON BEING JEWISH

Being Jewish has permeated all of my life. It's perhaps the most important thing in my life. When I grew up – before the Nazis came to power, and even though I was, of course, conscious of anti-Semitism in Germany – being Jewish just wasn't a big deal. That's what I was. I didn't give it too much thought.

Then, when I was about nine years old, I joined the Jewish (Zionist) Boy Scouts and became a very politicized Jew. Also at that time, partly because I believed having received a sign from God – remember how I found that one *mark* coin on the street – I also became quite religious. That, however, was a phase that passed fairly soon. But my ethnic sensitivity, my consciousness and my pride of being Jewish always remained.

I was so persuaded of my ethnic superiority – sort of a secular adaptation of the "chosen people" syndrome – that I was able to disdain the Nazis and all their hateful words and actions. I could not disregard them, of course, but I disdained them because I was so totally persuaded of their meanness and ignorance and of my personal and ethnic value. I felt much empathy with the blacks in America, especially in "the bad old days" in the American South, and I know how blacks, especially middle-class and intellectuals, must have felt about ignorant rednecks and white trash who were trying, usually successfully, to hold them down.

During the eight years that I spent in Bolivia, I had no contact at all with anything Jewish, though I did follow the constant struggles in Palestine with greatest interest, to the degree that I could find out about them from the occasional newspapers I got. Life in Bolivia was so rough, there were few Jewish people with whom I had any contact and, of course, no Jewish community with which to connect, certainly not in the mines where I worked.

I told you about how, on my first full day in the Untied States, I went for lunch to Morrison's cafeteria and found that platter with matzos. They were displayed quite unselfconsciously and no one seemed to pay any special attention to them. It was Passover, and some Jewish customers, perhaps even some gentiles, took the matzos instead of the bread. It was an emotional shock for me.

But even after that and even though I joined a Jewish fraternity while at the Missouri School of Mines at Rolla and my short involvement with the Jewish community in Tyler, Texas, I had little contact with Jewish matters or with any Jewish community. I did not belong to any congregation. There was no congregation to belong to. And, of course, during my eight years in the Arkansas oil fields and while I was living in Magnolia, I had no contact with Jewish people at all.

I did become electrified in 1948 when the State of Israel was founded. I followed events with the keenest interest. But that was just about all.

Oddly, the real reawakening of my serious interest in Judaism seemed to have begun when and after I married Priscilla. In good faith and with an open heart, she converted to Judaism. She became a Jew by choice. But she knew very little about it, except the rudimentary instruction that she had received from Rabbi Lefkowitz in Shreveport. It wasn't very much. So, I had to try to show her by example what to do and how to conduct a Jewish home. I didn't know too much about that myself. I know that she would have done anything within reason that I would have suggested. We joined a congregation. We sent the children to religious school. We celebrated the holidays, with Passover being a yearly important family event. What I did neglect to do, and I regret it deeply, was to light Shabbat candles and say Kiddush every Friday night. It would have been a good example for the children. It would have anchored their faith and their sense of identity and belonging. It might have persuaded them to have the same important rituals in their own homes.

I believe I made one major mistake. About five or six years after we were married, I came home one day and found a Christmas tree in our living room, with the children and Priscilla decorating it. I was appalled. To me, the Christmas tree was a symbol of Christianity. There was nothing wrong with it, of course, but it didn't have any place in a Jewish home, as far as I was concerned. It was almost to me (though not quite) as having a crucifix in the home. My mistake might have been in not saying anything about it. I just did not want to hurt Priscilla's feelings. She had so lovingly bought the tree and had decorated it, and I did not want to disappoint the children. But, after that, and as long as the children were little, the Christmas tree was a holiday fixture in our home. I never could get used to it. And, of course, the children picked it up and now have it in their own homes. Well, that is that.

One thing we did do, however, was at all times to have a *mezuzah* at our door, both in San Francisco and in our second home in Tahoe. I just could not be comfortable without it.

In subsequent years I became a major activist in Jewish causes, especially my founding of FLAME, an organization, which now has about 30,000 supporters and about an equal number of affiliates. Then, I took on the other job of being President of Friends of the Danish Jewish Museum. I give much effort – all of it on a pro bono basis – to those two projects. For the last fifteen years or so, and even though I was running a fairly substantial business, they have taken about fifteen or twenty hours a week of my time.

Derek, Rachel's husband is "technically" Jewish – his mother, though totally alienated and uninterested, is Jewish. Partly because of self-identification, but also I suspect to please me, they maintain a nominally Jewish household. Our grandson Zaddy goes to religious school, preparatory to his bar mitzvah, but I don't thing that there's any real spirit in it. It seems to be more of a chore than a pleasure to him. His "reading" (correctly) is that his parents are not too interested in Judaism and he understandably takes his cue from them. During the holiday season, the Christmas tree plays a primary role in their home. I conduct a Chanukah service, but it is perfunctory. I realize that. There is no *mezuzah* at the door. That's just the way it is; I don't like it, it hurts me, but I have to accept it.

I don't know about Joe. He married a Catholic girl and I don't know what pledges they had to give to the rabbi and to the priest, respectively, prior to their interfaith wedding. I have never asked them and they haven't told me. And, not surprisingly, there is no *mezuzah*, the inevitable symbol of a Jewish home, on their front door either.

All that is a little sad to me, but I have come to accept it. I realize, with some bemusement, that what two thousand years of persecution and suffering of the Jewish people had not been able to accomplish, a few generations of opportunities and of the good life in this blessed country may accomplish, namely reducing Jews to a small and quite unimportant minority in the United States, perhaps in just a few generations. Jews in this country may, eventually, be reduced only to the ultra-orthodox, who are now concentrated mostly in Brooklyn. After the terrible events of the Holocaust, in which six million Jews were murdered, while the world (except perhaps for the Danes) did not lift a finger to help them or to save them, the hope for the future of the Jewish people lies in Israel. It is, unfortunately, the only country in the history of the world, the legitimacy of which has been questioned since its creation, which has been constantly under the threat of destruction, and extermination and the future of which is still not clear at all.

I have an almost mystic feeling about the role of American Jews in the history of Judaism. Because American Jews are politically active and are financial contributors to the political process much beyond their proportion of the U.S. population, and also much assisted by fundamental Christians, American politics are usually pro-Israel – quite in contrast to those of Europe, which almost succeeded in wiping out Jews and Judaism altogether. As long as this political influence in the United States continues and it, too, may decline and eventually disappear in a couple of generations, we in America are able to foster the State of Israel until it will be able to totally stand on its own feet and will not be dependent economically or militarily on the good will of others. It may take a little time.

Jews, the Jewish destiny, and the survival of Israel are my major preoccupations.

REFLECTIONS ON BOLIVIA

I lived in Bolivia for eight years and though I have visited a few times since, I haven't lived there or have been there for any length of time, for almost sixty years. I spent the formative years of my life in that impoverished country. I arrived there as a boy and left being a man. I learned the virtue of hard work, in the most primitive possible environment, and living all those years at altitudes as high as 16,000 feet. I enjoyed my stay in the country, the wonderful people I met and, of course, my sexual awakening.

Most of all, of course, I am deeply grateful to the Bolivian people and the Bolivian government of that time for having given me and so many others generous *acogida*, an embracing welcome, to their country, in the hour of greatest need. They also gave such welcome to my parents, although they ultimately decided not to stay. I love Bolivia and I love the Spanish language, of which I am still a fluent speaker. I regret never having fully learned the Indian dialect Aymara, which was spoken all around me. I never could find a textbook and the Indians could not explain their difficult language to me in Spanish. I did the best I could, had a working knowledge, and could say what was necessary. But I never learned it fluently or to read and write.

One week every year, the first week of August, the Sixth of August being Bolivia's Independence Day, I fly the Bolivian flag from the flagpole in our home. It is my expression of gratitude and affection for the country. I have expressed my thanks in writing to the government of Bolivia. It is a very poor country, not favored by nature, and with an unhappy history that has deprived it of much of its land and of access to the sea. But what wonderful people! They deserve a better fate and a way out of their poverty. I hope that some day soon they will succeed.

REFLECTIONS ON THE UNITED STATES

I love the United States, where I have now lived for over sixty years. I am deeply grateful to this country for having given me so many opportunities, of some of which, I am afraid, I have not taken full advantage.

I feel utterly at home and have helped raise an American family – children and grandchildren.

My enduring regret is that I did not serve my adopted country in the War and did not do my small share to defeat the Nazis. But I couldn't do it because I wasn't here. I was still in Bolivia when the War ended. I console myself with the knowledge that I did my part by working in the tin and tungsten mines and therefore contributed by producing materials indispensable for the War effort.

Being Jewish in the United States is a wonderful experience. It began with my first full day in the country, when I saw those matzos on display at Morrison's Cafeteria. It continues until today, when Jewish organizations and institutions prosper and where Jews are prominently represented in leadership positions in virtually every field of activity, including the highest reaches of government.

I still cannot quite make myself refer to "the fathers of our country." It just doesn't quite seem to refer to me. But I am filled with admiration to those founding fathers for, it seems, having envisioned what the United States was going to be like and going to be about more than two hundred years after they drafted those incomparable documents: the U.S. Constitution and the Bill of Rights.

But not all is perfect. I remember my second full day in the country when, for the first time, I was confronted with the ugly reality of racism, when that red-faced railroad employee threw me and Sergio out of the "colored" waiting room. And I continued to be distressed and dismayed about that for years after. We did not have a single black student at the Missouri School of Mines (and, sad to say, not at the Harvard Business School either, except for that Ethiopian prince); and I lost my first job in Abilene, Texas, when I foolishly tried to change or at least protest against the prevailing social order.

I am so happy that this ugly stain on America's escutcheon has largely been removed.

Two other things concern me. First: it is still almost incomprehensible to me that a country as advanced and as prosperous as the United States has not been able to solve the problem of extreme poverty, of the homeless, and of the uninsured. To see people sleeping in the streets of great American cities, begging for food and relieving themselves is a shameful spectacle. One does not see that in even the poorest countries of Europe. May those shameful conditions perhaps partly be due to the American aversion to paying taxes?

Second: Even after all these years, I cannot understand that a civilized country would not only allow, but would actually encourage citizens to arm themselves, virtually at will. It is most unusual and unique in the developed world.

But those are really only quibbles, though I don't think of them as "minor" ones. They are serious ones, but I am confident that the generous spirit and the good sense of the people of this great country will successfully deal with those issues, just as they have (almost!) vanquished the ugly dragon of racism.

I am confident that the 21st century, just like the 20th, will be the American century, and that America will use its preponderant position in the world, its position as the only superpower, to bring the blessings of democracy and the blessings of liberty to those areas of the planet that are still suffering under tyranny and economic slavery.

——————————————— • ———————————————

Dear Friends,

Thank you for your patience in accompanying me on this trip through my life and for listening to my story. I hope you found it interesting and perhaps even rewarding.

I am now over eighty years old. I plan on coming out with a follow-up volume by the time I am a hundred years old – in about twenty years from now. I certainly hope that you will be my companion in that second volume as well.

Thank you, good bye, and God speed.

Gerardo Joffe

anagraphics® #1047

There Always Seems To Be a Spoiler

From the clues given, solve each of the following word pairs. They are anagrams — same letters in different order.

King David's specialty

Beverly Hills trees
Read carefully

Dough in India
Menaces, warning

Break into pieces
Does what Gutenberg invented

Short distance burst
Gall, chutzpah

Better late than that

Now, take the "dotted" letters and form another pair of anagrams. The cartoon will give you clue to surprise answer.

WHY THINGS DIDN'T WORK OUT IN THE GARDEN OF EDEN.

BECAUSE THE

WAS

I told you that, somewhere in this book, I would show you a sample of ANAGRAPHICS, the word puzzle that I developed. Here it is. It was not as successful as I hoped. Could it be that it was too difficult? You be the judge!

799   Joffe, Gerardo
JOF   Weaned on Carrot Juic